Nicholas N Patricios is Professor and Dean Emeritus of Architecture at the University of Miami. His previous books include *Kefallinia and Ithaki: A Historical and Architectural Odyssey* (2002).

'Architecture takes central stage in this intriguing take on hugely important questions around the interaction of art, liturgy and symbolism in the Byzantine church. The book brings together a mass of information and detail to formulate new approaches to the classification and understanding of Byzantine ecclesiastical architecture in a broad social and religious context.'

Liz James, Professor of Art History, University of Sussex, author and editor of *Light and Colour in Byzantine Art* and *A Companion to Byzantium*

'This very handsomely illustrated book will be welcomed by many people interested in the art, architecture and history of Byzantium, treated here in a wide reach from Italy – with special attention to Rome – to the eastern part of the empire. Employing evocative and sometimes lyrical language, the author describes and gives rich context to ecclesiastical buildings and their decoration in ways that will pull readers into an historical past that has left such powerful, ghostly traces. The author employs a novel taxonomy for these buildings and their art that opens up the whole range of building types and functions across the empire and within its cultural orbit. And the liturgical life of these buildings, so often underplayed by scholars, is brought out fully so that readers will catch the scents, sounds and wonder of that world between the lines.'

Glenn Peers, Professor of Early Medieval and Byzantine Art, The University of Texas at Austin, author of *Subtle Bodies: Representing Angels in Byzantium* and *Sacred Shock: Framing Visual Experience in Byzantium*

THE SACRED ARCHITECTURE OF BYZANTIUM

ART, LITURGY AND SYMBOLISM
IN EARLY CHRISTIAN CHURCHES

NICHOLAS N PATRICIOS

I.B. TAURIS
LONDON · NEW YORK

Published in 2014 by I.B.Tauris & Co Ltd
6 Salem Road, London W2 4BU
175 Fifth Avenue, New York NY 10010
www.ibtauris.com

Distributed in the United States and Canada Exclusively by Palgrave Macmillan
175 Fifth Avenue, New York NY 10010

Copyright © 2014 Nicholas N. Patricios

The right of Nicholas N. Patricios to be identified as the author of this work has been asserted by him in accordance with the Copyright, Designs and Patent Act 1988.

All rights reserved. Except for brief quotations in a review, this book, or any part thereof, may not be reproduced, stored in or introduced into a retrieval system, or transmitted, in any form or by any means, electronic, mechanical, photocopying, recording or otherwise, without the prior written permission of the publisher.

Library of Classical Studies: 4

ISBN: 978 1 78076 291 3

A full CIP record for this book is available from the British Library
A full CIP record is available from the Library of Congress

Library of Congress Catalog Card Number: available

Printed and bound in China

TO EM

St Gregory of Nazianzus, in monk's garb, writing his liturgical homilies in a spectacular imaginary architectural composition. Manuscript illustration, Monastery of St Catherine, Sinai

CONTENTS

	Prologue	ix
	Preface	xi
	Acknowledgements	xvii
1	CHURCH AND STATE	1
2	SACRED ARCHITECTURE	38
3	SPLENDID CHURCHES	88
4	SPIRITUAL ART	245
5	PLACES OF SPLENDID SPIRITUAL ART	278
6	LITURGY OF THE EUCHARIST	373
7	SYMBOLISM IN ARCHITECTURE AND ART	389
	Epilogue	405
	Notes	407
	Further Reading	409
	Bibliography	413
	Illustrations, Credits and Sources	419
	Index	439

PROLOGUE

My Village Church on the Ionian Island of Ithaka

The peal of church bells sweeps through the valley. It is Sunday morning and it is the first of three bells to be rung during the church service. As I struggle to awaken the image of the priest performing the *Orthros,* or daybreak service prior to beginning the Divine Liturgy, flits in and out of my mind. I have never been to church early enough for the preparation, the *proskomedia*, of the bread and wine for communion. When I eventually make my way up the pathway to the church at the top of the hill, I know I am tracing the steps my father took, and his father before him, on their way to *Taxiarchis,* the church of the Archangels. As I enter the open ironwork gate into the forecourt the easterly sun peeks over the roof and I have to shade my eyes as the light is bright even this early. Up a few steps and I am in the shady portico. Through the open central doors I hear the chanting from within. I enter the barrel-vaulted narthex and naos (nave) space, light a candle and kiss the icon on the stand. I walk to the right aisle, the side of the men, and find an empty fold-up stall-seat against the side wall. I take a stall at the back of the wall lined seats and hope I shall not be embarrassed if one of the elders arrives and finds I am in his unmarked but traditional place! There are not any men yet except for two ushers. As I stand alone in the aisle I look through the columns on my side to the opposite aisle and see all the stall seats are taken up mostly by grey-haired women dressed all in black. I know the space between the two arcaded aisles will soon fill up with women arriving late but who will have to stand as by tradition there are no pews or chairs in the middle of the naos. While the small congregation fills the back half of the church the front half always remains empty dominated by a narrow passageway formed by velvet ropes strung between slender posts leading from the central door of the holy bema (the sanctuary), to the centre of the naos.

I look around at the familiar visual spectacle of paintings covering most of the wall space. At the same time the aroma of sweetly scented incense reaches me. I listen carefully to the chant of the *psaltes* to judge where we are in the liturgy. Yes, they have just begun the liturgy of the catechumens in which litanies and antiphons follow one another. I look to the front of the church which is completely taken up by an elaborate icon screen, the *iconostasis*, which extends from the floor almost to the ceiling and separates us from the holy bema that is behind. The screen is filled with tiers of icons except for the central doors and one door at each end. From inside the bema the priest emerges into the naos through the left-hand door of the *iconostasis* holding a silver covered book of Gospels. He is preceded by an usher with a lighted candle. They take a few steps towards us before the priest turns and proceeds along the roped-off passageway entering the holy bema alone through the central doors and then placing the book of Gospels back on the Holy Table (altar). The usher in the meantime enters back through the same left-side door. This procession is simple in my village church but back in my hometown church of St Andrew in Miami the procession includes a deacon and altar boys with candles and liturgical fans. I do not really miss the choir from my Miami church as the *psaltes* in the village church have superb even angelic voices. As there is no deacon for my small village church one of the *psaltes* proceeds with an Epistle reading that I have difficulty in following not only because it is in Byzantine Greek but he is a fast reader. He is followed by the priest reading the Gospel passage for this Sunday. I understand this reading much better as I am familiar with the passage and the priest pronounces the words very clearly. Then the part that inevitably intrigues me, the exclamation: 'The doors! The doors! Guard the doors.' I had always wondered about this until one time a priest explained to me that in the old days the catechumens, those wanting to be Christians but not yet baptized, had to leave the service at this point and the doors were closed as they were not allowed to remain for the second part of the liturgy. But the exclamation has still remained as part of the liturgy today even though catechumens as such have disappeared.

The service continues with some litanies and a hymn after which the priest emerges again from the left-hand door carrying a veiled chalice and paten towards us before returning along the roped-off passageway to the bema entering through the central doors. If altar boys had been present they would have headed the procession with their candles and fans but this is a small village church so an usher carrying a candle stands in. After entering the bema the priest closes the central Holy Doors and begins the mystery of consecration hidden from our view. His voice is inaudible. I notice that only the *psalti* recites the Creed and later the Lord's Prayer whereas in the Greek Orthodox churches in North America the whole congregation participates in their recital. It is time for communion. Only a few of the elderly women go forward. The rest of us are left to share the *antidoron*, the Eucharist bread not consecrated, at the end of the service. There is no sermon, which is common in village churches. Instead the priest hands out a four page printed leaflet, the *Foni Kyriou,* for us to take home and read.

As I walk down the hill back home, past the ageless olive trees, I ponder how traditional the liturgy is, how it has remained essentially unchanged for centuries. I wonder about how the liturgy developed from the first century onward and especially the interplay between it and sacred space, the architecture of the church building and spiritual art – the icons. That was the inspiration for this book, to answer that question.

In a lyric poem he called *At Church* the great modern Greek poet Konstantine Kavafy has managed to capture the essence of the sensory experience of an Eastern Orthodox Sunday church service when he wrote in 1912 (my translation):

> I love the church – its cherub icons,
> the silver of its sacred vessels, its candlesticks,
> the lights, its icons, its ambon.
>
> There as I enter, into a church of the Greeks,
> with its incense so fragrant,
> with its liturgical and symphonic voices,
> the majestic presence of its priests
> and in every one of their movements solemn rhythm –
> most splendid in their vestments so adorned –
> my mind goes to the high honours of our people,
> to our glorious Byzantine tradition.

PREFACE

Crossing the sea, I arrived at Constantinople a city with a teeming population, giving thanks to Christ our God who deigned to give me such grace, unworthy and undeserving as I am, for He had deigned to give me not only the will to go, but also the power of walking through the places that I desired. On my arrival I went to the holy bishop of the city; Nektarios, a truly devout man, received me willingly and said: 'My daughter, I can see what a long journey this is on which your faith has brought you – right from the other end of the earth. So now please let us show you all the places Christians should visit here.'

Forthwith a monk took me to the church Constantine built first, Hagia Eirene, in the same walled courtyard to Hagia Sophia completed by his son Constantius. The next place he showed me was a striking building in the form of a Greek cross, the Church of the Holy Apostles, in the centre of a large courtyard with baths and halls all around. We entered the church and walked reverently to the crossing where in the soft light I gazed upon the altar that contained the relics of the Apostles Andrew, Luke and Timothy and where once had been the porphyry sarcophagus of Constantine now in the circular room at the east end.

The next day, the Lord's Day, I returned to Hagia Eirene entering through the grand gateway into a courtyard that had a shady portico all round. Above the church at the far end I could see the sky begin to lighten as it was before cockcrow. At this greater church built by Constantine a whole multitude was already assembled outside the doors, where lights are hanging for the purpose. And for fear that they should not be there at cockcrow they come beforehand and sit down there. Hymns as well as antiphons are said, and prayers are made between the several hymns and antiphons, for at the vigils there are always both priests and deacons ready there for the assembling of the multitude, the custom being that the holy places are not opened before cockcrow.

Now as soon as the first cock has crowed the bishop arrives in procession with priests and deacons and they assemble in the narthex. All the five doors are opened with the bishop, priests, and deacons entering through the centre Royal Doors while the whole multitude enters through the other doors. Inside countless lights are already burning. And when the people have entered, they stand men on the right and women on the left. The bishop takes his place on the throne behind the altar and the priests and deacons seat themselves on circular benches on either side of him in the apse. A priest comes forward and says a psalm to which all respond, and afterwards prayer is made; then one of the deacons says a psalm and prayer is again made, a third psalm is said by one of the clergy, prayer is made for the third time and there is a commemoration of all. A reader recites from the Prophets and then the bishop from within the rails first says a prayer for all, mentioning the names of those whom he wishes to commemorate; he then blesses the catechumens, afterwards he says a prayer and blesses the faithful. A deacon takes the book of Gospels from the altar and comes forward along a *raised passageway to the ambo in the centre and reads a passage. After the reading of the Gospel there are hymns and again a psalm is said and prayer is made. The custom here is that of all the priests who take their seats, as many as are willing, preach, and after them all the bishop preaches, and these sermons are always on the Lord's Day, in order that the people may always be instructed in the Scriptures and in the love of God. After three psalms and three prayers are ended, censers are brought so that the whole basilica is filled with aromas. The catechumens are dismissed and then the bread and wine are brought by the deacons in ceremony to the altar for the oblation to be made and a thanksgiving prayer said. The bishop offers the oblation there, and all communicate. And when the bishop comes out from within the rails, everyone approaches his hand, and he blesses them one by one as he goes out, and the dismissal takes place, by daylight.*

The church is very great, very beautiful and of new construction, well worthy to be the house of God. Shiny marble columns separate the central area from the side aisles and above are the decorative rails of the galleries. At one end of the gallery is the place for Emperor Theodosius and his court when they attend the liturgy. And what shall I say of the decoration of the fabric itself, which Constantine decorated with gold, mosaic, and costly marbles, as far as the resources of his kingdom allowed him. In the apse like an earthly emperor on his throne is Lord Jesus Christ, his right hand raised in blessing, with six apostles in white robes seated on either side of him. The walls are adorned with paintings of fruits, flowers, birds and fish. You see there nothing but gold and gems and silk seen in the light from the high windows. For if you look at the veils, they are made wholly of silk striped with gold, and if you look at the curtains, they too are made wholly of silk striped with gold. The floor is of black and white marble tiles. On the raised platform of the holy altar there are church vessels too, of every kind, gold and jewelled, are brought out on that day. Indeed, who could either reckon or describe the number and weight of the candles on tall candlesticks or of the lamps for burning oil, or of the lanterns or of the various vessels?

The narrative above is a rare firsthand account of the liturgy, architecture and art of the late fourth century. Most of the sentences are gleaned from scattered parts of a long letter that survives only in fragmentary form written by a pilgrim named Egeria.[1] I have taken the liberty of adding my own sentences, hopefully in her style, to connect the sentences and so create a coherent and unified account. Egeria, most probably a nun, travelled from somewhere in Gaul to the Holy Land and Constantinople between 381 and 384. She wrote an account of her journey in a long letter to a circle of women back home which survives only in fragmentary form in a later copy now called the *Itinerarium Egeriae*, or the Travels of Egeria.

Egeria's experiences and those of my own in the village church in Greece are the inspiration for this book. As an architect my focus is naturally on the architecture of churches, specifically the origin of the early Christian churches and their development over the following centuries during the Byzantine era. As religious art is an integral part of Byzantine church architecture the topic of wall paintings and icons is significant and important. Before describing church architecture and religious art there is a need, however, to set the historical background under which Christian religious edifices were designed, built and decorated with art. Thus Chapter 1, 'Church and State', outlines the beginnings of Christianity in the Roman Empire and how it was given official recognition in 313 and then later in the fourth century was made the official religion of the state. With the slide of the Western Roman Empire into the centuries of the so-called 'Dark Ages' the Eastern or Byzantine Roman Empire remained vibrant with the building of numerous churches. These were decorated with beautiful mosaics and wall paintings under the Macedonian, Komnenian and Palaiologan dynasties until the Fall of Constantinople in 1453 and the end of the Byzantine Empire.

Against this background I discuss in Chapter 2, 'Sacred Architecture', the beginnings of Christian church building and how in the early centuries there was a variety of architectural forms for churches. After an analysis of 370 congregational church plans I have arrived at a distinctive approach to the classification of the numerous forms and that is to describe Byzantine churches by type. I then describe the characteristics of each. The seven types are the basilica, cross-in-square, cruciform, centralized, domed basilica, converted temple and Athonite. Independent of form, architectural space in Byzantine congregational churches is always divided into three distinct parts: the narthex or vestibule, the central naos or nave, and the holy area of the bema (pronounced *véma* in Greek) or sanctuary. In addition to these three key places I describe other spaces that may be found along with them and these are the open forecourt, the solea (a kind of passageway), the 'pastophoria' or side chambers adjacent to the bema, transepts and galleries. An account of the sacred architecture of Byzantine churches would not be complete without descriptions of architectural fixtures that include the Holy Table (altar), synthronon (clergy benches), iconostasis or icon screen and ambo (pulpit). The chapter concludes with a discussion of a major feature of Byzantine churches, that of orientation.

With an understanding of the general characteristics of Byzantine sacred architecture it is now possible to depict in detail how these broad features came to be realized in specific church buildings. That is the purpose of Chapter 3, 'Splendid Churches'. As there are hundreds and hundreds of Byzantine churches and it would be overwhelming to depict them all I have focused only on the splendid churches in influential centres. These centres are the capital cities of Rome and the new capital of the Roman Empire, Constantinople; the Holy Land as it was the heart of Christendom; and the regional capitals of Thessaloniki and Ravenna. In Rome there are more than 50 early Christian churches that can still be seen today. Of these I describe 22 of them some in more lengthy detail than others. Some readers may be surprised to learn that all of these early Christian churches in Rome were of the basilica type, except three. As can be expected Constantinople also had a large number of churches but in contrast to Rome these can only be seen today as converted mosques or museums in Istanbul, as the city is now named. Another difference between the churches of the two capital cities is that all six architectural types, perhaps all seven, are evident in the 25 former churches in Constantinople that can still be seen today. There is no doubt that the presence of so many types of church forms in the capital city of the Eastern Roman Empire was a reflection of the variety of churches in the eastern region as a whole. In the Holy Land the two churches of significance are the ones connected to the birth and death of Jesus Christ. Thessaloniki in northern Greece was known as the 'co-capital' along with Constantinople during the Byzantine era. Today the splendid and functioning churches of Thessaloniki are mostly in very good condition, making it a treasure house of Byzantine churches. I describe eleven of these grouped under the seven types. I follow on then to describe four splendid Christian religious structures in Ravenna, a former Byzantine city located in the northeast region of Italy, then the notable monastery churches on Mount Athos, at Meteora and Mystras. The chapter concludes with a detailed account of the domed basilica church of St John at Ephesus in Asia Minor, where all the typical Byzantine sacred architectural components can still be clearly seen and appreciated today.

Chapter 4, 'Spiritual Art', covers in depth the elaborate decorative programme of stylized images in mosaic, wall paintings and icons that makes Byzantine church interiors so sumptuous. The art of the early Christian period was naturally influenced by contemporary Roman art but by the fourth century Christian art emerged with its own distinct character. After Christianity became the official religion of the Roman Empire toward the end of the fourth century there was a golden age in spiritual art of about two centuries. Then there was a new era when images were overthrown in what is called the Iconoclastic period. When this era ended in the middle of the ninth century religious art entered a second golden age that continued for a time until the Fall of Constantinople in the fifteenth century and the end of the Byzantine Empire. In the Chapter I outline how the decorative scheme of Byzantine churches was integrated with and related to the architectural spaces. Under the topic of iconography I explain the themes of Byzantine spiritual art, as well as stylization, the use of inscriptions, the various media used, and who some of the famous iconographers of the time were. The Chapter concludes with some selected texts that provide a firsthand account of how people at the time saw and explained church art.

Just as the chapter on splendid churches built on the foundations of the chapter on Sacred Architecture, the specific following the general, so I do the same with Christian art. Chapter 5, 'Places of Splendid Spiritual Art', contains detailed descriptions of specific, superb images based on the broad artistic principles explained in Chapter 4. As there are hundreds if not thousands of images in the churches I narrowed my selection to describing splendid art in important places of the Byzantine Empire. So rather than a chronological account I follow a geographical arc that starts in Rome, sweeps across northern Italy, the Balkans, Greece, Asia Minor, the Near East, Egypt and then, almost completing the circle, that ends in Sicily. In Rome and Italy I describe the beautiful mosaic images in the churches of Rome, Milan, Ravenna, Venice, Aquileia and Istria before proceeding to those in Ohrid and Thessaloniki. I go on to explain the spiritual art of the churches of Mount Athos, Meterora, Hosios Loukas, Mystras and Athens in Greece, most of which is to be found in monasteries. Even though it is only a proportion of what once existed, the spiritual art of the former churches in Constantinople is still today overwhelming in terms of quantity and quality. To begin to capture some feeling of the remarkable church art of the city I have lengthy depictions of the most significant images. My descriptions continue by following the arc in Cappadocia, Dura-Europos, Madaba, Jerusalem, Crete, Sinai, Bawit and Sakkara, before concluding in the splendid and overpowering number of images in the cathedral of Monreale in Sicily.

As the architecture and art of Byzantine churches provide a setting for the liturgy, an understanding of the ritual actions of the service will provide a deeper appreciation of their sacred architecture and spiritual art. Chapter 6, 'Liturgy of the Eucharist', thus provides a sketch of the history of the liturgy, its shape and content, in the Orthodox East and the continued interaction between architecture and liturgy during the Byzantine era. The first three centuries after the death of Jesus Christ were formative ones for the new religion of Christianity. I outline the development of the Eucharist liturgy from a simple, common meal of the faithful to a ritual service held every Sunday and the places where they were held. With the official acceptance of Christianity in the fourth century, handbooks of church teaching and practice were prepared to assist clergy scattered throughout the different regions of the Roman Empire. By the seventh century the liturgy in the East involved movement and actions with entrances and exits that related to specific architectural spaces and fixtures in Byzantine churches. In the eleventh century changes to the liturgy included elaboration of the preparation of the bread and wine for the Eucharist that required the use of a permanent space or chamber adjacent to the bema known as the prothesis. By the fourteenth century the Byzantine liturgy reached its full development and has remained virtually the same since then in the form of the Eastern Orthodox liturgy. I conclude the chapter with a summary of the interpretations by prominent Byzantine religious scholars from the third century to the fifteenth century as to the meaning of the liturgy.

In Chapters 2 to 5 inclusive I touch on symbolism in Byzantine sacred architecture and spiritual art, and because it is of such a significant characteristic I devote the entire Chapter 7, 'Symbolism in Architecture and Art' to the subject. Instead of attempting to interpret the meaning of symbols from a modern point of view I use extracts from the original texts of twelve different ancient documents to decode, so to speak, the meanings or significance of objects, events or relationships in Byzantine church architecture and art. Text extracts are grouped in the same order in which sacred architecture was explained in Chapter 2. The first two groups are about symbolism in the spatial division of the church and laying the foundations. Following are texts on the symbolism involving the forecourt or courtyard, the narthex, naos, aisles, Holy Bema, apse, Holy Table and ciborium, the diaconicon, synthronon, templon and iconostasis, solea, ambo, and finally orientation. There are also extracts related to art. In the second half of the chapter I have further reflections on relationships beginning with the preparation of the gifts and the prothesis and diaconicon. Other symbolic relationships I look into are those between the entrance procession and narthex; relics and the central plan and dome; mystery and the iconostasis and Holy Table; teaching and the synthronon; the second coming of the Messiah and orientation; and, lastly, religious symbolism in spiritual art.

I have been fortunate that over the years I have had the opportunity to visit many countries and studied most of the churches that I describe in this book and viewed a great number of the mosaics and wall paintings. A word needs to be said about terminology as there is no generally agreed manner in translating Greek names and words into English and on the use of technical terms in Byzantine architecture and art. As the intention of this book is to be as accessible to as many readers as possible the word saint is abbreviated to St instead of the authentic *Agios* or *Agia* that it would be in Greek. An exception is in the name Hagia (*Η Αγία*) for the churches of Sophia (*Σοφία*) and Eirene (*Ειρήνη*) as these two names are so well known in this form. For churches in Italy the words *San* or *Santa* are retained in their names. As in the Byzantine world the Mother of Jesus Christ was referred to as the *Theotokos* (literally 'God Bearer') or sometimes *Panagia* ('All Holy') these are the terms to be use throughout the book, whereas in the West she was known as the Virgin Mary. For Byzantine architectural terms I try to stay as close as possible to the original Greek word as this brings us closer to the minds of those who used the original terms during those times. In the chapters I have omitted footnotes and limited endnotes to keep the passages straightforward. Instead I list suggested further readings for each chapter that are grouped at the end of the book. The Bibliography incorporates all of these readings and includes in addition specialized references. In Chapters 3 and 5, which describe many Byzantine churches, place by place, the names of the churches are in a bold font to enable the reader to easily distinguish the written depictions of diverse buildings in each place.

ACKNOWLEDGEMENTS

I am most grateful to the American Academy in Rome and the Director, Professor Carmela Franklin, for the Visiting Scholarship that I was granted in 2009 which enabled me first, to visit and study 27 early Christian churches in the city and, second, to make use of the Academy's vast library and photographic archives. I wish to thank the United States Educational Foundation for my Fulbright Fellowship to dwell on the Ionian Islands of Kefallinia and Ithaka in 1990 to study traditional architecture that first exposed me to close contact with Byzantine churches and monasteries. Also, I appreciate the prior travel grants from the University of Miami Research Council that enabled me to visit the other Ionian Islands and in particular Venice where my researches included the study of the Basilica of St Mark's.

I am especially grateful to my colleague and dear friend, Professor Aristides Millas, for sharing with me his bibliography on Byzantine architecture. Many thanks to Father Peter Chamberas for his advice on the liturgy and Fathers Eudokimos and Aristides, Deacon Gustavo Alfonso, and chanters Vassilis Kokorelis and George Jenetopulos for their encouragement. My visits to the monasteries of Mount Athos would not have been possible without Christos Gonidis, guide and companion. For their spiritual insights and information I thank profusely Fathers Efthemios, Akakios, Philemon, Jeremiah, Theonas, Ioachim and especially Eirenaus, monks of Mount Athos.

Chapter 1

CHURCH AND STATE

Millennium. That is at least how long the State of the Byzantine Empire lasted, ruled from its capital Constantinople. The actual period was an astonishing 1,123 years from AD 330 to 1453. In historical narratives it is highly unusual to have such precise dates but is it known that the ceremonial inauguration of Constantinople as the New Rome took place on 11 May 330 and its capture by the Ottoman Turks occurred on 29 May 1453. Some scholars argue for an earlier starting date than 330 for the Byzantine Empire, that of 324, when Emperor Constantine I (reigned 306–337) began to reconstruct the Greek city of Byzantium on the Bosphorus as the new capital of the Roman Empire. The 330 date, however, is marked by a dedication ceremony and the erection in the city's main square of a stone pillar with an engraving of the imperial decree that Byzantium was to be renamed *Nova Roma Constantinopolitana* or New Rome. In popular speech the city was called *Constantinopolis* in Greek, the City of Constantine, and in English thus came to be named Constantinople. Yet other scholars maintain a later starting date of 395. This was after the death of Emperor Theodosius I (r. 379–395) when the single empire was divided into eastern and western parts. Each part was ruled by one of the sons of Theodosius but the brothers were bitter rivals. Arcadios (r. 395–408) ruled the Eastern Roman Empire from his capital in Constantinople while Honorius (r. 395–423) presided over the Western Roman Empire with Ravenna as capital.

1. Constantine Augustus. Head of the emperor in the courtyard of the Palazzo dei Conservatori, Rome

The term 'Byzantine' is recent, coined in the sixteenth century but only came into general use in the nineteenth century. Nowadays it is generally accepted that the terms *Byzantine* or *Byzantium* are used to designate the architecture, art, religion and other features of the Eastern Roman Empire from the fourth to the fifteenth century. The Eastern Roman or Byzantine Empire as it was also known was Christian, from about the fifth century Eastern Orthodox in form, and essentially Greek-speaking. In contrast the Western Roman Empire was Latin and Catholic in religion. While modern authors label the people of the Eastern Roman Empire 'Byzantines'

2. The Byzantine world under Justinian I in the sixth century

3. Byzantine Empire territory before and after Justinian I

4. Byzantine Empire territory in the ninth century

the inhabitants and most of their neighbours understood themselves as *Romäoi* ('Romans') and their Empire as *Romania*. As the East became more Greek, Emperor Herakleios (r. 610-641) adopted the title *Vasiléos* (*Basileus*) and thereafter each Byzantine Emperor regarded himself as a *Vasiléos Romanós* ('Roman Emperor').

Although Emperor Theodosius separated the former unified Roman Empire into halves, at the end of the fourth century each half shared a common world view, at least initially. This changed when barbarian invasions began to conquer the Western Roman Empire. According to Edward Gibbon's influential work *The Decline and Fall of the Roman Empire*, published in five volumes between 1776 and 1787, the West succumbed to 'barbarism and religion', declined and ceased to exist after 476. His view of the waning of the West as well as his dismissal of the Byzantine civilization in the East Empire has largely prevailed. Hence the common perception, first, that the Western Empire withered and experienced the so-called 'Dark Ages' for three or four centuries and eventually faded away and, secondly, ignorance that the Eastern Empire was dynamic, flourished, remained essentially intact and culturally unified, and survived for a millennium from the fourth to the fifteenth centuries. Modern historians have re-evaluated Gibbon's picture of a long slide of the West into oblivion and his contention that Christianity was a cause of Rome's decline. Around the eighth or ninth centuries the paths of West and East diverged. In the Western Empire as most barbarians converted to Christianity, church architecture and art, and the liturgy, developed differently than that in the Eastern Empire. In the East architecture and art were influenced by the new religion of Islam that swept across central Asia, parts of Persia, all of Asia Minor, North Africa, and Spain with raiders penetrating as far as Gaul (modern day France). Instead of the 'Dark Ages' the period is now seen as one of a great transformation, a reordering of the once mammoth Roman Empire into three great civilizations: the Byzantine Empire, Medieval Europe, and the Islamic Caliphate. Hence, the period from the fifth to the ninth centuries has been renamed 'Late Antiquity' by historians.

5. Emperor Constantine with a model of the city of Constantinople

6. Emperor Justinian with a model of the church of Hagia Sophia

In the Byzantine Empire Church and State were intertwined. From the time the Christian religion was officially recognized by imperial decree at the beginning of the fourth century until the Empire ceased to exist emperors involved themselves directly in church affairs. They convened and presided over church councils and had a direct influence on church architecture and art. Outlined below are crucial and relevant political and religious events that are essential information to fully appreciate Byzantine architecture, art, liturgy and symbolism in the context of Church and State. This appreciation applies not only for the period of Late Antiquity but for the prior era of early Christianity as well as for post-Late Antiquity until the demise of the Byzantine Empire with the Fall of Constantinople in 1453.

7. Church and State. The cross of Emperors Romanos II and Basil II

Early Christianity

After the death of Jesus his followers consisted of small and obscure groups that did not attract much attention from Roman authorities. Although there is a noticeable lack of information about the early growth of Christianity it is known that Christians in the first century began to meet in homes and had little public presence. By the end of the first century, though, Christianity had gained a foothold in Syria and by the second half of the third century Christians were a major force in Antioch then the third city of the Roman Empire. By 320 there were several churches in the city and as a centre of Hellenic culture with schools of learning and its central location, Antioch, was an intermediary between East and West. It was from the Syrian city of Edessa, however, that there was a dissemination of Christian teachings, in particular a compilation of the four Gospels. St Paul was instrumental in spreading Christianity by taking the 'good news' (the literal meaning of gospel) throughout Cilicia, Asia Minor, Macedonia and Achaia (modern Greece). He set up Christian churches in each place he visited while others were founded after his death. By 325 the region was covered by a network of bishoprics with Ephesus second only to Antioch as a Christian city. Cities with major churches were the Holy City of Jerusalem and the capital cities of Constantinople and Rome.

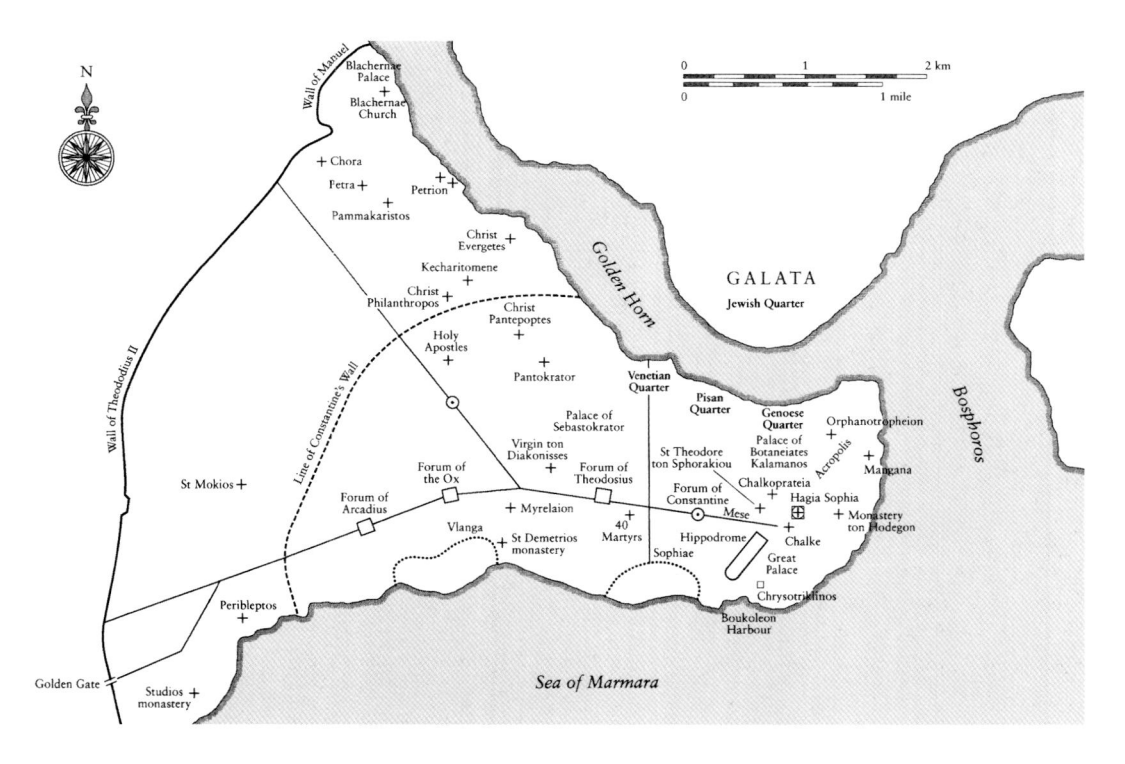

8. Map of Byzantine Constantinople. Location of churches and monasteries

9. Byzantine Constantinople. Artist's view of the Great Palace (bottom, in front of the Hippodrome), Hagia Sophia (on the right) and Hagia Eirene (further right)

10. Mosaic map of the Holy City of Jerusalem

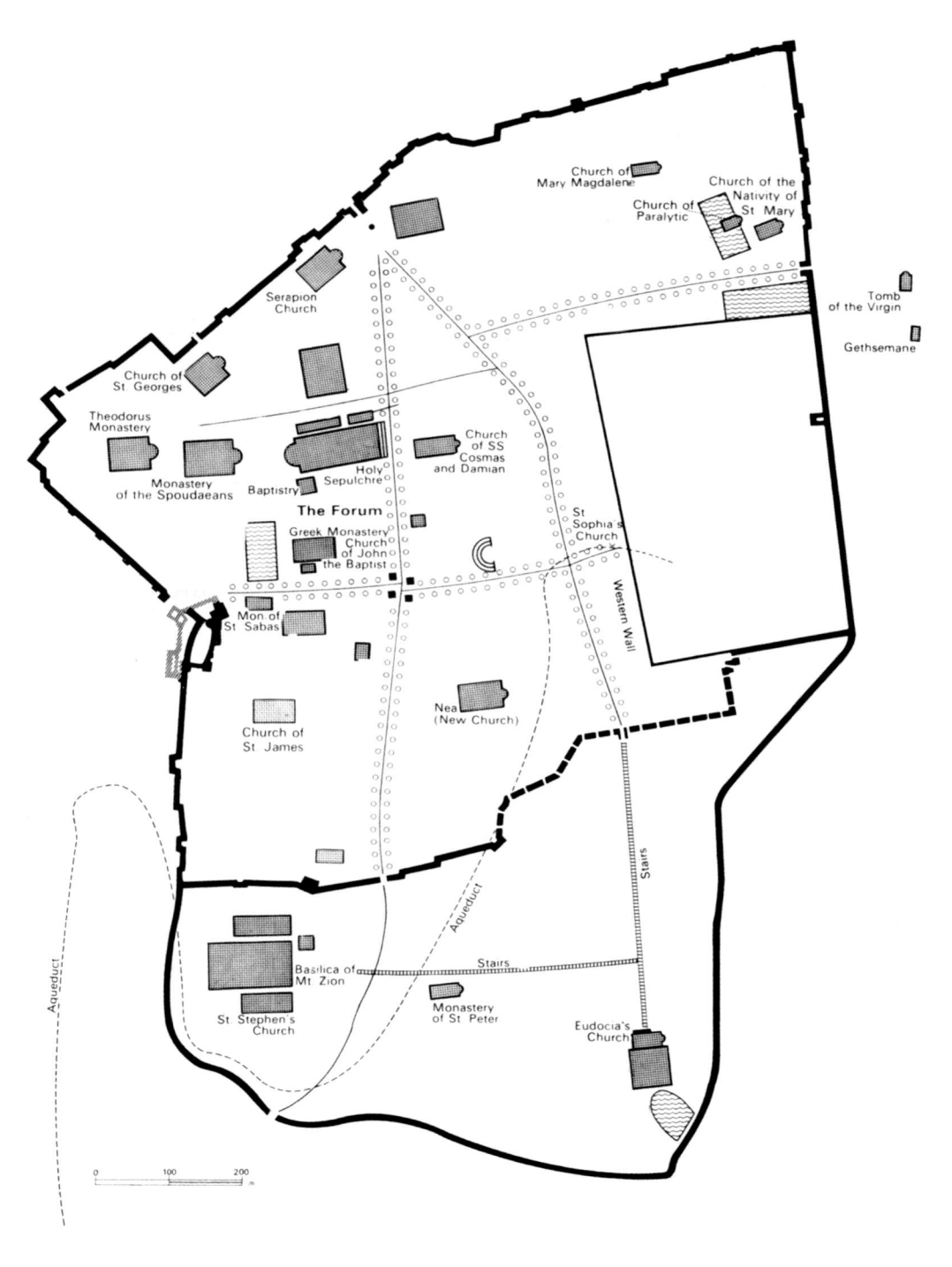

11. Map of Jerusalem. Location of churches and monasteries

In Greece, Christianity had a firm footing only in the cities of Corinth and Salonika. In Rome there were many Christians as early as AD 64 when Nero crucified St Peter and persecuted the Christians as alleged perpetrators of the disastrous fire in the city. At the church council meeting, a synod, held in Rome in 250–251, 60 bishops from Italy were present, an indication of the remarkable increase in the number of Christians. To handle the growth of the faithful the dioceses, under metropolitan authority, were organized with parishes and allowed to have their own churches.

West of Italy Christianity was established on the coast of Gaul and in the Rhone valley by the middle of the second century. By the time of the Council of Arles in 314 many bishoprics had been created and by 450 the Roman population in Gaul was largely Christian. The history of the Spanish church begins in the third century with Christian centres at Leon, Astorga, Merida and Saragossa. In North Africa Christian communities were to be found in Carthage, Mauretania and other places and the size of the Christian community can be gauged by the fact that by the time of a synod around 218–222 some 70 bishops could attend. The church architecture of North Africa was Eastern, quite possible via Egypt, rather than from Rome. Alexandria as a great Hellenistic city was the centre of Christianity in Egypt but Christians were present even in remote villages. By the middle of the fourth century there were nearly 100 bishoprics in existence, the Scriptures had been translated into Coptic, and by the sixth century Ethiopia (Abyssinia) was Christianized.

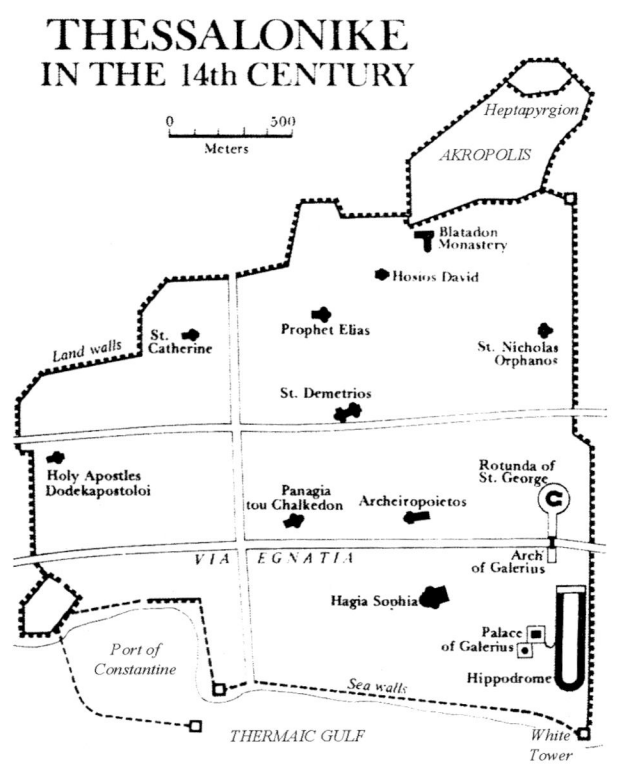

12. Map of Thessaloniki. Location of churches and monasteries

Even with all this growth in the first three centuries after the death of Christ, Christianity was still a minority religion in the Roman Empire. It stood out as being 'strange and unlawful', strange because of the religion's beliefs and practices were so different to the others and unlawful as Christians refused to venerate the emperor. Despite this characterization Christianity grew, perhaps, as people in the Roman Empire were looking for new religious forms for comfort in the so-called 'Age of Anxiety'. They saw Christianity as an eastern mystery religion that brought the initiated into close contact with the deity, was exclusive, promised great rewards and was thus highly attractive.

Christians in the Roman Empire enjoyed long periods of peace with freedom to assemble without subterfuge but still led a precarious life. Though most of the time they lived quietly there were periods of persecution which were not the result of any consistent or coherent state policy. Persecutions were sporadic, first under Nero in AD 64 that was limited to Rome and then under Emperor Domitian from 81 to 96. There were local persecutions during the reigns of Septimius Serverus (r. 193–211) and Maximinus

(r. 235–238) but under Decius (r. 248–251) there was a serious attempt against all religious believers throughout the Empire, not only Christians. Decius, to preserve his fragile regime and divine authority, ordered everyone to prove their loyalty to the state by sacrificing to the Roman gods or face death. Refusal of the Christians to acknowledge the state gods in the eyes of the authorities threatened the public order. Roman persecutions of Christians, however, remained occasional and politically motivated. There were further persecutions under Valerian (r. 253–260) and Diocletian (r. 284–305) who in his attempt to re-establish political order decreed that churches were to be razed to the ground, Christian scriptures to be destroyed by fire, and those who continued to profess Christianity to be deprived of their liberty. Although popularly believed that persecutions led to secret Christian burials in catacombs this belief has been demystified by scholars. The burial tombs in the catacombs of Rome are important for early Christian art as these contain the majority of examples from the first few centuries of the Christian era.

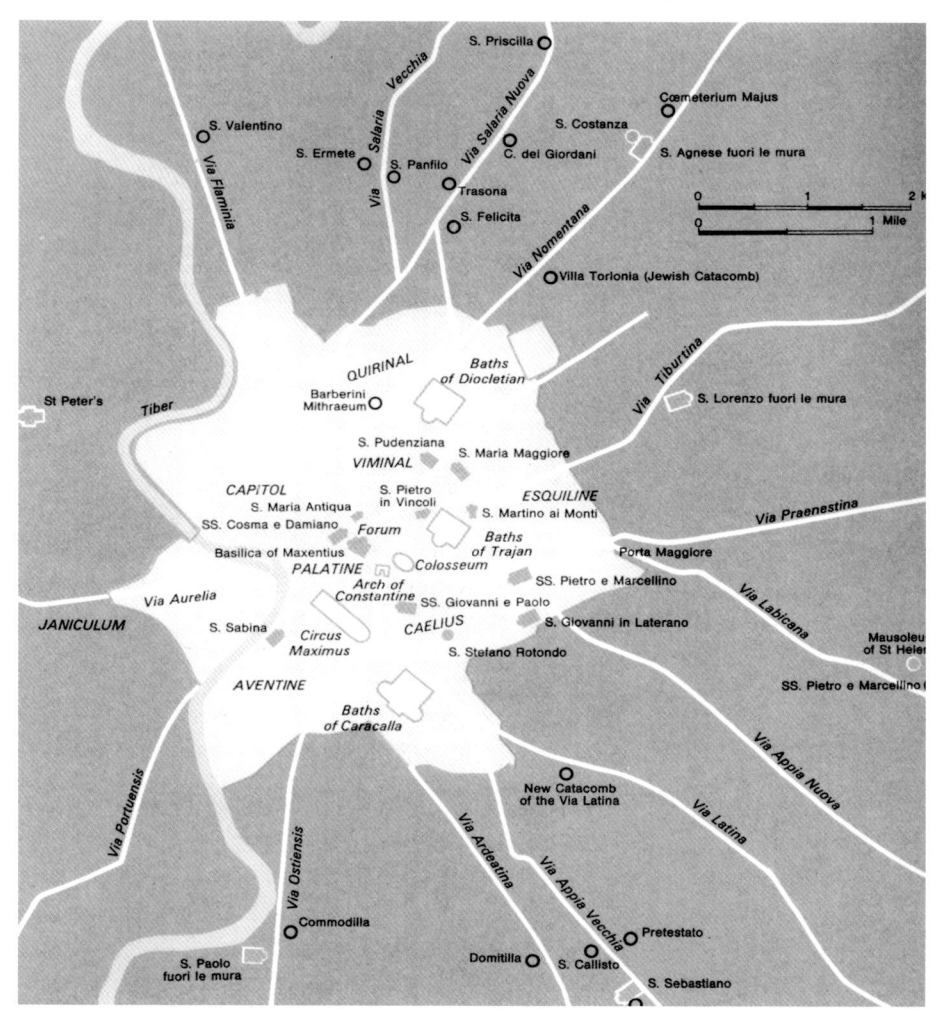

13. Map of Rome. Location of early Christian churches

Late Antiquity

The history of Late Antiquity, or Early Byzantine as the period is sometimes called, is linked to the rise and expansion of Christianity, which had a major impact on the Roman Empire. Besides the effect of Christianity the other influence on Late Antiquity was political. Emperor Diocletian considered the Roman Empire was too vast to be ruled by one man and so in AD293 he established a system of government in which power was divided among four individuals, known as the *tetrarchy* from the Greek 'leadership of four'. Under the system there were two emperors with the title *Augustus*, one for the West and one for the East, each with a subordinate or junior associate as future successors with the title of *Caesar*. In 312 Constantine as one of the Western *Augusti* became sole emperor in the West after the death in battle of the usurper Maxentius. In the following year Licinius defeated Maximin Daia to become sole emperor of the East.

14. Tetrarchy emperors in red porphyry stone. External corner, Treasury Building, St Mark's, Venice

Religious and political forces came together in 312 with the recognition of Christianity by the state. It all started, as is commonly understood, on the eve of the battle at the Milvian Bridge on 28 October. Constantine, according to his biographer Eusebius, 'about midday, when the sun was about to decline,

15. Battle of Milvian Bridge. Constantine and symbol of the cross

he saw with his own eyes the trophy of a cross of light in the heavens, above the sun, and bearing the inscription "In this sign, you shall conquer" (Εν Τούτω Νίκα).' Constantine had his soldiers place the sign on their shields and in the ensuing battle successfully defeated Maxentius. He attributed his victory to the use of the sign. There is no agreement on what the sign was but it was a Christian symbol, either the simple cross or the monogram-like cross *Chi Rho* (XP, the first two letters of the Greek spelling of the word Christ superimposed).

The following year, on 13 June 313, the co-emperors Constantine and Licinius met in Milan to discuss matters pertaining to the 'benefit and security of the state' following which they issued their 'Edict of Milan' also known as the Edict of Tolerance. The first action in the edict was to 'grant to Christians (*christianis*) and all others free authority to follow whatever religion anyone chooses … and everyone who bears a desire to observe the religion of the Christians may now finally and plainly do just that without annoyance or molestation'. The Edict went on to order the return to Christian corporations, that is, their churches (*ecclesiarum*), properties previously confiscated and the restoration of 'places at which they were formerly accustomed to assemble'. Despite their joint action relations between the two co-emperors deteriorated. In 324 Constantine defeated Licinius and went on to reunite the eastern and western halves of the Roman Empire. He declared himself the sole *Augustus* ruler. In the domain of Christian doctrine Constantine convoked a Council of all the bishops of the Empire at Nicaea in 325. He presided over

16. Mummy panel, Hawara

17. Funeral portrait, Egypt

deliberations to resolve doctrinal disputes that raged in Christendom. Constantine thus helped move Christianity from the fringe to the mainstream of Roman religions. With imperial recognition of the Christian Church bishops were accorded the status of senior officials. Like them, bishops wore the dress of the Roman upper classes and came to be preceded by candles and incense in official processions. In the catacombs of Rome, carved into the soft tufa rock, the earliest Christian images appear. Not surprisingly Christian wall paintings in the small chapels and tombs shared the pagan art style of the time but in content the subject matter consisted of meaningful spiritual images, one of the most popular being that of the 'Good Shepherd'.

18. Tomb of the Aurelii, Rome. Christ and apostles shown without halos at early stage of Christian art

19. Catacomb Coemeterium Majus, Rome. Mary and Christ Child with *Chi Rho* symbol (on the left)

20. Catacomb SS Pietro e Marcellino, Christ between SS Peter and Paul

21. Catacomb fresco of Christ

CHURCH AND STATE

22. Catacomb Commodila, Rome. Enthroned Virgin Mary and Christ Child flanked by the widow Turtura and SS Adauctus (left) and Felix (right)

23. Santa Maria Nova, Rome. Virgin Mary

24. Santa Maria Antiqua in Forum, Rome. Fresco remains of Virgin Mary and Christ Child

25. Santa Maria Antiqua in Forum, Rome. Crucifixion fresco

26. Santa Maria Domnica Apse, Rome. Mosaic with Virgin Mary and Christ Child

27. Good Shepherd statue, Rome. Lateran Museum

After the Edict of Milan was issued Christians were now free to worship in public. Up to this time Christians had assembled in private houses and in converted buildings. Now they could gather in large, purpose-built buildings – churches – without fear. Constantine began a programme of building Christian churches that was continued by his successors. Imperial resources from money to architects, masons and artists were made available to build magnificent churches in capitals and leading cities. Christianity became the sole and official religion of the Empire under the pious Emperor Theodosius I (r. 379–395) when he closed down the pagan temples and made the Christianity as practiced in Rome the state religion. From then on imperial patronage had profound consequences due to the influence exerted by the emperor on both church architecture and worship. The authority of the emperor on the Christian religion became all-encompassing, which is at odds with the modern idea in the West of separation of church and state.

With Christianity as the official religion of the Roman Empire, state and church became intertwined as never before. In 381, Theodosius called together bishops and leading theologians to meet as a Council in Constantinople to define orthodox ('right-thinking') Christian belief. Although Constantinople was the capital of the Eastern Roman Empire it absorbed its liturgy from Antioch primarily through the transfer of several bishops to the capital. Other centres of liturgical influence in the fourth century besides Antioch were Rome, Alexandria and Jerusalem. But Constantinople as the New Rome eventually became the centre of architectural and liturgical influence. The liturgical rite of the main church in

New Rome, the Great Church of the Holy Wisdom, gradually spread to become by the twelfth century virtually the only rite in what came to be known as the Eastern Orthodox churches. Theodosius I and his dynastic successors spent large sums building churches, including in places such as Milan and Ravenna, and adorning them on a lavish scale. Although these cities benefitted the most from imperial generosity, towns such as Thessaloniki, Ephesus, Alexandria and those in Syria and elsewhere in the Near East also gained.

28. Thessaloniki, early Christian cemetery. Tomb relocated to the Byzantine Museum, Thessaloniki

29. Thessaloniki, early Christian cemetery. *Chi Rho* symbol

30. Thessaloniki, early Christian cemetery. The cross as a dominant symbol in tomb iconography

31. Thessaloniki, early Christian cemetery. Ancient motifs as Christian symbols of paradise

While the Eastern Empire remained stable and provided a continuously safe environment for the building of churches the same cannot be said for the Western Empire which experienced periods of uncertainty. In 410 Rome was sacked by Alaric the Visigoth, and by the Vandals in 425 and 455. According to tradition Roman authorities pleaded with the Visigoth leader not to destroy the ancient city or murder its inhabitants. Alaric agreed and the gates of Rome were thrown open to him and his men spared the apostolic churches and allowed people to seek asylum in them. The Vandals in their second raid did, however, plunder the city and looted great amounts of treasure.

A new group of Goths entered imperial territory in 473. They were the Ostrogoths from across the Danube but they had good relations with Byzantine authorities. Emperor Zeno (r. 474–491) in fact adopted their leader Theodoric who spent a decade living in Constantinople. In the meantime, in 476, the last Western Emperor, Romulus Augustulus, was deposed by another Ostrogoth, Odoacre. The year 476 is thus considered by most scholars as the end of the Western Roman Empire. Due to the unsettled situation in the West Theodoric was sent to Italy in 488. After a four year struggle he managed to gain the upper hand and brought peace, order, and security to Italy – something unknown for decades. He engaged in an extensive public works programme in Ravenna, Rome and elsewhere. The Ostrogoths were Christian converts and showed respect for the city's churches and shrines. With the Roman secular administration dismantled the Bishop of Rome assumed a central role in the preservation of *Romanitas*. Revenues from the church's holdings in North Africa enabled it to continue to build new churches and to convert 'house churches' into large churches. In 590 Gregory I (the Great) became pope and within five years he reorganized the western liturgy into the so-called *Gregorian Sacramentary* and introduced singing that is known today as the 'Gregorian Chant'.

In the Eastern Roman Empire the sixth century was a golden age in Byzantine history. It was the 'Age of Justinian' that included the reigns of Justin I (518–527), Justinian I (527–565) and Justin II (565–578). Justinian I ruled for 38 years and his reign is regarded as the most illustrious of any Byzantine Emperor. As Emperor of the Eastern Empire he conquered Italy to reunite the western part to achieve his vision of a unified Roman Empire. He extended the areas of the Empire to North Africa and Spain turning the Mediterranean into an imperial lake. He was served by very able and loyal generals and ministers and advised by a remarkable wife, Theodora. His very capable general, Belisarius, between 532 and 534, destroyed the Vandal kingdom that had lasted for a number of decades.

Justinian I, seeing himself as a new Constantine, initiated a vast building programme, including many churches, that are described by Procopius of Caesarea (*c.*500–*c.*565) in his book *Edifices* ('Peri Ktismaton')

32. Emperor Justinian I (r. 527–565)

written between 553 and 555. Although the book was more a flattering work on the building programme of the emperor it is no exaggeration that the 'Age of Justinian' still represents the high point of Early Byzantine church architecture. When most of Constantinople was destroyed by fire during the Nika Rebellion (from shouts of 'Victory' by rebels) in 532 Justinian himself was nearly toppled. He, however, seized the opportunity and rebuilt the city with astonishing speed that included rebuilding churches and adding new ones, 33 according to Procopius. Besides the riots the other dramatic event of Justinian's reign was the plague that raged in Constantinople from 542 to 544, which it is estimated killed half the city's population. Justinian himself was infected and was gravely ill for some time but he was fortunate to be one of the few to recover. His reign also saw a concerted attack against the remnants of Hellenistic paganism in the empire. The University of Athens was closed in 529 and exclusively Christian learning and culture was promoted.

33. Empress Theodora, wife of Justinian I

Monasticism

A major feature of the Byzantine world was monasticism. In Egypt at the beginning of the fourth century St Anthony (250–357) became the inspiration for embracing an ascetic life. As not many could follow his difficult way St Pachomius (c.292–346) founded the first community based arrangement, known as cenobitic monasticism, in which monks lived in religious hamlets, the first monasteries proper. Each of these monasteries had a church, a refectory, huts and an enclosing wall. In their hamlets the Pachomian monks arranged separate huts in parallel lines separated by a space. This arrangement became known as the *lávra*, the ancient Greek word for lane or passage. St Basil of Caesarea (330–379) was the great monastic founder in the East and prominent as one of the greatest church fathers. He wrote the rules for a community monastic life that became the standard in the Byzantine and later Eastern Orthodox world. After the expansion of hundreds of monasteries in the late fourth and during the fifth centuries in the Nile Valley in Egypt monasticism spreading to Palestine, Syria and Anatolia. By the sixth century the idea of religious communities living in monasteries was widespread with hundreds of monasteries being founded in Asia Minor and Greece. In Constantinople alone there were about 100 monasteries.

Monasticism was about individuals who sought withdrawal from the urges of worldly society to lead a truly religious life. Underlying monasticism was the desire of the monk (*mónos* or alone in Greek) for union of mind and heart with God through prayer. To achieve this aim a monk sought separation from the attractions and distractions of the world. Spiritual solitude could be achieved in one of three ways – the physical solitude of a hermit ('one who dwells in the desert'), isolation of an anchorite ('one who retires or withdraws'), or the communal life of a monastery which most preferred known as the cenobitic (*koinóvion*) way of life. Justinian encouraged monastic life and founded the famous Monastery of St Catherine in the Sinai desert, built between 550 and 565. An example of the new emphasis on Christian values was the book *Ladder of Divine Ascent* written in the seventh century by John Klimakos, a monk at the monastery of St Catherine at Sinai. This work became one of the most widely read books of the time and not only among monks. The *Ladder*, with Jacob's Ladder as an analogy, describes how to raise one's body and soul to God through acquiring ascetic virtues.

In Byzantine monasticism an abbot, called *igoúmenos* or *kathegoúmenos*, headed each monastery. A foundation charter (*typikón*) laid down the procedures for his election which was normally confirmed by the local bishop. Monks in the monasteries lived under fixed practices and the rule of a superior, the *igoúmenos,* and centred their lives on day and night services of the Divine Liturgy. Time was also set aside for instruction and private devotion. Each monk, in addition, shared in the monastery's daily tasks of administration and special duties. These obligations included care of the poor or supervision of medical services. Monasticism in the Eastern Church began and remains today a lay movement. In the West St Benedict of Nursia (480–547) wrote the rules for Latin-speaking monasteries.

The sixth-century monastery of St Catherine in the Sinai is of great significance as it is one of the oldest and is well preserved. Mount Athos, however, was and remains today the major monastic centre of Eastern Orthodoxy. In 885 Emperor Basil I (r. 867–886) issued a chrysobull that proclaimed the peninsula in northeast Greece as a Holy Mountain and a place for monks. The monk Athanasios arrived on Mount Athos in 958 and built the first monastery of Megistis Lavra. Over the following centuries many other monasteries were built and 20 still function today. Many monasteries were funded by emperors and wealthy individuals. Megistis Lavra was built in a fortified manner with monks' cells and other functions forming a perimeter defensive like wall.

34. Heavenly ladder of St John Klimakos

35. St Athanasios. Founder of Megistis Lavra Monastery, Mount Athos

36. Emperor Nikephoros Phokas (r. 963–969). Patron of Megistis Lavra Monastery, Mount Athos (Painting by Theophanes)

37. Emperor John Tzimiskes (r. 969– 976). With a model of the *katholikon* (main church) of the Megistis Lavra Monastery (Painting by Theophanes)

38. Monastery of Megistis Lavra, Mount Athos. Imaginary representation of the walled complex with the *katholikon* in the middle (Watercolour)

39. Monastery of Panteleimon, Mount Athos. *Katholikon* and two other churches in the central courtyard (Lithograph)

40. Monastery of Stavronikita, Mount Athos. Religious procession progressing out of the gate (Copperplate)

41. Monastery of St Catherine, Sinai. Walled complex with monks' cells forming the rear wall

42. Monastery of Dionysiou, Mount Athos. Dramatic cliff location

43. Monastery of Docheiariou, Mount Athos. *Katholikon* in the centre of the enclosed courtyard

44. Monastery of Kastamonitou, Mount Athos. *Katholikon* dominates the courtyard

45. Monastery of Koutloumoussi, Mount Athos. Central location of the *katholikon*

46. Monastery of Panteleimon, Mount Athos. Central complex and surrounding supporting buildings

47. Monastery of Xeropotamou, Mount Athos. *Katholikon* in a clear courtyard

48. Monastery of Zografou, Mount Athos. View from the west (Rendering)

49. Monastery of Megistis Lavra, Mount Athos. Refectory wall paintings

In the centre of the monastic complex was a central open courtyard dominated by the main church of the monastery, known as the *katholikon*. This arrangement became the model for the other monasteries on Mount Athos and elsewhere in the Byzantine world. The architecture and religious art of the monasteries is one of the greatest contributions to the Byzantine world.

Iconoclasm

The Late Antiquity or Early Byzantine period, no matter how it is labelled, came to an end during the seventh and eight centuries as Byzantium faced triple threats – Arabs in Anatolia, Avars and Slavs in the Balkans, and Lombards in Italy. The loss of a large amount of territory was a traumatic turning point in Byzantine history. During the first two decades of the seventh century the whole Near East of Mesopotamia, Syria, Palestine and Egypt fell to the Persians. Soon afterwards Muslim Arabs conquered all these areas, destroyed the Persian kingdom and captured Jerusalem. The Byzantine Empire had already faced crises further west when the Avars and Slavs invaded the Balkans in 586 and then Greece after 602. Constantinople itself was attacked by the Avars in 626 and by the Arabs between 673 and 678 and again between 705 and 707. Ravenna fell to the Lombards in 751, essentially reducing Byzantine presence and influence in Italy.

By the early eighth century the once mighty Byzantine Empire was reduced in size to the eastern part of Greece and western Asia Minor. In addition, a decline in population and outbreaks of plague transformed life. Provincial cities either shrank or disappeared leaving the capital Constantinople, the 'Queen of Cities', with its impregnable walls as the centre of cultural life. In these perilous times a new dynasty of emperors, the Isaurians ('Syrians'), from 717 to 802, achieved some military successes, brought about economic stability, and completed the reforms of the administrative structure of the empire. A new municipal organization was introduced to replace the previous Hellenic political and financial organizations. Under the new arrangement inhabitants lost their distinctive characteristics as they where no longer members of a *polis*, such as Athens, or leagues like Achaia. This was the end of the classical city. Greek was officially declared the language of the administration and everyone regarded themselves as a Romaic Greek.

50. Iconoclasts obliterating an image of Christ with whitewash

51. Iconoclastic mosaic cross. Apse of Hagia Eirene, Constantinople

The rule of the new Isaurian dynasty, however, will be forever associated with religious turmoil, *iconoclasm* (the ban on the making and worship of icons) that shook the Byzantine Empire between 726 and 843. The Iconoclastic ('image breaking' but in Greek texts *eikonomachia* literarily 'icon battle') movement began simply as a Christian reaction to their losses to Muslim 'non-believers'. The belief grew that Christians had sinned by falling into idolatry that was expressly condemned by the Second Commandment. They further became convinced that the icons were idols and because they venerated them God visited the people with war, pestilence, famine and death. When in 726 the pious Emperor Leo III (r. 717–741) initiated the ban it seemed to be validated by his military successes, and those of his more radical son Constantine V (r. 741–775) against the Arabs and Bulgars. Constantine instituted a reign of terror that forced monks, the supporters of icons, in the capital to flee. Those that did not escape were imprisoned, some tortured, and others executed. Also, the volcanic eruption on the island of Thera (Santorini) produced tidal waves and spread ash over much of the empire, leading pious people to believe them as punishment from God. When Constantine died he was succeeded by his son Leo IV (r. 775–780) who increased the persecutions of the believers in icons and went as far as to confiscate the treasure of churches and monasteries.

Reverence of icons was prohibited and the only decoration allowed was to be the cross. In some churches and palaces flora and fauna scenes were the only decoration allowed. The Council of Hieria, in 754, declared iconoclasm as Eastern Orthodox doctrine. Strong opposition to the banning of icons developed, with the supporters known as *iconodules*. John of Damascus, one of the iconodules, wrote vast theological treatises defending icons as inspiring the memory of Christ, the Theotokos (Mother of God), or the saints. When Emperor Leo IV died in 780 his wife Eirene, a remarkable and capable woman, became regent for their nine-year-old son, Constantine VI (r. 780–797). He grew up to become a weak ruler, extremely cruel, and unpopular and was apparently assassinated in 797. Eirene was then crowned Empress of the Byzantine Empire and ruled until 802 as *Basileus*, the only woman in Byzantine and Roman history to do so. She, as an iconodule, was instrumental in convening the Seventh Ecumenical Council at Nicaea in 787 that restored the veneration of icons and reversed iconoclasm. But after her death a second period of iconoclasm was introduced in 815

52. Emperor Leo V (r. 813–820) crowned by Michael I Rangabe (r. 811–813)

53. Emperor Theophilos (r. 829–842) flanked by two bodyguards and his court

by Leo V the Armenian (r. 813–820) and continued by his successors, such as Theophilos. The opposition to icons ended in 843 when the 'Triumph of Orthodoxy' was declared under the reign of Regent Theodora and her infant son Michael III (r. 842–867). Iconoclasm was condemned as heresy. A thanksgiving ceremony celebrating the return of sacred images to the churches and monasteries of Byzantium was held on Sunday, 11 March 845, a ceremony continued to be celebrated today in the Eastern Orthodox Church.

The phenomenon of iconoclasm had an impact not only on religious art and theology but on the state's political structure as well. According to Byzantine tradition the emperor was the chosen of God and both the secular and religious leader of his subjects. When opponents of iconoclasm regarded the emperors Leo III and those that followed as heretics, imperial authority in spiritual matters was questioned. Iconoclasm and its aftermath further differentiated the East as Greek in culture and Orthodox in religion and the West as Latin and Catholic. In the year 800 the contrasts were apparent. In the East Empress Eirene ruled the Eastern Roman or Byzantine Empire from her capital in Constantinople. In the West Pope Leo III, displaying the power of the papacy, crowned Charlemagne emperor on Christmas Day in Rome's Basilica of St Peter's. The coronation, however, was furiously contested by the Byzantines. In the Islamic world, the Muslim empire, called the *caliphate*, stretched from central Asia to Spain. A great caliph of the Abbasid dynasty ruled from the empire's newly founded capital of Baghdad.

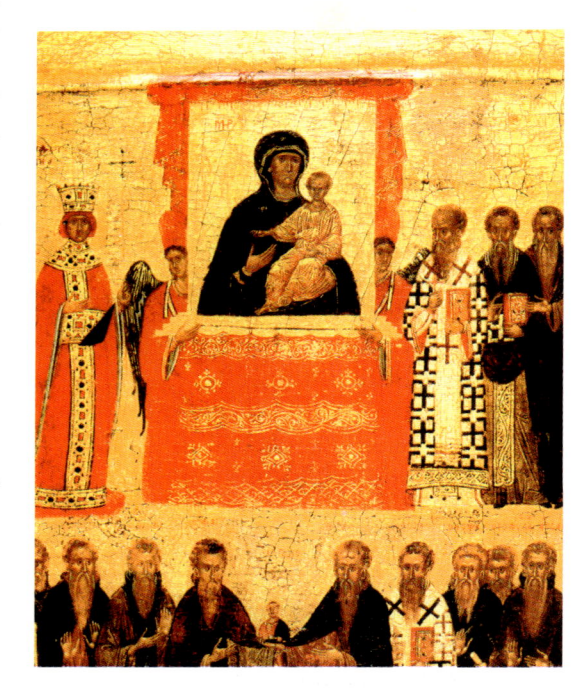

54. Triumph of Orthodoxy Icon. Empress Theodora and son Michael III (r. 842–867) (left) with Patriarch Methodios (right) officiating and in attendance iconodules (below)

Restoration

When Basil I (r. 867–886) came to the throne he established the so-called Macedonian dynasty that included Emperors Leo VI, Alexander, Michael V and Constantine IX, and that lasted until 1056 when Empress Theodora, the last member of the dynasty, died. During the first period up to 1025 there were brilliant military successes with the territories of Northern Syria and Eastern Anatolia regained and the empire extended as far as the Danube in the west.

55. Emperor Leo VI (r. 886–912) prostrating himself before Christ

56. Emperor Alexander (r. 912–913)

Italy and Sicily were conquered in 875 and remained in Byzantine hands until 902. During the rule of the Macedonian dynasty the Byzantine Empire expanded, population rose, the economy grew, and it culturally reached great heights with the preservation and copying of ancient texts. Many new churches were built and graced internally by brilliant mosaics. Other prominent Macedonian emperors were Leo VI, named the Wise (r. 886–912), who continued the cultural revival begun by Basil I. Leo's brother and successor Alexander (r. 912–913) is remembered as the first Byzantine emperor to use the title *aftokrátor* ('autocrat'). Younger son of Leo VI, scholar-emperor Constantine VII Porphyrogennetos (r. 945–959), in his handbook *On the Administration of the Empire,* presented the Byzantine Empire as the supreme power of the Mediterranean and beyond with Constantinople at its hub. Empress Zoe Porphyrogenita ('born into the purple') was noted, among other things, for her obsession to continue the Macedonian dynasty.

The greatest emperor during the Macedonian period was Basil II (r. 976–1025) who further extended Byzantine territory by annexing the Kingdom of Bulgaria. It was at this time that Russia converted to Orthodox Christianity following the Bulgarians and Serbs who had converted in the ninth century. The Byzantine Empire became the richest and most sophisticated state in the West.

57. Emperor Michael IV Paphlagon (r. 1034–1041) after his defeat of the Bulgars

58. Emperor Constantine IX Monomachos (r. 1042–1055) in full imperial regalia holding a bag of gold coins to place on the Holy Table of Hagia Sophia during Holy Week. The halo is not meant to indicate sanctity but supreme importance

59. Crown of Emperor Constantine Monomachos depicting Theodora, Constantine and other imperial rulers

In Greece a period of relative security and prosperity for the next three centuries saw the founding of an increasing number of churches. Among the noted actions of Macedonian emperors was the restoration of the Church of the Holy Sepulcher in Jerusalem by Constantine IX Monomachos (r. 1042–1055) who was also a patron of the arts and literature. Following the 'Triumph of Orthodoxy' figurative art returned and became the essential identifying feature of Byzantium church decoration during Macedonian period.

After the death of Basil II the Empire plunged into crisis under his inept successors. The Empire gradually disintegrated beginning with the conquest of Sicily by the Normans in 1061. Ten years later the Normans took Bari and Byzantium lost southern Italy. In the same year, 1071, the Seljuk Turks defeated Romanos IV Diogenis at Manzikert that began Turkish domination of all of Anatolia within ten years. The West responded by sending out the First Crusade in 1096, recapturing Jerusalem and establishing a Latin Kingdom there in 1099. Over the next century the Normans attacked Thessaloniki, the Crusaders lost Jerusalem, and there were more Crusades.

60. Empress Zoe (1042) 'The Most Pious Augusta' and written on the scroll are the words 'Descendant of Constantine'. The halo is not meant to indicate sanctity but supreme importance

61. Emperor Nikephoros Botaneiates (r. 1078–1081)

The crises led to the ascension of a new Byzantine dynasty, the Komnenoi that lasted until 1185. They were a military and wealthy family from Adrianopolis. Isaac I was the first Komnenian emperor but after a turbulent period ruled by rebellious usurpers, such as Nikephoros, it was Alexis I Komnenos (r. 1081–1118) who was responsible for beginning a period of cultural and artistic creativity. The Komnenoi emperors after him oversaw a dazzling recovery in prosperity and the building of churches. John II, who succeeded his father Alexios I, was noted for his pious nature and his integrity, both rare qualities in Byzantine emperors. There was a notable increase in the growth and expansion of cities in Greece such as Athens and Corinth but especially Thessaloniki, the second city of the Empire, which hosted a famous summer fair that attracted traders from far afield. The Komnenoi sponsored the revival of classical arts and letters and ensured that books from the imperial libraries were copied. At the same time

62. Emperor Nikephoros Botaneiates (r. 1078–1081), whose name was added and that of Michael VII Doukas (r. 1071–1078) erased, between John Chrysostom (left) and Archangel Michael (right)

63. Emporor Alexios I Komnenos (r. 1081–1118) blessed by Christ

64. Emperors John II (below left) and Alexios I (below right) Komnenoi (r. 1081–1143) crowned by Christ flanked by the figures of Justice (left) and Charity (right)

65. Empress Eirene, wife of Alexios I Komnenos

66. Emperor Alexios II Komnenos (r. 1180–1183)

books on the lives of various saints were widely circulated. The style of church art of Constantinople spread to the provinces and Byzantine religious art reached the West through Norman Sicily and Venice. During the Komnenian period there was contact with the newly created Crusader states and many Italian traders, particularly Italian, became resident in Constantinople. This helped the spread of Byzantine art, literature and technology throughout the West. Unfortunately the restoration of the Byzantine Empire under the Komnenoi was undermined by their weak successors, the Angeloi emperors (1185–1204).

Latin Interlude

In 1204 the active political antagonism between East and West reached a high point when the Latin soldiers of the Fourth Crusade, on their way to Jerusalem, diverted and unforgivably sacked the eastern capital of Constantinople. Christian attacked Christian that poisoned relations and left a legacy of hate and distrust between Greek Orthodox and Latin Christians. Intrigue, treachery and greed are some of the expressions that were used to describe the Crusaders' unprovoked attack. The unexpected assault was on the pretext of restoring order to the Byzantine throne that left Greek and Muslim inhabitants living in the capital city aghast at the Crusaders' orgy of looting and massacres. Constantinople lost many of its treasures from its palaces and churches, many going to St Marks's in Venice, Sainte-Chapelle in Paris and other places in Europe. The Greek historian Niketas Choniates (*c*.1155–1215/16) in his book *History* vividly describes the destruction of 'sacred wealth and of so great and infinite splendor' and the stealing of precious ornaments and relics that took place. He was either an eyewitness of events or of which he heard firsthand.

After the capture of Constantinople by the Crusaders the territory of the Empire became a patchwork of Latin and Greek states. Byzantium was reduced to two small entities, the Trebizond Roman State on the Black Sea and the Nicaean Principality. Leaders of the French and Venetian crusaders partitioned the entire remaining territory of *Romanía* into six domains. One of the six was named the Latin Empire of Constantinople. It was headed by a new Latin emperor, Baldwin, whose political power was confined to the city of Constantinople, its hinterland and Thrace. Another one of the domains, the former Roman province of Achaia (Morea), the Peloponnese, was given to the Franks and designated a principality that lasted from 1204 until 1432. In the southwest Peloponnese the introduction of the feudal system by the Franks brought about a fragmentation of governmental authority. The new rulers built many fortifications with settlements growing beneath or around the castles. Under the deed of partition Venice received the Ionian Islands, Crete and many islands in the Aegean. The Latin occupation lasted until 1261 when the Byzantines managed to take back the city of Constantinople.

67. Latin Emperor Baldwin. Decorative letter B (r. 1204–1205)

68. Portraits of a Palaiologos prince and princess

69. John Katakouzenos as emperor (left) and monk (right) after his abdication (r. 1347–1354)

Resurgence

In 1261 Michael VIII Palaiologos (r. 1259–1282) retook Constantinople and restored Byzantium as a regional power. He reinstated many monasteries and undertook the construction of public works such as markets, baths, hospitals and streets, and strengthened the defence wall of the capital. Despite the chaos in the Empire – wars, religious conflicts, social unrest, numerous earthquakes, and bubonic plague epidemics – under the Palaiologos dynasty there was a resurgence in arts and letters, the revival of the classical philosophy of Plato, a new approach taken to the classical past, and the writing of histories in the manner of the ancient historian, Thucydides. Patrons of the arts included the rich Byzantine statesman Theodore Metochites (1280–1332) who remains famous for his restoration and decoration of the monastery church of St Saviour in Constantinople. Byzantines began to arrive in the West, scholars made Latin translations of Greek texts they brought with them, and Byzantine painters and architects spread their styles facilitating the Renaissance in the West. Mixed populations of Orthodox and Catholics during the Palaiologos period brought a Western influence into painting with the emphasis on greater naturalism. Amongst icon painters the most prolific was Angelos Akotantos (fl. *c.*1425–50) and Andreas Ritzos (1421–1492) of Crete. The adoption of Western elements was so extensive that the noted Byzantine art historian, Kurt Weitzmann, was led to the conclusion that the impressive number of icons from the thirteenth century at St Catherine's in the Sinai were painted by Crusader artists. The Palaiologos dynasty, the longest lasting in Byzantine history, endured until the fifteenth century when Constantinople fell to the Ottoman Turks in 1453 after a siege by Mehemet II the Conqueror. Gunpowder and artillery made the once impregnable walls of the city obsolete. Large number of Greek scholars and artists fled Constantinople and sought refuge in Italy, accelerating the Renaissance.

70. Theodore Metochites holding a model of St Saviour in Chora. Patron of the interior mosaic and mural decoration (1316–1321)

71. Chief of the army, Theodore Komnenos Doukas and wife Evdokia

Church History

Eusebius, Bishop of Caesarea (c.AD263–339), is regarded as the Father of Church History. He was a prolific author including the monumental work partially based on earlier sources, *Ecclesiastical History*, penned sometime between 313 and 339. His account begins with the period of the apostles and includes the reigns of Roman Emperors, bishops and other church teachers, the relations with the Jews and portrayals of Christian martyrs. He is also the author of the *Life of Constantine*, which is more a flattering celebration of the emperor's life than a level report.

During the second and third centuries there were a number of competing Christian sects attempting to appeal to people who lived in a world that had old, deep pagan beliefs. There were, for example, the followers of Marcion whose theology was based on differentiating the God of the New Testament and thus Christ from the God of the Old Testament. Then there were the Gnostics who believed Jesus of Nazareth was a supreme being who became human to bring 'knowledge' for salvation from the material world. The so-called Apologists argued for certain doctrines mostly to differentiate Christianity from Judaism or to identify similarities with classical culture. These descriptions are extremely simplified and in no way capture the teaching of each sect.

Official Christian church doctrine began to emerge when certain bishops took the lead to fix rules and establish some religious discipline. The bishop of Lyon, Irenaeus, advocated the idea that bishops descended from the apostles and retained the authority that Christ had assigned to them. In his *Against Heresies* (c.180) he wrote about the need for a definitive canon of scripture. As a result Christianity developed a recognized body of authoritative religious texts that was not something any

72. Evangelist Matthew

73. Evangelist Mark

74. Evangelist Luke

75. Evangelist John

pagan cult in the Roman Empire had. Nor did any have an advanced administrative system such as that had by the Christians. By the year 250 the apostolic churches of Rome, Alexandria and Antioch were recognized as the supreme centres of Christian doctrine. In 367 Athanasius (c.293/98–373), Bishop of Alexandria, declared which 27 Christian books were to make up the Book of Gospels or New Testament. Only the Gospel accounts attributed to the evangelists ('bearers of good news') Matthew, Mark, Luke and John were included. From then on until the present day his list of books was to remain as a 'closed canon' of the Christian church everywhere. In later art images each evangelist was by identified by a winged symbol but at first they were seen as scholars who were held in high esteem in the classical world.

Despite Constantine's efforts at Nicaea religious controversy still persisted after his death. First his three sons, who reigned in succession from 337 until 361, professed Arianism, a belief that Christ was created by God the Father and thus inferior to him. Then Constantine's nephew, Julian 'the Apostate' (r. 361–363) attempted to restore the pagan gods for the last time in Roman history. During those post-Constantinian decades controversy between different Christian sects led each to accuse the other of 'heresy'. This did not end even when Theodosius I (r. 379–395) declared Christianity the official religion of the Roman Empire. In the next century great debates raged between Monophysites, Chalcedonians and Nestorians regarding the two natures of the person of Christ, human and divine. Points were reached when one group would declare their view the right one, or orthodox, and label their rivals as heretics – those holding an unorthodox religious view.

Following the example set by Constantine many emperors after him intervened in doctrinal issues by holding Ecumenical Councils, conferences of the bishops of the whole Christian Church. The deliberations and decisions of the Ecumenical Councils are another source of church history besides that derived from Eusebius. The word Ecumenical derives from the Greek *oikouméne* meaning 'inhabited world'. Between the fourth and eighth centuries a total of seven Ecumenical Councils were convened to discuss and settle matters of Church doctrine and practice in an attempt to reach consensus and establish a unified state church of the Roman Empire. Certain doctrinal decisions are particularly relevant to understanding the spiritual art of Byzantium that will be described in a later chapter. Emperor Constantine I convened the First Council in 325 that was held in Nicaea in the church of Hagia Eirene. Among the significant decisions made by the Council was the adoption of the original Nicene Creed; granting Constantinople precedence over all other churches except Rome; and elevating the rank of the bishop of New Rome to archbishop. The Nicene Creed was modified and reaffirmed by the Second Council held

76. First Ecumenical Council. Emperor Constantine (in red) presiding, an open book of Gospels in the centre and a Holy Table with ciborium at the top (Painting by Michael Damaskinos)

in Constantinople. It was convened by Emperor Theodosius I in 381 and also held in the church of Hagia Eirene. At this Council it was determined that Jesus Christ was equal to God the Father and co-eternal. Theodosius as an unwavering Christian during his reign issued a total of eighteen edicts. One squashed what he regarded as breakaway religious sects, another banned all pagan worship and practices, and yet another allowed pagan temples to be destroyed or converted into churches. At the Third Council held in Ephesus and called by Emperor Theodosius II (r. 408–450) in 431, Mary, mother of Jesus, was proclaimed the *Theotokos* (in Greek 'God-Bearer' but more usually translated as 'Mother of God'). In 451 Emperor Marcian convened the Fourth Ecumenical Council which was held in the church of St Efimia in Chalcedon. This Council declared that Christ had two natures, human and divine, which existed in one person, Jesus, without being blurred. In addition the Council established Constantinople as a patriarchate with jurisdiction over Asia Minor. The Fifth Council was called by Justinian and held in Constantinople in 553. At the Sixth Council, held in 680–681 and convened by Constantine IV, it was affirmed that Christ had both human and divine wills. The Seventh Council, held in 787 at Nicaea, restored the veneration of icons under the wishes of the Empress Eirene and repudiated iconoclasm. Icons had been condemned at the Council of Hieria summoned by the strongly iconoclastic Emperor Constantine V in 754 but the Eastern Orthodox and Roman Catholic Churches later rejected the council as ecumenical.

77. Second Ecumenical Council, Constantinople. Emperor Theodosius I, church elders, enthroned book of the evangelists

78. Seventh Ecumenical Council, Nicaea

Parallel with the Ecumenical Councils were the writings of the church thinkers, the 'church fathers', as they were called who were highly influential in their day and continued to be so over the centuries. Among the most influential Greek church fathers were Origen of Caesarea, St Gregory of Nyssa, St Gregory of Nazianzus, St Basil, and St John Chrysostom. Origen (184/5–253/4) brought Christian theology to new heights and was the first to seriously provide an explanation of the Trinity. St Gregory of Nyssa (c.335–after 394), who was also bishop of Nyssa, made a major contribution to the doctrine of the Trinity and his spiritual theology on the infinity of God laid the foundation for future theologians. St Gregory of Nazianzus (c.329–389/90) also made a significant impact on Trinitarian theology and was noted as one of the great orators of his time. St Basil of Caesarea, also known as

St Basil the Great (330–379), was Bishop of Caearea, brother of Gregory of Nyssa and a close friend of Gregory of Nazianzus. St Basil was a well regarded theologian, a famous preacher, who in addition wrote the guidelines for monastic life that centred on community life, liturgical prayers and manual labour. During his time there many liturgical prayers which he wrote down so they could be remembered. One of the two Divine Liturgies of the Eastern Orthodox Church used today bears his name. St John Chrysostom (*c*.349–407) was given the name Chrysostom from the Greek *chrysóstomos* meaning 'golden mouth' because of his eloquence in preaching and public speaking. Not only was he Archbishop of Constantinople but his sermons were so famous they were written down, and his writings had long-lasting influence. His lasting legacy, however, was his revision of the prayers of the Divine Liturgy so that to this day the typical celebration of the Divine Liturgy in the Eastern Orthodox Churches is that of St John Chrysostom.

79. St John Chrysostom

80. King William crowned by Christ

81. King William II offering a model of the cathedral to the Theotokos

Across the Byzantine Empire the Orthodox Christian faith united people of different cultures, ethnicity or languages. Christianity was a shared identity and the centre of Byzantine life apparent from the large number of churches that still exist and the volumes of ecclesiastical texts produced. In Byzantine churches architecture, art and liturgy came together to celebrate the divine in very symbolic ways that took separate paths from those in the West. A rare example of East-West convergence occurred in Sicily in the twelfth century. The Norman King of Sicily, William II (r. 1166–1189), built the cathedral of Monreale (1172–1176) which still today remains as an architectural masterpiece filled with golden style Byzantine mosaics (Figures 80–88). Depicted on the vast area of the interior walls of the cathedral, all in mosaics, is the history of the world according to the Bible, from Creation to the Acts of the Apostles. Ecclesiastical, theological and political conflicts and disputes between East and West continued though until relations finally broke down in 1054. The two formally split in what is called the Great Schism dividing the state church of the Roman Empire into a Greek eastern part, the eastern Orthodox Church, and a Latin western part, the Roman Catholic Church, which continue as such until the present day.

82. Creation of light

83. Separation of the waters

84. Creation of dry land

85. Creation of the stars

86. Creation of the fish and birds

87. Creation of the animals and humankind

88. The Creator rests

Chapter Two

SACRED ARCHITECTURE

In the first three centuries before Emperor Constantine issued the Edict of Tolerance in AD313, which recognized their religion, the Christian faithful assembled in private houses. When houses grew too small Christians converted larger buildings such as tenements and warehouses to meet in. Knowledge of these early places of Christian worship is scarce due to their destruction but it is accepted they had no fixed architectural form. In the fourth century Constantine began the process of constructing brand new buildings, churches to provide an architectural setting for the liturgy, the celebration of the Eucharist. The sacred architecture to be described here is that of the congregational church and does not include accounts of the separate buildings for baptisms, the baptisteries, or the *martyria*, used for burials of saints and martyrs, although these will be mentioned.

Christian religion differed drastically from others in the Roman Empire in not having bloody sacrifices, cult images of a god or goddess, or buildings sanctified by the presence of a divinity. Instead in the first century when Christians assembled they carried out the ritual of the *agápe* meal, a ceremony that could not be more different than in any other religion. The meeting would take place after an evening meal in the dining room, or *triclinium*, of a private house which usually could accommodate only about a dozen persons. The *Acts* (II, 46) tell of the first Christians 'breaking bread' in private houses and there is a record of St Paul sending greetings to prominent believers, such as Aquila and Prisca, assembled in 'the church which is their house' (*Romans*, XVI, 5). As the size of the groups of believers increased the meetings would be held in the courtyard. In the second century when the number grew even larger, it became necessary to meet in a bigger space. Christian communities then began to convert entire houses for their meeting place. These are known as house-churches or *domus ecclesiae* (οἶκος εκκλησίας). The term *ecclesia* (εκκλησία) in Greek means 'assembly' that came to mean the Christian assembly. Later still it was translated as the *place* of assembly – the church building – and then became the English adjective ecclesiastical 'of the church'.

In Rome the large private house was known as a *titulus*, a legal term derived from the marble slab that contained the name of the owner and recognized title to a property. By the time of Constantine there were 25 Christian *tituli* in Rome, one such being the *titulus Clementis*. Over the succeeding centuries the *tituli* were replaced by regular church buildings that usually incorporated parts of the older structure; for example, the *titulus Byzantii* beneath the church of SS Giovanni e Paolo.

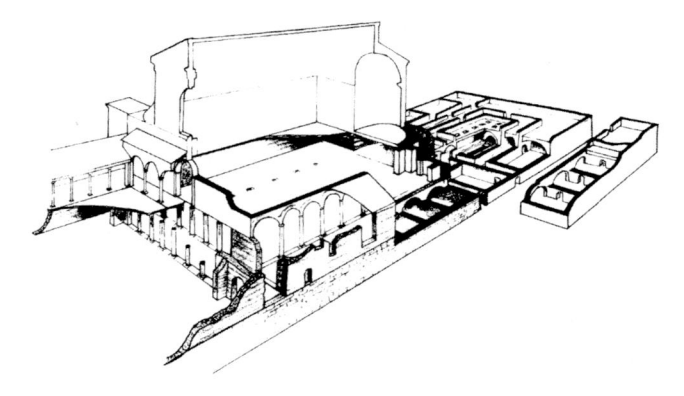

89. Titulus San Clemente, Rome. Reconstruction

The largest surviving Christian building of the pre-Constantinian period in the city is the *titulus Esquitii* as the basilica of San Martino ai Monti was constructed alongside it and not above it. In Rome, where the largest Christian congregations were to be found, even converted houses became too small. It became necessary to convert parts of tenement buildings (*insulae*), small bath-houses (*thermae*) or warehouses into Christian religious spaces. Large hall type assembly spaces are known as *aula ecclesiae* or *horrea ecclesiae*. Little physical trace remains of these early *ecclesiae* or churches whether they were private houses or larger community buildings. In Rome it was reported that there were over 40 churches at the beginning of the fourth century including the 25 *tituli*.

In the East there is also early evidence of Christian buildings. A written document records that Bishop Isaac (r. 123–36) was responsible for building that he called a 'church'. Another manuscript chronicles that in the city of Edessa a *templum ecclesiae Christianorum* was destroyed by a flood in 202. Archaeological evidence points to the transformation of a private house in Dura-Europos on the Euphrates into a Christian place of worship around 232. While the exterior of the house remained the same the interior rooms of this house were altered. Around a central open courtyard one room was enlarged for an assembly of about 50 people with a dais on the east wall for the bishop. Another room for about 30 people was most likely set aside for the catechumens. A third and smaller room became the baptistery with walls decorated with murals. It is also known that a church was built in Neocaesarea in 258, that a 'church building' at Antioch was referred to by the Emperor Aurelian

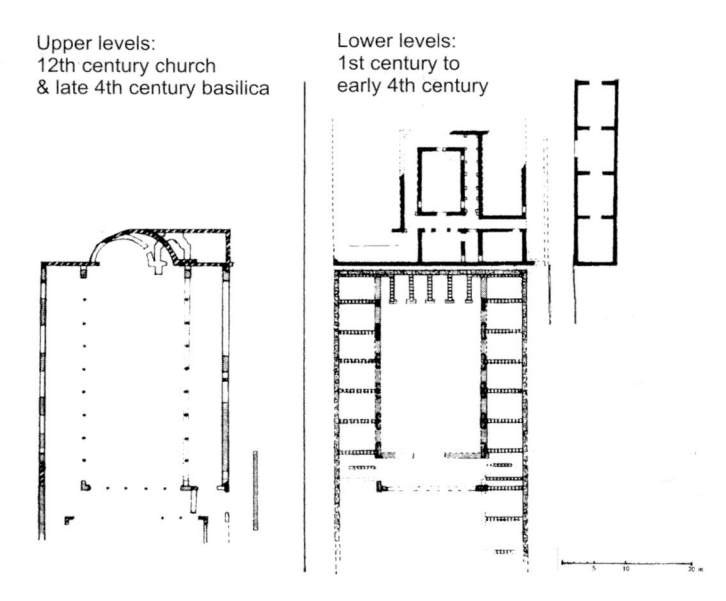

90. Titulus San Clemente, Rome. Stages of construction second to fourth centuries

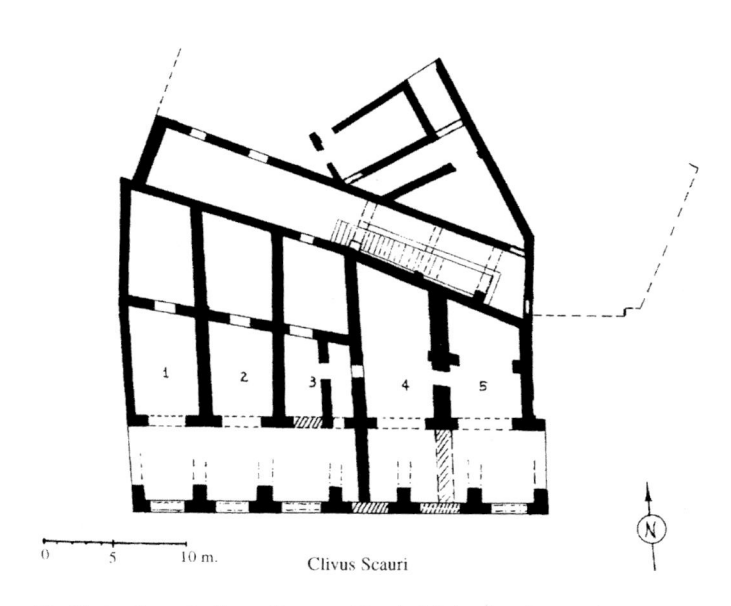

91. Titulus Byzantis, Rome. Renovated insula third to fourth centuries

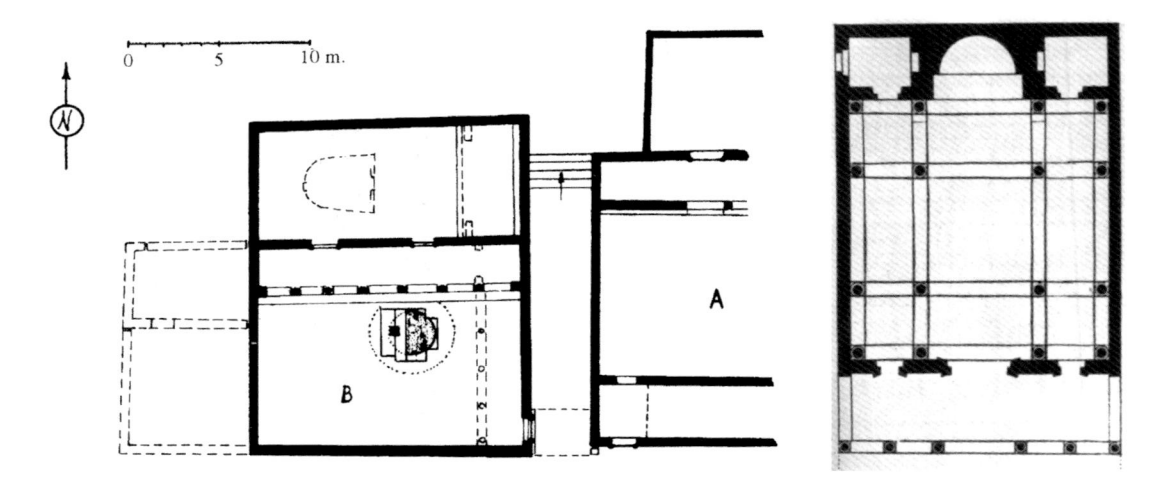

92. House-church, Qirqbize, Syria. Reconstruction

93. Hall-church, Musmiyeh, Roman Syria. About year 400 with clear narthex and pastophoria

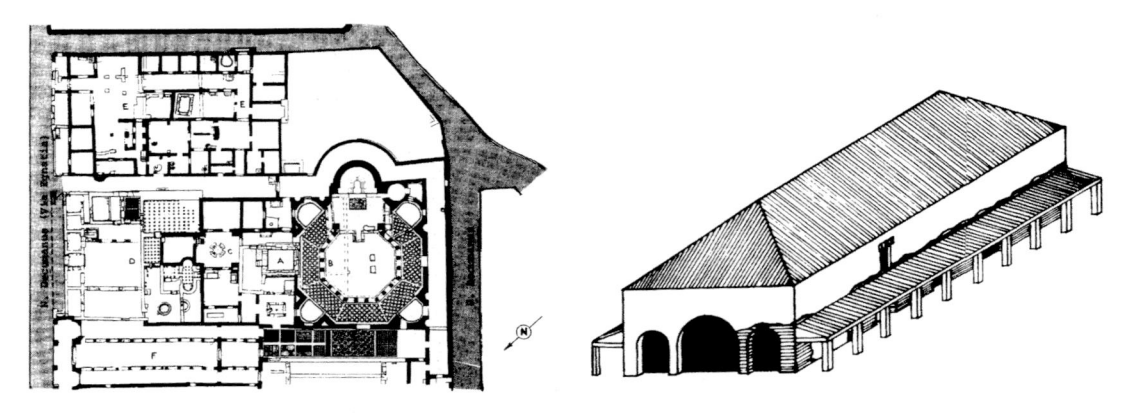

94. Octagonal hall-church, Philippi, Greece

95. Aula Ecclesiae, San Crisogono, Rome. Reconstruction of first church building

in 270, that three churches were built at the end of the third century at Etchmiadzin, and that Diocletian ordered the destruction of the church at Nicomedia.

Eusebius, Bishop of Caesarea, in his *Ecclesiastical History* written in the early part of the fourth century notes quite graphically: *'But how can anyone describe those vast assemblies, and the multitudes that crowded together in every city, and the famous gatherings in the houses of prayer; on whose account, not being satisfied with the ancient buildings, they erected from the foundation large churches in all the cities... feasts of dedication in the cities and consecrations of the newly built houses of prayer took place, bishops assembled, foreigners came together from abroad, mutual love was exhibited between people and people, the members of Christ's body were united in complete harmony.'*[1]

96. Aula Ecclesiae, San Crisogono, Rome. Stages of construction fourth to sixth centuries

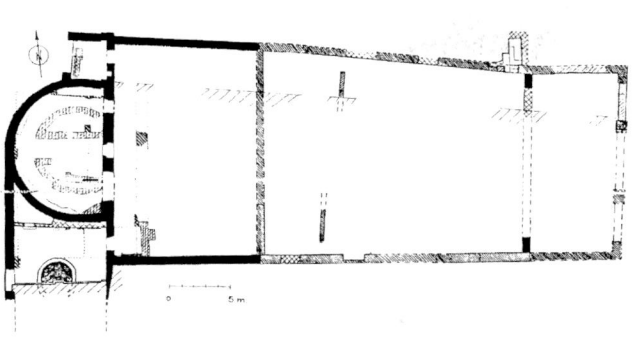

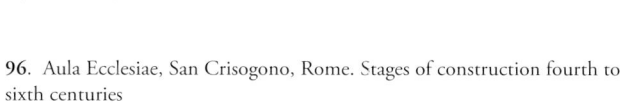

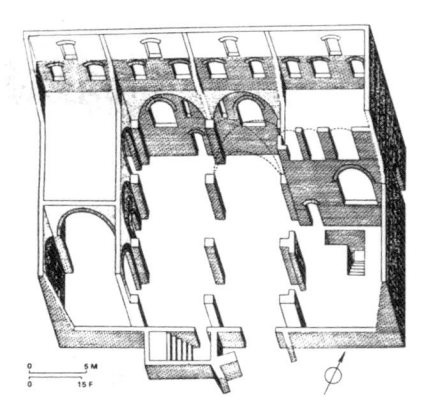

97. Aula Ecclesiae, St Martino ai Monti. The original church

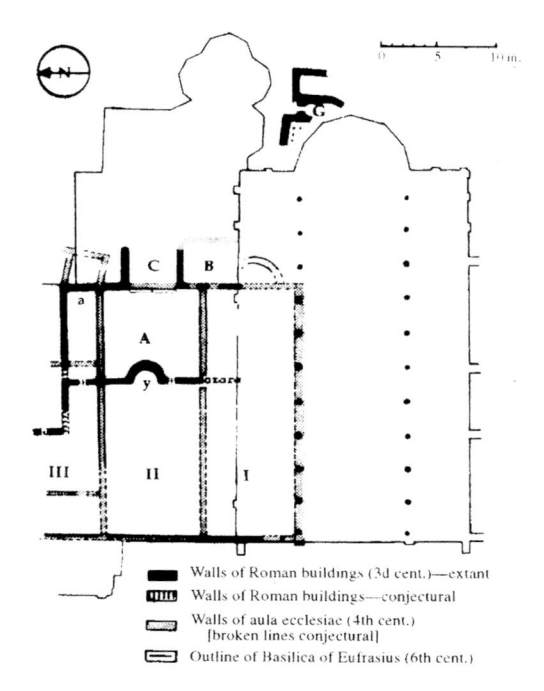

98. Aula Ecclesiae, Basilica Eufrasiana, Parentium. Roman buildings beneath the basilica

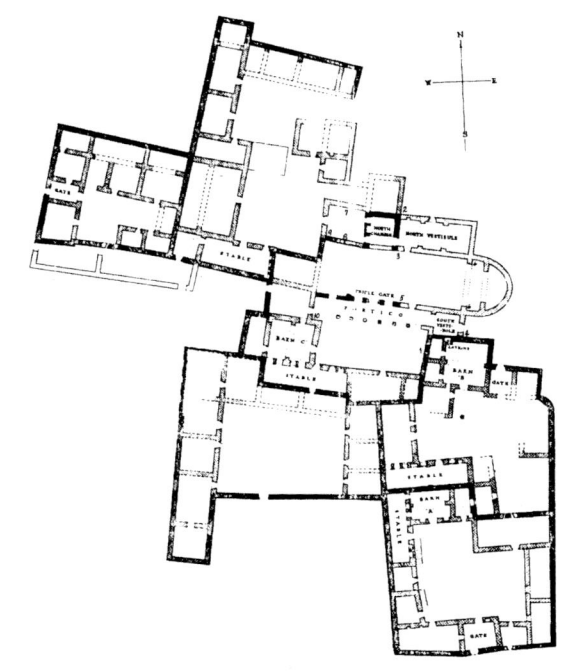

99. Insula-Church 'Julianos's', Umm el-Jimal, Syria. Church building in centre with semi-circular apse

100. Insula-church 'Julianos's', Umm el-Jimal, Syria. Plan restoration in stages third to fifth centuries

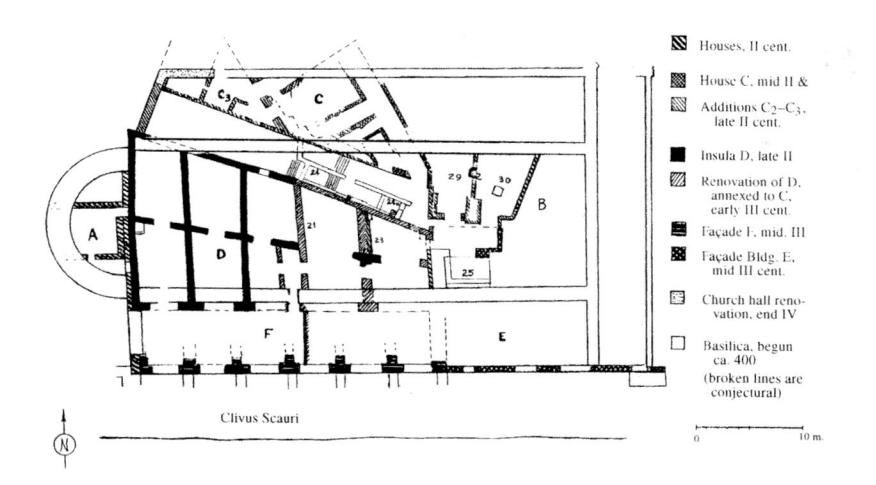

101. Insula-church, SS Giovanni e Paolo, Rome. Plan restoration third to fifth centuries

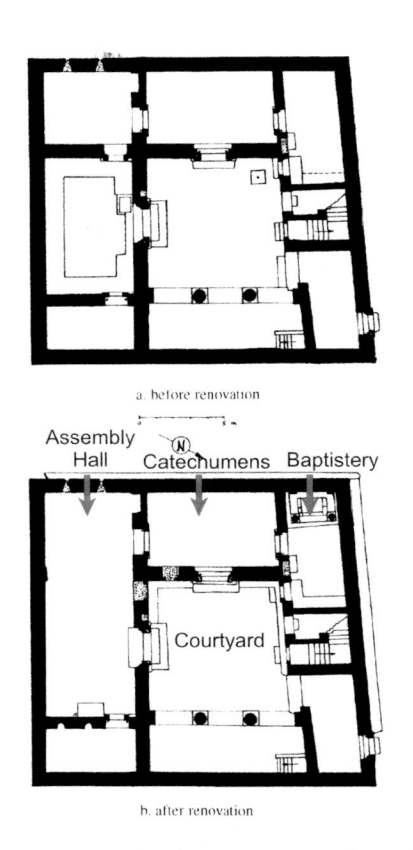

102. House-church, Dura-Europos. Before and after restoration (see also Figures 103 and 104)

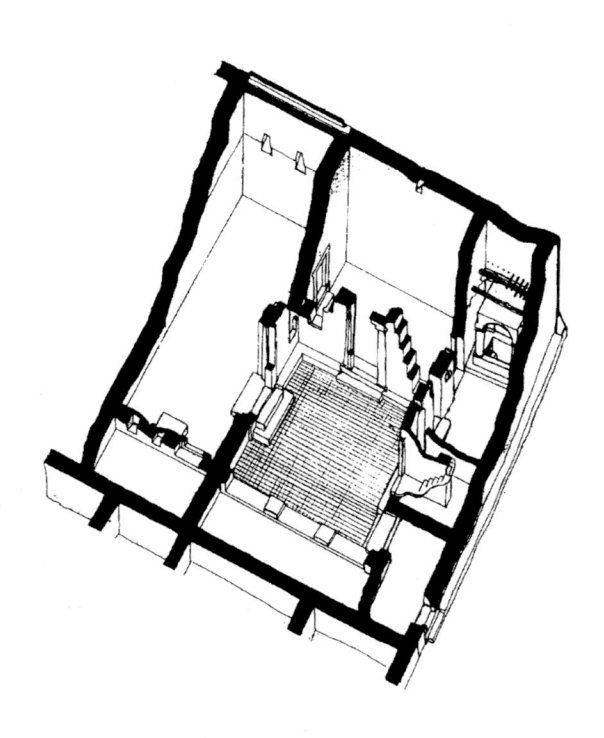

103. House-church, Dura-Europos. Reconstructed view

The exterior of converted buildings, large and small, were deliberately undistinguished so as not to draw attention to them during the early perilous times for Christians. The spaces in the *domus ecclesiae* later become the three-part spatial division of the typical church building – the entry porch becomes the narthex, the pillared courtyard or atrium turns into the roofed naos or nave, and the raised dining area (*tablinium*) and stone table develops into the holy bema or sanctuary with the Holy Table or altar. The terms narthex, naos, and bema for the three major spaces of Byzantine churches will be used in this book to contrast them with the equivalent terms porch or vestibule, nave and sanctuary in Western churches. Also the term Holy Table (αγία τράπεζα) will be used instead of altar as this is the way it is termed in Byzantine religious literature. Even at this

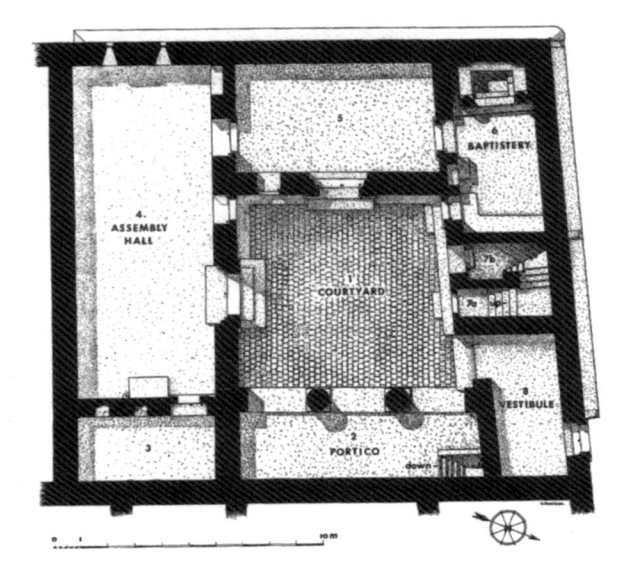

104. House-church, Dura-Europos. Cutout view

early stage in the converted buildings or *ecclesiae* only the bishop and presbyters were allowed onto the raised platform while the faithful were confined to the remaining space. Early altars or Holy Tables were of wood and were not fixed. A wood railing in front of the Holy Table separated the clergy on the platform from the lay people in the room. The railing in time became more elaborate as a low parapet known as the templon and later as a taller partition, the iconostasis in Byzantine churches. On the walls of the *ecclesiae* in these first few centuries there were no paintings, which were to be found only in the catacombs.

Written information about the first churches at the beginning of the fourth century comes mainly from the book *Ecclesiastical History* by the church historian Eusebius and from the *Liber Pontificalis* ('Book of the Popes') that was started in the third century. From these sources it is known that the first official and monumental church built by Constantine was the Basilica Constantiniana (312–319), also known as the Basilica Lateranensis or the Lateran after its location in Rome. The second church constructed by Constantine was St Peter's (after 320), known as Old St Peter's as it was demolished at the beginning of the sixteenth century to make way for the current building. In 324 Constantine rebuilt the Greek city of Byzantium on the Bosphorus which at first he named as New Rome (*Nova Roma*) but in 330 renamed it *Constantinopolis* ('Constantine's City') or Constantinople. Scholars have termed the style of church architecture produced from this time until the Fall of Constantinople in 1453 as Byzantine and after that time as Eastern Orthodox. Constantine founded churches in New Rome as well as in the holy city of Jerusalem and in Bethlehem. But as Eusebius noted Christians 'were no longer satisfied with the buildings of olden times, and would erect from the foundations churches of spacious dimensions throughout all the cities'. Emperor Constantine issued edicts to governors around the Roman Empire to build churches using imperial funds.

Constantine and his architects faced a problem when he decided to build the first purposefully designed churches after he recognized the Christian religion at the beginning of the fourth century.

From the start he wanted his new churches to match the magnificence of existing Roman buildings and a way to proclaim the new faith. The Christian need for a large indoor space for assembly precluded the adoption of the Greek or Roman temple as the purpose of these was to house a cult statue. Furthermore, pagan religious rituals occurred outside, around an outdoor altar and not inside the building. Another reason for avoiding existing religious building types could have been the reluctance to use a pagan architectural form. The new religious building of the Christians needed to be conceived as an architecture of the interior rather than of the exterior and one that had meaning in the Roman world. After also rejecting precedents such as the Roman bath or villa, the decision was made to follow the basilica as a model.

105. Model of centralized temple of Minerva Medica, Rome

106. Basilica Constantiniana (Lateran), Rome. Cross section showing double aisles, clerestory lighting, looking toward apse

107. Basilica Ulpia, Rome. Restored interior

108. Basilica Maxentius, Forum Rome. As seen today

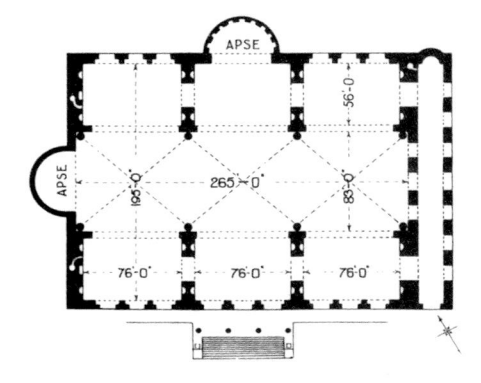

109. Basilica Maxentius, Rome. Plan with a portico, wide aisles and semi-circular apses

The Roman basilica as a law court consisted of a rectangular hall with colonnades separating it from aisles on either side. On the one short wall there was an entrance and at the opposite end wall there was an apse that formed in most cases a semi-circular projection. In the apse sat the magistrate who presided over the proceedings. The basilica also had the advantage in that the name meant 'royal house' (βασιλικόν) formerly the name of the dwellings of a king derived from Solomon's palace where people assembled to hear judgments.

110. Basilica of Constantine, Rome. Reconstructed interior 307–312

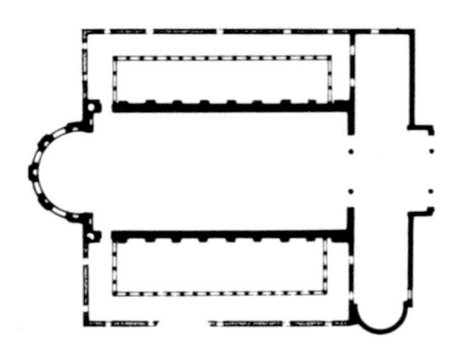

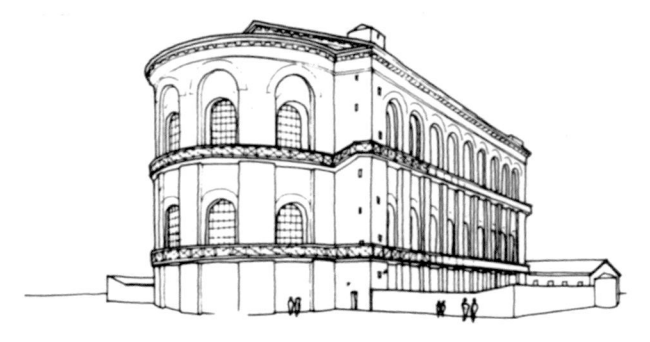

111. Trier Basilica of Constantine. Plan and exterior view

It is possible that the model for the basilica was not the law court but the imperial palace which had large reception halls rectangular in shape. Constantine in fact had built a hall without aisles in his palace complex at Trier in present day Germany, which in Roman times was called Augusta Treverorum and capital of the vast province of Gallia Belgica. In the hall Constantine would sit on a throne in the apse to receive visitors. The palace hall at Trier was converted into one of the first Christian basilica churches.

The Constantinian churches, in adapting the basilican form, incorporated the evolving bema, naos and narthex spaces of the *ecclesiae* but so arranged as to have an architecturally and spatially unified whole. The bema (βῆμα in Greek meaning step or pace) became the raised area in Byzantine

112. Trier Basilica of Constantine. Interior view, looking toward apse

churches directly in front of the apse containing the Holy Table and occupied the east end of the naos. At first the bema was marked off from the naos by a simple railing, later an elaborate screen or templon, and eventually by a highly decorative icon screen (iconostasis). Also later, a canopy supported by four or more columns, a baldachino or ciborium, could be added to cover the Holy Table to give it greater prominence. The naos (ναός, literally 'temple') as the main space of the basilica as a church was a timber-roofed rectangular hall with colonnaded side aisles and an apse containing the bema at one end facing the narthex entrance at the other end. Even from early times in some churches the wooden roof trusses were hidden by ceilings, often painted in gold and with sunken panels, floors were covered with marble or mosaic, and the church splendidly decorated with silver and silk. From the beginning more attention was paid to the adornment of the interiors of the churches rather than their exteriors. In the colonnades that divided the naos from the side aisles the arch was often used to span between piers or columns which were frequently reused, unmatched marble columns from earlier Roman buildings. The rectangular form of the basilica could be varied in length and precise shape but was limited in width by the spanning capacity of the timber roof. As the side aisles were lower in height than the main hall windows could be placed in wall above the roof of the aisles to create clerestory lighting to light up the interior. The narthex functioned as a transition space from the outside world to the interior religious area and had the same width as the naos. Outside the narthex there was, in most cases, a courtyard or forecourt that was an open space similar to that in front of pagan temples.

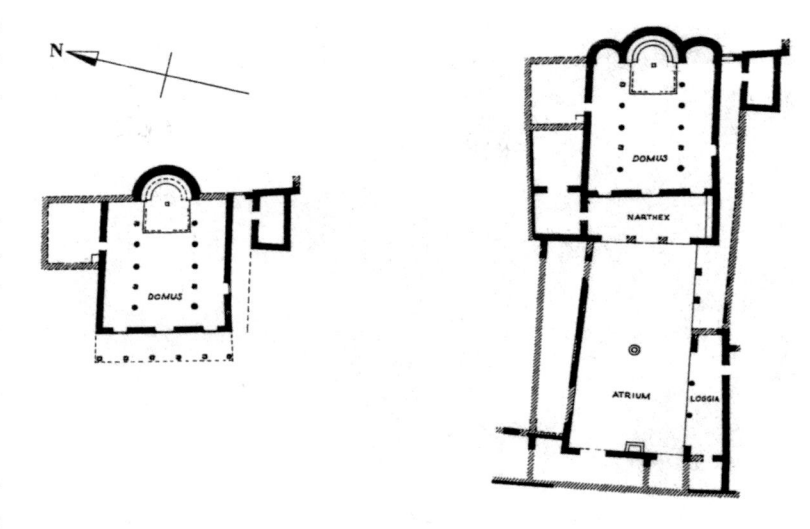

113. Church Kh. el-Karak, Lake Tiberius. Development of spatial components: courtyard, narthex, diaconicon and bema

Approach to Byzantine Architecture

In the popular image a Byzantine church is a building with a large dome or perhaps one with a dominant dome and some smaller ones. But as just described, the first Christian churches were basilican in form, that is, rectangular in shape with pitched timber roofs and no domes. In reality Christian churches over the centuries, both in the eastern and western parts of the Roman Empire, display a bewildering number of architectural forms but more so in the East. Perhaps this is the reason that there are so many different approaches to describing Byzantine church architecture.

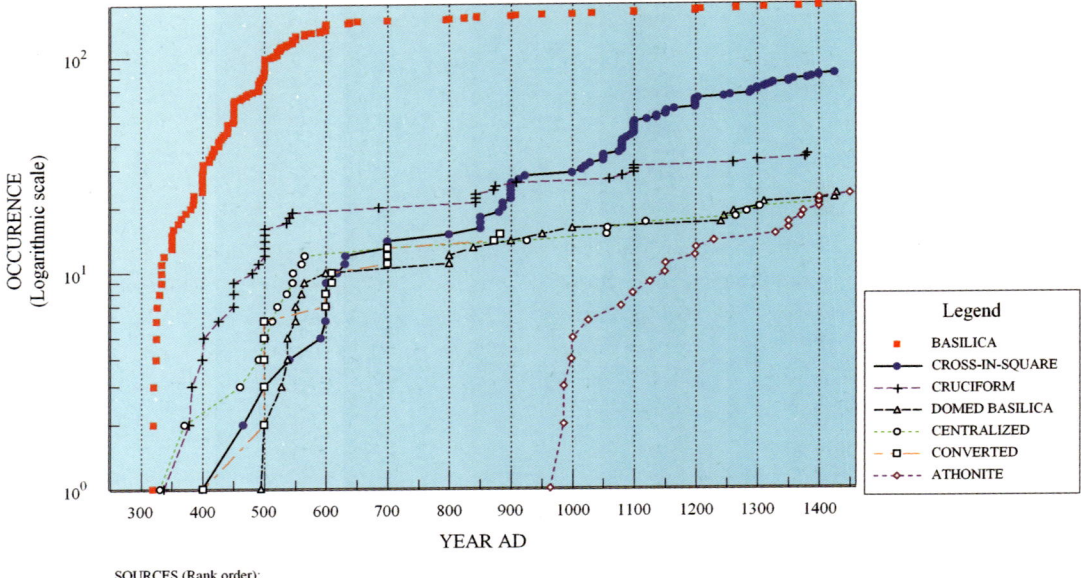

114. Timelines chart of the seven Byzantine church types AD 300–1453

SOURCES (Rank order):
Krautheimer, Bouras, Buchwald, Freely, Plakogiannakis, Peeters, Mango, Mastrogiannopoulos, Mathews, Van Milligen, Molho, Webb, Ousterhout, Acheimastou-Potamianou, Doig, MacDonald, Camp, White, Wybrew, Davies, Dupre, Grundmann, Tsigarides

One approach is to depict specific churches. While this is interesting in learning about individual churches it does not lead to an understanding of the reasons for the variety of architectural forms and particularly their relationship to the liturgy. So a more common approach adopted by scholars is the chronological one. In this approach churches are distinguished according to the time periods in which they are built, whether Early, Middle or Late Byzantine. This follows the model of other periods of architecture such as Gothic or Renaissance architecture. Another approach is to portray Byzantine architecture by eras as defined by the ruling emperor or dynasty in Constantinople. In this method the major imperial epochs are identified as the Constantinian, Justinian, Macedonian, Komnenian and Palaiologan. The churches built in each era are then illustrated. Another different line to describing Byzantine church architecture is to write about the churches by geographical region such as those in the Aegean Coastlands, the Inland Countries, the Latin West, the Borderlands and the Balkans. A major problem that these and other approaches have is that they do not account for the parallel development of multiple and unrelated architectural forms that do not follow a sequential development. Another problem is that each form of Byzantine church has a different rate of development, appearing at different points in time, lasting for some time and then disappearing from use.

An analysis of the development over time of each architectural form of Byzantine church leads to the conclusion that a more distinctive approach than the individualized, chronological, epochal or geographical is needed. This distinct approach is to describe the architectural form of Byzantine churches by type. An examination of 370 published architectural descriptions and plans of dateable and significant congregational churches (excluding *ecclesiae*) amassed from the work of 23 scholars leads to the identity of seven distinct architectural types of Byzantine churches built between 318 and 1453. The identified types are the basilica, cross-in-square, cruciform (cross), domed basilica, centralized, converted temple and Athonite (see Timelines chart).

The Church Types Overall

Based on the chart data by far the most prevalent type in terms of the number built (47 per cent) and period of time covered is the basilican type church that is found in virtually every geographical region across the Empire and persists from the beginning to the end of the Byzantine era. While a significant number were constructed during the fourth century the following two centuries experienced the heaviest occurrence of the basilica type. From the seventh century onward only a few were built. The next dominant type is the cross-in-square (22 per cent), which began to be built in the fifth and sixth centuries with a spurt at the beginning of the seventh century. There was a lull until there was another surge in the ninth century. Then from the eleventh century until the end of the Byzantine age a large number of the cross-in-square types were built to become almost the only sort erected. The less dominant types each account for less than ten per cent of the churches listed. They are the cruciform (9 per cent), domed basilica (6 per cent), centralized (6 per cent) and converted temple (4 per cent). The cruciform type had a strong showing in the fifth century while the centralized, domed basilica and converted types occurred in significant numbers in the sixth century. All these less dominant types tailed off in the seventh century with the converted temple type discontinued after the ninth century. The Athonite type (6 per cent) emerged in the tenth century and lasted well after the fifteenth century with the Fall of Constantinople and the end of the Byzantine Empire as more and more monasteries were built. The dramatic reduction in the amount of church building in the seventh to ninth centuries, the so-called 'Dark Ages', was no doubt impacted by the plague that swept through the Empire and the loss of the territory in the Near East and Egypt to Arab invaders. A common architectural feature of all the Byzantine church types except the basilica, and some converted temples, was the dome.

Not surprisingly the fourth to the sixth centuries was the period when there was the greatest surge of church building, with the acceptance of Christianity. The sixth century was the era of greatest productivity, mainly due to the vast building programme of Emperor Justinian. This building boom was followed by a dramatic decrease in church construction with the decline of cities, internal crises in the empire and foreign wars from the seventh to the ninth centuries. Much of the construction activity in these centuries was in the form of preservation and repair. Building began anew with the relative stability brought about with the ascension of the Macedonian dynasty in the middle of the ninth century. For the next few centuries the building of churches reached a high point in Greece but with a difference. Churches were smaller in size and inevitably the cross-in-square type with multiple domes. With the addition of adjoining chapels to existing main churches this resulted in a multiplicity of domes. In the fourteenth and fifteenth centuries and into the sixteenth much of the building activity took place in Thessaloniki and the monasteries on Mount Athos, at Meteora, and Mystras in Greece.

The reasons for the launching of each type has given rise to a continued and unresolved debate among scholars as to why a particular type was introduced, why it was launched at a specific point in time, and why at a certain place. In one instance the eminent Byzantine scholar, Cyril Mango, has made the intriguing suggestion that the inspiration for the centralized church was probably the palace audience hall where the metaphor of the earthly monarch surrounded by imperial courtiers and their rituals was transferred to the idea of the heavenly King in His habitat encircled by clergy and laity participating in the liturgy. He further notes that the cruciform type is obviously a symbol of the cross upon which Jesus Christ was crucified and that the basilica is a reflection of Roman grandeur.

While the classification of Byzantine churches is a major challenge the problem does not end there. Within each of the seven types there is no standard plan so it is difficult to illustrate a typical church form, such as a basilican or cross-in-square Byzantine church, the two dominant types. The same applies to the five less dominant architectural types of church. Although regional difference are to be expected the main reason for the divergences within each type are the different ways in which the narthex, bema and other spatial pieces are related to the naos.

115. Dome of Hagia Eirene, Constantinople AD307–312

116. Central and subsidiary domes, St Saviour in Chora, Constantinople

117. Hagia Sophia, Constantinople. Interior dominated by the dome

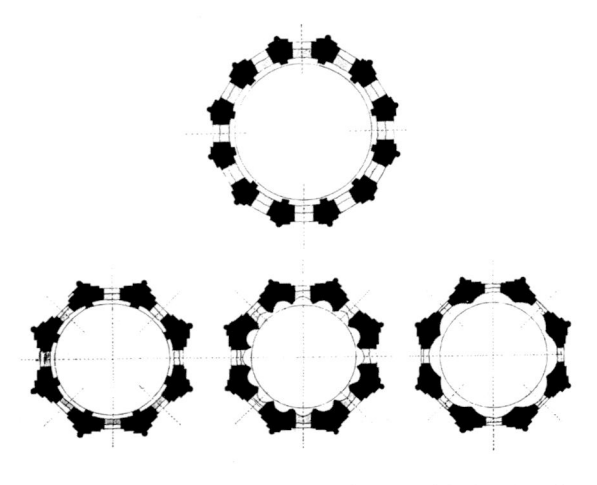

118. St Theodore, Constantinople. Central (top) and narthex domes (bottom) – Circular interiors but polygonal or circular exteriors

The dome turned out to be the most spectacular architectural feature in the Byzantine church whether in the cross-in-square, the cross, the central or Athonite type. Anyone that enters a space covered by a large central dome cannot but be overwhelmed by a vault that seems 'suspended by a golden chain from heaven' as so aptly depicted by the Byzantine court historian Procopius (c.500–565). The sublime space that seems to expand like a sail opening up against the wind, resting on arches and piers, and with closely spaced windows around its base, gives the appearance that the dome floats on a ring of light. The hovering hemisphere reveals a vertical axis that draws the eye upward. In traditional churches a large circular chandelier of brass, called a *horos*, usually hangs below the dome. In larger churches there are multiple domes, a large central dome and a number of smaller half-domes covering side spaces. The upward direction of the central dome contrasts with the linear axis of the rectangular basilica which emphasizes a horizontal thrust from courtyard and narthex to the holy bema.

In Byzantine domed churches the impression given is that the central dome, a hollow upper half of a sphere, floats above a cubical space. The challenge to Byzantine architects was how to fit a circular shape, the dome, onto the square base at the top of the cube that occurs in non-basilican type churches. There were two problems. First there was a structural problem, how to support the dome. If the cube base is four solid walls this does not do as it closes off the centre of the church, the naos, from the narthex and the bema. The solution was to replace the solid walls with four round arches whose piers or columns formed the four corners of the cubical space. Secondly, how was the circular bottom of the dome to sit on the square base at the top of the cube. Only four short, opposite arcs of the circular rim of the dome can rest on the top of the arches that form the sides of the cubical space. In other words, the problem was how to provide a continuous base for the circular rim at the bottom of the dome when it sits over a square shape. The key was to fill the curved spaces between the upper parts of the arches to provide a complete base for the dome to sit on. The initial solution was the use of what are called squinches formed by corbelling, that is by bricks or stones built out in courses with one course projecting beyond the one below. A better solution was the introduction of pendentives, inwardly curving triangular surfaces that fill the spaces between the arches. Thus the four squinches or four pendentives became the means of blending a circular form, the dome, with the four sides of the cubical space bounded by the four supporting arches. The top of the squinches or pendentives along with the top of the arches provided a continuous rim on which the bottom of the dome could rest. In churches with a central dome the vertical supports of the arches can take two forms. In the first form the supports are thick piers at the four corners of the central cubical volume embedded in the walls of the surrounding bays. The second form gives a more open feeling of space and freedom of movement as the vertical supports of the arches are slender freestanding columns. This arrangement is known as a four-column or pillared kind of church.

119. First approach circle to square [the slab at corners]

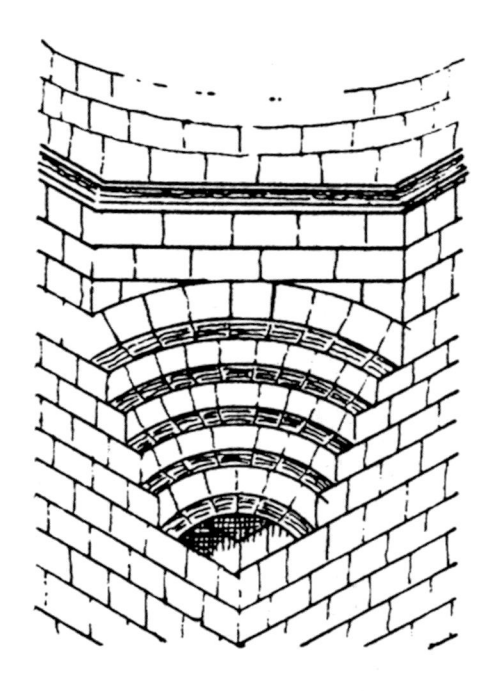

120. Second approach circle to square [the squinch. Corbelled rows of stones]

121. A squinch

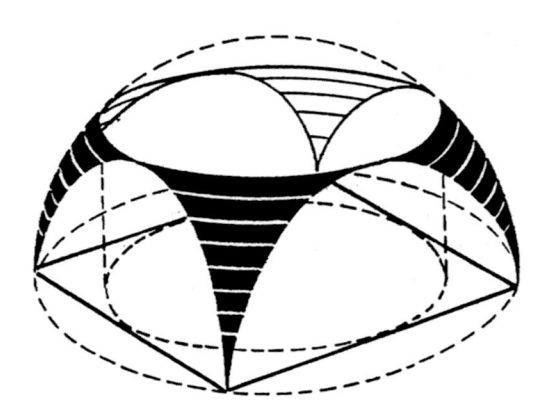

122. Third approach circle to square [pendentives]. Inwardly curving triangular surfaces

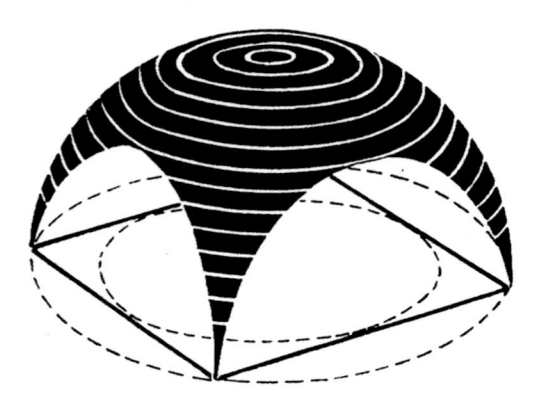

123. Pendentives merged with dome [cupola]

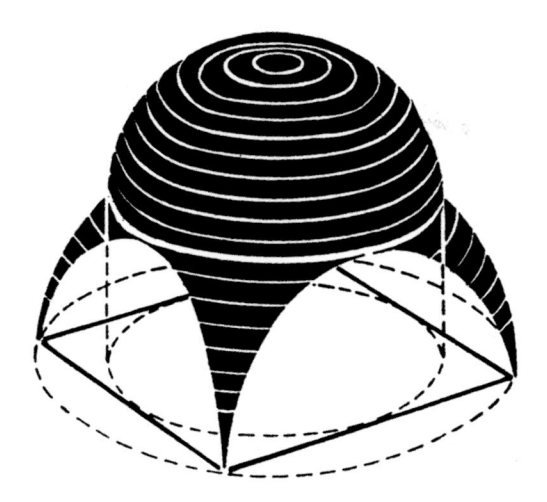

124. Pendentives surmounted by semi-circular dome [cupola]

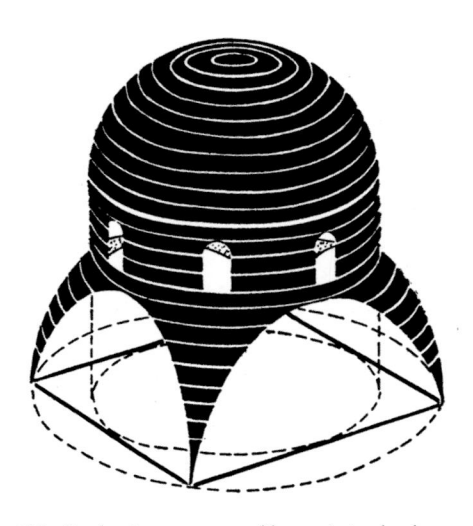

125. Pendentives surmounted by semi-circular dome [cupola] on a drum

To increase the sense of height the dome in many churches was raised so that it sat on a drum which itself was supported by the arches and squinches or pendentives. The drum was usually in the shape of a cylinder but could also be polygonal, usually eight-sided. The drum not only provided for additional height in the centre of the church but could be pierced by windows to provide light to the interior. Semi-circular apse spaces were usually covered by a semi- or half-dome. Strictly speaking in architectural vocabulary a cupola is a spherical roof cover over a circular, polygonal or square space whereas a dome is a covering over only a circular and polygonal space and not a square or cubical area. However, the association of domes with Byzantine church architecture is so entrenched in everyone's mind that the term dome will be retained.

The magnificent dome of the Byzantine church of Hagia Sophia (reconstructed 557–562) in Constantinople has a diameter of 107 feet. This is smaller than the dome with the largest diameter in the ancient world, the Pantheon (AD118–126) in Rome, which is 150 feet. Unable to repeat the magnificent feat of the Romans in constructing the Pantheon dome, the Renaissance architect Filippo Brunelleschi came up with a brilliant solution to build an internal octagonal cupola of 138 feet diameter at Santa Maria del Fiore (1420–1436) in Florence without scaffolding and covering it with a light exterior protective shell. This design became a model for Michelangelo in his design for the dome of the new St Peter's in Rome which has a diameter of 136 feet. Work on the dome began in 1547 but was only completed in 1590 by Giacomo della Porta.

The horizontal shape of the basilica type has the advantage of perspective as the narthex, naos and apse that contain the holy bema are lined up in a straight line or axis. From the entrance to the naos, the narthex, and in the naos itself, the focal point of the interior is the Holy Table in the semi-circular apse where the momentous ritual of Eucharist consecration mystery takes place. In the other architectural types, the cross-in-square, the cross, the central and Athonite domes have the advantage in that the vision of the faithful ends in the large dome where the image of Christ as the Ruler of All is depicted. The only church type to attempt to have the advantages of both horizontal and vertical emphases was the domed basilica building. In general, the churches in the Latin West remained conformist influenced by the prominent basilicas of Rome, whereas in the Hellenized East there was more innovation in the new capital of Constantinople and particularly in places such as Syria and Anatolia. From Constantinople, the centre of imperial administration, architectural ideas and buildings components such as columns, capitals and church furniture were 'exported' to territories throughout the Byzantine Empire.

126. San Saba, Rome. The horizontal axis of the basilica focuses on the Holy Table in the apse

Church Types and their Architecture

Basilica

When Constantine as emperor or *basileus* (βασιλεύς) adopted the rectangular building plan of the Roman basilica for his first churches the term *basilica* came to be associated with the early plan form of Christian churches. The first purpose-built churches thus had the stamp of imperial approval. The basilican type consists of a rectangular space, the naos, a narthex the width of the naos on one of the short ends and an apse, usually semi-circular in shape, on the other end, and in nearly all cases the east end.

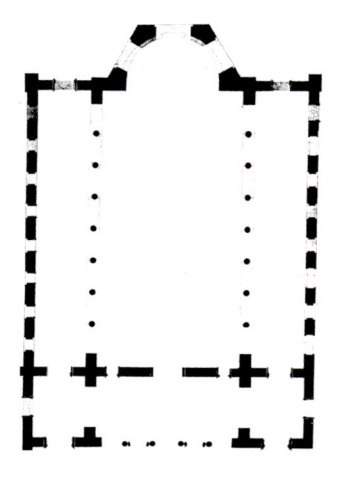

127. Basilica plan type – St John Studios, Constantinople. Narthex (bottom), side aisles and projecting bema apse

128. Basilica type – Santa Sabina, Rome. Naos looking at apse, arcades with Corinthian columns and wood panel ceiling

129. Basilica type aisles – Santa Maria Maggiore, Rome. Colonnade with Ionic column capitals and decorated barrel vault

130. Mosaic showing a basilica, Tabarka, Tunisia. 'Ecclesia Mai E Valentiain' 'R I Pacea'

Most basilican forms have two side aisles, occasionally these are double aisles on each side, or in a few small churches no aisles at all. Rows of columns in the form of a colonnade or arcade divide the naos from the aisles. Often unmatched columns and capitals from Roman buildings were reused. As the ceiling and roof of the naos are higher than the side aisles windows in the walls provide light to the interior.

As Buchwald points out the basilica type is characterized by clear, geometrical forms – the rectangle, square and semi-circle. The narthex, naos, aisles and bema tend to be symmetrical in form and separated from one another by pierced walls, colonnades or arcades, and screens. The roof over the naos is covered by the gable sort while those over the side aisles and narthex are the shed type. Regional variations were determined by the materials available. An advantage of the basilica form was that it could be extended in length when the space was later judged to be inadequate, as happened in a few cases.

Cross-in-Square

The cross-in-square type consists of a Greek cross shaped plan enclosed in a square form with the space between the arms of the cross and the square filled in. The origin of this inscribed cross form is not known. As seen from above the cross is clearly visible as it is higher than the four, lower filler spaces on the corners, each of which has its own roof. Internally the major space is the central bay of the Greek cross which is crowned by a dome that rests on four piers or columns. The four bays that surround the central bay are the arms of the cross, each equal in size, and are usually each covered by a barrel vault. The four corner bays that form the filler spaces usually have a cross vault or small dome covering each. Geometrically the ground floor level of the church is a series of cubes while the level above is cruciform with a dome resting at the crossing point of the arms of the cross. The cubical shapes in the plan of the cross-in-square church form nine square bays or compartments, all equal in size except for the larger central space over which the dome rests. In later centuries the exterior wall surfaces of the church are ornamented by intricate brickwork or stonework patterns.

There are two variations to the standard four-pier, cross-in-square type. First, there is the so-called four column type where the usually bulky piers are replaced by slender columns that create a more

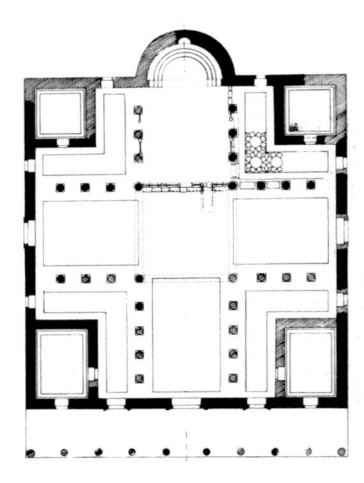

131. Cross-in-square plan type – Prophets, Gerasa. Narthex porch (bottom) and projecting semi-circular apse (top)

132. Typical cross-in-square church, Greece. Dome covered with tiles and arms of the cross with gable roofs

spacious naos as they take up less floor space. In addition the visual impression is that space seems to flow one into another, from the central naos into each of the four arms of the cross. Secondly, there is the compressed cross-in-square type. In this variation the arms of the cross are so compressed they are more like shallow extensions of the central naos space. While the compressed cross form may be visible in the plan drawing of a church the spatial experience in practice is more of a centralized type. For this reason churches with compressed cross forms will not be classified as cross-in-square types but as centralized ones. As in both variations the arms of the cross are less defined and become more interconnected, almost like a passageway, the term ambulatory has been applied to these variations in the literature on Byzantine church architecture. However, as ambulatories or walkways around the central naos did not have a liturgical function in Byzantine or Eastern Orthodox services (even the processions) the term will not be used but instead the side spaces of interconnected cross arms will be referred to as wide aisles. Justification for this comes from experience of services in churches on Mount Athos and village churches in Greece where the naos is kept open and free during regular services with congregants standing on the sides in the aisles. Wider aisles would thus provide more space to accommodate a larger congregation.

133. Cross-in-square column type – Theotokos Pammakaristos, Constantinople. Interior looking east at apse

SACRED ARCHITECTURE

134. Cross-in-square column type – Theotokos Pammakaristos, Constantinople. Interior looking north

135. Cross-in-square column type – Theotokos Pammakaristos, Constantinople. Interior looking west at narthex entrance

136. Cross-in-square column type – Theotokos Pammakaristos, Constantinople. Interior looking south

137. Cross-in-square compressed type – St Saviour in Chora, Constantinople. Naos looking east at apse

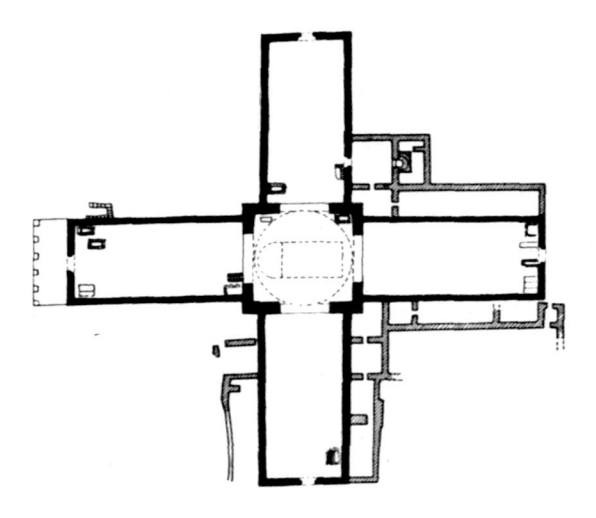

138. Cruciform plan type – St Babylas, Antioch. Bema (dotted lines) at the crossing point of the cross and a narthex porch (left)

139. Cruciform type – Mausoleum of Galla Placidia, Ravenna. View of a side arm of the cross with a sarcophagus

Cruciform

In the free standing cruciform type church the shape of the cross is visually clear both in the interior and the exterior of the building. In Byzantine churches the Greek cross is used in which all four of the arms are all equal in length whereas in the Latin cross the arm that contains the entrance is longer than the remaining three arms. Over the crossing point of the cross there is a dome and each arm of the cross is covered by a barrel vault. The dome may be raised on a drum to increase its height and become a more dominating structure in the city or countryside. The cross form was first used as a shape in subterranean tombs in the Roman catacombs and in many eastern rock tombs to symbolize the Christian belief in the resurrection of the body. Buildings with cross plans are small and mostly sepulcher chapels rather than churches for public worship.

Centralized

From the funerary mausoleums of the Romans the Christians developed the idea of a centrally-planned church. The central type plan was usually

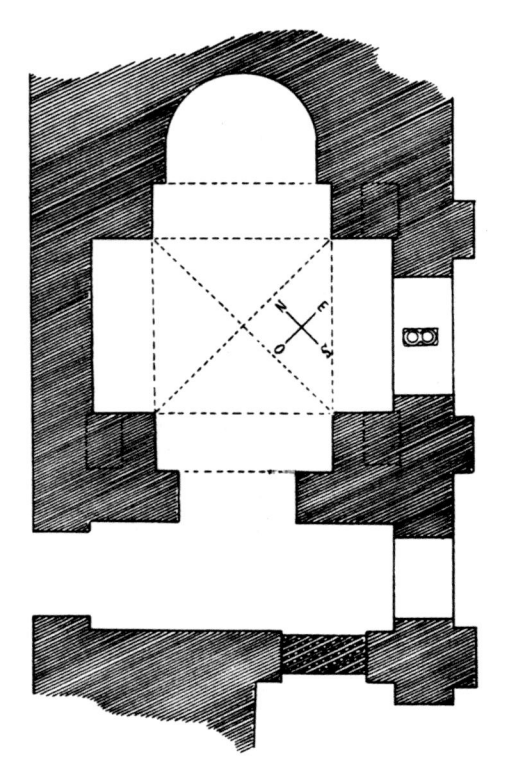

140. Cruciform type – Archiepiscopal Chapel, Ravenna. Central space covered by a cross vault

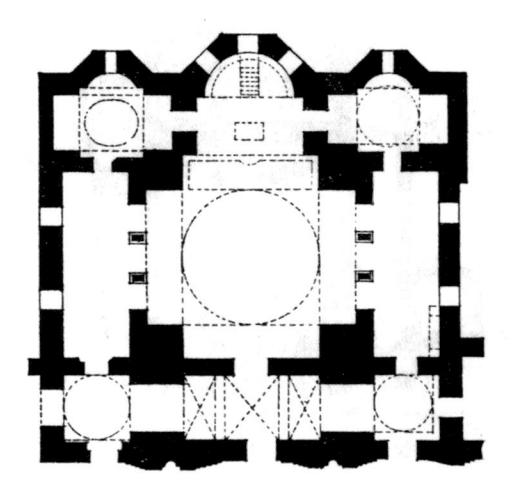

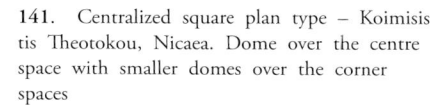

141. Centralized square plan type – Koimisis tis Theotokou, Nicaea. Dome over the centre space with smaller domes over the corner spaces

142. Centralized circular type – Santo Stefano, Rome. Clear expression of inner and outer circles

a simple geometrical form such as an octagon, circle or sometimes a square but could be a more complex form, consisting of four lobes and known as a tetraconch plan. A lobe or conch is a semi-circular space or niche surmounted by a semi-dome. The simpler forms have a central space alone but elaborate ones are enveloped all around by a wide aisle that can also act as a passageway. Pierced walls, colonnades or arcades with columns or piers separate the domed central space from the surrounding wide aisle which is usually covered by a barrel vault. In the fourth century the central type was used as a memorial building or *martyrium* to mark the tomb of a saint in a cemetery or to mark a place in the Holy Land associated with Jesus Christ. The circular building erected over the supposed tomb of Christ in Jerusalem, the *Anastasis* (Resurrection in Greek), became most influential as Christians elsewhere wished to replicate the *martyrium* of Christ.

During the fifth century the relics of saints and martyrs were allowed to be moved from the cemeteries and enshrined in churches dedicated to an individual saint or martyr. This led to the creation of the centralized church plan. The attraction of this form was that it enabled the sarcophagus of the saint or martyr to be at the centre of the space and thus the focal point of the church. When adapted for congregational services the problem was where to locate the Holy Table as access to it was limited to the clergy. In some cases the Holy Table was placed to one side in an apse but this tended to compromise the shape of the circle, octagon, or square and its centrality. In other cases both the tomb and Holy Table were left in the centre but with the tomb placed below the floor level and accessed by a stair.

60   THE SACRED ARCHITECTURE OF BYZANTIUM

143. San Vitale, Ravenna. Interior of centralized nave

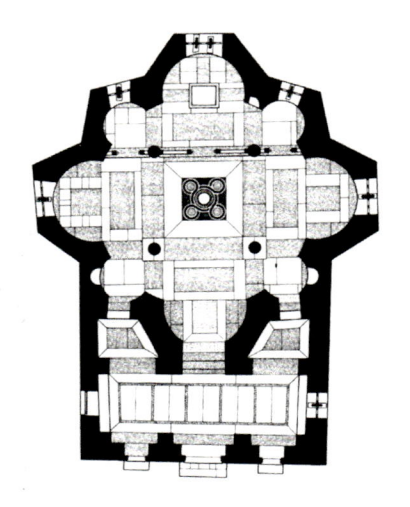

144. Centralized tetraconch plan type – Holy Apostles, Athens. Four large semi-circular apses and two semi-circular smaller apses that serve as the pastophoria

145. Centralized type – Holy Apostles, Constantinople. Sectional rendering viewing Holy Table and large cross behind it in the multi-domed church

146. Centralized type – detail from the icon of SS Peter and Paul combining front view of the hexagonal exterior and the iconostasis in the interior with *despotikaí* icons and a visible Holy Table

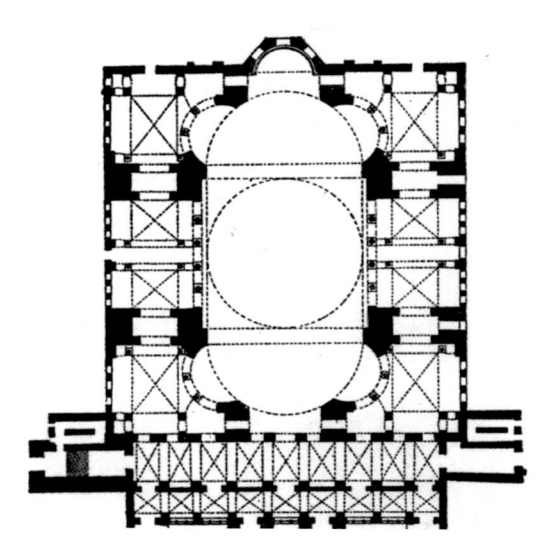

147. Domed basilica plan type – Hagia Sophia, Constantinople. Rectangular shaped naos with rounded corners covered by a central dome flanked by semi-domes

148. Domed basilica type – Hagia Sophia, Constantinople. Central dome with a semi-dome beyond looking at the apse

Domed Basilica

In Asia Minor and the Balkans dissatisfaction with the lack of centrality of the rectangular basilica form led to the creation of a hybrid type, the domed basilica, where a dome was placed over the centre of the rectangular naos. In the domed basilica the horizontal and vertical axes are thus merged so that there is both a focus on the Holy Table where the consecration mystery of the Eucharist occurs and attention centred on the dome where the image of Christ as the *Pantokrator* or Ruler of All resides. The domed basilica type never fully flowered due to the inherent problem of integrating a vertical feature, the dome with its supports, into the horizontal colonnaded structure of the basilica.

Converted Temple

Pagan temples converted for use as churches constitute another but rare type. The converted temple type can be explained as a practical measure to make use of an existing structure and save on the cost of building a new church. In some cases the conversion was simply the division of the pagan cella space into a narthex, naos and bema, leaving the exterior of the temple intact. In other cases the outside walls incorporated the exterior columns, changing the appearance of the building completely.

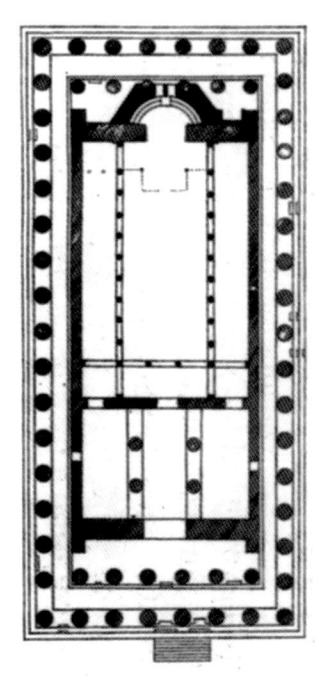

149. Converted plan type – Parthenon, Athens. Apse with synthronon inserted into back porch (top) with an outline of the bema templon (dotted line)

150. Converted type – Duomo Siracusa, Ortegia (former Temple of Athena). Doric columns incorporated into entrance wall

151. Converted type – Duomo Siracusa, Ortegia (former Temple of Athena). Doric columns in the side wall

Athonite

The main church of an Eastern Orthodox monastery, known as a *katholikon,* is a freestanding building, located in the centre of an enclosed courtyard. The word *katholikon* is a modern Greek term to designate the main church in a monastic complex and does not appear in Byzantine sources where it was referred to as the *naos* or *ekklesia*. Since the liturgy can only be said once a day in an Orthodox church, monasteries often contained several small churches or chapels to allow the conduct of additional services. The *katholikon* was often dedicated to the patron saint of the monastery. The distinctive architectural style of the *katholikon* is named 'agioreitikos', that is the Mount Athos monastic or Athonite type established in the tenth century. It is thus the last type of church plan to be created. The overall plan of the Athonite type church is a cross-in-square but with two additions. First, the arms of the cross as a rule are covered with barrel vaults that end, except for the entrance arm, in semi-domed apses forming what is known as the 'three-shelled' or three-conch church. In the two arms at right angles to the arms of the entrance and sanctuary the space there is reserved for the chanters (*psáltes*). The space is referred to as the *chorostasía*. The central space of the naos is where all the arms of the cross meet and is covered by a large dome that usually sits on a tall drum punctured by large windows. These windows are the main source of light for the interior although there is some contribution from the narrow windows in the three apses. The corner spaces between the arms of the cross are square in shape and covered with small domes or cross (groin) vaults. The second addition to the traditional cross-in-square takes the form of two narthexes in front of the entrance arm compared to the single narthex in all other types of churches. The inner narthex is known as the *liti* and has a special liturgical function.

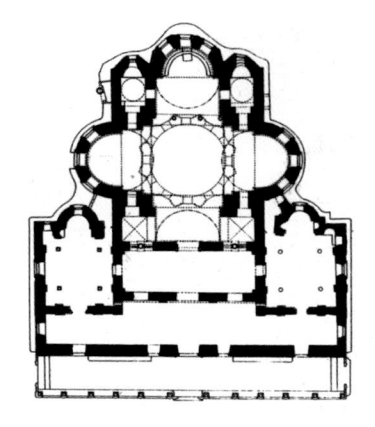

152. Athonite plan type – *Katholikon* of Megistis Lavra, Mount Athos. Entrance porch, outer narthex, inner narthex (*lití*) flanked by *parekklesia*, central space covered by a dome with a *chorostasía* on either side, pastophoria covered by small domes and bema apse

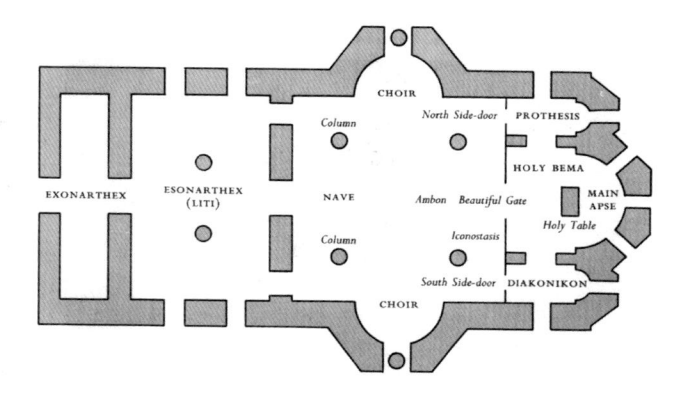

153. Typical Athonite spatial components, Mount Athos. Key spaces labelled

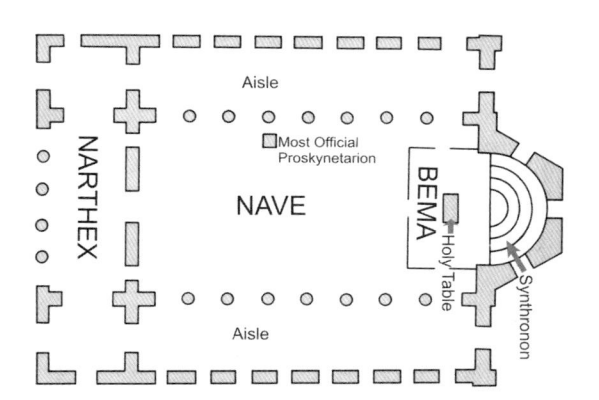

154. Typical basilica spatial components – St John Stoudios, Constantinople. Key spaces labelled

155. Athonite type *Chorostasía* – Prophet Elijah (Elias), Thessaloniki. A *horus* or large chandelier hangs down from the central dome, a marble bishop's throne (right) and *prokynetária* (left)

So while the Athonite type of church has a cross-in-square plan what makes it different are the two lateral apses of the *chorostasíes* and the double narthex. This is the pure Athonite form which is modified by the addition of chapels, the *parekklésia*. In these cases the chapels are positioned at either end of the inner narthex. Otherwise the interiors resemble lay churches, where the bema is separated from the naos by a wooden or marble iconostasis and the walls filled with wall paintings. On Mount Athos every one of the 20 monasteries, in addition to their main church, the *katholikon*, has many chapels, the *parekklésia*. These are located around the courtyard and are in addition to those attached to the *katholikon*.

These monastery churches are not only a specific type of church plan but have a different function to the other types considered, serving a congregation of monks instead of lay people. While there may be one or two services a week in a lay congregational church, in a monastery the monks have services every day and night of the week. In dependencies of monasteries, such as a *skéte* (a secondary monastery), the main church is called a *kyriakón* instead of a *katholikon* but have the same kind of plan.

156. Athonite type. Wooden model of the north side of the *katholikon*, Monastery of Xeropotamou, Mount Athos. Semi-circular apse and square prothesis (left), semi-circular *chorostasía* (centre left), rectangular *litî* (centre right) and original narthex portico (right)

Division of Space

As indicated previously the three main spaces in a Byzantine and Eastern Orthodox Church are the narthex, naos and bema. An early depiction of the formal layout of the church building is gained from the description given by Eusebius concerning the order from a judge for Marinus, a Christian soldier, to renounce his faith. Given time to reconsider his refusal to do so, a bishop, Theoteknos, took Marinus by the hand and led him into the church building (εκκλησίαν) and the sanctuary (αγιαστήριον – literally 'holy base') itself, to assist him to make a decision. The text clearly presupposes a defined holy space within the building.

The difficulty in describing the narthex, naos or bema in more detail is that each of their shapes varies depending on whether they are a component in a basilica type church or one of the other types that are not rectangular in form. Some generalizations are possible and will be made with variations explained. Besides these major spaces other spaces found in Byzantine and Eastern Orthodox churches are the forecourt or courtyard, solea, pastophoria, transepts and galleries. Byzantine and Eastern Orthodox churches in addition have a number of architectural fixtures that will be identified and described later. While the descriptions below attempt to present a clear depiction of these architectural spaces in reality the addition of enveloping spaces results in more elaborate forms. In Byzantine architecture the addition is mostly in the form of a side chapel or chapels, the *parekklésion* or *parekklésia*. These were secondary sacred spaces that have a great variety of forms and functions. Then there was the exedra, a semi-circular niche or recess crowned by a semi-dome, found extensively in centralized plan types. Exedrae were carried on arches supported on columns or piers that allowed free passage through them from the central space to the surrounding aisles.

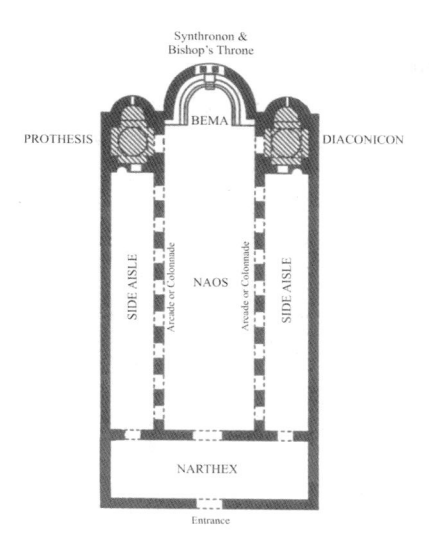

157. Typical spatial division – basilica type shown. Narthex, naos, side aisles, bema, prothesis and diaconicon

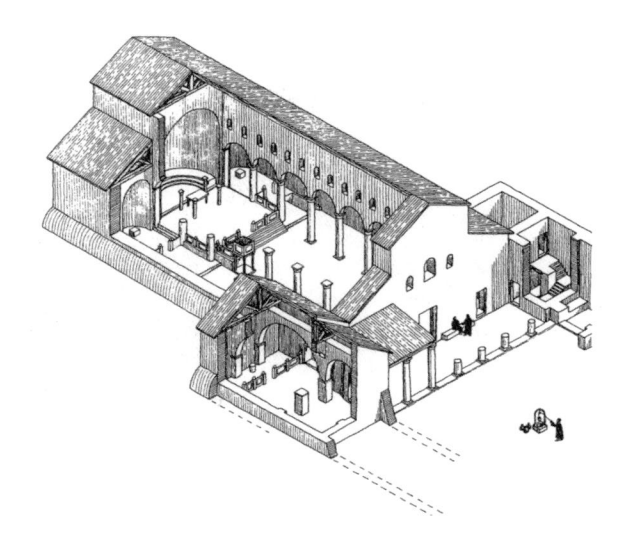

158. Typical basilica (cutout). Synthronon is semi-circular apse, holy bema, naos and side aisles separated by arcades, narthex porch, forecourt (left to right)

159. Typical bema. Bishop's throne, synthronon, Holy Table with baldachin, templon enclosed by low panels and open colonnade, ambo with two stairs (left to right)

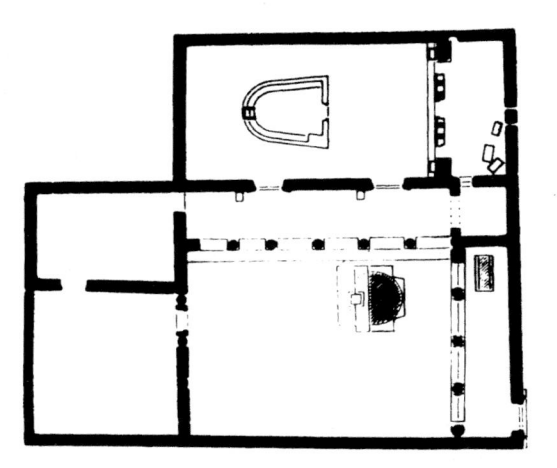

160. Qirk-Bizzeh, plan of church. Courtyard and narthex portico (bottom) and 'bema' unusually in centre of naos (top)

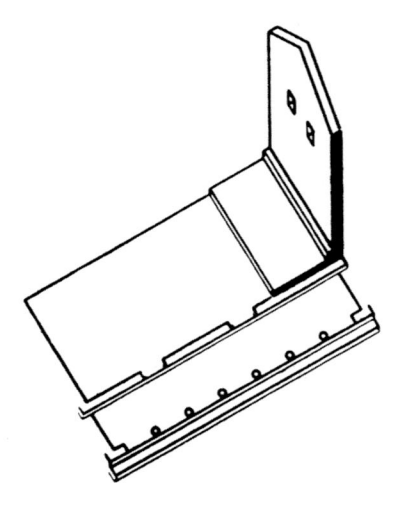

161. Qirk-Bizzeh, stage I. View of narthex portico (foreground) and holy area platform (right)

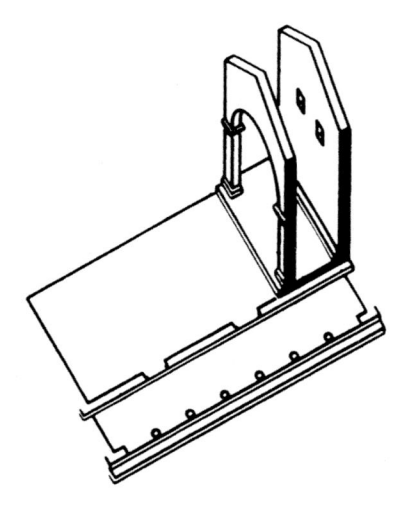

162. Qirk-Bizzeh, stage II. Insertion of triumphal arch

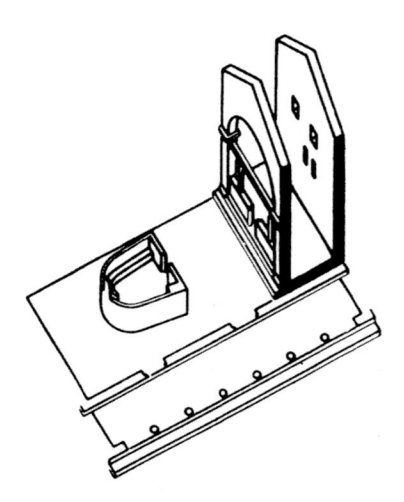

163. Qirk-Bizzeh, stage III. Completion of templon and bema in the naos

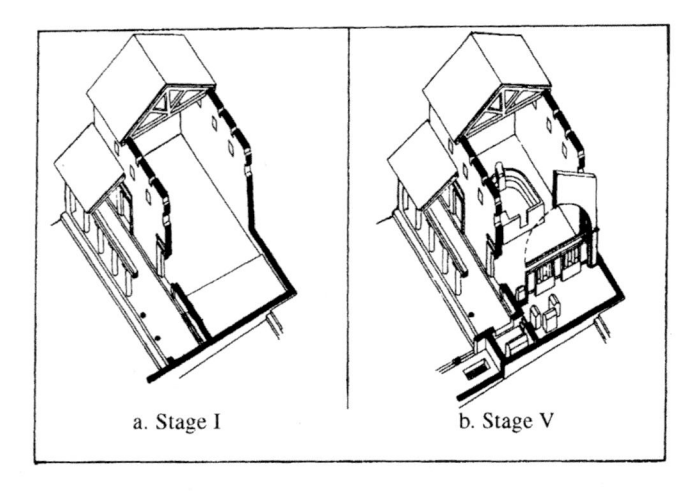

164. Quirk-Bizzeh. Development stages I to V

Forecourt and Courtyard
Most external spaces known as forecourts have disappeared and hardly any can be viewed today. When they did exist they inevitably were enclosed on all sides by a colonnaded portico. Entrance to the forecourt would be through an elaborate gateway in direct line with the central entrance to the church. Sometimes there would be a fountain, cistern, or well in the centre of the forecourt. In monasteries, instead of a

forecourt there is a central courtyard dominated by the main church, the *katholikon*. As can be seen in many Byzantine monasteries today the *katholikon* is conspicuous, imposing, with the area around the building kept clear. The courtyard is completely enclosed by a peripheral building that contains monks' cells, chapels, a refectory, and other spaces. The building constitutes a continuous multistorey barrier against the outside world, giving the appearance of a fortress. The shape of the building is rectangular or irregular depending on the contours of the topography. In monastic courtyards where there is space there is a large fountain called a *fiali* (φιάλη) that contains holy water. The fountain structure generally is octagonal in shape enclosed by a low wall with a font in the centre and covered by a small, decorated dome supported on columns.

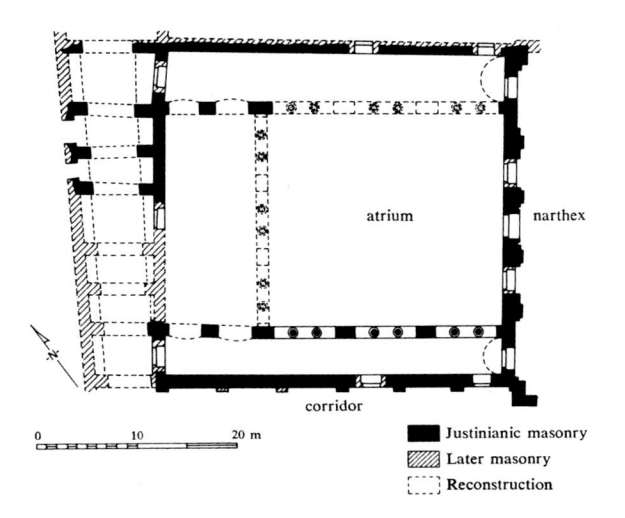

165. 'Atrium'. The forecourt of Hagia Eirene, Constantinople

166. Forecourt. San Clemente, Rome. Narthex portico (left) and original monumental gateway (right)

167. Reconstruction of monumental gateway entrance to forecourt. Hagia Sophia, Constantinople

Narthex

The narthex is a covered entrance space on the west end of a Byzantine church that extends the full width of the church in the basilica type. In other types the width of the narthex is adjusted to fit the shape of the non-rectangular naos. A narthex can take the form of a portico but in most cases is an enclosed vestibule. A central door provides access from the exterior, ideally from a forecourt or courtyard. The narthex is separated from the naos by a wall which normally contains three openings or doors that in many cases match the positions of those in the external wall to the forecourt. The central doorway from the narthex

168. Outer narthex, Hagia Sophia, Constantinople. Cross vault ceiling, holy water font, with entrance doors to the inner narthex (left)

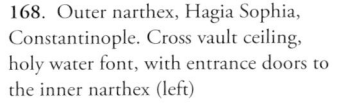

169. Inner narthex, Hagia Sophia, Constantinople. Looking south with doors (left) leading into the naos

into the naos is known as the Royal Doors. The name came about from the first churches built in Constantinople as the emperor would enter the church through this doorway with the patriarch. The congregants would enter through the two doors flanking the central one.

Besides its physical features the narthex is considered a symbolic space that connects the outside material world with the spiritual world of the church interior. In Byzantine churches the narthex has distinct liturgical and spiritual functions compared to Western churches, where if it exists the space is more of a practical vestibule. There are certain rites which are conducted in the narthex such as the exorcisms that precede the sacrament of baptism, the betrothal at weddings in some Orthodox communities, and the prayers of churching after birth. The Orthodox faithful when entering a narthex light a candle and venerate the icons there.

In the Byzantine world a church with two narthexes is rare, except for the main churches of the monasteries on Mount Athos, where they appeared first, and then in other monasteries elsewhere in Greece. What is unique about these main churches is that they have double narthexes. The outer narthex or *exonarthex* is similar to those in the traditional Byzantine church but the inner narthex or *esonarthex* is reserved for special liturgical services. The monks call this inner narthex a *litī* (λιτή).

170. Inner narthex, Hagia Sophia, Constantinople. Central higher royal doors into naos

Naos

The naos is the largest interior space in the church as it needs to accommodate the assembly of the faithful. In size the naos can be very large as in the early imperial churches built by the emperors Constantine and Justinian to the very small as in village churches. In shape the naos can be rectangular, cruciform, octagonal, square and even circular. Generally the naos would be bordered entirely or partially by a colonnade or arcade of some sort with vertical supports as either columns or piers. In wealthier communities of the Byzantine world columns were of marble with capitals that displayed an endless variety of patterns that departed from classical forms. Popular themes of capitals were basket forms or windblown acanthus but also included animals such as the lion, lamb and eagle.

171. Byzantine column capital topped by an 'impost' decorated with a cross supporting arches. San Vitale, Ravenna

172. Byzantine column capital with floral decoration. San Vitale, Ravenna

173. Byzantine column capital with imperial monogram. Hagia Sophia, Constantinople

174. Naos column capital with imperial monogram. St John, Ephesus

175. Nave column capital with 'impost' above. Santa Costanza, Rome

176. Transept Ionic type column capital (remains). St John, Ephesus

177. Typical Byzantine Corinthian type column capitals with Christian symbols on the 'imposts'

178. Corinthian style column capital. Sant'Agnese Fuori le Mura, Rome

In traditional Byzantine and Eastern Orthodox churches there were no seats or pews in contrast to Western churches. The faithful were meant to stand before God with men on the right (south side) and women on the left (north side). In some churches there is seating along the side walls in the form of lift-up wooden seats with high arms known as *stasídia*. The division of men and women persisted in Rome through the early Middle Ages as evident from the *Ordines Romani* (protocols for papal services and ceremonies) and implied in the *Liber Pontificalis*. In modern Eastern Orthodox churches the practice has been altered and there are pews with men and women seated together.

179. *Stasídia*. Lift-up wooden seats lining wall

SACRED ARCHITECTURE

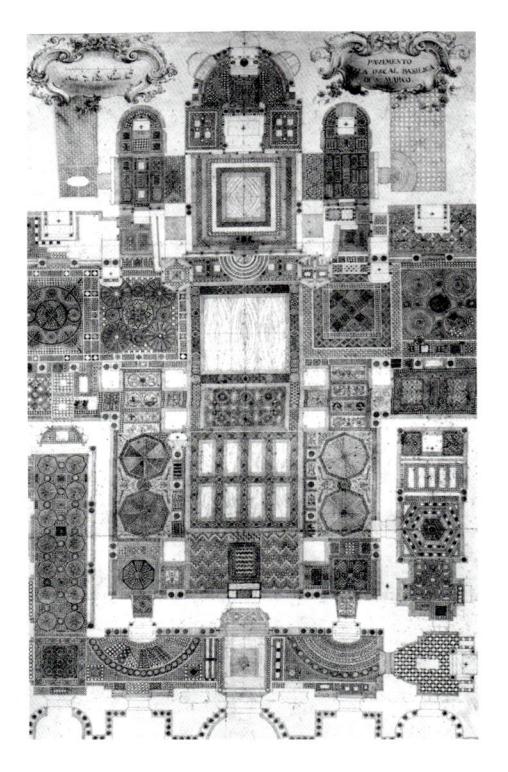

71

180. Marble floor with intricate geometrical patterns. St Mark's, Venice

181. Detail of marble floor pattern. St Mark's, Venice

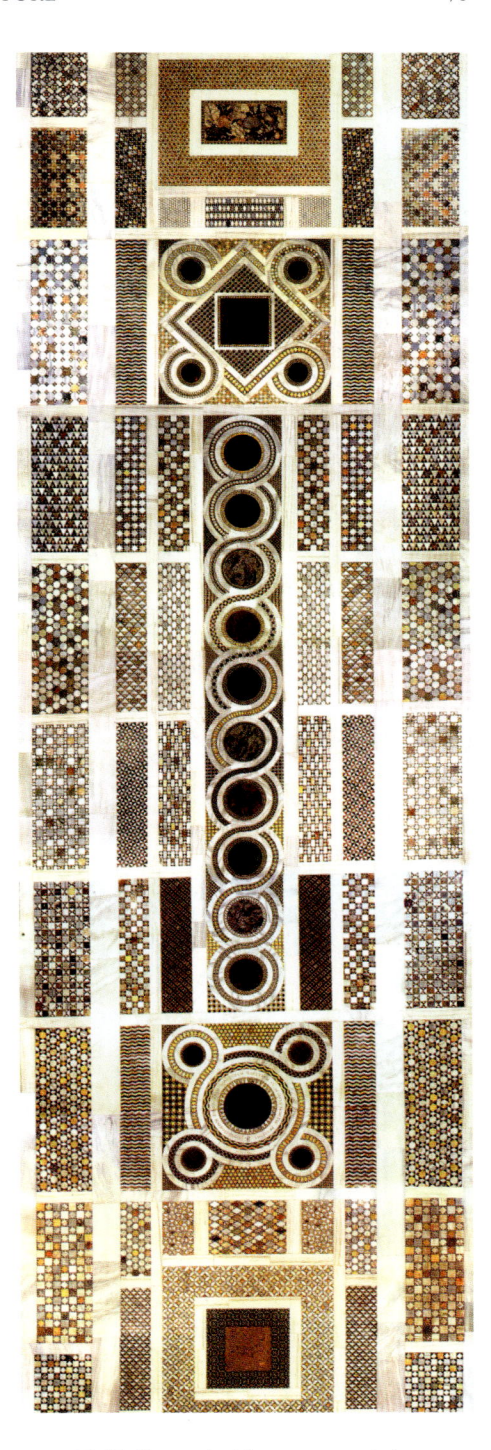

182. Marble floor with elaborate geometrical patterns. Santa Prassede, Rome

183. Interior marble wall surfaces and floor. Hosios Loukas, Stiris

184. Marble panelled wall. Hagia Sophia, Constantinople

What makes Byzantine churches distinctive is that almost the entire interior wall surfaces are covered from floor to ceiling with wall paintings or icons with plain surfaces in marble, mosaic or painted plaster. The floors are marble, typically laid out with black and white or coloured marbles inlays in geometric patterns. In some cases instead of marble floors are in mosaic. Exterior surfaces of churches (naos, narthex and bema) are generally plastered or exposed stone but kept simple. Around the twelfth century the tendency was to finish the exterior in brick which was laid in intricate patterns such as zig-zags or key-designs to create a decorative effect. It may be that the custom was derived from the East as similar decoration is found in many Persian buildings. Bricks were also used to form complicated floral motifs and in a few cases old Arab script known as cufic. A popular decoration is known as *cloisonné* in which small stone blocks are framed by bricks placed vertically and horizontally in single or double courses.

Bema
The bema is an internal raised platform and an important architectural and liturgical feature in Byzantine churches. The area occupied by the bema is also referred to as the *presbytérion* or *hieratéion* and can be viewed as the Christian equivalent of the 'Holy of Holies' in the ancient Jewish temple. A precedent for the platform was from ancient Athens where orators would address the citizens and courts of law from a raised stone dais. Cyprian, Bishop of Carthage, stated that to ascend the raised platform indicated ordination and a symbol of the power and authority of the clergy. In basilica type churches the bema is located in an apse at the one end of the naos, inevitably at the eastern end. The apse is crowned by a half-dome or a conch ('mussel shaped shell') and normally framed on the naos side by a triumphal arch. This is usually decorated with shimmering mosaics depicting narrative scenes from the Bible, or single figures against stylized landscapes, or plain gold background. Apses are either semi-circular or

185. Bema with low templon screen showing behind the covered Holy Table and synthronon

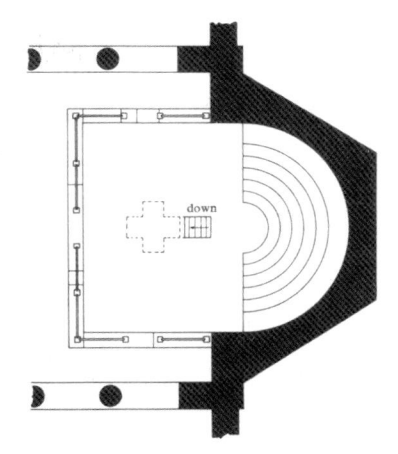

186. Reconstructed plan of bema with semi-circular synthronon, stairs down to the cross-shaped tomb below and enclosing templon with three gates. St John Stoudios, Constantinople

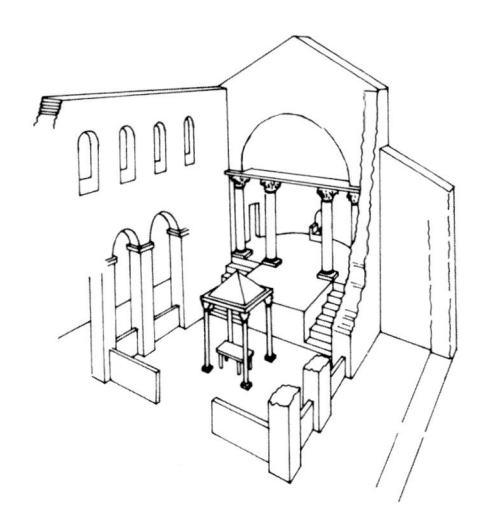

187. Diagram of a North African bema. Low templon panels, baldachin over Holy Table. Unusual stairs up to apse with bishop's throne

188. Diagram of a North African bema. Tall baldachin over Holy Table

polygonal projections or are inscribed within the flat end walls. In the non-basilica type church the bema space is usually located in the centre of the naos. The bema became a standard item in Byzantine and Eastern Orthodox churches, functioning as a stage for the Holy Table and clergy, and is equivalent to the sanctuary in Western churches.

Solea

Inside the Byzantine church the solea provides a passage for the clergy to go unhindered between the bema and ambo (pulpit) in a crowded naos. To achieve this, the solea (meaning an elevated place) is an extension out from the bema to the ambo or ambos (when there are two) in the form of a protected, raised walkway. To separate the space of the solea from the naos there is some form of barrier on either side of the passageway that could be as simple as a row of brass posts joined by a velvet rope to stone slabs set into pillars. In early churches the walkway was narrow and seemed like an arm extending out to the middle of the naos. When the ambo at some point in time was moved from the middle of the naos to the side and nearer the bema the solea changed shape. Instead of extending out at like a finger at right angles from the bema it now formed a narrow space parallel to the bema. The solea ran the full length of the bema and appeared to be an extension of it except it was a step down. The solea itself would have one or more steps down to the level of the naos.

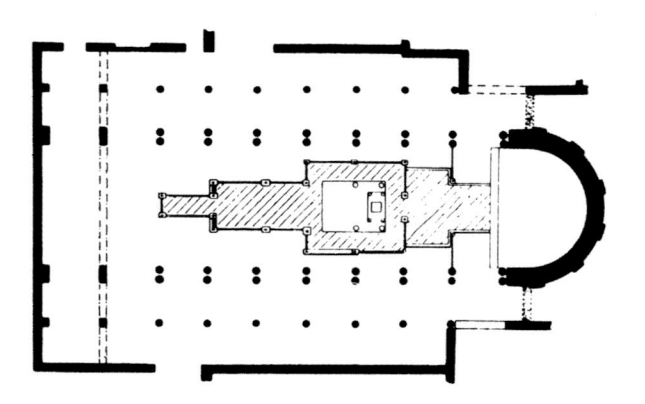

189. North African solea and central bema. Dermech Basilica, Carthage

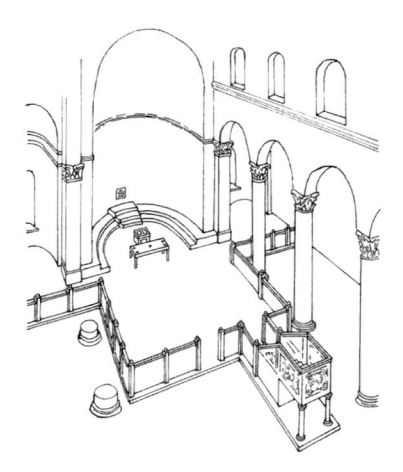

190. Broad solea and ambo. SS Peter and Paul, Gerasa, Jordan

191. Solea with central ambos on both sides. *Schola cantorum*, San Clemente, Rome

Pastophoria

The term pastophoria is from the Old Testament where it denoted the treasury and the priests' quarters in the Temple of Solomon. In Christian texts pastophoria are first mentioned in the fourth century Apostolic Constitutions and described as a sacristy at the eastern end of a church building. In scholarly literature on Byzantine churches the term pastophoria is used to designate two spaces, the prothesis and the diaconicon, that flank the central bay of the bema and Holy Table. Before pastophoria were introduced, probably in the second half of the sixth century, the preparation of the Gifts, or bread and wine, the *proskomedía* ('offering'), for the Divine Liturgy in the pre-Constantine era took place on a small table placed against the northern wall of the bema. Later, in the first Byzantine churches, the preparation took place in a special room outside the naos. Sacred books, priestly robes and various religious objects were also kept there. This special room known as the *skevophylákion* meant that precious Christian artifacts could be locked away in a safe place until needed for a service. During the Divine Liturgy separate ceremonial processions began from the *skevophylákion* carrying the Gospels and Gifts into the naos and then to the bema.

192. Exterior of the *skevophylákion* northeast view. Hagia Sophia, Constantinople

193. Interior of the *skevophylákion* looking south. Hagia Sophia, Constantinople

By the ninth century the functions of the *skevophylákion* were transferred inside the church itself. With the preparation of the gifts taking place in its own chamber, the prothesis, on the north side of the bema, this led to the disappearance of the *skevophylákion*. Clerical vestments, books and other religious items used in the Divine Liturgy were then kept in another separate chamber, the diaconicon, on the south side of the bema. In basilica type churches the prothesis and diaconicon are contained in separate apse spaces each lit by a narrow window and usually covered by a semi-dome. In small churches niches replace the prothesis and diaconicon chambers.

194. Triple apse array, Constantinople churches. Variety of semi-circular and polygonal forms

195. Remains of triple semi-circular apses. Sbeita, Tunisia. Side apses with niches in the exterior semi-circular wall

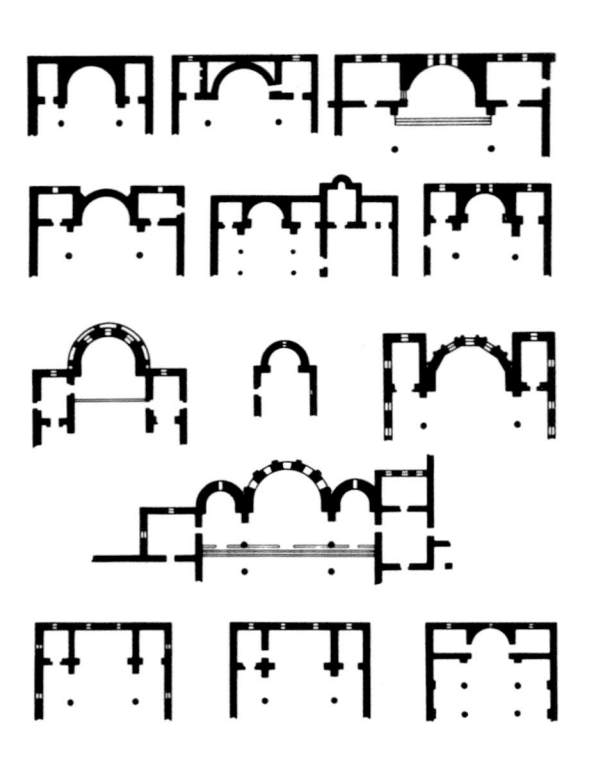

196. Variations in apse layouts – semi-circular or rectangular, enclosed or projecting. North Syria

The triple apses of the large bema space in the centre flanked on either side by the smaller spaces of the prothesis and diaconicon form what is known as a tripartite sanctuary. To some the triple apses came to represent the newly influential symbol of the Trinity. In the basilica type church the tripartite sanctuary, with its three separate curved apses, extends out and on the outside gives the appearance of three half cylinders, the centre one larger, attached to the rectangular end of the naos. Instead of the half-cylinder shape, later churches display the three sides of a hexangular projection. In Asia Minor there was a preference for a tripartite sanctuary with its two symmetrical side chambers flanking the central apse and opening into the side aisles to be enclosed by a single eastern wall thus preserving the overall rectangular shape of the basilica type. An exception to the symmetrical arrangement was where the side chambers were of a different size. The larger one would open onto the inside aisle with an arch while the smaller chamber would be closed off with a wall that contained a small door. It would appear the larger chamber was a *martyrium*, a chapel for the relics of a martyr or saint and influenced by the cult of saints that took place in the East beginning at the beginning of the fifth century. In the cross-in-square and Athonite type churches the spaces adjacent to the bema in the corner of the square are used as the prothesis and diaconicon. In the most prominent Byzantine churches built in Ravenna during the fifth and sixth centuries it appears that the side chambers did not serve a liturgical function but were used variously as chapels for the relics of martyrs, or even as libraries or storerooms. This was not the case later, after the ninth century, when they had specific uses as part of the liturgy.

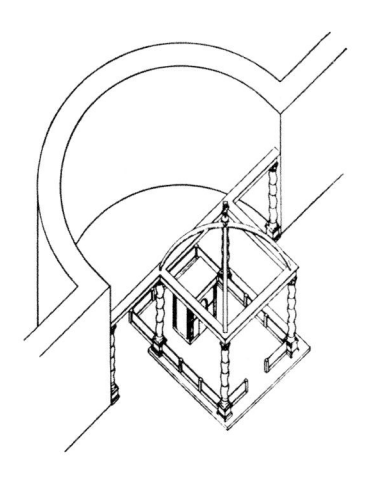

197. Martyrium, shrine or *tropaion*. St Peter's, Rome. Reconstruction *c.* AD350

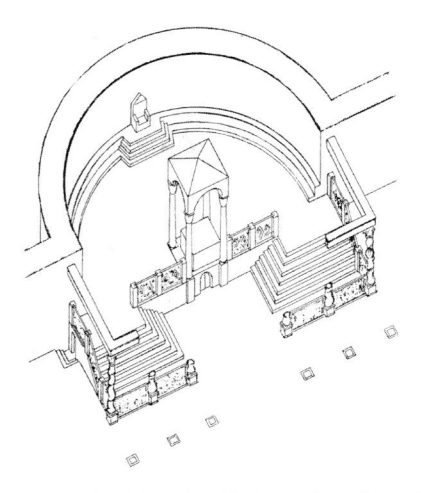

198. Holy Table with baldachin with *confessione* below. St Peter's, Rome. Reconstruction *c.* AD600

Transept

The transept or wing sometimes appeared as a feature in a few basilican type churches of the fifth and sixth centuries. Symmetrically shaped transepts or wings were spaces that protruded at right angles from and beyond the line of each side aisle. The transepts were positioned either at the termination of the aisles at the bema end or near the end. When the transepts were at the actual end against the bema, the rectangular basilica took on the shape of T. When, however, the transept was set in from the bema end the church took the form of a long cross. The transepts were usually separated from the aisles by some form of screen, colonnade or other architectural feature. Either barrel vaults or semi-domes are used to cover the transepts. If the wings are kept within the line of the side aisles they are not considered transepts but end chambers if connected to the aisles.

Galleries

Galleries if present would be either above the side aisles or the narthex, opening fully onto the space of the naos. Sometimes they extended over the both the side aisles and narthex to form a U-shape. Access to the galleries was usually by a stair outside the church. Although some contend that the galleries were for women, as men only occupied the floor of the naos, it is more likely that the galleries were for the catechumens and other special groups who are distinguished from the believers. That the gallery was commonly called the *catechoúmenon* from the seventh century would seem to confirm this. When the catechumen class eventually disappeared the gallery was put to

199. Galleries of St Demetrios, Thessaloniki. Separation from naos space by small arcade on either side

other uses such as places for private prayer or converted to rooms for various purposes. In the churches of Constantinople space was reserved in the gallery for the emperor.

Architectural Fixtures

Holy Table

The focus of the liturgy is the consecration of the Eucharist on the Holy Table. The absence of examples of Holy Tables from the early centuries is due to the use of perishable wooden tables. They were ordinary, of no particular size or shape. In some catacomb frescoes a three-legged table seemed popular. The Holy Table is usually free-standing to allow the priest, and deacons if present, to circulate around it during certain portions of the liturgy. Holy Tables were initially modest and of limited size but over time they came to be made of stone or marble, or even precious metals, instead of wood, with rich coverings, usually heavy brocade. In the larger churches from the fourth century onward a structure was placed over the Holy Table to emphasize it architecturally. In the East the structure took the form of a cupola carried on four pillars, known as a ciborium (from κιβώριον a cup), whereas in the West it was more usual to find a baldachin, a canopy with a conical or pyramidal roof.

200. Holy Table. St Mark's, Venice. Elaborate carved columns support a ciborium with the *Pala d'Oro* visible behind

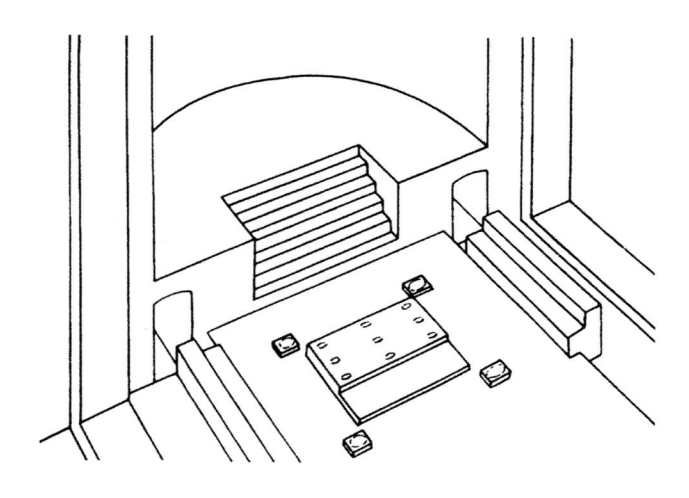

201. Holy Table. Remains of support platform and column bases, Basilica B, Nikopolis

During the fifth century the practice of bringing sacred relics within the congregational basilica brought about changes in the spatial arrangement of the church. One change that resulted from the cult of relics was that Holy Tables were transformed from the open table type to the solid box-like kind. The Tables were placed above the tomb of a saint or martyr with a vertical shaft to where the body lay in a small vault. The opening to the shaft was on the side of the Holy Table and closed by a grating of stone or metal. In some churches there was access to the vault by means of steps inside the shaft. When the body of a saint to whom the church was dedicated was elsewhere relics of the saint would be enclosed in a case called the *katathésis* in a special compartment in the Table itself. By the eighth century relics became indispensable for the inauguration of a church. The other change was when relics were placed not under or in the Holy Table but in a side chamber or chapel flanking the apse, usually on the south side. Entrance to the chapel was marked by an arch and a hanging oil lamp with curtains to close off the chapel. The relics were contained in a reliquary that usually took the form of a miniature stone sarcophagus with a gable lid. This practice came to an end in Byzantine churches when the Second Council of Nicaea in 787 required a uniform approach and ordered the placing of relics beneath all Holy Tables or embedded inside them usually at the time the Table was consecrated.

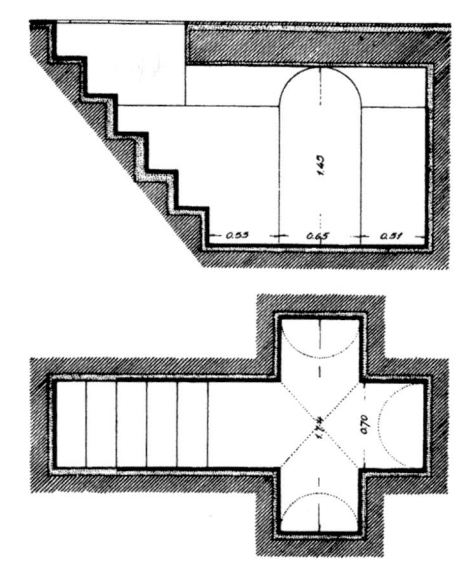

202. Tomb below the Holy Table. St John Stoudios, Constantinople. Steep steps down to cross-shaped tomb

In various commentaries the Holy Table has been viewed as Christ's tomb, or the table of the Last Supper, Golgotha, or the heavenly altar and other interpretations. On top of the Holy Table toward the back and in the centre is the tabernacle in which the Eucharist is stored in a small ark reserved for communion of the sick and dying. The tabernacle is made of brass or silver and is often shaped like a model of a church building. In front of the tabernacle is the book of Gospels most often with a decorated metal cover. Behind the Holy Table is a seven-branched candle stand which recalls that of the Old Testament Tabernacle and Temple in Jerusalem. Behind the stand is a golden processional cross and on either side of this are liturgical fans which represent the six-winged Seraphim. Against the wall behind the Holy Table is a large cross with a flat icon of a crucified Christ which can be moved during the 50 days following *Páscha* (Easter).

Synthronon

In the early churches a synthronon ('with throne' from the Greek σύν and θρόνον), a semi-circular bench for the clergy to sit on when the scriptures were read during the Divine Liturgy, lined the back wall of the apse in basilican type churches. The synthronon could take two forms. First, the bench could be at the top of a number of semi-circular steps. Secondly, the synthronon could be more than one bench and instead could be a concentric series of semi-circular benches above a step. In the centre of either form of synthronon, and placed higher than the benches, was the bishop's chair. Eusebius uses the expression tall throne (θρόνος ὑψηλός) to designate the episcopal chair. This followed the tradition in civil basilicas where the judge or president sat above the scribes and assessors. There was a functional reason for the bishop's throne to be at the top of the synthronon. It was so that he could both be seen and see above the Holy Table during the service. From his throne the bishop would preach, seated flanked on either side by clergy. This arrangement followed the description in the Book of Revelation

203. Synthronon. Hagia Eirene, Constantinople. Former seven-level synthronon is semi-circular apse still visible today

204. Synthronon. St Nicholas, Myra. Ten-stepped well preserved synthronon with base for the bishop's throne visible in the centre

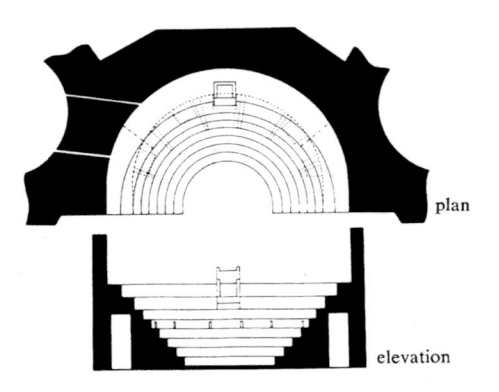

205. Synthronon, plan and elevation. St Efimia, Constantinople. Seven-stepped synthronon with bishop's throne and platform at the top

206. Synthronon and bema. St Efimia, Constantinople. Remains of the synthronon

(4, 2-10) where God is on His throne with 24 elders in white robes disposed on either side of Him. It appears that at about the same time as the triple apses were introduced the synthronon was abandoned. The bishop's throne was then relocated to a position on the south side of the solea.

Initially the bishop delivered the sermon while seated on his throne following the Jewish custom. When this position at the back of the apse was found inconvenient it is likely that a portable chair, most likely of wood, would be placed in the front of the bema. Some bishops, the famous example being Chrysostomos, preached from the ambo in the naos so that the congregation could hear him with greater ease. A revealing representation in Byzantine art of a bishop preaching from the synthronon is contained in the Paris manuscript of Gregory of Nazianzus (c.329–389/90). It also shows the apostles seated on a semi-circular bench each holding a gospel or scroll and gesturing vigorously.

Early bishop's thrones may have been portable. In her pilgrimage diary Egeria mentions that at Jerusalem after the morning service at the Anastasis building '(i)mmediately a throne is placed for the bishop in the major church, the Martyrium', and during Holy Week when the bishop comes to the major church '(t)o the rear, at the apse behind the altar, a throne is placed for the bishop …'. In the West the word *cathedra* (derived from the Greek word for chair, καθήδρα) was used in place of throne (θρόνος) to indicate a chair with a straight high back. Christian cathedrae were made of wood or marble compared to the Roman senatorial ones that were veneered in ivory. The episcopal church received the name *ecclesia cathedrae*, from which is derived the designation of a church which is a cathedral.

207. Ivory paneled throne of Archbishop Maximian, Archiepiscopal Chapel, Ravenna

Templon and Iconostasis

A screen in the form of templon in early churches or an iconostasis in later churches separated the naos from the bema. The templon was at first a low wood rail or screen that eventually came to consist of short stone columns or colonnettes supporting a decorative beam (architrave) on top of them. This meant that the congregation had a clear view of the bema and the clergy activity there. At some stage slabs were placed between the colonnettes which created more of a visual and physical barrier between the naos and bema. About the middle of the fifth century the templon developed into an elaborately decorated and much higher screen or iconostasis (icon stand) that supported icons. The appearance of the iconostasis as it appears today was completed toward the end of the eleventh century. The effect of the solid iconostasis that completely fills the archway of the apse is to cut congregants off both from hearing the most important prayers and seeing the vital actions of the liturgy. The idea behind this was the belief that the mystery of the consecration was too holy for the laity and only the clergy by virtue of their ordination could hear, see and touch the mysteries.

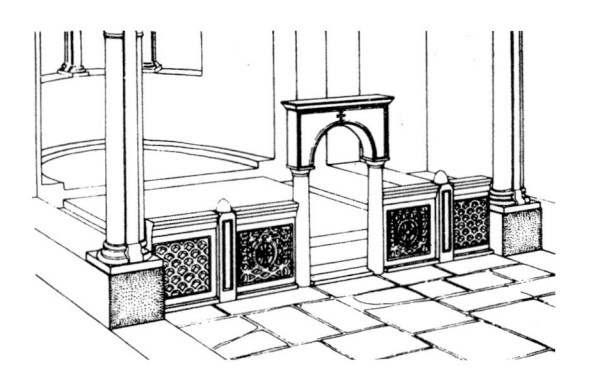

208. Templon with decorative panels and arched bema entrance. Basilica, Olympia

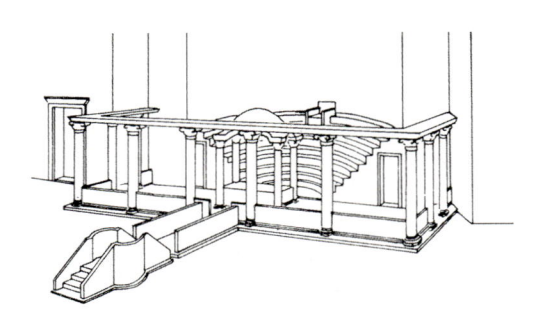

209. Reconstructed templon with low panels, columns and architrave, St Efimia, Constantinople. Enclosed solea leads to ambo in the naos

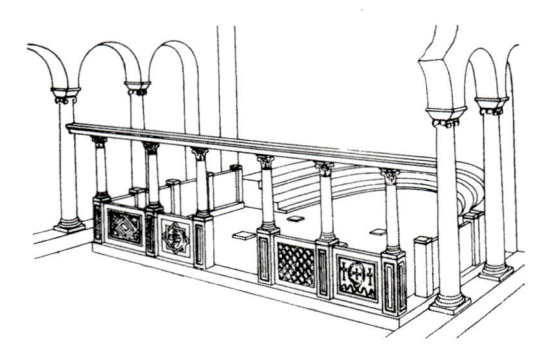

210. Templon with decorative panels, colonnettes and architrave. Aphendelli, Lesbos

Usually there will be three doors in the iconostasis, one in the middle and one on either side, or only one central door in small churches or chapels. In the group of three doors the central one is called the Beautiful Gate and can only be used by the clergy. The most common image on the two doors of the Gate is the Annunciation. During certain parts of the service a curtain is drawn or the doors of the Beautiful Gate are closed. The doors on either side of the centre are called the Deacons' Doors or the Angels' Doors and have depicted on them the Archangels Michael and Gabriel. Although the iconostasis separates the space of the naos from that of the bema symbolically it can be sensed in two different ways. In one sense it marks the border between the terrestrial naos and the heavenly Holy Bema but in another way it connects the faithful in the naos to the Holy of Holies and the Holy Table through the holy persons represented by the icons.

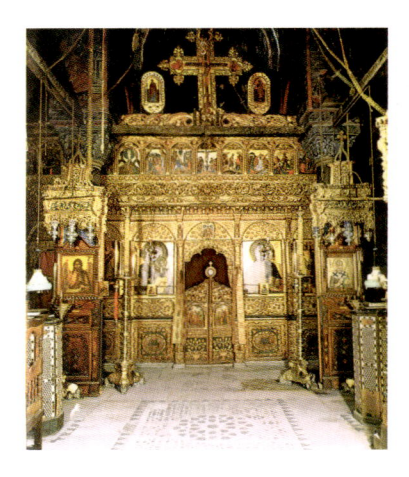

211. Iconostasis. *Katholikon*, Monastery of Stavronikita, Mount Athos. Typical of a small naos are two '*despotikaí*' icons on either side of the Beautiful Gate, partial view of additional icons on either end, one tier of icons above and the large cross at the top. On the right-hand *proskynetárion* is the famous icon of St Nicholas 'Streidás'

212. Short Iconostasis with four icons, three doors, and one tier of icons above. From an Ionian Island, the Byzantine and Christian Museum, Athens

213. Iconostasis. Koimisis tis Theotokou, Anogi, Ithaka. Elaborate iconostasis with three levels of icons

214. Iconostasis. St Nicholas, Svoronata, Kefalonia. Highly ornate, three-level iconostasis that reaches the ceiling

215. The Beautiful Gate. Chapel of the Five Martyrs, Monastery of St Catherine, Sinai. A stunning depiction of the Annunciation

216. The Beautiful Gate. Byzantine Museum, Thessaloniki. Highly wrought doors depicting the Annunciation (top centre), imperial figures, possibly Justinian and Theodora, and four Fathers of the Church (bottom)

217. The Beautiful Gate. Byzantine and Christian Museum, Athens. The Annunciation with an architectural background, and two figures above with the lettering crossing over the two scrolls

Ambo

From a liturgical point of view the ambo (raised pulpit) and the bema are the two focal points in a Byzantine church. Processions back and forth between the two took place along the solea or pathway connecting the two. The ambo derived its name from the fact is had had to be ascended (αναβαίνειν) by a flight of steps.

First introduced into churches in the second half of the fourth century the ambo came into universal use by the ninth century and reached its full development in the twelfth. There was no standard position for the ambo in the naos. It could be found in the middle of the naos or to one side of the naos. As Davies relates, the ambo in Greece went through three stages of development. At first it consisted of a monolithic pedestal and a rounded platform reached by three or four steps. In the second stage the pedestal became a semi-circular structure with two short flights of steps leading up from the same side to a low platform. Occasionally there was a baldachin. Finally, the ambo took the form of a high platform, with or without a baldachin, approached by two flights of steps, one on the east and the other on the west. The ambos were usually built of white marble and richly decorated with ornamental panels of coloured marbles and enriched with carvings. As noted earlier, in Byzantine churches the separate structure of the ambo, or ambos, was connected to the bema by the solea. In the fourteenth century the ambo gradually fell out of use and was largely superseded by simpler pulpits.

218. Ambo sketch. Hagia Sophia, Thessaloniki

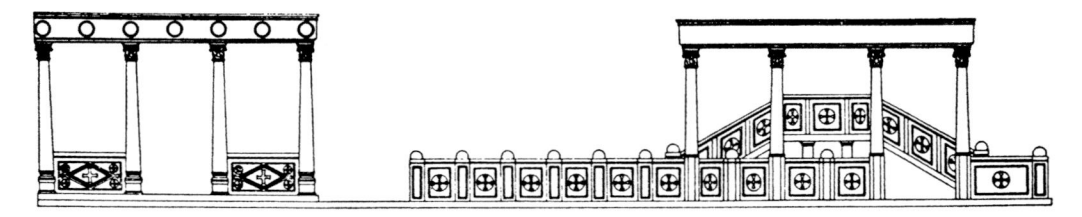

219. Ambo side view, Hagia Sophia, Constantinople. Holy Table with columns and architrave, solea, covered ambo with stairs on both sides (left to right)

220. Gospel ambo, San Clemente, Rome

221. Ambo. Basilica A, Beyazit, Constantinople

From the ambo the scriptures were read by deacons or sub-deacons sometimes called lectors. The method of reading was most likely taken from the practice in synagogues where rabbis used a kind of desk. When the ambo had two flights of steps the lector would read the Epistles from the eastern steps facing the Holy Table whereas the Gospels were read from the western steps with the deacon facing the congregation. When there were two ambos flanking the bema on either side, one was for the reading of the Epistles and the other for the Gospels.

222. Ambo. San Lorenzo Fuori le Mura, Rome

Baptismal Fonts
The ritual of baptism changed over the centuries, beginning with the baptism of Jesus Christ in the River Jordan by John. The Christians paralleled what many religions believed – that the immersion in water was a ritual of symbolic cleansing. Baptism ($\beta\alpha\pi\tau\iota\zeta\epsilon\iota\nu$, 'to dip') of people initiated into Christianity during the first two centuries was by triple immersion in natural pools of water such as lakes or rivers. After Constantine's Edict of Tolerance in 313 allowed Christians to practice openly the need to baptize throngs of new converts called for separate buildings, baptisteries, to be erected. Early baptisteries were most often separated from the main church building to protect the privacy of converts who were baptized naked. Typically the baptisteries had antechambers where converts could undress, while in a separate room there would be a baptismal pool with glittering mosaics.

The first baptisteries had a pool sunk into the floor with steps to allow easy descent and ascent into the water for immersion in the baptismal ritual – passage from life into death and into a new life. Pools were in the shape of a cross to connect the ritual of baptism to Christ's death and resurrection. Around the seventh century above-ground pools came into use in which a convert would stand or kneel while being doused with holy water. Until the Middle Ages baptisms were intended for adults only as it followed a lengthy process of purification and understanding of the profundity of the ritual. The increase in infant deaths during the Middle Ages led to the desire to have a child baptized as soon as possible with the fear that death before baptism would mean eternal damnation without the absolution of original sin. With the practice of infant baptisms in the Middle Ages, pools for baptisms were replaced by pedestal fonts as infants were baptized by the sprinkling or pouring of holy water of their head. An exception was in Eastern Orthodoxy, which still today continues the early practice of full immersion of an infant in a basin font. Fonts came to be located in separate chapels or areas in the church itself as the need for a separate baptistery disappeared.

Orientation

The custom in ancient Greek and Roman temples was to have the main doors open to the east – that is, oriented eastward – so as to herald sunrise. This allowed the rays of the rising sun to light up in a dramatic fashion the statue of the deity located at the end of the temple nave and to awe the onlookers. This special event – the rising sun shining directly through the entrance doors – occurred only on one day of the year, the festival day of the god or goddess to whom the temple was dedicated. The term to *orient* is derived from the Latin word *oriens* translated as rising or rising sun and thus east.

Early churches followed the pagan temple custom of entrance doors on the east. This meant that the apse was at the other end of the naos, oriented west. But the Christians had a different purpose in mind. As the theologian Tertullian (*c*.160–220) pointed out many pagans believed the Christians worshipped the sun because they met on *dies solis* (from the Greek *eméra elíou*), that is Sunday, and that they prayed towards the east. Another association, a very early one, is displayed in a tomb below St Peter's in Rome that shows a captivating image of Christ as the sun god Apollo in a four horse chariot hurtling toward the sun. The Christian theologian, Clement of Alexandria (*c*.150–215), wrote about this mosaic scene depicting Christ driving his chariot across the sky like the Sun God. More directly Origen Adamantius, a third-century Christian scholar and theologian, wrote that the significance of the eastward-facing entrance was that is where the rise of the true light, Christ resurrected, will occur at the end of days and appear as the sign of the son of man, the cross, in the sky. The fourth-century church historian, Eusebius, in his descriptions of churches built by the bishop of Tyre and the bishop of Nola, noted that each had their main entrance on the east. The apse at Tyre thus faced west as did those of other basilicas such as St Peter's, St Paul's and San Lorenzo in Rome and the Church of the Resurrection in Jerusalem. In these churches, then, the bishop on his throne in the apse looked outward to the congregation and toward the east.

It is worth recording a little more of the description Eusebius wrote about the basilica at Tyre as it is the oldest depiction of an early Christian church. It comes from his address of extravagant praise to the Bishop of Tyre, Paulinus, on the dedication of the basilica, probably around 317. Eusebius begins his description by noting the fortified wall Paulinus used to secure the courtyard. Then he writes how Paulinus placed in the wall a high and great gateway (πρόπυλον) 'toward the very rays of the rising sun'. Within these gates he encloses the four sides of a quadrangular courtyard with colonnades (στοαίς) so that there remains in the middle an atrium 'for beholding the sky, providing it with airy brightness, open to the rays of light'. In front of the main façade of the 'temple' he places fountains as symbols of holy purification and to provide cleansing for those who will proceed to the interior of the sacred enclosure. The entry into the 'temple' was by means of three doors, the middle one wider, higher and more heavily decorated with ornaments and embossed compared to the other two, 'once again under the rays of the sun'. The interior space of the basilica, the Royal House (βασίλειον οίκον), had a similar arrangement as the courtyard with colonnades on each side and openings above them to provide light. The interior was decorated with lavish materials and with a floor of ornate marble and cedar of Lebanon 'placed above these'. No expense was spared. There were also 'lofty thrones in honor of the presidents' along with an altar in the 'holy of holies' and benches all of which were 'inaccessible to the masses … fenced … with wooden latticework adorned with the craftsman's utmost artistry so as to present a wonderful scene to the beholder'. Outside the 'temple' were covered arcades or halls (εξέδρας) and large buildings on either side joined to the Royal House with openings to allow communication into the central building.

Sometime in the fifth century the orientation arrangement was dramatically reversed so that the entrance was now on the west end of the church and the apse with the Holy Table on the east end. It is not clear why this extraordinary change occurred and what brought it about. The idea now held was that it was necessary for the priests and faithful to pray facing east as the second coming of Christ

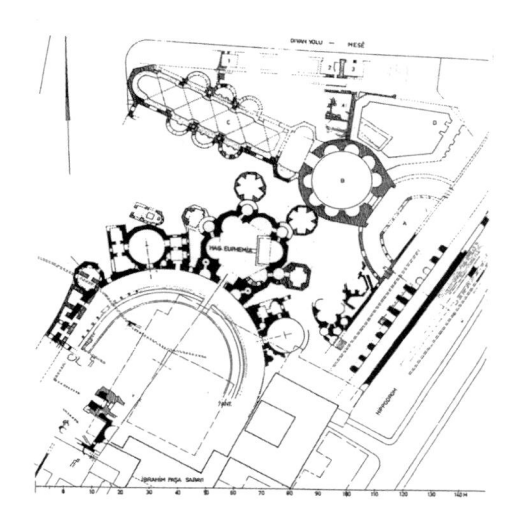

223. St Efimia, Constantinople in the centre of the complex with an entrance from the semi-circular Sigma courtyard

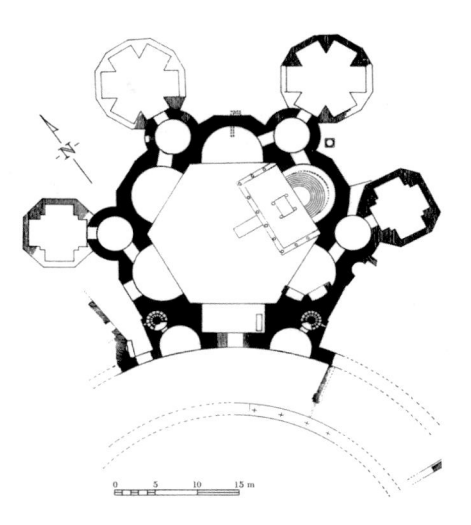

224. St Efimia, Constantinople reoriented with bema and synthronon placed due east with new entrance directly opposite

would be from the east at sunrise. The eastern apse becomes the rule in the churches of Ravenna and Byzantine churches throughout the East and remains so in Eastern Orthodox churches until the present day.

The conversion of a particular Roman building into a church is of great interest as it shows the importance attached to correct orientation. The building in question is the small palace north of the hippodrome in Constantinople constructed during the second or third decade of the fifth century. The original palace building was a six-sided hall with an entrance from a semi-circular courtyard known as the Sigma Court. In the sixth century the interior of the Roman palace was converted into the Christian church of St Efimia. In the conversion it would have been logical to place the bema and Holy Table on the side of the hexagon opposite the existing entrance into the hall, creating an axis from the courtyard through the entrance of the hall and terminating at the bema. If this had been done, however, it would have meant that the bema would not be oriented due east. To attain the correct orientation the bema was placed in a niche on one side off the axis so that the priest would face east during the Divine Liturgy. Left like this the bema would not be on axis with the entrance doors. To address this problem a new entrance was opened up next to the existing one, which was walled up, so that there would be a direct line between it and the bema. This arrangement allowed the new Christian space to be centred on an east-west axis.

Chapter Three

SPLENDID CHURCHES

The general description of the sacred architecture of the Byzantine church in the previous chapter provides a scaffold to represent individual churches in detail. There are hundreds of fascinating early Christian and Byzantine churches that still exist throughout the former Byzantine Empire but to describe them all would be too encyclopedic and require a volume in itself. To take the Greek Islands for example, there must be over 1,000 urban and rural Byzantine churches that still exist today, as attested in the work of the art historian, Nigel McGilchrist, in his magisterial 20-volume series covering 70 islands. On Naxos alone there are more than 130 important churches which constitute a greater concentration and spread over time than the largest Greek island, Crete. Then again, in a book about the islands of Kefallinia and Ithaki off the west coast of Greece by this author, over 30 monasteries and numerous village churches on the two islands were studied. So the approach adopted in this chapter is to be highly selective and describe only the splendid churches located in the old influential centres – the capital cities of Rome and New Rome or Constantinople, the Holy Land as it was the heart of Christendom, and the regional capitals of Thessaloniki and Ravenna. The reasoning is that they became models for churches built elsewhere. Of the churches in these centres the emphasis will be to depict those which can still be seen today in one form or another. This approach also enables examples of all the seven architectural types of church to be described. The art work in the selected churches is described separately in a later chapter. In the illustrations of church plans walls are shown as solid black lines, or hatched, or unfilled, each indicating a different date of construction.

Rome

The city of Rome is where one can still see today in one place many early Christian churches as there are such a large number of them, at least 50. They have been described superbly in separate books by Matilda Webb and by Hugo Brandenburg and in an overall book on the architecture of Rome edited by Stefan Grundmann. The challenge is how to capture this wealth of information in a brief manner. Although all the churches are of the basilica plan type, except three, this does not simplify the problem as the most of the basilica churches were conversions of earlier buildings or built on top of previous structures. The kinds of building that were converted or built over included houses, mansions, apartment buildings (*insulae*), halls, bath houses (*thermae*) and other types of Roman edifices. To depict concisely early Christian churches in Rome the solution adopted here is to group them into four categories: Original, Converted, Superimposed and Eastern. In each group only a typical or intriguing church of the group, or sometimes more than one, that displays many visible early Christian architectural and art features will be described in detail. In virtually every church side chapels have been added to the pure basilica form in later times but these will not be mentioned in the descriptions. As far as possible what is known of the original forms of each church will be depicted without adding information about all the remodelings or restorations that occurred

225. San Giovanni in Laterno, Rome. Baptistery colonnade around a central font

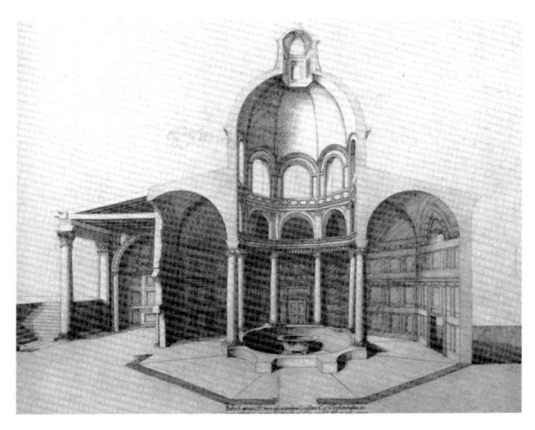

226. San Giovanni in Laterno, Rome. Baptistery cross section

later. As an introduction, the first two churches built by Emperor Constantine will be explained in detail as they were the originals or prototypes and no doubt influential on the design of churches that followed. It should be noted that after Constantine other emperors as well as popes and wealthy private individuals sponsored the building of churches.

The first official and monumental church building of Christianity built by Constantine was the **Lateran Church**. The presumed ground-breaking foundation took place in the year 314 during the pontificate of Sylvester (r. 314–335) and the likely completion date was 324. The building was known at first as the *Basilica Constantiniana* after its founder, or *Basilica Lateranensis* after its location. At the consecration it was called the *Basilica Salvatoris* (Saviour) and only in the early Middle Ages was it designated *Basilica S. Iohannis* (S. Giovanni in Laterno) as it is known today. Beneath and around the church are the remains of a mansion and barracks. The mansion was the *Domus Faustae* that belonged to Constantine and which was used in 313 for meetings of the church presided over by Pope Miltiades (r. 311–314). Frescoes depicting scenes from the New Testament dated to the second half of the fourth century have been found in a porticoed structure of the mansion. Barracks that belonged to the Constantine's mounted Imperial

227. San Giovanni in Laterno. Original bronze doors from the Curia in the forum of Rome

Guard and the mansion were razed and their basements filled in to create a platform and foundations for the church. The church underwent several repairs and minor additions over the centuries and then extensively remodelled in the seventeenth century by the renowned architect Borromini. Only part of Constantine's edifice was preserved. The inscription on the façade reads: *Omnium urbis et orbis Ecclesiarum Mater et Caput* (Mother and first of all churches of the cities of the world) in recognition of its status.

The original building had a nave and aisles on either side of lower height (Latin instead of Byzantine terminology such as nave instead of naos for the churches in Rome will be used). The double aisles on either side were of almost equal width. Inner aisles were the same length as the nave but the outer aisles stopped short in low chapels or annexes at the apse end. The apse was semi-circular in shape the full width of the nave which was brightly lit by clerestory windows. There was probably a forecourt on the eastern end and a porticoed porch from which three portals opened onto the nave. The exterior of the building was plain and austere and was notable only for the central bronze doors that were the original doors from the Roman Curia in the Forum. In contrast the interior was very elaborate with columns of red granite and green marble, a colourful marble floor, and wall paintings with scenes from the Old and New Testaments. Golden mosaic covered the half-dome of the apse. A colonnade with a pediment (*fastigium*) over the central arch, an allusion to triumphal architecture, separated the sanctuary from the nave. In the pediment there were almost life size figures of Christ and the Twelve Apostles. Constantine embellished the interior with fabulously rich decorations and gifts.

The second church built by Constantine is known as **Old St Peter's**, a funerary basilica over the apostle's shrine on the Vatican hill. The basilica also served as a congregational church. Adjacent to the shrine were numerous Christian tombs known as the Necropolis. To create a level platform for the vast basilica the builders had to cut deeply into the rock on one side and place the tons of excavated earth on the other side which meant that the Necropolis and everything in it was completely covered up to provide a level area for the church. Work was begun in 318 and the church completed in 324. A porticoed forecourt preceded the basilica which consisted of a nave, flanked by two aisles on each side, ending in a transept and apse. The altar was placed above the shrine of St Peter. As with the *Basilica Salvatoris,* Constantine richly decorated the interior with gold and silver lighting fixtures and covered the apse with gold foil. Column bases, shafts and capitals were reused from Roman buildings. The Necropolis was rediscovered in 1940 and excavations carried out to reveal two rows of mausolea, the cemetery and the shrine of St Peter.

By the fifteenth century the Old St Peter's church building showed signs of collapse that led to a series of rebuilding efforts by various popes. In 1506 much of the old St Peter's was dismantled by Pope Julius II and the task of designing a new basilica was handed to the prominent architect of that time, Bramante. His design was a Greek cross plan with an enormous central dome about the same size as the Pantheon which would have made it a more spectacular cruciform type church than that of St Mark's in Venice which was built later. The plan of St Peter's was changed to a Latin cross and only finished in the first half of the seventeenth century and involved many famous architects, including Raphael and Michelangelo. In 1656 the building of the splendid and enormous forecourt of the Piazza San Pietro was initiated under the direction of the renowned architect Bernini.

Hugo Brandenburg in his book points out that in the first half of the fourth century the papal and private church foundations took second place to those founded by Emperor Constantine. But in the second half of that century the growth in the number of believers including wealthy members of the upper classes and senatorial aristocracy, as well as the suppression of pagan religions, transformed Rome into the centre of the Christian world. The church received many gifts, legacies and donations and was thus able to embark on an extensive building programme from the late fourth century until early in the following

228. Old St Peter's on the Vatican hill, Rome. Basilica form, double aisles and clerestory lighting

229. Old St Peter's, Rome. Drawing of forecourt (now disappeared) and drum of the central dome under construction

century. Pope Damasus (r. 366–384) in particular was active founding five new community churches in Rome to serve the rapidly growing number of Christians. Brandenburg further notes that in the middle of the fifth century popes such as Sixtus III (r. 432–440) and Leo I (r. 440–461) competed with imperial authority in the foundation of church buildings. In this period church architecture reached a new height with architectural achievements such as the great papal basilica of Santa Maria Maggiore and churches such as Santa Sabina. Despite the sack of Rome by Alaric in 410 church buildings continued to be erected. In the period after the Vandals under their king Genseric occupied and plundered Rome in 455 church buildings were built smaller and less lavishly furnished than in the preceding half-century. Brandenburg provides a list of the ten *martyria* and memorial churches in

230. Old St Peter's, Rome. Just before its demolition early in the sixteenth century

the age of Constantine, the four churches that were the first community churches in Rome, and the names of the papal, private and community church foundations in the late fourth, fifth and sixth centuries.

Original Basilicas
After St Peter's the other original basilica type churches were Sant'Agate dei Goti, San Vitale, and San Sisto Vecchio all erected in the fifth century. Those built later were Santi Quirico e Giulitta and San Silverstro in Capite (sixth century), Sant'Angelo in Pescheria (eighth), and Santa Maria Nova (ninth). Unfortunately all of these were so altered later that few early Christian features are visible today.

EARLY CHURCHES IN ROME
ORIGINAL BASILICAS

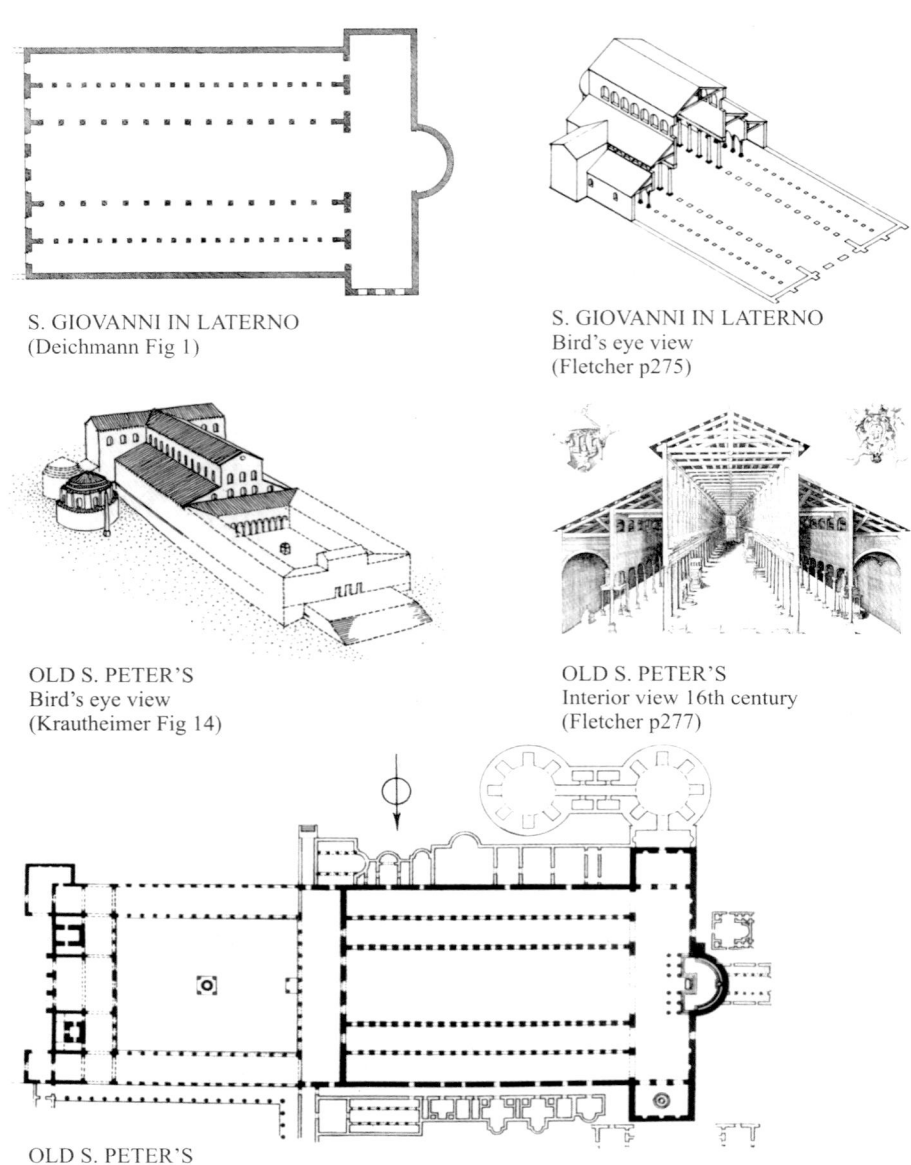

S. GIOVANNI IN LATERNO
(Deichmann Fig 1)

S. GIOVANNI IN LATERNO
Bird's eye view
(Fletcher p275)

OLD S. PETER'S
Bird's eye view
(Krautheimer Fig 14)

OLD S. PETER'S
Interior view 16th century
(Fletcher p277)

OLD S. PETER'S
Plan
(Grabar, 1968 Fig 180)

231. Rome, plan type – original basilicas I

EARLY CHURCHES IN ROME
ORIGINAL BASILICAS

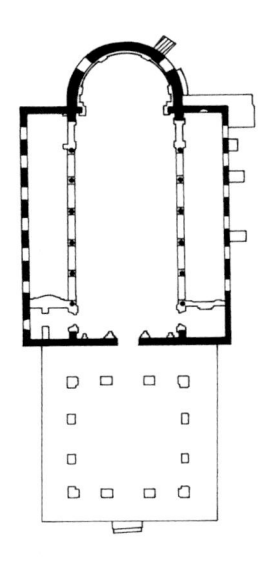

S. AGATE GOTI
(Webb p79)

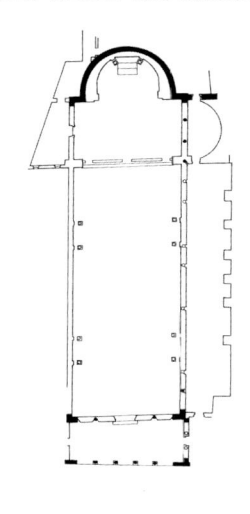

S. VITALE
(Webb p81)

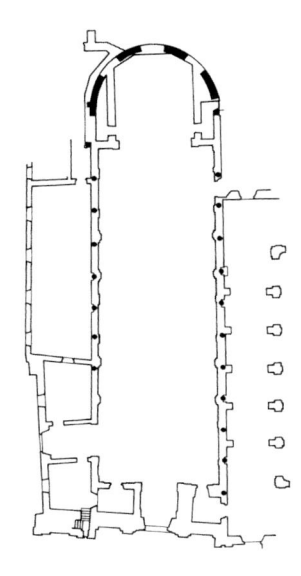

S. SISTO VECCHIO
(Webb p204)

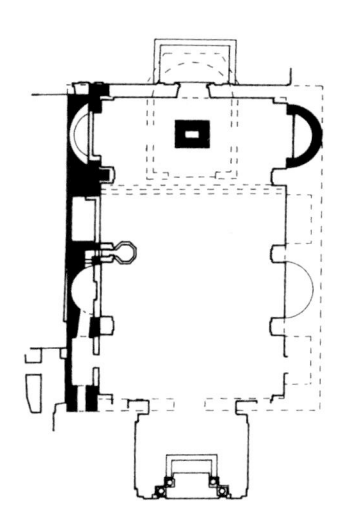

SS. QUIRICO E GIULITTA
(Webb p134)

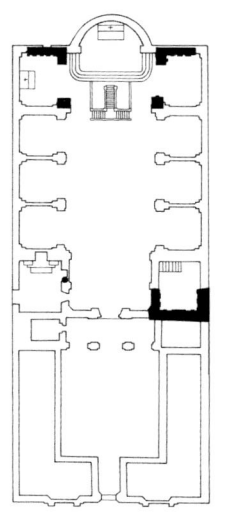

S. SILVESTRO IN CAPITE
(Webb p159)

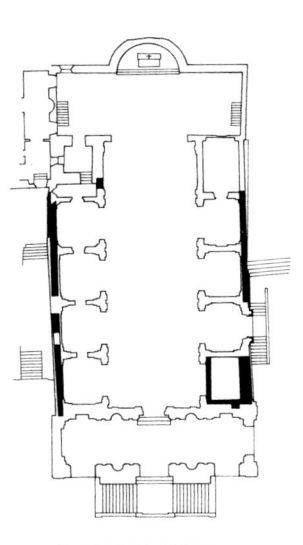

S. MARIA NOVA
(Webb p131)

232. Rome, plan type – original basilicas II

EARLY CHURCHES IN ROME
CONVERTED BUILDINGS

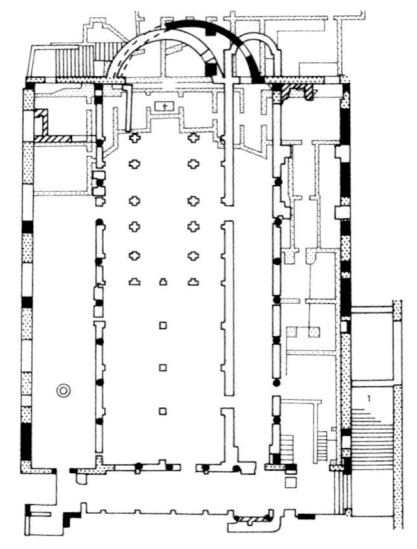

S. CLEMENTE LOWER CHURCH
(Webb p90)

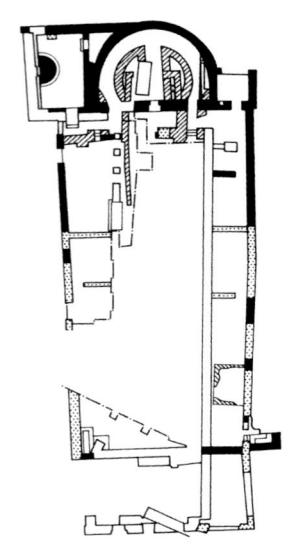

S. CRISOGONO LOWER CHURCH
(Webb p264)

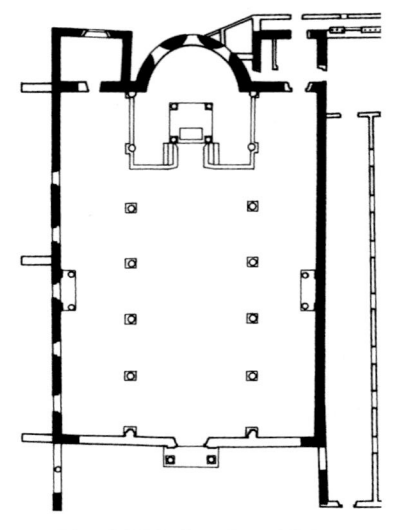

SS. NEREO ED ACHILLEO
(Webb p199)

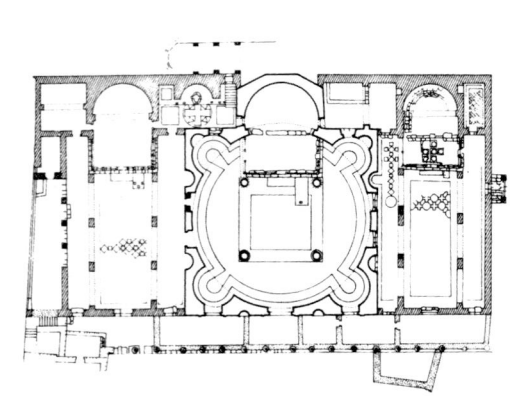

SS. COSMAS E DAMIANO
(Mango Fig 22)

233. Rome, plan type – converted buildings I

EARLY CHURCHES IN ROME
CONVERTED BUILDINGS

S. CLEMENTE
Interior of upper 12th century basilica
(Peeters Fig 31)

234. Rome, plan type – converted buildings II

EARLY CHURCHES IN ROME
CONVERTED BUILDINGS

Restored entrance view (north facade)

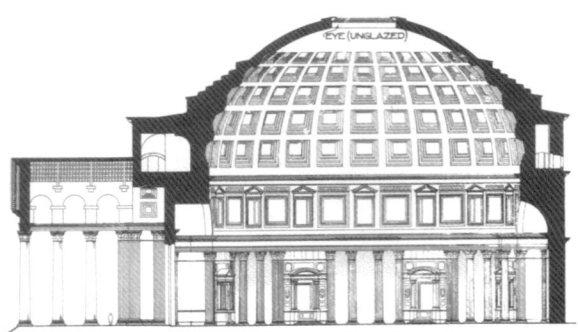

Section through portico & altar apse (north-south)

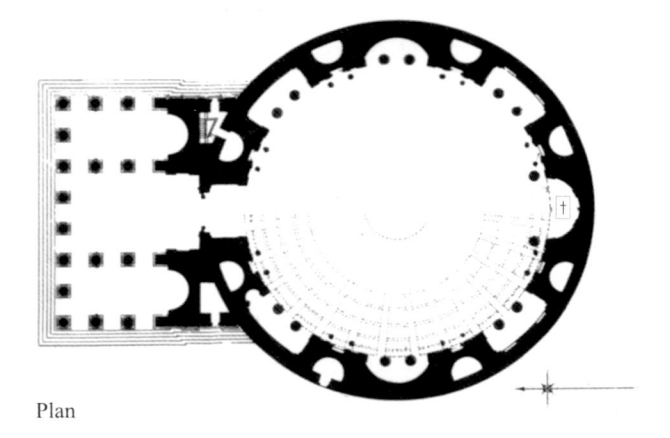

Plan

S. MARIA AD MARTYRES (PANTHEON)
(Fletcher p235)

235. Rome, plan type – converted buildings III

EARLY CHURCHES IN ROME
CONVERTED BUILDINGS

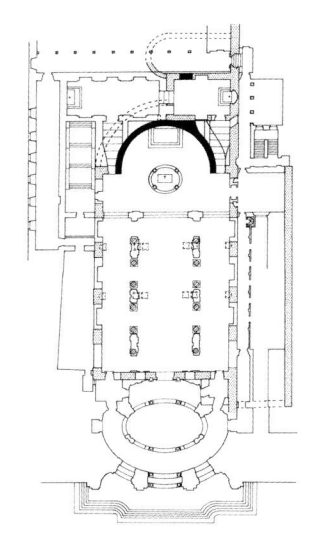

S. CROCE IN GERUSALEMME
(Webb p53)

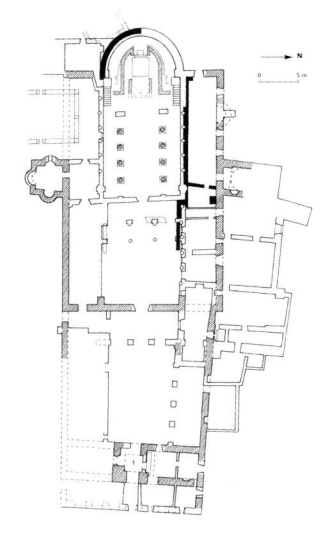

S. QUATTRO CORONATI
(Webb p94)

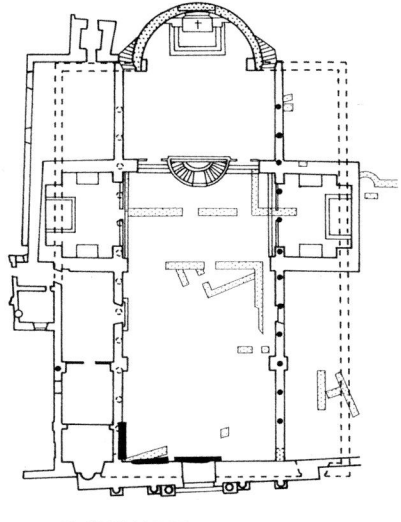

S. SUSANNA
(Webb p83)

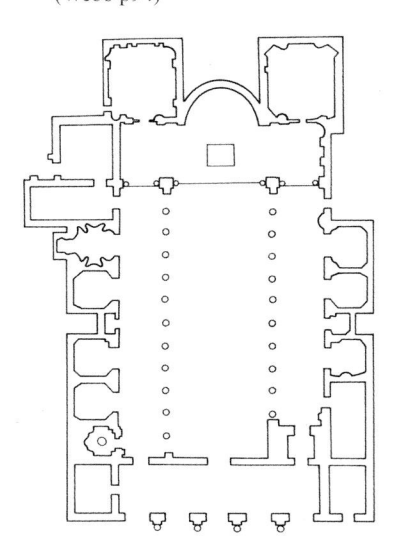

S. MARIA TRASTEVERE
(Webb p271)

236. Rome, plan type – converted buildings IV

EARLY CHURCHES IN ROME
CONVERTED BUILDINGS

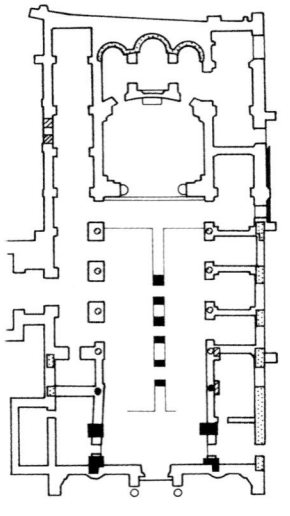

S. PUDENZIANA
(Webb p66)

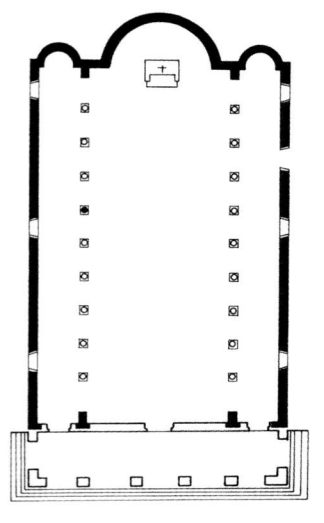

S. MARIA DOMNICA
(Webb p100)

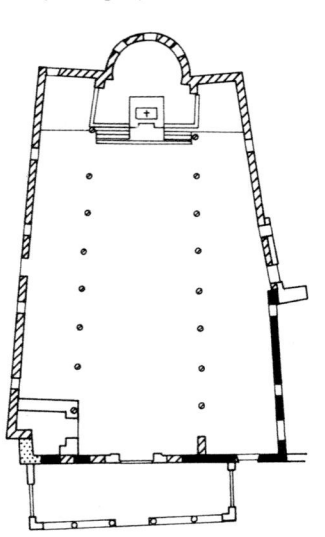

S. GIORGIO IN VELABRO
(Webb p183)

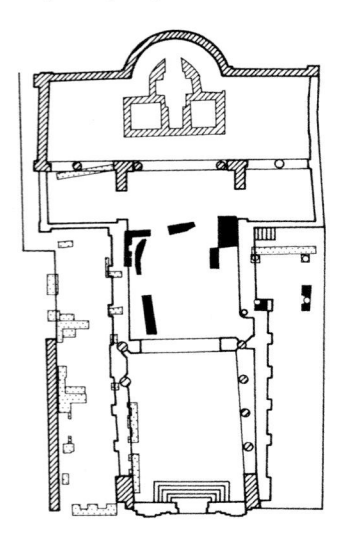

S. STEFANO ABISSINI
(Webb p37)

237. Rome, plan type – converted buildings V

Some notable individual attributes are, for example, that at Sant'Agate dei Goti the standard basilica form of a nave, two side aisles, and a semi-circular apse are still discernible as well the forecourt. Noteworthy features in other churches are the colonnaded narthex of San Vitale; the prominent forecourt of San Silverstro in Capite decorated with sculptural fragments from the catacombs along with two eighth or ninth-century inscriptions on the narthex piers, one of which lists female saints and the other male saints; the triple apses of Sant'Angelo in Pescheria, a basilica church built adjacent to the Roman structure of the Porticus of Octavia; and the seventh-century large icon of the Virgin Mary and Child as well as the twelfth-century apse mosaic in Santa Maria Nova, also known as Santa Francesca Romana, located in the Forum.

Converted Buildings

Most of the early Christian churches in Rome fall into this group, the converted building type. By far the most common building converted into a basilica church was a hall. Before the fourth century these halls were considered a Christian assembly room or an *aula ecclesiae* but after the Edict of Milan these halls were more fully transformed for Christian use. In the fourth century these converted churches were Santa Balbina, the lower church of San Clemente, San Crisogono, Santa Croce in Gerusalemme (from the Sessorian palace hall), and Santi Quattro Coronati and in the sixth century Santi Cosma e Damiano. A late conversion from a hall into a basilica was that of Santa Susanna in the eighth century. Basilicas converted from houses were Santa Maria in Trastevere in the fourth century and Santi Nereo ed Achilleo in the fifth century. Other structures transformed into basilicas were Santa Pudenziana from a bath building (*thermae*) in the fourth century, from barracks (Santa Maria in Domnica), a market building (San Giorgio in Velabro), and a mausoleum (Santo Stefano degli Abissini), all in the ninth century.

The lower church of **San Clemente** is fascinating as it is the earliest basilica type that survives in Rome and that can be visited. A large hall, the *titulus Clementis*, built in the third century for early Christian worship was turned into a basilica form in the following century by Pope Siricius (r. 384–399). The conversion consisted of the additions of a forecourt, narthex, a semi-circular apse and two arcaded colonnades in the nave to create the side aisles. As these are all Byzantine architectural features the church could quite easily be placed in the Eastern-influenced category. This kind of overlap points to the difficulty of clearly classifying the early Christian churches in Rome. The decorative programme of the nave, however, consists almost entirely of frescoes of the ninth to eleventh centuries and they only partially follow a Byzantine programme. There are a few faded frescoes from an earlier period with Byzantine characteristics on the walls of what was once the hall and now the outer walls of the right-hand-side aisle. Apparently there was no triumphal arch between the nave and sanctuary. To further complicate the issue of classification is the fact that the third-century hall was built over an *insula* and a mansion, that in turn were constructed over earlier structures destroyed in the great fire of AD64, which would then place the church in the superimposed category. To complete the picture in the twelfth century Pope Paschal II (r. 1099–1118) abandoned the earlier church and built a completely new basilica over the old nave and left aisle. It is an extraordinary experience today to visit all four levels – the first-century Roman remains with rooms of beautifully preserved brickwork and a corridor with the sound of water gurgling somewhere underground; the remnants of a third-century hall; the fourth-century lower church; and the twelfth-century upper church with its well-preserved colonnaded forecourt (now well below existing street level), entrance porch, an enclosed choir area (*schola cantorum*) in the nave, and mosaic decorated triumphal arch and half-dome of the apse.

238. Santa Balbina, Rome. Side view of the hall-church

239. Santa Balbina, Rome. Black and white marble floor decoration of a dove

240. Santa Balbina, Rome. Black and white marble floor geometrical decoration

241. Santa Balbina, Rome. Black and white marble floor decoration of zodiac signs

242. Santa Balbina, Rome. Proclamation indicating that the mosaic fragments (in the floor of the church) are from a first century necropolis and restored in 1939

243. Santa Balbina. Rome. Traditional bishop's throne in a niche at the rear of the semi-circular apse

244. Santa Balbina, Rome. On display Roman vessels discovered in building renovations

245. San Giorgio in Velabro, Rome. Elegant arcade separating nave from side aisle

246. San Giorgio in Velabro, Rome. Holy Table canopy (left) with bishop's chair in front of vertical marble panels on semi-circular apse wall (right)

247. San Giorgio in Velabro, Rome. Corinthian-type column capital I

248. San Giorgio in Velabro, Rome. Corinthian-type column capital II

249. San Giorgio in Velabro, Rome. Corinthian-type column capital III with a snake symbol

San Crisogono is similar to San Clemente in that an early fourth century large hall was converted into an aisleless basilica church later in the century and a new twelfth-century church built over it. Although the lower church has not been completely excavated it is interesting to explore. The hall was subdivided by a screen into a large space, the nave for the congregation and a smaller space for the sanctuary. A narthex and an apse were added as well as a few frescoes. In addition on the left side of the apse a baptistery, including a font, were attached. Among the early frescoes, much faded, are a depiction of a cross, the *Chi Rho* Christ symbol, hanging draperies, and in the apse ornamental frescoes representing marble.

250. San Giorgio in Velabro, Rome. Corinthian-type column capital IV

251. San Giorgio in Velabro, Rome. An ancient Roman column left for display

252. San Clemente, Rome. Courtyard looking at the church entrance

253. San Clemente, Rome. Partial view of the portico colonnade

Santi Nereo ed Achilleo is mainly of interest as part of the original sixth-century narthex walls with faded frescoes can be seen in the present portico built in the sixteenth century. Furthermore, it appears that the narthex may have been two stories with access to galleries (no longer visible) over the aisles. The first Christian building on the site was the fourth- or fifth-century *Titulus Fasciolae*, the name which is inscribed over the main entrance doorway.

There were five churches converted from earlier Roman temples. The most famous is the **Pantheon**, so well described by Judith Dupré. The earlier circular structure was rebuilt between AD 118 and 123 by the emperor Hadrian. Bronze letters across the façade spell out homage to Marcus Agrippa who built the original temple. In 609 Pope Boniface IV (r. 608–615) consecrated the Pantheon as the church of

254. San Clemente, Rome. Ionic column capital in portico

255. San Crisogono, Rome. Excavated area of original basilica

256. San Crisogono, Rome. Extensive arch support system in the original basilica

257. San Crisogono, Rome. An early Christian sarcophagus which includes classical figures

Santa Maria ad Martyres, more popularly known as Santa Maria Rotonda. It is one of the best-preserved Roman buildings, although stripped of its gilded bronze tiles from the dome and the bronze from the porch. Originally the Pantheon was approached from a square colonnaded court through a central triumphal arch. Although these have disappeared, the splendid temple portico with its 16 one-piece granite columns from Egypt can still be appreciated. The most dramatic moment, though, is on entering through the immense bronze doors into the circular interior and being overwhelmed by the beautiful hemispherical dome with its row upon row of square, decorative sunken panels. The dome, as wide as it is tall, merges perfectly with the cylindrical wall below. Above at the centre of the dome is a circular opening, an *oculus*, that allows the sun to stream in and lighten the interior. The vast space is unaltered from ancient times except for an altar that has been set up in the niche opposite the entrance doors, Christian saints who have replaced Roman deities in the niches, and the tombs of the Renaissance painter Raphael and the Italian kings Victor Emmanuel II and Umberto I.

Located in the Forum of Vespasian, also known as the Forum of Peace, is the basilica church of **Santi Cosma e Damiano**. The building had been dedicated as the temple of Romulus in 309 then converted into a church in 527 by Pope Felix IV under the reign of Theodoric the Ostrogoth king. Cosmas and Damian were two Greek brothers, physicians, who were martyred for their Christian faith in 287 during the persecution of Diocletian and began to be venerated as saints by the fourth century.

The third Roman temple transformed into a church was **Santa Maria Egiziaca**, undertaken by Pope John VIII (r. 872–882). The original temple was built in the fourth century BC, reconstructed at the beginning of the second century BC, and restored by Julius Caesar between 48 and 31 BC. The deity to whom the temple was dedicated is unknown but the temple goes by the name *Fortuna Virilis* and may have been dedicated to Portunus, the god of harbours. Although a wall now joins the exterior fluted columns their Ionic architectural order is still very prominent. The temple stands on a large podium with the columns at the front left free to retain the open portico. The frescoes inside the building are of significance as they show a Byzantine influence and are among the few that survive from the ninth century. Twenty seven fragments of the frescoes have survived and scholars have classified them into three major groups. The first major group shows mainly scenes about the life of the Virgin Mary, the second the apostles, and the third saints and martyrs. Outside of Rome the other notable Roman temple that was converted into a church is the Duomo or Cathedral of Ortegia in Syracuse, Sicily where the splendid Doric columns are very prominent in the interior.

258. Santa Maria Egiziaca, Rome. Walls built between the columns of the Roman temple form an enclosed space for the sanctuary

The fourth converted temple in Rome was the small, circular Temple of Hercules Victor (*Tempo di Ercole Vincitore*) in the Forum Boarium. The second century BC temple is completely encircled by a colonnade of 20 Corinthian columns still standing today although the roof is not the original one. By 1132 the temple had been converted into the church of **Santo Stefano alle Carozze** (St Stephen 'of the carriages') but rededicated in the seventeenth century to Santa Maria del Sole (St Mary of the Sun).

San Nicola in Carcere (St Nicholas in Prison), the fifth conversion, was built on the ruins of three temples from the third and second centuries BC in the Forum Holitorium. The central ruin was fully incorporated into the church. Reused Roman marble columns support the arcades that separate the nave from the side aisles. On the exterior of the church, six columns from the Temple of Juno Sospita are built into each of the side walls and are clearly visible today beyond the Renaissance front façade. It seems that the present building dates from the tenth century, certainly the twelfth from the date 1128 on a plaque, and built on the site of an earlier sixth-century church. The designation 'Prison' was added in Byzantine times when the ruins were converted into a prison that later became the lower or underground level of the church.

259. San Saba, Rome. Graceful arcade separating the nave from the side aisle

260. San Saba, Rome. Marble floor with geometrical patterns

261. San Saba, Rome. Remains of a classical frieze with egg-and-dart and dentil motifs

262. SS Giovanni e Paolo, Rome. Entrance façade with colonnaded portico

Superimposed Basilicas

In Rome the number of basilicas superimposed over existing buildings was large. The most frequent structure built over was a house, houses or mansion. In the fourth century superimposed basilicas included that of San Marco and in the fifth century Santa Cecilia, Santa Prisca, Santa Sabina and San Pietro in Vincoli. In the sixth century San Martino ai Monti and San Saba were each constructed over a hall. Basilicas built over apartment buildings were Sant'Anastasia in the fourth century, and in the fifth century San Lorenzo in Lucina and Santi Giovanni e Paolo. There were three basilicas built over catacombs or a mausoleum. These were San Valentino (fourth century), San Pancrazio (fifth) and Santo Stefano in Via Latina (fifth).

SPLENDID CHURCHES

263. SS Giovanni e Paolo, Rome. Ionic column capital in portico

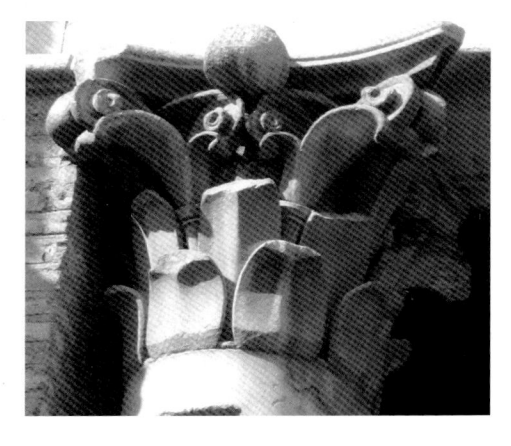

264. SS Giovanni e Paolo, Rome. Unusual simplified Corinthian capital in end column of portico

San Marco is interesting from two historical points of view. First, the original church was laid out before the middle of the fourth century and built over a mansion, possibly belonging to the family of Pope Mark (r. 336), and is the earliest known example of a church with a basilica type plan in central Rome. This church burnt down and a second was built on the same site probably in the sixth century. Second, a passageway similar to a solea is part of the remains of this second church and is evidence of the introduction of Eastern features into Rome during the sixth century. The current church took the place of the collapsing second structure when it was demolished by Pope Gregory IV (r. 827–844).

265. San Martino, Rome. Interior with ancient marble Corinthian columns and sixteenth-/seventeenth-century additions – ceiling, balconies and apse decoration. The stairs in the centre lead down to a third-century chapel from the original church house 'titulus di Equitii'

The attractive church of **Santa Cecilia** has an appealing forecourt, portico and well-proportioned interior with a perfectly semi-circular apse. In fact, the church today is very popular for wedding services. The church was built in the ninth century by Pope Paschal I (r. 817–824) superimposed over a second-century Roman *domus* and bathhouse. Below the floor of the sanctuary is the crypt containing the tomb of Santa Cecilia and above at the front of the sanctuary there is a sixteenth-century statue of her by Stefano Maderno. On the triumphal arch above the sanctuary traces of a mosaic can be seen.

EARLY CHURCHES IN ROME
SUPERIMPOSED CHURCHES

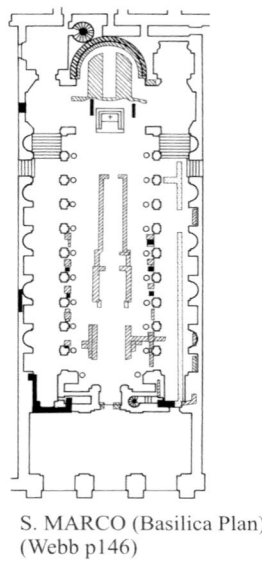

S. MARCO (Basilica Plan)
(Webb p146)

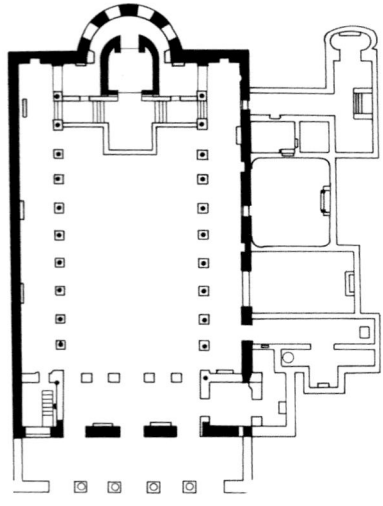

S. CECILIA (Basilica Plan)
(Webb p267)

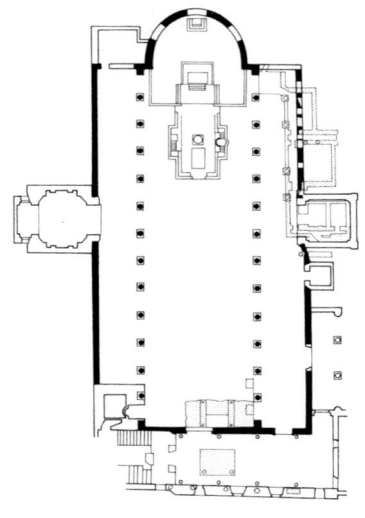

S. SABINA (Basilica Plan)
(Webb p170)

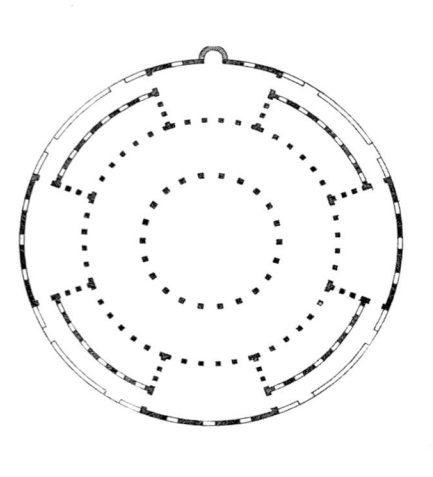

S. STEFANO ROTONDO (Centralized Plan)
(Deichmann Fig 9)

266. Rome, plan type – superimposed basilicas I and one exception

EARLY CHURCHES IN ROME
SUPERIMPOSED BASILICAS

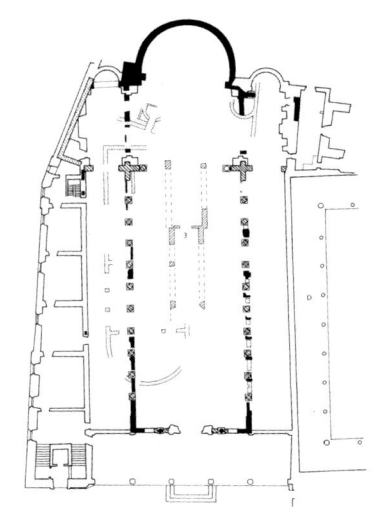

S. PIETRO IN VINCOLI
(Webb p76)

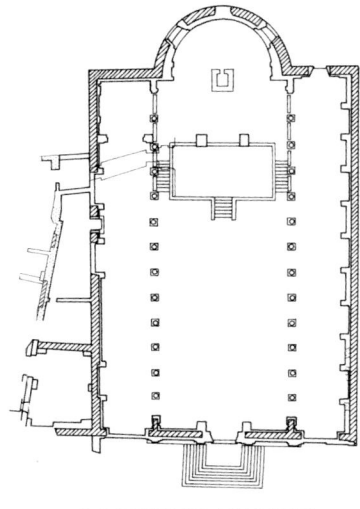

S. MARTINO AI MONTI
(Webb p73)

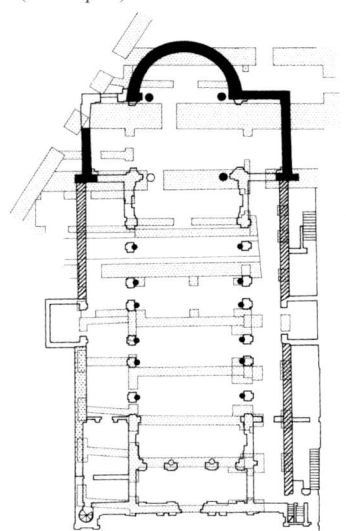

S. ANASTASIA
(Webb p189)

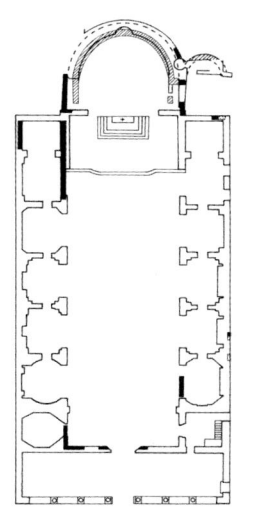

S. LORENZO IN LUCINA
(Webb p162)

267. Rome, plan type – superimposed basilicas II

110　THE SACRED ARCHITECTURE OF BYZANTIUM

EARLY CHURCHES IN ROME
SUPERIMPOSED BASILICAS

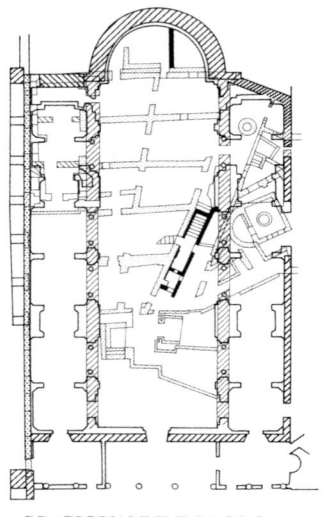

SS. GIOVANNI E PAOLO
(Webb p102)

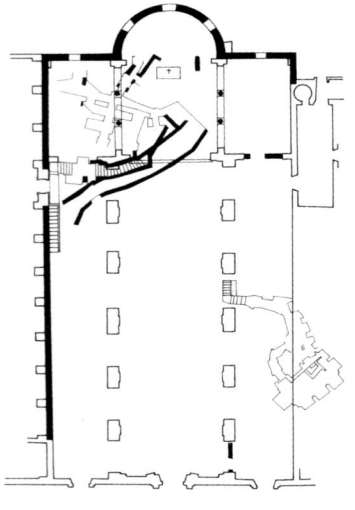

S. PANCRAZIO
(Webb p274)

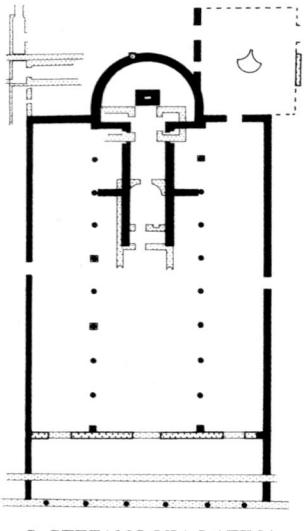

S. STEFANO VIA LATINA
(Webb p286)

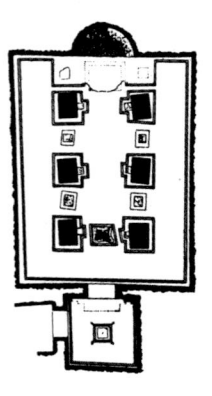

UNDERGROUND BASILICA
Near Porta Maggiore, Rome
(McDonald Fig 4)

268. Rome, plan type – superimposed basilicas III

269. Santa Sabina, Rome. Exterior of sanctuary apse

270. Santa Sabina, Rome. Nave, looking at the triumphal arch with a sixteenth-century replacement of the apse mosaic that followed the original fifth-century composition

271. Santa Sabina, Rome. Interior with low screen of marble panels enclosing the solea with two ambos

272. Santa Sabina, Rome. Arcade of superb, reused fluted Corinthian columns separating side aisle from the nave

Santa Sabina on the Aventine hill is one of the best examples of an early Christian basilica church that has remained largely unchanged. A highlight of the vast space of the interior is the 24 exquisite white marble fluted columns of the Corinthian order reused from a Roman building. They form an arcade of round arches that divides the nave from the side aisles. The church is brightly lit by large round-arched clerestory

273. Santa Sabina, Rome. Close-up of arcade columns and arch

274. Santa Sabina, Rome. Matching arches of the arcade and upper windows

275. Santa Sabina, Rome. Rear wall of nave with an inscription extending the full width of the space dating, most likely, from the time of the rededication of the church, AD425–432

276. Santa Sabina, Rome. Superb fifth-century carved, cedar wood door with decorative panels showing scenes from the bible

windows that make the polished marble floor sparkle. There is no solea but the choir area with barriers and an ambo on either side extends five bays into the nave. Unfortunately much of the original decoration is lost except for a large mosaic on the back wall of the nave. The church was built over a *domus* and adjacent *insula*, one that is assumed to have been the *titulus Sabina* to which the title of Saint was added (originally the *Sanctae Savinae*). The narthex contains pieces of early Christian sarcophagi and architectural fragments. Although reconstructed from their original sections the enclosed choir (*schola cantorum*) is a beautiful ninth-century example which includes within it a bishop's chair and a pair of ambos on either side.

Santo Stefano Rotondo is a superimposed non-basilican church of the fifth century built over the remains of some Roman barracks. As the name implies the church is of the centralized type, in fact circular and perhaps modelled on the Church of the Holy Sepulcher in Jerusalem. The church was built by Pope Simplicius (r. 468–483) as a martyrium to St Stephen whose relics were only found at the church in 1973. The function of the building is unclear. Originally the church consisted of a central rotunda surrounded by two concentric rings. The outer one was divided into eight sections of which four served as entrances and the remaining four as chapels. Four chapels projected above the rings to form the arms of a Greek cross. The middle ring acted as a circular aisle and was separated from the innermost circle, which formed the nave, by a colonnade of Ionic columns with round-arched clerestory windows above. As it is assumed that the slight

277. Santa Sabina, Rome. A panel in the cedar door depicting an angel and seven other figures

columns could not have carried a dome then the original roof was most probably a light conical roof. Pope Innocent II (r. 1130–1143) added the five arched entrance portico with its simple Tuscan columns. Then in 1450 or 1453 Pope Nicholas V carried out alterations which destroyed the form of the Greek cross. In the seventh century a small apse with a mosaic and an altar were added to the original fifth-century northeast chapel. The mosaic depicts a huge jewelled cross in the centre, flanked by two martyrs SS Primus and Felicianus, and surmounted awkwardly by a roundel containing the bust of Christ, and with an inscription in Latin.

Eastern-Influenced Basilicas
Basilicas in Rome that showed a distinct Eastern influence will be described in more detail because of their direct relevance to this book. Eastern features were primarily a triumphal arch that framed the sanctuary on the nave side and mosaic decoration on the arch and in the apse that followed a Byzantine programme. Detailed descriptions of the mosaic programmes in these churches will be found in a later chapter describing *Places of Splendid Spiritual Art*. In the fourth century the Eastern influenced basilicas were Sant'Agnese Fuori le Mura and San Lorenzo Fuori le Mura, both built over catacombs, also San Paolo Fuori le Mura and San Sebastiano which were each constructed above a cemetery. Completed early in the fifth century was the original basilica of Santa Maria Maggiore. Then in the sixth century there was San Giovanni a Porta Latina that was also an original basilica, Santa Maria Antiqua built in a courtyard and Santa Maria in Cosmedin erected over a hall. In the ninth century Santa Prassede was constructed over a decaying fifth-century church. Each of the above will be described because evidence of the influence of Byzantine church design from the East can still be seen today. San Sebastiano will not be described as later additions and alterations severely obscure its early Christian architectural features. This church is mainly of interest for the large number of Christian mausolea and catacombs that were once on the Via Appia Antica.

278. Santo Stefano Rotondo, Rome. Drawing of reconstructed exterior

279. Santo Stefano Rotondo, Rome. Low screen wall in the centre encloses the sanctuary and large tabernacle

280. Santa Prassede, Rome. The triumphal arch

281. Santa Prassede, Rome. Marble floor pattern

Just like St Peter's, **Sant'Agnese Fuori le Mura** is an example of a basilica built over the shrine of a Christian martyr, in this case St Agnes. The first church on the site was constructed around the year 400 and replaced by the present church by Pope Honorius I (r. 625–638). The earlier church was built partly into the catacomb where St Agnes was buried and partly above ground. From an architectural point of view the basilica is of great interest and displays Byzantine influences. First of all there is forecourt (the present piazza, a peaceful space with cypress trees and brick paving, was created in 1603), a narthex, a triumphal arch, an apse half-dome both with mosaic decoration, and something rare – galleries. The bottom part of semi-circular walls of the apse are covered with seventh-century vertically-laid marble slabs and the mosaic in the half-dome has three full-length figures. From the narthex there is a monumental staircase that leads into the catacomb. Fragments of inscriptions from the catacombs line the stairway.

282. Santa Prassede, Rome. Geometric floor pattern in marble with inscription 'Conditorium Reliquarum Sanctorum Martyrum in Aedibus Sanctae Praxidis' (The sarcophagus of other Martyrs in the Building of Holy Praxidis)

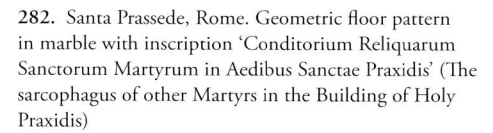

283. San Sebastiano, Rome. Model

The arcades that separate the nave from the two side aisles have columns that are reused Roman marble columns which are unmatched, some fluted and some reddish in colour and veined. The galleries are fronted by smaller arcades with clerestory windows above them. At the end of the right-hand aisle there is an entrance to the crypt which houses the tomb of St Agnes and a silver reliquary below the altar that contains her relics.

San Lorenzo Fuori le Mura has a complicated history. Emperor Constantine built a funerary hall outside the hill in which lay a catacomb with the grave of the martyr, San Lorenzo (Lawrence). In time the vast basilica-shaped hall functioned as a covered cemetery as many wished to be buried near the martyr's tomb. In the sixth century Pope Pelagius II (r. 579–590) built a church at the site close to Constantine's hall. As he wanted the church to be directly over the shrine of St Lorenzo, which was located in a catacomb chamber inside the hill, a large space had to be cut out of the hill so that the tomb of the saint would be upstanding in the centre of the nave. This meant that the northern and eastern sides of the basilica were actually walls without windows built against the side of the hill. The entrance to the interior of the basilica was thus forced to be, unconventionally, in the southern wall. In the centre of the northern wall there was a small door that led into the catacombs. What is noteworthy is that against the interior of the eastern wall there was a narthex to accommodate the Byzantine design concept although in this case the space could not act as an entrance because the outside wall was built into the hill. This indicated the length to which builders would go to satisfy the incorporation of Byzantine elements. Other Eastern features of the basilica are the triumphal arch and a sixth-century mosaic, though extensively restored in later centuries, it is still impressive today, the semi-circular apse, and galleries above the side aisles. The columns in the nave to both the side aisles and galleries are reused Roman marble columns, and some of the most impressive in the city. A visitor to the basilica today can still make out the sixth-century basilica form and features despite the great alteration carried out by Pope Honorius III (r. 1216–27) in which he destroyed the apse, added a large new basilica on the west side at a higher level and with a new entrance thus reversing the orientation of the whole. In the centre of the modern nave there are two traditionally designed and striking marble ambos opposite one another.

EARLY CHURCHES IN ROME
EASTERN INFLUENCED BASILICAS

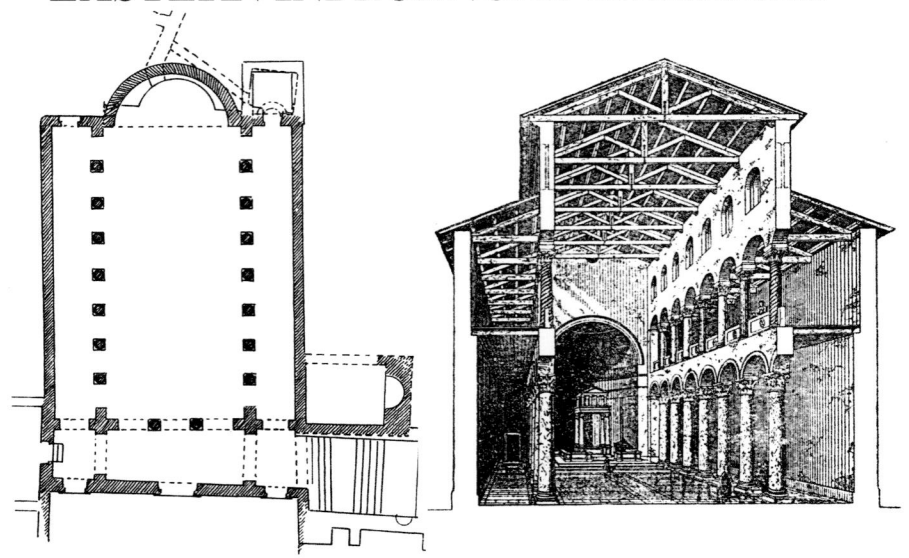

S. AGNESE FUORI LE MURA
Ground plan
(Deichmann Fig 10)

S. AGNESE FUORI LE MURA
Cross section
(Deichmann Fig 10A)

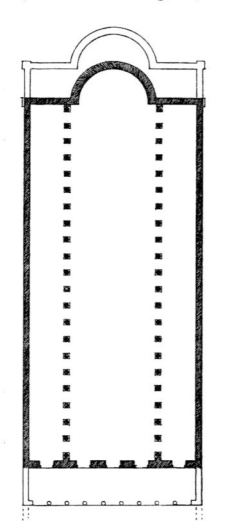

S. MARIA MAGGIORE
(Deichmann Fig 6)

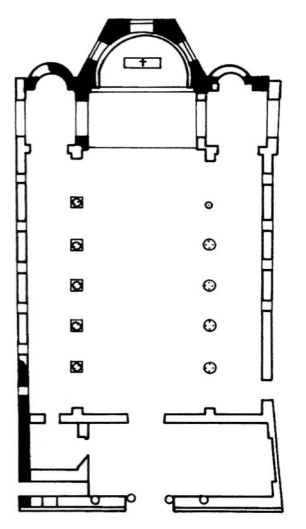

S. GIOVANNI A PORTA LATINA
(Webb p202)

284. Rome, plan type – eastern-influenced basilicas I

EARLY CHURCHES IN ROME
EASTERN INFLUENCED BASILICAS

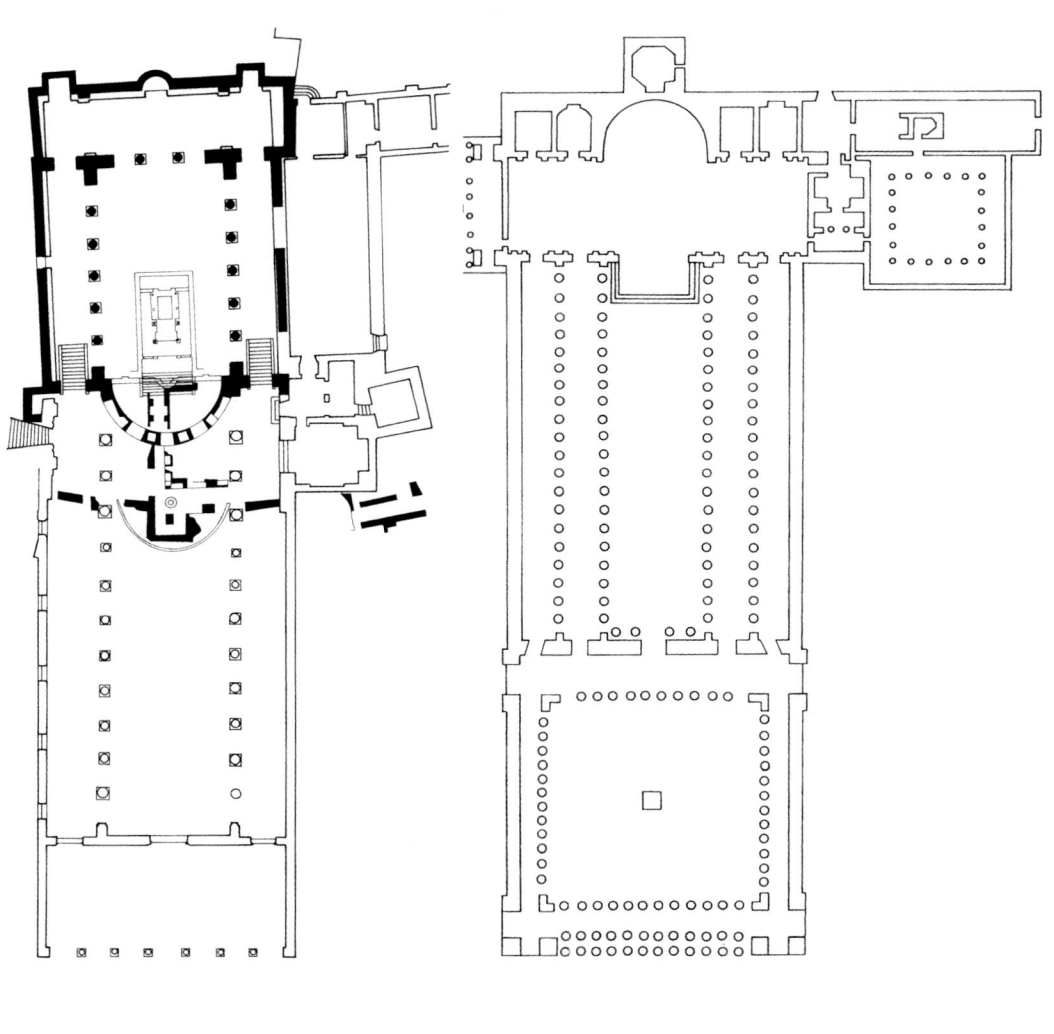

S. LORENZO FUORI LE MURA
(Webb p241)

S. PAOLO FUORI LE MURA
(Webb p208)

285. Rome, plan type – eastern-influenced basilicas II

EARLY CHURCHES IN ROME
EASTERN INFLUENCED BASILICAS

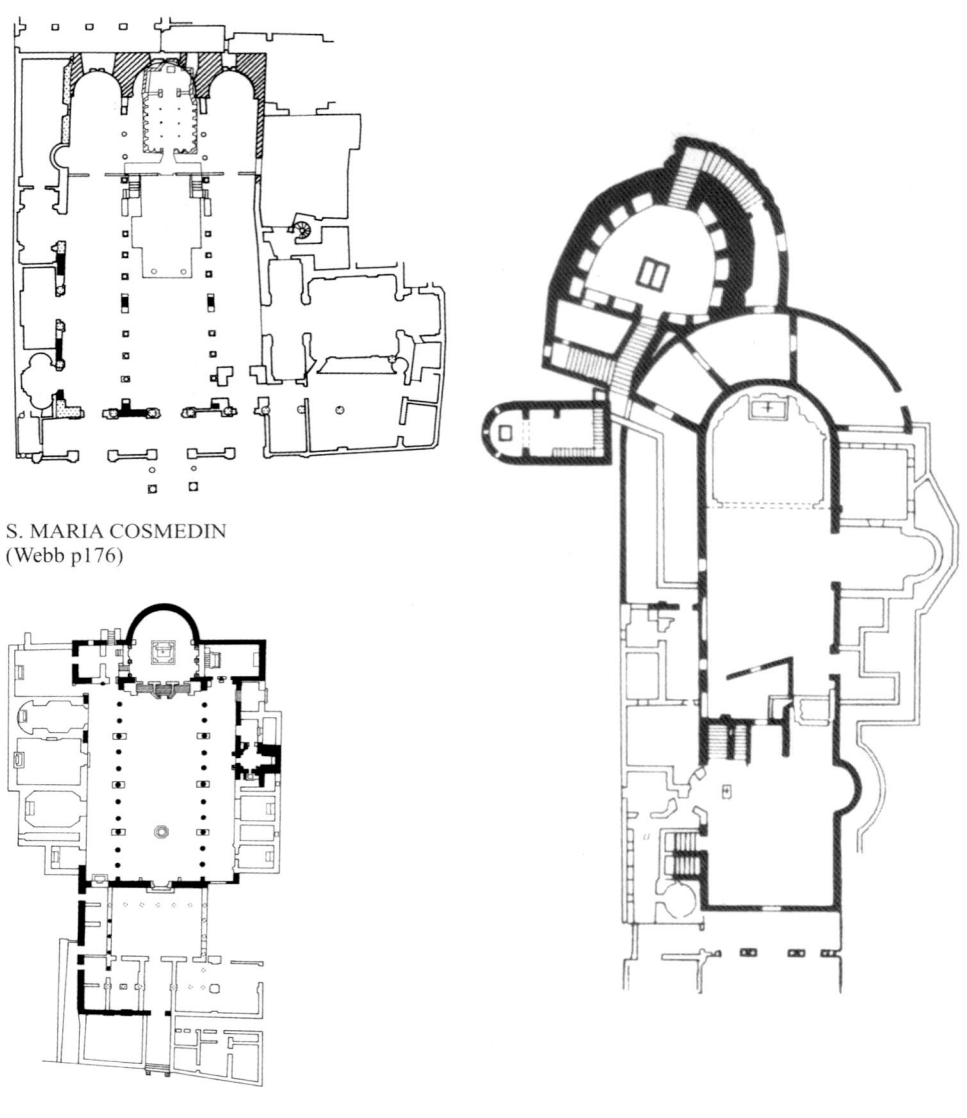

S. MARIA COSMEDIN
(Webb p176)

S. PRASSEDE
(Webb p69)

S. SEBASTIANO
(Grabar, 1968 Fig 182)

286. Rome, plan type – eastern-influenced basilicas III

287. Sant'Agnese Fuori le Mura, Rome. From the nave looking at the triumphal arch and apse

288. Sant'Agnese Fuori le Mura, Rome. Side aisle and gallery arcades

The basilica of **San Paolo Fuori le Mura** creates a dilemma. It was built at the end of the fourth century but mostly destroyed by fire in 1823 and a new church built on the same site. The rebuilding incorporated some of the surviving structure but followed the original plan, building dimensions, and mosaic decoration re-created based on old artists' prints. To all intents and purposes it is the original structure rebuilt. So a description of the church is included here as, despite being a reconstruction, it provides a present day experience of a vast early Christian basilica with its immense space and mosaic decoration. At St Peter's Emperor Constantine built the original basilica church over the shrine of an apostle but in this case it was the Western Emperor Honorius (r. 395–423) who completed a basilica over the shrine of the Apostle Paul. An inscription in the north portico is dedicated to Pope Siricius (r. 384–399) who was in office at the time the original church was constructed. The basilica San Paulo is approached through a large, square porticoed forecourt. Bronze doors lead into a nave whose vast space is accentuated by its openness and lack of pews, the glittering marble floor, the gilded ceiling, and the flood of sunlight from the large clerestory windows.

289. Sant'Agnese Fuori le Mura, Rome. Variety of reused Roman marble column shafts

290. San Lorenzo Fuori le Mura, Rome. Portion of the entrance portico colonnade

291. San Lorenzo Fuori le Mura, Rome. Nave with colonnade, two ambos, the triumphal arch, steps up to the sanctuary flanking the crypt holding the tomb of San Lorenzo

292. San Lorenzo Fuori le Mura, Rome. Triumphal arch mosaic with Christ in the centre shown sitting on a globe blessing in the Byzantine manner. On his right is St Peter, St Lorenzo (Laurentius) holding an open book and St Pelagius holding a model. On the left side of Christ is St Paul, St Stephen holding an open book and St Hyppolitus holding a martyr's crown

293. San Lorenzo Fuori le Mura, Rome. At the bottom left of the triumphal arch is a representation of the Holy City of Jerusalem

The nave is separated from the double aisles on either side by arcades of marble Corinthian columns. The eastern end of the nave terminates in an imposing triumphal arch that frames the altar and semi-dome of the apse beyond. Both the triumphal arch and half-dome depict Christ in colourful mosaic scenes. The triumphal arch mosaic survived the fire, was taken down and restored in place. Between the top of the arches of the arcade and the bottom of the windows there is a mosaic frieze. The original frieze was begun in the fifth century and depicted the busts of popes from St Peter up to Pius VII (r. 1800–1823), the pope who reigned at the time of the fire, was re-created and is now up to date.

294. San Lorenzo Fuori le Mura Rome. At the bottom right of the triumphal arch is a representation of the Holy City of Bethlehem

295. San Lorenzo Fuori le Mura, Rome. Partial view of crypt under the sanctuary

296. San Lorenzo Fuori le Mura, Rome. Partial view of the arcaded gallery above the side aisle

297. San Lorenzo Fuori le Mura, Rome. Side aisle with magnificent Corinthian columns

298. San Lorenzo Fuori le Mura, Rome. Entrance to the catacomb and in the pediment a variation of the *Chi Rho* symbol, the first and last letters of the Greek alphabet α and ω and on either side two doves. Above an early Christian inscription which includes the words 'IN PACE' (In peace) and the *Chi Rho* sign

299. San Lorenzo Fuori le Mura, Rome. Geometrical pattern of the marble floor

300. San Lorenzo Fuori le Mura, Rome. Unusual column capital with figures

301. San Lorenzo Fuori le Mura, Rome. A beautiful example of a Corinthian column capital with Roman-type acanthus leaves

In early Christian Rome the basilica of **Santa Maria Maggiore** on the summit of the Esquiline hill was one of the primary pilgrimage churches. Although completed by Pope Sixtus III (r. 432–440) the church was founded by a previous Pope, Liberius (r. 352–366), and a wealthy citizen, Giovanni Patrizio. According to legend the Virgin Mary appeared to both men and instructed them to build a church over the exact spot on the Esquiline hill which would be covered by snow the following morning. For this reason the church was first named Santa Maria ad Nives after the snowfall. It was later renamed Santa Maria Maggiore being the largest of 26 churches in Rome dedicated to the Virgin Mary. Even today entering the church is striking because of its magnificent and grand interior. The original basilican form is distinctive with its tall, wide nave separated from flanking aisles by splendid marble columns, clerestory

302. San Lorenzo Fuori le Mura, Rome. A two-sided view of the column capital with figures

303. San Lorenzo Fuori le Mura, Rome. A different, two-sided view of the column capital with figures

304. San Paolo Fuori le Mura, Rome. A view of the interior prior to the fire

305. San Paolo Fuori le Mura, Rome. After the 1823 fire: the triumphal arch and one side wall, still standing

windows, and a semi-circular apse at the end defined by a triumphal arch. Mosaics of the fifth century cover the triumphal arch. A series of mosaic panels high up on the nave wall run the full length of the interior on both sides. The triumphal arch mosaics show scenes from the life of Christ, the panels biblical scenes, and the apse mosaic from the thirteenth century the Coronation of the Virgin.

The basilica **San Giovanni a Porta Latina** is of special note because of its tripartite sanctuary that was added sometime in the sixth century. In the centre of the sanctuary is the Holy Table which is situated in the middle of the apse. In plan the apse is semi-circular inside but polygonal in shape on the outside. Two spaces that flank the apse are the pastophoria that are entered from

306. San Paolo Fuori le Mura, Rome. Restored nave showing the triumphal arch and apse beyond

307. Santa Maria Maggiore, Rome. The fifth-century nave with the original, fourth-century marble columns and the sixteenth-century gilded, coffered ceiling

308. Santa Maria Maggiore, Rome. Intricate marble floor pattern with the row of individual mosaic panels visible below the windows depicting scenes from the life of Abraham through to Esau on the left wall and of Moses and Joshua on the right side

309. Santa Maria Maggiore, Rome. Detail of a floor motif

310. Santa Maria Maggiore, Rome. Detail of an elaborate geometric floor figure

both the platform in front of the apse and the side aisles. The floor of the ninth-century platform is of coloured marble. Selenite, small sheets of crystalline gypsum, make up the panes in the three sixth-century apse windows and filter the sunlight to produce a warm golden glow internally. The shafts of the columns of the arcades in the nave are all different as they are reused from ancient Roman buildings. Above the arcade there are frescoes from the twelfth century which are fragmented but scenes from the Old and New Testaments can be detected. There is no ceiling but when viewed through the open wooden roof trusses the underside of the roof tiles form a varied pattern. A brick arcade of five arches with unmatched Ionic columns of marble and granite separate the narthex from a walled courtyard that contains an old well.

311. San Giovanni a Porta Latina, Rome. Entrance portico with reused, ancient columns of different lengths

312. San Giovanni a Porta Latina, Rome. Nave arcade with different, reused Roman columns

313. San Giovanni a Porta Latina, Rome. Nave looking at the triumphal arch and apse

314. San Giovanni a Porta Latina, Rome. Glowing triple windows of the apse

315. San Giovanni a Porta Latina, Rome. Selenite window pane pattern

316. San Giovanni a Porta Latina, Rome. Rear and side walls with a band of faded, twelfth-century wall paintings

317. San Giovanni a Porta Latina, Rome. Former diaconicon converted into a modern chapel with an old wall painting, above, of the Theotokos holding the Christ Child

318. San Giovanni a Porta Latina, Rome. Incomplete inscription 'TIT*S JOANNIS ANTE PORTAM LA' refers to the location of the church on the titulus of John that is situated before the gates [of Latina]

Santa Maria in Domnica is worthy of note as it displays two Eastern influences. The first is the two side apses, the pastophoria, and the second is the ninth-century mosaic decoration of the half-dome in the apse and the triumphal arch. The church was founded at least by the seventh century on the remains of a Roman fire station and rebuilt and decorated by Pope Paschal I (r. 817–824). He brought in Greek artists to execute the mosaics. In the apse mosaic the Theotokos is shown with the Christ child, with Paschal kneeling below them, who has a square halo or nimbus of the living according to Byzantine convention. Green fields with wild flowers form an unusual background which also includes angels in pale blue. On the glittering and colourful mosaic triumphal arch Christ is shown being approached by the apostles with Moses and Elijah below. The aisles are separated from the nave by antique columns in grey granite with Corinthian capitals. In 1513–14 Pope Leo X added the elegant five, arched portico designed by the renowned Renaissance architect, Andrea Sansovino. The church is sometimes known as Santa Maria della Navicella after the striking Roman stone boat turned fountain placed in front of it by Pope Leo whose arms are carved on the base.

In the sixth century the courtyard of a five-century-old Roman building in the Forum was transformed into the church of **Santa Maria Antiqua**. The colonnades were incorporated to define the side aisles of the church. Traces of a narthex, ambo, sanctuary screen, sanctuary, triumphal arch and apse can be seen. There are extensive frescoes from the eighth century on the apse, sanctuary back wall, triumphal arch and side walls of the aisles.

Santa Maria in Cosmedin has a fascinating history. A seventh-century Christian hall which served as a *diaconia* was extended by Pope Hadrian I (r. 772–795) to create a large church with Byzantine features. These were a narthex, nave with two aisles, a triumphal arch, three apses, and galleries above the aisles. Signs of the galleries have disappeared but the two side apses are each closed off from the side aisles by an open marble screen and gate. Early frescoes are still visible on the semi-circular walls at the back of the apses. In front of the central apse there is an enclosed choir area with traditional marble ambos on the sides. The church with its decorated marble floors came to be called *ecclesia Grecorum* as it was given to Greek monks fleeing from the Iconoclastic persecutions in the east. In the next century it became more popularly known as Santa Maria in Cosmedin, its present name, from the lavish embellishments made by Hadrian I as *cosmedin* comes from the Greek meaning decoration.

319. San Giovanni a Porta Latina, Rome. Exposed ceiling with a view of the gable roof trusses and underside of the roof tiles

320. Santa Maria Domnica, Rome. Triumphal arch depicts Christ seated on a throne flanked on each side by a standing angel and six apostles each carrying a symbol. The broad, semi-circular apse is decorated with a ninth-century Byzantine style mosaic with the Theotokos as the central figure. The arcade is composed of grey, granite column shafts and marble Corinthian capitals mostly from old Roman buildings

321. Santa Maria in Cosmedin, Rome. Faded wall paintings in the former diaconicon

322. Santa Maria in Cosmedin Rome. Faded wall paintings in the former prothesis

323. Santa Maria in Cosmedin, Rome. Arcade from former church incorporated into the later construction

324. Santa Maria in Cosmedin, Rome. Open templon in front of the former prothesis

325. Santa Maria in Cosmedin, Rome. Marble panels of the sanctuary screen

326. Santa Maria in Cosmedin, Rome. Ambo with two stairs

Not far from Santa Maria Maggiore is the small church of **Santa Prassede**. It was built in the ninth century by Pope Pascal I (r. 817–824) to replace an older fifth-century church. The design was based on the basilica-transept model of St Peter's but with the transepts in the form of chapels at the end of each aisle. Granite columns and piers that support architraves made from Roman fragments make up the two colonnades that separate the nave from the side aisles. Mosaics cover the triumphal arch and the half-dome of the apse and are part of the original ninth-century decoration. The present-day forecourt, although below street level and with a sixteenth-century front façade to the church, still provides some indication of the former approach to the building.

327. Santa Maria in Cosmedin, Rome. Geometric marble floor pattern

Although not a congregational church the building of Santa Costanza is of historical, architectural and artistic value. According to tradition Emperor Constantine built the structure as a royal mausoleum for his daughter Constantina, also known as Costanza, who died in 354. In the Middle Ages it was dedicated as a church to Santa Costanza. The centralized, domed architectural form followed Roman precedents for a building that was to honour a person as the sarcophagus was to be placed in the centre of the space. Perhaps the most important aspect of Santa Costanza is that it represents a prime example of early Christian art, epitomized by its surviving mosaics. Interestingly enough the fifth- or sixth-century church of Sant'Angelo in Perugia has a similar rotunda form with sixteen ancient columns.

In brief, other churches in Italy outside of Rome displayed a variety of types: basilica, cross-in-square and even cruciform. The most remarkable is the Greek cross plan of St Mark's in Venice that was rebuilt a few times. Its present basic form is from 1063 with a narthex and new façade added in the first half of the thirteenth century.

328. Mausoleum, Santa Costanza, Rome. Exterior view of the dome

329. Mausoleum, Santa Costanza, Rome. Interior view (Drawing by Piranese)

330. Mausoleum, Santa Costanza, Rome. Corinthian-style column capitals

331. Mausoleum, Santa Costanza, Rome. Holy Table in the centre with a sarcophagus visible in a niche beyond

332. Sant'Angelo, Perugia. Interior of rotunda

OTHER EARLY CHURCHES
ITALY & REGION

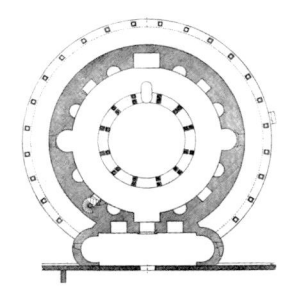

ROME, S. COSTANZA
Ground Plan (left) &
Cross section (right) from altar niche to the portico
(McDonald, Fig 14)

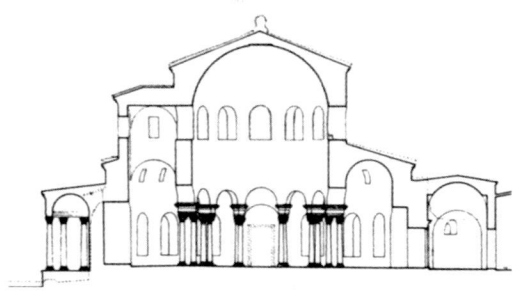

By tradition the 4th century church is regarded as a mausoleum built by Constantine for his daughter Costanza

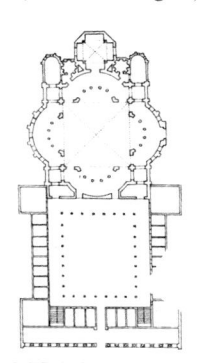

MILAN
S. Lorenzo
(McDonald Fig 37)

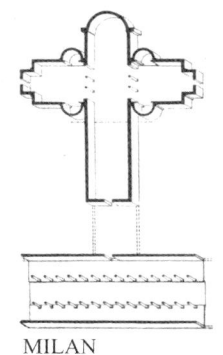

MILAN
Holy Apostles
(Krautheimer Fig 21)

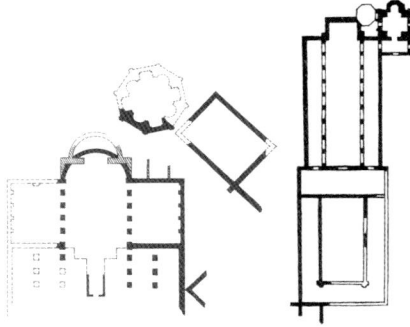

MILAN
S. Tecla
(Krautheimer Fig 22)

VICENZA
SS. Felice e Fortunaro
(Krautheimer Fig 54)

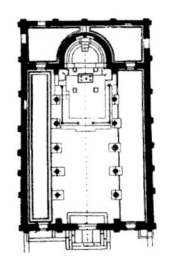

GRADO
S. Maria
(Peeters Fig 37)

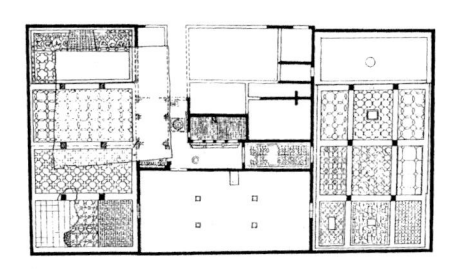

AQUILEA
S. Theodore double basilica
(White Fig 13)

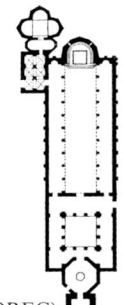

PARENTIUM (POREC)
Basilica Eufrasius
(Stewart p32)

333. Italy and region, early churches I

OTHER EARLY CHURCHES
ITALY & REGION

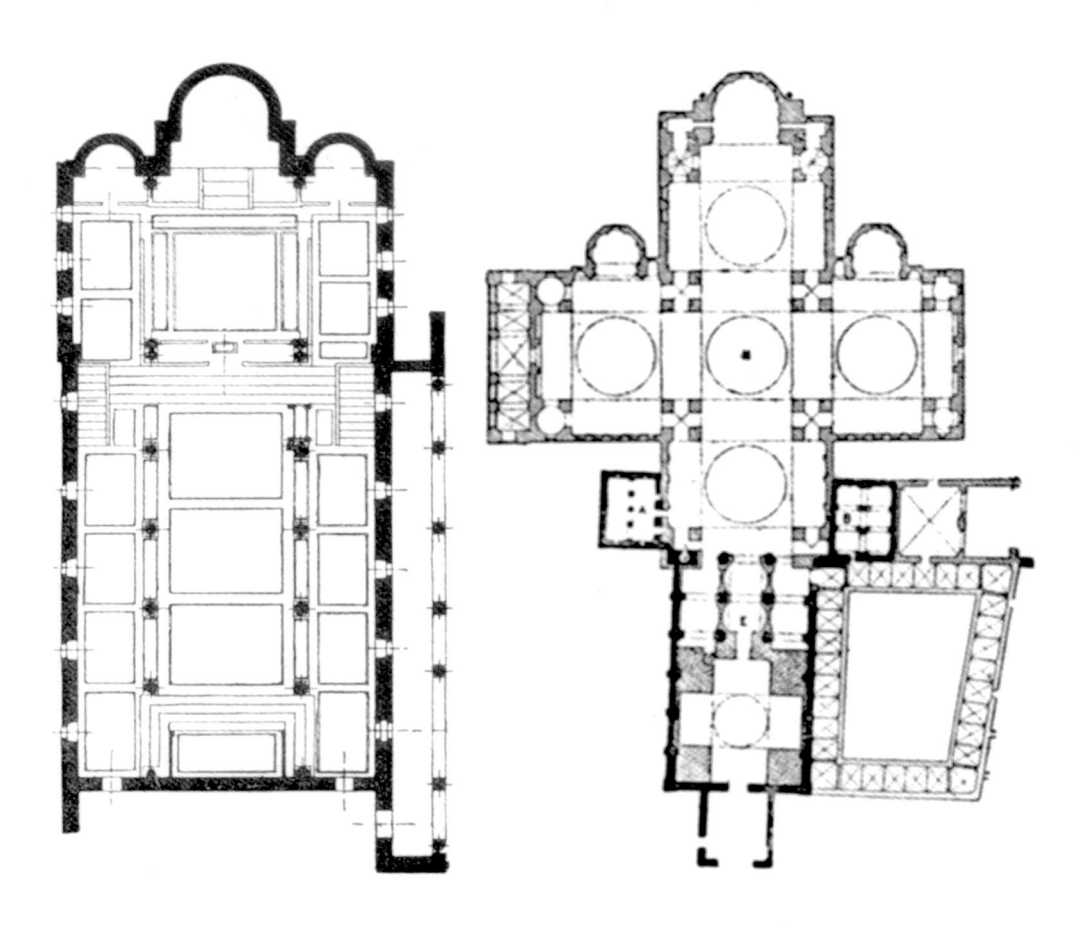

PALERMO
Cappella Palatina
(Hamilton Fig 43)

PERIGUEUX
S. Front
(Hamilton Fig 45)

334. Italy and region, early churches II

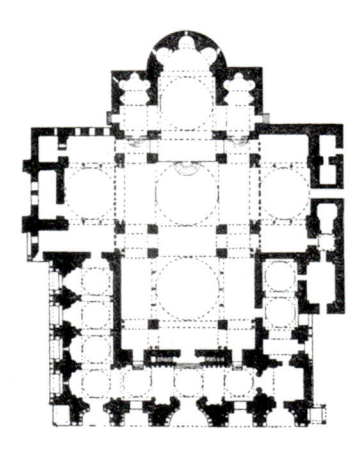

335. Plan of St Mark's, Venice. Clear Greek cross form with U-shaped narthex and chapels

336. St Mark's, Venice. Entrance façade facing Piazza San Marco

337. St Mark's, Venice. Nave looking east at apse

338. St Mark's, Venice. Iconostasis, apse mosaic with an enthroned figure of Christ and eastern half of the Immanuel cupola with the central figure of the Theotokos and two others

New Rome / Constantinople

As in Rome the first churches built in New Rome/Constantinople were by the Emperor Constantine (r. 324–337). In addition to erecting churches he adorned the public spaces of his new capital with ancient statuary and built a public square – the forum that was dominated by a porphyry column that carried a statue of himself. After Constantine the other emperor who undertook a major building programme was Justinian (r. 527–565). His programme covered the renovation, rebuilding and founding anew of countless churches not only in Constantinople but in other places in the Byzantine Empire. After the end of the Iconoclastic period there was resurgence in the building of some new churches under the Macedonian, Komnenian, and Palaelogoi emperors.

A difficulty in describing the Byzantine churches of Constantinople is that they are in present-day Istanbul where virtually all the churches have been converted into mosques, with restricted access, except for three churches that are now museums and one that is a concert hall. In most cases the conversions did not involve structural changes so that the architectural character of the original church in many cases can still be appreciated today even though the Christian spaces, such as the naos, bema, narthex and pastophoria, are not used as such any more. Naturally, all Christian liturgical fixtures and fittings have been removed. The substantial change to the churches is in the art work. After the Fall of Constantinople mosaics were whitewashed or plastered over, and a few were destroyed, as Islam prohibits the depiction of human and animal figures. Some images have now been restored but can only be seen in churches turned into museums. Another complication in describing Constantinople's Byzantine churches is that even before their conversion into mosques many of them underwent successive rebuilding or remodellings making it difficult to identify the original architectural forms. Despite these stumbling blocks four books in particular help to identify the Christian architectural features of these structures and in many cases earlier plans. These are the works of Alexander Van Millengen, Thomas Mathews, Robert Ousterhout, and Freely and Cakmak.

In the Istanbul Archaeological Museum there is a huge aerial type map of the Great Palace area of Constantinople as it may have looked in the year 1200. Buildings in the map are shown in three dimensions and are all computer reconstructions (www.byzantium1200.com). All the monuments are shown on the assumption that they were properly maintained in the previous centuries, which of course was never the case. Nevertheless, the aerial map is of great interest as the physical form of the buildings is based on extensive research and the assistance of Byzantine experts. Thirty churches are shown on the map spread out on the eastern side of the hippodrome with the adjoining churches of SS Peter and Paul and SS Sergius and Bacchus anchoring the southern end and Hagia Eirene the northern end. Whereas in Rome virtually all the churches were of the basilica type with pitched roofs the documented churches of Constantinople span all seven church types as will be seen in the descriptions below.

Of the 30 churches in the Great Palace area 13 (43 per cent) are of the basilica type, nine (30 per cent) cross-in-squares, five (17 per cent) are centralized, two (7 per cent) are domed basilicas, and there is one (3 per cent) cross type. This distribution in the capital city reflects that in the Byzantine Empire as a whole in which the basilica type dominated. It should be kept in mind that the Great Palace division is based on viewing the reconstructed building shapes and roof plans in the map and may not be entirely accurate, particularly as it is not possible to discern the converted or Athonite types even if they did exist. An exciting finding is that 25 of the 30 churches are shown as having an eastern orientation, with four of the remaining five pointing in a southeastern direction and the fifth with the apse facing the southwest. Only a handful of the Great Palace churches survive. There were many churches built outside the Great Palace area as will be seen.

BYZANTINE CHURCHES IN CONSTANTINOPLE
BASILICA TYPE

S. JOHN THE FORERUNNER STOUDIOU
(Mango, 1985 Fig 43)

THEOTOKOS CHALKOPRATEIA
(Mathews Fig 12A)

CHURCH A, BEYAZIT
(Mathews Fig 37)

SARAY
(Mathews Fig 18)

S. POLYEKTOS
(Freely Fig 35)

339. Constantinople, plan type – basilicas

Basilicas

Even though the early churches built in Constantinople were of the basilica type as in Rome none exist to be seen today. The first church built by Constantine I (r. 324–337) in Constantinople, or more likely enlarged and embellished, was the *Palaia Ekklesia* ('Old Church') of Hagia Eirene (*Holy Divine Peace*). Little is known about the church but certainly it was basilican in form. His son Constantius II (r. 337–361) followed by constructing the first church of Hagia Sophia (*Holy Divine Wisdom*) consecrated in the year 360. The basilica form was used in other churches of Constantinople but only until the end of the sixth century. There was also the rebuilding of the second Hagia Sophia by Emperor Theodosius II (r. 408–450) in 415 on the same spot as the first church. In the fifth century still another basilica type church of note was that of the Theotokos in Chalkoprateia (450–460). At about the same time, 449, the monastery and church of St John the Forerunner Stoudiou was founded by the Roman patrician and consul John Stoudios. During the reign of Justin I (r. 518–527) Princess Anicia Juliana sponsored the building of the church of St Polyektos (512–527).

It is commonly assumed that Justinian I (r. 527–565) built only domed churches but he also constructed traditional, basilica-type churches. The architectural character of these early basilica churches of Constantinople, however, has to be reconstructed from written sources and archaeological studies. These churches were, for example, SS Peter and Paul (527–565), which shared a common forecourt and a continuous narthex with the adjoining church of SS Sergius and Bacchus, Basilica A (so named by archaeologists) in the Beyazit complex (532–565), the Saray basilica (532), and the first Theotokos basilica at Blachernai (518–527), remodelled with a transept by Justinius II (r. 565–578).

The **first Hagia Sophia** was known as the *Megáli Ekklesía* ('Great Church') because of its size and the name remained even after the rebuilding of the basilica. The church had a wooden roof, possibly four aisles, galleries, and was preceded by a forecourt. Adjacent to the church was a baptistery building, called Olympas, and a treasury building where the sacred liturgical vessels were kept, the *skevophylákion*. Nothing remains of this first Hagia Sophia as it was destroyed in a fire to the Great Palace set by the populace in 404 when they learned that their beloved patriarch John Chrysostom had been sent into exile by Emperor Arcadius for his sermons condemning the immorality of the empress Eudoxia. A new, **second Hagia Sophia** also in the form of a basilica was in turn destroyed during the Nika Riots in 532. It was replaced by the present building completed by Justinian in 537.

Today the **Stoudios church of St John the Forerunner** (Imrahor Camii) and monastery are in ruins. The monastery was once the centre of not only religious life of the city but also intellectual and artistic life housing about seven hundred monks in its prime. During the first three decades of the ninth century when St Theodore was *igoúmenos* (abbot) the Stoudios monastery was the most powerful and influential in the empire. He was the leader against iconoclasm and was banished three times from Constantinople. The monks of the monastery were renowned as scholars, painters of icons, illuminators of manuscripts and composers of hymns. Their laws and customs were taken as models in the Orthodox world particularly by the monks of Mount Athos.

In 1204 the Crusaders destroyed the monastery which was not fully restored until 1290 but then destroyed again by the invading Ottoman Turks in 1453. After fire and an earthquake damaged the monastery buildings and church in the eighteenth and nineteenth centuries the complex was abandoned. What can be seen today from the outside is the imposing silhouette of part of the roofless naos. Remains of the original large and porticoed courtyard are now part of a walled garden.

The church had a simple basilica form, a narthex with three doorways into a wide naos and separate doors into each of the two aisles. The doorways were framed with marble columns of the Corinthian

340. St John Stoudios, Constantinople. Remains of the naos and bema

341. St John Stoudios, Constantinople. Narthex entrance portico with Corinthian columns

order. Colonnaded galleries once extended above the aisles and narthex. In the remains of the semi-circular apse there are signs of a six or seven tiered synthronon and a bema platform that projected out into the naos. The bema was separated from the naos by a low screen that consisted of colonnettes in the front and four on the side, with an entryway in the front and on each side, and parapet slabs between the colonnettes surmounted by a tie beam. Steps led down to a crypt. The floor of the naos was paved in the Roman style with shaped tiles and designs of animals and scenes from classical mythology. According to a fifteenth-century visitor to the church 'the walls are of mosaic work very richly wrought, in which are depicted many histories'.

The church at **Chalkoprateia** ('Copper Market') was one of the most important churches dedicated to the Theotokos in Constantinople until the church at Blachernai overtook it in significance. Most scholars attribute the building of the Chalkoprateia church to Empress Pulcheria, granddaughter of Theodosius I. Among the historical events associated with the church is its use by Justinian (r. 532–567) as the patriarchal seat for five years (532–537) from the destruction of the Theodosian Hagia Sophia in the fires of the Nika revolt until the completion of the Justinian Hagia Sophia church. Another event linked to the church of Chalkoprateia was in 553 when it was the venue for the meeting of the Ecumenical Council. Although few parts of the church are preserved today it was clearly of a basilican form with two aisles, a western narthex, an eastern three-sided apse, and galleries over the aisles and narthex. The church was approached through a large porticoed forecourt. The remains of the Byzantine church are difficult to view as the foundations have been overbuilt with houses and a ramshackle mosque, Acem Aga Mescidi.

The church of **St Polyektos** was founded by the princess Anicia Juliana, daughter of Augusta Galla Placida, after her disappointment arising from her husband's refusal of the throne. So as to emphasize her imperial lineage she built a huge church to rival the Theodosian Hagia Sophia and dedicated it to St Polyektos when the church was completed in 527. It was the largest church in Constantinople before the building of the third Hagia Sophia. The church of St Polyektos was destroyed by the Fourth Crusaders in their sack of the city in 1204 and is now a preserved archaeological site. Excavations reveal that the church had a two-aisled basilican form with a large square forecourt, a narrow narthex, eastern apse, and an ambo in the centre of the naos. An unusual feature was the difference in level between the forecourt and church which required a great staircase up to the narthex. Some scholars believe there is evidence of a dome classifying it as the first domed church before SS Sergius and Bacchus and Hagia Sophia were built a few years later by Justinian.

Domed Basilica

The best known of all churches not only in Constantinople but in the Byzantine world was the third Hagia Sophia (532–537). It is a domed basilica. A precedent may have been the second church of Hagia Eirene built just before (532). The other two known, domed basilicas were built later – the aisleless St Thekla (1057–1059) and the middle church of St Saviour Pantokrator (1118–1141).

Hagia Eirene is separated from Hagia Sophia by the outer defence wall of the palace and is one of the few Byzantine churches in Constantinople not converted into a mosque; it is today used as a concert hall. Emperor Justinian had Constantine's earlier church restored after it was damaged during the Nika Riots in 532 and it was completed at about the same time as the rebuilt Hagia Sophia. Not only are the two churches closely linked spatially, they were served by the same clergy and share, in Greek, an attribution as the churches of Divine Peace (*Eirene*) and Divine Wisdom (*Sophia*).

The second church of Hagia Eirene retained the layout and main structure of the first: a basilica but remodelled as a domed basilica. In addition to the naos there was an apse, a narthex with five doors, and side aisles that ended in small square spaces, most likely the pastophoria. A gallery extended above the narthex and side aisles. The entrance to the church was from a large forecourt surrounded on four sides by a colonnade. An exceptional feature of the interior of Hagia Eirene is the well-preserved six-tiered synthronon in the apse which is semi-circular inside and five-sided on the outside. The shallow dome is carried by a high drum pierced by windows that is supported by massive piers. The position of the Holy Table is indicated by the stones in the apse floor.

Justinian had the interior decorated with wall paintings and mosaics. During the Iconoclastic period it seems all the mosaics covering the bema arch and the semi-dome of the apse were removed and in the semi-dome replaced by a large cross. The large mosaic cross has a black outline set against a gold background with a geometric border. The cross has flared ends and stands on a pedestal of three steps placed on a green band extending around the base of the semi-dome. It is not clear if the cross replaced an earlier image which would have been either a Theotokos *Platytéra* or Christ Pantokrator.

The **third Hagia Sophia** (*Holy Divine Wisdom*) is the most famous Byzantine church of Constantinople and the mother church of Eastern Orthodoxy – the former patriarchal basilica of Hagia Sophia (in Greek the full name is *Naós tis Agias tou Theoú Sofías* / 'Church of the Holy Wisdom of God'). The church, which is the supreme example of a domed basilica, was built on the orders of Emperor Justinian on the site of the previous church destroyed by the Nika rioters. The designers of Hagia Sophia, Anthemius of Tralles, a mathematician, and Isidorus of Miletus, a physicist, are each referred to by Procopius as a *mechanikos* and not as an *architekton*. At that time a *mechanikos* had a broad academic education, was highly skilled in mathematics, and had experience in the design and construction of buildings. On the other hand an *architekton* would have had a technical training in building rather than a theoretical one. The title *mechanikos* disappeared in the medieval period probably because he no longer received an academic and theoretical education.

The new building was consecrated in 537 but the mosaic decoration in the interior only completed later during the reign of Justin II (565–578). Procopius, in his book *Edifices*, lauds Justinian as the ideal

BYZANTINE CHURCHES IN CONSTANTINOPLE
DOMED BASILICA TYPE

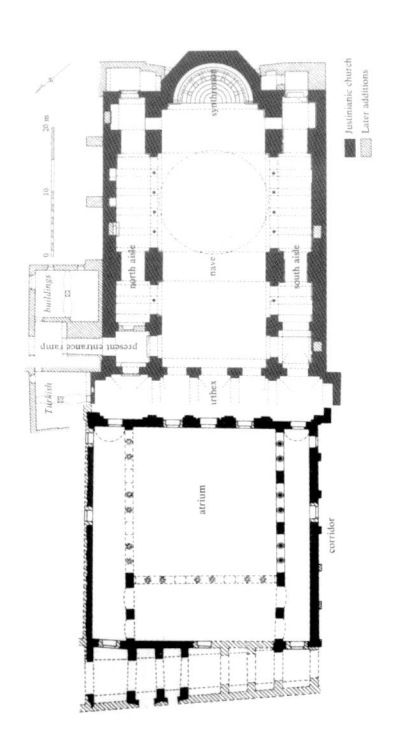

HAGIA EIRENE
(Mathews Fig 38)

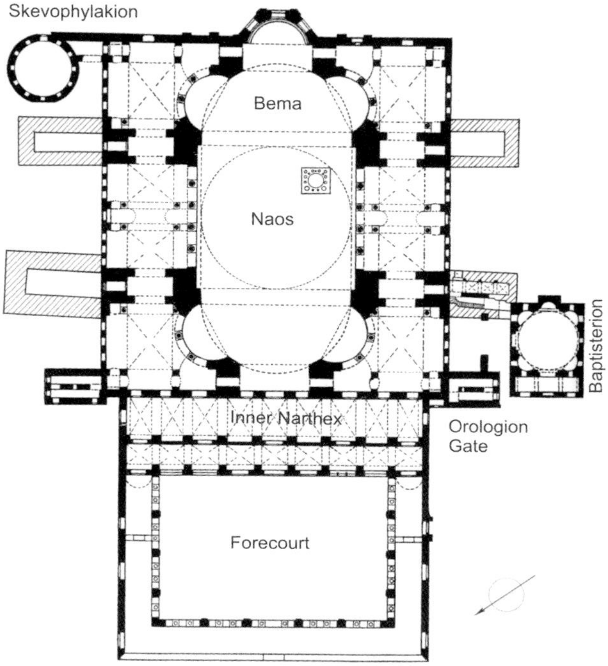

HAGIA SOPHIA III
(After Grabar, 1967 p. 88)

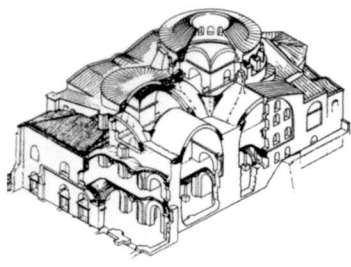

HAGIA EIRENE
3-dimensional view from the west
(McDonald Fig 61)

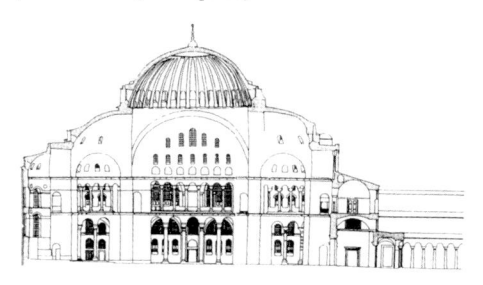

HAGIA SOPHIA III
Bema to Narthex Section
(Freely Fig 41)

342. Constantinople, plan type – domed basilicas

343. Hagia Eirene, Constantinople. Apse elevation

344. Hagia Eirene, Constantinople. North elevation with the apse on the left and narthex on the right

345. Hagia Eirene, Constantinople. Bird's-eye view with the courtyard (left), narthex and cutout viewpoint of the shallow western dome, and central dome over the naos (right)

346. Hagia Eirene, Constantinople. Cross section looking east at apse and synthronon

Christian emperor who built churches to the glory of God. His lengthy praise of Justinian's Hagia Sophia reads in part: 'So the church has become a spectacle of marvellous beauty, overwhelming to those who see it … For it soars to a height to match the sky … For it proudly reveals its mass and the harmony of its proportions, … its interior is not illuminated without by the sun, but that its radiance comes into being within it, such an abundance of light bathes this shrine'. He goes on to describe how material from all over the Byzantine Empire, including ancient Corinthian columns, were brought in to construct the church which became the largest in Christendom and remained so for centuries. The interior decoration of granite, marble, mosaics and porphyry was so magnificent Justinian is reported to have exclaimed 'I have overseen the completion of the greatest cathedral ever built up. Solomon, I have surpassed thee!'

The description of the forecourt of Hagia Sophia in Constantinople by Paul the Silentiary would be typical of most Byzantine churches. He wrote that the court, as he termed it, was 'surrounded by four stoas or colonnaded walks; one is joined to the narthex *[exonarthex]* and the others open, and various

347. Hagia Eirene, Constantinople. Windows in the western end of the naos

348. Hagia Eirene, Constantinople. Apse end with Ottoman dome

349. Hagia Eirene, Constantinople. Typical double window and Byzantine column

350. Hagia Eirene, Constantinople. Close-up of Byzantine column with a *bas-relief* carving of a cross in the plain capital

351. Hagia Eirene, Constantinople. Interior view of the naos and apse

352. Hagia Eirene, Constantinople. View of northeast corner and edge of the synthronon

paths lead to them. At the center of the court stands a spacious fountain *[phiale]* … from it a burbling stream of water leaps into the air'. The large rectangular colonnaded forecourt is now destroyed.

From the forecourt there was an entrance to the outer narthex which does not have any architectural or decorative features. Five doors made of wood and covered with bronze lead from the outer narthex to the inner narthex, the walls of which are covered with coloured marble panels and has nine cross-vaults covered with geometrically patterned mosaics. The door at the northern end opens onto a ramp that leads to the gallery above. The door at the southern end is called the 'Orologian Gate' due to the presence of a timekeeper in that corner in times past. There is also a ramp there to the upper gallery. Besides the historic bronze doors of the *Orologian Gate* this was the place through which emperors entered the church. But the most significant feature is the mosaic above the doors. As described in detail in a later chapter the mosaic depicts Constantine I holding a model of Constantinople, Justinian I holding a model of Hagia Sophia, and both models being offered to the Theotokos. From the inner narthex there are nine doors into the naos but in practice only three were used. The central or Royal Doors were restricted for entry into the naos by the emperor and clergy only, and the side doors flanking them for the faithful to enter into the side aisles of the church. Also described later is the famous mosaic above the centre Royal Doors of an enthroned Christ with the figure of an emperor prostrate at his feet.

The central feature of the architecture of Hagia Sophia is the enormous central dome in the naos with its 40 arched windows at its base resting on pendentives and large semi-circular arches supported by four massive corner piers. The pendentives were an innovation and spurred the building of domes in other churches. On the east and west side of the central dome are semi-domes that create the rectangular space of a basilica. As the central dome is without a drum it merges with the two semi-domes to give the appearance of one large elliptical dome and the feeling of a large, soaring space. The top of the dome is high enough that an 18-storey building could fit underneath. The central dome of Hagia Sophia was damaged by an earthquake in 557 and rebuilt 20 feet higher than the original. In 1204 Hagia Sophia was desecrated and looted by the Crusaders and over the centuries there were further repairs and restorations to the structure of the building. The church was converted into a mosque in 1454, the mosaics were

353. Hagia Sophia, Constantinople. East view of the apse

354. Hagia Sophia, Constantinople. Looking east at apse with dramatic shafts of sunlight penetrating the naos

355. Hagia Sophia, Constantinople. Central dome overhead looking east at apse with Ottoman ornamentation

356. Hagia Sophia, Constantinople. View of the southeast corner and gallery

357. Hagia Sophia, Constantinople. Typical decorative arch in the arcade separating naos and aisle

358. Hagia Sophia, Constantinople. Highly wrought naos capital with imperial monogram

359. Hagia Sophia, Constantinople. Marble clad inner narthex looking south toward the *Orologian Gate* at the mosaic of the Theotokos with the Christ child, Emperors Justinian (left) and Constantine (right)

360. Hagia Sophia, Constantinople. Outer narthex with marble floor and walls and doors to the inner narthex

briefly uncovered between 1847 and 1854, and then restored in 1932. The building opened as a museum in 1934.

The naos is separated from two wide, side aisles by arcades of green marble columns with striking Byzantine basket type capitals. The capitals throughout the church are splendid and are of different types but similar in the way the acanthus and palm foliage is carved to produce a white lace effect. Above the aisles and narthex in the form of a U are galleries with their own arcades looking down upon the naos. The south gallery is closed off by a marble screen with a door opening in the centre creating a private space for the emperor where 'seated on his customary throne gives ear to the sacred books' as portrayed by Paul the Silentiary.

361. Hagia Sophia, Constantinople. Original raised basin in baptistery

The empress and her entourage had their own area known as a Loge in the well-lit west gallery above the narthex. There they could overlook the naos and have a majestic view of the Holy Table and bema. A circle of green marble apparently marks the position of her throne. The whole interior of the church is brightly lit by two-tiered windows in the two side arches in addition to the arched windows at the base of the dome. The floor of the naos is paved in marble slabs inset by broad bands of dark green marble.

Paul the Silentiary provides a lengthy description of the liturgical fixtures and fittings, all of which have now disappeared. At the back of the bema apse ran a seven-tiered synthronon providing seats for the clergy with a patriarch's throne in the centre. From other sources it is recorded that in the first half of the seventh century the number of clergy was 600, divided into 80 presbyters, 150 deacons, 40 deaconesses, 70 sub-deacons, 160 readers, 25 singers and 75 doorkeepers. Paul goes on to mention the great arch framing the bema on the naos side and below it a three-sided iconostasis that projected out into the naos space. In the centre of the bema was the Holy Table covered by a canopy in the form of an eight-sided ciborium, which was of silver. The Table itself was of gold set with precious stones. The front side of the iconostasis was arrayed with six columns with four on each of the two sides (counting the corner columns twice), making a total of 12 columns. There were doors on each of the three sides with the Holy Gate in the centre of the front side surmounted by a round arch. Between the columns was a low wall topped by a tie beam all sheathed in silver decorated with incised, sacred images and the monograms of Justinian and Theodora. From the Holy Gate the solea, a raised walkway with a low parapet of marble slabs, extended out to the ambo. This was a monumental structure that stood under the great dome, not directly under its centre but slightly toward the bema. Paul the Silentiary describes the ambo as 'reached by two flights, one of which stretches towards the west, but the other towards the dawn. So they are opposite to one another, and both lead to a space formed like a circle'. The circular platform was supported by eight gilded columns and finished in a variety of coloured marbles while the stairs were shielded by parapets sheathed in silver.

Outside of the main church building there was the baptistery (*baptistérion*) located just beyond the Orologion Gate. The baptistery had an octagonal shape inside and was covered with a dome. Inside the baptistery a large baptismal basin with three steps down into it can still be seen. On the northwest corner of Hagia Sophia there was the circular *skevophylákion* or treasury building also covered with a dome.

Cruciform

The complex dedicated to the **Holy Apostles** in Constantinople consisted of two buildings. The first was a circular mausoleum erected by Constantine in 330 while the second building, a cruciform shaped church, was added afterwards by his son and successor Constantius II (r. 337–361). Together the buildings were known as the *Apostoleíon* dedicated to all the apostles. The church was one of the most famous of its time, second only to Hagia Sophia, but the two buildings of the Holy Apostles do not exist today. Eusebius (*c*.263–339) described Constantine's church building as having a dome 'entirely encompassed by a fine tracery, wrought in brass and gold that reflected the sun's rays with a brilliancy which dazzled the distant beholder'. There was a large forecourt with porticoes on all four sides and the interior walls were lined with fine marble slabs of various colours. Constantine prepared the mausoleum with 12 empty caskets to receive the relics of the Twelve Apostles. In the end only the relics of one apostle, Andrew, and the two saints Luke and Timothy, were acquired. Constantius also buried his father's remains there. Later the relics of the great fathers of the Church, St John Chrysostom and St Gregory the Theologian, were placed in caskets on either side of the Holy Table.

Justinian did not consider the *Apostoleíon* grand enough so he demolished the old structures between 534 and 540 and rebuilt them larger and grander. The rotunda and cruciform forms for the mausoleum and church buildings respectively were retained. The church building is of interest for two reasons. It was the only cruciform church in Constantinople and also because it was designed by Anthemius of Tralles and Isidorus of Miletus, the architects of the third Hagia Sophia. In the *New Apostoleíon*, as it is known, Justinian's domed rotunda which replaced the old mausoleum became the burial place of almost all the emperors for the next five centuries. It was a free-standing structure in the centre of an open courtyard surrounded on all sides by colonnades. On the west side of the courtyard stood the new church, the design of which Procopius in his book *Edifices* describes as follows: 'Two straight lines were drawn, intersecting each other in the middle to form a cross, one extending east and west and the other which crossed this running north and south. ... At the crossing of the two straight lines, that is to say about the middle, there was set aside a place which may not be entered by those who may not celebrate the mysteries: this with good reason they call the "sanctuary" ...' He goes on to write that above the sanctuary there was a dome set on a drum pierced with windows 'resembling the Church of Sophia, except that it is inferior to it in size'. The four arms of the cross each had their own dome but not pierced by windows. This cross plan was used by Justinian in the building of the church of St John at Ephesus, except there the western arm is longer and covered by two domes instead of one. The *Apostoleíon* church plan was copied in the Basilica of San Marco, Venice built in 1063.

`A splendid image of Justinian's building in vibrant colours, one of which is in the Vatican Codex of 1162, shows five domes with figures assembled in the narthex. The image confirms the description by the Procopius who depicts the church as having the shape of a cross with the 'sanctuary' located at the crossing point bounded by four arches that support a circular drum pierced by windows and a dome above which 'seems to float in the air and not rest upon solid masonry'. He goes on to describe how the four arms of the building were roofed with smaller domes but were not pierced by windows. There is disagreement among scholars as to the shape of the bema at the eastern end. It seems, though, that in the apse there was a semi-circular synthronon containing a bishop's chair and a railing separating the bema from the naos.

Justinian's rebuilt structures were described somewhat later by Nicholas Mesarites in his book *Ekphrasis on the Church of the Holy Apostles* composed between 1198 and 1203. He noted the Greek cross plan, the double narthex at the western end, and a synthronon behind the Holy Table which was

BYZANTINE CHURCHES IN CONSTANTINOPLE
CRUCIFORM & CONVERTED TYPES

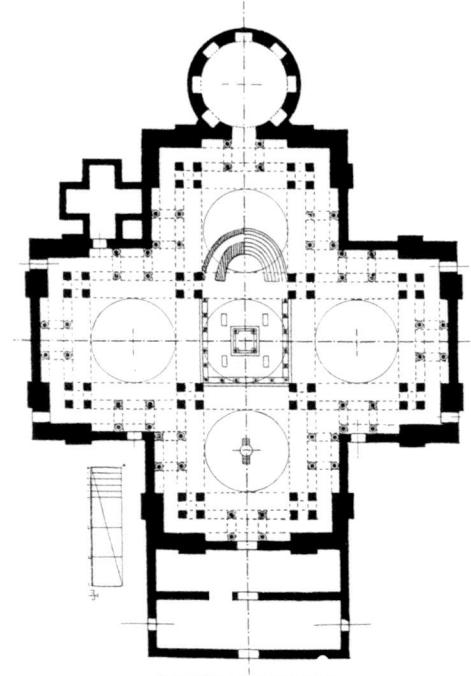

HOLY APOSTLES
(Mango 1993 V, Fig 1)
[Reconstructed plan by G. A. Soteriou]

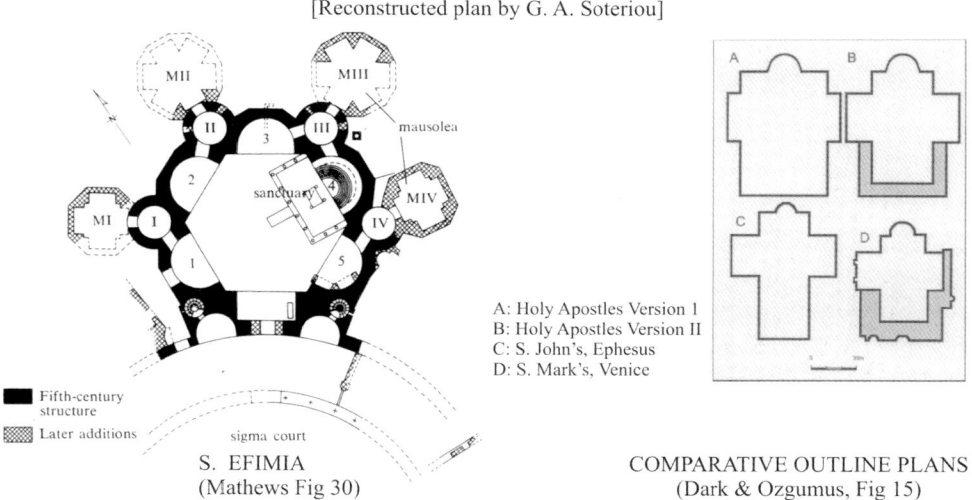

S. EFIMIA
(Mathews Fig 30)

A: Holy Apostles Version 1
B: Holy Apostles Version II
C: S. John's, Ephesus
D: S. Mark's, Venice

COMPARATIVE OUTLINE PLANS
(Dark & Ozgumus, Fig 15)

362. Constantinople, plan type – cruciform and converted

located at the crossing of the arms of the cross. He observed that attached to the eastern end of the church was a rotunda that contained the Mausoleum of Constantine the Great. The Mausoleum of Justinian himself was a small cross-shaped structure joining the eastern and northern arms of the larger Greek cross.

Until the eleventh century the courtyard of the *Apostoleíon* was the imperial cemetery for the graves of emperors and for the Patriarchs of Constantinople. The church and imperial tombs were looted during the Fourth Crusade in 1204 and some of the treasures were taken to Venice and are still in St Mark's basilica today. In 1461, eight years after the Fall of Constantinople, Sultan Mehmet II demolished the church of the Holy Apostles and built the Fatih (Conqueror) mosque over its foundations.

Cross-In-Square

From the ninth century onward the domed, cross-in-square church became the dominant type in Constantinople and from there the popularity of the form spread throughout the Byzantine Empire. Most notable of the ninth-century cross-in-square type were the churches of SS Peter and Mark, St John the Forerunner Troullo (*Agios Ioánnis o Pródromos en to Troúllo* – St John the Forerunner with-the-Dome), St Theodosia, and the *New Ekklessia* ('New Church'). The best-known cross-in-square type built in the tenth century was the church at the monastery of Myrelaion. Renowned cross-in-square type churches of the eleventh century were the North church of the Theotokos Panachrantos, the monastery churches of Theotokos Pammakaristos and that of St Saviour Pantepoptes, and the church dedicated to St Theodore. Twelfth-century cross-in-square type churches were the Theotokos Kyritoissa and the two known as the 'Earliest' and 'Latest' churches at the monastery of St Saviour Pantokrator.

Of the ninth-century edifices the church of **SS Peter and Mark** (Hoja Atik Mustapha Camii) is one the smallest and simplest of all the cross-in-square churches in Constantinople. There is, however, no general agreement whether the church is that of SS Peter and Mark. It may have replaced an older one said to have been founded by two patricians of Constantinople, named Galbius and Candidus, in 458 during the reign of Leo I (457–474). In the ninth century building the cross shape in the square is perfectly clear and there is only one dome – that over the crossing point. Large piers and arches support the dome that is without a drum or windows. Typical of the period, the three apses are each semi-circular within but polygonal on the outside with three sides of equal width.

The church of **St John the Forerunner Troullo** was part of a monastery of the same name built in the twelfth century but possibly earlier. It is the smallest Byzantine church in Constantinople and very charming. The building is reasonably preserved as the Hirami Ahmet Pasha Mescidi. It is an example of a perfect cross-in-square type which is very much in evidence in the interior but especially in the exterior in its three dimensional form. In the centre there are four columns that support a dome which rests on a drum, octagonal with ribs on the interior and circular on the exterior, pierced by eight arched windows. The cross arms, each covered by a barrel vault, have triple windows in the north and south arms. The central apse and the smaller side apses are semi-circular both within and without and all project out from the east wall. Three windows separated by pilasters with carved capitals provide light to the bema while the side apses, which have barrel vaults, each have one window. The narthex is entered unusually from the south (it is not known if this was a later change) but has the entrance into the naos from the central of its three bays. The exterior appears to have been altered in parts but the original alternating bands of brick and stone can still be seen.

St Theodosia, or *Agia Theodosia en tois Dexiokrátous* (a district named after the owner Dexiokrates), to give the church its full name but scholars disagree on the Christian identity of the building. It may have

BYZANTINE CHURCHES IN CONSTANTINOPLE
CROSS-IN-SQUARE TYPE

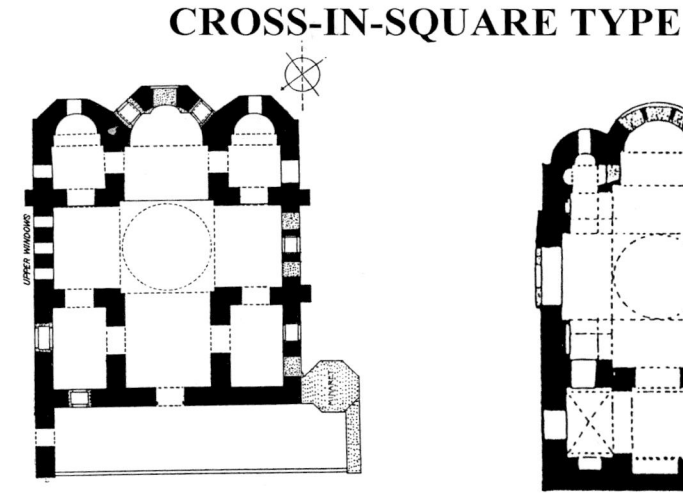

SS. PETER & MARK
(Van Millingen Fig 64)

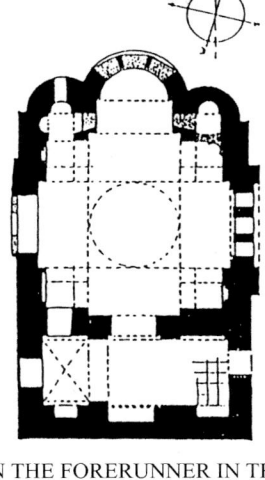

S. JOHN THE FORERUNNER IN TROULO
(Van Millingen Fig 70)

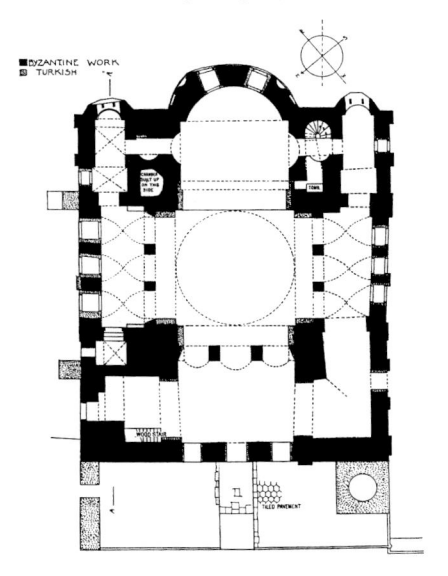

S. THEODOSIA
(Van Millingen Fig 56)

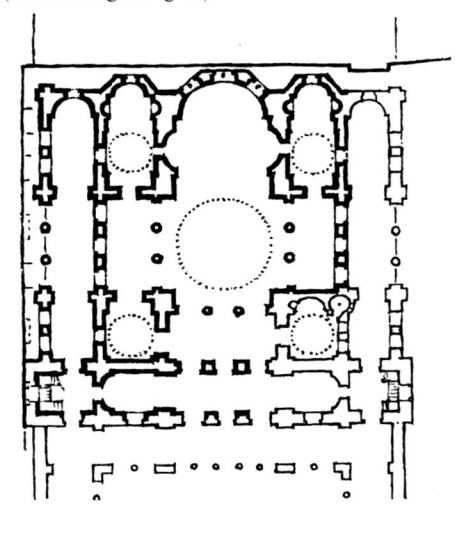

NEA EKKLESIA RESTORED PLAN
(McDonald Fig 67)

363. Constantinople, plan type – cross-in-square I

BYZANTINE CHURCHES IN CONSTANTINOPLE
CROSS-IN-SQUARE TYPE

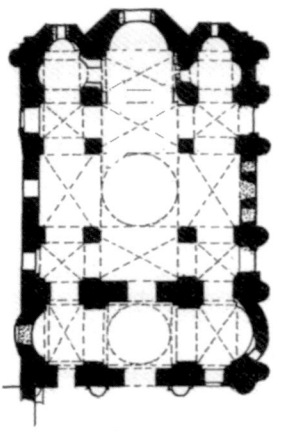

MYRELAION
(Redrawn by author
from Krautheimer Fig, 90)

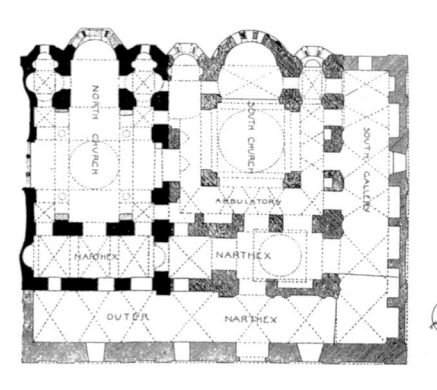

THEOTOKOS PANACHRANTOS
(Van Millingen Fig 44)

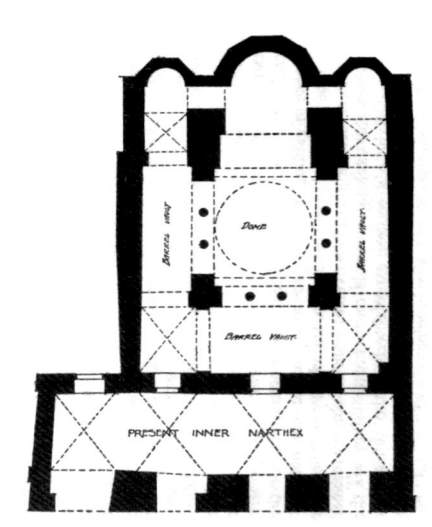

THEOTOKOS PAMMAKARISTOS
Probable Original Plan
(Van Millingen Fig 47)

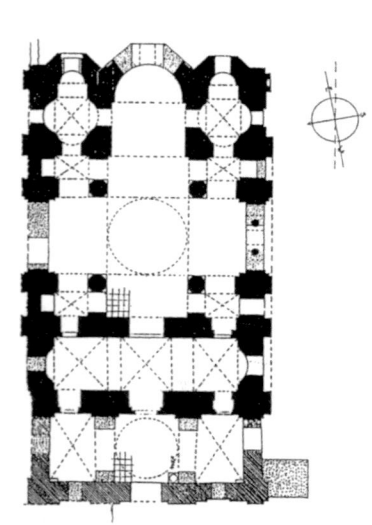

S. SAVIOR PANTEPOPTES
(Freely Fig 100)

364. Constantinople, plan type – cross-in-square II

BYZANTINE CHURCHES IN CONSTANTINOPLE
CROSS-IN-SQUARE TYPE

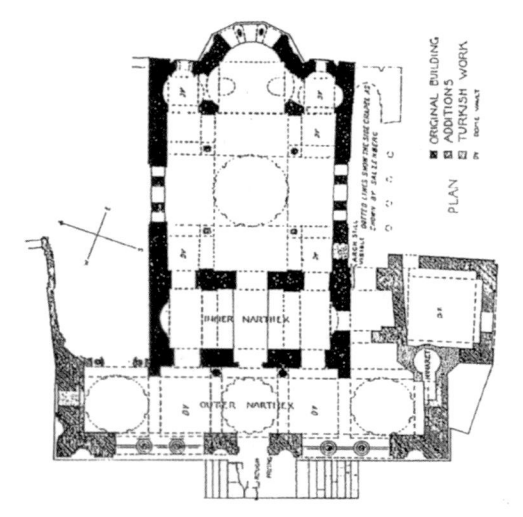

S. THEODORE
(Van Millingen Fig 84)

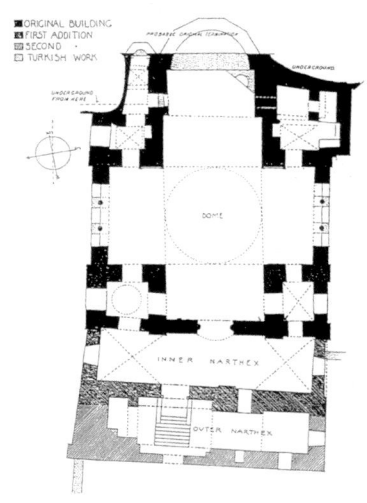

THEOTOKOS KYRIOTISSA / DIACONISSA
(Van Millingen Fig 61)

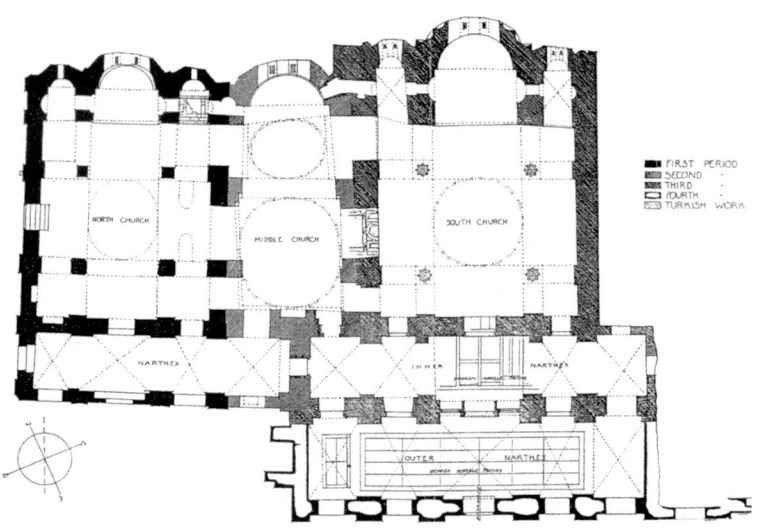

S. SAVIOR PANTOKRATOR
(Van Millingen Fig 77)

365. Constantinople, plan type – cross-in-square III

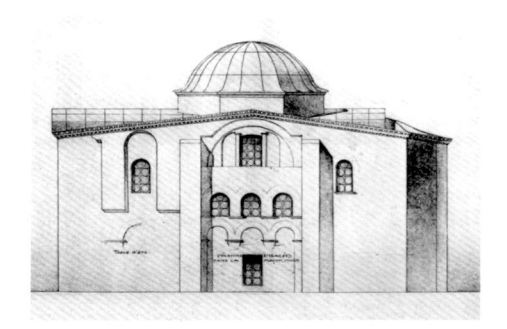

366. SS Peter and Mark, Constantinople. South elevation with upper right window lighting the diaconicon

367. SS Peter and Mark, Constantinople. Section through central apse (left), naos and dome (centre) and narthex (right)

368. SS Peter and Mark, Constantinople. View of the three apses (right) at the eastern end with stone finishes

369. SS Peter and Mark, Constantinople. Central dome with Ottoman decoration

been originally dedicated to *Agia Efimia en tou Petriou* and rededicated sometime after the building was constructed during the reign of Basil I (867–886). Then, perhaps, it could have been dedicated to Christ Evergetes because of the adjoining monastery of the same name. It is identified by some as the present day Gul Camii. The building has undergone three building phases and was considerably altered in Ottoman times.

Although ostensibly a cross-in-square church the impression is more of a domed basilica due to the longer east and west cross arms and the shorter north and south arms. Over the centre there is a dome with a low drum, without any windows, that is supported by four immense piers, arches, and the pendentives. The dome is not original and the arches are pointed Ottoman ones. Between each pair of immense piers there are two small square piers of a triple arcade except on the bema end. In the bema there are bold projecting polygonal apses. At the opposite end of the naos there is a low narthex covered by a barrel vault with a triple arcade separating the narthex from the tall space of the naos. A gallery extends above the narthex and side aisles and is accessed by a wooden stair at the northern corner of the narthex. Passageways link the bema and the former pastophoria chambers each of which was covered by cross vaults. The chapels in the galleries directly above the pastophoria are domed. What distinguishes the exterior of the church is its elongated appearance due to the high naos and side aisles spaces but in particular the tall gallery space.

After the end of the Iconoclastic period Emperor Basil I (r. 867–886), who regarded himself a new Justinian, built a church named the **Nea Ekklesia** ('New Church') to signify the beginning of a new era. At the consecration in 880 the church was dedicated to Jesus Christ, the archangel Michael, the Prophet Elijah, St Nicholas and the Theotokos. It later was just called the *Nea Ekklesia of the Theotokos*. After the Ottoman conquest the church was used for gunpowder storage so when the building was struck by lightning in 1490 it was destroyed.

Descriptions of the church are thus based on written sources and some maps. Most scholars consider the church to have been a cross-in-square type with a central dome and smaller domes over each of the four corner spaces of the square. In an unusual arrangement porticoes ran the full length of the northern and southern sides of the church. Perhaps the reasons were that the northern portico opened to the polo field (*tzykanistérion*) and the southern portico faced the sea and

370. SS Peter and Mark, Constantinople. Barrel vault over northern arm of the cross and tall archway into the former prothesis

371. St John the Forerunner Troullo, Constantinople. Clear cross-in-square form

372. St John the Forerunner Troullo, Constantinople. Naos with partial view of dome overhead looking at semi-circular apse

lighthouse tower. Beyond the southern portico there was probably a *skevophylákion* building. The forecourt on the western side was decorated with two fountains of marble and porphyry. On the east side of the church between the apses and the hippodrome was a garden known as the *mesoképion* ('middle garden'). Ousterhout in his book the *Master Builders of Byzantium* records the description of the church given by Emperor Constantine VII Porphyrogenitus (r. 945–959), the grandson of Basil I (r. 867–886):

373. St Theodosia, Constantinople. View of polygonal-shaped apses with the larger bema apse in the centre, prothesis (right) and diaconicon (left)

This church, like a bride adorned with pearls and gold, with gleaming silver, with a variety of many-hued marble, with compositions of mosaic *tesserae*, and clothing of silken stuffs, he [Basil] offered to Christ, the immortal Bridegroom.Its roof, consisting of five domes, gleams with gold and is resplendent with beautiful images as with stars, while on the outside it is adorned with brass that resembles gold. The walls on either side are beautified with costly marbles of many hues, while the sanctuary is enriched with gold and silver, precious stones, and pearls. The barrier that separates the sanctuary from the naos, including the columns that pertain to it and the lintel that is above them; the seats that are within, and the steps that are in front of them, and the holy tables themselves – all of these are of silver suffused with gold, of precious stones and costly pearls. As for the pavement, it appears to be covered in silken stuffs of Sidonian workmanship; to such an extent has it been adorned all over with marble slabs of different colours enclosed by tessellated bands of varied aspect, all accurately joined together and abounding in elegance …[1]

In 920 Emperor Romanos I Lekapenos (919–945) built a palace and a nearby church at **Myrelaion** (place of myrrh – a dried resin used in both incense and in holy anointing oil). He and other members of the Macedonian and following Komnenian dynasties were buried in the basement chapel of the church changing the tradition of imperial burials in the church of the Holy Apostles. The funerary chapel was converted from part of the vaulted substructure of an immense fifth-century cistern known as the Rotunda. The roof of the chapel is supported by four columns crowned by beautiful capitals and forms a platform over which the church is built. In the 1980s the remaining section of the Rotunda was converted into a subterranean shopping mall. Before his deposition and exile the Emperor converted his palace into a nunnery. After the Ottoman conquest the complex was converted into the Bodrum Camii, Bodrum meaning a subterranean hollow that refers to the cistern.

The most distinctive aspect about the church is its exterior which has a striated appearance created by thin, horizontal brick courses separated by thick mortar joints. Furthermore half-cylindrical buttresses, also of the same brick pattern, project out from the sides of the building creating interesting shadow patterns on the wall. Internally the church has a very clear cross-in-square plan of the four column type represented by plain piers. While the dome and drum on the inside are segmented into eight sections each penetrated by a round headed tall window, on the outside the drum has a polygonal shape with decorative brick window arches and a shallow saucer dome above. Each arm of the cross is roofed by a cross vault. At the east end the main apse of the bema was flanked by the smaller apses of the pastophoria

374. Myrelaion, Constantinople. Model of original church above the cistern (Photograph in the former narthex)

375. Myrelaion, Constantinople. View of the northern side with arched windows piercing the drum of the dome

376. Myrelaion, Constantinople. Thin bricks with courses separated by thick mortar joints

377. Myrelaion, Constantinople. Central dome with Ottoman decoration

each semi-circular internally and three-sided externally. There were three tall windows in the central apse and single narrow ones in each of the two side apses. The narthex was divided into three bays with a shallow dome over the centre bay and cross vaults over the side ones.

Soon after the construction of the *Nea Ekklesia* Constantine Livos (also known as Lips), a patrician in the time of the Greek Emperor Leo VI the Wise (r. 886–912) founded a Nunnery known by his name (*Moní tou Lívos*) at a place called *Merdosangaris*. He also built a church there on the remains of a sixth-century shrine and dedicated it to the Theotokos. Known as the church of the **Theotokos tou Livos,** it also has the designation of **Panachrantos** ('Immaculate') and was actually two churches side by side. The two were built at different times but joined together by a double narthex.

The first church built by Constantine Livos was in 907 and served the convent founded at the same time. After falling into disuse the monastery was re-founded by Empress Theodora, widow of Michael VIII Palaiologos (r. 1225–1282), in 1287 when she also added another church with its own narthex to the south of the existing church. Later in 1303 she attached to the two adjoining churches an outer narthex and at its south end a chapel, a *parekklesion*, dedicated to St John the Forerunner, actually to *Agios Ioannis Prodromos Livos* (after the Greek name of the founder of the Nunnery).

The first church was of the cross-in-square type but the four columns and semi-circular arches were removed in the Ottoman period and replaced by piers and the pointed arches seen today. Due to the wider east and west arms of the cross the internal impression is more one of a domed basilica. The apse has a barrel vault instead of a semi-dome and the small side chapels were clearly the original pastophoria. The apse has lofty triple windows while the pastophoria have single, plain, narrow windows. The second

378. Myrelaion, Constantinople. Original marble column and Corinthian capital in the former cistern converted to a chapel

church is more clearly a cross-in-square type but with arches between large piers supporting the dome creating in effect wide side aisles around three sides – the fourth side being the bema. The apse here is semi-circular both inside and outside. The remains of an inscription on the apse refer to 'O Immaculate One' and for this reason the church is also known as the Theotokos Panachrantos. The chapel dedicated to St John became a place of burial beginning with the Empress Theodora herself followed by several members of the Palaiologoi imperial family. An outer narthex with a gallery above joins the north and south churches.

On the exterior of the church alternating courses of brick and stone create an attractive pattern. When the two churches were converted into the Fenari Isa Camii the buildings were much altered. The buildings were destroyed by fire twice but thoroughly restored in the 1970s and 1980s. The interior today lacks the original marble and mosaic decoration but its unplastered domes, vaults and walls allows the superb brick craftsmanship of the Byzantine builders to be revealed and appreciated.

Towards the end of the eleventh century Emperor Michael VII Doukas (r. 1071–1078) built the monastery of the Theotokos Pammakaristos. Nothing remains of the monastery buildings. The associated church of **Theotokos Pammakaristos** ('All-Blessed'), however, does exist. The church is a complicated structure with three sections built at separate times. In the centre is the main church and around the north, west and south sides of the main church there are wide aisles, the second section. On the south side the wide aisles extend only just past the end of the narthex as the remainder of the south side is taken up by a *parekklesion*, the third section. The main church was built between 1081 and 1118 by the brother of Alexios I Komnenos, Adrian-John and his wife Anna, to contain their

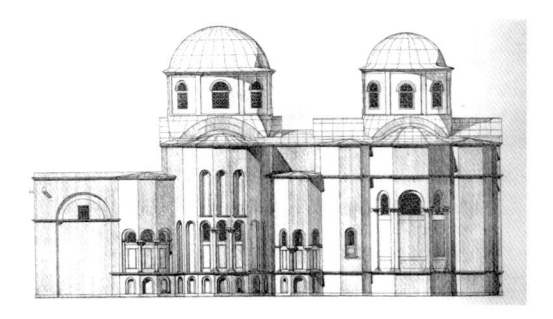

379. Theotokos Panachrantos, Constantinople. Apse elevation of the two adjoining churches with the *parekklesion* (chapel of St John) on the extreme left

380. Theotokos Panachrantos, Constantinople. North-south section through the two Churches (left) and the *parekklesion* (right)

381. Theotokos Panachrantos, Constantinople. Circular cylindrical drums and semi-circular domes of the two churches

382. Theotokos Panachrantos, Constantinople. The smaller drum and dome of the north church

tombs and those of their family. The *parekklesion*, dedicated to Christ the Word (*Christós O Lógos*), was added in 1320 by Maria the widow of Michael IX Palaiologos as a funerary chapel for her departed husband. Later in the fourteenth century the wide aisles, the second section, were added around the main church.

When the main church and wide aisles were converted into a mosque in 1587, the Fethiye (Victory) Camii, the interior spaces were radically altered and lack any architectural coherence. The church was a cross-in-square type with three apses on the east side and a narthex on the west side. The central square space was covered with a lofty dome on a drum and the sides by barrel vaults. Four chapels, the second section, took up the full north side of the original church.

One of the finest Byzantine walls of decorative brick and stone in the city is displayed on the exterior of the *parekklesion*, the third section. The decoration is a succession of narrow and wide arches, slender niches, and concave roundels. Internally the *parekklesion* is a perfect cross-in-square with the central dome supported by four marble columns with superb capitals. An unusual feature of the monolithic columns is their pattern of greenish swirls. The hemispherical dome is divided into 12 segments

383. Theotokos Panachrantos, Constantinople. Side wall of the *parekklesion* showing a stair down from present day ground level

384. Theotokos Panachrantos, Constantinople. Restored but left unfinished semi-circular dome, drum with windows and pendentives of the south church

385. Theotokos Panachrantos, Constantinople. Complex meeting of a cross vault (top) and semi-circular dome (bottom)

386. Theotokos Panachrantos, Constantinople. Dome, drum, pendentives and supporting arches

separated by flat, narrow projecting ribs which continue down and likewise divide the drum into 12 sections with an arched window in each section. Cross vaults cover each of the four arms of the cross and the bema and pastophoria apses while each of the small corner spaces of the square is covered by a small dome. The apses are semi-circular on the inside and polygonal on the outside with the central apse pierced by a triple window with carved shafts and capitals between the lights of the window. The two smaller pastophoria apses have a single window each. The *parekklesion* has its own narthex, which

387. Theotokos Panachrantos, Constantinople. Dome (top) and barrel vault (bottom) of the north church

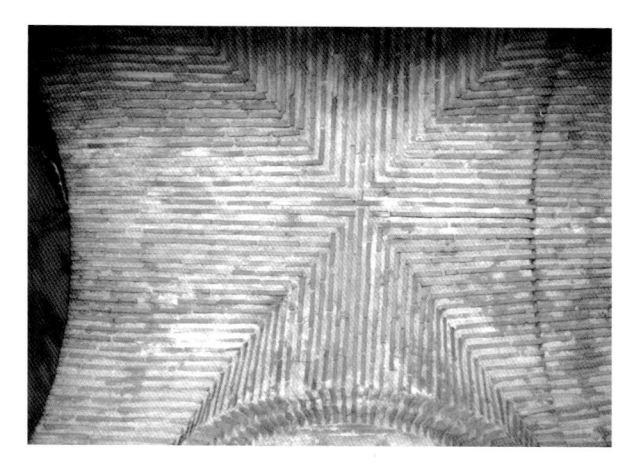

388. Theotokos Panachrantos, Constantinople. Restored and left unfinished cross vault that displays the construction technique employed

has three bays covered in cross vaults, with a small gallery above approached by a narrow stairway in the corner of the narthex. After the conversion of the main church into a mosque the *parekklesion* was neglected and the mosaics were whitewashed over. They were only restored in the 1940s. Today the chapel is a museum that exhibits among the most exquisite mosaics in the city. Travelers to Constantinople in earlier centuries described with admiration the mosaics they saw in the chapel.

The church of **St Saviour Pantepoptes** ('All Seeing') belonged to a monastery of the same name built sometime before 1087

389. Theotokos Panachrantos, Constantinople. Remains of a Byzantine column capital

by Anna Dalassena, mother of Alexios I Komnenos (r. 1081–1118), and the power behind the throne. St Saviour Pantepoptes is one of the most carefully built of the later churches of Constantinople and an excellent example of a cross-in-square structure and is the only eleventh-century Byzantine church building in the city that is still intact. It was converted by the Ottomans in 1453 into the Eski Imaret Camii.

The exterior of the church is dominated by a beautiful circular dome carried on a 12-sided high drum which has decorative brickwork and arched windows. The round top of the windows cut into the roofline creating a scalloped look. Attractive brickwork, with Greek key decoration, also distinguishes the walls even though parts are severely damaged or deteriorating and although the building is hemmed in on two sides by surrounding houses. The interior is a very good example of a symmetrical cross-in-square church plan with a square central bay, equal width south-north cross arms, and equal width east-west arms.

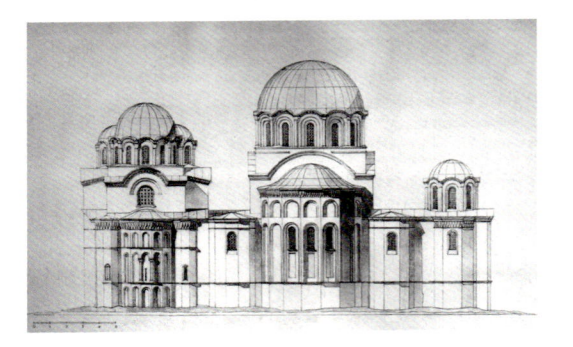

390. Theotokos Pammakaristos, Constantinople. East elevation of church apse (centre) and *parekklesion* (left)

391. Theotokos Pammakaristos, Constantinople. Cross section through church and *parekklesion* (right)

392. Theotokos Pammakaristos, Constantinople. South side with side view of the *parekklesion*

393. Theotokos Pammakaristos, Constantinople. Superb brickwork on the apse of the *parekklesion*

The arms of the cross are covered with barrel vaults while the two pastophoria chambers have cross vaults. The four columns of the central bay have been replaced by piers but otherwise the interior still retains most of its original characteristics. The central apse and former pastophoria apses are semi-circular on the inside and three-sided on the outside. Both the narthex and gallery above, which would have been reserved for the empress Anna Dalassena, are covered in cross vaults. Still to be seen today are the finely carved marble jambs and lintels that frame the doors and portals but the marble slabs that once covered the bottom of the walls have now vanished.

394. Theotokos Pammakaristos, Constantinople. The *parekklesion* naos looking at the apse with the large figure of a seated Christ in the semi-dome

SPLENDID CHURCHES 161

THEOTOKOS PAMMAKARISTOS, CONSTANTINOPLE
FOUR COLUMN CROSS-IN-SQUARE PARAKKLESION

NORTHEAST CORNER (Former Prothesis)

SOUTHEAST CORNER (Former Diconicon)

NORTHWEST CORNER

SOUTHWEST CORNER

395. Theotokos Pammakaristos, Constantinople. Images of each of the four columns of the cross-in-square *parekklesion*

The small and graceful church of **St Theodore**, now the Vefa Kilise Camii, has been assigned to the ninth or tenth century and may even be later. The outer part of the church was apparently rebuilt early in the fourteenth century around the original core in an attractive exterior design of alternating layers of brick and stone with marble decoration. The careful brickwork on the outside of the building is a good example of the greater interest taken in the outside appearance of churches. On the outside a double flight of steps leads up to the doors of the central portal which is flanked by triple arcades each with finely carved capitals and that are filled by windows and decorative marble panels.

396. Theotokos Pammakaristos, Constantinople. Marvelous Byzantine column capital

397. St Saviour Pantepoptes, Constantinople. South elevation with apse on the right

398. St Saviour Pantepoptes, Constantinople. Cross section through apse (left), central dome (centre) and two narthexes (right)

399. St Saviour Pantepoptes, Constantinople. From the southeast with the arched windows of the central dome

400. St Saviour Pantepoptes, Constantinople. Close-up of the arched windows in the southern arm of the cross-in-square plan

The exonarthex is famous for its domes. The space was added in the rebuilding and is unusual in that it has five bays with the end bays extending beyond the side walls of the inner narthex and naos. The central and end bays of the exonarthex are each covered by domes on tall drums which on the outside have fine-looking polygonal forms in brick with superbly decorated arches around the windows. In the south dome there is small patch of mosaic which gives some indication as to the splendid mosaics that once covered all the domes but which have now vanished.

All the doors leading from the outer narthex to the inner narthex have marble frames and the one on the north is flanked by two columns with Corinthian capitals all of which appear to have been reused from the earlier fifth- or sixth-century church. The naos is a perfect cross-in-square of the four column type although the Ottomans replaced the columns with piers. The central bay of the cross is covered with a dome supported by a drum that is punctured by 12 windows while the cross arms have barrel vaults and the corner spaces of the square have small domes. The bema apse is a shallow semi-circle while the former pastophoria chambers do not project beyond the face of the eastern wall. A triple window lights the bema and a tall, thin window each of the flanking chambers.

401. St Saviour Pantepoptes, Constantinople. Merged central dome and drum divided into 12 segments with Ottoman inscriptions on the pendentives and barrel vault over the arm of the cross

The dedication of the church of **Theotokos Kyriotissa** ('Enthroned') is based on the discovery of a donor wall painting in the building. The church may have also been the one dedicated to the Theotokos Diaconissa ('Deaconess') because of its rich and beautiful decoration and imperial connection. It was built around 1200 on the ruins of overlaying structures: a fourth- or early fifth-century Roman bath adjacent to the Valens Aqueduct, a sixth-century church, and a seventh-century church, known respectively as the North and Bema churches, and once surrounded by monastery buildings. The new thirteenth-century church is of the cross-in-square type but with some irregularities (walls are not parallel and the corners are not right angles) due to the pre-existing structures. The central bay is covered by a dome on a drum, the cross arms by barrel vaults, and the small corner chambers of the square by cross vaults. Internally the dome and drum are merged and provide a spectacular appearance and appears to be floating as the each of the sixteen arched windows is slightly wider than the tapered ribs on the side of each window. Triple arcades fill in the ground floor between the central bay and cross arms except for the bema end. A gallery extends around the three sides of the church. In the bema there is evidence that there was once a four-tier synthronon around the edge of the apse. Round headed doorways in the flanking walls of the bema lead to side chambers, the former pastophoria. A rare feature for a Byzantine church is that the majority of the exterior windows are original each made up of small rectangular grids. Many of the column capitals are reused from the earlier churches. The most notable aspect of the interior praised since earlier travellers arrived in Constantinople is the 16 different varieties of marble in panels that cover the walls. The panels are carefully laid out so that the colours and veinings match. The mosaics discovered in the church have been removed to the Istanbul Archaeological Museum. There is a cycle of thirteenth-century wall paintings in the diaconicon but are hidden behind the locked doors of the chamber in what is now the Kalenderhane Camii.

402. St Theodore, Constantinople. Entrance façade with the three narthex domes at the front and the central dome at the back

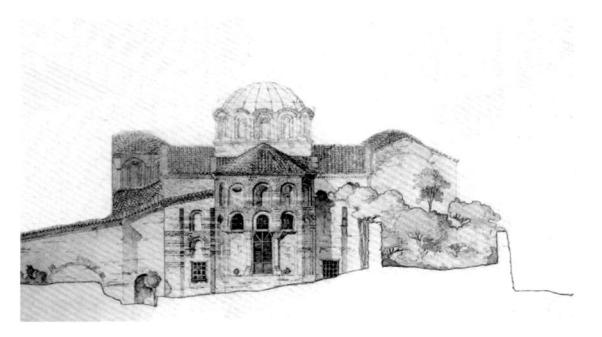

403. St Theodore, Constantinople. East façade with the triple windows of the bema apse

404. St Theodore, Constantinople. North elevation with central dome (left) and outer narthex dome (right)

405. St Theodore, Constantinople. Longitudinal section through the outer narthex with its three domes, looking west at the entrance door in the centre and the flanking external windows

406. St Theodore, Constantinople. Section through the two narthexes (left), naos and central dome (centre) and bema apse (right)

407. St Theodore, Constantinople. Entrance double stair

408. St Theodore, Constantinople. South end of the entrance façade

409. St Theodore, Constantinople. Naos dome looking at the entrance from the inner narthex – originally a triple entrance but now the two outer entrances blocked off

410. St Theodore, Constantinople. Narthex dome and drum with original Christian figures faintly visible

411. St Theodore, Constantinople. A narthex dome with some windows in drum blocked

Between 1118 and 1124 the Empress Eirene Komnena built a monastery and church dedicated to **St Saviour Pantokrator**. The monastery of Pantokrator with its hospital and hospice was of great renown in its time but all its buildings have disappeared. After her death in 1124 her husband Emperor John II Komnenos (r. 1118–1143) built another church to the south of the first and dedicated it to the **Theotokos Eleousa** ('Merciful'). After its completion he then built a middle church, really a mortuary chapel, dedicated to the **Archangel Michael,** to connect the two existing churches through arched openings. The chapel was to serve as a resting place for members of the Komnenian imperial family, beginning with the reburial of the Empress Eirene followed by John himself and his successors. The chapel also came to serve as a mausoleum for the following Palaiologoi dynasty with the last two emperors of Byzantium buried there, Manuel II in 1425 and John VIII in 1448. As it was built on a prominent hill the complex of buildings is a prominent landmark in the city.

412. St Theodore, Constantinople. Original column capital in narthex

413. Theotokos Kyriotissa, Constantinople. View from the southwest showing the clear cross-in-square form along with cylindrical drum, its arched windows and the dome

414. Theotokos Kyriotissa, Constantinople. Triple layer of windows lighting up an arm of the cross-in-square

The two outer (north and south) churches are of the cross-in-square type each with three polygonal apses while the middle is a simple aisleless basilica with two domes and a large apse. All the domes are on drums pierced by narrow arched windows. A long inner narthex connects all three churches but the outer narthex only extends in front of the south and middle churches. There is a gallery above the inner narthex accessible from the south side. Venetians looted the icons, sacred vessels and holy relics from the churches during the Latin occupation (1204–1261) to enrich St Mark's in Venice. In 1453 Sultan Mehmet II converted the monastery into an Islamic school (*madrasah*) and the churches into the Zeyrek Camii. The whole complex is currently undergoing a very substantial reconstruction.

415. Theotokos Kyriotissa, Constantinople. Drum, pierced by 16 windows and dome with Ottoman decoration

416. Theotokos Kyriotissa, Constantinople. Various patterned marble panels on interior wall

417. Theotokos Kyriotissa, Constantinople. Northwest corner of the naos looking at the entrance from the narthex

418. Theotokos Kyriotissa, Constantinople. Southeast corner looking at the former diaconicon

Centralized

The only clear-cut centralized model that survives of the handful of this church type built in Constantinople is the sixth-century church that was dedicated to SS Sergius and Bacchus. Two other surviving examples, St Saviour in Chora and St Andrew in Krisei, are considered centralized types even though they have ambiguous forms. When seen on drawings their plans appear to be of the cross-in-square type but the north and south arms of the cross shape are so compressed they appear to be more like wide aisles. The spatial experience reinforces this impression of a dominant square central space with side extensions.

The church of **SS Sergius and Bacchus**, still known as the 'little Hagia Sophia' (Kucuk Aya Sofya Camii), was begun by Emperor Justinian in 527 before he embarked on the 'Great Church' (Hagia Sophia). The church of the two saints is a good example of a well-preserved centralized type. The ideal design was for an octagon inscribed within a square. In reality both are irregular in shape but this is not obvious inside the building. The irregularity was most probably due to the fact that the church was built between two buildings, the Palace of Hormisdas and the church of SS Peter and Paul, both of which disappeared in the medieval period. The two churches seemed to have shared a narthex.

419. Theotokos Kyriotissa, Constantinople. Northeast corner looking at the former prothesis

The interior of the dome of SS Sergius and Bacchus is unusual in that it is without a drum and instead has a scalloped surface created from 16 sections, eight flat pierced by windows and eight concave. The dome is supported by an octagon of eight superb semi-circular arches and their grand polygonal piers. Between the piers there are marvellous green–veined, paired columns of marble on octagonal bases. While the paired columns and the decorative beam above, the architrave, are level with the piers on the west, north and south sides of the octagon, at each of the four corners of the octagon the paired columns are set back in a semi-circular niche or exedra. Shorter, paired columns of the same coloured marble front the gallery add to the unified appearance of the interior, accentuating its centrality.

420. St Saviour Pantokrator, Constantinople. Arched entrance façade of the outer narthex (foreground), small dome over the inner narthex, large dome over the south church (right), lower dome of the middle church (centre) and dome of the North church (left)

421. St Saviour Pantokrator, Constantinople. East elevation with three apses – south church (left), middle church (centre) and north church (right)

SPLENDID CHURCHES

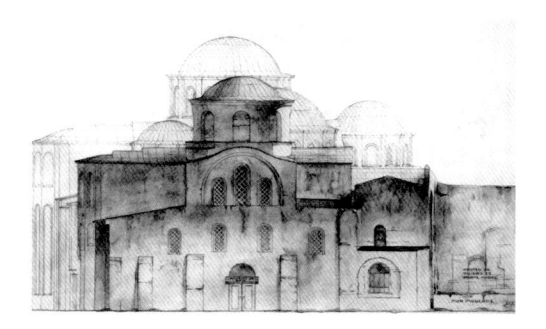

422. St Saviour Pantokrator, Constantinople. North elevation showing side entrance into north church (centre), narthex (right wide arch window) and outer narthex further back (far right)

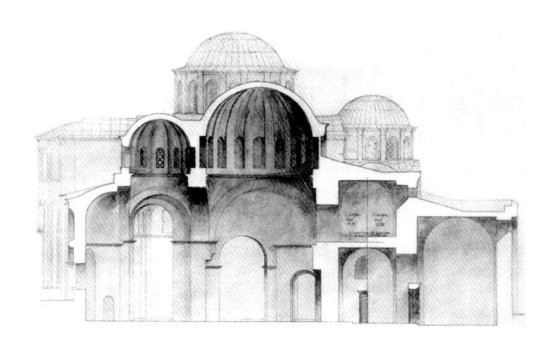

423. St Saviour Pantokrator, Constantinople. Section through middle church – apse (left) small dome over bema, large dome over naos and two narthexes (right)

424. St Saviour Pantokrator, Constantinople. Section through north church – narthex (left), drum and dome over naos centre with side entrance door visible, and apse (right)

425. St Saviour Pantokrator, Constantinople. View from the east showing the three apses and reconstructed drum and dome over the north church (right)

A broad stair at the south end of the narthex provides access to the gallery which continues all round the church except on the east side where the bema apse is located. Between the octagon and the enclosing square there is a passageway in the form of wide aisles that are covered by a series of barrel vaults. The bema was distinguished from the niche and aisle spaces by a raised floor or platform. The capitals of the columns throughout the church are exquisitely carved with deep undercuts that create beautiful shapes that produce intricate shadow patterns.

426. St Saviour Pantokrator, Constantinople. Central dome (partial view) and west end of south church

BYZANTINE CHURCHES IN CONSTANTINOPLE
CENTRALIZED TYPE

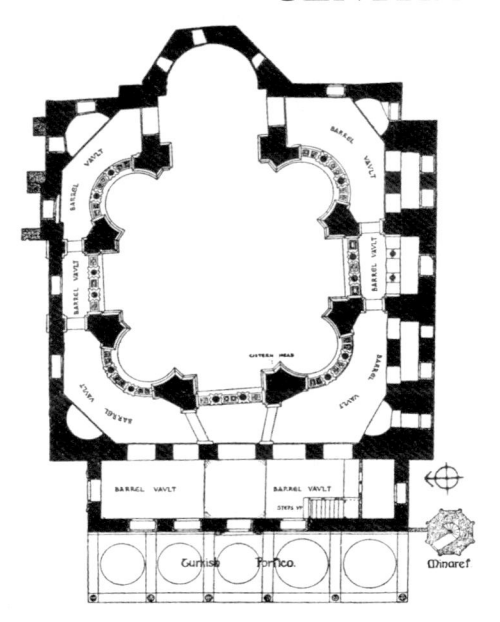

SS. SERGIUS & BACCHUS
Ground Plan
(Van Millingen Fig 23)

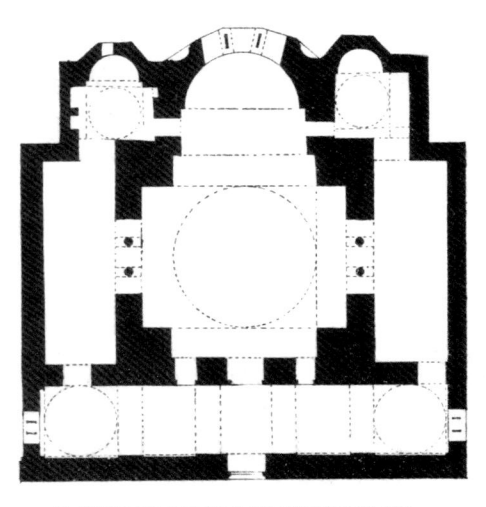

S. SAVIOR CHORA FIRST CHURCH
(Van Millingen Fig 102)

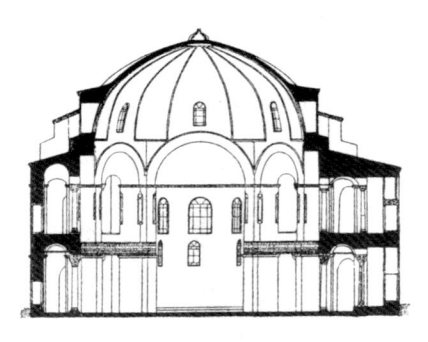

SS. SERGIUS & BACCHUS
North-South Cross Section
(Van Millingen Fig 26)

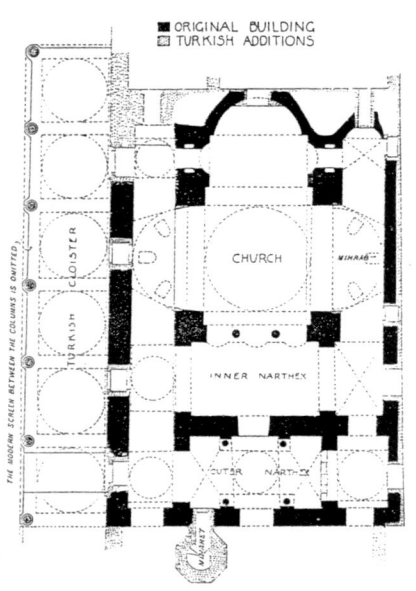

S. ANDREW IN KRISEI
(McDonald Fig 36)

427. Constantinople, plan type – centralized

428. SS Sergius and Bacchus, Constantinople. Entrance façade showing the pointed arches of the Ottoman portico (foreground)

429. SS Sergius and Bacchus, Constantinople. Apse elevation

430. SS Sergius and Bacchus, Constantinople. North elevation with apse (left) and narthex (right)

431. SS Sergius and Bacchus, Constantinople. Section through apse (left), naos and dome (centre) and narthex (right)

432. SS Sergius and Bacchus, Constantinople. Section through Ottoman portico (left), narthex, naos and dome (centre) and apse (right)

433. SS Sergius and Bacchus, Constantinople. View from the northwest of the entrance

434. SS Sergius and Bacchus, Constantinople. Ottoman portico

435. SS Sergius and Bacchus, Constantinople. View of apse from the southeast

436. SS Sergius and Bacchus, Constantinople. Drum and dome with Ottoman decoration

437. SS Sergius and Bacchus, Constantinople. View of former bema apse from the southwest gallery

Today nothing remains of the original interior decoration. According to Procopius, its marbles 'were more resplendent than the sun, and everywhere it was filled profusely with gold'. The pointed arch entrance portico on the western side is a later Muslim addition.

The church of SS Sergius and Bacchus was one of the churches in Constantinople to which the emperor paid a yearly visit. After his arrival he would proceed to the part of the gallery overlooking the holy bema where he would light tapers. He would then go the chapel of the Theotokos, also in the gallery, for private devotions and finally take his official place in the gallery, the *parakýptikon*, where he could have a view over the bema and the services at the Holy Table.

438. SS Sergius and Bacchus, Constantinople. Colonnade (bottom) and arcade (top) in the northern niche

439. SS Sergius and Bacchus, Constantinople. North archway in former bema and probable prothesis beyond

440. SS Sergius and Bacchus, Constantinople. South archway in former bema and probable diaconicon beyond

441. SS Sergius and Bacchus, Constantinople. Beautiful marble columns and Byzantine basket capitals

442. SS Sergius and Bacchus, Constantinople. Barrel vault over side passageway

443. SS Sergius and Bacchus, Constantinople. Attractive Byzantine column capital

The exterior and interior of the church of **St Saviour in Chora**, (*Agiou Sotiros en ti Chora* [Countryside]), also known as Holy Saviour in Chora, are of immense interest because of the striking architecture and magnificent mosaics and wall paintings that make it an outstanding Byzantine building. The original church and adjoining monastery were erected by Emperor Justinian (r. 527–565). After partial destruction of the church during the Iconoclastic period it was rebuilt between 1077 and 1081 by Maria Dukaina, the mother-in-law of Emperor Alexios I Komnenos (r. 1081–1118). In the sixteenth century the church was converted into a mosque and the mosaics and wall paintings covered with plaster and wooden panels. These were removed between 1945 and 1958, the images restored, and the building converted to a museum, which it remains today.

444. SS Sergius and Bacchus, Constantinople. Byzantine column capital incorporating classical Ionic volutes

A century later after the church was rebuilt in the eleventh century the apses on the eastern end collapsed and remodelled by Maria Dukaina's grandson, Isaac Komnenos. He added the present wider central apse that is covered by a semi-dome and took the opportunity to erect a larger central dome in the naos. A further phase of construction resulted in the addition of new narthexes, the *parekklesion*, the complete redecoration of the church with mosaics, wall paintings, and marble wall panels paid for by Theodore Metochites, a Byzantine statesman, patron of the arts, scholar and much else, between 1315 and 1321.

The spatial impression of the former naos is of a centralized cubical space with each of the four sides framed by wide arches that seem like shallow barrel vaulted spaces and which are the extremely compressed arms of a cross. These spaces appear as thin extensions of the naos. A semi-circular apse covered with a semi-dome is attached to the east side. Flanking the wide central apse are small spaces, formerly the pastophoria chapels, each covered with a small dome. The chapels were once connected by short passages to the bema (the one from the diaconicon is now walled up). Although the dome, semi-dome and arches are all unplastered from the restoration, the richly coloured marble slabs cover the bottom half of the naos walls that are a reminder of the once lavish naos. The whole interior is flooded with bright light from both the large, triple-arched window in the central apse wall and the arched windows in the large central dome. A fascinating suggestion has been made by scholars that the unusual annex adjoining the north side of the former naos, with a door into the prothesis at one end and the narthex at the other end, was the *skevophylákion* where the liturgical and sacred objects of the church were kept for safekeeping. The upper floor of the two story annex may have been the library of Theodore Metochites who had a celebrated collection of books and manuscripts.

The *parekklesion* on the south side had its own exonarthex and narthex, each a square space. An arched opening with two columns and splendid capitals leads into the chapel itself which is a small-scale, domed basilica space. The dome is ribbed and carried on a 12-sided drum with a window in each side. The bema was contained in a semi-circular apse covered with a semi-dome that projects out beyond the east wall of the church. The art work was restored from 1948 to 1958 after centuries of having being covered in plaster when the building was converted into a mosque at the end of the fifteenth century and is, today the Kariye Mosque Museum.

An attraction of the building is that it one of the few that is free-standing which allows the visitor to walk around the entire exterior of the church and absorb the sculptural qualities of its architecture – the domes on high, the walls punctured by arched windows, and the alternating bands of colourful brick and roughly dressed stone. The entrance still remains in the centre opening of the exonarthex but the remaining four openings have been walled in but leaving an arched window at the top of each opening. A sixth bay at the south was the former entrance into the *parekklesion* which extends the full length of the southern side of the church. There is only one central door leading from the exonarthex into the esonarthex in which the central and end bays are covered with small domes. The end domes are carried on drums perforated with windows to provide natural light into the esonarthex. There were once three doorways from the inner narthex into the naos which is covered by a large dome on a high drum pierced by 16 windows that required the addition of supporting piers in the corners of the naos.

The church **of St Andrew in Krisei** (from the district named Krisis) was part of a monastery. It was rebuilt three times and had a dedication change. The first church building most likely followed the basilica form common at the time built under the orders of the Princess Arcadia, sister of the Emperor Theodosius II (r. 408–450). The original dedication was to the Apostle St Andrew. After Andrew of Crete was martyred in 766 due to his opposition to the Iconoclastic policies of Emperor Constantine V (r. 741–775) he was buried at the church. As a result of his popularity after the end of the Iconoclastic movement the name of the church was changed to St Andrew in Krisei. Emperor Basil I (r. 867–886) wholly rebuilt the church which was again rebuilt around 1284 by Princess Theodora Raoulaina, niece of Michael VII Palailogos (r. 1259–1282).

The Byzantine monastery buildings have now disappeared. Drastic alterations to the church building when it was converted into a mosque, the Koca Mustafa Pasha Camii, in the sixteenth century make it difficult today to appreciate the original form of the church. The centralized square of the church was covered by a dome. On the east side of the square the shallow space is covered by a crosswise barrel vault, as were once the spaces on the north and south sides that now have semi-domes.

445. St Saviour in Chora, Constantinople. View from the south of narthex (left) and *parekklesion* (right)

446. St Saviour in Chora, Constantinople. East end of *parekklesion* (left) and diaconicon (right)

447. St Saviour in Chora, Constantinople. Striking triple window and arched drum at east end of *parekklesion*

448. St Saviour in Chora, Constantinople. Restored central dome of the naos

Attached to the eastern space was the bema with a semi-circular apse covered by a semi-dome all of which projected out beyond the wall of the building. This is all one large open space today without any fixtures in it. The eastern ends of the north and south spaces end in small apses that were once the prothesis and diaconicon. Slightly larger spaces are on the western end. While the two end spaces on the north side are each covered by a small dome those on the south side have cross vaults. All in all the interior experience today is of flowing space from the large central domed area to the side spaces on all sides.

449. St Saviour in Chora, Constantinople. Eye-catching marble panels on interior naos wall

450. St Andrew in Krisei, Constantinople. View from the east of the polygonal shapes of the apse drum (foreground) and central naos drum (background)

451. St Andrew in Krisei, Constantinople. Ottoman enclosed portico on the north side

452. St Andrew in Krisei, Constantinople. Central naos dome with Ottoman decoration

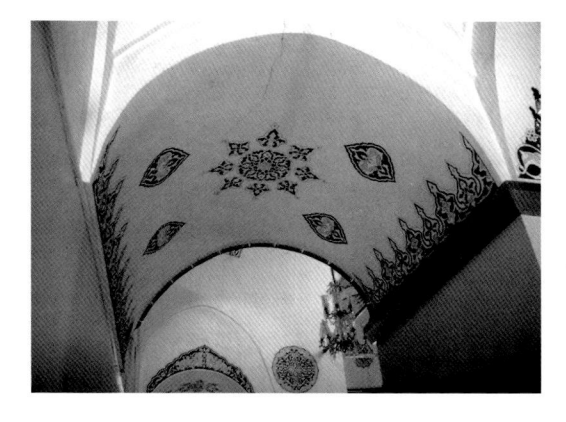

453. St Andrew in Krisei, Constantinople. Barrel vault over side space with Ottoman decoration

The dome and drum in the central space and the semi-domes over the side spaces are Ottoman replacements. Originally the dome of the central bay rested on pendentives rising from four columns with beautiful sixth-century capitals.

The inner and outer narthexes, though, still convey the previous spatial qualities of the church, particularly the outer narthex with its five bays. While the bays at each end are each covered by a small saucer dome, the central bay is covered by a same diameter dome but hemispherical in shape. Cross vaults cover the two bays separating the central bay from the two end bays. The inner narthex had a long central bay, corresponding to the three bays of the outer narthex, and covered by a barrel vault.

454. St Andrew in Krisei, Constantinople. Former bema apse

455. St Andrew in Krisei, Constantinople. Former archway into prothesis from bema apse converted into the new entrance to the building

456. St Andrew in Krisei, Constantinople. Former diaconicon

457. St Andrew in Krisei, Constantinople. Inner narthex looking south

458. St Andrew in Krisei, Constantinople. Marble Byzantine columns in outer narthex framing entrance to inner narthex

459. St Andrew in Krisei, Constantinople. Central dome in outer narthex

In the thirteenth-century rebuilding a long, wooden six-bay enclosed portico was added on the northern side, creating a new entrance for the mosque in what was formerly the prothesis. The original narthex entrance has been blocked off. In addition to this reorientation the triple arcades between the central space, the former naos, and north and south side spaces were removed but the arcade on the west is still in place.

Converted

As far as it is known the only Roman building in Constantinople converted into a church was that of **St Efimia** of Chalcedon. It is located in a converted Roman hall, a *triclinium*, in the Palace of Antiochus. The church was destroyed around 1520 but excavations, which are not open to the public, reveal the features of the church. It was a centralized type church with a hexagonal central space surrounded by five semi-circular apses and a sixth which was rectangular in shape that served as the entrance. Around the outer edge of the eastern apse there was an eight-tiered synthronon. The iconostasis consisted of six colonnettes in the front and three on the sides (counting the corner columns twice) and the spaces in between enclosed with low parapet slabs. Sockets in the floor in the apse identify the four corners of the square and the position of the columns supporting the ciborium over the Holy Table. Wall paintings depicted scenes from the life and martyrdom of St Efimia.

Athonite

As has been seen, there were once a number of monasteries in Constantinople and several points can be made about them. First, these monasteries were unusual in that they were located in or just outside the city whereas monasteries elsewhere were mostly situated in isolated and relatively inaccessible places. Second, there is no known evidence as to whether the main monastery churches were called *katholika* as in Greece. Third, there is lack of evidence whether the addition of a second narthex in some churches, thus creating inner and outer narthexes, was for liturgical reasons. These questions are not addressed even in a detailed study such as that in *The Monks and Monasteries of Constantinople, ca. 350–850* (2007) by Peter Hatlie although his time frame is restricted to a period prior to the development of the Athonite model in the tenth century.

Evidence of Athonite type churches, those with liturgically significant choir apse spaces and double narthexes, in Constantinople is suggestive rather than definitive. While there are no choir apse spaces in the city's surviving churches there is written evidence of the addition of lateral apses to two churches. First of all there is the statement by Theophanes in his *Chronographia* that Justin II (r. 565–578) 'added to the church of the Holy Theotokos of the *Blachernae* the two apses, the one to the north and the one to the south' turning the church into 'a cross-like shape'. This action of Justin's was confirmed by another writer, Giorgios Kedrenos, and in an epigram in the so-called 'Palatine Anthology'. Later Basil I (r. 867-886) carried out a similar project in adding 'light-bearing apses' to the church of the Theotokos at Chalkoprateia as recorded by George the Monk. The purpose of adding lateral apses in both cases seem to be to transform the shape of the churches into a cross but it is not clear if this was just for 'enlargement' and 'beautifying' them or for symbolic reasons. Also in doubt is whether they had any liturgical function as the two churches were not part of any monastery in which case the apse spaces would be used by monks for chanting.

The other characteristic of the Athonite type church is the double narthex. As seen in the descriptions above of the churches in Constantinople, a number of them have an inner and an outer narthex. Due to questions on the dating the construction it is difficult in most cases to assert if the double narthex was part of the original design or if the outer narthex was a later addition. Compounding the problem is the lack of information as to whether the inner narthex was a *liti* with a liturgical function as in a true Athonite type church. When the churches were converted to mosques the double narthex turned out to have a benefit. This was the use of the narthexes as an ablution facility for Muslim men to wash their feet in ritual purification and for the temporary storage of their shoes or sandals on racks or in lockers as they have to enter the carpeted prayer hall unshod. For this reason where churches only had a single narthex often a second was added in the conversion to a mosque.

Existing Greek Orthodox Churches
There are three churches in Istanbul which were never converted into mosques and remain in use as Greek Orthodox churches. Empress Pulcheria, granddaughter of Theodosius I (r. 379–395) built the first church, the **Blachernitissa** ('Our Lady of Blachernae' / *Panagia ton Blachernon*) in the fifth-century shrine around a sacred well, a *hagiasma*. She led a very chaste life founding two other churches in Constantinople: the Theotokos Hodegitria which has now disappeared and the Theotokos at Chalkoprateia which is a ruin. The original two-aisled basilican type church of Blachernitissa was destroyed by fire in 1434 and thereafter rebuilt many times. The present structure dates from the nineteenth century and has a naos that is a simple, non-descript rectangular hall entered from the north through a narthex that runs the length of the naos. On the right-hand side of the iconostasis the sacred spring is visible as a luminous cave. According to tradition, in 626 the sacred robe and mantle of Panagia, then housed in the church the Blachernitissa, saved the city of Constantinople from an attack by the Avars. A seventh-century icon known as the Blachernitissa is the visible symbol of the Theotokos as a protectress of the city. The icon is made of wax and is unusual in that it is not flat but formed in bas relief. As the original icon is in a gallery in Moscow there is a copy of the icon in front of the iconostasis on the right side. Every year to commemorate the event a thanksgiving service, the

haunting Akathistos liturgy, is held at the church led by the Ecumenical Patriarch. In memory of the seventh-century miraculous event that took place on a Friday the church has dispensation to hold the weekly liturgy service, most unusually, on Fridays instead of Sundays as elsewhere in the Christian world. During the Iconoclastic period, the final session of the Council of Hieria which condemned the cult of the images took place in the church. As a consequence of that decision, Emperor Constantine V ordered the mosaics of the interior to be destroyed, and replaced them with others representing natural scenes with trees, birds and animals.

The second Greek Orthodox church is the small Byzantine church of **Panagia Mouchliotissa**, which is of historic interest rather than of any architectural value. It is named Mouchliotissa because it was founded or rebuilt about 1282 by Maria Palaelogina who had married the great khan of the Mongols ('Mouchlos' in Greek). She lived for about 15 years at the court in Persia and returned to Constantinople after the death of her husband. Along with the church she also founded a convent where she spent the last years of her life as a nun. Later reconstructions and the addition of secondary buildings unfortunately have obscured what would have been a unique church type in the city, a domed, tetraconch structure: a square centre with semi-circular spaces or large niches on all four sides, just like petals on a flower. The square centre is covered with a scalloped dome and the discernable semi-circular niches by semi-domes. As the eastern niche is the bema it is separated from the naos by an elaborately carved wooded iconostasis. The entire complex is enclosed in a courtyard with a high wall with the circular drum supporting the dome peaking above it.

St George in the Phanar serves as the home of the Ecumenical Patriarchate since the end of the fifteenth century. When the original church was destroyed by fire in 1720 the current neoclassical style building was built from the foundations up. This occurred in 1726 after which there were several restorations especially after severe damage by fire in 1797. Little is known of the original church except that it was

460. St Andrew in Krisei, Constantinople. Cross in centre of column capital partially obliterated

461. Panagia Mouchliotissa. View from the east of the cylindrical drum

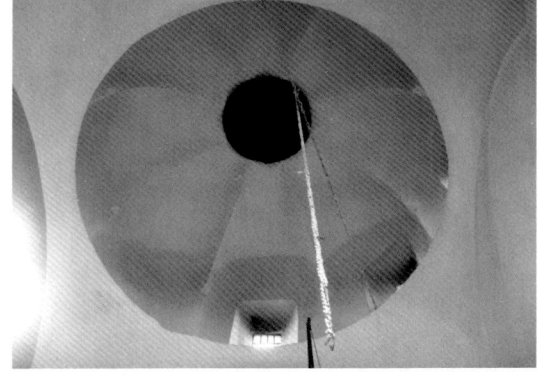

462. Panagia Mouchliotissa. The courtyard

463. Panagia Mouchliotissa. Segmented central dome of naos

formerly a convent church and that it was rebuilt many times. It would be expected that the principal church of the Greek Orthodox Church would follow the trend of Hagia Sophia and other churches and have a dome with a cross-in-square or other form but instead it has a basilica plan. The reason for this is that after the Fall of Constantinople it was forbidden for Christian buildings to have domes. The interior follows the traditional basilica type with three apses on the east side, side aisles and a narthex. At the front of the naos on either side of the iconostasis there is a long row of stalls reserved for hierarchs, visiting clergy and dignitaries. The non-Byzantine front façade dates from 1835–1840 as part of a restoration to raise the height of the roof of the church.

Bethlehem and Jerusalem

The first Christian structures in the Holy Land were built on the orders of Constantine at the behest of his mother Augusta Helena, a pilgrim in 326–327 at the grand age of 80. The structures were the Church of the Nativity in Bethlehem and the Church on Golgotha in Jerusalem. These two structures are exceptional first, because they were directly connected to the birth, crucifixion, and burial of Jesus Christ and, secondly, they each had two types of buildings joined together – a congregational basilica and a centralized martyrium. Two smaller Constantinian churches are only known from excavations. These are the basilica at the Oak and Spring of Mamre near Hebron, south of Bethlehem, and the Eleona basilica on the Mount of Olives in Jerusalem where Jesus was believed to have instructed his disciples about the end of the world and his second coming (Matthew 24).

At Bethlehem the **Church of the Nativity** was built at a grotto believed to be the birthplace of Jesus of Nazareth. Construction was under the supervision of Bishop Makarios of Jerusalem and completed in 333. The present building is a sixth-century replacement by Emperor Justinian after the first church was burnt down in the Samaritan Revolt of 529. Only the huge foundation blocks of stone and the colourful mosaic floor were preserved from the original structure. From descriptions by ancient travelers a plan of the original complex can be reconstructed. On the western end there was an enormous public space that could have served as a resting place for pilgrims and trades people serving their needs. Next was a colonnaded forecourt from which three doors led into the basilica. Inside, the naos was flanked on either side by two, colonnaded aisles with reused columns – most certainly the shafts as the Corinthian capitals are copies. Clerestory windows provided light to the nave. At the centre of the eastern end of the nave instead of the typical semi-circular apse there was a large octagonal space flanked on either side by smaller chambers. The central space, which was raised up seven steps from the naos, and the chambers, were separated from the naos by arches. In the centre of the octagonal space three steps led up to a railing which protected a circular opening that pierced the rock ceiling of the grotto, the cave where according to tradition Jesus was born. Natural light may have been from an opening in the centre of the roof over the octagon. The position of the Holy Table is unknown but possibly it was a movable wooden altar placed at the foot of the steps leading to the octagon. The relatively small basilica space probably was adequate in size for the small congregation of Christians in Bethlehem in the fourth century. Today visitors can descend to the grotto by winding stairways on either side of the octagon.

At about the same time the Church of the Nativity was under construction in Bethlehem the Bishop of Jerusalem also had an imperial order from Constantine to build in Jerusalem 'a basilica more beautiful than any on earth' at Golgotha, the place where Jesus had been crucified and buried, henceforth the **Church of Golgotha**. The pagan temple of Aphrodite, erected by Emperor Hadrian (r. AD117–138) on the site had to be demolished and excavation of the cave identified as the tomb of Christ overseen by Constantine's mother, Helena. Under the supervision of the architect Zenobius and the presbyter Efstathios construction of the Christian building was began in 328 with the consecration taking place in 336. As in Bethlehem, little remains today of Constantine's original building complex but the description by Eusebius is reasonably clear. On the rocky cliff of Golgotha Christ's sepulcher was isolated and the builders cut it into a conical shape and created over it a small protective structure (an *aedicule*) of 12 columns supporting a canopy or baldachino. In front of the entrance to the sepulcher that faced the rising sun the ground was levelled to create a large paved courtyard and space for the basilica. A porticoed courtyard was created to enclose the cone-shaped sepulcher at the western end where the semi-circular colonnade seemed to embrace the sepulcher building. The courtyard also enclosed the Rock of Calvary upon which the crucifixion cross of Christ was believed to have once stood. The Rock was located in the southeast corner of the courtyard and was shaped into a cube. The entire eastern end of the courtyard was closed off by the basilica building. The Jerusalem church was similar to the church at Bethlehem with four aisles and a colonnaded forecourt. Instead of a traditional semi-circular apse at the eastern end of the basilica the Jerusalem church had a centralized domed structure, known as the Martyrium that extended into the sepulcher courtyard. Internally the domed structure was, to quote Eusebius, 'encircled as a wreath by 12 columns, like the number of the apostles'. There were apparently galleries over the aisles but no clerestory windows.

The entire complex was a succession of architectural structures beginning at the eastern end with the forecourt, followed by the rectangular basilica, the centralized domed structure or Martyrium, and in the courtyard or *triportico* the cubical Rock and conical Sepulcher or rotunda all serving to commemorate the crucifixion, burial, and resurrection of Jesus Christ. The rotunda is known as the Church of the Resurrection or the *Anastasis*. The Jerusalem building complex was damaged in 614, demolished in 1009, and the current rotunda reconstructed later in the eleventh century and rebuilt many times over the centuries. The courtyard has been filled with small chapels and all that remains of the basilica itself is the Chapel of St Helena constructed by the Crusaders. However, the church built by Constantine features prominently in the famous sixth-century floor mosaic known as Madaba Map in the church of St George in Jordan. Design of the Map was based on earlier, mainly Christian sources and clearly shows a stairway ascending from an ordinary street of shops to three entrances of a colonnaded forecourt. From there three entrances lead into the double-aisled naos. The golden dome of the rotunda is prominent in the Madaba Map which also depicts a number of significant structures in Jerusalem identified by Greek letters. These include the basilica type New Church of the Theotokos built by Justinian in 543 after its namesake in Constantinople.

The access to the Golgotha church of Constantine from the street is mentioned by Egeria in her pilgrimage diary when she travelled from somewhere in Gaul to the Holy Land between 381 and 384. She wrote that when the bishop, in procession, enters, he does so through 'the great doors which are on the market street side'. Eusebius confirms that the great doors were in the form of a *propylaeum,* similar to the important gateways entrances in front of ancient Greek sacred precincts. From Egeria's references a plan of the Golgotha complex can be reconstructed. She wrote that where the main portals opened up from the middle of the market street there was the major church of the city. She variously calls the complex either the church built by Constantine, the church on Golgotha, or the Martyrium. Egeria does not mention the forecourt between the market street entrance and the church building. Behind the church building she refers to the inner open-air courtyard (called the *Ante Crucem*) in which stood the rock of Calvary and a chapel (the *Post Crucem*) where special services were held. At the other end of the courtyard she mentions many times the *Anastasis* (Sanctuary of the Resurrection) where the divine office was celebrated daily. Apparently, then the liturgy was celebrated twice at the Basilica of the Holy Sepulcher on Sundays, once in the Martyrium and once in the *Anastasis*.

464. Golgotha – Holy Sepulcher Jerusalem. Restoration as of *c.*348 showing the Anastasis Rotunda (right) without the basilica

Egeria mentions other important churches in Jerusalem. These were the Church of Sion within the walls and the churches of Imbomon and the Eleona on the Mount of Olives. Very little remains of these churches. The oldest surviving building is the fifth-century crypt of St John Prodromos now below street level. It has three apses and on the western side a long narthex. The dome over the centre is supported by four piers. All that remains of the monumental *Nea Ekklesia tis Theotokos* ('New Church of the Mother of God') built by Emperor Justinian in 543 are the apse and foundation walls. The church was so huge an artificial platform had to be constructed on its hilltop to support it. The size and grandeur of the church extended to the guesthouse (*xenodóchion*) which could, it was said, accommodate 3,000 visitors. After Egeria's visit to Jerusalem the church of St Stephen the Protomartyr, whose relics were claimed to have been found in 415, was built by the Empress Eudocia along with an adjoining monastery just outside the city walls. The complex was begun in 438 and completed in 460. The church and monastery became the largest in Jerusalem until the *Nea Ekklesia* was built in the sixth century but were destroyed by the crusaders in the twelfth century. Many of the churches had already been destroyed by the invading Persians in 614.

CONSTANTINIAN CHURCHES
HOLY LAND
Reconstructions

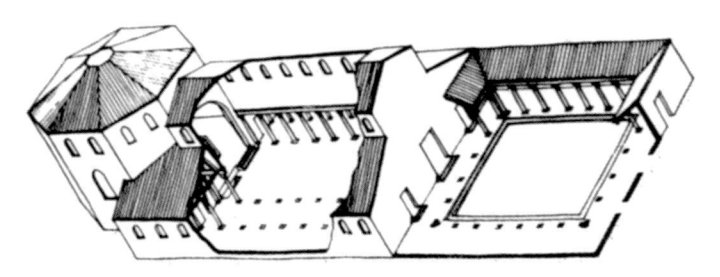

CHURCH OF THE NATIVITY, BETHLEHEM
View from the north
(After Fletcher p275)

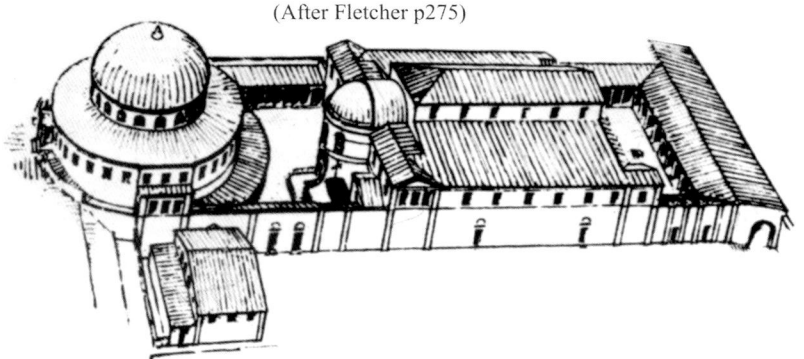

CHURCH OF GOLGOTHA, JERUSALEM
View from the south
(After McDonald Fig 9)

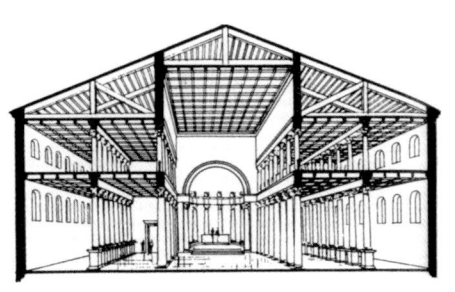

CHURCH OF GOLGOTHA, JERUSALEM
Cross section through basilica
(Krautheimer Fig 17)

465. Holy Land. Constantinian churches I

CONSTANTINIAN CHURCHES
HOLY LAND
Reconstructed Plans

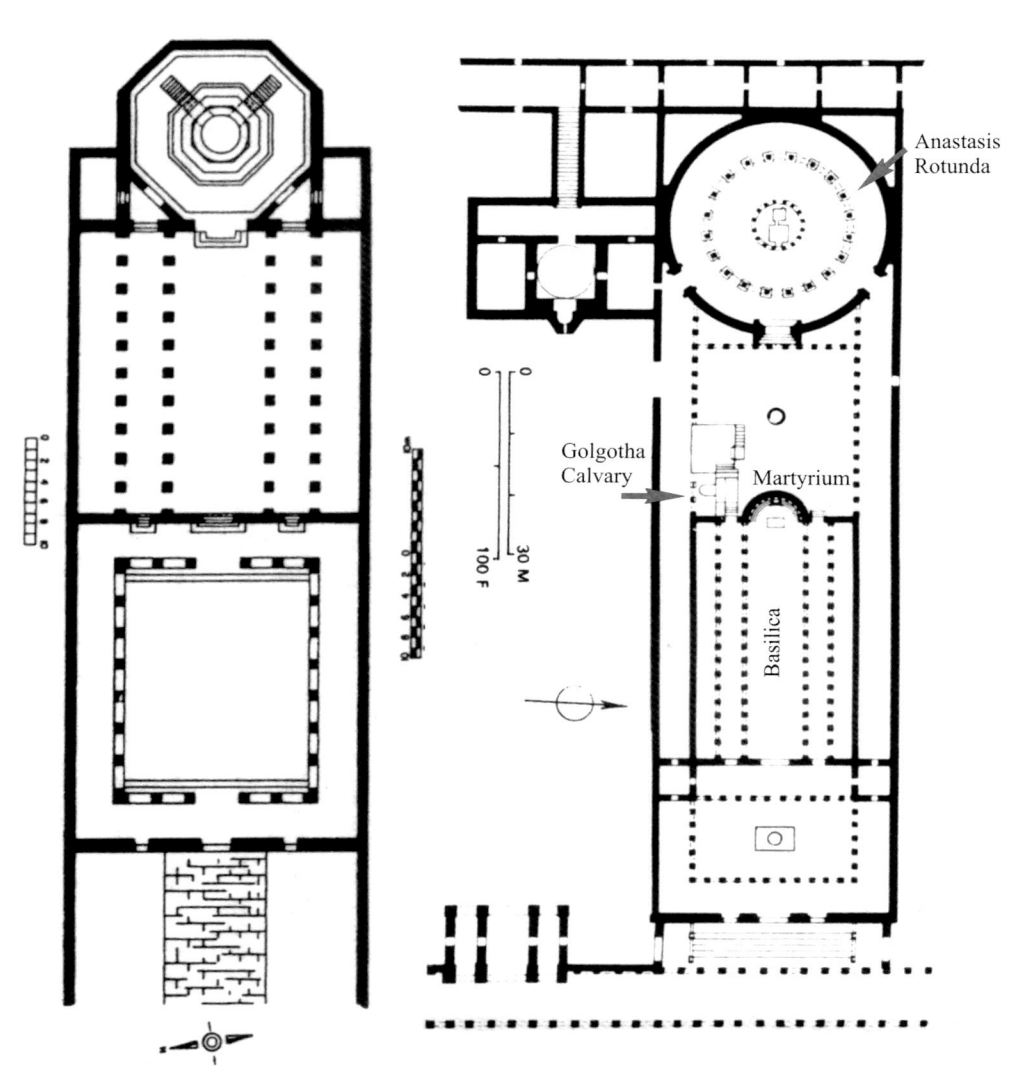

Anastasis Rotunda

Golgotha Calvary

Martyrium

Basilica

CHURCH OF THE NATIVITY
BETHLEHEM
(Armstrong, Fig 21)

CHURCH OF GOLGOTHA
JERUSALEM
(After Grabar, 168 Fig 170)

466. Holy Land, Constantinian churches II

SPLENDID CHURCHES

467. 'New Church' Tokalikilise, Cappadocia. Naos wall paintings from the ninth century depicting scenes from the life of Christ

468. Sivri cross-in-square church, Cappadocia. Remains of clear cross-in-square form

469. Basilica, Der Turmanin, Syria. Restored exterior with impressive entrance

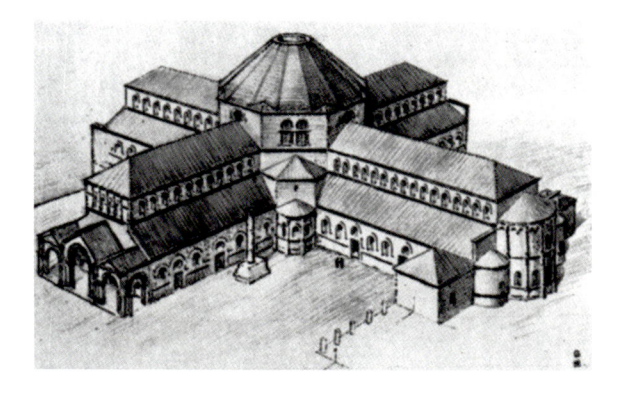

470. St Simeon Church, Aleppo, Syria. Restored exterior of cruciform shaped building with a narthex portico (left)

Outside of the these churches in Bethlehem and Jerusalem the other churches in Palestine, Jordan, Syria, Turkey and North Africa from the Byzantine era are nearly all in ruins. From the documented archaeological remains of about 90 structures it can be ascertained that the vast majority are of the basilica type, mainly aisled. Of the remainder about equal numbers are of the cross-in-square, cruciform and domed basilica forms and just a handful are centralized and converted temple types. The reconstructed plans of the churches from these regions are well recorded in the works of Krautheimer, Davies, Buchwald and Peeters. In Krautheimer's book *Early Christian and Byzantine Architecture*, pure forms of each of five of the six church types can be seen. These are the 'White Monastery' Basilica at Deir-el-Abiad (*c*.440), the cross-in-square Church of the Prophets, Apostles, and Martyrs at Gerasa (465), the cruciformed St Babylas in Antioch (378), the centralized octagon Church of the Theotokos at Mount Garizim (484), and the domed basilica of St John at Ephesus (second church *c*.565). A good example of the converted church type of the fifth century is former temple of Aphrodite at Aphrodisias (Buchwald).

In Lalibela in central Ethiopia there are 11 extraordinary Orthodox churches, most probably constructed in the thirteenth century. They are astonishing for being hewn out of rock, cut in one piece, to form subterranean churches in the shape of a Greek cross. The most refined is that of Beta Ghiorghis (House of St George) which sits in a small courtyard on a stepped platform. The Lalibelan churches are different to the cave churches in Cappadocia, Turkey in that they were made by chiseling down into a single block of volcanic rock with tunnels for entrances as there were no staircases leading down into the churches. The interiors of the churches were made by cutting inward from the main western door and hollowing out from the inside. At the upper level of each arm of the cross there are three, small key-shape windows making a total of 12 which provide light into the interior. As described by Judith Dupré, the impression in the dark depths of the church is one of divine illumination.

471. Alaban, Cilicia. Regular arches (right) and Syrian type horseshoe arches (left)

Thessaloniki

During the Byzantine Empire the city of Thessaloniki was known as the 'co-capital' (*symprotévousa*) alongside Constantinople. It was also an important episcopal centre and, according to tradition, was created by St Paul. After the conquest of Bulgaria to the north by Basil II (r. 976–1025) the city of Thessaloniki became a major economic and cultural centre and developed a cosmopolitan atmosphere. As can be expected, there are numerous notable churches and monuments of the Byzantine era in Thessaloniki; in fact, the city is a treasure house of Byzantine churches. Not only are all seven church type plans present, but all of the churches described here are active except one. Another reason to visit the city is that it has been called a great Byzantine museum as it contains monuments from all Byzantine periods. The churches have all been restored to Christian worship after they were converted to mosques during the Ottoman Turk occupation of Thessaloniki from 1430 until 1912.

Basilicas

There are four churches in Thessaloniki with basilica plans. Those of St Demetrios and the Theotokos Archeiropoietos deserve a detailed description. **St Demetrios** is a splendid example of a doubled-aisled basilica, with magnificent mosaics. The first church was built sometime in the ten years after the martyrdom in 303 of the young Demetrios in Thessaloniki during the persecution of Christians by Diocletian and Galerius. Later, around 412 or 413, a larger church was built on the site by Leontius, a ruler of the Roman province of Illyricum. This church was rebuilt after a fire in the seventh century and again after a destructive fire in 1917, and then only finished in 1948. The plan seems to have remained the same through both reconstructions. Four arcades at the lower level divide the space into a central naos and four aisles which terminate in transepts.

BYZANTINE CHURCHES
NEAR EAST
BASILICAS

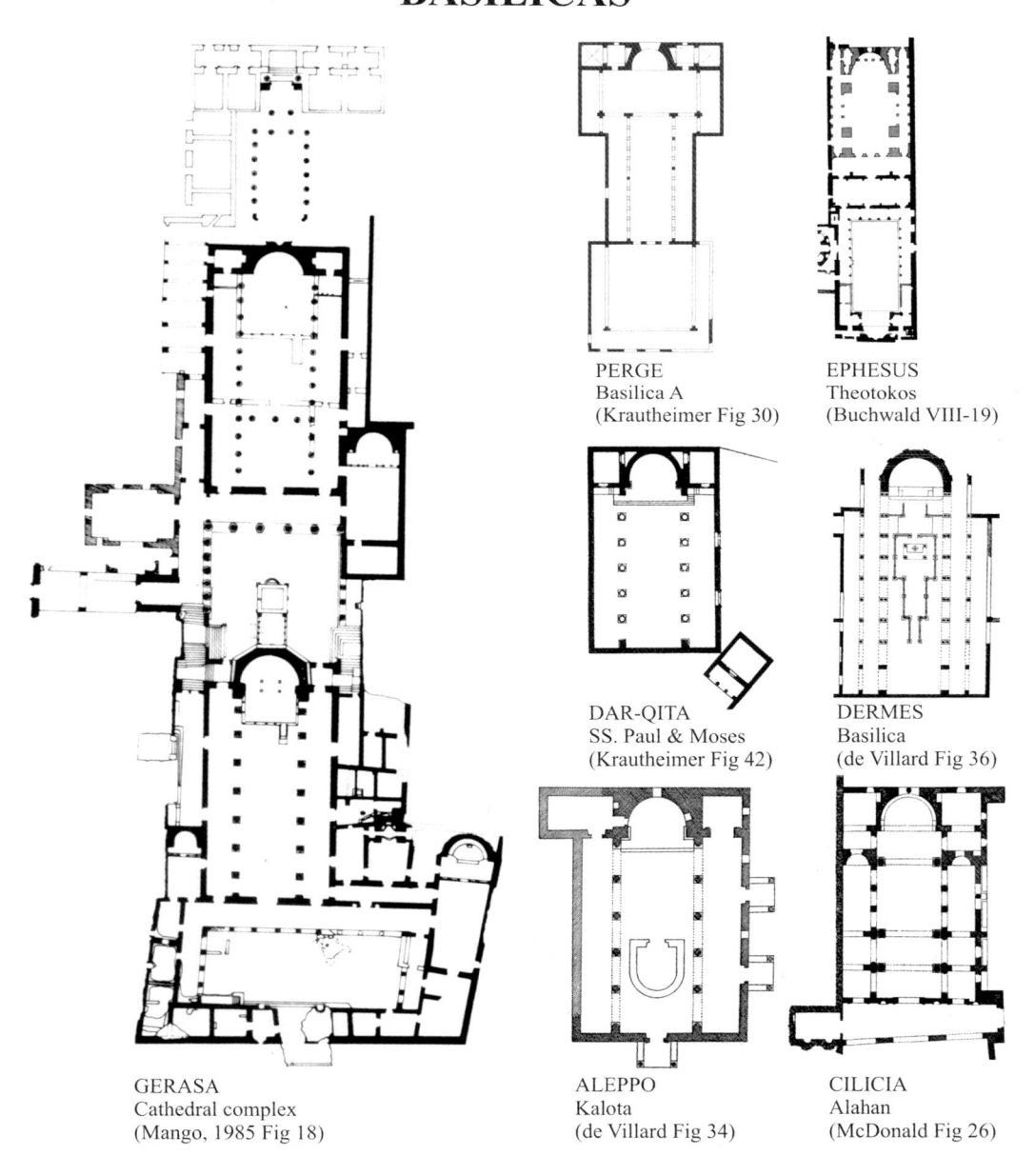

PERGE
Basilica A
(Krautheimer Fig 30)

EPHESUS
Theotokos
(Buchwald VIII-19)

DAR-QITA
SS. Paul & Moses
(Krautheimer Fig 42)

DERMES
Basilica
(de Villard Fig 36)

GERASA
Cathedral complex
(Mango, 1985 Fig 18)

ALEPPO
Kalota
(de Villard Fig 34)

CILICIA
Alahan
(McDonald Fig 26)

472. Near East, plan type – basilicas

BYZANTINE CHURCHES
NEAR EAST
CROSS-IN-SQUARE

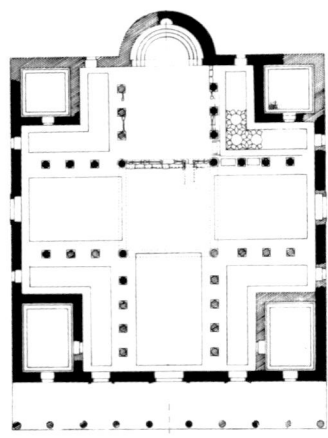

GERASA
Prophets, Apostles & Martyrs
(Mango, 1985 Fig 22)

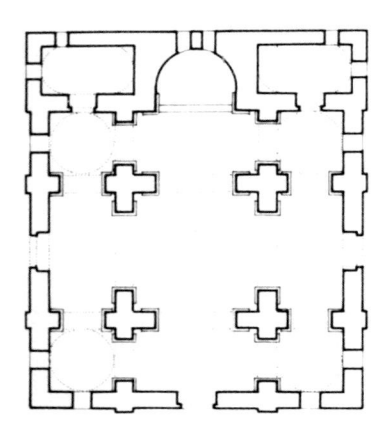

SERGIOPOLIS
S. Sergius
(Mango, 1985 Fig 75)

CROSS-IN-SQUARE / COMPRESSED

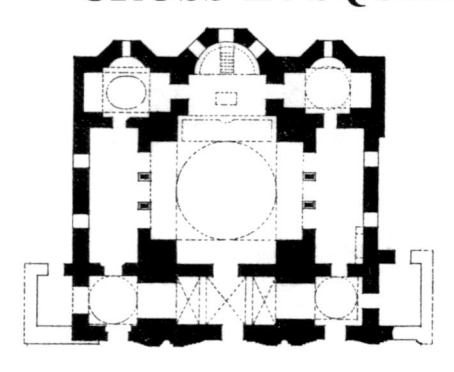

NICAEA
Koimesis tis Theotokou
(Van Millingen Fig 5)

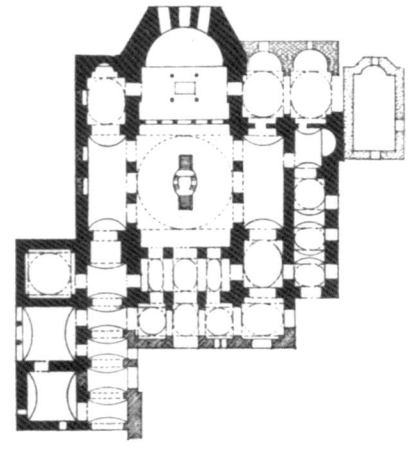

MYRA
S. Nicholas
(Van Millingen Fig 4)

473. Near East, plan type – cross-in-square

BYZANTINE CHURCHES
NEAR EAST
CENTRALIZED

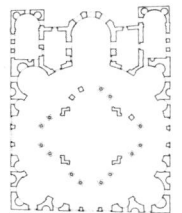

BOSRA
Church
(Mango, 1985 Fig 68)

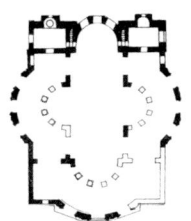

SERGIOPOLIS
Church
(Krautheimer Fig 74)

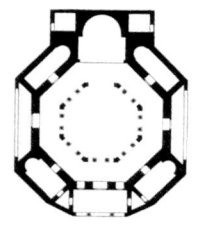

MOUNT GERIZIM
Theotokos
(Krautheimer Fig 47)

CRUCIFORM

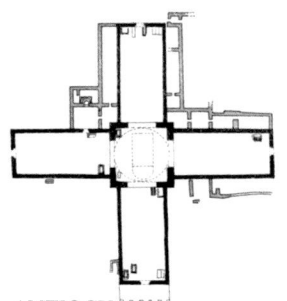

ANTIOCH
Babylas martyrium
(Krautheimer Fig 19)

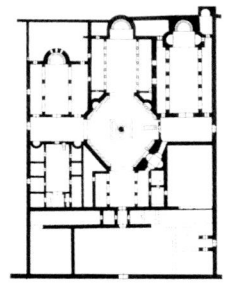

ALEPPO
Simon Stylitis martyrium
(Mango, 1985 Fig 16)

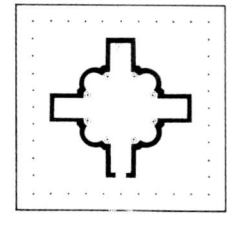

NYSSA
Martyrium
(Mango, 1985 Fig 15)

DOMED BASILICA

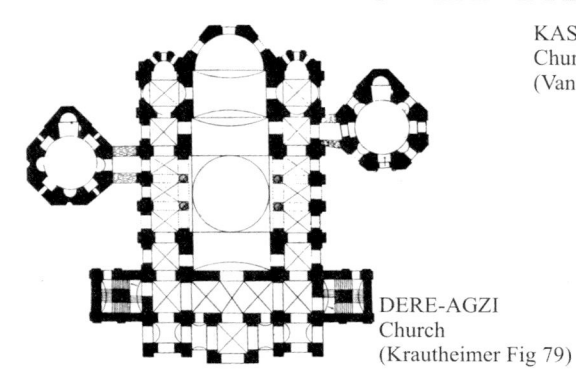

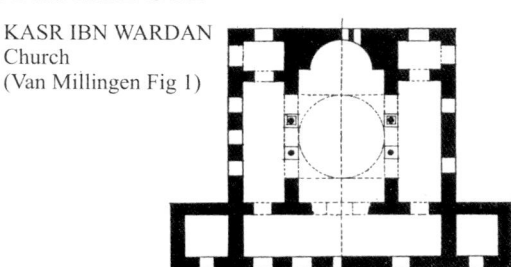

KASR IBN WARDAN
Church
(Van Millingen Fig 1)

DERE-AGZI
Church
(Krautheimer Fig 79)

474. Near East, plan types – centralized; cruciform; domed basilica

BYZANTINE CHURCHES
NORTH AFRICA

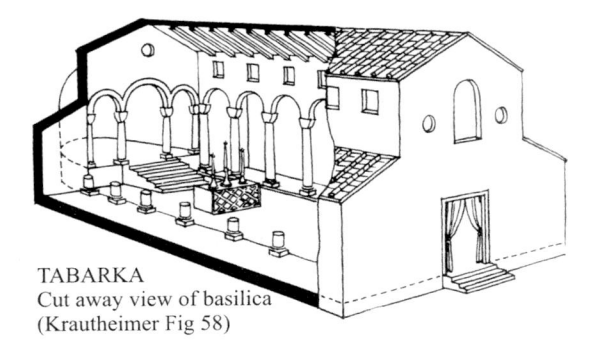

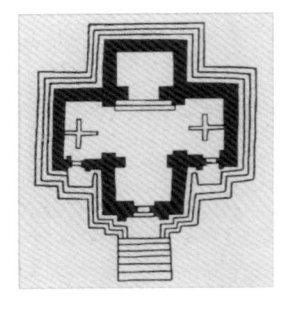

TABARKA
Cut away view of basilica
(Krautheimer Fig 58)

ETHIOPIA
Beta Ghiorghis
(Dupre Fig 40)

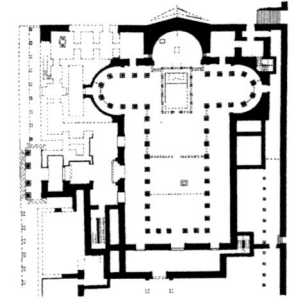

HERMOPOLIS
Cathedral transept basilica
(Krautheimer Fig 32)

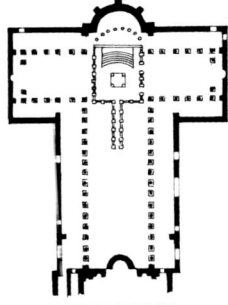

MENAPOLIS
Abu Mina Basilica
(Peeters Fig 10)

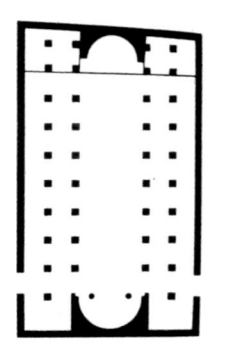

CASTELLUM TINGITATUM
S. Reparatus
(Grabar 1968 Fig 94)

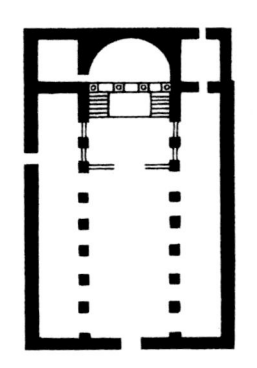

BENIAN
Basilica
(Peeters Fig 44)

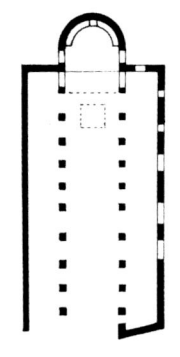

HIPPO REGIUS
Basilica Pacis
(Peeters Fig 43)

475. North Africa, Byzantine church plans

BYZANTINE CHURCHES IN THESSALONIKI
BASILICA TYPE

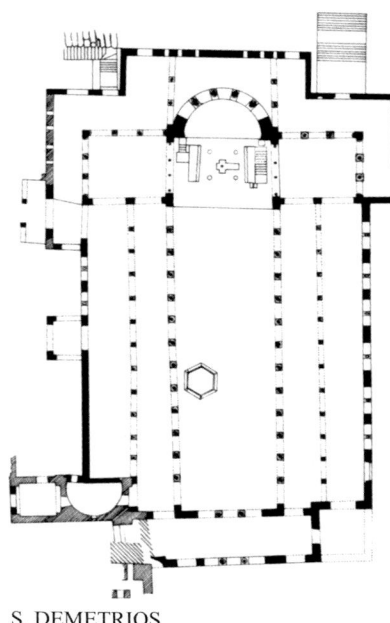

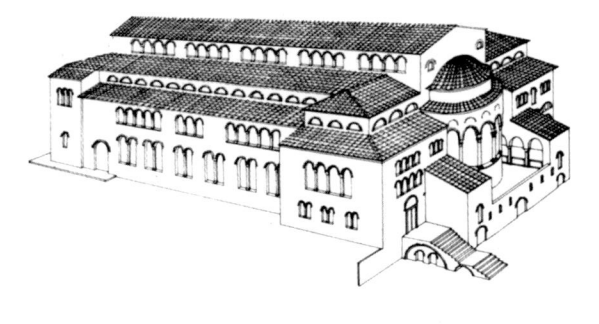

S. DEMETRIOS
Restored ground plan
(Mango, 1985 Fig 55)

S. DEMETRIOS
View of the apse from the southeast
(Mango, 1985 Fig 56)

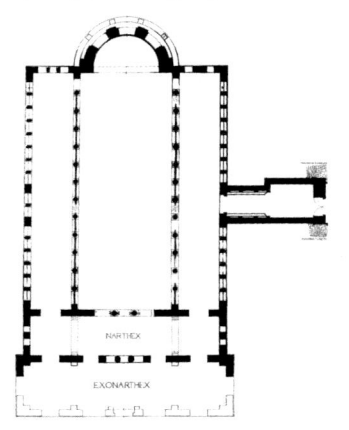

THEOTOKOS ARCHEIROPOIETOS
(Gerstel Fig 19 p63)

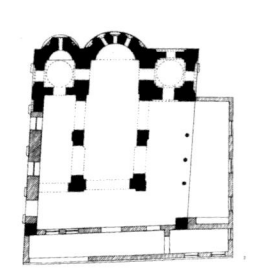

TAXIARCHES
(Molho Fig 246)

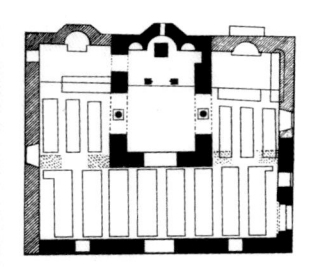

S. NICHOLAS ORPHANOS
(Mohlo Fig 257)

476. Thessaloniki, plan type – basilicas

477. St Demetrios, Thessaloniki. Naos with arcaded side aisles and galleries looking east at bema apse

478. St Demetrios, Thessaloniki. Arcaded side aisle

479. St Demetrios, Thessaloniki. Arcaded gallery

480. St Demetrios, Thessaloniki. early Christian structure containing a font for holy water in the lower crypt level

Two smaller arcades at the upper level separate the galleries from the naos space. The sumptuous columns of the arcades are reused from earlier Classical structures and include various materials and colours, such as white marble from Marmara, red-purple granite from Egypt, and green marble from Thessaly. The various capitals of the columns are particularly noteworthy, especially the Theodosian ones from the late fourth century with their variety of ornaments and forms.

Architectural features include a narthex, a single apse with a mosaic decorated half-dome, and colonnaded galleries that run above the narthex and aisles. The entire church is filled with light from the numerous windows above the galleries and in the aisle walls. There is a large crypt below the bema and transepts that contains a small chapel some believe to be the first church, a number of basins, a font of holy water, and a number of graves.

A remarkable feature of the **Theotokos Archeiropoietos** is the Roman mosaic floor found under the northern aisle. The name of the church is probably because it houses an icon of the Theotokos *Archeiropoíetos* ('Not-Made-By-Human-Hands'). The colourful and geometrically patterned mosaic was from a Roman public bath, only part of which was built over by the basilica building. According to a mosaic inscription dated after 447/8 in the church, the donor was a Father Andreas that makes the building one of the oldest early Christian churches anywhere still in use. The basilica is very spacious with beautiful arcades of Corinthian columns at the lower level separating the naos from the two, flanking aisles, a narthex, and single apse, lit by three large semi-circular windows, rows of sizable clerestory with aisle arched windows that create a brightly lit interior, and an open truss wooden roof. The galleries above the side aisles are separated from the naos space by elegant arcades. Reconstructed plans by scholars show that at one time there was an outer narthex and a forecourt.

The two other basilicas in Thessaloniki that are from the fourteenth century are the small churches of Taxiarches (*Archangels*) and St Nicholas Orphanos with its magnificent and vivid wall paintings, almost untouched through the centuries.

481. St Demetrios, Thessaloniki. Remains of a classical column capital in crypt

482. Theotokos Acheiropoietos, Thessaloniki. Western view of entrance

483. Theotokos Acheiropoietos, Thessaloniki. Eastern end of side aisle with apse just visible (right)

484. Theotokos Acheiropoietos, Thessaloniki. Typical triple arched windows

485. Theotokos Acheiropoietos, Thessaloniki. Naos looking east at the iconostasis and semi-circular bema apse

486. Theotokos Acheiropoietos, Thessaloniki. Interior before the restoration showing Ottoman decoration

487. Theotokos Acheiropoietos, Thessaloniki. Arcade separating naos from side aisle with marble Corinthian columns and 'imposts' decorated with a cross

488. Theotokos Acheiropoietos, Thessaloniki. Harmonious arcades

489. Theotokos Acheiropoietos, Thessaloniki. Gallery arcade

490. Theotokos Acheiropoietos, Thessaloniki. Elaborate wood carved iconostasis (left side chapel)

491. Theotokos Acheiropoietos, Thessaloniki. Roman mosaic below the church floor

492. Taxiarchis, Thessaloniki. New entrance addition (right) and original church (left)

493. Taxiarchis, Thessaloniki. Intricate stonework on bema apse

494. Taxiarchis, Thessaloniki. Fine brick pattern

495. St Nicholas Orphanos, Thessaloniki. View from the east of small naos and projecting bema apse

Cross-In-Square
The cross-in-square type church became popular in Thessaloniki after the first one, **Panagia Chalkeon** ('Virgin Mary of the Coppersmiths'), was built in 1028. The date is precise as it is incised on the marble lintel of the main entrance to the church as 6537, a Byzantine date, converted to 1028 in the modern calendar. Also inscribed on the lintel is the name of the founder, Christophoros, a royal dignitary, along with his wife Maria and three children. Internally the space of the church is a perfect Greek cross with a large dome on a drum over the centre supported by columns with barrel vaults over each of the four arms. The centre apse is semi-circular on the inside, polygonal (three-sided) on the outside, lit by three narrow windows. The side apses, the prothesis and diaconicon, are relatively small and semi-circular both inside and outside. The narthex has three bays, each with a door to the outside and corresponding ones into the naos, with the centre bay and doors being wider than the ones on either side. There is a gallery but it extends only over the narthex. Small domes surmount the side bays of the narthex and galleries above. Although the extensive wall paintings are not in very good condition, the Ascension of Christ surrounded by 16 prophets, in the main dome, is clear. The exterior of the church is dominated by the octagonal drum of the main dome and the whole edifice is richly decorated with ornamental brickwork.

The church of the **Holy Apostles** has one of the most richly and attractively brick-decorated exteriors anywhere. In plan it is similar to the Panagia Chalkeon except for the wide aisle running around the three sides, that is all sides except the bema side where there is the traditional three apses. The appearance of the monograms of the founder, Patriarch Nefon, indicates that the church was built in the years 1312–1315. The monastery to which it once belonged has long disappeared. The interior of the church is splendidly decorated with mosaics and wall paintings that represent the culmination of Byzantine artistry. Although all the gold background from the mosaic scenes was removed during the Ottoman period the depiction of the Transfiguration of Christ is still dramatic. He is shown standing on a rock with his right hand extended in blessing against the backdrop of an elliptical disk radiating beams of light. On the right side of Christ is the Prophet Elijah and on the left side is Moses holding the Commandments.

SPLENDID CHURCHES

BYZANTINE CHURCHES IN THESSALONIKI
CROSS-IN-SQUARE TYPE

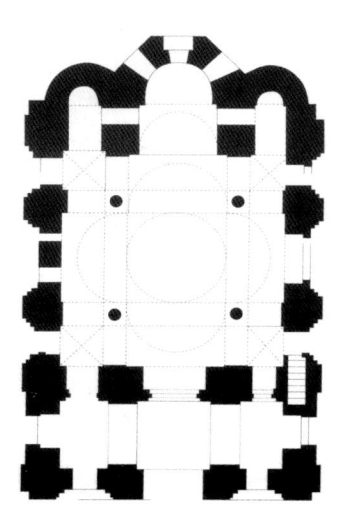

PANAGIA CHALKEON
(Mohlo Fig 189)

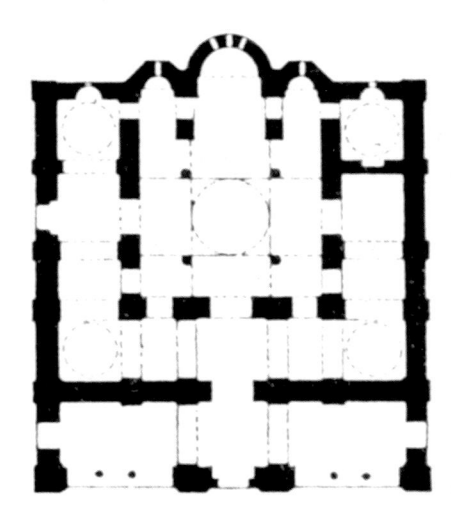

HOLY APOSTLES
(Stewart p104)

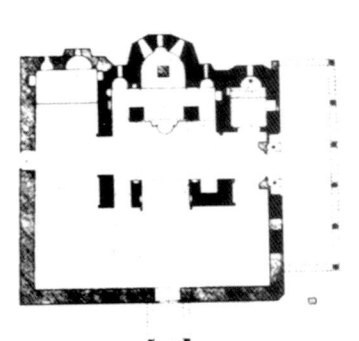

METAMORPHOSIS OF THE SAVIOR
VLATADES
(Mohlo Fig 276)

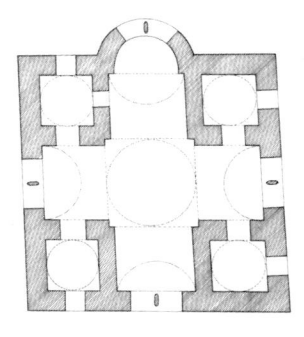

CHRIST SAVIOR LATOMOU
(OSIOS DAVID)
Reconstructed plan
(Tsigarides Fig 1)

496. Thessaloniki, plan type – cross-in-square

497. Panagia Chalkeon, Thessaloniki. South side with projecting apse (right), polygonal drum of central naos dome (centre) and narthex domes (left)

498. Panagia Chalkeon, Thessaloniki. West entrance end with the two narthex domes above

499. Panagia Chalkeon, Thessaloniki. Brick pattern in window arch

500. Panagia Chalkeon, Thessaloniki. Drum and dome with faint surface decoration

501. Panagia Chalkeon, Thessaloniki. The Beautiful Gate with small rendition of the Annunciation on the carved wooden doors, embroidered curtain behind and *despotikaí* icons on either side

502. Holy Apostles, Thessaloniki. View from the northwest showing central entrance doorway (right) drums of the narthex domes above and the tall drum of the central naos dome (background)

503. Holy Apostles, Thessaloniki. View from the east with projecting bema apse (centre)

504. Holy Apostles, Thessaloniki. View of south side with polygonal shaped drums of diaconicon dome (right) and inner narthex dome (left)

505. Holy Apostles, Thessaloniki. View from the southwest corner with polygonal shaped drums of the various domes

506. Holy Apostles, Thessaloniki. Superb brickwork patterns of a typical drum

507. Holy Apostles, Thessaloniki. Superlative brickwork at the top of the of the semi-circular bema apse and top of the drum of the central naos dome

508. Holy Apostles, Thessaloniki. Detail of the brick pattern at the top of the semi-circular bema apse

509. Holy Apostles, Thessaloniki. Detail of intricate brick pattern in the bema apse

510. Holy Apostles, Thessaloniki. Narthex looking north with arched entrance doorway (left) and archway to inner narthex (right)

511. Holy Apostles, Thessaloniki. North *parekklesion* with overflow seating for naos (open archway centre right)

512. Holy Apostles, Thessaloniki. South *parekklesion* with overflow seating for naos (open archway centre left)

SPLENDID CHURCHES

513. Holy Apostles, Thessaloniki. Central dome of naos with a faint Christ Pantokrator at the centre

514. Holy Apostles, Thessaloniki. Roped off solea extends from the Beautiful Gate of the bema to the inner narthex

515. Holy Apostles, Thessaloniki. Classical type column capital

516. Holy Apostles, Thessaloniki. Geometrical marble floor pattern

The other fourteenth-century cross-in-square church is the small *katholikon* of the monastery of **Vlatades** dedicated to the Transfiguration of the Saviour. The monastery and church were built by the Vlatades brothers who arrived from Crete and became monks in Thessaloniki. As it has been much altered the true shape of the church is only apparent from old drawings which show a single dome on a polygonal drum over the centre of the cross with barrel vaults over the arms. Similarly, the shape of the *katholikon* of the former monastery of **Latomou** cannot be fully seen today as the west side of the church has been destroyed leaving three arms of the cross and two corner spaces of the square. The cross-in-square form was apparently from the fifteenth-century rebuilding of a fifth- or sixth-century church, most probably a square, dedicated to Christ the Saviour which in turn was constructed over an older Roman building. During the 1920s the church was renamed Osios David.

BYZANTINE CHURCHES IN THESSALONIKI
CRUCIFORM / ATHONITE TYPE

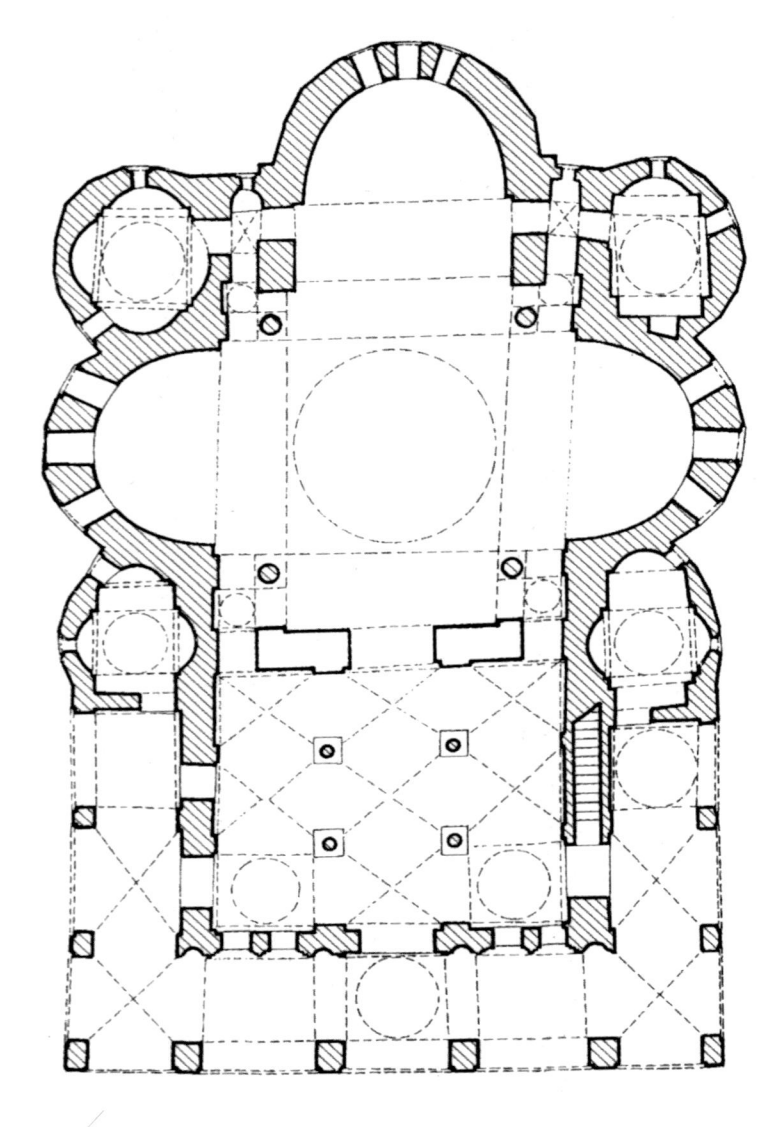

PROPHET ELIJAH
(Bouras Fig 17)

517. Thessaloniki, plan type – cruciform / athonite

518. Prophet Elijah, Thessaloniki. View from the northeast corner showing three sides of the prothesis drum and dome (centre front) and tall arched drum of the central naos dome (centre back)

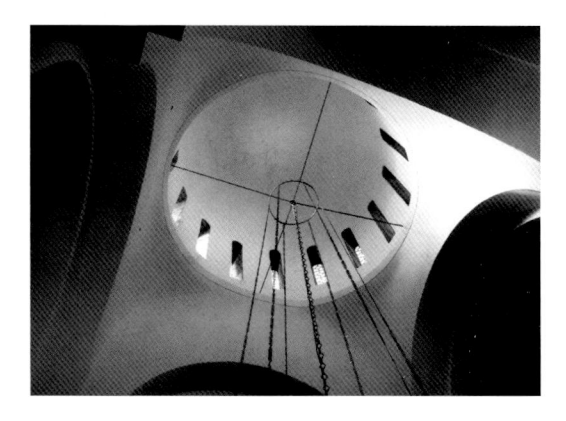

519. Prophet Elijah, Thessaloniki. Undecorated restored dome of the naos

520. Prophet Elijah, Thessaloniki. Short iconostasis with four icons and two *proskynetária* in front

521. Prophet Elijah, Thessaloniki. The spacious *lití* with fragments of old wall paintings

Cruciform / Athonite
At the church of the **Prophet Elijah** the cruciform shape is clear both from the outside and inside. Instead of the normal rectangular or square shape for the arms of the Greek cross they are equally sized semi-circles, except for the western arm which forms a square shaped inner narthex. The exterior of the church is dominated by the high, polygonal drum of the dome over the central space of the cross. Due to its height, supporting buttresses were added at one stage that disrupts the otherwise pure external form of the cross. The wall surfaces on the outside of the church are of striking decorative brickwork and the drum is composed of narrow recessed arches, also in brick, each pierced by a thin window. Inside the dome is supported on four narrow barrel vaults (actually wide arches) that stood originally on four columns. Apparently the building was erected in 1360 as the church of the Theotokos. Although not certain it seems the church's original cruciform shape was modified when it became the *katholikon*

of the new monastery of Nea Moni, founded later in the fourteenth century by the monks Makarios and Gabriel. The transformation of the cross shape into an Athonite-type church occurred when the square narthex became the *lití*, a U-shaped outer narthex added, the northern and southern arms of the naos became the choir spaces for the monks, and pastophoria chambers constructed. In the centre of the large space of the *lití* there are four columns supporting a gallery above that is accessed by a narrow internal stair inside the south wall. The space of the *lití* is almost as large as the centre space of the naos under the dome.

Centralized
The one clearly centralized-type church in Thessaloniki is the small chapel-like building dedicated to the **Transfiguration of the Saviour**. The interior consists of a central square surmounted by a drum and dome supported by four arches. The sides of the square are extended out into broad niches. The whole is contained within an outer square structure of walls from which a rectangular narthex space extends on the western side. The exterior is of brick.

522. Prophet Elijah, Thessaloniki. Reused classical column and lower portion of original arch left exposed

Along with the Panagia Chalkeon and Holy Apostles the churches of St Panteleimon and St Catherine (*Agia Aikateríni*) are architectural gems, all with attractive exteriors in decorative brickwork. St Panteleimon and St Catherine are very similar and are considered here as centralized types. It has been argued that they are instead cross-in-square forms, but against this is the fact that the arms of the cross are extremely shallow, that is so compressed that they are in fact more like broad archways. From the outside it can be seen that the central square is dominant and the so-called arms are short projections on the sides of the square. Both churches are small but excellent examples of the striking decorative brickwork of late period Byzantine edifices. **St Panteleimon** is the earlier church assigned to the thirteenth century. It has a central dome supported by four barrel vaults resting on four columns, a wide central apse, and two very narrow side chambers of the prothesis and diaconicon. The half-dome over the bema is almost the same diameter as that of the central dome while the diameter of the dome over the middle of the narthex is slightly smaller. There was once a wide aisle that ran the entire perimeter of the three sides of the church, excluding the side of the bema. The aisle was removed by the Ottomans when the building was converted into a mosque.

Whereas St Panteleimon is overall a rectangular shape, **St Catherine** is square. The reason for this is that the narthex is incorporated into the aisle that surrounds the three sides of the church. Another reason St Catherine is a perfect form is that each of the four corners of the outer square has a small dome over it. Seen from the outside the perfectly proportioned central drum and dome sit on a cube that is supported on all four sides by windowed decorative arches. At the four corners of the building the shallow domes are supported by exquisite polygonal drums. The exterior walls below are adorned with arches. The church of St Catherine is dated to the end of the thirteenth century.

BYZANTINE CHURCHES IN THESSALONIKI
CENTRALIZED TYPE

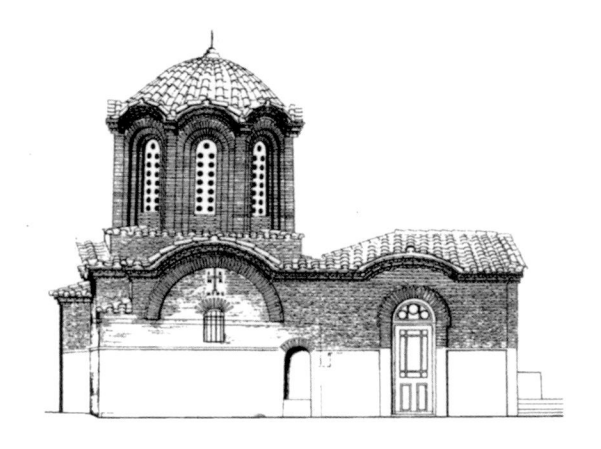

TRANSFIGURATION OF THE SAVIOR
Plan
(Mohlo Fig 252)

TRANSFIGURATION OF THE SAVIOR
Side view
(Mohlo Fig 253)

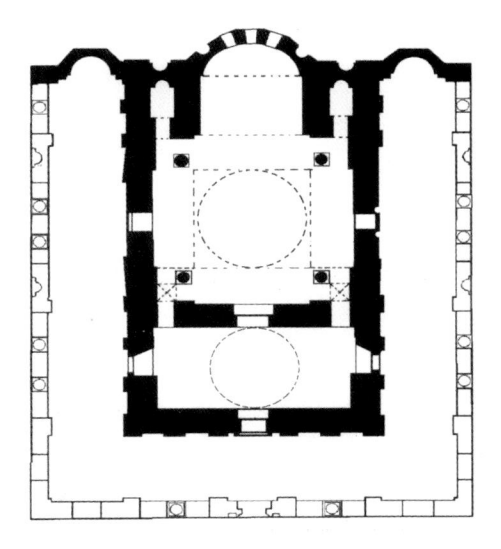

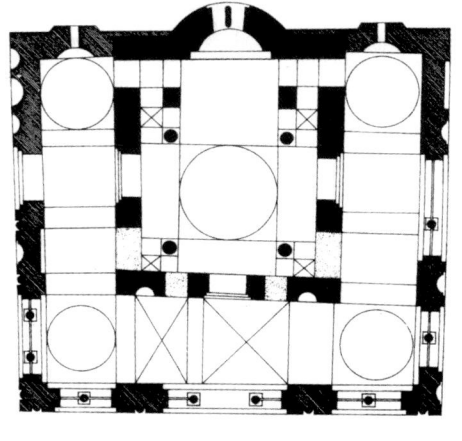

S. PANTELEIMON
(Mohlo Fig 240)

S. CATHERINE
(Mohlo Fig 206)

523. Thessaloniki, plan type – centralized

524. St Catherine, Thessaloniki. West end with entrance doors in the centre

525. St Catherine, Thessaloniki. Typical double window

526. St Catherine, Thessaloniki. East end with projecting semi-circular bema apse (left) and polygonal drum of the prothesis dome (right)

527. St Catherine, Thessaloniki. Narthex looking north with entrance door (left) and archway to naos (right)

528. St Catherine, Thessaloniki. South *parekklesion* with overflow seating for naos (open to the left)

529. St Catherine, Thessaloniki. Simple marble iconostasis with a curtained Beautiful Gate and marble naos floor

BYZANTINE CHURCHES IN THESSALONIKI
CONVERTED TYPE

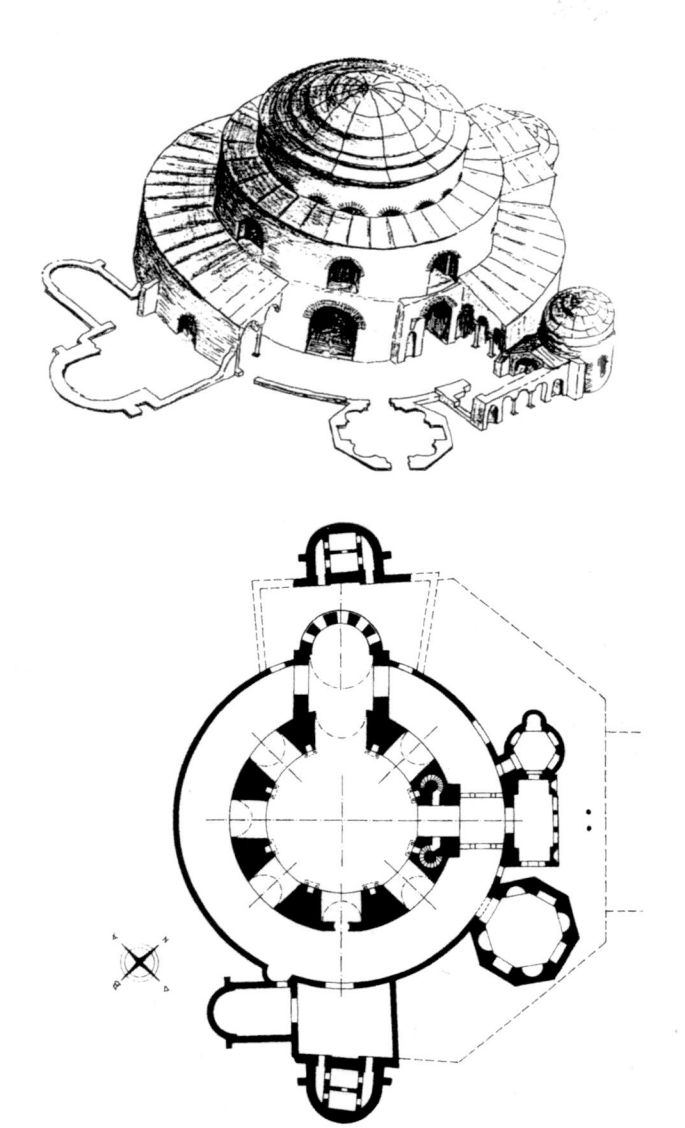

ROTUNDA OF S. GEORGE
View of the entrance from the southeast & ground plan
(Mohlo Figs 62 & 63)

530. Thessaloniki, plan type – converted

531. St George Rotunda, Thessaloniki. View from the west

532. St George Rotunda, Thessaloniki. Original Roman wall with partially destroyed Christian mosaic band above the windows

533. St George Rotunda, Thessaloniki. View looking southeast at iconostasis and bema apse windows behind

534. St George Rotunda, Thessaloniki. Classical column capital and Christian 'impost' above

Converted Hall / Centralized Plan

The building called the **Rotunda** is one of the famous monuments of Thessaloniki. The original building was constructed around 300BC under Emperor Galerius (*c.*260–311), one of four rulers of the Roman Empire, in the tetrarchical system established by Diocletian in 293. The large circular building was built exclusively of brick. Whether it was intended as a palace hall or mausoleum or temple is not known but it was part of the palace complex of Galerius. The central space of the rotunda is surmounted by a dome about 80 feet in diameter and whose weight is carried down by a 20-foot thick circular wall. Cut into the wall are eight recesses or niches each with its own barrel vault. The interior of the building was once lined with slabs of coloured marble. Around AD400 the building was converted into a church dedicated to the Archangels (*Taxiárches*), sometimes also known as the *Asómati* ('Incorporeal Beings'), and some changes made to the original form. As the building was not aligned to the cardinal points the southeast recess was enlarged and extended outward to form an apse for the bema. Then the entrance was transferred from its original southwest position to the northwest recess to be exactly opposite the apse. A small, rectangular narthex was added to the new entrance. Also, the inside of the dome and barrel vaults were decorated with mosaics.

This intervention of the bema apse disturbed the structural balance of the building and as a result the eastern portion of the dome and apse collapsed after an earthquake, possibly at the beginning of the eleventh century. In the reconstruction, to solve the problem it was decided to build a completely new supporting wall around the original structure at a horizontal distance of 26 feet and about three-quarters the height of the old circular wall. The space between the old and new walls became a wide aisle with its own roof. The seven recesses on the perimeter of the existing wall were opened up to allow movement between the central circular space of the naos and the new aisle. As a result the original thick wall now became a series of large piers. The bema apse was also rebuilt at the same time. The name Rotunda was attached to the building by travelers of the eighteenth century and at some stage it was given the name St George by which it is known today. It is not an active church but an exhibition gallery.

Domed Basilica
The church of **Hagia Sophia** in Thessaloniki replaced a large, early fifth-century Christian five-aisled basilica dedicated to St Mark destroyed in the great earthquake of AD618. It is believed the Hagia Sophia was built between 690 and 730, perhaps during the reign of Leo III the Isaurian (717–741). The naos consists of a rectangular space with a dome, a wide central apse, and two flanking apses whose centres atypically do not line up with the side aisles. The central apse is semi-circular on the inside and three-sided on the outside, whereas the two smaller apses are semi-circular both in and out. The narthex runs the entire width of the church and there are galleries over both the narthex and side aisles. The present day paved terrace in front of the church has replaced the forecourt that once existed there but it does give some idea of its once large size. A very unusual feature of the church is that the short drum on which the dome rests is not a perfect circle but rather a square with rounded corners. When seen from the outside, however, it is clearly square in shape. Various theories have been suggested as to why this is and whether it was due to defective construction. There are three arched windows on each side of the square drum that provide light to the interior. Another unusual feature is that unlike the earlier Hagia Sophia in Constantinople, whose dome is supported by system of arches, the Hagia Sophia in Thessaloniki has barrel vaults supported on four large square piers as in the cross-in-square type churches.

Side Aisle Chapels
To avoid repetition a feature common of all the churches with side aisles that has not been noted above is that at their eastern ends, that is adjacent to the bema, there are chapels. In some cases they are the prothesis and diaconicon as in the churches of St Demetrios and Hagia Sophia. In other cases they are independent spaces with their own icon screen, usually with a central door and two flanking icons such as at Holy Apostles and St Catherine.

BYZANTINE CHURCHES IN THESSALONIKI
DOMED BASILICA TYPE

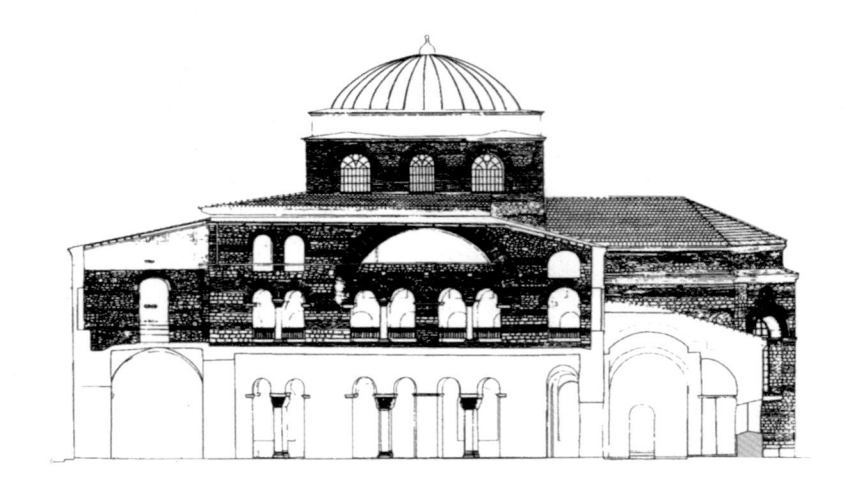

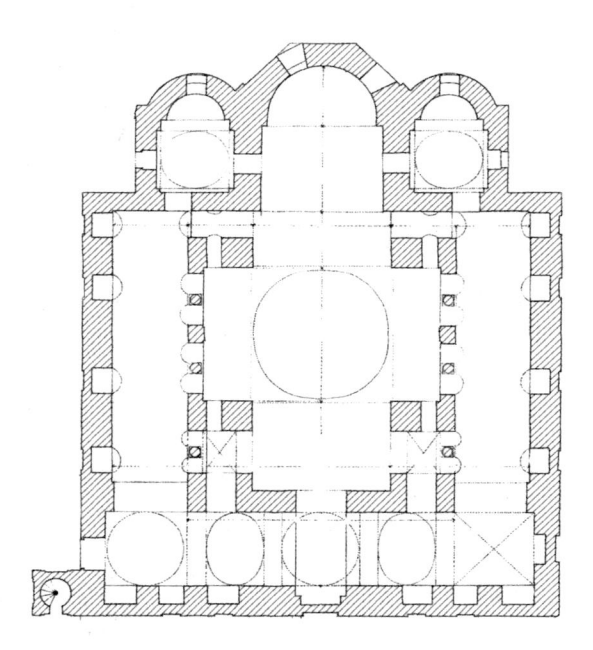

HAGIA SOPHIA
Cross section through narthex and apse; Ground plan
(Mohlo Fig 171; Bouras Fig 3)

535. Thessaloniki, plan type – domed basilica

536. Hagia Sophia, Thessaloniki. View from the west of entrance and (modern) forecourt

537. Hagia Sophia, Thessaloniki. View from the northeast of prothesis apse (foreground), polygonal shaped bema apse (left) and square drum of central dome

538. Hagia Sophia, Thessaloniki. Aisle and gallery arcades on the north side of the naos

539. Hagia Sophia, Thessaloniki. Wide south aisle used as a chapel

540. Hagia Sophia, Thessaloniki. *Platytéra* on the semi-dome of the bema

541. Hagia Sophia, Thessaloniki. Elaborate iconostasis with four large icons, curtained Beautiful Gate and in the tier above 12 medallions each containing a bust of an apostle

542. Hagia Sophia, Thessaloniki. Decorative Byzantine column capital

BYZANTINE CHURCHES
GREECE & BALKANS

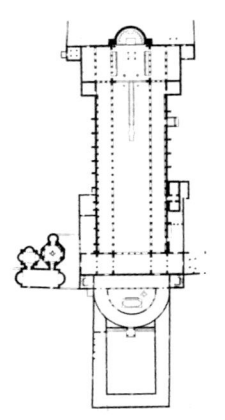

CORINTH - LECHAION
S. Leonidas
(Krautheimer Fig 38)

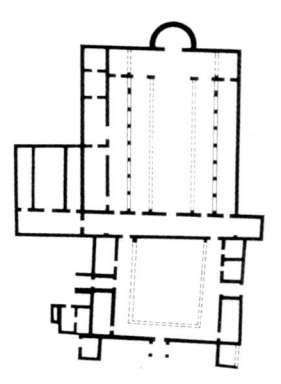

EPIDAVROS
Basilica
(Grabar, 1968 Fig 190)

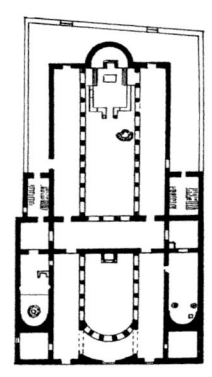

NEA-ANCHIALOS
Basilica A
(Krautheimer Fig 35)

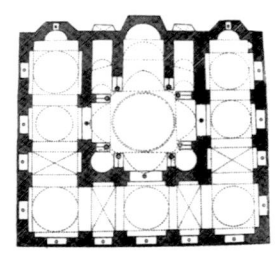

ARTA
Cross-in-Square church
(Buchwald VIII-21)

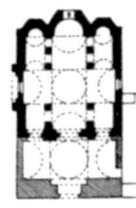

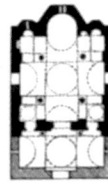

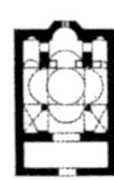

HYMETTOS, Kaisariani katholikon
HYMETTOS, S. John the Theologian
LIGOURIO, S. John
(Krautheimer Fig 103)

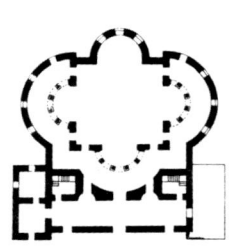

ATHENS
Church, Hadrian's stoa
(McDonald Fig 38)

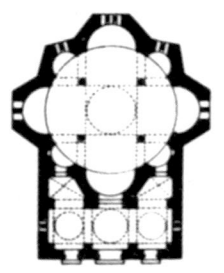

ATHENS
Holy Apostles
(Krautheimer Fig 102)

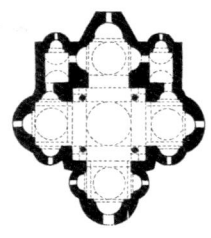

PERISTERA
Tetraconch church
(Krautheimer Fig 101)

543. Greece and Balkans, Byzantine church plans I

BYZANTINE CHURCHES
GREECE & BALKANS

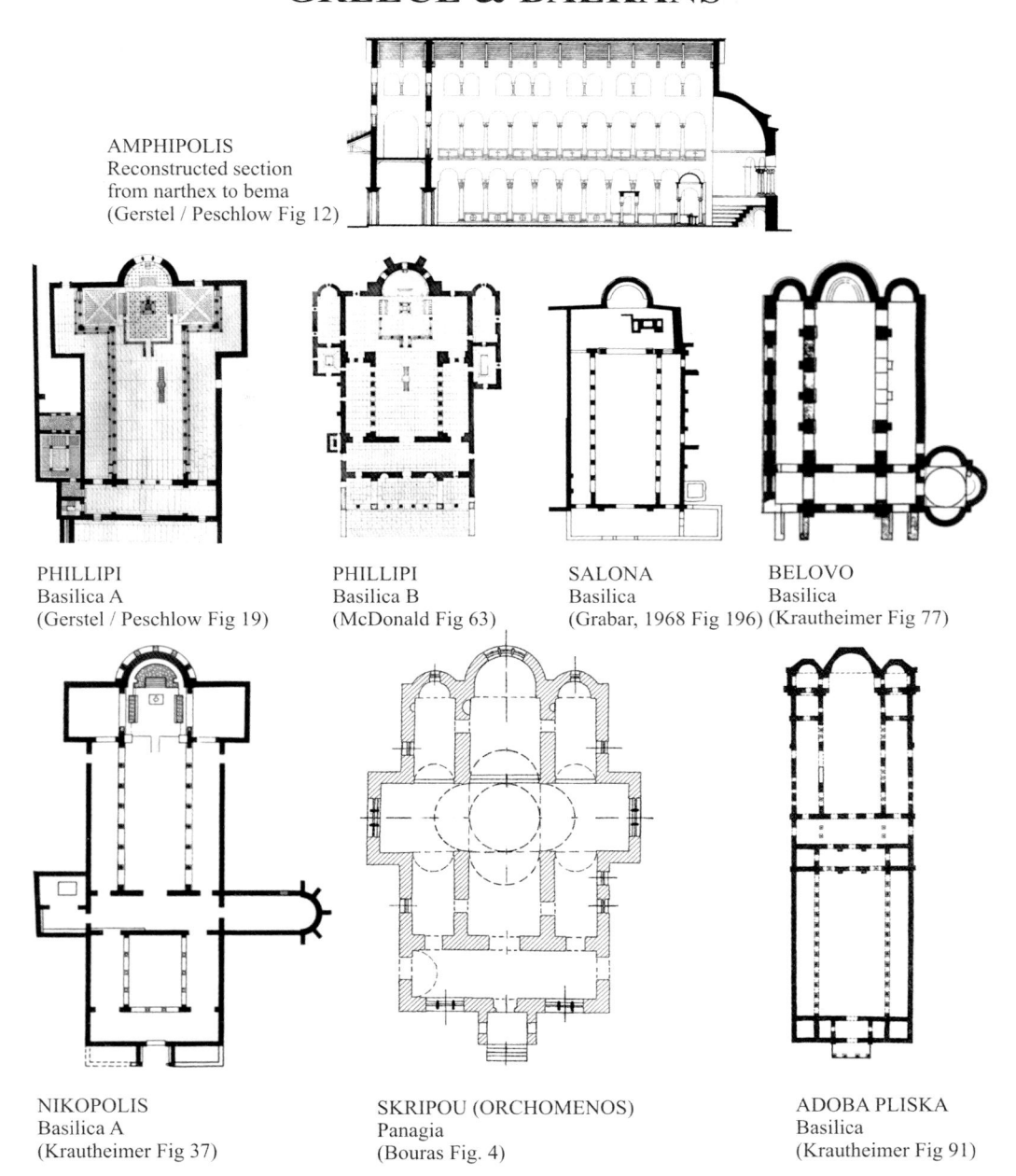

AMPHIPOLIS
Reconstructed section
from narthex to bema
(Gerstel / Peschlow Fig 12)

PHILLIPI
Basilica A
(Gerstel / Peschlow Fig 19)

PHILLIPI
Basilica B
(McDonald Fig 63)

SALONA
Basilica
(Grabar, 1968 Fig 196)

BELOVO
Basilica
(Krautheimer Fig 77)

NIKOPOLIS
Basilica A
(Krautheimer Fig 37)

SKRIPOU (ORCHOMENOS)
Panagia
(Bouras Fig. 4)

ADOBA PLISKA
Basilica
(Krautheimer Fig 91)

544. Greece and Balkans, Byzantine church plans II

545. Athens, Panagia Kapnikarea. View from the south with naos dome (centre), bema apse dome (right) and visible sunken entrance level (left)

546. Athens, SS Theodorii. View from the northwest of the entrance (right) and central naos dome

547. Athens, Theotokos Goroepikoos aka St Eleftherios or Little Metropolis. View from the west of the entrance

548. Athens, Holy Apostles. In the ancient agora view of the south side with projecting apse (centre), gable roof of the narthex (left), diaconicon and bema apses (right)

549. Athens, Holy Trinity. View from the northwest

550. Parigoritissa, Arta. View from the northeast

Other Places Elsewhere

As mentioned in the introduction to this chapter there are innumerable Byzantine churches elsewhere in Greece and also the Balkans that are covered in exceptional detail in other books such as that by Charalambos Bouras. Because of this the description of splendid churches in this chapter has been restricted to one city, Thessaloniki. There are, however, a few exceptional examples outside Thessaloniki, such as at Arta, Ohrid and Parentium and these are illustrated here.

551. Parigoritissa, Arta. View from the northwest

552. Hagia Sophia, Ohrid. Arcaded entrance façade

553. Basilica Eufranius, Parentium (Porec). Restored interior looking toward the bema

Ravenna

Two events established Ravenna as an important centre. The first was when Emperor Honorius (r. 395–423) transferred the capital of the Western Roman Empire from Milan to the inaccessible and heavily defended city of Ravenna in 402. The second event was when Archbishop Apollinaris of Antioch in Asia Minor built a large church at Classe, the port of Ravenna. During Roman times Classe had a large harbor and was a cosmopolitan community with numerous churches belonging to various Christian groups from the east. Most of the churches have disappeared or are in ruins and the area is now an archaeological park. When Rome fell to the Visigoth Alaric in 410 Ravenna remained untouched and prospered with the building of the Basilica of St John the Evangelist, the Neonian or Orthodox Baptistery, and the Mausoleum of Galla Placidia. In 479 the Eastern Emperor Zeno (r. 474–491) allowed his adopted son, Theodoric the Ostrogoth king, to become ruler of the Western Roman Empire based in Ravenna. Theodoric made possible an era of religious tolerance among Eastern Orthodox and Arian Christians, Latins and Goths. During his reign the archiepiscopal chapel, the Theodoric Mausoleum, the Arian Baptistery, and the churches of Sant'Apollinare Nuovo and the Holy Spirit were built in Ravenna. In the sixth century when Emperor Justinian embarked on his campaign to retake Italy his general, Belisario, captured Ravenna in

554. Mausoleum of Theodoric, Ravenna. View of the entrance

555. Orthodox Baptistery, Ravenna. View of the entrance (bottom right)

556. Orthodox Baptistery, Ravenna. Baptismal pool and highly decorated mosaic interior

557. Orthodox Baptistery, Ravenna. Looking east at Holy Table niche

558. Orthodox Baptistery, Ravenna. Hexagonal baptismal pool

540. Justinian began a programme to decorate the churches in Ravenna with mosaics, plus those of San Vitale, Sant'Apollinare in Classe, and part of the church of Sant'Apollinare Nuovo. The city remained under Byzantine influence until 741 when Ravenna was conquered by the Lombard king Astolfo.

The so-called **Galla Placidia Mausoleum** was built between 425 and 430 in a cruciform shape, in the form of a Latin rather than a Greek cross, with a dome over the centre and barrel vaults over the arms. The building was originally an oratory dedicated to St Lawrence and part of the Holy Cross complex. Even though there is doubt that it is the mausoleum of Galla Placidia, the building retains her name. Beautiful mosaics cover completely the interior and are described in detail in a later chapter, as are those of the other churches in Ravenna. Aelia Galla Placidia (392–450) was the daughter of the Emperor Theodosius I and a major force in the political life of the time. For a short time, 425–437, she was regent of the Western Roman Empire.

SPLENDID CHURCHES

559. Mausoleum of Galla Placidia, Ravenna. Clear view of cross-in-square form (apse in foreground)

560. Mausoleum of Galla Placidia. View of entrance (left)

561. Mausoleum of Galla Placidia, Ravenna. Three arms of the cross-in-square visible from the fourth arm

562. San Vitale, Ravenna. Bird's-eye view of centralized form with dominant central dome (top) and smaller domes of the bema and pastophoria apses (bottom)

Begun under Gothic domination in 527, the church of **San Vitale** was completed in 547 under Byzantine control by Bishop Maximianus. The overall outline of the church is in the form of an octagon as is the exterior of the dome which internally is spherical in shape. The dome is supported by eight large piers that have niches in-between with two columns at the back separating the niche spaces from the passageway or wide aisles that surrounds the church, except at the bema end. Between the central circular space and the bema instead of a niche there is a large arch. There is a gallery above the wide aisles that is

563. San Vitale, Ravenna. Exit door on the northeast corner

564. San Vitale, Ravenna. View of bema apse

565. San Vitale, Ravenna. View from behind the present day altar

566. San Vitale, Ravenna. View in the naos of the tall arches supporting the central drum and dome looking at the beam apse

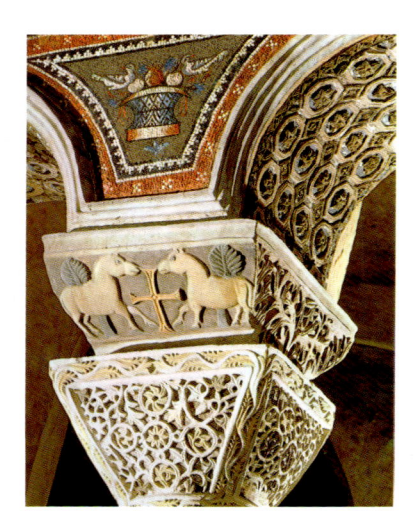

567. San Vitale, Ravenna. Decorative Byzantine column capital and Christian symbols – cross on the 'impost' and doves in the mosaic panel above

accessed from an external circular stairway tower. Attached to one side of the building is a long rectangular narthex, which makes an awkward fit with the diagonals of the two octagon sides. On the opposite end there is a polygonal apse with side chambers for the prothesis and diaconicon. The original arcaded forecourt is now part of the National Museum.

Churches of the basilica type in Ravenna are St John the Evangelist, built after 425 by Galla Placidia, Sant'Apollinare in Classe, consecrated in 549, and Sant'Apollinare Nuovo constructed by King Theodoric sometime in the sixth century. These Ravenna churches are of the single-aisled basilica type without galleries and are notable for their early mosaics. The church of St John has suffered from several

SPLENDID CHURCHES

568. Sant'Apollinare in Classe, Ravenna. Naos looking at triumphal arch and bema apse with arcades separating the aisles, clerestory lighting and open roof with exposed, wood trusses

569. Sant'Apollinare in Classe, Ravenna. Arcade of marble columns and band of medallions on opposite wall

570. Sant'Apollinare Nuovo, Ravenna. Naos looking at restored bema apse

571. Sant'Apollinare Nuovo, Ravenna. Arcade with mosaic frieze panel of figures leading toward an enthroned Theotokos (right)

572. San Giovanni Evangelista, Ravenna. Naos looking at bema apse with arcades separating the aisles, clerestory lighting and open roof with exposed wood trusses

rebuildings and has a fourteenth-century Gothic entrance portal. **Sant'Apollinare in Classe's** interior is extraordinary, with its two arcades of magnificent Greek marble columns, the open wooden roof, the brightness from the plentiful clerestory and aisle windows, and a naos terminating in a triumphal arch that frames the semi-circular apse with its half-dome. Unfortunately, when the floor was raised above the original, as in the church of St John, the proportions of the arcades were disfigured. The narthex and bell tower are later additions.

BYZANTINE CHURCHES
RAVENNA

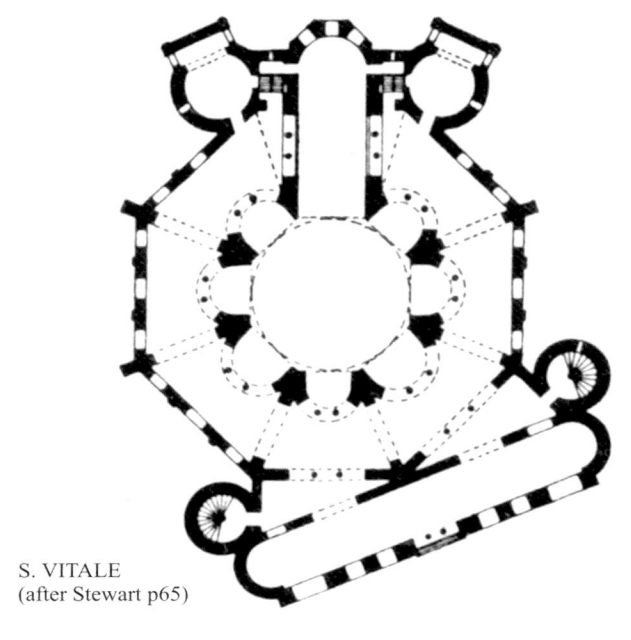

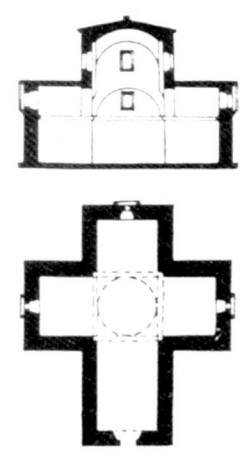

S. VITALE
(after Stewart p65)

GALLA PLACIDIA
(after Stewart p61)

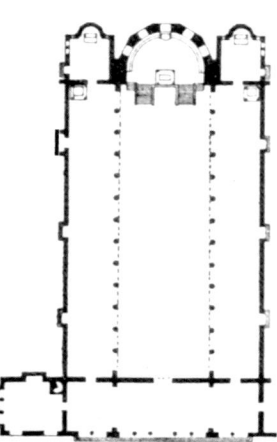

S. APOLLINARE IN CLASSE
(after Stewart p30)

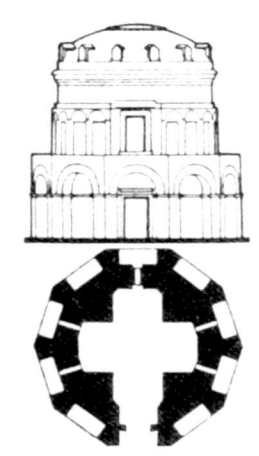

MAUSOLEUM OF THEODORIC
(after Stewart p62)

573. Ravenna, Byzantine church plans

Sant'Apollinare Nuovo has a beautiful basilica interior with arcades of Greek marble columns and Corinthian capitals separating the naos from the side aisles. The church was originally dedicated to Christ the Redeemer by the Ostrogoth king Theodoric as his palace chapel in 504. In 561 the church was re-consecrated under the rule of Justinian (527–565) and renamed in 856 St Apollinare when the relics of the saint were transferred from the basilica Sant'Apollinare in Classe.

Monasteries

As there are too many Byzantine monasteries to describe the focus here will be on three centres in Greece where there are groups of monasteries that still exist and are active. These centres are Mount Athos[2] in the northeast, Meteora[3] in Thessaly in central Greece, and Mystras[4] in the centre of the Peloponnese. An exception will be made in describing an individual monastery and that will be St Catherine in the Sinai in Egypt because of its historic significance. The monastery was never conquered, damaged or destroyed as it was recognized as the sacred biblical site of the burning bush of Moses and thus protected after the Byzantine era by Arab, Turkish and Egyptian rulers. The first structure was a church erected by Helena, mother of Emperor Constantine in 330. In the sixth century at the request of local monks Emperor Justinian ordered the building of a great, walled monastery-fortress around the small church. The new *katholikon* was dedicated to the Theotokos and recorded on a roof beam are the names of Justinian, his wife Theodora, and the architect Stephanos. The outer walls of the monastery complex are six to nine feet thick and vary between 30 and 60 feet in height. Initially the interior space was taken up by a central courtyard dominated by the main church, basilican in form with aisles and which incorporated Helena's small structure, chapels and monks' quarters.

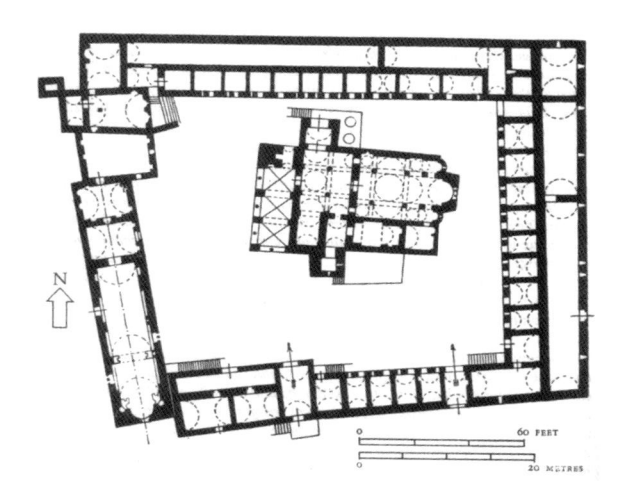

574. Plan of a Typical Monastery – Hosios Meletios, Mt. Kithairon. *Katholikon* in open courtyard surrounded by a wall of supporting spaces

Mount Athos, a high, pyramid-shaped mountain, is at the southern end of a peninsula that is some 37 miles in length and varies between five and seven miles in width. The monk Athanasios founded the first monastery of Megistis Lavra about 963 with funds provided by the Emperor Nikephoros Phokas. A charter (*typikon*) was granted in 971/2 which still governs life on Athos today. Further monasteries, large and small, were added during the tenth century, eventually reaching 180 in number. The 20 that still exist and are active today provide firsthand experience of Athonite architecture and art but also monastic life as little has changed over the ages.

BYZANTINE CHURCHES
MONASTERIES

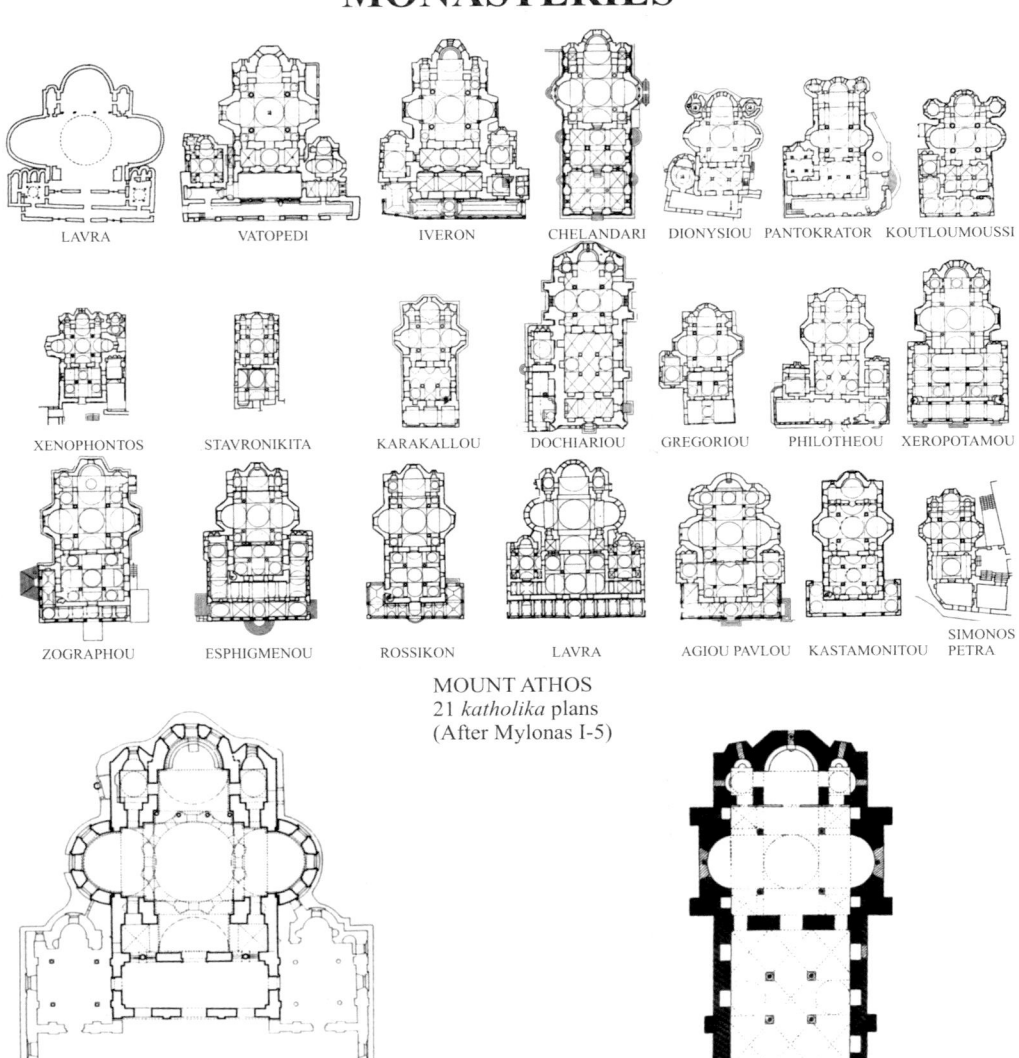

LAVRA — VATOPEDI — IVERON — CHELANDARI — DIONYSIOU — PANTOKRATOR — KOUTLOUMOUSSI

XENOPHONTOS — STAVRONIKITA — KARAKALLOU — DOCHIARIOU — GREGORIOU — PHILOTHEOU — XEROPOTAMOU

ZOGRAPHOU — ESPHIGMENOU — ROSSIKON — LAVRA — AGIOU PAVLOU — KASTAMONITOU — SIMONOS PETRA

MOUNT ATHOS
21 *katholika* plans
(After Mylonas I-5)

MOUNT ATHOS
Great Lavra *katholikon*
(Ousterhout Fig 4.26)

MOUNT ATHOS
Dochiariou *katholikon*
(McDonald Fig 83)

575. Byzantine Monasteries – *Katholika* Plans I

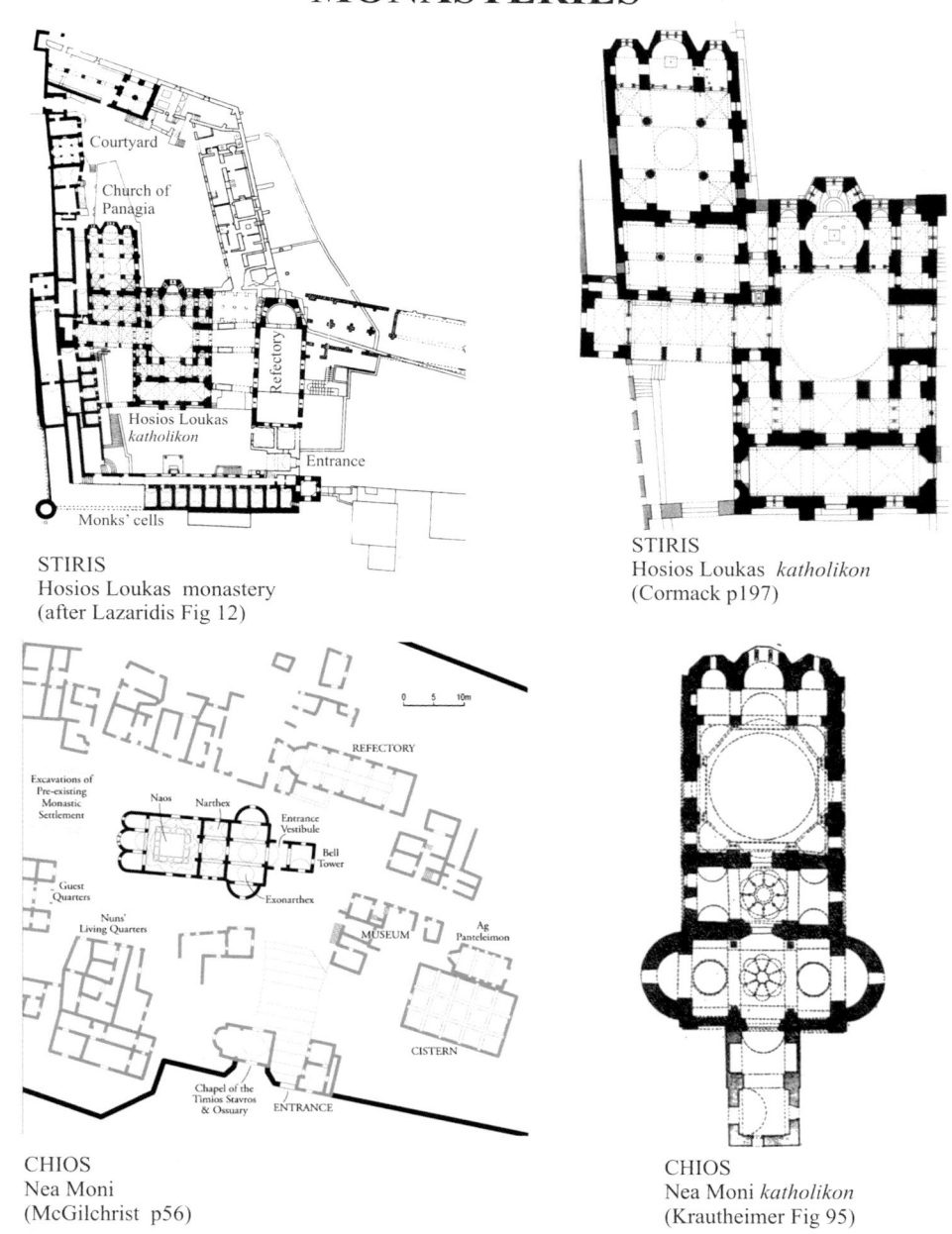

BYZANTINE CHURCHES
MONASTERIES

STIRIS
Hosios Loukas monastery
(after Lazaridis Fig 12)

STIRIS
Hosios Loukas *katholikon*
(Cormack p197)

CHIOS
Nea Moni
(McGilchrist p56)

CHIOS
Nea Moni *katholikon*
(Krautheimer Fig 95)

576. Byzantine Monasteries – *Katholika* Plans II

BYZANTINE CHURCHES
MONASTERIES

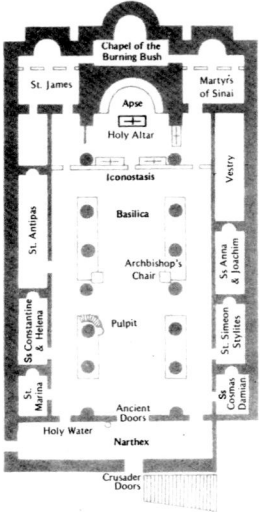

SINAI
S. Catherine *katholikon*
(Evans p18)

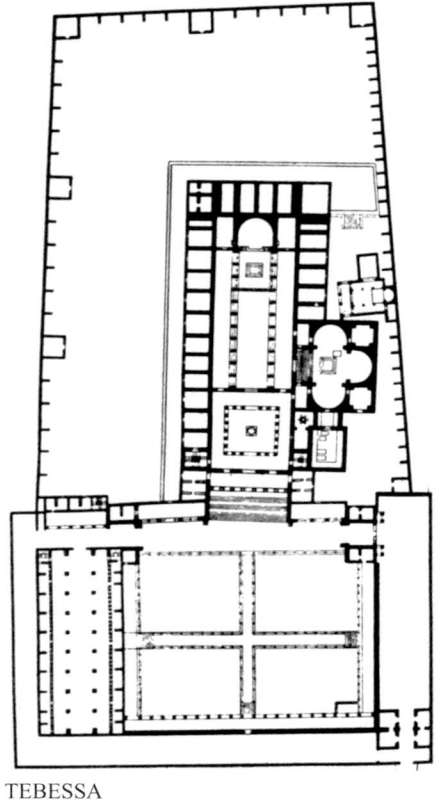

TEBESSA
Monastery
(Krautheimer Fig 59)

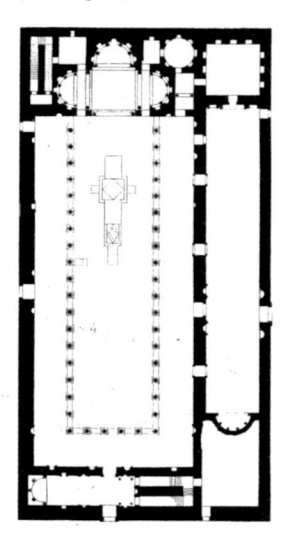

DEIR-EL-ABIAD
"White Monastery"
(Krautheimer Fig 33)

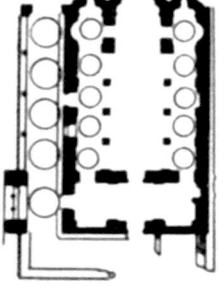

MYSTRA
Pantanassa *katholikon*
(Krautheimer Fig 107)

577. Byzantine Monasteries – *Katholika* Plans III

BYZANTINE CHURCHES
MONASTERIES

CHIOS
Nea Moni entrance elevation
(McGilchrist p60)

578. Byzantine Monasteries – Chios. Entrance view with three narthex domes (front) and tall arched drum of the central naos dome (back)

579. Monastery of St Catherine, Sinai. High perimeter wall and *katholikon* in centre crowded by other buildings

580. Mount Athos, Church of the Protaton. East side with projecting semi-circular apses, the bema in the centre with the pastophoria on either side

581. Mount Athos, Church of the Protaton. A special service

582. Mount Athos, Chelandari. Entrance to the *katholikon*

583. Mount Athos, Chelandari. Stone courses of the monks' wing

584. Mount Athos, Dionysiou. West view to the sea

585. Mount Athos, Esfigmenou. Entrance to the *katholikon*

586. Mount Athos, Iveron. Sea frontage

587. Mount Athos, Iveron. Fortress-like walls

588. Mount Athos, Karakalou. Location on plain

589. Mount Athos, Karakalou. *Katholikon* entrance with bell tower

590. Mount Athos, Koutloumoussi. Outer narthex

591. Mount Athos, Megistis Lavra. *Katholikon* painted in typical blood-red colour

592. Mount Athos, Megistis Lavra. Octagonal shaped *phiale* with font of holy water

593. Mount Athos, Panteleimon. *Katholikon* with arched drums and semi-circular domes

594. Mount Athos, Pantokrator. *Chorostasiá*

595. Mount Athos, Pantokrator. Monk's wing with stone and brick decoration

596. Mount Athos, Simonos Petra. Location on coastal bluff

SPLENDID CHURCHES

597. Mount Athos, Stavronikita. View from the east

598. Mount Athos, Stavronikita. View from the south with terraced garden (foreground)

599. Mount Athos, Stavronikita. Aqueduct

600. Mount Athos, Vatopedi. *Katholikon* entrance façade onto courtyard

601. Mount Athos, Vatopedi. Monks' wing

602. Mount Athos, Vatopedi. Bronze entrance door to *katholikon* from portico

603. Mount Athos, Vatopedi. Marble throne in portico on right side of entrance door

604. Mount Athos, Vatopedi. Double eagle symbol floor slab in portico

605. Mount Athos, Xenophontos. Coastal location

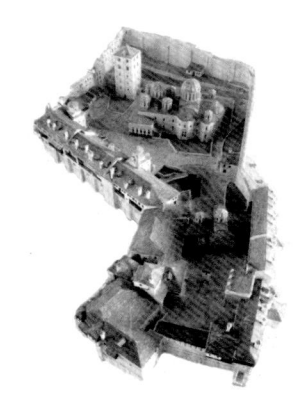

606. Mount Athos, Xenophontos. Model of monastery complex with the new *katholikon* (top) and old *katholikon* (bottom), Museum in Ouranoupolis

Only that of Megistis Lavra will be described as it was the first monastery built on the peninsula and became the model for those that followed on Athos and elsewhere. According to the biography of Athanasios, he first constructed the defensive wall, followed by the main church or *katholikon* in the middle of the enclosed space, and finally the monks' cells and refectory. The church was built from the beginning as a cross-in-square type with a double narthex and *parakléssia* on either side of the inner narthex, the *lití*. Later semi-circular apses were added to the northern and southern arms of the cross to form the choir spaces for the monks. The central crossing point of the cross is covered in a large dome with smaller ones over the pastophoria spaces and the *parakléssia*. Semi-domes cover the *chorostasíes*. Over the inner narthex there is a central barrel vault flanked by small domes while the reverse occurs in the outer narthex – a central small dome with barrel vaults on either side.

607. Mount Athos, Xenophontos. Old *katholikon*

608. Mount Athos, Xenophontos. New *katholikon*

609. Mount Athos, Xenophontos. Model of new *katholikon* from the northeast, Museum in Ouranoupolis

610. Mount Athos, Xeropotamos. Monks' wing

611. Mount Athos, Zographou. External view of the *chorostasiá*

612. Mount Athos, Skete Profiti Ilias. From approach road looking at southeast corner

613. Mount Athos, Drum and Dome Roof I. New *katholikon* of Xenophontos

614. Mount Athos, Drum and Dome Roof II. *Katholikon* of Chelandari

615. Mount Athos, Drum and Dome Roof III. *Katholikon of* Iveron

616. Mount Athos, Drum and Dome Roof IV. *Katholikon* of Koutloumoussi

617. Mount Athos, *Phiale* I. Iveron

618. Mount Athos, *Phiale* II. Koutloumoussi

SPLENDID CHURCHES

619. Mount Athos, small chapel in courtyard. Koutloumoussi

620. Mystras, Metropolis. Northeast view of circular drum and dome (top) and projecting bema apse (bottom)

621. Mystras, Metropolis. Naos looking east at bema apse with stone plaque on floor where last Byzantine emperor was crowned

622. Mystras, Aphendiko. View from the southeast

Outside the main entrance to the church stands the circular domed *phiali* structure (basin of holy water), the largest on Athos. Other structures added to the complex inside the walls were the treasury, which is very rich and a library that contains over 2,000 valuable manuscripts.

The most dramatic sight at Meteora is the natural slender, vertical stone pillars like extended fingers of a hand reaching for heaven. At the peak of these pillars, some over 500 feet tall, perched like bird's nests, are the monasteries. First Doupiani was built in the eleventh century, and within three centuries later there were 24 in number. Only six are preserved and active today. Because of the shape and size of the pillars of stone the monasteries are small and compact. Despite that they each have a *katholikon*, other chapels, monks' cells and a refectory. An architectural characteristic of the Meteora monastery churches is that the drums of the large domes tend to be tall polygonal cylinders pierced by windows with a segmented, tiled roof covering a shallow dome.

236 THE SACRED ARCHITECTURE OF BYZANTIUM

623. Mystras, Hodegetria. View from the northeast

624. Mystras, Hodegitria. Central drum and dome

625. Mystras, Pantanassa. East side with projecting apses of bema (centre) and pastophoria on either side

626. Meteora, Roussanou. Spectacular location atop a stone outcrop

At Mystras the monasteries were once part of the hilltop Byzantine city of the same name. From 1262 until 1460 the city thrived as the capital of the Morea (Byzantine Peloponnese) with 20,000 inhabitants at its height. Regretfully, today only one church and one monastery exist and are active in the deserted city. The remaining church buildings are empty shells, but still visible are their remarkable architectural features and wall paintings. Saint Demetrios, known as the Metropolis church and still active today, was built in 1262 in basilica form with two aisles. A narthex and portico were added later and front onto a courtyard. In the fifteenth century galleries were added in such a way that the outward appearance of the church looked as if it was a cross-in-square type with a large central dome and four smaller domes around it.

627. Siris, Hosios Loukas. View from the east of the *katholikon* (left) and church of the Theotokos (right)

628. Daphni, Koimisis tis Theotokou. View from the northeast

The other churches of Mystras have an outwardly clear cross-in-square form with dressed stone exterior walls and clay tile roofs. Pantanassa is the only functioning monastery in Mystras today.

St John at Ephesus

The church of St John at Ephesus is special for two reasons. First, it is the place where the apostle preached, lived and died, and, second, it is one of the few churches anywhere where all the typical Byzantine architectural components can still be seen clearly today. Ephesus was a major Roman city in Asia Minor and is reputed to be the place that the Apostle John and Mary, the mother of Jesus, arrived there sometime between the year 50 and 54, when they could no longer remain in Jerusalem. According to the Gospel of St John (19:26–7): 'When, on the cross, Jesus saw his mother and the disciple whom he loved standing beside her, he said to his mother, "Woman, here is your son." Then he said to the disciple, "Here is your mother." And from that hour the disciple took her into his own home and never separated again.' During the Christian persecutions by the Emperor Domitian (r. 81–96) John was taken to Rome where he survived attempts to kill him. He was exiled to the island of Patmos, and after Domitian's assassination in 96 John returned to Ephesus. It has been argued that he is the author of the Gospel of John and the Book of Revelation but scholars cannot agree on the dates when they were written. When John died around the year 100 a martyrium was built over the apostle's tomb just as had been done over those of Peter's grave and Paul's, both in Rome. The martyrium building at Ephesus was in the form of a large square space with huge piers at the corners supporting a dome. During the reign of Theodosius II (408–450) a basilica was built around the martyrium. A bema was added on the eastern side of the square structure, a rectangular space and narthex with a forecourt on the western side, and transepts on the northern and southern sides.

The church was toppled by an earthquake and its rebuilding was included by Emperor Justinian in his vast building programme. It was probably completed before 548 but then partially destroyed in the earthquake of 1361. The first excavations were carried out in the 1920s and the re-erection of the columns and restoration of the walls and religious fixtures completed in the 1970s. The presence of a large-scale model (1:100) on the site of the partially reconstructed building provides a complete appreciation of the forecourt and the church exterior with its six major round domes and smaller domes over the narthex and side spaces. Open-air services are still held at the church on the festival day of the saint in the first week of May.

The church of St John has a spectacular setting. On the northern outskirts of the medieval city of Ayasuluk (Selcuk today) is a hill with an old castle and citadel enclosed by a long, thick fortification wall forming a precinct in the shape of an elongated ellipse. Outside the wall to the southwest are the remains of one of the largest temples of antiquity, the famous Artemesion, also the fourteenth-century Mosque of Isa Bey, and beyond them the ancient city of Ephesus. The fortification wall has 20 towers and three gates. The best-preserved and most monumental of the gates is the Gate of Persecution, located at the south end of the enclosed precinct. This Gate was built by Christians early in the fourth century, as a symbol of the persecutions carried out by the Romans at the nearby stadium adjacent to the Vedius Gymnasium. The Gate structure consists of an arched entrance flanked by two square towers. On the inner side of the gateway arch are faded frescoes of Christ in the middle and apostles on either side of him, but the figures can barely be seen. At the exit of the gateway there are steps at the head of a paved marble pathway which cuts across the courtyard that slopes up to the south side of the church. This is highly unusual as the approach to Byzantine churches is inevitably from the west. The reasons why this was not the case here were no doubt practical. First, the church is located on a sloping hill with a very steep incline on the western side which precluded an approach from that direction without a monumental staircase. Second, the requirement of an east–west axis meant that the church could just fit in the narrow area between the two opposite sides of the fortification walls. Thus there was not enough space for an approach from the west as the two ends of the church building, the forecourt on the west and apse on the east, actually touch the fortification wall. Aerial photographs reveal a diagonal path from the southern gateway of the precinct to the eastern corner of the forecourt as an entry approach.

The forecourt, which archaeologists have concluded belonged to the original church, is large, over 152 feet long and 113 feet wide. Arcades paved in marble, each with eight Corinthian columns, surround the central space on three sides with a narthex on the fourth or eastern side. An unusual feature is an eight-foot-wide walkway with balustrades on the outside of the three arcaded sides of the forecourt. Because of the steep slope the forecourt is supported on a huge substructure which is more than 30 feet high off the ground at its highest point. This provides for impressive views from the raised walkway. No trace has been found of a fountain in the forecourt that was typical of Byzantine churches. Three central doorways lead from the eastern arcade of the forecourt into the narthex. Two outer doorways open directly into the side aisles, one on the north end and the other at the south end of the narthex. At these two ends there are also side doors into the aisles from the outside that were added for easier access from the difficult terrain. In typical manner three doors connect the narthex to the naos. There are in addition doors at each end of the narthex, making five all together, that lead directly into each side aisle. Each of the five bays of the narthex was covered by a small dome.

In form the church was a domed basilica like Hagia Sophia in Constantinople, except that it had a longer western arm that called for two domes. If, however, the end bay in the western arm is ignored the remainder of the church would form a perfect Greek cross. With the addition of the western end bay the church becomes a domed basilica. It has transepts as well. Of the completed church Procopius wrote in his book *Edifices* that it was 'so large and beautiful, that, to speak briefly, it resembles very closely in all respects, and is a rival to, the shrine which he [Justinian] dedicated to all the apostles in the imperial city …'. As described previously the church of the Holy Apostles in Constantinople was of the cruciform type.

BYZANTINE CHURCH
S. JOHN AT EPHESUS
(After Buyukkolanci, pp 43, 49, 51, 58)

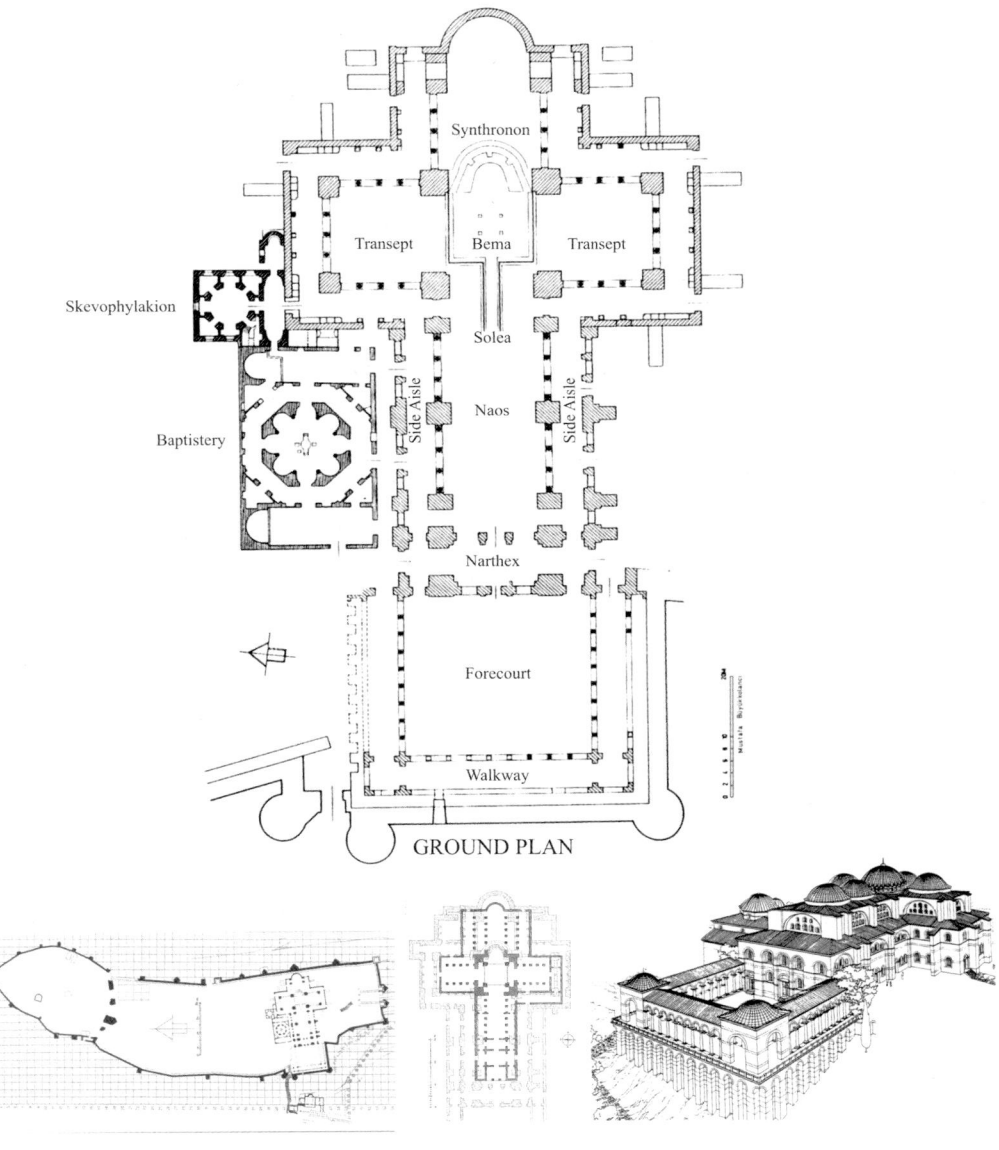

GROUND PLAN

CITADEL

THEODOSIAN & JUSTINIAN PLANS

VIEW FROM THE SOUTHWEST

629. St John at Ephesus. Plans

630. St John at Ephesus. Model from the southwest

631. St John at Ephesus. Actual view from the same angle as the model

632. St John at Ephesus. From bema looking west at the remains of the solea and naos

633. St John at Ephesus. From bema looking at solea foundations

On entering the naos from the narthex the first impression would have been of two domes supported by thick piers over the rectangular basilica space rather than the expected flat ceiling or exposed wooden trusses, or even a barrel vault. The domes were supported by large piers. Between each pier there are four columns that once supported a gallery above each of the two aisles. The position of the stairs to the galleries is not known. The columns between the piers are made of the famous marble from the island of Marmara (*from the Greek mármaron for marble*), known in ancient times as Prokonnesos where Byzantine royalty built their palaces. The capitals of the columns bear the monograms of Emperor Justinian and his wife Theodora on the side facing the naos. Traces of wall paintings on the arches between the formerly marble clad brick piers supporting the domes means that the arches and domes were at one time decorated.

634. St John at Ephesus. Ciborium columns with grille set in the floor covering stair down to the tombs in the crypt

635. St John at Ephesus. Forecourt column capital

636. St John at Ephesus. Capital with monogram of Justinian

637. St John at Ephesus. Capital with monogram of Theodora

638. St John at Ephesus. Transept capital with cross motif

639. St John at Ephesus. Transept capital with simple cross motif

Before describing the central area of the church it should be noted that the square bays of the north and south transepts are the same size as each of the two western bays of the naos. This meant that the domes over the transepts and the two over the western bays were all the same size. The transept domes were each supported by four large marble clad brick piers but had three instead of four Prokonnesian marble columns as in the naos. The capitals are of the Ionic order as in the naos but with Greek cross motifs in circles.

At the eastern end of the rectangular basilica space in the middle of the naos there was a large marble ambo which had two flights of steps, one on the east side and one on the west. Today, only fragments on the floor show the position of the once prominent ambo with its curved balustrades. Behind the ambo the raised solea led to the bema and is still very much evident. The square-shaped bema is located exactly at the intersection of the rectangular basilica space and the transepts. The floor of the bema is higher than that of the naos and transepts, and sections of its once rich, geometrically patterned marble surface can still be seen. On the northern and southern edges of the bema there were columns and balustrades to separate the clergy space from the laity in the transepts. The only signs of the iconostasis on the western end of the bema are some columns that are still in position and a tie beam between them. A stepped synthronon, once faced with pink marble, occupies the entire eastern end of the bema with a place for the bishop's throne in the middle of the synthronon. In the centre of the bema is a raised marble platform, square in shape, with short columns at each of the four corners that once supported the canopy or ciborium over the Holy Table. The bema was surmounted by a dome larger than the others and had a windowed drum. Behind the synthronon there is another domed bay with a semi-circular apse. It is possible that this area was used as the pastophoria.

Immediately behind the east side of the Holy Table platform there is an iron grille set into the floor. This grille closes off a narrow staircase that leads down into the crypt where archaeologists have unearthed four empty tombs directly beneath the Holy Table platform. It is assumed the larger tomb was that of St John the Apostle and evangelist. In the crypt there are large brick piers believed to be those of St John's martyrium and on which later the Holy Table platform of the first church was built.

In the northwest corner of the northern transept there is a door through which the liturgical processions of the Little Entrance and Great Entrance must have come, as directly outside the doors is the *skevophylákion*. A complete *skevophylákion* is a rarity in Asia Minor as the only other one is at Hagia Sophia in Constantinople. At Ephesus the *skevophylákion* is a small building, about 46 by 38 feet, and is attached to the church. The building consists of two spaces, a narrow narthex that connects to the church's northern transept and a large circular domed room set in a square structure. Between the circular room and the outer square small chambers fill the space. A barrel vault forms the roof of the narthex and its floor is paved in marble. The ends of the narthex are semi-circular in shape with doors. The eastern door opens into a small chapel and the western door to the baptistery. Originally the eastern chapel of the narthex had a small semi-circular pool set into the floor with a fountain, most likely used by the clergy for religious cleansing purposes before entering the main room of the *skevophylákion*. In the apse of the eastern chapel there is a wall painting of three standing figures – Christ in the middle, St John to his right, and another figure to his left, perhaps Timothy the first bishop of Ephesus. The other walls of the chapel also have wall paintings. In the large circular room four of the surrounding chambers are so arranged so as to form a cross, the southern chamber in fact is the access doorway from the narthex. The three remaining corner chambers have niches in their walls with marble shelves where the treasures of the church were kept.

Equally impressive is the baptistery building adjacent to the *skevophylákion* and attached to the northern side of the church. It is a large building about 110 by 70 feet, separated from the church by a covered aisle with two doors into the naos. Outside access to the baptistery is from the north door of the church narthex. The baptistery building consists of three spaces, a large central octagonal-shaped room with a dome over flanked on either side by a narrow hall (about 17 by 65 feet) each with semi-circular ends. The octagonal room is divided into two separate spaces; an inner octagon is enclosed by a thick wall separating it from the outer octagon and forming a surrounding corridor. There are eight semi-circular niches in the wall facing the inner octagon. Access to the surrounding corridor is from doorways in the four niches that are on the north, south, east and west sides which form a cross. This cruciform shape is accentuated by a cross shape in the marble floor-pattern. The four remaining niches on the diagonals have windows in them. In the centre of the inner octagonal space there is a small, sunken, circular baptismal pool with steps down on the east and west sides. On either side of the circular pool there are smaller square water basins set into the floor. The high dome over the inner octagonal room was decorated with mosaic while the walls and floor were finished with marble. It is not known how the corridor was roofed but it seems it would have been lit by clerestory windows.

640. St John Ephesus. Remains of the *skevophylákion*

641. St John at Ephesus. Remains of the baptistery

The outer octagon was contained in an enclosing square structure. It seems that the four triangular rooms at the corners between the outer octagon and square were used for changing clothes and other functions. It appears that those to be baptized, mostly adults in the early centuries, would gather in the church narthex or western hall, then proceed to undress in one of the triangular shaped rooms, continue into the inner octagonal space, be immersed in the baptismal pool accompanied by a ceremony, get dressed, and end up in the eastern hall which contained a small Holy Table in the apse. The neophyte Christians were now eligible to participate in the full Divine Liturgy.

I. Typical Domed Byzantine Church. Artist's concept of Holy Apostles, Constantinople

II. Rome, Sant'Agnese Fuori le Mura. Nave looking toward triumphal arch and semi-dome of bema apse

III. Rome, San Lorenzo Fuori le Mura. Nave looking toward triumphal arch and raised sanctuary

IV. Rome, Santa Sabina. Nave looking toward triumphal arch and semi-dome of sanctuary apse

V. Ravenna, San Apollinare in Classe. Semi-circular sanctuary apse and semi-dome

VI. Constantinople, Hagia Sophia. Mosaic of the Theotokos with Emperors Constantine and Justinian over south door of inner narthex

VII. Constantinople, Hagia Sophia. View from the south of central dome and flanking semi-domes

VIII. Constantinople, Hagia Sophia. Platytéra in semi-dome of bema apse

IX. Constantinople, Hagia Sophia. View of domed interior and bema apse from the western loggia

X. Constantinople, Hagia Sophia. A Byzantine column capital

XI. Constantinople, Hagia Eirene. Central dome and apse semi-dome with Iconoclastic cross

XII. Constantinople, Theotokos Pammakaristos. East elevation of the *parekklesion*

XIII. Constantinople, Theotokos Pammakaristos. Interior of column type cross-in-square form

XIV. Constantinople, Theotokos Pammakaristos. Central dome with Christ Pantokrator mosaic

XV. Thessaloniki, St Demetrios. Naos looking toward triumphal arch and semi-dome of bema apse

XVI. Thessaloniki, Acheiropoietos. Naos looking toward semi-dome of bema apse and iconostasis

XVII. Thessaloniki, Holy Apostles. East side with projecting apses of bema and pastophoria

XVIII. Stiris, Hosios Loukas. Naos looking east at entrances to bema and pastophoria

XIX. Stiris, Hosios Loukas. Platytéra in semi-dome of bema apse

XX. Mystras, SS Theodoroi. View from the southeast

Chapter Four

SPIRITUAL ART

A distinctive feature of a traditional Byzantine church is the sumptuous adornment of the interior with stylized images of holy figures in murals, mosaics or icons. The images are not merely art objects but are a sacred representation meant to transport the faithful to the spiritual realm. Specifically, the images are reminders of another reality beyond the physical world. Byzantine art was not only a religious but a didactic art, to teach the Christian religion to the uneducated. Because religious images had to attract the interest of the spectator they had to be satisfying aesthetically as well. For this reason the best artists were employed to produce the art to go with the sacred architecture. As the Byzantine cultural historian Leslie Brubaker so aptly wrote 'Words and images communicate differently: words describe, images show.' Ideally, then, a display of images without accompanying text in this book should be sufficient to convey the spiritual art of Byzantium. But in the modern world images by themselves, however, cannot stand without text to both describe and explain the character and meaning of the images. Thus the reason for this chapter and the following one.

The character of Byzantine church art is captured in the words of St Gregory of Nyssa (c.335–after 394) who wrote that 'While silent on the wall, painting speaks many and more useful things.' The essence of Byzantine art is its 'content' rather than its 'form' and cannot be comprehended through Renaissance or modern ideals. Insight into Byzantine spiritual art requires an understanding of the liturgical and theological significance of different forms, colours, and gestures. The art is not to be interpreted subjectively, by personal taste and desires, or even aesthetically even though their beauty is what attracts many people. The purpose of Byzantine church art from the beginning was spiritual as it was considered that Jesus Christ, the apostles, saints and martyrs were present in image form to inspire, to guide, and to encourage the faithful to reach perfection.

During a liturgical service in a Byzantine church the faithful worshipper not only experiences a spiritual awareness but a profound impact on all the physical senses. There is not only the overwhelming richness of visual images, but the feel and swish of the silky texture of the priestly vestments, the flickering of candles, the sounds of harmonious chanting, the tinkling of the censer, the aroma of fragrant incense, and the taste of the communion bread and wine.

The spiritual art of the Byzantine church is commonly understood to describe the artistic products of the Byzantine Empire from about the fourth century until the Fall of Constantinople in 1453. Byzantine spiritual art also refers to the art of Eastern Orthodox states which were contemporary with the Byzantine Empire and were culturally influenced by it, without actually being part of it (the so-called 'Byzantine commonwealth'), such as Bulgaria, Serbia and Russia as well as the art of the Republic of Venice and Kingdom of Sicily, which had close ties to the Byzantine Empire despite being in other respects part of western European culture. To cover such a vast region would go beyond the scope of this book so this chapter and the following will concentrate on the Byzantine Empire itself, from the fourth to the fifteenth century and the period preceding and leading to it.

642. Tomb of Aureli, Rome. Face of an apostle

643. Cemetery below St Peter's, Rome. Christ as the Sun God on a chariot

644. Catacomb of SS Pietro e Marcellino, Rome. Christ healing a woman

645. Catacomb of SS Pietro e Marcellino, Rome. The raising of Lazarus from the dead

Epochs

The Early Christian Period

Byzantine spiritual art did not emerge fully formed in the fourth century but developed from early Christian art of the second and third centuries. This early Christian art conformed to the tastes and techniques of contemporary Roman art which in turn had been influenced by the earlier classical Greek and Hellenistic art. Classical Greek artists had perfected their ability to create ideal human figures while their Hellenistic successors extended this to the whole world of natural appearances. Roman art built on this foundation as is evident in their realistic portraits and paintings which created the illusion of spatial depth. Early Christian art began as a minor part of the art of Late Antiquity. It was not a new form

646. Catacomb of Goirdani, Rome. An orant

647. Catacomb Commodila, Rome. Enthroned Theotokos holding the Christ Child

648. Catacomb of Trasona. Portrait of a woman

of expression but one that existed side by side with pagan art. While Christian art later developed antique art declined and eventually disappeared leaving the art of the Christians triumphant. Unfortunately little of the Christian art of the first few centuries remains for art historians to make any generalizations except that they were a continuation of the arts from the previous centuries, above all that of Rome.

It appears that in the first two centuries little emphasis was given in early Christian art to images. But for some reason this changed around the year 200 which means that they must have had a specific Christian purpose which is unclear today. These early paintings are important, then, as they throw light on the religious values assigned to images. The first Christian paintings

649. House of the Scribes, Dura-Europos. Portrait of Heliodoros

and, more rarely, mosaics, began to appear on the walls and ceilings of the catacombs and subterranean walk-in tombs in Rome. Sculpture in the form of reliefs was confined to stone or marble coffins or sarcophagi and engraved tombstones. The first painted frescoes in the catacombs of Rome were used for burials with appropriate funerary themes. Catacombs continued to be the normal burial places of well-off Christians until they were given up in the second half of the fifth century in Rome although they continued in other places such as Naples. Christians adorned their tombs with wall paintings that had deliberate choice of figures and events. These were intended to convey a message – deliverance and a new life beyond the grave. Outside of Rome the first examples of Christian imagery found by archaeologists are the wall paintings in a house-church in the little Roman garrison town of Dura-Europos on the Persian frontier. The murals had to do with baptism and were not in the hall used for the Eucharist liturgy.

The largest number of preserved third- and fourth-century Christian paintings is to be found in the catacombs in Rome as the above-ground decorations have disappeared along with the buildings themselves. Overall, the paintings of the fourth century do not depart much from the third-century types. The difference was that the art of the fourth century frequently had heavily painted frames and larger and more realistic figures. As the centuries progressed, the number and variety of pictorial representations increased becoming more stylized.

From the available evidence it is clear that Christian art was limited in the second and third centuries. There were no large-scale church buildings to be decorated since Christians performed their ceremonies in house-churches. That changed with the ascension of Constantine at the beginning of the fourth century. His Edict of Toleration of Christianity brought about the so-called Peace or Triumph of the Church. The result was a new orientation in art as well as in religious beliefs and practices. He was the first emperor to support Christian art on a large scale, mainly in the adornment of new church buildings. He and his family founded churches in Rome, the cities of Jerusalem and Bethlehem in the Holy Land, in his new capital of Constantinople at Byzantium on the Bosphorus, and elsewhere. The early art in these churches has been largely lost with their demolition or reconstruction. It appears that the similarities in the limited Christian art in widely separated regions of the Roman Empire would indicate that unification in subject matter and style was encouraged. Yet, each region – Rome, Sicily, Antioch, Syria – varied in some respects to reflect local traditions.

The first initiatives on Christian art in churches came strangely enough from the imperial palace. Emperors had established a tradition from antiquity of putting representations of themselves on coins and medals. They were shown seated on a throne in majesty and in the Christian era the hand of God was added, blessing or crowning the emperor. The image was meant to convey that the emperor ruled by divine authority and was the symbol on earth of the Lord of the Divine Kingdom. In the fourth century this became the model for representations of Christ enthroned as the ruler of the universe. At first, such images of Christ alone, or surrounded by angels and saints, or handing out a scroll of authorization, were often placed in the half dome of the apse in basilican churches.

Byzantine Age of Splendour
The first golden age of Christian art is represented by the works produced during the fifth and sixth centuries. This age of splendour began under the bold and active religious policies of the Theodosian dynasty in elevating Christianity to a State religion and closing down the pagan temples. Theodosius I (r. 379–395) and his dynastic successors spent large sums building churches, including in places such as Milan and Ravenna, and adorning them on a lavish scale. In Rome, Pope Leo I (r. 457–474) realized how art could serve the religion and began a programme to decorate the apses of the great basilicas. Although the capital cities benefitted the most from imperial generosity, various towns such as Ephesus, Alexandria and those in Syria and elsewhere in the Near East also gained. Bishops and wealthy private patrons followed the emperor's example and thus many churches adorned with art work were built throughout the vast Roman Empire. The Arab invasions of the seventh century interrupted the development of Christian art but it continued later as practiced by Eastern Orthodox and Western Catholic churches.

The favoured medium for the fifth and sixth centuries was mosaics, especially in Rome, as seen in the apses of Santa Pudenziana and Santi Cosma e Damiano, the triumphal arch and nave walls of Santa Maria Maggiore, the nave walls of San Vitale and Sant'Apollinare in Classe in Ravenna, and the narthex of Hagia Sophia in Constantinople. Wall paintings still continued to be made during this period as they were simpler, less expensive and speedier to complete. Only fragments remain of the paintings from these

650. Santa Pudenziana, Rome. Christ in apse mosaic with a Latin inscription 'Dominus Conservator Ecclesiae Pudentianae' (The Lord Preserves the Church of Pudenziana)

651. SS Cosma e Damiano, Rome. SS Peter and Cosmas in the apse mosaic

652. SS Cosma e Damiano, Rome. A close-up of the figure of Christ in the centre of the apse mosaic

653. Santa Maria Maggiore, Rome. Figures before the temple at the meeting of the infant Jesus (upper right side of the triumphal arch mosaic)

654. Santa Maria Maggiore, Rome. The Virgin Mary close-up (upper right side of the triumphal arch mosaic)

655. Hagia Sophia, Constantinople. Inner narthex south entrance with the famous mosaic above the doorway of the emperor Justinian (left) presenting a model of the church to the enthroned Theotokos and emperor Constantine (right) presenting a model of the city of Constantinople

centuries in the churches of Rome compared to the number preserved in the darkness of the catacombs. Outside of Rome early Christian paintings in Palestine, Syria, Asia Minor and North Africa were destroyed by Moslem invaders. Some wall paintings, though, have survived in the Coptic monasteries of Egypt and in the Christian caves of Cappadocia.

Overthrow of the Images

By the end of the seventh century, certain images of saints had come to be viewed as 'windows' through which one could communicate with the figure depicted. The veneration of *acheiropoíeta*, or holy images 'not made by human hands', became a significant phenomenon. *Proskýnesis* or prostration before images is also attested in texts from the late seventh century. This type of veneration of icons by lighting candles and burning incense in front of them came under attack in the early eighth century. An intense debate developed over the proper role of art in worship.

At the Quinisext Ecumenical Council, or Council of Trullo as it is often called, held under Justinian II (r. 685–695) in 692 at Constantinople, canons were passed several of which were attempts to eliminate certain festivals and practices, many because there were regarded of pagan origin. Three canons related specifically to art: the prohibition of the representation of the cross on church pavements; Christ as a lamb; and 'pictures … which attract the eye and corrupt the mind, and incite it to the enkindling of base pleasures'. During the early part of the 720s some local bishops in Asia Minor began to ban religious images an action taken up by Emperor Leo III (r. 717–741) in 726. He issued an edict that condemned the making and veneration of icons as idolatry and as contrary to the second commandment. His son, Constantine V (r. 741–775), at the Council of Hieria in 754, fully launched the Iconoclastic movement in which the depiction of personal images in traditional Christian art of the previous five centuries or so was overthrown. This led to the removal of some earlier apse mosaics and destruction of portable icons.

An Iconoclast was literally one who attacked and sought to overthrow traditional ideas, that is, one who destroyed religious images, from the Greek word *eikonklastés*, icon breaker. In Iconoclastic art the cross became a frequent feature and the only representations allowed were animals, birds, plants and trees. The argument of the Iconoclasts was that because the Church Fathers had not left behind any prayer for the hallowing of images the painted representations implied heresy. They argued that the only permissible figure was Christ, whose body and blood were symbolized in the bread and wine of the Eucharist.

The monasteries became strongholds against Iconoclasm with monks organizing an underground network to support the veneration of icons. Prominent among the monks was John of Damascus, living in Syria, located in Muslim territory, and far enough away from the emperor not to suffer retribution. Defenders of the making and veneration of icons clashed fiercely with the Iconoclasts. There was a brief period of respite when the regent Eirene convened the Seventh Ecumenical Council, the second to be held in Nicaea, in 787 to

656. Hagia Eirene, Constantinople. Iconoclastic cross (Contemporary use as a concert hall)

657. Empress Theodora and Son Michael III. Presiding at the ceremony on the restoration of the icons

658. Christ. Monastery of St Catherine, Sinai

659. Theotokos. Monastery of St Catherine, Sinai

reverse the previous decrees. The Council did not accept the claims of the Iconoclasts and affirmed that veneration of icons was not worship but an honouring of a holy person through his or her image. At the same time the Council established a hierarchy of icons with Christ first, then that of the Theotokos ('Mother of God'), followed by angels, apostles, martyrs and other saints. Despite the decisions of the Council Iconoclasm revived in the early part of the ninth century. In 815 Leo V (r. 813–820) instituted a second period of Iconoclasm but in 843 the regent Theodora proclaimed the restoration of the icons at a new church Council. From 726 to 843 the Iconoclastic ban on icons led to large-scale destruction of icons particularly in Constantinople.

Triumphant Era
In 845 the final restoration of the icons came to be celebrated, and is still today in Eastern Orthodoxy, on the first Sunday of Lent as the Victory of the Icons. After the downfall of Iconoclasm, Christian spiritual art developed with great vitality. The first phase of the second golden age of Byzantine art emerged after the ban on icons was lifted and coincided with the advent of the new Macedonian dynasty (867–1056). The second phase began with the following Komnenoi dynasty (1081–1185) and the final flowering occurred during the Palaiologoi emperors (1259–1453). There was a temporary disruption when the Fourth Crusader's captured Constantinople in 1204. Artists fled the city to safe havens such as Crete and even further afield to Serbia and probably Bulgaria. With the Latin's sack of Constantinople, and even after the Byzantines retook Constantinople in 1261, a new dialog between Byzantine and Western art took place.

From the time of the Victory of the Icons Christian art in the Byzantine Empire was influenced largely by the monastic spirit that cultivated the study of ecclesiastical and apocryphal writings. Icon images came to be understood as a 'prototype'. Henceforth three basic principles of church decorations governed the development of iconography:

1. Persons and events must be clearly recognizable; the image must have a clear identity. They were to be identified by a title.
2. The image had to be presented frontally so that there could be a real meeting between the image and the beholder.
3. Each image had to occupy its proper place in the hierarchical order of precedence.

Between the tenth to the twelfth centuries spiritual art came to portray dogmas and was dominated by the ascetic ideals of the victorious monks. The dogma of the Theotokos as truly the Mother of God, formulated by the Council in Ephesus in 431, for example, came to be depicted in the half dome of the apse. From the thirteenth to the fifteenth centuries, narrative art took over in which compositions contained many persons and depicted psalms and hymns, such as the Akathistos Hymn, and scenes from the Apocrypha. Narrative art is highlighted in the fourteenth century by what is known as the Macedonian School (not to be confused with the Macedonian dynasty of emperors). By the end of the fourteenth century, artists in Crete began receiving commissions from Venetians to paint in the Western style. The Cretans quickly adapted the Latin approach, and developed the flexibility to create in Latin or Greek style as the assignment required. Cretan art was much prized throughout Europe and demand increased after the Fall of Constantinople in 1453. After the Fall the Cretan School of iconography persisted for about a century mainly in the monasteries.

Shortly before the middle of the sixteenth century there was an amazing surge in the building of new monasteries in Greece and Macedonia and the renovation of wall paintings in existing ones especially on Mount Athos. This was prompted by the combination of privileges granted to the monasteries by the Ottoman authorities and the generous sponsorship of Greek hierarchs and Balkan princes. The flowering of monasticism was supported by the cult of 'neo-martyrs', a new group of canonized martyrs who made a stand against the Ottoman practice of forcing Christians to convert to Islam and also represented a

660. Macedonian style. The Theotokos bordered by scenes illustrating the 24 stanzas of the Akathistos Hymn. Monastery of Sission, Kefalonia

661. Cretan style. Koimisis tis Theotokou. Candia, Crete. Likely first work of Domenikos Theotokopoulos (El Greco)

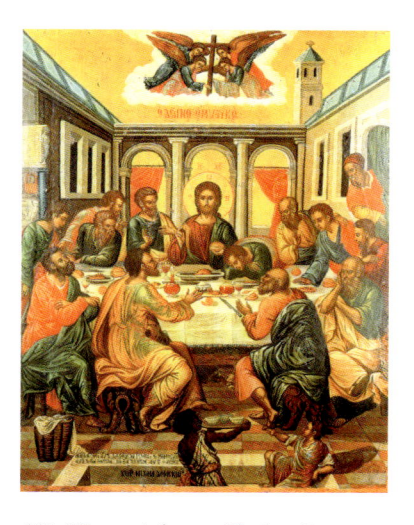

662. Western influence. The Last Supper painted by Michael Damaskinos

663. Ionian School, Kefalonia. Theotokos *Phaneroméni* painted by G. Matsoukas

664. Ionian School, Monastery of Sission, Kefalonia. Theotokos and Christ Child painted by Stephanos Tzankarolas

665. Ionian School, Kefalonia. Theotokos – detail from a portable icon

renewed interest in asceticism and religious fervor. The Orthodox Church allotted equal rank to the neo-martyrs to that of the established saints of the early years of the Christian era.

Westernization then Revival
After the loss of Constantinople to the Ottoman Turks in 1453 iconographers and others fled to places held by the Venetians, such as Crete and the Ionian Islands, and Venice itself. Crete became an

important centre of art production in the eastern Mediterranean as the Byzantine Empire declined and was renowned for the technical perfection and style of its icons. With the domination of the Near East and Greece by the Turks the traditional approach to iconography continued in isolated pockets and also in the Balkans and Russia. In Romania at the end of the fifteenth century, for example, Stephen the Great marked each of his 46 victories over invading Turks and others by constructing monasteries and churches with interiors adorned by works of Byzantine artists whose vivid murals are still stunning today. The main developments, however, occurred in Venetian held territory and Italy where Byzantine, now Eastern Orthodox iconography, was influenced by copying western models of the Renaissance. Copper engravings of western artists circulated widely during the Ottoman occupation and influenced church art.

In the Venetian-held Ionian Islands off the west coast of Greece, the settlement there of the greatest Cretan icon painters along with the multitude of portable icons that the refugees brought with them fleeing Turkish occupied Crete made a decisive contribution to the development of painting in the second half of the seventeenth century. In these Islands, above all in Zakynthos, in the eighteenth century, the merging of the Cretan school of painting and Western artistic trends culminated in the 'Ionian School' of religious painting. New subjects such as the scenes from the Old Testament appeared, but depicted naturally, as did non-religious themes in the work of painters of this school.

Following the Greek Revolution and independence from the Turks in the nineteenth century, lithographs from the West especially from Italy flooded Greece. In this context the thrust in religious painting was to 'correct' old Byzantine models on the basis of European art. Byzantine works, particularly in the main churches of Athens, were altered to be more 'natural' in terms of anatomy, perspective and other creative principles. This followed the artistic trend in the West, where since the Renaissance paintings had become increasingly naturalistic and realistic with the introduction of perspective. The contrast between the new approach of life-like Western religious images and traditional symbolic Eastern Christian figures became very sharp. In the 1850s King Otto, a Bavarian prince and the first monarch of a newly independent Greece, brought to Athens the German painter Ludwig Thiersch who introduced 'Nazarene' painting into Greece. The Nazarene movement that began in Vienna in the early nineteenth century created religious paintings in Italian Renaissance style combined with attributes from the contemporary movements of Neo-Classicism and Romanticism. Some Greek painters, however, such as Spyridon Chatzigiannopoulos, attempted to strike a balance between Nazarene art and traditional Byzantine painting.

666. The iconographer Fotis Kontoglou. St John the Theologian, Byzantine and Christian Museum Athens

In the early twentieth century the return to traditional Byzantine art began with Kostis Parthenis, a teacher at the School of Fine Arts in Athens who strongly influenced the next generation of artists such as Fotis Kontoglou. During the years between the two World Wars many artists went to Mount Athos to immerse themselves in that unchanging Byzantine world and study and copy the artistic treasures there. By the middle of the twentieth century more and more scholars and artists began to return to the traditional models, not only in Greece but in Europe and America. Following the fall of communism in 1998 wall paintings and mosaics in the Balkans and Russia are being cleaned and restored.

667. Narthex with wall paintings looking at the Beautiful Gate beyond. Church at Milopotamos, Mount Athos

668. Dome of the *katholikon,* Monastery of St Nicholas Anapafsis, Meteora. Christ Pantokrator

669. Apse semi-dome, Cathedral of Cefalu. Christ Pantokrator mosaic begun after 1145 by Byzantine masters from Constantinople with Greek and Latin inscriptions

670. Apse semi-dome, Cappella Palatina. Christ Pantokrator blessing in the Byzantine manner (somewhat) with a closed Gospels book, a twelfth-century mosaic

The Decorative Scheme

During the tenth and eleventh centuries the interior of the church came to be conceived as an image of the cosmos and a coherent scheme developed for the decoration of its spaces. In a traditional Byzantine church the images were arranged according to a scheme that began with the entrance to the church, the narthex, continued into the naos and culminated in the sacred bema. Accordingly, spiritual art in Byzantine churches is interrelated and organized according to the theology of the Eastern Orthodox Church, in contrast to Western churches where religious paintings that decorate the church are often unrelated with each other.

The major decoration in the narthex is over the main entrance doors, known as the Royal Doors (*Vasíleion Pýlin*), that lead into the naos. The most usual depiction is a bust of Christ as Teacher blessing with his right hand and holding a Gospels book in his left hand. On the open page of the book the most common written statement is from John. This is either 'I am the door. By me if any man enter in he shall be saved' or 'I am the light of the world. He that followeth me shall not walk in darkness but shall have the light of life' (John 10:9; 8:12). Other parts of the narthex are decorated with events from the life of the Theotokos, or Christian martyrs, or individual saints. Occasionally there may be a depiction of visions from Daniel or the Book of Revelations. From the thirteenth century onward it became customary to depict the seven ecumenical councils in the narthex. In the fourteenth century a new representation, the Last Judgment, was added as an image either in the narthex or side chapels.

The naos of a non-basilican type Byzantine church is dominated by a large dome that hovers over the middle of the space. In the centre of the dome is the figure of Christ as representing the *Pantokrator* (Ruler of All, the Almighty). The figure expresses the whole Christian theology of creation, salvation and judgment with the Pantokrator as Creator, Saviour and Judge. The image of a stern Christ as judge above sets up the space of the church below as a courtroom for judgment of the congregants. The figure of the Pantokrator is the largest and most impressive of all the images in the church and dominates the entire interior space. The image of Christ is rendered artistically possessing royal magnificence, active goodness and impartial austerity. He is shown in bust form, enclosed by a multicoloured circle, with a halo behind his head, holding a Gospels book in his left hand while blessing with his right hand. Sometimes Christ is supported by cherubim and seraphim or a procession of angelic deacons. In an outer ring beyond Christ and at the edge of the dome, or on the supporting drum if there is one, are the prophets such as Moses, David and Solomon. In some central domes there is an image of the Ascension instead of the Pantokrator. In that case the figures in the ring are the apostles instead of the prophets. Often there are windows in the dome or drum to provide natural light into the interior. The figures of the prophets or apostles then are placed between the openings, parallel to the windows, and symbolize sources of spiritual illumination as well as intermediaries between God in heaven and humanity on earth below. In some earlier churches the Pantokrator image was located in the semi-dome of the bema apse instead in the central naos dome.

On each of the four triangular curved surfaces, the pendentives, below the dome or drum, it is usual to depict one of the four evangelists. By custom Matthew and John are on the bema side, Matthew on the north pendentive and John on the south pendentive, while Mark and Luke are on the narthex side, Mark on the north and Luke on the south pendentive. They are presented seated, engaged in writing, and sometimes with their winged symbols: Matthew by a winged man, an angel; Mark by a winged lion, a figure of courage; Luke by a winged ox or bull, figures of strength and sacrifice; and John by an eagle, a figure of the sky that was believed to be able to look straight into the sun.

There are usually three parallel bands of wall paintings on the walls of the naos. On the upper band are depicted the Twelve Great Festivals (the *Dodekaórton*), in the middle band are the miracles and parables of Christ, and on the lower band individual saints and martyrs. Sometimes on this lower band there are also scenes from the life of a particular saint, perhaps the saint in whose honour the church is dedicated. The Twelve Great Festivals are the Annunciation, the Nativity, the Presentation of Christ in the Temple, the Baptism, the Metamorphosis (Transfiguration), the Raising of Lazarus, the Entrance into Jerusalem, the Crucifixion, the Resurrection, the Ascension, Pentecost and the *Koímisis* (Dormition) of the Theotokos. The back or west wall of the naos usually contains the Koimisis of the Theotokos whose life might be depicted also in the aisles, side-chambers, or in the narthex.

After the Pantokrator the most dominant image in the interior of the church is the Theotokos as *Platytéra*, which takes up the entire half dome of the bema apse. Her full name is actually *Platytéra ton Ouranón* or 'She who is wider than the Heavens', and she looks out above the Holy Table into the naos. She is shown either with only the upper part of her body with arms outstretched in prayer and the Christ child against her chest or as an entire figure enthroned with the Christ child in her lap. He is clothed in a magnificent gold robe and unlike an ordinary infant sits upright in his mother's lap as if on a throne. The holy child blesses with his right hand and holds a scroll in his left, or blesses with both hands. The Theotokos is no ordinary mother. She is seated on a throne and adorned regally with three gold stars embroidered upon her, one on each of the two shoulders and one above her forehead. Her gaze is outward to the faithful and not down at her child. Often the Theotokos is flanked on either side by the archangels Michael and Gabriel. In a domed church the floor symbolizes earth and the large dome heaven which are spatially united by the half dome of the apse. As it contains the image of the Theotokos she is regarded as the one who unites the upper world of heaven with the lower level of the earth by means of the divine child in her arms.

671. Festival icon. Four of the 12 Festival icons depicting the Annunciation, Baptism, Ascension and Koimisis tis Theotokou (from top left in anti-clockwise direction)

On the back wall of the apse, below the *Platytera* but visible above the Holy Table, the images are arranged in tiers. Immediately below the *Platytera* is a depiction of the Divine Liturgy with Christ clad in episcopal vestments and assisted by angels who are dressed as deacons. The arrangement includes the book of Gospels resting on the Holy Table, which is covered by a canopy, the ciborium. Holy Communion is represented by a paten and chalice on the Holy Table. Christ assisted by the two angel-deacons is shown offering the sacred elements to his disciples, on one side the consecrated bread and on the other from the chalice. Generally Peter is head of the group receiving the bread and Paul the other group receiving the wine. This painted setting mirrors the actual ceremony that takes place in the holy bema. Depicted in the lower tier of the back wall of the apse, facing the Holy Table, are the great fathers of the church in episcopal robes: St Basil the Great, St Gregory Nazianzus, St John Chrysostom, St Athanasios the Great and others. These great hierarchs with their liturgical scrolls are considered the editors of the

672. Bema apse. Hosios Loukas, Stiris. *Katholikon* looking east

Divine Liturgy. Rendered in three-quarter stance and with light coloured vestments against a receding blue background the impression given is that the painted celebrants appear to emerge and assist the clergy as they move around the Holy Table.

On the north side of the bema is the prothesis chamber or space where the Eucharistic bread and wine are prepared. The usual symbolic images in the prothesis are of the birth, death or burial of Christ. Sometimes the Divine Liturgy is depicted in the prothesis instead of below the *Platytera*.

673. Prothesis. Metropolis, Mystras. Holy hierarchs Babylas and Anthimos

674. Diaconicon vault. Metropolis, Mystras. Preparation of the Throne

The chamber or space on the south side of the bema, the diaconicon or sacristy, is often decorated with one of two images – Daniel in the Lions' Den or the Three Hebrews in the Fiery Furnace.

Between the naos and the bema there was initially a wooden or marble screen, the templon, but later when adorned with icons became known as the iconostasis. By the fourteen century the iconostasis assumed the form it has today. At the beginning the templon was a simple railing then developed as a colonnade with curtains. When images were added later they were confined to the horizontal beam. Then, when images began

675. Diaconicon apse semi-dome. Metropolis, Mystras. Christ the Merciful

to be placed between the columns it became the iconostasis (literally icon-stand). At first it was a low structure but over time increased in height and sometimes reached the ceiling of the church. Both templon and iconostasis are pierced by double doors in the centre. In long screens single doors area added at either end. The central doors in the iconostasis are referred to as The Beautiful Gate (*H Oraía Pýle*). The Annunciation is usually represented on the lower part of the hinged doors (*vemothýra*). In its taller form the decoration of the iconostasis is arranged in tiers just as are those images on the naos and apse walls. Typically, there are two tiers of icons on the iconostasis, a lower tier of large icons and an upper tier of smaller ones. The lower tier always includes the icons of Christ and the Theotokos holding the Christ child. The icon of Christ invariably flanks the right or south side of The Beautiful Gate while the Theotokos icon is always placed on the left or north side of the Gate. These two images are known as the Sovereign or *Despotikaí* icons. There may be additional images depending on the length of the iconostasis. The first of these would be the icon of St John the Forerunner who is placed next to Christ. The second would be an icon depicting the sacred person, persons or sacred event celebrated by the church and is in most cases is set next to that of the Theotokos. The figures of St John and the Theotokos are shown in a three-quarter stance pointed toward Christ indicating their role as intercessors for the faithful with Christ. If there are even more images these would be the images of the archangels mounted on the side doorways at either end of the iconostasis with Michael on the south door and Gabriel on the north door. In a very long iconostasis other icons would be included on the lower tier of the icon screen. The upper tier images are events in the life of Christ with the Last Supper immediately above The Beautiful Gate. It there is a third tier this would consist of smaller icons comprising representations of either the Twelve Apostles or the 12 Great Festivals. If there is a fourth tier it would contain the prophets with the Theotokos and the Christ child in the centre. Should the iconostasis not reach the ceiling then above the Beautiful Gate at the top of the iconostasis there is usually a cross with the figure of Christ crucified. Depicted on panels on the right side of the crucifix there is the Theotokos and on the left that of St John the Theologian.

Although the main concentration of images in the form of wood panels is on the iconostasis, icons are displayed in many places in a Byzantine church. Special panel icons are placed on a *proskynetárion* or icon stand and except in small chapels there is at least one with the icon of the sacred person, persons or sacred event to whom the church is dedicated. The special icon is usually contained in an elaborately decorated frame, and the *proskynetárion* on which it is displayed is always prominently located as the image is regarded as possessing a sacred power. In addition, there are often panel icons attached to the walls in various parts of the church.

676. Synthronon symbolism. Pentecost – sitting on the synthronon are the apostles in hierarchical order. Peter heads one group (left) followed by the evangelists Matthew and Luke (each holding a Gospel book), then Simon, Bartholomew and Philip; Paul heads the other group (right) followed by the evangelists John (a young man) and Mark (each holding a Gospel book), then Andrew, James and Thomas. Symbolism in the scene includes the rays of light above the groups that represent the Holy Spirit; the empty space between the groups the Teacher who has ascended to the heavens; and the aged king beneath them who personifies the world and who holds 12 papers wrapped in a cloth that denote the preaching carried by the 12 apostles to all the nations

There are many variations on the typical theme. For example, in basilican church plans, ones without a central dome, the *Platytera* would be replaced by the Pantokrator image. Then again the iconostasis can be very elaborate with many tiers. Another variation it that the general three zone scheme is in the narthex, naos and bema can differ according to the size of the church, with fewer representations in a smaller church, whether it is basilica or cross-in-square shape, the period in which it was decorated, and the region in which it was built. Before the tenth century there was quite a variation of schemes but after this century a definite order for the arrangement of holy figures in the church was established and this still remains in place today in Eastern Orthodox churches. The scheme represents the dogmatic cycle of Christ as Teacher at the entrance to the church, the Pantokrator in the dome, and the Theotokos in the holy bema.

677. Iconostasis. *Katholikon*, Monastery of St Catherine, Sinai

678. Iconostasis *despotikaí* icons. *Katholikon*, Hosios Loukas, Stiris

679. Iconostasis Beautiful Gate. St Stephen, Meteora

680. Miraculous panel icon. St Nicholas, *Katholikon*, Monastery of Stavronikata

681. Triumphal arch. San Lorenzo Fuori le Mura, Rome

Iconography

Iconography is the study of the themes along with the subject matter, stylization, symbols and media used in the decorative scheme. When the image is referred to as an icon strictly speaking this refers to a sacred image painted on a portable wood panel. In Greek the word icon (*eikon*) means image, likeness or representation. An icon is a symbol of a prototype or original which it represents and provides a means to go from the material world to the spiritual one, from the visible to the invisible. As St John Damascene remarked 'we are led by the perceptible icons to the contemplation of the divine and spiritual.' Icons are considered as lifting the faithful to a higher level of feeling and thought evoking a spiritual experience. They also instruct in matters relevant to the Christian faith, for example the life of Christ as the visual form is more vivid than the written one as avowed by St Photios, patriarch of Constantinople (858–867 and 877–886), and widely regarded as the most important intellectual of his time. Icons, in addition, wrote Niketas Stethatos an eleventh-century monk and theologian, beautify the church as they 'embellish like a bride'.

Subject Matter / Themes during the Early Christian and Byzantine Eras

Palace art initially influenced spiritual art in, for example, the stiffness of expression and stillness that typified later Christian representations. The purpose of the artist was to convey the elevated status of the emperor and his officials, clad in court dress, and their divine grace. There was also the style of official imperial portraits that came to influence Christian images. Imperial portraits were not meant to be portraits of individuals but rather of a person who held grand office. Likewise Christian portraits of saints and martyrs were not meant to be true portraits but depicting certain features attributed to the individual. As in antiquity these portraits were often enclosed within a circular medallion.

Prototypes of Christian figures were transpositions of Roman dignitaries – Christ and his mother, especially when enthroned, stemmed from portraits of emperors and empresses, and the apostles from those of consuls. The ancient tradition of venerating certain portraits passed into Christian hands in the form of reverence to their benefactors. About the year 400, at the time Christian art suddenly bloomed, portraits of Christ, the apostles or martyrs became more common and were venerated not commemoratively but religiously. Until the tenth century the early images of the Resurrection of Christ did not depict the actual event as this did not accord with the testimony of the evangelists. In keeping with the Gospels the resurrection was portrayed by the testimony of Mary Magdalene and Mary, the Mother of Jesus, or the conversation between them and the angel.

682. Portrait. Emperor Constantine

Christians used symbolic art in the first two centuries to decorate their tombs and the catacombs in Rome. In an era of intolerance of Christianity by Roman authorities, Christians hid the true meaning of their imagery in allegories or symbols. Common symbols used by early Christians were the dove as a sign of peace, the fish and shepherd as representing Christ, the peacock to denote the resurrection, the anchor to represent salvation followed by a safe arrival at the gates of heaven, and other symbols. Christ when depicted as the Good Shepherd carrying the lamb meant that he was saving a Christian soul. In pagan Roman art the figure of the shepherd carrying the lamb was a symbol of benevolence. The Theotokos is often depicted with three stars, one on her forehead and one on each shoulder to signify her perpetual virginity. The use of allegorical works continued for some time but was renounced at the Council of Trullo in 692 as the precise meanings of the allegories were difficult to define. They were abandoned in favour of representing the truth and from the end of the seventh century onward allegories were abandoned in Eastern Christian iconography. Inscriptions were to be added so that images might not be misunderstood or remain unknown.

683. Christ and his Mother

From the early Christian paintings that have survived it can be said that they seem to have followed a consistent pattern lasting about two centuries until about 395 (the separation of the Eastern and Western Roman Empires). Themes in art works up to that time were uniform throughout the Empire and appear to be confined to selected Christian doctrinal subjects. There was further

684. Scene of the Good Shepherd. Mosaic, Mausoleum of Galla Placidia, Ravenna

685. Symbol of the Good Shepherd. Mosaic, Cathedral of Bishop Theodore, Aquileia

686. Early Christian symbol, the *Chi Rho*. Grave of the Good Shepherd, Thessaloniki

687. Christian symbols: the anchor, fish and *Chi Rho*. Catacomb of San Sebastiano, Rome

688. Tree of Life. Apse mosaic, San Clemente, Rome

689. Three stars on the Theotokos image

uniformity in that artists, although spread out through the Empire, used the same imagery that would indicate there may have been some prescribed rules. Christian paintings of the fifth and sixth centuries in Rome began to show two new trends: one classical as a continuation of the imperial era, and the other more schematic with emphatic outlines and flat surfaces which were the more dominant. Good surviving examples of the schematic paintings are those in the chapels of the Coptic monasteries at Bawit and Sakkara in Egypt.

The decorative scheme had from the beginning a hierarchy of saints and saintly bishops. Ranking of saints was influenced by Roman and Greek models that grouped philosophers, ancestors and government officials. The first rank created in Christian art was the apostles and martyrs. Bishops appeared as 'ancestors' of the local church but also figure among the martyrs. When the image of Christ appeared in the apse he always had a central place but with a changing emphasis from universal emperor to universal father. In the fourth century the pictures adapted imperial imagery, for example the court of heaven was visualized as corresponding to the imperial court. At first the expectation was that the second coming of Christ would not be long delayed. As this hope receded it became clear that further divine intervention was needed. The Theotokos was adopted for this role and as early as the seventh century the *Theotokos Paráklesis* was represented. In addition, the intercession of saints became more important. From the ninth century onwards two chapels or spaces were regularly constructed on either side of the central apse; the prothesis and the diaconicon as the liturgy rite became more elaborate. With the decoration of these apses or spaces came a transformation of the apse decorative programmes.

The fourth-century apse programme of San Vitale in Ravenna and the mid-eleventh-century programme in Hagia Sophia in Ohrid provide a good depiction of the official imagery of the Byzantine Church. Both programmes focus on the relationship between the faithful and Christ. From the middle of the eleventh century there was a rapid development of the apse programme that began to feature Eucharistic scenes. By the eleventh century the decorative programme took on a specifically liturgical character. In the fourteenth century Patriarch Philotheos combined together previous ideas and wrote a book about them titled the *Diataxis*. With the introduction of printing and the ease of making copies his work became the authoritative text on decorative themes.

Approaches to Byzantine Art
Various influences shaped Byzantine art. At first these were Hellenistic concepts of idealism, balance and elegance, Syrian oriental expressionism, and the doctrines of the Christian church. The early Christians adapted Late Antiquity art to express themes from the Old and New Scriptures. An important aspect of this art was that of portraiture that became of great importance in the Eastern Christian tradition. It is probable that the early Christians painted portraits of distinguished and venerated members. It was not uncommon for portraits to be enclosed within a medallion, garlanded with flowers and having candles burnt in front of them. By the beginning of the fifth-century portraits of saints survived to become portable icons. Portraits of Christ were rare early on and if he was shown he was depicted seated among the apostles, a classical arrangement of a teacher surrounded by a group of learned men.

Byzantine art arose primarily in the capital city Constantinople and from there this manner of art spread throughout the Empire and then beyond its borders. Hand in hand with an order of arrangement of holy images established in the tenth century was the development of a traditional style of showing figures and events. Until the thirteenth century icons portrayed mainly single figures but from that century onwards an increasing number of sacred events were illustrated.

Two remarkable approaches emerged in the thirteenth and fourteenth centuries known as the Macedonian and Cretan schools of painting. These terms are used for convenience as the approaches did not originate in the area denoted by them and nor were confined to Macedonia or Crete. The Macedonian School built upon the traditional approach but differed by stressing Hellenistic idealism, colours, and landscapes. Human figures tended to be more natural but with idealistic characteristics. Colours were kept light with no sharp contrast between light and shade. The folds in the garments were made simple. As landscapes are not suited to panels the approach was used mainly to decorate large surfaces. Although the School grew up in Constantinople the centre was Thessaloniki, the second largest city of the Byzantium Empire. The approach of the Macedonian School spread and was more evident later in Mount Athos, the Balkans, and Mystras, the Byzantine city in the midst of Frankish Peloponnese. The Macedonian School petered out by the end of the sixteenth century, losing its original approach as it began to include more folk or popular elements.

690. Macedonian style icon. Crucifixion of St Andrew

The Cretan School followed the traditional approach more closely with tall and narrow human figures, closely repeated folds in the garments, dark colours, and sharp contrasts of light and shade. The School seems to have also originated in Constantinople, but later than the Macedonian style, and similarly spread to the Balkans and Greece with Mystras becoming the important centre. In the second half of the fourteenth century the style spread to Crete, Mount Athos and Meteora. As the Cretan style was suitable for both panels and wall painting it survived after the Fall of Constantinople in 1453 and became the dominant style of painting in the Eastern Orthodox Church. In the eighteenth and nineteenth centuries the influence of Western ideas such as naturalness, anatomical detail, physical beauty, perspective and the use of oil colours led to a break in Byzantine tradition. In the late twentieth century a revival has taken place with a significant return to the traditional style of icon painting.

691. Cretan style icon. Prophet Elijah, Monastery of St Catherine, Sinai

Stylization in Byzantine Art
Disregard of the material world by the artist and focus on the spiritual realm was manifested in many ways. The stiffness and gestures of the figures, their lack of apparent weight, no real contact with the ground, and the schematic space surrounding figures, were unlike real life. Bodies as a whole did not appear with lively movements and the face was shown forward. To achieve lifting thought and feeling to a spiritual reality beyond the physical, the Christian painters resorted to a type of distortion. A primary means of distortion was in the proportions of a figure or parts of the figure. The body was often elongated to 'dematerialize' it. The head may be depicted disproportionally large so that the face may be seen more distinctly. Eyes were shown larger than normal, sometimes almond-shaped, and animated as they have seen great things. Large, wide-open eyes were presumed to reveal the innermost being of the holy person since eyes were regarded as 'mirrors of the soul'. Ears were large so as to hear God's commandments and the nose was made rather thin, as it was not meant to smell things of the world but smell the fragrance of incorruption.

The mouth was shaped small to indicate that food and drink were to be limited and only that necessary for preservation was to be taken in. Smallness of the mouth was an indication of spirituality, of a bodily state materially not in need of food.

The sensory organs of the eyes, ears, nose and mouth were not rendered naturally or anatomically then but stylized as organs of the spirit that have been changed through having sensed and received divine revelation. Hands and feet were also stylized and not rendered naturally. Fingers were shown thin and elongated to present an external expression of the transfigured state of a saint whose senses have been spiritualized. Often fingers were disproportionately large, expressive of spiritual intensity. Sometimes the blessing right hand was made the same size as the head to signify that it was not a mere gesture but an expression of grace. The hands of Christ were usually shown large to signify tremendous power. The index finger of St John the Forerunner was also large pointing to an important person figure, the figure of Christ approaching, coming to be baptized. Legs were usually shown very slender with a hollowness of the soles of the feet with long toes, or sometimes flat-footed with a curved heel.

The right hand of Christ is shown blessing in one of two ways. In the first way the last two fingers touch the thumb that symbolize the Trinity while the forefinger and middle fingers are extended to signify his two natures, the human and the divine. In the second form of blessing the forefinger is extended straight, the middle finger curved slightly, the thumb and the ring finger are crossed, and the little finger curved slightly. This gesture forms the first and last Greek letters of the two words for Jesus Christ, **I C X C** (Ιησοῦς Χριστός, with C as the old letter for the later Σ formed by the curved fingers).

In pagan art the gesture of a figure with both arms raised symmetrically signified piety (*pietas; evséveia*). Christian art adopted the gesture, known as the *orant*, and it became a favourite way of expressing a figure in prayer or of bearing witness that accompanies the taking of an oath. In the paintings of the catacombs the gesture at first symbolized piety but was adapted later to show a pious person in a funerary portrait. Eventually the *orant* gesture was retained only for the portraits of martyrs, saints and especially in the various images of the Theotokos. In later Christian art the gesture was confused with benediction and thus retained a lasting place in religious works.

Along with the use of the frontal pose in Byzantine art the heads of holy persons and saints were encircled with a crown of light regarded as the centre of the spirit, thought and understanding. The crown, the halo, was represented as a light disk, usually gold or yellow in colour that helped to emphasize the face and meant to be seen as a radiance emitted from within. Missing from very early Christian representations the halo only later came to be a regular feature. A saintly person still living would have a square halo known as a nimbus. In Byzantine art holiness was indicated not only by the crown of light but by the entire form.

692. Elongated figures. The three hierarchs: SS Gregory, John Chrysostom and Basil (left to right)

693. Stylized facial features. Icon of St Basil

694. Christ blessing with his right-hand in the Byzantine manner and open Gospels book with an inscription in Greek

695. Orant. Theotokos, Lateran Baptistery, Rome

696. Halo. Icon of Moses, Monastery of St Catherine, Sinai

697. Nimbus. Pope Paschal in apse mosaic, Santa Prassede, Rome

698. Garment depiction. Two saints, Hosios Loukas, Stiris

Garments were also presented unrealistically as they were meant to project or signify spiritual bodies covered by them. Simple garment folds and their wider overlaps were not represented naturally and in some cases did not correspond to the covered members of the bodies. This was deliberate and not a sign of artistic inability. In earlier works the convention was that folding of the garments was to be in the form of vertical lines, often parallel, of a darker colour than the garment. Later the flat appearance of the clothes gave way to folds that were well curved and in relief somewhat resembling the draping garments on ancient Greek statues.

The anti-realistic lighting contributed to the spiritual grace of the clothing. Lighting was usually a whitish or a rose colour, lighter in tone than the colour of the garment, or sometimes a complementary colour placed in diagonal shapes or in spots at prominent points. Calculated lighting contributed to conveying the radiance of the spiritual world and along with careful colouring of garments contributed to the ethereal and transcendent characteristic of Byzantine spiritual images. Choice of colour was deliberate, with delicate shades of red, blue and green for the garments of Christ and the Theotokos, while the shades were less pronounced for other sacred persons. Jesus Christ mostly wears a reddish tunic and a bluish cloak, colours that signify his two natures, human and divine. On the Theotokos the colours are reversed with a bluish tunic to indicate the divine nature of Jesus whom she bore and the warm burgundy or brown cloak her humanness. Gold was chiefly used in the garments of Christ and purple only for imperial robes. Colour and form were merely a means to express a sublime meaning. White equates to heavenly glory, and paradise, black to death, green to the Holy Spirit and eternal life, red to life, blood, suffering, and martyrdom, and blue to revelation and heavenly wisdom. As St John Chrysostom acknowledged the goodness of an object was not from its colour and form alone but the 'service it renders'.

699. Mountains and trees. Meeting of Christ and John the Forerunner

Figures were surrounded by space which like the figures was not represented realistically. A city, buildings, mountains and trees were depicted abstractly with no attempt to imitate faithfully the physical world. As the emphasis was on the sacred person the mountains, trees, rocks or buildings in the background were always secondary to the holy figure. Mountains were depicted stair-like, stylized with sheer, sharp rocks intensified at the peaks. A city may be denoted by a few simple buildings surrounded by a fortification wall. A tree was represented by a trunk with a few branches. The relationship of a person to the surrounding space typically was not logical or correct according to the laws of perspective but was meant to be symbolic. Space was reduced to a minimum and spatial depth, natural light and colours were suppressed. Like a vision figures were depicted as two-dimensional with non-natural, mystical, colours. Human emotions such as grief and horror, such as in the crucifixion of Christ in some Western art, were replaced in Byzantine art by heavenly calm and grandeur.

In compositions the concern was to avoid natural reality to emphasize the spiritual realm. In scenes where there were many persons the figures and objects lying further away were drawn larger than the ones nearer which were drawn smaller. This was in fact reverse perspective. Also, a person or event of greater significance was presented on a larger scale than the other persons or events regardless of position in the composition. When two or more events that took place at different times were depicted and shown in one scene, the separate incidents were separated by folds in the ground. From the thirteenth century onward figures were portrayed more realistically with hierarchs, prophets, and saints as revered old men with strong wrinkles on their faces, expressive eyes, dense eye-brows, curved noses and heavy beards. Figures also were given more ample gestures and movement.

Inscriptions
Visual images were enriched with an inscription which identified the person represented, or the subject of the scene depicted, or was a quotation and fragment from gospel texts. In early Christian art inscriptions were rare as secret symbols recognizable only by those initiated into the faith were used.

700. Inscription IC XC. A Christ Pantokrator icon

701. Inscription O ΩN. Christ 'the One who Is'

After the Victory of the Icons in 843 one of the three basic principles of church decorations was, in part, that persons and events were to be identified by a title. From then on it became standard for an inscription to be added to denote the saint or event depicted. To ensure the aesthetic integration of inscriptions into images they were treated as decorative features and part of the usually symmetrical composition. Some inscriptions were abbreviated and became symbolic signs or mysterious seals, particularly those that accompany Christ or the Theotokos. This is in contrast to religious paintings of the West that regarded inscriptions in naturalistic art as unnecessary or out of place.

Before the Iconoclastic period, the images of Christ may be divided into three groups. The first group, which is the most common, consists of images of Christ, alone or with others, with no inscription. This first group is exemplified by the famous sixth-century icon of Christ at St Catherine in the Sinai. The inscription seen today on the image is a later addition. In the second much rarer group the images of Christ incorporate one of a small range of inscriptions. The most frequent inscription in the second group, AΩ, is a title rather than identifying a name. The reference is to Christ as the alpha and omega, the beginning and the end, as written in *Revelations* (1.8 and 1.17–18). This inscription can be seen in the ninth-century apse mosaic in the church of San Marco in Rome. In the third group Christ is depicted with others and everyone except Christ has a naming inscription. Christ does not need an inscription to be identified whereas the other individuals in the image do. One example is on the sixth-century triumphal arch in San Lorenzo fuori le Mura in Rome.

In the tenth century after the Triumph of the Icons the images of Christ increasingly came to be inscribed with IC XC, in which the IC are the first and last letters of Jesus' name in Greek (*I* ουσό *C*) and the XC the first and last letters of the Christ's name (*X* ριστό *C*). The letter C is the old form of the letter Σ (S). The significance of the inscription is that Jesus was his name as man and Christ as the anointed one – the inseparable union of his human and divine natures, according to Justin Martyr and others. Images of Christ sometimes contain the inscription ΙΧΘΥΣ, which in Greek means fish, an early Christian symbol for Christ himself. The word is derived from the first letters of the expression *Ιεσούς Χριστός Θεού Υίου Σοτήρ* – Jesus Christ Son of God and Saviour. On the halo of Christ traditionally there are three Greek letters, *O ΩN* or *o ων*, literally 'the One Who Is'.

This is an allusion to 'I Am Who I Am' the words God spoke to Moses and an indication that Jesus Christ and his Father are One. In the tenth century the icons of Mary, mother of Jesus, began to be inscribed as ΜΗΤΗΡ ΘΕΟΥ (Mother of God) rather than Η ΑΓΙΑ ΜΑΡΙΑ (St Mary), even though she had been proclaimed Theotokos in 431. Most often on the images of the Theotokos the inscription is a pair of Greek letters, *MP* and *ΘY*. These represent the first and last letters of two words, ΜΗΤΗΡ ΘΕΟΥ, Mother of God. When texts are included it is usually either of a hymn, or a quote from scripture, or perhaps a writing or prayer associated with the saint depicted on the icon.

In the Christian world the longevity of interest in Mary, mother of Jesus Christ, in Rome is unrivalled. The earliest surviving image of her anywhere is a mural in the Catacomb of Priscilla dated to the second quarter of the third century. Her name was given to the imposing basilica of Santa Maria Maggiore constructed by Pope Sixtus III (r. 432–440) and her image lavishly dressed in court costume was prominent in mosaic decorations of the time. Her artistic glorification reached its peak in her image called *Maria Regina*, with crown and purple robes of the empress of Byzantium that appeared in many churches in Rome during the fifth and following four centuries, such as on the triumphal arches in Santa Maria Maggiore, Santa Maria Cosmedin and Santa Maria in Trastevere. In another church dedicated to her in Rome, Santa Maria Antiqua, she is shown as *Maria Regina*, elevated to the status of queen of heaven. In the composition the portrait of the sponsor, Pope Hadrian I (r. 772–795), with a nimbus (square halo), is included at the far left.

In Byzantine spiritual art Theotokos images are often inscribed with an epithet or title the most common of which is *Hodegétria, Eleoúsa* or *Glykophiloúsa*. In each case the poses of the Theotokos and the Christ child, the inclination of their heads, and the position of their hands follow general rules. Each artist introduced his own minor variations such as in the dress and halos, but never to the extent that the faithful would not clearly recognize the Theotokos type whether there was an inscription or not. In the *Theotokos Hodegétria* the Christ child is held on the left arm of the Theotokos. She gazes out benevolently to the worshipper, hears his or her prayers and passes them on to her son as depicted by her right hand that is raised in front of her and pointing toward him. This gesture is meant to indicate that Christ is the only way to salvation and provides the stem of the name *Hodegétria* (literally 'The Guide' or 'The Instructress'). Christ is depicted in a frontal position, blessing with his outstretched right hand while his left holds a closed scroll resting upon his knee. The *Theotokos Eleoúsa* ('Compassionate') is depicted in half-length holding the Christ child

702. Inscription MP ΘY. Theotokos ivory panel, Utrecht

703. Maria Regina. Regal Theotokos in apse mosaic, Santa Maria in Trastevere, Rome

704. Theotokos *Hodegétria*    705. Theotokos *Eleoúsa*    706. Theotokos *Glykophiloúsa*

on her left arm. Her left hand gently touches the shoulder of the child whose cheek touches that of his mother while he holds a scroll with both hands. This Theotokos type was well known before the Iconoclastic period after which it became better known as the *Glykophiloúsa* (literally 'Sweet-Kissing' but translated as "Tenderness'). Although their cheeks touch, their heads inclined to one another, their gazes avoid each other, as if she foresees the Passion of Christ that brings sadness to her face. In contrast to the *Hodegétria* in the *Eleoúsa* and the *Glykophiloúsa*, the Theotokos in most cases is shown holding her son on her right arm while the child tenderly touches his mother's face with one hand and with the other holds the closed scroll.

On Mount Athos there are over 20 icons of the Theotokos that are regarded by the monks as miracle-working, too many to describe in detail here. Each icon has a title derived from a particular miracle. While most monasteries have one of these icons the Monastery of Vatopedi has five. These are the *Elaiovrýtissa* associated with the marvellous overflow of olive oil from dry jars; the *Esfagméni* from the curing of a disturbed monk who damaged the icon with a knife; the *Ktitórissa* or 'Foundress' an icon that survived for decades in a well after the monastery was looted by Arabs; the *Paramýthia* from a tradition that the icon saved the monks from pirates; and the *Pyrovolítheisa* from the divine retribution on a Turkish soldier that dared to shoot at the icon and damaged the right hand of the Theotokos.

Iconographers rarely signed their names on their paintings. If a painter did add a signature he used the phrase *XEIP* ('By the hand of') before his name. For a portable icon, it was common practice for many centuries for the iconographer to sign or write his name on the back of the icon. Sometimes there was, in addition, a reference to the person or family who commissioned the icon. Portable Greek icons in monasteries may have an inscription in small lettering of the name of the monastery where the icon was painted and the year the icon was painted, often in the old Greek numbering system. Outside of the monasteries patronage was rarely acknowledged. If it was the wording would be *Δωρεά* ('Gift of') and the name of the donor (individual, couple or family). A variation would be *Εἰς μνήμη* ('In memory of') with or without the donor's name.

707. Theotokos *Paramýthia*. Monastery of Vatopedi, Mount Athos

708. Theotokos *Foverá Prostasía*. Monastery of Koutloumousiou, Mount Athos

709. Theotokos *E Geróntissa*. Monastery of Pantokratora, Mount Athos

710. Theotokos *Koúkou*. Monastery of Megistis Lavra, Mount Athos

711. Theotokos *Tríche*, Monastery of Chelandari, Mount Athos

712. Theotokos *Nicopeía* (Bringer of Victory). Now in St Mark's, Venice originally in the Monastery of St John the Theologian, Constantinople

Media

Various media were used by Christian artists in creating spiritual art. At an early date in the catacombs of Rome wall paintings in the form of frescoes were used by Christians. In terms of technique it was natural that these early Christian paintings imitated the decoration of pagan tombs. Most of the paintings of the third century were restricted to a few splashes of colour and the figures or objects treated in a very summary fashion. The simple decoration of both Christian and pagan tombs replaced the more elaborate and illusionist art on the walls of the villas in Pompeii of two centuries earlier that was now out of fashion.

Christian artists took over the art of mosaics from the Greeks and Romans who used mosaics, made from small square stones called *tesserae*, chiefly for pavements. Christian mosaic artists used tesserae of tinted or gilt glass and placed them on walls and apses instead. They also altered the subject matter depicting sacred figures and events. The smallness of the tesserae enabled the curves of arches and vaulted ceilings to be decorated easily. The early, rather limited Christian mosaics of the fourth century gave way to the very finest of mosaics from the fifth century on, particularly in Constantinople where the best mosaic-workers were to be found. This medium was used extensively until the fourteenth century when the impoverished state of the Empire made mosaic decoration too expensive. Although mosaics were used mostly for wall decoration they were also used in very small size panels.

In addition to murals and mosaics, icons on panels were made using the technique known as tempera, an egg base with colour pigments added. In most cases the icon was painted on a prepared wood panel or on a fine linen canvas that was then attached to a wood panel. The earliest icons, portable images painted on wood, date back to the sixth or seventh century. Most of these are still to be found in place the

713. XEIP. Signature of iconographer Ieremias in letters bottom left

714. Media – mosaic. Head of Christ

715. Media – mosaic. St Peter, San Clemente, Rome

716. Media - mosaic. Empress Theodora, San Vitale, Ravenna

717. Media – wall painting. Refectory, Monastery of Pantokratora, Mount Athos

Monastery of St Catherine in the Sinai. Many have found their way into various museums. Icons painted in the encaustic technique involved mixing the pigment into melted wax and while still warm applied to a thin wood panel. Afterwards the surface was smoothed down with a metal instrument.

When mosaics were used extensively they covered the upper surfaces of the church interior. Lower walls were then usually faced with marble. In the basilicas where vast stretches of wall had to be filled mosaic and marble gave way to plastered interiors entirely covered with the cheaper medium of mural painting. As the previous hierarchical, sacramental could not be reproduced successfully in such churches, narrative themes were used. Often the narrative sequences spread throughout the building and took little notice of the spatial divisions of the church.

Iconographers
Byzantine art developed a so-called canon, a system of signs and approved ways to represent holy figures and events. Iconographers, then and now are not completely free to express themselves but some over the centuries have made considerable contributions. The artists were generally anonymous, a few became renowned, but little is known about them. The earliest iconographer specifically identified is Manuel Panselinos (*c.*1300), who was known as one of greatest artists of wall paintings, most of which are to be found in the Protaton Church on Mount Athos. Another known and famous icon painter was Andreas Ritzos (*c.*1422–1492) whose work created the foundation of the so-called Cretan school of painting.

In the sixteenth century two of the great iconographers were Theophanes Strelitzas Bathas (died *c.*1559) and Michael Damaskinos (1530/35–1592/93). Theophanes the Cretan, as he was also known, was the most important figure in Byzantine religious wall painting in the first half of the sixteenth century. He was active from about 1527 to 1548 and trained several iconographers, including his two sons Simeon and Neofitos, the Cretans Antonios and Tzorzis, and the Theban Frangos Katelanos. Theophanes' earliest work was for the churches at Meteora and then in the monasteries of Mount Athos. He is not only considered a prominent representative of the Cretan School but one who preserved traditions and was not influenced by Western art. The works of Damaskinos, on the other hand, show influences from Venetian painting. He was famous for his portable icons and had his workshop most probably in the monastery of Vrontissi in Crete. Damaskinos is a major representative of the Cretan School and worked mainly in Crete and the Ionian Islands. His use of paler flesh tones became a stylistic feature of his paintings and proved to be highly influential among other iconographers of the sixteenth century. He signed his works in Greek with the words either 'By the hand of Michael Damaskinos' or 'Creation of Michael Damaskinos'. Colleagues of Michael Damaskenos included Domenikos Theotokopoulos, Nikolaos Tzafouris, Andreas Pavias, Giorgios Klontzas, and Donatos

718. Media – encaustic. Theotokos and Christ Child

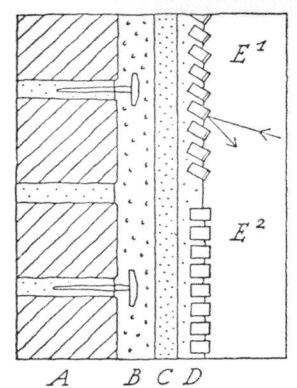

719. Media construction – mosaic. Tesserae on plaster layers

Plaster layers and tesserae

A Brick wall. *B* Coarse plaster with binding nails. *C–D* Finer layers of plaster. E^1 Gold tesserae, tilted. E^2 Normal setting of tesserae.

720. Iconographer Manuel Panselinos. Theotokos and Christ Child, Church of Protaton, Mount Athos

721. Iconographer Andreas Ritzos. Enthroned Theotokos and Christ Child

722. Iconographer Theophanes. Koimisis of St Nicholas, Monastery of St Nicholas Anapafsis, Meteora

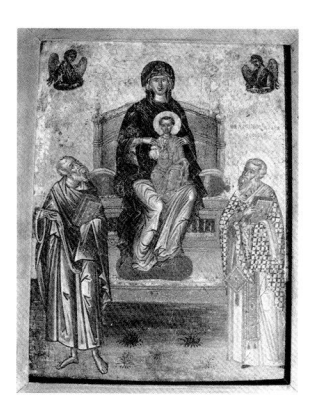

723. Iconographer Michael Damaskinos. Enthroned Theotokos and Christ Child between St James (left) and St John (right)

Bitzamanos. Other noted iconographers whose work appears in Crete, the Ionian Islands, or Venice were Stephanos Tzakarolas, Angelos Akotantos, Theodoros Poulakis and Emmanuel Tzanes.

Outside of the Balkans and Russia these were the last famous Byzantine iconographers. After them, Western influences in religious art led to the virtual disappearance of traditional spiritual art in Eastern Orthodoxy as mentioned before and with them iconographers in the area occupied by the former Byzantine Empire. After the Second World War the painter and writer Fotis Kontoglou (d. 1965) in Greece and the Russian Leonid Ouspensky then living in Paris led a return to traditional painting of Byzantine religious

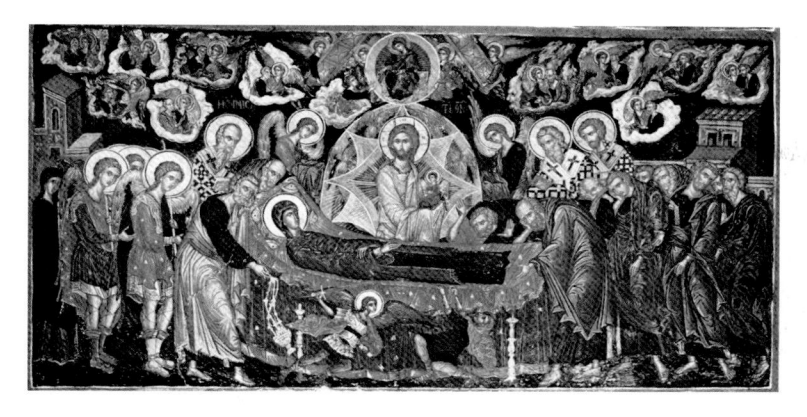

724. Iconographer Frangos Katelanos. *Koimisis tis Theotokou*, Monastery of Varlaam, Meteora

725. Iconographer Stephanos Tzankarolas. Christ as a high priest

726. Iconographer Angelos Akotantos. Theotokos *Kardiótissa*

727. Iconographer Theodoros Poulakis. Panagia reading and inspired by the Holy Spirit (in the form of a dove) and God the Father

728. Iconographer Emmanuel Tzanes. Christ enthroned

art. Since then and despite initial opposition the acceptance of a more authentic approach became evident in the religious art commissioned by Eastern Orthodox churches.

While the focus of spiritual art in this chapter has been on wall paintings, mosaics and images on wood panels, the icons, one should not forget the art of manuscript illustrations, reliefs on sarcophagi, or on objects such as ivories, medallions and textiles. The topics of illuminated manuscripts, sculpture (statues, figure reliefs, ornamental ivories), metal work (silverware, reliquaries, jewellery), glassware and figured textiles have not been included here as there they do not have a strong connection to the architecture of sacred spaces.

Texts

There is a lack of early writings on specifically religious art in the first few centuries of the Christian era. Strangely enough the spiritual attributes of the figures in early Christian art can be ascertained, though, from the pagan writers of Late Antiquity, particularly the writers known as the Neo-Platonists. Above all there was Plotinus (204–270) who in his *Enneads* justifies a way of seeing with the 'inner eye' that disregards the natural appearance of objects, their dimensions or colours. He wrote that the apprehension of the essence of things could be obtained when they are almost transparent and devoid of substance and weight. Then there was Gregory of Nyssa (*c.*335–after 394), along with his brother Basil the Great of Caesarea, and Gregory of Nazianus, who attempted to establish Christian philosophy as superior to Greek philosophy. Gregory of Nazianus' argument was that as God is infinite He cannot be comprehended. It may be for this reason that God is rarely represented as a human figure in Byzantine art. Interesting textual fragments of other writers include a rare letter from about 400 in which St Nilus charges the Eparch Olympiodorus in Constantinople to have the Cross represented in the apse of the church and Old and New Testament scenes in the naos. He also rejects the representation of animals and images of hunting and fishing.

During the time Leo III issued edicts against the worship of images the Patriarch of Constantinople was Germanos (r. 715–730). As Patriarch he naturally defended the veneration of icons. In one of his letters that has survived he worried that a ban on icons would prove that the Church had been in error for a long time, an unacceptable position. In another letter he envisaged the church building as an 'earthly heaven wherein the heavenly God dwells and walks about'. He argued that Orthodox iconography was developed to support this idea so that the faithful could apprehend it. Another defender of icons was St John Damascene (*c.*676–749) whose arguments took the form of three separate publications. These played an important role and carried considerable weight in the deliberations of the Second Ecumenical Council of Nicaea. In addition, his summary of the dogmatic writings of the early Christian Fathers, *An Exact Exposition of the Orthodox Faith,* provides valuable knowledge about early Orthodox beliefs.

The Seventh Ecumenical Council that took place in Nicaea in 786 is also known as the Second Council of Nicaea. The primary purpose was to end the disputes between the Iconoclasts, the 'icon-smashers' and the Iconodules, the 'venerators of icons'. In the end the Council upheld the position of the Iconodules and clarified the role of the artist in Byzantine iconography: To the painter belongs the art but the fundamentals, the tradition, belong to the holy fathers of the Church. From this position the Church declared that the form of the divine Christ was not to be represented as any natural man's. In this way the stylized images of Christ in Byzantine art came to contrast with the purely humanly 'beautiful' images of Christ in Western art. The Byzantine dogma for depicting holy persons was also extended to the Theotokos and the saints and martyrs.

Dionysios of Fourna (1670–*c.*1745), a monk at Mount Athos, set forth the system of arrangement of religious decoration in Byzantine churches in his *Explanation of the Art of Painting* (*Hermeneía tes Zographikés Téchnes*). Written about 1730 the work was based on several earlier anonymous writings. In his book he explains how murals and icons are to be executed, how each saint or scene is to be depicted, and how the icons are to be arranged in basilicas or domed churches. Fotis Kontoglou, in his book *Explanation of Orthodox Iconography* (*Ekphrasis tes Orthódoxou Eikonographías*) published in 1960, is based on the work of Dionysios of Fourna, but he also refers to older writings. The explanations have the benefit of Kontoglou's own experience as a modern Greek iconographer and restorer of Byzantine paintings.

Both Dionysios and Kontoglou explain the decorative scheme of dividing a Byzantine church into three decorative zones, an arrangement that became established sometime after the tenth century. They write that the first zone of domes, high vaults, and the half dome of the apse are to contain images of Christ, the Theotokos, and angels as these areas are considered to represent heaven. Near or in the bema are to be the patriarchs of the Old Testament and the hierarchs and teachers of the church. The main dome might contain one of three representations within a medallion: the Pantokrator, the Ascension or Pentecost. As already seen, the Pantokrator was in practice the predominant of the three images. Radiating out from the medallion is to be images of angels, apostles or prophets. The half dome of the apse in the bema is the place for the Theotokos shown either sitting enthroned or standing against a gold background. As mentioned earlier, before the Iconoclastic controversy Christ was represented in the apse instead but also later in churches without domes. Side apses other than the prothesis or diaconicon generally are to contain images of St John the Forerunner or of Joachim and Anna representing the preparation for the coming of Christ. So much for the first zone. In the top tier of the second zone, the naos walls below the heavenly domes and vaults, the scenes to be represented are the cycles of great festivals such the Annunciation, the Nativity and the Baptism. The full cycle is to contain 12 scenes altogether that exemplify key aspects of the life of Christ. The middle tier of the second zone is intended to relay the miracles and parables of Christ. The lowest tier is reserved for individual saints, selected according to local preference, arranged in hierarchical order. In the third zone, the narthex, images of persons are to be shown standing to emphasize that they and the worshippers belong to the same community. In small spaces they could be shown as half-figures or busts in medallions.

Entrance into the narthex of a Byzantine church is regarded as a transitional space as it is where the faithful person takes the first step in the passage from the physical world to the spiritual realm of the naos. There the spiritual experience is enhanced by keeping the level of light low so that the eye struggles to make out the forms of the images on the walls and vaults. When light flickers over the gold in the mosaic icons a magical, mystical moment is created. The glimmering glow gives the impression that the images are the source of light itself. As Theodore the Stoudite wrote the Gospel was 'writing in words' but the golden rays glitter from the gilded tesserae icons are 'writing in gold'.

Chapter Five

PLACES OF SPLENDID SPIRITUAL ART

As described in the previous chapter, Early Christian art in the Late Classical period up to about the middle of the fourth century was naturally centred in Rome. Limited evidence remains today of this early art from other cities or towns except for Dura-Europos and Aquileia. Whether the churches built in the Constantinian era in Jerusalem were adorned and in what form is not known as these have disappeared and there is a lack of a written record. In the second half of the fourth century there was increased activity in the artistic decoration of church interiors. This was the beginning of the Age of Splendour which culminated in the magnificent Byzantine art of the sixth century. Major centres of magnificent spiritual art in this Age were Rome, Constantinople and Ravenna. Significant Christian art was also to be found in churches throughout the Empire from Egypt, to Syria to Greece. Among the most admired of the surviving art are the fifth and sixth-century mosaics in Ravenna and the sixth-century painted images in the isolated Monastery of St Catherine in the Sinai desert.

The seventh century saw major changes in the social and religious roles of images within the Byzantine Empire as the debate about the role of images in church art intensified. The eighth century saw the launching of the Iconoclastic movement in which the depiction of personal images in traditional Christian art of the previous five centuries or so was overthrown. In the middle of the ninth century an imperial proclamation led to the restoration of the icons. The renewal of figural images in church art was celebrated with installation of a new *Platytéra* in the apse of Hagia Sophia in Constantinople in 867. During the stable eleventh and twelfth centuries the Komnenoi dynasty (1081–1185) was a great patron of the arts. Byzantine artists began to depict their subjects with greater humanism and emotion. Perhaps the finest Byzantine mosaic work of this period was carried outside the Empire in Sicily (Cefalu, Monreale and Palermo) and in Venice and Torcello.

During the thirteenth century there was a brief interruption after the sack of Constantinople by the Fourth Crusaders in 1204. After the recapture of the city in 1261, Byzantine art flourished again under the Palaiologoi dynasty. Cultural exchanges with Italian artists led to an interest in landscapes and rustic scenes. Crete, ruled by the Venetians since 1211, became a hub for Byzantine painting but one with western influences, exporting large numbers of painting to the West. It became the centre of Byzantine art after the Fall of Constantinople in 1453 and remained so until the capture of the island by the Ottoman Turks in 1669. With the Fall of Constantinople Orthodox Christianity and Byzantine art spread to the Balkan countries of Bulgaria, Serbia and Romania as well as to Russia.

The places of splendid spiritual art up to the middle of the fifteenth century were spread throughout the eastern Mediterranean basin. Faced by the countless number of images that still exist to be seen and can be depicted, only extremely selected ones in a few chosen places will be covered here. Images will be described based on their location that follows a geographical arc rather than a chronological order. Thus the virtual journey begins with Rome, then northern Italy and from there the sequence of places follows a sweeping arc eastward through the Balkans, Greece, Asia Minor, the Near East, Egypt and then, almost completing the circle, ending in Sicily.

729. San Giovanni in Via Latina, Rome. Depiction of one of the three wise men

730. Santa Costanza, Rome. One of the first examples in Christian art of Christ portrayed like an emperor but sitting atop a blue sphere, a symbol of the world, handing keys to Peter

731. Santa Costanza, Rome. Decorative barrel vault of the peripheral passageway with Roman images

732. Santa Costanza, Rome. Late eighth-century depiction of God presenting the Laws of Moses

Rome

In the second century, among the first Christian religious decorations were those on sarcophagi, richly carved stone or marble coffins, in underground chambers. The decorations were usually a mix of New and Old Testament scenes. Then early in the third century wall paintings began to appear in the **Catacombs of Rome** such as in the Catacomb of Domitilla and at the beginning of the fourth century in the Catacomb of Priscilla, the so-called Greek Chapel. In the Catacomb of Domitilla, Christ is shown among the Twelve Apostles while in the Catacomb of Callistus he is shown as the Good Shepherd. An early depiction of the Christ child in the arms of his mother, Mary, is in the Catacomb of St Priscilla. The transition from pagan to Christian art is clearly reflected in a mosaic found in a small burial chamber in the cemetery beside the **Via Cornelia**, the future site of the Constantinian basilica of St Peter in the Vatican. The figure of Christ is shown with the attributes of Apollo as the sun god riding a chariot of four horses. From a nimbus or luminous frame around the head of Christ spring seven rays of light that

733. Santa Costanza, Rome. Late eighth-century image of Christ

734. San Giovanni in Laterno. Restored apse mosaic of Christ in heaven with angels and below on either side of the cross the Theotokos, SS Peter and Paul (left) and SS John, John the Forerunner, James and Andrew (right)

735. San Giovanni in Laterno. Close-up of Christ in the restored apse mosaic

736. Santa Pudenziana, Rome. Mosaic of the apse probably the oldest in a church in Rome going back to the time of Siricius (384–399). Enthroned Christ between two groups of apostles and two females that personify *Ecclesia ex Circumcisione* (Church of the Jews) and the *Ecclesia ex Gentilibus* (Church of the Gentiles). At top cross of Golgotha, symbols of the evangelists and a view Jerusalem and its Christian churches. The mosaic appears incomplete as it was 'trimmed' in the sixteenth century

allude to Christ as the personified Sun or the 'light of the world'. An underground gallery under the **Via Latina** in Rome that dates to the middle or second half of the fourth century has wall paintings of high stylistic quality of both pagan and Christian scenes. Art restorers have recently discovered what are believed to be the oldest paintings of the apostles in a tomb in the Santa Tecla catacomb. The faces are those of the Apostles Andrew, John, Peter and Paul and date from the second half of the fourth century or the early fifth century.

Until the Peace of the Church in 313 above-ground artistic representations were limited as Christians worshiped privately in homes or specially converted houses. The wall paintings that were once in buildings such as the Titulus Equitti (249–261) and other residences, and in the great churches founded by Constantine in Rome, have virtually all disappeared along with the buildings themselves. A rare example of the new adornment can be seen in **Santa Costanza**, the only fourth-century church that has survived more or less intact from that time. Mosaics in the church of Santa Costanza are of ornamental design as little place was given as yet to Christian images. An unusual survival is a mosaic of Christ in the church of **San Giovanni in Laterno**. Built in 318 by Constantine as the first Christian basilica in Rome it was embellished with fabulous rich decorations and gifts. In the refurbishment carried out at the end of the thirteenth century the fourth-century image of Christ was salvaged and incorporated into the magnificent mosaic in the half dome of the apse. The image is of a bust of Christ borne by a cloud. The features are of a serious face, realistic almost like a portrait, of a man with a beard, shoulder length hair, sallow cheeks, furrowed brow, and piercing eyes. What distinguishes the figure from being a portrait of a mere mortal being is the golden halo behind the head.

737. Santa Sabina, Rome. The exterior wood cedar doors

There are two famous early apse mosaics in Rome, those at Santa Pudenziana (384–399) and Santi Cosma e Damiano, in the Roman forum (527). The apse mosaic of **Santa Pudenziana** has an image of Christ as an earthly emperor with the apostles seated beside him dressed as Roman senators arranged in a symmetrical composition. Two female figures represent the Church of the Jews and the Church of the Gentiles crowning Peter and Paul. This mosaic is the earliest surviving Christian figure representation and combines Classical style with early Christian symbolism. In the sky float the four-winged symbols of the evangelists: the angel of Matthew, the lion of Mark, the ox of Luke, and the eagle of John. Behind the figures the background consists of an array of Roman buildings. Another fifth-century church with an impressive mosaic is **Santa Sabina**. On the back wall of the nave stretching the full width of the space is a mosaic composed of a long inscription in large gold letters on a blue background flanked by two female figures. One figure represents the Church of the Jews and the other the Church of the Gentiles. The inscription records the founding of Santa Sabina by a presbyter, Petrus of Illyria, during the papacy of Celestine I (r. 422–432) and thus the date of its construction. The entrance doors below the mosaic are made of cypress wood and date to the fifth century and are famous for the 18 panels carved with scenes from the scriptures.

738. Santa Sabina, Rome. A panel from the wood doors

At **Santi Cosma e Damiano** the apse mosaic depicts the *Parousía* or Second Coming of Christ with Christ standing on billowing red clouds of dawn dressed in golden robes and on one side is his monogram, the letter **I** (from the first letter of his name in Greek *Ἰησοῦς*). His right hand is outstretched and in his left hand he holds the scroll of Law. On Christ's right are St Paul and Damian, then Pope Felix IV (reigned 526–30) who offers a model of the church he founded. On the left side of Christ are St Peter, who is introducing Cosmas and on their outside is St Theodore. The figures are standing on the bank of the River Jordan and at each end there is a palm tree with a phoenix, the symbol of resurrection. Below are the Twelve Apostles represented by sheep on a hillock ranged on either side of the Lamb of God identified by a silver halo. At one end is an image of Bethlehem and on the other one of Jerusalem. On the triumphal arch there is an elaborate sixth-century mosaic centred on an enthroned Lamb of God.

739. SS Cosma e Damiano, Rome. The sixth-century mosaic in semi-dome of the apse. Christ is in the centre among red-tinged clouds.

740. SS Cosma e Damiano, Rome. A full-length figure of Christ with his right arm fully extended and holding a scroll in his left hand

741. SS Cosma e Damiano, Rome. San Cosmas

742. SS Cosma e Damiano, Rome. San Damian

After the sack of Rome in 425, Pope Sixtus III (r. 432–440) commissioned the rebuilding of the interior of **Santa Maria Maggiore** with mosaic decoration on the triumphal arch and mosaic panels on the nave walls. The 27 surviving mosaic panels, each about 5 feet by 7 feet in size, are attached to the nave walls on both sides and follow classical antiquity designs. Depicted are individual scenes from the Old Testament, such as God protecting Moses and his companions, but the panels do not represent

PLACES OF SPLENDID SPIRITUAL ART 283

743. Santa Maria Maggiore, Rome. Triumphal arch with mosaics from the renovation by Pope Sixtus III 432 to 440. At the summit of the arch is the inscription XYSTVS EPISCOPVS PLEBI DEI ('Sixtus, bishop of the people of God')

744. Santa Maria Maggiore, Rome. Baroque altar and apse mosaic that dates from the thirteenth century

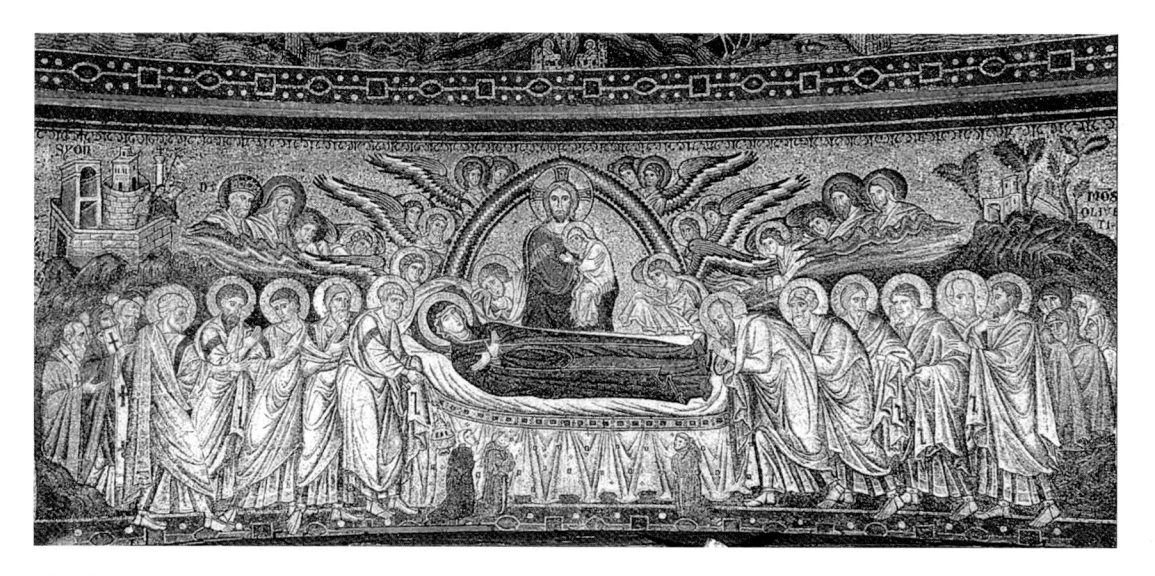

745. Santa Maria Maggiore, Rome. Koimisis tis Theotokou on the back wall of the apse below the semi-dome

episodes in a continuous story. Single scenes taken from the New Testament are on the triumphal arch which separates the nave from the sanctuary. The mosaics on the triumphal arch illustrate the life of Christ from legends rather than the Gospels and are arranged in four superimposed tiers. Just as the panels on the nave walls reflect a Classical influence so do the scenes on the arch in the allusion to scenes on the triumphal monuments of Roman emperors. Significantly, the elevation of the mother of Jesus as the Theotokos at the Council of Ephesus in 431 is evident in the apse mosaic where she is depicted as an *Augusta*, a Roman empress Her regal status is indicated also in a sixth-century fresco,

746. Santa Maria in Domnica, Rome. Enthroned Theotokos holding the Christ Child in her lap. They are surrounded by adoring angels with a kneeling Pope Paschal I, a square nimbus indicating that he was still living

747. Santa Maria Antiqua, Rome. Santa Giuleta

748. San Paolo Fuori le Mura, Rome. The original, fifth-century composition of the triumphal arch retained despite numerous restorations over the centuries

749. San Paolo Fuori le Mura, Rome. Enormous bust of Christ at the summit of the triumphal arch with rays darting from his head

later overlaid with another image, in **Santa Maria Antiqua al Foro Romano**, where she is shown between two archangels adorned as a Byzantine empress and with the inscription *Regina Coeli* (Queen of Heaven). Santa Maria Antiqua also contains fragments of many frescoes from the eighth century on the sanctuary walls, on the triumphal arch, on the aisle walls, on pillars and columns, and in the two small chapels. The colossal figure of Christ in the apse, blessing with his right hand, and with the four symbols of the evangelists on either side, dominates the interior.

In **San Paolo Fuori le Mura** (initial foundation 324) the restored fifth-century mosaic on the triumphal arch contains an inscription along the edge that mentions the donors Emperor Theodosius and the Dowager Empress Galla Placidia. In the centre of the arch is a bust of Christ with his right hand raised in blessing almost in the Byzantine manner – thumb touching the fourth finger and the second, third and fifth fingers raised upright. On either side of him are the symbols of the evangelists and below them are portraits of SS Peter and Paul, the latter pointing a finger at his tomb below.

750. San Paolo Fuori le Mura, Rome. Twelve elders in robes each offering their jewelled crowns to Christ with the symbols of the evangelists Luke and Matthew above and an angel kneeling before Christ (left side of triumphal arch)

751. San Paolo Fuori le Mura, Rome. Twelve elders in robes each offering their jewelled crowns to Christ with the symbols of the evangelists Mark and John above and an angel kneeling before Christ (right side of triumphal arch)

752. San Paolo Fuori le Mura, Rome. An enthroned Christ at the centre of the apse semi-dome

753. San Paolo Fuori le Mura, Rome. Close-up of the enthroned Christ blessing almost in the Byzantine manner and an open Gospels book with a Latin inscription

Other superb mosaics of the fifth and sixth century in Rome churches are to be found in the churches of Santa Cecilia, Sant'Agnese Fuori le Mura and San Lorenzo Fuori le Mura. At **Santa Cecilia** the apse mosaic shows Christ at his Second Coming blessing with his right hand, holding a rolled up scroll in his left, and with the Divine Hand of God above his head. On the right side of Christ are the figures of St Paul, St Agatha, and Paschal I who has a square halo and is holding a model of the church. On the left of Christ are SS Peter, Valerian, and Cecilia who are holding martyr's crowns. Below the figures, which are shown in a meadow with flowers and palm trees, there are 12 lambs and on either side images of Bethlehem and Jerusalem.

In the half dome of **Sant'Agnese Fuori le Mura** three full-length figures are depicted. In the centre is St Agnes standing on a platform, or possibly a funeral pyre, holding in her hands a scroll sealed with a cross, a crown on her head and wearing a purple robe and jewelled vestments. On her left is (probably) Pope Symmachus (r. 498–514) holding a Gospel book and on her right Pope Honorius I who is holding a model of the church.

At **San Lorenzo Fuori le Mura**, besides the triumphal arch the other Eastern feature is the mosaic in the semi-circular apse, still impressive today despite extensive restoration in later centuries. In the centre of the mosaic is the figure of Christ seated on the blue globe of the sky. On one side is St Peter with Pelagius, who is holding a model of the church, and St Lorenzo who is holding a book with an inscription in Latin. On the other side of Christ are St Paul, St Hyppolitus, who is holding martyr's crown, and St Stephen who is holding a book also with an inscription.

754. Santa Cecilia, Rome. A full figure of Christ flanked by three figures on each side in the apse semi-dome

755. Santa Cecilia, Rome. Below the apse mosaic 12 sheep, representing the apostles, proceed from the cities of Bethlehem and Jerusalem to the Lamb on the Mount in the middle from which flow the Four Rivers

Some idea of the nature of the wall paintings from the seventh to the ninth centuries can be discerned from those in the lower levels of **Santa Maria in Via Lata**. Those paintings from the thirteenth century in the basilica of **San Paolo Fuori le Mura** were painted in the old style by Pietro Cavallini. The Cavallini paintings were destroyed in a fire in 1823 but are known from copies. The present basilica was rebuilt after the fire reproducing the early Christian church in its proportions, materials, and colours. In 1291 Cavallini also executed mosaics in the lower portion of the sanctuary apse of **Santa Maria in Trastevere** that show scenes from the life of the Theotokos. In an unusual gesture Christ has his right arm around the shoulder of the Theotokos whose richly embroidered garment and jewelled headdress give her a regal bearing.

Santa Prassede is known as the best example of a ninth-century basilica in Rome with its mosaics intact. The mosaics cover the triumphal arch, the arch of the apse wall, and the apse half dome. In this dome is the Second Coming of Christ that is similar in composition to that at SS Cosma e Damiano.

756. Santa Cecilia, Rome. In the apse mosaic a row of standing figures (from left to right): Pope Paschal with a square nimbus, Sant'Agnese, St Paul, Christ, St Peter, St Valerian and Santa Cecilia holding a crown

757. Santa Cecilia, Rome. The figures on the left side of the apse mosaic

758. Santa Cecilia, Rome. Pietro Cavallini fresco of Christ

759. Santa Cecilia, Rome. Peristyle of Roman domus below the basilica

760. Santa Cecilia, Rome. Rooms of the Roman domus below the basilica

Christ is shown with his right arm outstretched and holding a scroll in his left hand. The hand of God appears above him. The most remarkable mosaics are those that cover the interior of the small, cross-shaped chapel of San Zeno on one side of the nave. Above the entrance to the chapel from the nave the composition consists of medallions set in the form of two concentric arcs, the inner with the Theotokos and ten saints and the outer with Christ and the Twelve Apostles. Inside the small chapel the Christ Pantokrator mosaic in the dome is simply overwhelming.

761. Sant'Agnese Fuori le Mura. The three figures of the apse mosaic: Pope Honorius (left), Sant'Agnese (centre) and Pope Symmachus (right)

762. Sant'Agnese Fuori le Mura. The full length figure of the saint wearing a crown and jewels holding a scroll in her hands and a sword and flames at her feet signifying the manner of her martyrdom

763. Sant'Agnese Fuori le Mura. The full length figure of Pope Honorius (r. 625–639) with a model of the basilica in his hands

764. Sant'Agnese Fuori le Mura. The full length figure of a pope holding a closed Gospels book with a jewelled cover

He is accompanied by the four archangels Michael, Gabriel, Rafael, and Uriel. Around the walls various saints are depicted. Another Pantokrator mosaic that survives also from the ninth century is in the apse of the church of **San Marco**. Christ is in the centre flanked in this case by saints and popes, each one standing on a decorated mat upon which their names are written. Christ holds in his left hand a book upon whose open pages are written in Latin 'I am the Light. I am the Life. I am the Resurrection.'

PLACES OF SPLENDID SPIRITUAL ART

765. San Lorenzo Fuori le Mura, Rome. St Peter holding a key in his right hand

766. San Lorenzo Fuori le Mura, Rome. Early Christian symbols – dove and *Chi Rho* sign

767. Santa Maria in Trastevere, Rome. Magnificent apse mosaic by Pietro Cavallini with Christ and his mother enthroned together and the hand of God reaching down above them

768. Santa Maria in Trastevere, Rome. Christ and Theotokos at the centre of the apse mosaic

769. Santa Maria in Trastevere, Rome. An enthroned Theotokos with the Christ Child

770. Santa Maria in Trastevere, Rome. The nativity in apse mosaic by Pietro Cavallini, one of four scenes between the windows below the apse

771. Santa Prassede, Rome. Nave looking toward the triumphal arch and sanctuary beyond both with ninth-century mosaics

772. Santa Prassede, Rome. Triumphal arch divided into two zones, an upper and a lower, separated by an arch. In the centre of the upper field is Christ between two angels and six apostles on either side of them. The lower field is filled with a great company of saints

773. Santa Prassede, Rome. Sanctuary apse mosaic with Christ in the centre surrounded by clouds and three figures on either side

774. Santa Prassede, Rome. Pope Paschal I (left), Santa Prassede (centre) and St Paul (left side of the apse mosaic)

775. Santa Prassede, Rome. St Peter (left), Santa Pudenziana (centre) and San Zeno (right side of the apse mosaic)

776. Santa Prassede, Rome. Triumphal arch lower field

777. Santa Prassede, Rome. Procession of the lambs with the Lamb of God in the centre

778. Santa Prassede, Rome. Apostles Peter and Paul with an archangel between them on the triumphal arch (right side)

779. Santa Prassede, Rome. Pope Paschal I holding a model of the basilica

780. Santa Prassede, Rome. Geometrical marble floor pattern

PLACES OF SPLENDID SPIRITUAL ART 293

781. Santa Prassede, Rome. Intricate marble floor pattern

782. Santa Prassede, Rome. Entrance portal to Chapel of San Zeno. A series of medallions of the 12 apostles arranged in the form of an outer arcs with Christ as the keystone and an inner arc with the Virgin at the centre of ten saints, eight female and two male

783. Santa Prassede, Rome. Central vault, Chapel of San Zeno. A medallion of Christ supported by four angels each of whom springs from a corner of the chapel

784. Santa Prassede, Rome. Close-up of the Christ medallion, central vault, Chapel of San Zeno

785. Santa Prassede, Rome. SS Theodora, Prassede, the Theotokos and Pudenziana (left to right)

786. San Marco, Rome. The apse mosaic with Christ at the centre and San Marco on his left

PLACES OF SPLENDID SPIRITUAL ART

The present day church of **San Clemente** is distinctive as four layers from different construction periods, from the first to the twelfth centuries, can be visited. Numerous frescoes from the fifth to the twelfth centuries can still be seen, some faded. In the half dome of the twelfth-century sanctuary apse of the upper church is a mosaic with a crucifixion scene in the centre surrounded by a vast vine studded with figures. At the top of the triumphal arch there is a figure of Christ holding a closed Gospels book in the left hand and blessing with his right hand but not quite in the Byzantine manner as his thumb does not touch the fourth and fifth fingers. Below him is Christ's Greek monogram XP and with the Greek letters A and W (which really should be an Ω). Other churches with notable mosaics, wall paintings and ancient inscriptions are those of **Santa Balbina, Santa Maria Cosmedin, San Crisogono, San Giorgio in Velabro, San Giovanni a Porta Latina, Santi Neroe ed Achilleo, San Pietro in Vincoli,** and **San Saba**.

787. San Clemente, Rome. *Schola Cantorum* (seventeenth-century drawing)

788. San Clemente, Rome. Apse mosaic showing the Crucifixion

789. San Clemente, Rome. Christ in a medallion at the centre of the triumphal arch blessing with his right hand

790. San Clemente, Rome. SS Peter and Clemente on the triumphal arch (upper right side)

791. San Clemente, Rome. SS Methodios and Kyrillos, contemporary mosaic in traditional Byzantine style

792. Santa Balbina, Rome. Christ in a medallion blessing (almost) in the Byzantine manner

793. Santa Balbina, Rome. Theotokos sitting on a high-backed throne holding the Christ Child

794. Santa Maria in Cosmedin, Rome. Adoration of the Magi in mosaic

795. San Crisogono, Rome. Portion of a wall painting in the original basilica

796. San Crisogono, Rome. Portion of a painted cross still visible in the original basilica

797. San Giorgio in Velabro, Rome. Early inscriptions in Greek displayed on the wall of the portico

798. San Giorgio in Velabro, Rome. *Chi Rho* symbol merged with, most likely, a compass sign: N (Notios – South in Greek) and B (Boreas – North)

799. San Giovanni a Porta Latina, Rome. Figure of a young, beardless Christ (centre)

800. San Giovanni a Porta Latina, Rome. Wall painting on the rear wall of the nave with a faint figure of Christ in a medallion

801. San Giovanni a Porta Latina, Rome. Group of youthful figures

802. SS Nereo ed Achilleo, Rome. Faded frescoes on the former inner wall of the entrance portico

803. SS Nereo ed Achilleo, Rome. 'Titulus Fasciolae' inscribed above the entrance door

804. SS Nereo ed Achilleo, Rome. Nave, aisle arcades, triumphal arch and apse semi-dome with Renaissance canopy over the altar. The mosaic of the arch is from the time of Pope Leo III (795–816) and at its centre is the scene of the Transfiguration of Christ, Moses and Elijah on either side and the prostrate figures of three apostles. The mosaic of the apse was replaced later by a fresco

805. San Pietro in Vincoli, Rome. San Sebastiano, a seventh-century mosaic

806. San Saba, Rome. Enthroned Theotokos and Christ Child

807. San Saba, Rome. The raising of Lazarus with Greek inscription

Milan and Florence

In fourth-century Milan **St. Ambrose** built his basilica next to the martyrium of San Vittore, a small memorial church which he renovated. In the eleventh century the mosaics of glittering gold from the early basilica were incorporated into a rebuilt building. The mosaics include a portrait of St. Ambrose made not long after the saint's death (397), so it may reflect his actual appearance. The central scene of the apse mosaic is of a blessing Christ in the Byzantine manner and dates from the late thirteenth century. In the interior of the Cappella di Sant'Aquilino in **San Lorenzo Maggiore** the highlight among the fourth-century Byzantine mosaics is one that depicts a beardless Christ.

The **Baptistery of San Giovanni** (eleventh to thirteenth century) in Florence is remarkable for two reasons. First, the simple and elegant octagonal shape of the building is clad in polychrome marble with an outstanding geometrical design. The four bronze entrance doors are world famous for their artistry. Second, the lavish interior of marble has an apse arch and dome decorated with Byzantine-style mosaics completed mostly by craftsmen from Venice.

808. Baptistery San Giovanni, Florence. Iconographical scheme of the dome

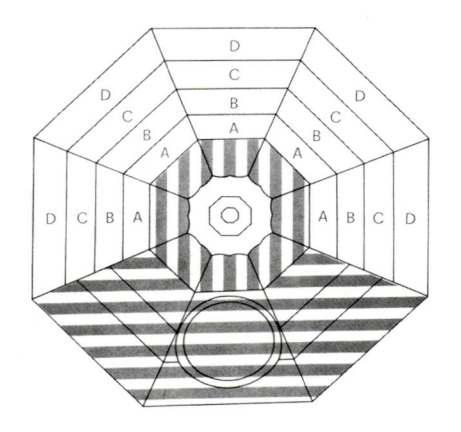

PLAN OF BAPTISTERY DOME MOSAICS
- Last Judgement
- Heavenly Hierarchy
- A Stories from Genesis
- B Stories from the Life of Joseph
- C Stories from the Life of Christ & Madonna
- D Stories from the Life of John the Baptist

809. Baptistery San Giovanni, Florence. Mosaic in octagonal dome

810. Baptistery San Giovanni, Florence. Christ as Judge dominates the dome

811. Baptistery San Giovanni, Florence. St John – a detail from the dome mosaic

812. Baptistery San Giovanni, Florence. Figures from the Last Judgment panel (second row on the right of the Christ figure)

Ravenna

Ravenna reached the height of its splendour and wealth when Emperor Honorius moved the capital of the Western Roman Empire there from Milan in 402. At the same time he also transferred the Christian centre from the harbour town of Classe to Ravenna. During the next few decades, while Rome was occupied by the Visigoths, Ravenna enjoyed a peace that enabled major Christian buildings to be erected. Even after the Western Roman Empire fell to the Ostrogoth Odoacre, Ravenna remained safe under the Goth Theodoric. He made it possible for Greek Orthodoxy to coexist with Christian Arianism and for Goths and Latins to live together. There was a spurt in religious building in Ravenna after 540 when the Eastern Emperor Justinian I (r. 527–565) conquered Italy to reunite the divided Roman Empire.

Executed between 425 and 430, the mosaics in the interior of the **Mausoleum of Galla Placidia** are the oldest and most complete in Ravenna. The background of the long barrel vault is a deep blue colour and is decorated with stylized flowers. The same blue background colour is on the dome but the decoration is stars rather than flowers. In the centre of the dome there is an image of a

813. Mausoleum of Galla Placidia, Ravenna. The Good Shepherd mosaic vault

814. Mausoleum of Galla Placidia, Ravenna. The Good Shepherd

golden cross with the base turned towards the east. On the four triangular areas below that support the dome, the pendentives, there are the golden, winged symbols of the four evangelists – Matthew, Mark, Luke and John. On the drum are figures of the apostles in white tunics on a blue background. Christian symbols such as doves, fish and palms abound. Inside, above the entrance door, there is a young beardless figure of Christ as the Good Shepherd dressed in a golden tunic and purple mantle. There is a golden halo behind his head and in his left hand he grasps a long cross. The background contains six small sheep set in a calm landscape rich in plants and flowers.

In the basilica of **Sant'Apollinare Nuovo** built by Theodoric in the sixth century mosaic decoration

815. Mausoleum of Galla Placidia, Ravenna. Doves at the fountain of salvation

covers both walls of the nave and is organized in three tiers. The first is directly above the arcade that separates the nave from the side aisles and contains a procession of figures. In the second tier above there are windows and between them are stately figures of saints and prophets. Above the windows but below the ceiling is the third tier which consists of a narrow band containing small panels of scenes from the life of Christ. The procession in the first tier on the left nave wall is of 22 named virgins led by the Three Wise Men, also named, bearing gifts to an enthroned Theotokos. On the right hand wall the first tier procession is composed of 26 named martyrs heading toward Christ who is seated on a jewel encrusted throne flanked by two angels on either side of him. Also shown are views of the palace of Ravenna and its port, Classe.

816. Sant'Apollinare Nuovo, Ravenna. Procession of the Virgins in arcade mosaic frieze panel proceeding toward the enthroned Theotokos

817. Sant'Apollinare Nuovo, Ravenna. Depiction of the palace

818. Sant'Apollinare Nuovo, Ravenna. The Last Supper

819. Sant'Apollinare Nuovo, Ravenna. The miraculous abundance of fishes

820. Sant'Apollinare Nuovo, Ravenna. Enthroned Christ between angels

821. Sant'Apollinare Nuovo, Ravenna. Enthroned Theotokos between angels

Later, during the reign of Justinian I, a series of great mosaics were created in the city's churches and especially famous are the two sanctuary apse mosaics, those of San Vitale (532–547) and Sant'Apollinare in Classe (549), which are equal to those in Rome. At **San Vitale** the splendid mosaics that cover the interior of the octagonal-shaped church display some clear differences among themselves. Those in the sanctuary are of Hellenistic-Roman influence, as can be seen in the naturalistic faces and green landscape backgrounds, whereas those in the apse are more Byzantine in their plain, golden backgrounds. In the bowl-shaped vault of the apse Christ is shown enthroned and flanked by two angels and on either side of them are San Vitalis and Bishop Ecclesius. Christ is shown as young and beardless sitting on a celestial globe and in the act of handing the crown of the glory of martyrdom to San Vitalis.

At the bottom of the apse vault are two renowned mosaic panels depicting Byzantine liturgical rituals (see Figures 1104 and 1105). On the left side panel the Emperor Justinian is shown with his attendants and on the right panel the Empress Theodora is depicted with her attendants. Despite the focus on the imperial couple neither Justinian nor Theodora actually ever visited the church. The first panel with the Emperor is a representation of the First Entrance procession in early Orthodox liturgy. Bishop Maximianus is shown leading the procession holding a cross with two members of the clergy on his left, one deacon carrying the gospel and the other incense. To the right of the bishop is Emperor Justinian with purple mantle, a halo, and wearing his crown (which normally would be removed in the narthex but probably left by the artist to identify him) accompanied by three high court officials and a military guard.

822. Sant'Apollinare Nuovo, Ravenna. Enthroned Christ blessing in the Byzantine manner

823. San Vitale, Ravenna. View of apse and its semi-dome

824. San Vitale, Ravenna. Apse mosaic with a youthful Christ sitting on a blue globe flanked by angels and at the ends San Vitalis (left side) and San Ecclesius (right) holding a model of the church

825. San Vitale, Ravenna. Christ medallion at the summit of the sanctuary arch

826. San Vitale, Ravenna. A deacon in the Emperor Justinian procession mosaic

The Emperor carries a shallow golden bowl, or paten, a gift that was a regular part of his participation in the ceremony. In the second procession panel the Empress Theodora is shown wearing a golden embroidered dress and a diadem; she is accompanied by two chamberlains and two ladies-in-waiting followed by a crowd of women. The Empress is carrying a chalice which she extends in a gesture of presentation. The fountain in the foreground implies that the group is entering from the forecourt before proceeding into the church through a door-curtain drawn by one of the chamberlains.

High up on the centre of the triumphal arch in **Sant'Apollinare in Classe** there is a bust of Christ with a halo and his right hand in a gesture of blessing. On both sides of him among a multitude of coloured clouds are the winged-symbols of the four evangelists. Below the group 12 sheep representing the apostles ascend toward Jesus and are shown coming out of painted models of the cities of Jerusalem and Bethlehem. The tall palm trees in the composition are a symbol of martyrdom.

827. San Vitale, Ravenna. Peacock symbol

In the apse the top part of the half dome is dominated by a large golden and jewelled cross enclosed in a blue coloured circle filled with numerous stars. At the crossing point of the cross is a bust of Christ. Above the cross are the Greek words ΙΧΘΥΣ ('Fish'), translated as Jesus Christ Son of God Saviour. At the ends of the arms of the cross are the first and last letters of the Greek alphabet, alpha and omega. These indicate the beginning and end of the course of the man's life. Around the cross and circle at the top are clouds from which

828. Sant'Apollinare in Classe, Ravenna. Apse mosaic dominated by a large cross contained in a medallion

829. Sant'Apollinare in Classe, Ravenna. Christ symbolized by the cross above the figure of San Apollinaris with God's hand pointing down from the clouds and on the side the figure of Moses and Elijah

830. Sant'Apollinare in Classe, Ravenna. Medallion of Christ blessing (almost) in the Byzantine manner and holding a closed book

831. Sant'Apollinare in Classe, Ravenna. Lambs as symbols of the apostles

the hand of God emerges. On either side among the clouds are Moses and the Prophet Elijah. In the bottom part of the half dome Sant'Apollinare is shown with outstretched arms set in a green meadow full of birds, flowers and plants, with a row of sheep right at the bottom. Other buildings in Ravenna with striking mosaics are the Archiepiscopal Chapel, the Arian Baptistery and the Orthodox Baptistery.

832. Archiepiscopal Chapel, Ravenna. Apse mosaic of the cross in a starry heaven and in the arch a youthful Christ flanked by SS Paul (left) and Peter (right) and other apostles: Iaocobus and Johanus (left) then Andreas and Phillipus (right)

833. Archiepiscopal Chapel, Ravenna. Dome mosaic centred on Christ's monogram 'IX' supported by four angels springing from the corners and symbols of the four evangelists between them

834. Archiepiscopal Chapel, Ravenna. Apostle Paul

835. Archiepiscopal Chapel, Ravenna. Ivory throne of Bishop Maximian. In the panel St John the Forerunner in the middle flanked by the evangelists and the bishop's monogram (top middle)

836. Arian Baptistery, Ravenna. Dome mosaic of the baptism of Jesus in the centre encircled by the figures of the apostles each holding a crown

837. Arian Baptistery, Ravenna. Dome mosaic of the baptism of Jesus in the River Jordan by John attended by God the Father (seated figure left) and the Holy Spirit (dove above)

838. Orthodox Baptistery, Ravenna. Baptism of Jesus by John in the River Jordan in the presence of God the Father and the Holy Spirit

839. Orthodox Baptistery, Ravenna. Interior showing the bands of decoration

840. Orthodox Baptistery, Ravenna. Three circle scheme of the dome mosaic with the baptism scene at the centre, followed by the figures of the apostles and on the outside various non-figurative scenes

841. Orthodox Baptistery, Ravenna. Close-up of SS Paul (left) and Peter (right) in the second circle of the dome mosaic

Venice

The present day **Patriarchal Basilica of St Mark** was consecrated in 1094 with the narthex and new façade constructed later in the first half of the thirteenth century. Both the exterior and interior of the Basilica were covered with bright mosaics containing gold, bronze and a great variety of stones. The mosaics in the interior followed an iconographic programme but one that is a Latin interpretation and translation of Byzantine tradition. The extensive art programme of the Basilica is difficult to grasp owing to the considerable alterations and renovations carried out over the first five centuries of its existence.

842. St Mark's, Venice. Portal mosaic in the Porta di Sant'Alipio (north entrance) depicting the transfer of the relics of St Mark with the former façade of the church as background. It is the only surviving thirteenth-century mosaic on the church's exterior

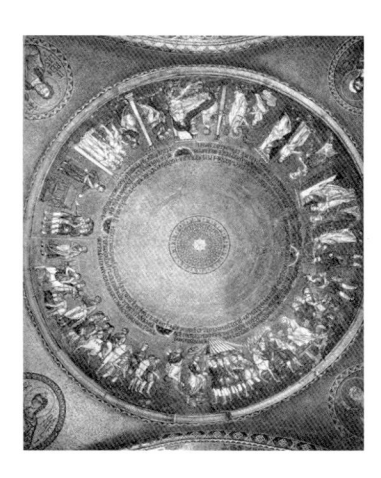

843. St Mark's, Venice. Narthex dome – Life of Abraham (left side of entrance with the Creation dome on the right)

844. St Mark's, Venice. Narthex dome – Life of Moses (at the Porta dei Fiori, north narthex)

845. St Mark's, Venice. Narthex dome – Life of Joseph I (at the northwest corner of the narthex)

Because of this only an outline description will be attempted here with an emphasis on the early work and the Byzantine character of the vast and superb mosaic decoration of the Basilica.

The mosaic decoration begins with the half domes of the entrances followed by the domes in the narthex. At St Mark's the decorative programme in the narthex begins with scenes from the Old Testament arranged in a time sequence. A local workshop produced the mosaics between 1225

310   THE SACRED ARCHITECTURE OF BYZANTIUM

846. St Mark's, Venice. Narthex dome – Life of Joseph II (north narthex east of Joseph I)

847. St Mark's, Venice. Sequence of vaults and domes showing scenes from the life of Christ (top), the Ascension (centre), God's Promise to Humanity (part of the Emmanuel dome) and Christ Pantokrator (apse semi-dome)

848. St Mark's, Venice. Pentecost dome (west)

849. St Mark's, Venice. Ascension dome (centre)

and 1285. The interior of the church itself takes the form of a Greek cross with a central dome over the crossing point and smaller domes over each of the four arms. Of the five domes the three significant ones are those over significant points on an imaginary straight line drawn from the entrance of the church to the sanctuary where the Holy Table is located. The first dome is over the western arm of the Greek cross and is encountered on entering the nave from the narthex. A mosaic of the Pentecost executed in the first half of the twelfth century by Byzantine craftsmen is depicted in this dome. The second dome is located over the meeting point of the arms of the Greek cross and is decorated with a mosaic of the Ascension completed in the last quarter of the twelfth century. Below on the pendentives the evangelists are depicted. They are shown along with the rivers of the Garden of Eden to convey the message that divine revelation flows to humanity through the Holy Scriptures. The third dome is over the eastern arm of the Greek cross that contains the sanctuary. On the inside of

850. St Mark's, Venice. Emmanuel dome (east)

the dome there is a mosaic of the prophets who are expressing God's promise that a Saviour would be born to a Virgin. Byzantine craftsmen also executed this mosaic, which is from the twelfth century. The half dome of the sanctuary apse is decorated with a golden Christ Pantokrator with the Greek letter IC XC at the top and in small letters at the bottom Petrus MCCCCCVI (1506), the signature of the iconographer and the date he created the mosaic. Of the two remaining domes the one over the northern arm of the Greek cross contains the mosaic figure of St John the Evangelist while the dome over the south arm contains the figure of St Leonard, a king who became a saint. The Eastern practice of accompanying figures of prophets, apostles and saints with an inscription

851. St Mark's, Venice. Christ Pantokrator in the apse semi-dome and the baldachin over the altar

852. St Mark's, Venice. The altar and *Pala d'Oro* behind

bearing the figure's name was followed but in Latin words. In scenes with texts the majority are in the Latin tongue sometimes written in abbreviated form. Elsewhere in the interior scenes from the New Testament are to be found on the walls, on piers, in the overhead vaults that are between the domes, in the chapels and in the Baptistery.

Regarded by many as the most precious and refined object in the Basilica of St Mark is the *Pala d'Oro* (Altarpiece of Gold), made in Byzantium on the order of Doge Orderlaffo Falier in 1102. The altarpiece is located in the sanctuary behind the Holy Table itself and is exceptionally ornate, covered in precious stones, gold and enamels. The *Pala d'Oro* contains three distinct rows of decoration. A large figure of an enthroned Christ surrounded by the evangelists is in the centre of the altarpiece and dominates the bottom two rows. The third and upper row is made with enamels looted during the Fourth Crusade. These are among the numerous collections of objects made for churches and palaces in Constantinople, plundered and brought back to Venice. The most venerated of these objects is an image of the Theotokos known as the *Nicopeía* ('Bringer of Victory'), a beautiful tenth-century icon framed in gilded silver, enamel and precious stones, probably that belonged to the Monastery of St John the Theologian.

Aquileia

Aquileia, located at the head of the Adriatic Sea, is one of the earliest surviving Christian churches. It was dedicated in 313 and has a basilican form. The nave and two side aisles of the church still retain an exceptional mosaic pavement from the fourth century, with geometric and floral patterns in addition to birds and fish. On the floor after the Christ monogram XP is a Latin inscription set in a circular frame that reads 'O happy Theodore. With the help of almighty God and the flock which was given to you by heaven, you did make everything happily to be gloriously consecrated.' In 1031 Pope Poppo built a cathedral on the site of the earlier church. It in turn was rebuilt about 1379 in Gothic style. The frescoes vary from those of the fourth century in the chapel of St Peter to those of the eleventh century in the apse. In the crypt there are twelfth-century frescoes, now largely faded, depicting the origins of Christianity in Aquileia and the first bishop of the city, St Hermagoras.

Istria

Along the shoreline of ancient Parentium (Porec), on the Istrian coast, today part of Croatia, there is the small, three-aisled basilica of **Eufrasiana** which forms the heart of a well-preserved episcopal ensemble. Substantial colourful sixth-century mosaic images survive in the main apse and on the triumphal arch of the basilica. Dominant images are Christ and the apostles in a horizontal band above the triumphal arch, while the Theotokos with the Christ child flanked by archangels, martyrs and other figures on each side, command the half dome of the main apse.

853. Basilica Eufrasiana, Parentium (Porec). Triumphal arch and *Platytéra*

854. Basilica Eufrasiana, Parentium (Poreč). Close-up of the Theotokos and Christ Child in the *Platytéra*

855. Basilica Eufrasiana, Parentium (Poreč). St Susanna

Ohrid

Ohrid, originally the Greek Lychnidos 'city of light', was a significant cultural and economic centre during the Byzantine period and the episcopal centre of the Slav Orthodox Church. During the eleventh century artists from Thessaloniki, the cultural centre of Greece and the Balkans, travelled north to create religious wall paintings of exceptional quality at the cathedral of Hagia Sophia in Ohrid, a city now in the former Yugoslav Republic of Macedonia.

The church of **Hagia Sophia**, the fourth basilica built on the same spot, is one of the largest in the Balkans. The interior of the church conforms overall to the Byzantine programme of wall paintings but there are local variations. The half dome of the sanctuary apse is dominated by a scene of a procession of angels bowing to the Theotokos who is seated on a richly decorated throne. Below in a middle zone are friezes with angels, scenes of the Ascension of Christ and the Communion of the Apostles. The left side of the lower zone contains a rarely depicted scene, that of 40 Roman soldiers who were left to freeze and became martyrs when they refused to give up Christianity. On the right side there are portraits of about 50 prominent patriarchs, archbishops and Eastern Orthodox wise men. Included are portraits of two Slav saints, Cyril and Clement. Wall painting continued to be done throughout the remainder of the church until the fourteenth century. Today the completed paintings constitute one of the largest compositions of preserved murals of any Orthodox church anywhere.

Altogether there are fourteen churches in Ohrid with well preserved murals many painted during the fourteenth century. After Hagia Sophia the other eleventh-century church with numerous beautiful wall paintings

856. Ohrid. Silver icon of the Theotokos (Museum of Icons, Ohrid)

is **St Clement** (St Bogorodica Perivlepta). At this church the two iconographers from Thessaloniki who did the paintings are known as they signed or initialled their work. They were Michael Astrapas and Eftychius who together dominated Balkan wall painting for nearly three decades from the end of the fourteenth to the beginning of the fifteenth centuries. At St Clement they followed the traditional Byzantine arrangement with Christ Pantokrator surrounded by angels in the central dome. Below them are scenes from the Festivals. In the narthex is a cycle of paintings about Christ, his miracles, actions and sufferings. Scenes of the Eucharist ceremony are painted on the back wall of the bema apse along with scenes describing the life of the Theotokos. The individual approach of Michael and Eftychius is seen in their depiction of the Last Supper in which they filled the background with architectural objects instead of leaving it plain. They also painted a more realistic treatment of figures; instead of thin and austere faces and bodies they presented young men as healthy, chubby and with red cheeks. Their influence can be seen in some of the numerous portable icons that date between the eleventh and fifteenth centuries now collected and displayed in the Icon Gallery of Ohrid.

Thessaloniki

The Apostle Paul established a Christian church in Thessaloniki in northern Greece around the year 50 during the Roman era when the city was capital of the province of Macedoniae. In recent years many early Christian vaulted graves with wall paintings have been found dating from the end of the third century to the beginning of the fifth century. While they demonstrate Hellenistic and Roman decorative designs the wall paintings also include Christian symbols. On the wall of one vault, for example, a fisherman refers to Christ who rescues people from the sea of wickedness while on the other walls in the same vaults are fruit, flowers and birds that symbolize paradise. A dominant feature in tomb decoration from the sixth century onward was the cross, a Christian symbol of an invincible weapon against death.

When the Christians converted the Roman building known as the **Rotunda** into a church, around the year 400 they decorated the dome and eight side recesses of the converted building with marvellous mosaics. The mosaic that was in the centre of the dome has disappeared except for some heads which probably were those of angels supporting a figure of Christ within a circle, a typical figure in the central dome of a Byzantine church. Below the dome there are superb portraits of various saints while the scenes in the recesses are of fruits, flowers, birds and geometric designs. The most common bird depicted is the peacock, a symbol of immortality.

One of the most beautiful mosaics in the city is in the bema apse of the small *katholikon* dedicated to **Christ the Saviour** of the monastery of Latamou. It is a fifth-century mosaic composition that shows Christ in the centre within a circle seated on a multicoloured hemicycle representing a rainbow. He is shown beardless wearing a dark red mantle with his right hand stretched out as if to speak, while in his left hand he holds a scroll with the inscription 'Here is our God in whom we hope and rejoice at the expectation of our salvation. For he will give peace into this House.' Christ is surrounded by four-winged beasts against a landscaped background which also includes the Prophets Ezekiel and Habakkuk. Ezekiel is shown with an ecstatic look on his face while Habakkuk sits with his hand to his chin in contemplation. The beasts represent the four evangelists each holding a lavishly bound Gospel. Because of the period it was created the mosaic displays Hellenistic influences. On the side walls of the small church are very important twelfth-century wall paintings, one a superb depiction of Christ's baptism.

857. St George Rotunda, Thessaloniki. Faded *Platytéra* in apse semi-dome

858. St George Rotunda, Thessaloniki. Architectural scene of classical buildings in drum mosaic I

859. St George Rotunda, Thessaloniki. Architectural scene of classical buildings in drum mosaic II

860. St George Rotunda, Thessaloniki. Architectural scene of classical buildings in drum mosaic III

861. St George Rotunda, Thessaloniki. Architectural scene of classical buildings in drum mosaic IV

862. St George Rotunda, Thessaloniki. Cross symbol in an apse semi-dome

863. St Saviour Latomos, Thessaloniki. Apse mosaic – the Theophany

864. St Saviour Latomos, Thessaloniki. Apse mosaic – a beardless Christ

865. St Saviour Latomos, Thessaloniki. Apse mosaic – Angel as a symbol of the evangelist Matthew

866. St Saviour Latomos, Thessaloniki. Apse mosaic – Prophet Ezekiel

867. Saviour Latomos, Thessaloniki. Apse mosaic – Prophet Habakkuk

868. St Saviour Latomos, Thessaloniki. Apse mosaic – Close-up of Prophet Ezekiel

869. St Saviour Latomos, Thessaloniki. Apse mosaic – Close-up of Prophet Habakkuk

870. St Saviour Latomos, Thessaloniki. Nativity fresco – Joseph

871. St Saviour Latomos, Thessaloniki. Nativity fresco – Bathing of the infant Jesus

872. St Saviour Latomos, Thessaloniki. Nativity fresco – Close-up of the oldest Magus

873. St Saviour Latomos, Thessaloniki. Nativity fresco – Close-up of Joseph

874. St Saviour Latomos, Thessaloniki. Nativity fresco – Close-up of the midwife

875. St Saviour Latomos, Thessaloniki. Nativity fresco – Close-up of Salome

876. St Saviour Latomos, Thessaloniki. Nativity fresco – Close-up of the younger shepherd

877. St Saviour Latomos, Thessaloniki. Baptism – Close-up of St John the Forerunner

878. St Demetrios, Thessaloniki. The *Platytéra*

879. St Demetrios, Thessaloniki. Close-up of the young St Demetrios

880. St Demetrios, Thessaloniki. St Demetrios with halo flanked by the founders of the church each with a nimbus: Bishop Ioannis (left) and Governor Leontios (right)

881. St Demetrios, Thessaloniki. St Demetrios with two children

882. St Demetrios, Thessaloniki. Wall paintings in side chapel

883. St Demetrios, Thessaloniki. A young St Demetrios (right) and a cleric

Throughout the Byzantine Empire the seventh century was a quiet period in terms of the production of religious art. An exception was the rebuilding of the church of **St Demetrios** in Thessaloniki after a fire and the execution of exceptional mosaics, some still to be seen today even after the almost complete destruction of the church in another fire in 1917. Three of mosaics are noteworthy and can be seen on the pillars of the bema. One of these mosaics shows the youthful full figure of St Demetrios with his hand on the shoulder of a cleric whose head is backed by a square halo, a nimbus. Another beautiful mosaic is again a youthful full length portrait of St Demetrios but this time between two children. A third mosaic is a full form of the saint between two figures who represent the officials who rebuilt the church after the destruction in the seventh century.

884. Hagia Sophia, Thessaloniki. The *Platytéra* in the apse semi-dome and cross on the barrel vault

885. Hagia Sophia, Thessaloniki. Close-up of the *Platytéra* figure

886. Hagia Sophia, Thessaloniki. Christ in the central dome sitting on a rainbow in a luminous globe of heaven supported by two angels and in an encircling ring the Theotokos flanked by angels and the 12 apostles

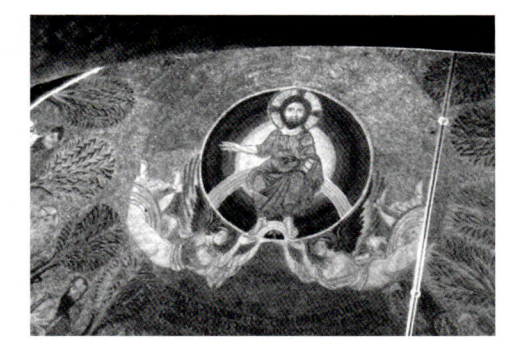

887. Hagia Sophia, Thessaloniki. Close-up of Christ seated on a rainbow in a globe of the world supported by two angels

When the church of **Hagia Sophia** in Thessaloniki was rebuilt in the eighth century the decoration followed the Iconoclastic rule of excluding figural art. In the Post–Iconoclastic period beautiful mosaics were added and still exist. In the apse of the bema there is a *Platytéra* – the sole figure of an enthroned Theotokos holding the infant Christ on her lap against a dazzling gold background. In the central dome there is a magnificent ninth-century mosaic of the Ascension. In the centre of the dome Christ is shown sitting on a rainbow within a circular frame of many colours held by two angels with extended wings. In a larger circle on the edge of the dome is the Theotokos, with her arms extended in prayer for mankind, standing between two angels pointing to the ascending Christ. The Twelve Apostles are arrayed in another circle with each apostle shown with an individual expression. A tree separates each apostle figure. Below the figure of Christ there is a lengthy inscription from the Acts of the Apostles that is written between the Theotokos, the standing angels and the flying angels. It refers to the apostles gazing up to Jesus in heaven.

888. Hagia Sophia, Thessaloniki. Icon of St John the Forerunner

889. Hagia Sophia, Thessaloniki. Icon of two saints

890. Hagia Sophia, Thessaloniki. Bottom rim of dome showing the Theotokos and two angels

891. St Catherine, Thessaloniki. Fragment of a faded wall painting

In the small eleventh-century church dedicated to **Panagia Chalkeon** notable wall paintings are those of the Holy Communion of the Apostles in the bema and the Last Judgment in the narthex. On the walls of the church and arches of the dome there are wall paintings of saints in full figure along with various scenes from the life of Christ and Panagia. In the church of **St Catherine** fragments of wall paintings of saints and gospel scenes from the end of the thirteen century still remain. Better preserved paintings from the beginning of the fourteenth century and that represent the last masterpieces of spiritual art of the Byzantine era are to be found in the churches of the **Holy Apostles, the Prophet Elijah,** and **St Nicholas Orphanos**. Accounting for the splendid art

892. Holy Apostles, Thessaloniki. Four prophets

893. Holy Apostles, Thessaloniki. Portrait of a saint

894. Holy Apostles, Thessaloniki. Figure of a saint

work was no doubt due to the imperial family of the Palaiologoi calling Thessaloniki their second home and making the city an important centre for religious art with a different sphere of influence from that of Constantinople.

Mount Athos

The monasteries on Mount Athos are wondrous to visit, as all Byzantine and Post-Byzantine wall paintings and icons are in their original positions in the churches and chapels in which services are still held today. In addition to the paintings and portable icons, there are also jewelled ornaments, embroidery, liturgical objects and illustrated manuscripts in the monastery libraries and treasuries (*skevophylákia*).

895. Vatopedi, Mount Athos. Exonarthex Deëis mosaic above the central entrance door

896. Ravdouchou *kélli*, Mount Athos. Apostle Peter

897. Ravdouchou *kélli*, Mount Athos. Apostle Paul

898. Vatopedi, Mount Athos. Mosaic of a saint above right-hand side door in a portico

899. Vatopedi, Mount Athos. Figure of Christ above portico window (immediately on right-hand side of entrance doors)

900. Vatopedi, Mount Athos. Figure of the Theotokos above portico window (immediately on left-hand side of entrance doors)

When the first large monastery, Megistis Lavra, was built on Mount Athos in 963 by St Athanasios, the peninsula had already been a refuge for hermits and small monastic communities for some centuries. Today Mount Athos is a self-governed monastic state recognized by international treaties and home to 20 inhabited Eastern Orthodox monasteries. Each one of the 20 main monasteries may own *skétes* or satellite monasteries, *kéllia* or spacious monastic dwellings much like a farmstead but with a small chapel, smaller *kalývia* also each with a chapel, and hermitages each occupied by a single monk.

The earliest surviving wall paintings on Mount Athos are from the twelfth century. They are found in the form of mosaic work in some portable icons and wall images in the *katholikon* (main church) of the monastery of **Vatopedi**. These are virtually the only mosaic work on Mount Athos and depict Jesus Christ, St Nicholas and the Annunciation. Wall paintings that survive from the twelfth and early thirteenth centuries are those of the Apostles Peter and Paul in the library of the monastery of Vatopedi and those in the Ravdouchou *kélli* of the monastery of Pantokrator near Karyes.

901. Vatopedi, Mount Athos. Figure of the archangel Gabriel above portico window (immediately to the left of the Theotokos window)

902. Vatopedi, Mount Athos. The Theotokos and Christ Child (niche at southern end of the portico)

903. Vatopedi, Mount Athos. Panel of saints on bottom tier of portico wall (left side of entrance doors)

904. Vatopedi, Mount Athos. A section of the four tiers of portico wall paintings I

905. Vatopedi, Mount Athos. A section of the four tiers of portico wall paintings II

906. Vatopedi, Mount Athos. Biblical scenes in the portico wall paintings

907. Vatopedi, Mount Athos. A portion of the portico wall paintings showing various scenes from the life of Christ I

908. Vatopedi, Mount Athos. A portion of the portico wall paintings showing various scenes from the life of Christ II

909. Vatopedi, Mount Athos. A portion of the portico wall paintings showing various scenes from the life of Christ III

910. Vatopedi, Mount Athos. Individual panel from the portico wall painting panels centred on the Theotokos I

911. Vatopedi, Mount Athos. Individual panel from the portico wall painting panels centred on Christ I

912. Vatopedi, Mount Athos. Individual panel from the portico wall painting panels tiers centred on Christ II

The greatest development, however, was in the fourteenth century beginning at Karyes, the capital and seat of the Mount Athos administrative assembly. Here stands the tenth-century church of **Protaton**, the oldest on the peninsula. It is without doubt one of the most important churches on Mount Athos for its ancient walls are adorned with wall paintings attributed to Emmanuel Panselinos, the last of the great mural painters from the so-called Macedonian School of Art at the beginning of the fourteenth century.

913. Vatopedi, Mount Athos. Individual panel from the portico wall painting panels centred on the Theotokos II

914. Church of the Protaton, Mount Athos. Head of the Theotokos in the Deësis portico wall painting

915. Church of the Protaton, Mount Athos. Head of St John the Forerunner in the Deësis portico wall painting

916. Church of the Protaton, Mount Athos. Head of Christ in the Deësis portico wall painting

917. Church of the Protaton, Mount Athos. The Deësis portico wall painting

918. Church of the Protaton, Mount Athos. SS Joseph and Athanasios the Athonite in portico wall painting

919. Church of the Protaton, Mount Athos. Four saintly figures in portico wall painting

920. Church of the Protaton, Mount Athos. SS John the Forerunner and Peter the Apostle

921. Church of the Protaton, Mount Athos. SS Theophanes and Gabriel in portico wall painting

922. Church of the Protaton, Mount Athos. SS Philotheos and Gennadios on portico wall

923. Chelandari, Mount Athos. Wall painting of Christ flanked by SS Savvas (left) and Simeon (right) above door to the refectory

924. Chelandari, Mount Athos. Individual panel in the refectory portico

His arrangement of the paintings in three thematic bands separated by frames became the model for the subsequent decoration of the churches of Mount Athos and beyond. While the wall paintings of the fourteenth century from the Palaiologan era have bright colours and dramatic movement there was little in the way of artistic production in the following century due most likely to uncertain political and economic times.

In the sixteenth century there was renewal of artistic expression as a result of a more stable period along with economic prosperity. Most of the great works of painting on Mount Athos are from this century and reflect a strictness of the ascetic life expressed in a monastic style that came to be called the Cretan School. The chief representatives of the School are Theophanes Strelitzas Bathas and his sons, the Cretans Antonios and Tzorzis, and the Theban Frangos Katelanos. The paintings of Theophanes in the

925. Esfigmenou, Mount Athos. Wall paintings above the main entrance to the monastery

926. Esfigmenou, Mount Athos. Prophet-King David

927. Esfigmenou, Mount Athos. Prophet-King Solomon (on front door panel at monastery entrance)

928. Philotheou, Mount Athos. Wall painting of a saint on arch at monastery entrance

929. Philotheou, Mount Athos. Wall painting of enthroned Theotokos and Christ Child on arch at monastery entrance

katholika of the monasteries of Megistis Lavra in 1535 and Stavronikita in 1546 are considered the best work of his mature period. At Stavronikita he was assisted by his son Simeon. There are three icons by Theophanes on the re-erected marble iconostasis of Protaton at Karyes, the original which is dated to the tenth century. There are wall paintings by Antonios (1544) in the narthex of original *katholikon* of the monastery of Xenophontos and others of the Cretan School in the esonarthex (1564) and exonarthex (1637). Murals by Katelanos are found in the chapel of St Nicholas at Megistis Lavra. The striking murals of the church of Dionysios executed in 1546/7 are by Tzorzis who later (1568) also painted the highly stylistic murals at Dochiariou. In the *katholikon* of Megistis Lavra the marble iconostasis is adorned with icons covered in gold and wreathed in precious stones that are the offerings of Byzantine emperors.

930. Megistis Lavra, Mount Athos. Mosaic icon of St John the Theologian

931. Mount Athos, Stavronikita. Enthroned St Nicholas with Christ and the Theotokos at his shoulders (wall painting at entrance to the *katholikon*)

932. Stavronikita, Mount Athos. Christ Pantokrator in the centre of the *katholikon* dome, encircled by a ring depicting the Divine Liturgy and in the outer ring prophets holding open scrolls with inscriptions

933. Stavronikita, Mount Athos. Crucifixion wall painting in the *katholikon*

934. Stavronikita, Mount Athos. Annunciation on the Beautiful Gate in the *katholikon*

935. Stavronikita, Mount Athos. Prophet Elijah painted by Michael Damaskinos

There are a very large number of portable icons in the monasteries of Mount Athos. Most icons are to be found on the iconostasis of the churches and the rest in small chapels or stored in the treasuries of the monasteries. As the monks especially revered the Theotokos it is not surprising to find her image as the most popular icon and are considered among the richest treasures of Mount Athos. On a special icon stand in the church of Protaton there is the historic tenth-century icon of *Panagias tis Karyótissas*, also known as the *Axion Estin*. There are over 20 icons of the Theotokos which are related to miracles. Besides the five in the Monastery of Vatopedi the most famous of all on Mount Athos, however, is the Theotokos *Portaïtissa* kept in a private chapel in the monastery of Iveron.

PLACES OF SPLENDID SPIRITUAL ART 329

936. Xenofondos, Mount Athos. St Demetrios mosaic

937. Xenofondos, Mount Athos. St George icon

938. Dochiariou, Mount Athos. St Nicholas wall painting in exonarthex portico

939. Dochiariou, Mount Athos. St Trifon wall painting in exonarthex portico

940. Dochiariou, Mount Athos. St George wall painting in exonarthex portico

941. Dochiariou, Mount Athos. Deësis wall painting in exonarthex portico

942. Dochiariou, Mount Athos. Archangel Michael wall painting in exonarthex portico

943. Mount Athos map cover signifying the holy peninsula as the 'Garden of Panagia'

944. Chelandari, Mount Athos. Portable mosaic icon of the Theotokos

945. Iveron, Mount Athos. Portable icon of the Theotokos *Portaítissa*

All of the icons include the Christ child except a rare full-length Theotokos *E Geróntissa*, in silver in the *katholikon* of the monastery of Pantokratoros.

There are hundreds of murals in the many churches, chapels as well in the *kyriakón*, the main church of the *skétes*, on Mount Athos but just too many to mention individually. It is worth noting, however, the extensive mural decoration of the outer narthex of the *katholikon* of the Monastery of Koutloumoussi. In addition, many monastery refectory interior walls were extensively decorated with wall paintings depicting religious scenes.

Unfortunately, most early murals on Mount Athos have been retouched even repainted over the centuries and their original character diminished or ruined.

The art of painting declined in the seventeenth century as the Cretan School had run its course. Murals dating from the eighteenth century can be found in some of the monasteries but many were influenced by western art. An exception was the work of the monk Dionysios of Fourna (*c*.1670 – after 1744) who taught a return to the techniques of Panselinos and wrote a manual of iconography, the so-called *Hermeneía*. His work can be seen in the chapel of St Demetrios in Vatopedi. Only in the second half of the twentieth century have painters on Mount Athos revived the original Byzantine style.

946. Megistis Lavra, Mount Athos. Portable icon of the Theotokos *Koukouzelíssa*

947. Stavronikita, Mount Athos. Refectory wall paintings by Theophanes

948. Megistis Lavra, Mount Athos. Refectory wall paintings by Theophanes

949. Koutloumoussi, Mount Athos. Exonarthex wall paintings at northern entrance

950. Koutloumoussi, Mount Athos. Exonarthex looking south with entrance to the inner narthex in the centre left

951. Koutloumoussi, Mount Athos. *Proskynetárion* of the Theotokos and Christ Child in the northwest corner of the exonarthex

952. Koutloumoussi, Mount Athos. Exonarthex with doors to the *parekklesion* guarded by the two archangels Michael (left) and Gabriel (right)

953. Koutloumoussi, Mount Athos. Christ in Glory in an exonarthex dome

954. Koutloumoussi, Mount Athos. The Theotokos and Christ Child on a cross in an exonarthex dome

955. Koutloumoussi, Mount Athos. The Theotokos *Foverá Prostasía* wall painting in the exonarthex

956. Koutloumoussi, Mount Athos. St Athanasios wearing a bishop's crown in a wall painting in the exonarthex

957. Koutloumoussi, Mount Athos. St Moses in a wall painting in the exonarthex

958. Koutloumoussi, Mount Athos. Archangel Gabriel in a wall painting in the exonarthex (right side of the door to the *parekklesion*)

Meteora

On a series of tall, gigantic rocky pinnacles in the centre of the Greek mainland are perched monasteries that make the monks feel close to the blue sky during the day and the bright stars at night. Some ascetics lived there in solitude before the first monastery of Doupiani was built in the ninth century. By the fourteenth century there were 24 monasteries mounted on the peaks of Meteora protected by imperial decrees and patriarchal privileges. Impressive art work can still be seen at six well-preserved and maintained monasteries. The oldest of the six is the monastery of St Stephen, started in the twelfth century, and it is also the most accessible. Of the remainder, three were founded in the fourteenth century.

959. Great Meteoron, Meteora. Narthex dome with multiple scenes

960. St Nicholas Anapafsis, Meteora. An angel deacon, *katholikon* dome

961. St Nicholas Anapafsis, Meteora. St Paxomios and angel wall painting by Theophanes

962. St Nicholas Anapafsis, Meteora. SS Anthony (left) and Efthymios (right) wall painting by Theophanes

963. St Nicholas Anapafsis, Meteora. SS John the Theologian (left) and Theophanes (right) wall painting by Theophanes

These are the Great Meteoron on the highest summit, St Nicholas Anapafsis ('Repose') and the Roussanou. In the fifteenth century the monastery of Holy Trinity was built on a secluded peak and the following century the monastery of Varlaam was built on its own mountaintop with a majestic *katholikon* dedicated to All Saints.

As the *katholikon* of the **Great Meteoron** was built and decorated in the fourteenth century its wall paintings are by Macedonian School artists. In the sanctuary the scenes are painted with realism, lively movement, and with dramatic action, such as the *Koímisis* of the Theotokos and the Martyrdoms of Saints. The Cretan School, with its more reserved approach, was prominent during the sixteenth century when much of the wall painting in the churches

964. St Nicholas Anapafsis, Meteora. Prophet Isaiah wall painting by Theophanes

965. St Nicholas Anapafsis, Meteora. St Nicholas wall painting by Theophanes

966. Varlaam, Meteora. SS Athanasios, the First Monk and Teacher of Meteoron (left) and Joseph, First Monk and Founder holding a model of the church (right), by Frangos Katelanos

at Meteora was done. Although the monastery **St Nicholas Anapafsis** was founded in the fourteenth century its *katholikon* was only built later during the first part of the sixteenth century. The interior was completely and wonderfully decorated with wall paintings by the Cretan iconographer Theophanes. These are his first paintings before he went on to do those on Mount Athos. In the narthex he signed his name under the large composition of the Last Judgment whereas his work at Mount Athos remained unsigned. Other inspired scenes in the narthex by Theophanes are the Death of St Nicholas, that of St Ephraim, and a vision of Paradise in which Adam names the different animals. Exceptional paintings in the *katholikon* of St Nicholas include the impressive Christ Pantokrator in the central dome of the naos and the icon of Extreme Humility by Emmanuel Tzanes in the bema. At the church of **All Saints in Varlaam** another famous Cretan iconographer, Frangos Katelanos, illustrated the naos and bema in 1548. The narthex was painted later, in 1566, by the Theban brothers Father Giorgios and Frangos Dikotaris. On the iconostasis there is a beautiful icon of an enthroned Theotokos draped in red holding the infant Jesus who has a robe of gold. Important sixteenth-century murals are also to be found in the *katholikon* of the monastery of Roussanou.

Hosios Loukas

Located at the ancient site of Stiris east of ancient Delphi is the monastery of **Hosios Loukas**. In the centre of the monastery's courtyard is a unique combination of two churches joined together. The first to be built, the Church of Panagia, was almost certainly the only one built in mainland Greece in the tenth century. Later, in the eleventh century, Abbot Philotheos built the adjacent church of Hosios Loukas that became the *katholikon* of the monastery. The narthex of the *katholikon* is covered in superb mosaics that centre on the figure of Christ in a semi-circular arch above the doorway to the naos. He is depicted with an open Gospel in his hand and an inscription that he is the light of the world.

PLACES OF SPLENDID SPIRITUAL ART 335

967. Hosios Loukas, Stiris. Mosaic of St Loukas

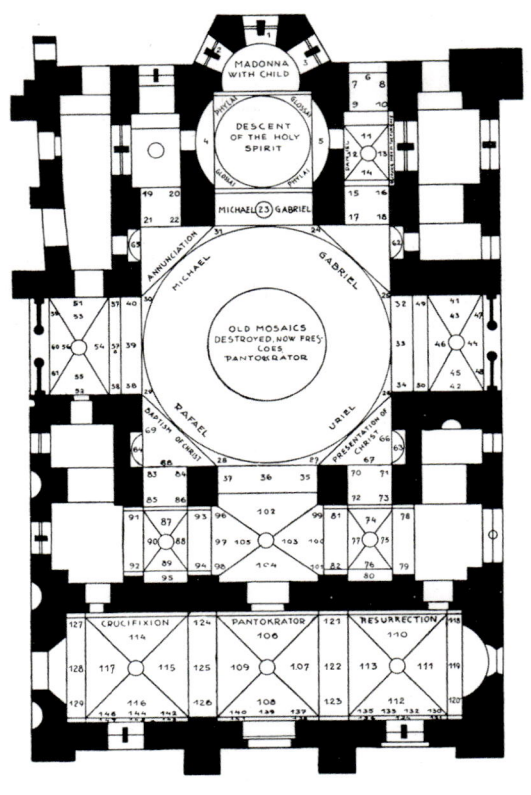

968. Hosios Loukas, Stiris. Location plan of 147 images (legend omitted)

969. Hosios Loukas, Stiris. Narthex cross vault of north door with Christ (bottom), the two archangels (centre) and St James (top)

970. Hosios Loukas, Stiris. Christ in the lunette above central narthex door to naos and in the cross vault the Theotokos, the two archangels and St John the Forerunner

971. Hosios Loukas, Stiris. St John the Theologian (narthex)

972. Hosios Loukas, Stiris. St Paul (narthex)

973. Hosios Loukas, Stiris. Christ washing the feet of the disciples (narthex)

974. Hosios Loukas, Stiris. Incredulity of Thomas (narthex)

975. Hosios Loukas, Stiris. The Resurrection (narthex)

976. Hosios Loukas, Stiris. The Crucifixion (narthex)

977. Hosios Loukas, Stiris. Christ Pantokrator in central dome of the naos

978. Hosios Loukas, Stiris. Presentation of Christ in the temple on northwest squinch (naos)

979. Hosios Loukas, Stiris. The Nativity on southeast squinch (naos)

980. Hosios Loukas, Stiris. Various saints on barrel vault, arch and northwest cross vault (naos)

In front and above him in the four sectors of the cross vault are depicted the Theotokos, St John the Forerunner, and the Archangels Gabriel and Michael. In the narthex there are in addition over 40 separate figures of apostles, saints, and martyrs and four scenes from the Gospels. The Crucifixion is a simple dramatic scene that shows Christ dead, head bowed, his eyes closed and face serene. On one side is his mother in a dark robe and sad face pulling at the edge of her mantle as if to raise it across her face, for she cannot bear to see the suffering of her son. On the other side is the Apostle John with a sorrowful expression on his face his cheek resting on his hand, a pose of weeping.

981. Hosios Loukas, Stiris. St John Chrysostomos (southeast niche in naos)

982. Hosios Loukas, Stiris. St Nicholas (southwest niche in naos)

983. Hosios Loukas, Stiris. Theotokos *Hodegétria* (wall painting in southern arm of the naos cross)

984. Hosios Loukas, Stiris. Prophet Daniel in the diaconicon

Except for a small number of mosaics the decoration in the naos itself is in the form of wall paintings. There are estimated to be about 150 figures of saints, martyrs, bishops and others depicted on the surfaces of the upper walls of the naos, side chapels and galleries. The original mosaic image of Christ Pantokrator inside the main dome and other mosaics in the dome were destroyed in the earthquake of 1593. As mosaic was expensive the image was replaced with a painting that imitated mosaic so successfully that viewers cannot tell that it is not real. The main apse of the bema depicts a *Platytéra* with the Theotokos enthroned within a vast golden heaven and with the infant Jesus on her knees. Until their theft in 1980 the iconostasis had at one time four icons by the famous Cretan iconographer, Michael Damaskinos. There are also fine wall paintings in the older Church of Panagia and in the crypt of St Barbara below the naos of the *katholikon*.

Fine elaborate, ornamental brickwork decorates the exterior of the Panagia church and in the interior the marble inlay floor is of particularly high quality.

The historic, walled monastery of Hosios Loukas is the largest of three monasteries that survive from the Byzantine period in Greece. The other two are those of Daphni (described later) and Nea Moni (New Monastery) on the island of Chios. The *katholikon* at **Nea Moni** is dedicated to the Theotokos. Among the fine mosaics in the church are those of Archangels Gabriel and Michael in two side apses in the sanctuary. The mosaic decoration that survives from the eleventh-century *katholika* of these monasteries provides a good idea of how the previous restrained iconographic decoration of churches had become more elaborate.

985. Hosios Loukas, Stiris. *Platytéra* in the apse semi-dome

Mystras

After the sack of Constantinople by the Fourth Crusaders in 1204 a castle was constructed at Mystras in 1249 and the fortified stronghold became the seat of Byzantine administration in the Peloponnese. In time its growth into a city led to Mystras becoming the centre of cultural and intellectual activity in southern Greece. As it sits on a sunny hillside overlooking the vale of Eurotas, the former capital city is a living museum that is impressive to walk through today, even though its castle, palaces, mansions, churches and monasteries, except one, are deserted. Splendid wall paintings can still be seen in the empty churches but more so in the still active metropolis (cathedral) dedicated to **St Demetrios** and the *katholikon* of the monastery of Pantanassa. The wall paintings in the metropolis church are from two separate periods. The first were completed between 1270

986. Metropolis, Mystras. Christ Pantokrator (*katholikon* central dome)

987. Hodegetria, Mystras. Theotokos and prophets (*katholikon* central dome)

988. Hodegetria, Mystras. Theotokos *Zoodóchos Pigí* (arch above entrance to the naos from the narthex)

989. Hodegetria, Mystras. The Holy Martyrs (northwest chapel)

and 1285 soon after the church was built. The exceptional paintings of this period are best seen in the diaconicon and prothesis of the metropolis church. In the second period the wall paintings are more narrative with scenes from the life of Christ and decorate the naos and narthex. They were completed between 1291 and 1315. On the floor in the centre of the naos is a marble slab with a double-headed eagle carved in relief an emblem of the Palaiologoi. According to tradition this was where Constantine XI, the last Byzantine Emperor, stood when crowned in 1449.

The early fourteenth-century murals of the church of **Panagia Hodegetria**, or Aphentiko (a reference to the ruler Theodore II buried here) as it is also known, are largely preserved. Their splendour is still apparent as is the programme they follow. Over the door of the narthex into the church and welcoming those that enter is Panagia, attended by her parents Joachim and Anna shown as the *Zoodóchos Pigí* ('Life-Bearing Source'), one of the first known depictions of scene. The remainder of the narthex is decorated with scenes from the life of Christ. Inside the naos apostles and disciples are depicted on the walls and holy martyrs and saints in the side aisles. In the bema there is an imposing procession of deacons and hierarchs. Up in the gallery are portraits of biblical patriarchs, prophets and kings. The composition in the central dome has been lost but the *Platytéra* in the half dome of the sanctuary apse is still imposing. Below her is the scene of the Communion of the Apostles. Scholars believe that the wonderful murals with their strong vibrant colours of the Aphentiko were the work of iconographers from Constantinople.

990. Hodegetria Mystras. St Gregory of Armenia (*katholikon* wall)

The *katholikon* of the monastery of **Perivleptos** ('Seen from all Sides') displays rich and colourful wall decorations that also follow a programme and date to the 1360s. Scenes from the life of Christ are splendidly depicted in the vaults that cover each arm of the Greek cross-shaped church. The bema contains a smaller than usual *Platytéra*, as well as scenes of the Communion of the Apostles and the Ascension. The Divine Liturgy itself is depicted with the sacred gifts carried in litany by angels dressed as deacons and presented to Jesus as the great high priest. Below the scene of the Divine Liturgy the great hierarchs, editors of the Divine Liturgy, with their liturgical scrolls are portrayed. The ethereal and spiritual qualities of the angels in Byzantine art can be compared to the naturalistic and physically beautiful angels depicted in Western art. The depiction of the liturgy supports the one purpose of Orthodox iconography – to depict the liturgy particularly the profound act of the Eucharist. The interior of the church is dominated by a magnificent Christ Pantokrator surrounded by eight scenes in the form of petals containing images of the Theotokos, Cherubim and Seraphim. Art historians believe the wall paintings of the Perivleptos are the work of four painters detectable in the way features were modelled, how colours were treated, and the manner in which the landscape was conceived. Despite that the compositions throughout are in harmony with one another.

991. Perivleptos, Mystras. Christ Pantokrator (*katholikon* central dome)

The monastery of **Pantanassa** ('Queen of the Universe') is located high up on the hill just below the walls of the crest-top castle. Founded in 1428 it was the last great church built at Mystras and whose murals represent the last years of the Byzantine era. The iconographers of the *katholikon* of Pantanassa were no doubt inspired by the wall paintings of the Perivleptos as they follow a similar decorative programme. They were not mere copyists as their creative independence is evident in their use of lighter, cool colours. Also, the religious scenes at Pantanassa tend to be larger and more crowded with architectural and landscape elements. The *Platytéra*, with the all-embracing Theotokos enthroned between the two archangels, is as vibrant today as it was in the past, and the Ascension in the vault of the sanctuary is a superb composition.

992. Pantanassa, Mystras. *Platytéra* (*katholikon* apse semi-dome)

In some of the other churches at Mystras only fragments of the murals are visible, such as at Evangelistria, SS Theodoroi, and Hagia Sophia. There are also about 20 small chapels that belonged to officials and aristocratic families, many with murals partially preserved. After the Fall of Constantinople, Mystras was occupied first by the Ottoman Turks then the Venetians. The medieval city was abandoned in the 1830s after the Greek War of Independence when the new town of Sparti was built nearby on the site of ancient Sparta.

993. Pantanassa, Mystras. The Ascension (apse vault)

994. SS Theodoroi, Mystras. A military saint (*katholikon* wall)

995. Metropolis, Mystras. Two of thirteen hierarchs (*katholikon* wall)

Athens

Among the oldest churches in Athens is that of **Panagia Kapnikarea**, with striking eleventh-century wall paintings as well as those in front of the iconostasis completed in traditional style by Fotis Kontoglou between 1930 and 1958. Original Byzantine works of the tenth and eleventh centuries can also be seen in the churches of **Agioi Apostoli** in the ancient agora, **Agia Triada**, and **St Catherine**.

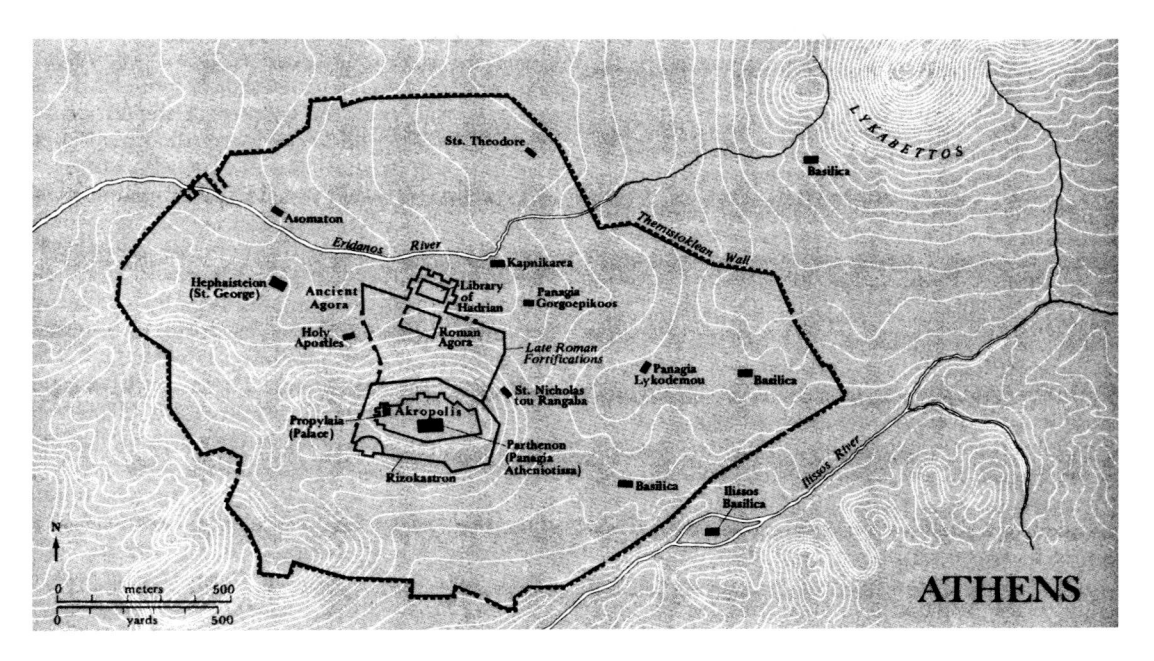

996. Athens. Map of Byzantine churches

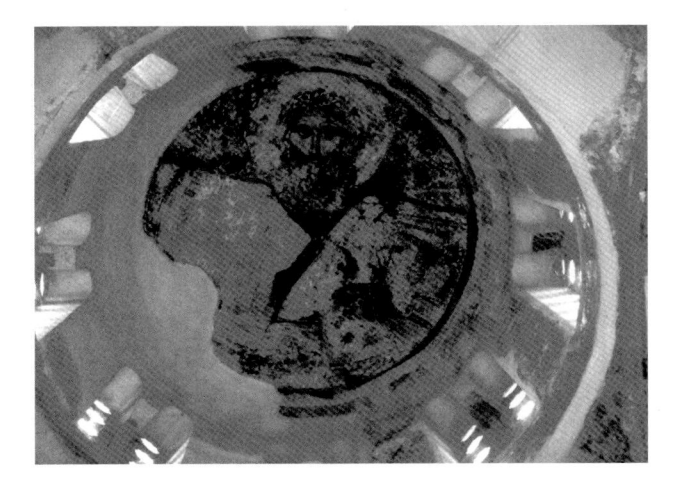

997. Holy Apostles, Athens. Christ Pantokrator (*katholikon* central dome)

998. Holy Apostles, Athens. Faded figure of a saint (*katholikon* wall)

There is an exquisite *Platytéra* in the apse of the small, thirteenth-century church of **Panagia Gorgoepikoos** that also goes by the name of St Eleftherios.

Just outside Athens is the ancient monastery of **Daphni**, dating back to the time of Emperor Justinian. The richly coloured mosaics of the *katholikon* built in 1080 are incomparable. The most famous is the masterpiece of a severe-looking Christ Pantokrator in the dome of the church, even though a small portion of the figure and some of the gold setting are missing. On the drum supporting the dome between the windows 16 prophets are depicted. In the four squinches below are representations of the Annunciation, the Nativity, the Baptism, and the Metamorphosis (Transfiguration) of Christ. In both the left and right arcades of the naos there are scenes from the New Testament. Also on the outskirts of Athens is the **Omorphe Ekklesia** (Beautiful Church) dedicated to St George whose interior is profusely adorned with thirteenth-century wall paintings. Although most are spoiled and covered in soot, the paintings that remain are an indication of the exquisite quality of the church's spiritual art.

999. Theotokos Gorgoepikoos, Athens. *H Platytéra ton Ouranon* (apse semi-dome)

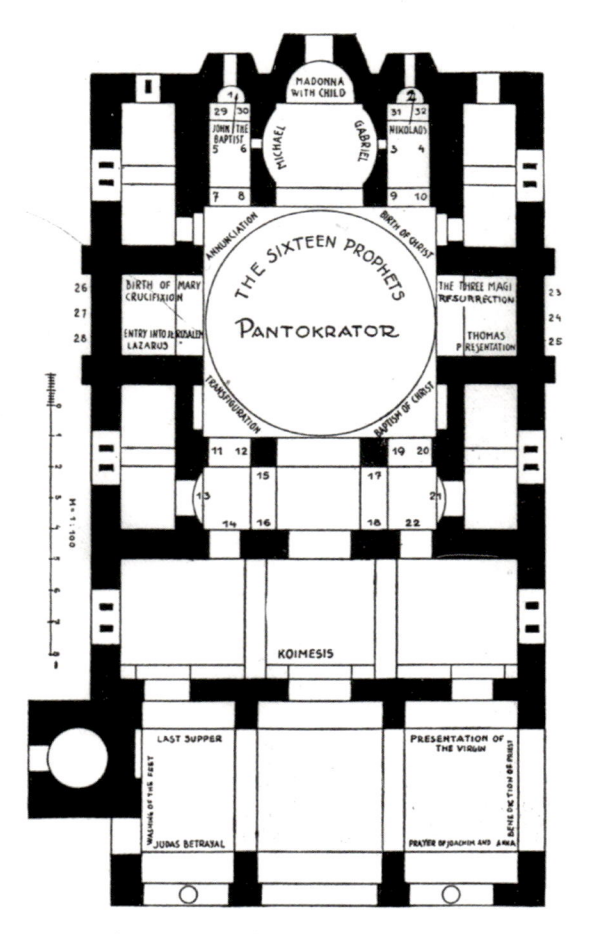

1000. Daphni, Athens. *Katholikon* iconographic programme (legend omitted)

1001. Daphni, Athens. Christ Pantokrator (*katholikon* central dome)

PLACES OF SPLENDID SPIRITUAL ART 345

1002. Daphni, Athens. The Nativity (*katholikon* squinch)

1003. Daphni, Athens. The archangel Gabriel from the Annunciation

1004. Daphni. Theotokos from the Crucifixion

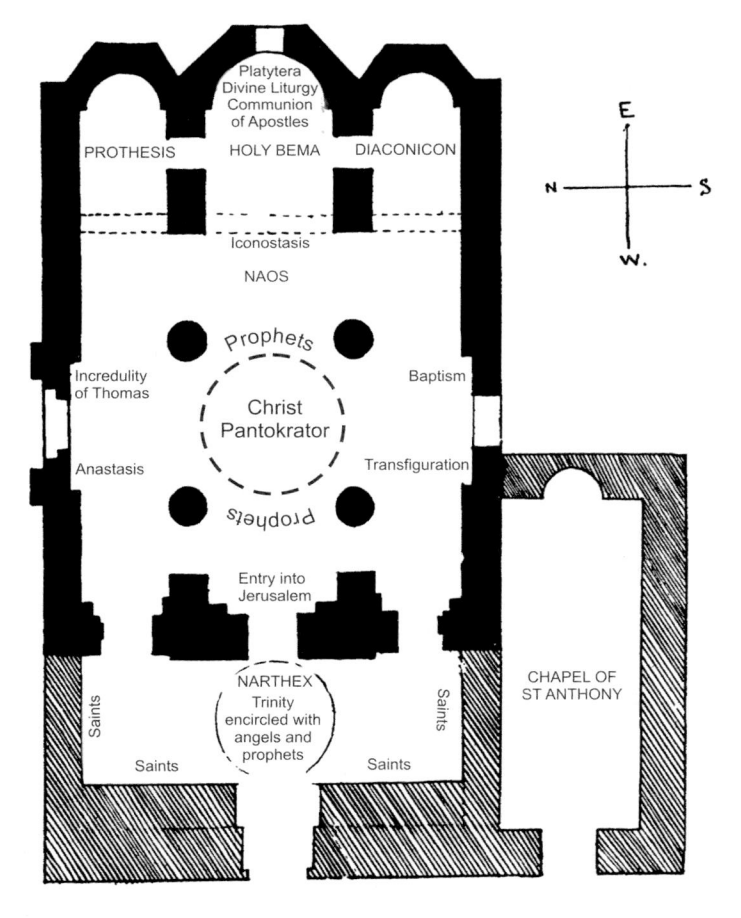

1005. Kaisariani, Athens. *Katholikon* iconographic programme

1006. Holy Trinity, Athens. SS Stephen and John the Theologian with Christ above (*katholikon* side wall)

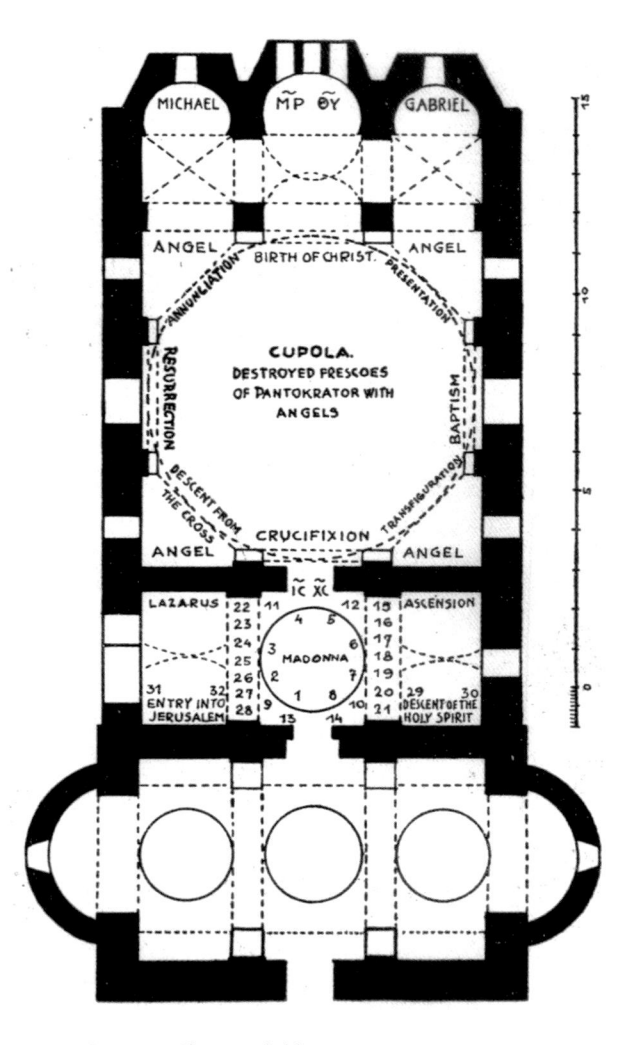

1007. Nea Moni, Chios. *Katholikon* iconographic programme (legend omitted)

Constantinople

As capital of the eastern empire Constantinople originally had the most splendid of Christian monuments. Justinian I (r. 527–565) built numerous churches as well as undertaking a significant rebuilding of the city, damaged by riots in 533. The Hagia Sophia was the largest church built by Justinian. Its interior was richly adorned with golden mosaics which were highly praised by those that saw them. Unfortunately virtually all the mosaics with figures were destroyed by the Iconoclasts during the eighth century and first half of the ninth century. The remaining golden mosaics in Hagia Sophia not destroyed by the Iconoclasts were shipped to Venice after the Fourth Crusaders sacked Constantinople in 1204.

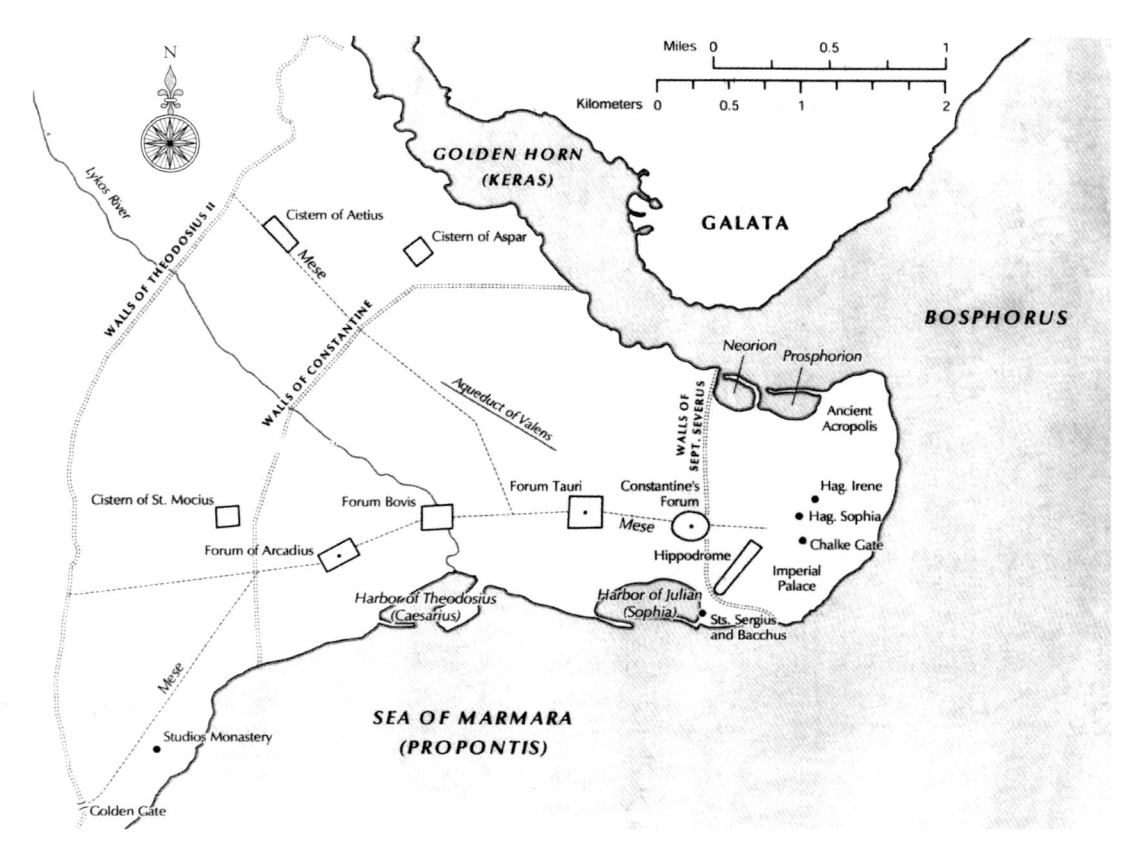

1008. Constantinople. Location of major landmarks

During the period of the Ottoman Empire the mosaics left were covered up with plaster and only restored in the middle of the nineteenth century.

Above the door from the Orologion Gate leading from the courtyard into the narthex of **Hagia Sophia** there is a striking middle tenth-century mosaic of a seated Theotokos holding the Christ child in her lap. She sits on a jewel encrusted throne but one without a back and with her feet resting on a pedestal. As usual she is identified with the letters MP ΘY. On her left is Emperor Constantine holding a model of the city of Constantinople. Along his side there is a vertical inscription that states 'Constantine, a Saint and Great Emperor'. On the right side of the Theotokos is the Emperor Justinian offering her a model of Hagia Sophia. Along his side is the vertical inscription 'Justinian, the Exalted Emperor'. Above the Royal Doors in the narthex that leads into the church there is a late-ninth- or early-tenth-century mosaic of Christ seated upon a magnificent throne adorned with jewels. In his left hand he holds an open book resting on his left knee and on the open page is the inscription 'Peace (be with you). I am the Light of the World.' His right hand is raised in a gesture of blessing. At the foot of the throne an emperor, either Leo V or VI, prostrates himself. On either side of Christ contained in roundels are the Theotokos on the right side and the archangel Gabriel on the left side. In the half dome of the sanctuary apse above five rounded windows set against a golden background is the figure of the Theotokos wearing a dark blue

348   THE SACRED ARCHITECTURE OF BYZANTIUM

1009. Hagia Sophia, Constantinople. Emperor Leo V or VI at Christ's feet with the Theotokos who holds her hands in intercession (medallion left) and an archangel (medallion right) (lunette above the Royal Doors)

1010. Hagia Sophia, Constantinople. Close-up of the *Platytéra* (apse semi-dome)

1011. Hagia Sophia, Constantinople. The Deësis mosaic (west wall of south gallery)

1012. Hagia Sophia, Constantinople. Christ from the Deësis mosaic (west wall of south gallery)

garment seated on a throne studded with precious stones. In an unusual gesture her right hand rests on the shoulder of the Christ child who sits on her lap. Edges of the mosaic are missing or are damaged as are the figures of the Archangels Michael and Gabriel on the bema arch.

Most of best-preserved and restored mosaics at Hagia Sophia are in the south gallery, some with holy figures and royalty together. An eleventh-century mosaic, for example, has the enthroned Christ, clad in dark blue robe, in the centre with the letters IC XC, and beside him the Empress Zoe and her third husband Constantine IX Monomachus in ornate imperial costume. Over his head there is an inscription stating that he is 'Constantine Monomachos, Autocrat and Pious Emperor of the Romans'. Above the head of the Empress is the inscription 'Zoe, the Very Pious Augusta (her official title)'.

It appears that the heads and names of the emperor and empress were replaced at some point by the heads and names of other holders of the imperial crown. In another mosaic composition, one from the twelfth century, the Theotokos is flanked by the Emperor John Komnenos and the Empress Eirene along with their eldest son Alexios, all wearing ceremonial garments. In both mosaics the emperor holds a purse that symbolizes an imperial donation to the church, and in each the empress offers a scroll document. The most famous mosaic and one widely considered by some to be the finest mosaic in Hagia Sophia, although fragmented, is the *Deësis* ('Entreaty' in Greek), because of the tones and the softness of the features of Christ, the Theotokos and St. John the Forerunner. The mosaic probably dates from 1261, reflects Western influence in the tenderness and kindness expressed in the face of Christ and the more realistic facial features of the Theotokos and St. John, and marks a departure from the traditional approach to Byzantine pictorial art. In the centre of the central dome it is known that there is the conventional Christ Pantokrator mosaic but is has remained covered in plaster. The mosaic is dated to the ninth century and replaced one of the cross that had been installed there during the Iconoclastic period.

1013. Hagia Sophia, Constantinople. Panagia from the Deësis mosaic (west wall of south gallery)

During the Iconoclastic period the church of **Hagia Eirene** was rebuilt following its destruction by an earthquake in 740. The apse, in keeping with the Iconoclastic principle that there should be no figural art, was redecorated with a large mosaic cross instead. Between 876 and 880 the Emperor Basil I built the first post-Iconoclastic church in Constantinople, the **New Church**, so-called as it implied a new beginning. Preaching at the consecration of the church in 881, Patriarch Photius commented on its spiritual art, specifically the Christ Pantokrator in the dome, symbolizing heaven, ruling the universe and looking down on the world that he created and redeemed. Photius remarked on the 'heavenly hosts of angels' in the cross-shaped sections around the dome crowding around Jesus to serve him. In the next highest space in the church, the apse in the sanctuary, he described the figure of the Theotokos as shining out with outstretched hands bestowing good fortune. Other spaces in the church were filled with the images of apostles, martyrs, prophets and patriarchs with saints in their due order placed on the upper parts of the walls.

1014. Hagia Sophia, Constantinople. St John the Forerunner from the Deësis mosaic (west wall of south gallery)

In the **Church of Holy Saviour in Chora** (the Country) a powerful Byzantine statesman, Theodore Metochites, endowed the church with magnificent mosaics carried out between 1315 and 1321. They represent an awesome and largest collection of surviving Byzantine spiritual art in the city. Most of the mosaics are in the outer and inner narthex and all the wall paintings in the *parekklesion*.

In the *parekklesion* there are 26 murals of various religious themes and persons. After walking through the triple archway of the *parekklesion* narthex what catches the eye first are the full-length

1015. Hagia Sophia, Constantinople. Christ flanked by Emperor Constantine IX Monomachos (r. 1042–1055) and Empress Zoe (mosaic in east corner of south gallery – inscriptions were added later)

1016. Hagia Sophia, Constantinople. Theotokos and Christ Child flanked by Emperor John II Komnenos (r. 1118–1143) and Empress Eirene (mosaic in east corner of south gallery)

figures of six Fathers of the Church set against a dark blue background at the far end of the *parekklesion* on the semi-circular back wall of the apse. The most eye-catching scenes, though, are those in the two domes and semi-dome. In the centre of the first dome from the narthex is the Theotokos with the Christ child in her lap encircled in a medallion from which 12 painted decorative ribs extend out to the edge of the dome. Between the ribs at the bottom of the dome there are large arched windows. In each segment between the top of the window and the central medallion there is a fine painting of a full figured angel. On the pendentives four gospel hymnographers are depicted. An archway separates this first dome from the next one which contains a representation of the Last Judgment. It is a complex scene with Christ sitting enthroned

1017. Hagia Sophia, Constantinople. Theotokos and Christ Child (central figure in east corner of south gallery mosaic)

1018. Hagia Sophia, Constantinople. An archangel

in the blue circle of heaven flanked by the Theotokos and St John the Forerunner interceding for humanity. The apostles are seated on benches on both sides and archangels fill the background. Most dramatic of all three scenes is the *Anástasis* (Resurrection), in the semi-dome of the apse. In the centre Christ is shown in an action pose, clad all in white within a blue and white oval frame ornamented with stars representing heaven, pulling Adam and Eve out of their sarcophagi.

1019. Holy Saviour in Chora, Constantinople. The *parekklesion*: view of apse, decorated wall and vaults of the naos space

1020. Holy Saviour in Chora, Constantinople. The Anastasis (*parekklesion* apse emi-dome)

1021. Holy Saviour in Chora, Constantinople. Close-up of the Anastasis (*parekklesion* apse semi-dome)

1022. Holy Saviour in Chora, Constantinople. Archangel Michael in front of the Anastasis scene (*parekklesion*)

Above them on either side pious groups of people are assembled. Under the feet of Christ are the broken gates of hell shown all in blackness. This powerful scene is accentuated by a large circle painted at the top of the broad arch in front of the apse semi-dome containing a bust of the Archangel Michael. Of the remaining wall paintings in the *parekklesion* perhaps the most poignant and sorrowful is that of the Theotokos *Eleoúsa* in muted colours at the bottom of the southern end of this broad arch.

In the outer narthex there are 18 mosaic scenes which do not appear to follow a specific programme. Over the arch of the entrance door is the Theotokos shown with outstretched arms and the baby Jesus in a circle in front of her chest. They are flanked by two angels. On the other side on top of the door leading into the inner narthex is a superb figure of Christ robed in dark blue

1023. Holy Saviour in Chora, Constantinople. Close-up of the archangel Michael (*parekklesion*)

1024. Holy Saviour in Chora, Constantinople. Full figure of the Theotokos *Eleoúsa* and Christ Child (south wall of the *parekklesion*)

1025. Holy Saviour in Chora, Constantinople. Christ in 'The Land of the Living' (lunette above door from outer to inner narthex)

1026. Holy Saviour in Chora, Constantinople. Theotokos with the Christ Child presented as a symbol of the universe (arch above entrance to outer narthex)

holding a jewelled book in his left hand and blessing with his right hand in the Byzantine manner. The inscription in the book reads 'The Land of the Living'. Beginning on the end or north wall of the outer narthex the series of scenes depicted on the walls in a clockwise direction are about the early life of Jesus. In the five vaults above there is the Young Jesus, John the Forerunner and Satan, the Miracle at the Wedding in Cana, Healing the Leprous Man, and Healing the Paralyzed Person. On opposite pilasters at the northern end are the figures of St Andronicus and St Trachos.

There does not seem to be a coherent programme in the 29 mosaics of the inner narthex either. But the two domes in this space each have a fabulous mosaic. The slightly larger dome of the end bay on the south side depicts Christ in the centre enclosed in a medallion. This recalls the description from the year 1200 of the mosaic of Christ in a dome of the Holy Apostles church (a building which no longer exists) by Nicholas Mesarites, a Byzantine writer.

1027. Holy Saviour in Chora, Constantinople. Christ 'Chalke' (in centre of a large, arched niche southeast corner of the inner narthex)

1028. Holy Saviour in Chora, Constantinople. Emperor Isaac I Komnenos (r. 1057–1059) (bottom left of the Christ 'Chalke' composition)

1029. Holy Saviour in Chora, Constantinople. Theotokos (left side of Christ in the 'Chalke' composition)

He visualized the scene of Christ framed by a rainbow-like circle as a portrayal of Christ looking out of a window of heaven. At Chora 24 triangular slivers spread out from the medallion to the edge of the dome. In the middle of each sliver is a figure of one of the ancestors of Jesus from Adam to Jacob. At the bottom of the dome there are nine arched windows and between them there are 15 figures representing the sons of Jacobs and others. In the dome of the end bay at the north end there is an equally matchless mosaic but in this case the central medallion has the typical figure of the Theotokos holding the Christ child in her lap. From the medallion 16 triangular wedges spread out each containing ancestors of Jesus but this time beginning with David and ending with Salathiel. As this dome is smaller than the southern dome there is space only for five windows and squeezed between and below them are 16 figures of an additional 11 ancestors of Jesus. The Theotokos mosaic in the northern dome has an ugly scar of a repaired crack across the one side that blemishes it. Fortunately the Jesus mosaic in the other dome is only slightly marred. On the barrel vaults between the domes and on the walls on the northern part of the inner narthex are scenes devoted to the life of Mary, the mother of Jesus. The theme of healing from the southern end of the outer narthex is continued in a number of scenes on the walls at the same end of the inner narthex.

1030. Holy Saviour in Chora, Constantinople. Christ and his ancestors (dome at south end of inner narthex above the Christ 'Chalke')

1031. Holy Saviour in Chora, Constantinople. Christ surrounded by his early ancestors from Adam to Jacob (dome at south end of inner narthex)

1032. Holy Saviour in Chora, Constantinople. Close-up of Christ in a medallion blessing with his right hand and holding a closed Gospels book in his left hand (dome at south end of inner narthex)

1033. Holy Saviour in Chora, Constantinople. Theotokos surrounded by Jesus' ancestors – 16 prophet-kings from David to Salathiel (dome at north end of inner narthex)

1034. Holy Saviour in Chora, Constantinople. Close-up of Theotokos and Christ Child in a medallion (dome at north end of inner narthex)

A significant highlight of the inner narthex is the doorway leading into the narthex. Above the doorway there is a figure of Christ as there is above the doorway from the outer to the inner narthex but with two major differences. First, Christ is shown sitting on a jewelled and cushioned throne, without a back, with his feet resting on a low stool. Second, is the remarkable figure of the sponsor of the mosaics and murals, Theodore Metochites kneeling on the right side of Christ and presenting him with a model of the church. On either side of the doorway are striking full-length mosaic figures of St Peter and St Paul, each looking inward toward the door and giving the appearance of guardians. St Peter is shown holding a scroll in his right hand and the 'keys of heaven' in the other.

PLACES OF SPLENDID SPIRITUAL ART

1035. Holy Saviour in Chora, Constantinople. *Katholikon* naos looking at apse

1036. Holy Saviour in Chora, Constantinople. *Koimisis tis Theotokou* (above entrance to naos from inner narthex)

1037. Parekklesion, Theotokos Pammakaristos, Constantinople. Christ Pantokrator surrounded by 12 prophets (naos dome)

1038. Parekklesion, Theotokos Pammakaristos, Constantinople. Close-up of Christ Pantokrator (naos dome)

St Paul is portrayed with a closed book of Gospels in left hand and blessing with his right but with a variation from the Byzantine manner in that only his thumb and fourth finger touch. On the east wall below the Jesus dome there are fragments of what must have been once a beautiful scene. Christ is shown in the middle with his hands across his body and on his right the bowed figure of the Theotokos with open hands pleading with her son. Below and to her left is the head and shoulder of the emperor Isaac I Komnenos (r. 1057–1059) looking up towards her. On the other side of Christ is the praying figure of a nun.

1039. Parekklesion, Theotokos Pammakaristos, Constantinople. Prophet Jeremiah (naos dome)

1040. Parekklesion, Theotokos Pammakaristos, Constantinople. Prophet Zephaniah (naos dome)

1041. Parekklesion, Theotokos Pammakaristos, Constantinople. Prophet Micah (naos dome)

Unfortunately only three mosaics remain in the naos itself. On the north pier of the apse arch in the naos is a somewhat deteriorated figure of Christ standing holding an open book of Gospels in his left hand and blessing with his right hand. To complete the symmetry on the south pier is a standing figure of the Theotokos *Hodegétria* in somewhat better condition. The most complete mosaic in the naos is the *Koímisis* (Dormition) of the Theotokos in a large, square format above the door from the inner narthex. At the bottom of the scene the Theotokos is shown stretched out on a red lined bier with hands crossed over her chest. On the left St Peter is shown with a censer and on the right the bent figure of St Paul venerating the deceased Theotokos. Behind the bier in mourning are the other apostles, holy men and women. As always in the Byzantine depiction of the Koimisis above the bier and in the centre of the scene is the golden, shining figure of her son, Jesus Christ, holding a baby that is intended to symbolize her soul. Christ is enclosed in a mandorla surrounded by four angels with the winged form of the Holy Spirit hovering above them all. The mandorla is a pointed and generally almond-shaped radiant shape indicative of the power of God.

1042. Parekklesion, Theotokos Pammakaristos, Constantinople. Prophet Zachariah (naos dome)

The *parekklesion* of the **Theotokos Pammakaristos** ('All-Blessed'), even though it is a chapel rather than a main church, has the third most surviving mosaics in the city after St Saviour Chora and Hagia Sophia. The mosaics of the *parekklesion* are simply superlative. As in most Byzantine religious buildings the central dome dominates the interior space which is accentuated in this case by a magnificent mosaic of Christ Pantokrator. As usual the figure of Christ is contained in a medallion in the middle and from which 12 decorative ribs extend out to the edge of the dome. Each rib ends in an arched window. In the spaces between the windows are depicted in full figure 12 named prophets from the Old Testament. Each holds a scroll with an inscription which read as follows:[1]

Isaiah: Behold, the Lord rideth upon a swift cloud
Moses: For the Lord your God is the God of gods, and Lord of lords
Jeremiah: This is our God, there is none to compare with him
Zephaniah: For all the earth shall be devoured with fire of my jealousy
Micah: The mountain of the house of the Lord ... shall be exalted above the hills
Joel: Fear not, O land. Be glad and rejoice; for the Lord will do great things
Zachariah: The mountain of the Lord of hosts
Obadiah: But upon Mount Zion shall be deliverance
Habakkuk: Oh Lord, I heard thy speech
Jonah: And may my prayer come in unto thee
Malachi: Behold! I will send my messenger
Ezekiel: And when the living creatures went

1043. Parekklesion, Theotokos Pammakaristos, Constantinople. Christ *Yperagáthos* (bema apse)

1044. Parekklesion, Theotokos Pammakaristos, Constantinople. Theotokos (left side bema niche)

1045. Parekklesion, Theotokos Pammakaristos, Constantinople. St John the Forerunner (right side bema niche)

After the mosaic in the dome the next mosaic to stand out is the sole figure of Christ *O Yperagáthos* in the half dome of the bema apse that is partially damaged on the lower right-hand corner. The epithet *Yperagáthos* ('the most benevolent') has not been found in other representations but appears mostly in the prayers for the Funeral Service which is appropriate for the *parekklesion* as it contained tombs of the Michael Glavas family. Christ is shown seated on a jewelled backless throne with a closed Gospels book resting on his knee with his left hand holding the top and blessing with his right hand in the Byzantine manner. Along the top are the letters IC XC. Around the edge of the apse is a half round cornice with a lengthy inscription that reads 'On behalf of her husband Michael Glavas, who was a champion and a worthy *Prostrator*, Martha the nun (has offered) this pledge of salvation.' Maria (whose name changed to Martha when she became a nun), wife of the general

1046. Parekklesion, Theotokos Pammakaristos, Constantinople. Close-up of St John the Forerunner (right side bema niche)

1047. Parekklesion, Theotokos Pammakaristos, Constantinople. Archangel Raphael (bema vault)

1048. Parekklesion, Theotokos Pammakaristos, Constantinople. South arm of naos cross looking west

1049. Parekklesion, Theotokos Pammakaristos, Constantinople. South arm of naos cross looking east at diaconicon

Michael Glavas Doukas Tarchaneiotes who had the military rank of *protostrátor*, built the chapel in memory of her late husband after the year 1310.

Of immense interest is the unusual arrangement on the side walls of the bema on either side of the Christ figure in the half dome. On the right hand side of Christ is an image of the Theotokos in a large niche and in the left niche St John the Forerunner.

PLACES OF SPLENDID SPIRITUAL ART 359

1050. Parekklesion, Theotokos Pammakaristos, Constantinople. St Efthymios

1051. Parekklesion, Theotokos, Pammakaristos. St Gregory of Armenia

1052. Parekklesion, Theotokos, Pammakaristos. St Ignatios Theophoros

1053. Parekklesion, Theotokos, Pammakaristos. St Anthony

1054. Parekklesion, Theotokos Pammakaristos, Constantinople. Close-up of St Ignatios Theophoros

1055. Parekklesion, Theotokos Pammakaristos, Constantinople. Close-up of St Anthony

1056. Parekklesion, Theotokos Pammakaristos, Constantinople. Close-up of St Antipas

1057. Parekklesion, Theotokos Pammakaristos, Constantinople. Close-up of St Gregory of Armenia

1058. Parekklesion, Theotokos Pammakaristos, Constantinople. Close-up of St Gregory of Agrigentum

1059. Parekklesion, Theotokos Pammakaristos, Constantinople. Close-up of St John Klimakos

This arrangement is unusual in that the figures are full length and they overlook the entire space of the bema. What is remarkable is that their role is that of intercessors as their outstretched hands indicate. Above the Theotokos is the Archangel Michael in the north groin of the cross vault that covers the bema and above St John is the Archangel Gabriel in the south groin. On the east and west groins are the Archangels Raphael and Uriel.

Originally the arches and small domes that covered the four corner spaces, partially supported by the free standing columns in the naos, were full of mosaics that also covered the vaults in the prothesis and

1060. Parekklesion, Theotokos Pammakaristos, Constantinople. Close-up of St Arsenios

1061. Parekklesion, Theotokos Pammakaristos, Constantinople. Close-up of St Efthymios

diaconicon. What remains are portrayals of seven bishops from Constantinople and Jerusalem, each in ornate attire and holding a Gospels book, in the northeast and southeast corners, and in the southwest corner six saint monks the most prominent of whom is St Anthony.

In an arched wall space in the southeast corner there is a wonderful depiction of the baptism of Jesus by John. Jesus is shown naked standing in the Jordan River and on his right side John is bending down with his hand over the head of Jesus. On the left side of Jesus are four angels one of whom is holding Jesus' folded garment in his hands. Directly over the head of Jesus are the symbols of the

Holy Spirit and God the Father. In the water of the river fish are shown and on one side there is a man in a shell pouring water and on the other side a young figure pointing up. In the narthex there are remains of wall paintings one of which is observable as that of the three Wise Men who are headed in the direction of the bema. They wear clothes in red, yellow, blue, green and black colours and each is bearing a gift.

Cappadocia

In eastern Anatolia, in the centre of present day Turkey, is Cappadocia. It has an alien-like landscape formed from eons of solidified volcanic ash layers eroded from wind and rain to create canyons and valleys and numerous striking cone stone structures. Early Christians took refuge here from Roman soldiers as did Christians between the seventh and thirteenth centuries when they sought a safe haven under threat from Muslim Arabs. When St Paul looked for a secure place after he was expelled from Jerusalem he came to Cappadocia and established the first Christian colony in this region with his followers.

1062. Parekklesion, Theotokos Pammakaristos, Constantinople. Baptism of Jesus

Over time Christians enlarged several Bronze Age underground cities in Cappadocia. Each city was many levels deep and housed thousands of people. Christians also created several below ground monasteries and carved hundreds of churches out of the rock formations in the area. Wall paintings in the rock-cut churches still retain their original freshness. The religious art is Byzantine in nature from both the pre- and post-Iconoclastic periods but with local touches. The **Tokali Church** is the largest in the area and consists of two main structures known as the Old and New Churches. The Old Church dates to the tenth century and is painted with scenes from the New Testament and depicts some saints with pale hues of red and green. In the New Church which was added at the end of the tenth century or early in the eleventh, the panels include the miracles of Christ and are dominated by a rich indigo colour obtained from lapis lazuli. Among the best-preserved paintings are those in the eleventh-century **Dark Church**. It was decorated with scenes from the New Testament including the Nativity, Last Supper, Crucifixion and Anastasis. Other interiors with superb wall paintings are in the Apple Church, the Church of St Barbara, the Snake Church and the Church with Sandals.

Dura-Europos

The location of Dura-Europos at the intersection of a major east-west route on the Euphrates River made it an important caravan city from its founding at the end of the fourth century BC. In a Christian house church discovered by archaeologists in the city remarkably preserved wall paintings dating from the year 235 were found. Among the surviving wall paintings in a baptistery room Christ is shown as the Good Shepherd, Healing the Paralytic, and walking on water with Peter. Interestingly enough there were no wall paintings in the main assembly room.

Madaba

The town of Madaba in Jordan was an important centre for making mosaics between the fourth and eight centuries. One of the significant mosaics is a map of the Holy Land (542–570) on the floor of the church of St George in Madaba. Mosaics in other churches, such as that of the apostles and the one of Prophet Elijah, depict indigenous fishes, birds, mammals and fruits. Another floor mosaic (530), this time on the baptistery floor of a monastery in the Siyagha area, depicts a natural scene of animals and plants. Other spectacular sixth-century mosaics of natural subjects are in the church of SS Lot and Procopius in Nebo village and in the nearby church of Preacher John. A seventh-century church at the birth place of the Prophet Elijah in a place known as Tell Mar Elias has a floor decorated with multicoloured mosaics of floral and geometric motifs. Geometrical designs are also a feature of the floor mosaics in other fifth- and sixth-century churches in the Jordan Valley.

Jerusalem

At one time Jerusalem probably had the most concentration of church mosaics but few have survived the many waves of destructions. Mosaic fragments are to be found in the remains of a fourth-century basilica (site of the Church of the Agony), the Basilica of St Stephen built in the fifth century by the wife of Theodosius II, Aelia Eudocia, and a fifth-century floor in the Monastery of the Cross on the location claimed to be the tree that gave its wood for the cross on which Christ was crucified. On Mount Olives the mosaic floor of the fifth-century monastery (today site of the Dominus Flevit Church) is richly decorated with intersecting circles and images of fish, fruit, leaves and flowers. In an unusual gesture the mosaicist was identified as Simon in a Greek inscription as he who 'decorated this place of prayer in honour of Jesus'. Early Christian mosaics are also preserved in the Church of St John the Baptist, Church of the Tomb of St Stephen and Church of the Seat of Mary (*Káthisma*). In all these churches, and others in Palestine and neighbouring areas, the floor mosaics have purely geometrical patterns.

Crete

After the sack of Constantinople in 1204 Crete became a Venetian possession. Stability and prosperity during the next two centuries was reflected in the number of churches and wall paintings created all over the island during this time. Cretan painting began to be shaped by the links still maintained with Constantinople and from collaborations with Venetian artists. Little is preserved from this time so the character of the painting from this period is difficult to reconstruct. Nevertheless, from the beginning of the fifteenth century icons painted in Crete have survived that display the now mature mixed style. After the Fall of Constantinople in 1453 and the Ottoman conquest of Mystras seven years later the stream of fleeing artists to Crete enabled the island to become the centre of Byzantine religious art. Sacred images were produced for the domestic market and exported to the eastern Mediterranean and Venice. A distinct school of the painting of sacred images emerged. Although the Cretan school created a new mode of painting it was still based on the traditional belief in their purpose – the expression of spiritual realities rather than the material depiction of the physical world.

Angelos Akotantos, in the first half of the fifteenth century, pioneered the merging of Byzantine and Western approaches to painting in Cretan icons. The style of icons came to be called *alla greca* that were sold in Greece and Venice but the demand declined in the sixteenth century. Perhaps for this reason Cretan artists travelled outside Crete to find work. Theophanes Strelitzas and his sons, for example, went to mainland Greece to paint churches and create icons. Others were attracted to Venice where there was a Greek confraternity, the Scuola di San Nicolo dei Greci, and the Church of San Giorgio dei Greci, where most of the icons on the iconostasis were by Michael Damaskenos. He was one of three Cretan artists to introduce features from Renaissance art into Cretan iconography. The other two were George Klontzas and Domenikos Theotokopoulos. Theotokopoulos' (1541–1614) initial training as a Cretan icon painter, his early experiments with Italian art and his subsequent unique career in Venice and then Spain, brought him onto the main stage of European painting where he is better known as 'El Greco'. Three icons discovered in different collections early in the twentieth century were authenticated as painted by him during his Cretan period. They all contain his signature in Greek. It is interesting to contrast these three icons with three known works he completed in Venice, before his move to Toledo, which show emergent changes in style and the use of oil instead of egg tempera. When he moved to Venice in his mid-twenties he altered his style substantially and developed his own distinctive way of painting traditional religious subjects.

Sinai

The **Monastery of St Catherine** is in the heart of the Sinai desert and is a foundation of Emperor Justinian I (r. 527–565). It is an exceptional complex with extremely well-preserved early Christian art which is fortunate as those elsewhere in Egypt have not survived very well due to the destruction of churches. Since its foundation, the Orthodox monastery of St Catherine has had a continuous life of over 1400 years protected over time from plunder by Arab caliphs, Christian Crusaders, Turkish sultans and even Napoleon Bonaparte himself. As the monastery has never been conquered, damaged or destroyed it represents an authentic and original image of the early Christian past. Its inaccessible location and that the Sinai was under Islamic control prevented any destruction by the Iconoclasts and eighth-century Byzantine emperors.

The first structure on the site was a small church dedicated to Panagia erected by Helena, the mother of Emperor Constantine in the year 330. A tower at the presumed spot of Moses' Burning Bush was to serve as a secure shelter for the monks. About two centuries later Justinian ordered the building of a great, walled monastery fortress around the earlier church and tower. The library became the second in importance only to that of the Vatican with its eventual collection of over three thousand items, from valuable manuscripts, early printed books, to documents bearing the seals of emperors, patriarchs, bishops and sultans.

Several decades after the building of the main church, the *katholikon*, also dedicated to the Theotokos, the magnificent mosaic of the Metamorphosis (Transfiguration) of Christ was created and fills the half

1063. St Catherine, Mount Sinai. Christ in a mandorla with Elijah (left) and Moses (right), Apostles Peter (at his feet), John (left) and James (right) (*katholikon* apse semi-dome)

1064. St Catherine, Mount Sinai. Enthroned Theotokos and Christ Child flanked by SS Theodore and George (icon)

1065. St Catherine, Mount Sinai. Theotokos and Christ Child (icon)

1066. St Catherine, Mount Sinai. St Peter (icon)

1067. St Catherine, Mount Sinai. St Antipas (icon)

dome of the sanctuary apse. In the centre is the imposing figure of a bearded Christ enfolded in a blue coloured oval known as a mandorla radiating light and set against a glowing golden background. On either side of him equal in size are Elijah and Moses and at his feet kneeling in awe and fear are John and James, and a just visible Peter. In the figure of Christ the artist has captured radiantly Matthew's description that 'His face did shine as the sun and His raiment was white as the light' (17:2). In the wide painted border of the Metamorphosis are medallions of the Twelve Apostles, 12 prophets, the abbot of the monastery at the time of construction of the mosaic, Longinus and the deacon John.

PLACES OF SPLENDID SPIRITUAL ART

The monastery has over 2,000 icons that are priceless and of immense spiritual, artistic and historic value and among the greatest treasures of the Orthodox world. From the sixth century there are 12 rare icons made in the coloured wax-melting or encaustic technique. Although difficult to identify any one of the 12 worthy of separate and special recognition three of them should be described. Each depicts faces in a naturalistic manner in the tradition of the Hellenistic art of Alexandria. The icon of Christ Pantokrator (actually seventh century) represents Jesus like a ruler holding in his left hand a closed richly ornamented Gospels book. His right hand blesses in the Byzantine manner. In the second icon the enthroned Theotokos holds the infant Jesus and is flanked by two saints, Theodore and George. Behind them are two angels each with a scepter looking upward. St Peter is depicted in the third icon holding the keys of the kingdom in his right hand and a long staff surmounted by a cross in his left hand. Above him are three small medallions with Jesus in the centre one, the Theotokos to his left, and an unidentified young man to his right. These three icons vary in size from 18" by 24" to 21" by 38".

Bawit and Sakkara

Christian art in Egypt is represented by the distinctive Coptic Art that was influenced by Hellenistic and ancient Egyptian works. In the early years of Christianity the wall paintings are described as unsophisticated but in a way attractive in their almost crude style. The Copts loved bright, clear colours and were extremely talented in mixing different dyes and powdered rock, often using the white of an egg to combine them. Samples of Coptic paintings can be seen in places such as Bagawat in the Kharga Oasis, St Simeon's Monastery at Aswan, in the temple of Luxor, the White Monastery at Sohag, the Monastery of St Makar in Wadi El Natroun, and the sanctuary of the Ethiopian St Takla Hemanout in the Church of Al Moallaka in Old Cairo. The monastery at **Bawit** is famous for its colourful murals from the sixth and seventh centuries. The decorated niches from both the monasteries of St Apollo at Bawit and St Jeremiah at Sakkara are now in the Coptic Museum in Cairo. In the upper section of one of the famous niches from Bawit Christ is shown enthroned in an enclosed oval, a mandorla, carried on wheels with

1068. Bawit, Egypt. Theotokos and Christ Child flanked by the apostles

1069. Bawit, Egypt. Christ with his protective arm around a holy monk, saint Apa Mena ('Abbot Menas')

flames thrashing at its base. At the side of the mandorla are the heads of the winged creatures associated with the four evangelists. In between the creatures are the Archangels, Michael on the left and Gabriel on the right. In the lower section of the niche the enthroned Theotokos is in the centre holding the infant Jesus and is flanked by the Twelve Apostles and two local saints.

In 420 Cyril I hung icons in all the churches of Alexandria and then decreed that they should be hung in other Egyptian churches as well. By the end of the century icon images changed from the naivety of the faces to a more spiritual expression influenced by the art of Palestine and Syria. Figures began to be drawn with more elegance, clerical garments were presented with richer adornment, and the backgrounds were filled with more gold. Egyptian artists did not seem to conform to the stylization elsewhere in the Christian world. The Archangel Gabriel, for example, would be painted sometimes with a cross at other times with a sword or even a trumpet. Then scenes of the Annunciation and the Nativity never seemed to be rendered the same way. Apart from the monastery of St Catherine, which was built by Emperor Justinian I, none of the other monasteries of Egypt attained the lavishness in their art work that took place elsewhere in the Byzantine Empire.

Monreale

In the town of Monreale (from the Latin *Mons Regalis* meaning Royal Mountain) just south of Palermo in Sicily is the cathedral **Santa Maria la Nuova**. The cathedral is unique as it represents the largest concentration of Byzantine, Arab and Norman art in one place. The splendid Byzantine mosaics cover virtually the entire walls of the interior and in area are larger than those of the splendid church of St Mark in Venice and perhaps more than any other Orthodox church anywhere else except Ohrid. Although far smaller in quantity the mosaics in the sanctuary of the twelfth-century cathedral of Cefalu in northern Sicily, or the more compact version of the Monreale cathedral mosaics in the Cappella Palatina in Palermo's Norman Palace, are noteworthy.

1070. Cathedral, Cefalu. Sanctuary apse and semi-dome

1071. Cathedral, Cefalu. Close-up of Christ Pantokrator blessing in the Byzantine manner (apse semi-dome)

The basilica-transept style cathedral in Monreale was built by William II who wished to impress Sicilian nobility and his subjects by ordering that the mosaic work be done by craftsmen from Constantinople. The mosaics were begun in 1176 and completed 13 years later. The ambitious aim was to depict in the art work the history of the world according to the Bible, from Creation to the Acts of the Apostles. For this reason there needed to be some organized way of presenting the story. The choice was to follow the traditional programme used in Byzantine churches. On the walls of both sides of the long nave and on the back wall there are 42 scenes from the Old Testament, starting with the Creation and

1072. Capella Palatina, Palermo. Christ Pantokrator

ending with Jacob's Fight with the Angel. The scenes are painted in two bands, the first above the arcade of pointed arches and the second above the first band and between the windows. Above the windows but below the decorated wood roof beams there is a row of medallions in the form of a frieze. The 48 medallions each depict the bust of an angel. Major events from the life of Jesus, from the Announcement to Zacharias to Pentecost are depicted in 49 scenes on the walls of the side arm spaces or transepts. On the walls of the side aisles and continuing on the back wall of the nave is a cycle of Jesus' miracles shown in 20 separate panels. Many of the scenes are accompanied by inscriptions in Greek or Latin.

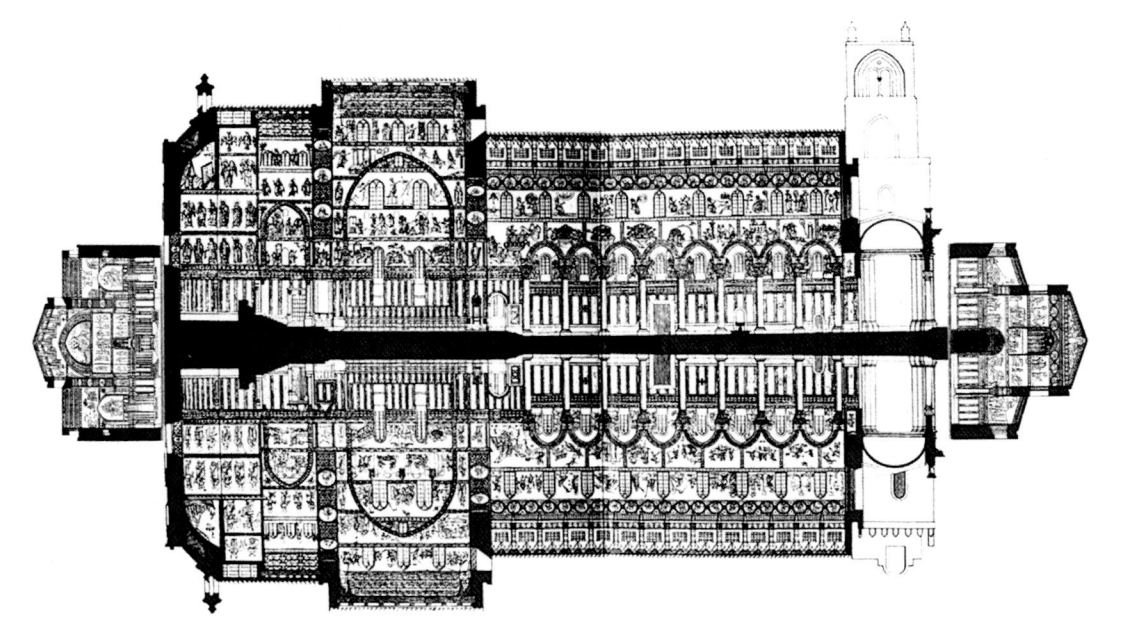

1073. Cathedral, Monreale. Interior elevations of the north and south walls (top and bottom), east and west end walls (left and right), showing full decoration

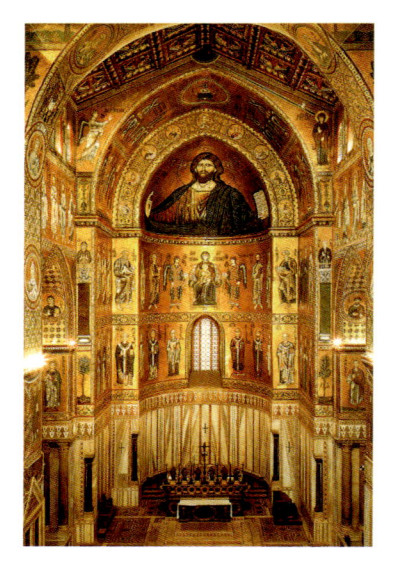

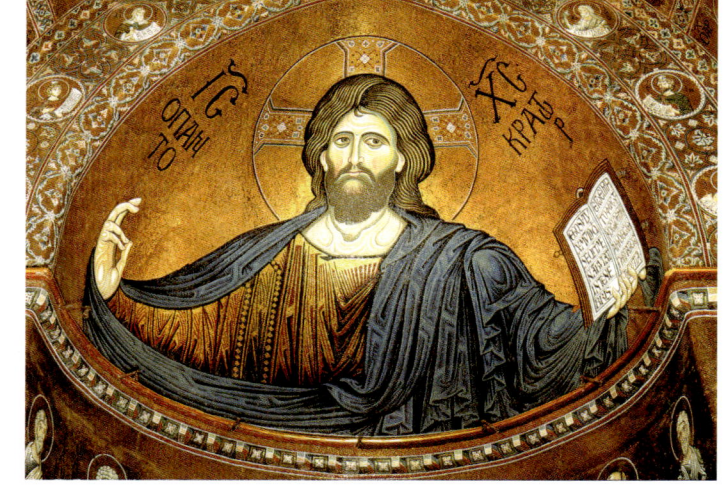

1074. Cathedral, Monreale. Nave looking at sanctuary apse

1075. Cathedral, Monreale. Close-up of Christ Pantokrator in sanctuary apse

Dominating the entire interior is the colossal mosaic of Christ Pantokrator located in the half dome of the central apse over the main altar. The right blessing hand of the Christ Pantokrator is curved rather than upright and the text on the open pages of the Gospels book are in both Latin and Greek scripts. This Pantokrator in the cathedral of Santa Maria la Nuova is not regarded by many as elegant as the one in the apse of Cefalu Cathedral. There, Christ, clothed in a luminous blue mantle and with sensitive facial features, is set against a glowing gold background. The right blessing hand of the Christ Pantokrator is also curved here and the Greek text in the circle around his bust is from the Book of Isaiah. Below the Pantokrator in the cathedral of Santa Maria la Nuova the two Archangels Gabriel and Michael appear below in a mosaic of the

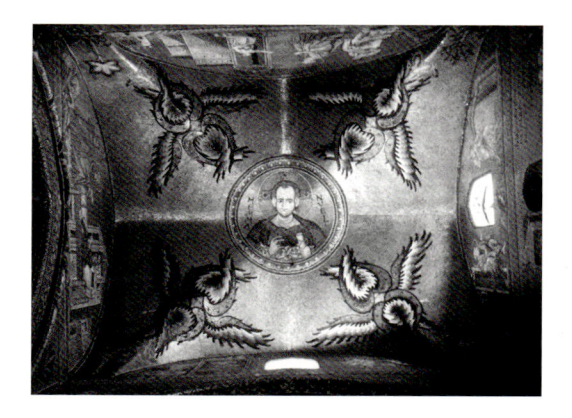

1076. Cathedral, Monreale. A beardless Christ as 'H Emmanuel'

1077. Cathedral, Monreale. Pentecost

Theotokos enthroned with the Christ child in her lap. Flanking the archangels are the apostles Peter, with keys and a cross, and James on one side and Paul and Andrew on the other. Below the mosaic of the Theotokos are the full figures of church fathers. Throughout the sanctuary area there are mosaics of angels, individual prophets, apostles and saints and scenes from the gospels. There are two notable scenes on the side – the one over the royal throne shows Christ crowning William II, while the one over the episcopal throne shows William II offering a model of the cathedral to the Theotokos. In the two side apses the mosaics depict the life of St Peter in one and St Paul in the other.

1078. Cathedral, Monreale. Theotokos enthroned

1079. Cathedral, Monreale. Scenes from the Lives of SS Peter and Paul

1080. Cathedral, Monreale. St Paul enthroned

1081. Cathedral, Monreale. St Peter enthroned

1082. Cathedral, Monreale. Animals enter the ark

1083. Cathedral, Monreale. God stops Abraham killing his son Isaac

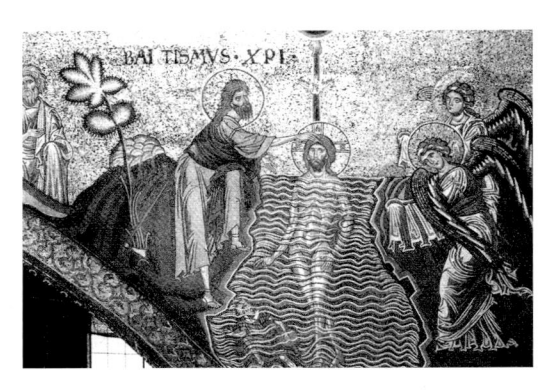

1084. Cathedral, Monreale. Baptism of Jesus

1085. Cathedral, Monreale. The Last Supper

1086. Cathedral, Monreale. Burial of Christ

1087. Cathedral, Monreale. Christ and Mary Magdalene

1088. Cathedral, Monreale. Ascension of Christ

1089. Cathedral, Monreale. The beheading of St Paul

1090. Cathedral, Monreale. Resurrection of Christ

1091. Cathedral, Monreale. Scene from the Life of Christ cycle

1092. Cathedral, Monreale. The Annunciation

1093. Cathedral, Monreale. Medallion of King Solomon

1094. Cathedral, Monreale. Theotokos and Christ Child

1095. Cathedral, Monreale. Corinthian column capital with added female bust

1096. Cathedral, Monreale. Interior view of the decorated roof trusses and underside of the tiles

XXI. Coptic icon. Athens, Byzantine and Christian Museum

XXII. San Cosma. Rome, SS Cosma and Damiano

XXIII. Theotokos and Christ Child icon. Rome, Santa Maria Maggiore

XXIV. Enthroned Theotokos and Christ Child. Ravenna, San Apollinare Nuovo

XXV. Christ from the Deësis mosaic. Constantinople, Hagia Sophia

XXVI. Theotokos *Hodegétria* icon. Constantinople now in Athens, Byzantine and Christian Museum

XXVII. Christ icon. St Catherine, Sinai

XXVIII. St Nicholas icon. St Catherine, Sinai

XXIX. Christ *despotikó* icon. *Katholikon*, Monastery of Stavronikita, Mount Athos

XXX. Theotokos *despotikó* icon. *Katholikon*, Monastery of Stavronikita, Mount Athos

XXXI. Christ portable icon. *Katholikon*, Monastery of Chelandari, Mount Athos

XXXII. The Crucifixion. Monemvasia now in Athens, Byzantine and Christian Museum

XXXIII. The Holy Trinity by Theophanes Bathas-Strelitzas. Athens, Byzantine and Christian Museum

XXXIV. Archangel Michael icon by Frangos Katelanos. Athens, Byzantine and Christian Museum

XXXV. Christ Pantokrator icon by Michael Damaskinos. Athens, Byzantine and Christian Museum

XXXVI. Theotokos *Hodegétria* icon by Michael Damaskinos. Athens, Byzantine and Christian Museum

XXXVII. Three Hierarchs icon by Michael Damaskinos. Athens, Byzantine and Christian Museum

XXXVIII. St Anthony icon by Michael Damaskinos. Athens, Byzantine and Christian Museum

XXXIX. Enthroned Christ icon by Emmanuel Tzanes. Athens, Byzantine and Christian Museum

XL. Enthroned Theotokos icon by Emmanuel Tzanes. Athens, Byzantine and Christian Museum

Chapter Six

LITURGY OF THE EUCHARIST

To obtain a deeper understanding of the sacred architecture and spiritual art of early Christian and Byzantine churches knowledge of the liturgy of those times is essential. As seen in the previous chapters the design of churches and their decorative programme had to meet specific liturgical requirements. There is, thus, no doubt that there was interaction between liturgical purpose, the shape and size of architectural spaces, fixtures and their relationships, and the position of specific religious images. Take the prothesis, for example, when a change in liturgical ritual had architectural implications. Once it was decided that the preparation of the bread and wine for the Divine Liturgy was to take place inside the church there were two architectural consequences. First, it became necessary to have an architectural space, whether a separate chamber or niche, inside the church for the prothesis, and, second, it led to the disappearance of the *skevophylákion* where the preparation of the gifts had traditionally taken place in early Byzantine churches. By necessity, then, the prothesis space had to be linked directly to the bema as this was where the Holy Table was located and where the Eucharist was consecrated. This in turn led to the need to develop a decorative programme for the prothesis space. The usual spiritual image used to decorate the prothesis became the birth, death or burial of Christ. These interrelationships and symbolic meanings will be further explored in the next chapter. In terms of the liturgy itself it took many centuries to develop from a simple ritual to an intricate ceremony.

The First Three Centuries

To start at the beginning. After the death of Christ the first few centuries were formative ones for the new religion. As there was no overriding authority during these times the various churches that were formed by believers in Christ had their own fixed order of worship or religious ceremony. Scholars have reduced these churches into six groups, named after the places where they originated and were used (and to the apostles to whom the ceremonies are attributed). These groups are Jerusalem (St James), Antioch (St Thaddeus), Alexandria (St Mark), Constantinople (St Basil and St Chrysostom), Ephesus (St John) and Rome (St Peter). Most of the churches belonged to Eastern groups that favoured ceremonies of greater variety compared to the Western which sought uniformity in organization and worship. The ceremony of Jerusalem is considered the oldest but this one and those of Antioch, Alexandria and Ephesus eventually went out of use. That of Constantinople came to form the Byzantine rite and later passed into the Eastern Orthodox churches. Today, repeated every Sunday, the symbolic drama of the life of Christ characterizes the Eastern Orthodox ceremony, accompanied as it is by symbolic acts of the priests and deacons and highlighted by processions, compared to the more instructive nature of the western Roman Mass.

For the first few decades after the death of Jesus believers came together on Saturday evenings to remember the Last Supper. The gathering took the form of a common meal in the dining room of the house of one of the believers. At the end of the meal the faithful shared in the breaking of bread and drinking from a cup of wine that became a distinctive Christian act. A precedent was a tradition in the Greco-Roman world where a fundamental form of social interaction was a communal or shared meal. Believers of Christ used this tradition to create cohesion within their new community. Over time the original simple act of breaking bread and drinking wine became an elaborate ritual with the addition of readings, ceremonies and prayers. But the essence of the ceremony of bread and wine always remained from the beginning to the present day the commemoration of the Last Supper of Jesus Christ and his 12 disciples at Passover.

From the common meal came the Christian Eucharist ceremony in which the bread symbolizes the body of Jesus and the wine his blood. St Paul, in his letter to the Corinthians in the year 52, claimed the command to break bread and drink from a cup of wine 'in remembrance of me' came from the Last Supper Jesus had with his disciples. The term Eucharist comes from the Greek word for thanksgiving (*efcharistía*). In the first century a prayer of thanksgiving was said over the bread and wine but there is no clear idea of its contents. It was probably modelled on the Jewish prayer of blessing, the *berakah*, such as used by Jesus at the Last Supper. The prayer came to be known as the Eucharistic prayer (*anaphorá*) or prayer of offering.

1097. Christ in a mandorla with symbols of the four evangelists at each corner

One of the earliest references to the term Christian is in the assertion that the 'disciples were called Christians first at Antioch' contained in the *Acts*, apparently written in Rome probably between the years 70 and 90, or even earlier. Another reference is by Tacitus (*c.*56–117), a historian of the Roman Empire, who recorded that the Emperor Nero blamed the 'Christians' for the Great Fire of Rome in the year 64. The common meal practice of Christians was mentioned by Pliny the Younger, a Roman governor of the Bithynia and Pontus province, in a letter to the Emperor Trajan in about 110 concerning his investigation of Christians. Pliny wrote that the customary practice of Christians was to assemble before daylight on a fixed day to sing hymns to Christ as God and bind themselves to one another with oaths. They would then depart 'to assemble again to partake of food'. It is not clear from Pliny's description on what day of the week these events took place. According to Tertullian, the 'Father of Latin Christianity' (*c.*160–220), the common meal that Christians enjoyed together was a dinner of love, an *agápe* meal, during which each person was called forward to sing to God from the divine scriptures. Pliny in his letter acknowledged Trajan's mandate and his own edict that Christians were to cease the practice of the common meal. This clearly did not happen.

It seems that by the end of the first century the act of the remembrance of Jesus was separated from the common meal for reasons unknown. The Eucharist ritual of bread and wine came to be attached to the synagogue service of scripture readings, sermon and prayers but held on Sunday mornings instead of Saturday, the Jewish Sabbath. The combined ritual and service soon became ordered as is evident from the epistle of Clement to the Corinthians about the year 96 in which he referred to 'the appointed rule' of the liturgy, as the ceremony was called, which 'we are bound to perform in due order'. In his epistle Clement uses the terms bishop (*epískopos,* overseer in Greek) and presbyter (*presbytéros,* an elder) for the higher order of ministers above deacons. His writing had authority as he was a leading member of the church in Rome in the latter part of the first century and may have known the Apostle Peter. By the end of the first century a collection of Christian writings had accumulated. A second-century bishop, Irenaeus of Lyon, asserted that the works attributed to the Apostles Matthew, Mark, Luke and John were *the* canonical Gospels. These four are also called the Evangelists from the Greek *evangélion* meaning 'good news'.

By early in the second century there were two forms of Eucharist services, the Sunday Eucharist and the one that involved baptism (not discussed here). An early account of the Sunday Eucharist is given by Justin Martyr (100–165) in his *First Apology* written about the year 160. He was brought up as a pagan, studied philosophy, converted to Christianity and suffered martyrdom in Rome under Emperor Marcus Aurelius (reigned 161–180). Justin begins his account by noting that on the day that is called the Day of the Sun persons from both the city and the countryside meet together in one place. The first activity is a reading by ordained lectors of the memoirs of the apostles or the writings of the prophets. The president (*proestós*), Justin's term but there is no doubt this referred to the bishop, then follows the readings with a discourse in which he exhorts the imitation of 'these good things'. When he finishes the assembled persons rise up in unison and offer prayers. After the prayers are finished bread and wine with water are brought out and the president offers prayers and thanksgiving to the best of his ability. As far as it is known there was no fixed text for the Eucharistic prayer at this time. The service is concluded by the congregation assenting with the exhortation 'Amen' ('so be it' in Hebrew). The deacons then distribute the bread and wine to those present and afterwards take them to those that are not there. These actions described by Justin followed the Jewish synagogue service of readings from the scriptures, a sermon, a prayer and perhaps concluded by the kiss of peace.

Justin also describes how the believers present in the assembly then give 'of his own possessions' each according to 'his own decision'. What is collected is entrusted to the president who uses what is collected to aid orphans, widows, the sick and others in need, prisoners, and to strangers who stay with him. The president is regarded as the patron (guardian) of all those who are in need. He is the 'one who has been proved from among the older men, an honor reached not by price, but by testimony (as to his character)' as wrote Tertullian in his *De idololatria* (*c.*196/7). In addition to the regular ritual conducted by the 'president of the brethren' he also performs the service of baptism that takes place in a separate place from the assembly area. Justin noted that it follows the regular ritual on the 'Day of the Sun' which actually was a pagan adulation of the sun that was recognized by the Christians.

It seems that the traditional themes of the Eucharistic prayer from these earliest times appeared in the thanksgiving recorded in the *Apostolic Tradition* composed by Hippolytus of Rome about the year 215. He was one of the most prolific writers of the early Church. The bread and wine used for the Eucharist were brought by people and handed over to the deacons who prepared enough for the service before the prayer of thanksgiving. How the people's gift of bread and wine was handled varied in the Western and Eastern parts of the Roman Empire. In the West people brought their gifts to the sanctuary barrier after the readings, sermon and prayers. The deacons collected the gifts and set aside enough needed for the Eucharist on the altar. In the East people handed in their offerings to a deacon on the way into church, either at a table near the entrance door, or in a small room just outside the church building. This is clear from the *Didascalia Apostolorum* which describes the role of the deacons as to 'let one stand always by the oblations of the Eucharist, and let another stand without by the door and observe them that come in; and afterwards, when you offer, let them minister together in the church'. The *Didascalia Apostolorum* is the title of a treatise which presents itself as being written by the apostles at the time of the Council of Jerusalem about the year 50, but most scholars agree that it was actually a composition of the third century, probably written in Syria in 230.

The word liturgy comes from the Greek *leitourgía* meaning 'public work' or 'work of the people'. In ancient Greece the word meant some public good which a wealthy citizen arranged at his own expense, either voluntarily or by law. The church use of the word comes from its frequent and historic use in the Greek text of the New Testament where it referred to a public and deliberate, well-defined ceremony, the Eucharist service. Also derived from the Greek is the use of the word *koinonía*, which means common or public to describe the sharing of the bread and wine, translated as communion. The preparation of the bread (*prósforon*,

1098. Book of Gospels cover. Gilded silver, enamels and precious stones

1099. Gospels book cover. Silver and precious stones

meaning offer) and wine for the Eucharist, the office of oblation, is referred to as the *proskomedía* (an offering) or sometimes the *prothésis* (setting forth). Nowadays the preparation in Eastern Orthodox churches occurs during the Orthros service which precedes the Eucharist liturgy. Orthros is from the Greek word *órthros* meaning morning, dawn or day break. The word *ekklesía*, literally call or summon out in ancient Greek, was the term used for the public assembly of citizens in the cities of Greece. In the Christian era the word was first used to describe an assembly of Christian believers and in time became the Greek word for church. In English the adjective ecclesiastical is derived from the Greek word.

Fourth to Sixth Centuries

When Emperor Constantine (r. 306–337) officially recognized Christianity at the beginning of the fourth century a great period of church building set in that continued until the end of the reign of Emperor Justinian (r. 527–565). At the same time the structure of the liturgy arrived at a basic form, a two-part service on Sunday morning, with variations within the various rites. The first part, derived from the Jewish synagogue ritual was first called the *Sýnaxis* or Liturgy of the Word but came to be called the Liturgy of the Catechumens (persons receiving Christian instruction from the Greek word *katechetís*, instructor). This part of the Sunday liturgy consisted of scripture readings, a sermon and a prayer. In the second part, the Liturgy of the Faithful called the Eucharist service, believers who had been baptized shared in the bread and wine after a thanksgiving prayer. By the middle of the fourth century the two parts of the service had been combined into one and known as the Eucharist liturgy.

The two-part liturgy became standardized but with some variations from region to region. Throughout the Roman Empire Christians living in cities participated in the liturgy at a church directed by the local bishop. In Rome with its large population this became difficult with the increase in the number of Christians. The Bishop of Rome, Dionysios (served 259–268), devised the parish system to solve this problem. Presbyters were put in charge of additional churches in the city 'under the bishop', a system that became common throughout the Empire.

One form of the liturgy was known as the Jerusalem rite. This rite was described by Cyril of Jerusalem, and perhaps by his successor John, in the fourth and fifth lectures of the *Mystagogical Catecheses* (oral instruction into the mysteries of religion). Cyril (*c*.315–386) was a distinguished theologian of the early Church who was bishop of Jerusalem from about 350. His famous 23 catechetical lectures (Greek *katechíseis*, literally to sound down or indoctrinate) that he delivered while still a presbyter in 347 or 348, contained instructions on the principal topics of Christian faith and practice for the catechumens to whom they were delivered. His last instructional addresses were called mystagogic (Greek *mystagogikaí*) as they dealt with the *mysteries* (*mystíria*), that is, the sacraments of baptism, confirmation and the Eucharist. The last of the lectures described the sequence of prayers in the liturgy. It is evident that there was a major departure from the previous centuries as there was more emphasis on the sacrifice of appeasement than one of thanksgiving.

The *Apostolic Constitutions*, a handbook of church teaching and practice for both clergy and laity during the last quarter of the fourth century, is the earliest complete description of the Eucharist liturgy. The account represents the usage of the Church of Antioch from which that of Constantinople was ultimately derived. In the fourth century the Eucharist liturgy as performed in Antioch differed from the Jerusalem or Alexandrian rites. What is significant about the ultimate rite of Constantinople is that the later Byzantine liturgy, the first surviving text of which dates from the end of the eighth century or the beginning of the ninth century, bears striking resemblances to that of Antioch.

In outline the fourth-century Antiochian rite, as described in the *Apostolic Constitutions,* is as follows: The liturgy begins with a call by the bishop for the assembly of the congregation. People are to gather in a rectangular-shaped building, pointing east, with sacristies on either side at the east end. The building is likened to a ship with the bishop as commander, the deacons as mariners, and the laity as passengers. There are no seats except for the elderly and very young with men and women segregated on different sides, with married, unmarried and elderly women grouped separately. Deacons have the responsibilities to direct people to their proper place and watch that they do not laugh, whisper or fall asleep. After the bishop has seated himself on his throne the liturgy proper begins with a reader reciting from the scriptures. At the end of the reading another person (probably the chanter) sings hymns with the people joining in at the last part of the verses. This is followed by readings from the *Acts* and the *Epistles of Paul*. Afterwards a deacon or presbyter reads from a Gospel in the centre of the naos, no doubt from an ambo. After the readings the bishop, still seated at his throne, delivers his sermon. Sometimes a presbyter may deliver a sermon before the bishop. Those not entitled to take part in the Eucharist itself, the catechumens and penitents, are then dismissed and the doors of the church closed. With only the faithful left, the service continues with prayers and litanies, the bishop's greeting of peace, followed by the exchange of the kiss of peace. Preparations are then made for the celebration of the sacrament with the deacons bringing the gifts of bread and wine to the bishop at the Holy Table. After the Eucharist prayer is uttered the gifts are consecrated at which point the bishop invites the people to come forward for communion. This in broad outline is a written description of the Antiochian Eucharist liturgy performed in the fourth century Syria and used elsewhere in the East.

The pilgrim Egeria, who travelled from somewhere in Gaul to the Holy Land between 381 and 384, describes in great detail the original fourth-century liturgies. She records that at the *Lazarium* outside Jerusalem at Easter time the service begins with hymns and antiphons, a reading from the Gospel regarding Lazarus' sister followed by a prayer, a blessing and then further singing. She notes that the hymns, antiphons and readings are all suitable to the day and place. For the dismissal a presbyter reads a Gospel passage and then announces Easter.

In Constantinople, capital of the Eastern Roman Empire, the liturgy was similar in structure to the Antiochian and others but differed in small respects. The Constantinople rite became the basis for the Byzantine and later Orthodox tradition and is linked to one of two Eucharistic ceremonies, that known as the Divine Liturgy of St John Chrysostom. He was a priest at Antioch from 386 to 398 and from his reputation as a preacher became known as John Chrysostomos ('golden-mouthed'). He served as Bishop of Constantinople from 398 until 404 during which time he was associated with liturgical reform. The second Eucharist ceremony that coexisted with that of St John Chrysostom was that of St Basil who was bishop of Caesarea around 370 and who is considered the patriarch of eastern monasticism. In Constantinople it was natural that the emperor would attend Sunday service. From early in the Christian era a tradition was established that he took part formally in the liturgy. He would arrive in procession to meet the assembled clergy in the narthex and both would enter the naos through the central doors, the Royal Doors. After passing through the central doors, the procession moved down the naos to the Holy Table where the emperor would leave as a gift a shallow bowl or paten before he took his special place in the gallery. While in the East the emperor and bishop led the entrance procession in the West the order was from the person of least status to those of greatest significance.

A written description of the entrance procession involving bishop John Chrysostom derived from different sources by Wybrew in his work *The Orthodox Liturgy* throws light on this important event. As the sources depict it the bishop enters the church from the porch (narthex) with his attendant clergy through the Royal Doors into the naos. Before him in the procession there is one deacon who carries a Gospels book and other deacons with lights and incense. When the procession reaches the bema the book is placed on the Holy Table. Bishop John Chrysostom then gives a peace greeting before he ascends his throne at the back of the apse. This is the signal for the scripture readings to begin. A reader narrates first from the Prophets, then from an Epistle followed by a reading from a Gospel. It should be noted that later, instead of a reader, it became the practice for a deacon, or priest, to read the Gospel, the most important of the readings. It is not clear from the different sources what happened between the readings. It is probable that a hymn was sung with the congregation singing the refrains between the verses. Next, according to the sources, there are sermons by priests, or any bishop who is present, and then by Chrysostom himself who as the senior bishop is the last with his homily or sermon. He follows the Jewish synagogue practice of preaching seated but is known to deliver the sermon not only from his throne at the back of the apse but seated at a chair at the ambo located more or less in the middle of the naos so he could be better heard. The action of sitting by the bishop was symbolic of Jesus who was said to have sat down to teach and also important in maintaining continuity in apostolic teaching. Prayers follow the sermons at which point the catechumens and the penitents are dismissed. It is then that the gifts of bread and wine are brought in for the Eucharist. At the Holy Table the bishop and the clergy, facing east and thus with their backs to the congregation, recite prayers of preparation before beginning the Eucharistic prayer. This prayer is said or chanted aloud and the bread and wine consecrated. Prominent persons, living or dead, ranged with clergy first followed by the laity, are commemorated with their names read from two hinged plates, which could be folded when not in use. These plates with the inscribed names, known as diptychs, are kept together with the sacred vessels. After the Eucharistic prayer a litany may have followed as well as the Lord's Prayer, absent from earlier liturgies.

1100. Paten. Alabaster with central figure of Christ in enamel and with jewelled rim

1101. Chalice of Emperor Romanos I. Silver gilt with enamelled figure insets

1102. Triptych. Ivory showing the Crucifixion (centre panel) and depiction of various saints (side panels)

1103. Paten. Christ distributing communion to the apostles on both sides (known as the Riha paten)

The clergy in the sanctuary receive the consecrated gifts first before the bishop invites the people to communion. The faithful come forward to receive the consecrated bread and wine which are given separately. The separate distribution is clearly illustrated on the Riha paten, as it is called in the Dumbarton Oaks Collection, Washington, DC. This sixth-century paten shows Christ distributing bread and wine separately to the apostles.

In the time of Chrysostom the bread and wine were carried to the Holy Table with little ceremony, with the simplicity of practical action, unaccompanied by chant or ritual according to the description. This was strikingly different to what later became the pomp and splendour of the Great Entrance in the Byzantine liturgy. A famous account of the entry of the gifts is that by bishop

Theodore of Mopsuestia in his *Mystagogical Cathecheses* written at the end of the fourth century. He describes how deacons bring in the oblation contained in the sacred vessels, the patens and chalices, and are placed on the Holy Table. As the Holy Table is considered a sort of sepulcher other deacons had already spread linens on the Holy Table to represent the linen clothes of burial. The deacons stand around the Holy Table and fan the air to prevent anything falling onto the oblation. Theodore depicts the ritual as 'awe-inspiring' and to be looked at 'in recollection and fear'. This interpretation of the entry of the bread and wine laid stress on the procession itself.

The Eucharistic prayer as the principal prayer of the service had always been recited aloud in the early centuries and still is in the Western Mass. It appears that sometime in the middle of the fourth century the bishops and priests began the practice of saying the prayer in a manner inaudible to the faithful. The practice appeared in Eastern Syria first and slowly spread westward. The reason for reciting the prayer inaudibly is not clear but seems to be linked to the growing recognition of the attitude of awe and fear in the presence of the mysteries. Reference to the consecrated sacrament as 'awful' or 'terrifying' and the 'language of fear' appeared first in the *Mystagogical Catecheses* of St Cyril. The exclusion of the laity from the common thanksgiving and offering of the gifts so concerned Emperor Justinian that in 565 he ordered all bishops and priests to say the prayers in a voice that could be heard by the faithful in the congregation. He was unsuccessful. By the latter part of the sixth century the central prayer of the Eucharist liturgy passed out of hearing except for the clergy in the sanctuary. By the eighth century the prayer was said silently as is present Orthodox practice and read 'mystically' by the priest as holy drama.

During the first three centuries the faithful regularly received communion at the end of the Eucharist liturgy. But there was a difference between West and East according to St Ambrose. He was Bishop of Milan and one of the most influential ecclesiastical figures of the fourth century. In one of his lectures around the year 380 he mentioned that in the West frequent communion was typical, a practice that survived for several centuries more. He observed that in the East they took communion infrequently, just on rare occasions and even to once a year. The infrequency of communion had a profound consequence on the Eastern liturgy. By the end of the fourth century as communion decreased in importance in the Constantinople rite more attention came to be given to adding splendour to the entry of the bread and wine than to the significance of the gifts themselves. The Eucharistic liturgy began to be understood in a more dramatic rather than sacramental way. During the fifth and sixth centuries the Eucharist liturgy became more ceremonial and steadily received additional prayers.

The fifth and sixth centuries were a period of doctrinal controversies, some of which were resolved in the meetings of the Ecumenical Councils. After the first Council was held in Nicaea in 325, attended by according to one account 220 and another 318 members, the second was held in Constantinople in 381. The third Council that met in Ephesus in 431 is noted for the affirmation of Mary, the mother of Jesus, as *Theotókos* (Mother of God). In 451 the Fourth Council of Chalcedon proclaimed the union of the divine and human natures of Jesus Christ as it appeared in text form in the Nicene Creed. For doctrinal reasons the Armenian, Syrian and Coptic churches seceded and each took on an independent existence. Further matters were decided at the Fifth Council of Constantinople in 553 and at the Sixth Council in 680–1, which was also held in Constantinople. The Seventh Council recognized by Eastern Orthodoxy was the second Council of Nicaea held in 787.

Seventh to Fifteenth Centuries

From the middle of the seventh century right up to the fifteenth century and the Fall of Constantinople to the Ottoman Turks, the Byzantine Empire experienced a number of political upheavals. During this period changes in the Eucharist liturgy, though, were more one of consolidation, of adjustments and elaborations reaching a uniform order in the fourteenth century. At the beginning of the seventh century the Eucharist liturgy apparently still preserved at its core the early simplicity of structure even with secondary elements, actions and prayers added. This is learnt from Maximus the Confessor (c.580–662), a Christian monk, theologian and scholar who gave up a distinguished career in the imperial service to become a monk. His is the first full-scale description of the Eucharist liturgy and is contained in his *Mystagogia*, written in the first half of the seventh century. As he describes it the liturgy still begins with the entry of the clergy and the people flocking into the church. The clergy are led by the bishop who is preceded by a deacon carrying the book of Gospels and other deacons carrying candles and incense. At first accomplished in silence in the sixth century it was now embellished with a prayer of entry and chanting by clergy and choir as they entered the church. This procession, called 'entrance of the people with the bishop' or 'entrance of the Gospel' or the First Entrance by Maximus, later developed into what came to be called the **Little Entrance** with introductory antiphons and litanies. The readings follow immediately after the entry, the first still from the Old Testament and the second from the Epistles. The reading from a Gospel, though, takes on a more elaborate and splendid aspect. By this time the book of Gospels is richly covered with precious metals and stones. It is carried in solemn procession by a deacon escorted with candles and incense from the Holy Table to the ambo located in the middle of the naos. It is worth noting here a depiction by Paul the Silentiary (d. 575 or 580), who wrote hundreds of epigrams and one sometime after 538 of how people strove to touch the book as the deacon returned to the Holy Table after the reading. Maximus does not mention in his *Mystagogia* whether or not a homily or sermon follows the readings as in fifth century. It appears that by this time sermons are preached only occasionally. After the readings, or a sermon if there is one, prayers for the catechumens are said before they are dismissed and the doors of the church closed. Then there is a procession of deacons bearing the gifts, which Maximus calls the Entrance of the Holy Mysteries and by the twelfth century known as the **Great Entrance**, accompanied by singing. In the meantime the bishop and presbyters with him at the Holy Table wash their hands as a gesture of purity and say the prayers of preparation. Once the gifts are placed on the Holy Table by the deacons the bishop gives his greeting of peace. The kiss of peace is then exchanged by both the clergy and laity.

Some observations can be made about this description by Maximus of how the liturgy was celebrated in the first half of the seventh century. Prayers for the penitents have now been dropped as by this time the discipline of penance has fallen into disuse. Also by now the number of catechumens must have been very few. Even so, when the catechumenate disappears, eventually the redundant prayers of dismissal still remained. In the Eastern Orthodox liturgy today it is quite strange to hear the deacon declare that the doors be closed or guarded at this point in the service. It has been argued by some that the Nicene Creed, which is a significant element of the Eucharist liturgy in Eastern Orthodoxy, was introduced into the service right away in 325, by others in 471 or later in 511. When it did secure a permanent place in the rite of Constantinople it was sung by the whole congregation. The Great Entrance, as Maximus points out, had become a prominent feature of the liturgy but it had reached the point that critics decried the misplaced devotion to the entrance of the gifts.

A new custom introduced by the end of the sixth or the beginning of the seventh century was the pouring of hot water into the consecrated wine (a ceremony known as *zeon* from the same word meaning literally 'hot' in Greek). It has been suggested that this signified the warm blood of Christ and stood for the new life of the resurrection. It was held that the mixing of the water with wine in the chalice along with the leaven bread symbolized the humanity of Christ. The Armenian Church differed with this view and used unleavened bread and unmixed wine as they believed these to be signs of the immortality of Christ.

In the sixth century the Eucharist liturgy ended with a prayer of thanksgiving before the dismissal of the faithful. This differed from early centuries when the liturgy ended after baptized believers had received communion and the deacon had dismissed them. Early in the seventh century a hymn was added to the prayer of thanksgiving and by the end of the eighth century the bishop recited a final prayer 'behind the ambo' as the people streamed out. Not much is known about the concluding rite in the early church but indications are that there was a return procession of the clergy making an exit back through the naos of the church and the general dispersal of the congregation. This assertion is supported by the presence of the last prayer of the liturgy, a prayer said 'behind the ambo' pronounced by the celebrant when he reached the ambo that often was halfway down the centre of the naos. Written sources do not provide any details on the

1104. First (Little) entrance procession with Emperor Justinian

1105. First (Little) entrance procession with Empress Theodora

form of the procession of clergy exiting the church. The presumption is that men of rank preceded the common people, and that men preceded women. In the present day liturgy the clergy disappear into the sanctuary as the congregation leaves the church.

The most significant additions after the seventh century were the *prothesis*, which was more a formalization of the preparation of the elements than an addition, the inclusion of three prayers or antiphons, and a litany (the *synapte*) at the beginning of the liturgy. These changes are recorded in the *Ecclesiastical History and Mystical Contemplation* written by Germanos, Patriarch of Constantinople (served 715–30). Another written source about the liturgy is the Codex Barberini that dates from about 800 and is the earliest text, not a description, of the Byzantine liturgy that is known. Certain scholars who have compared this text with what is known about the earlier forms of the liturgy consider that additions to the service began to obscure the primary emphasis of the service. With regard to the concluding rite the Codex confirms that the clergy processed out and that the bishop stopped to say a prayer, which by the fourteenth century had become a single fixed prayer, behind the ambo. It is noteworthy that there is no mention in the Codex of adding a little hot water to the wine in the chalice (the ceremony of *zeon*). This ritual was not performed everywhere and even in fourteenth-century manuscripts there is no reference to it. It is not known exactly when the custom of putting bread into the chalice and giving communion to the laity with a spoon began but it seems to have been introduced sometime in the eighth century.

By the end of the eighth century a dramatic change in the liturgy had taken place that influenced church architecture. The spectacular Procession of the Gospels and the Procession of Gifts from the outside the church naos were no more. They were replaced by muted internal and smaller processions that began inside the bema, went out into the naos and then returned to the bema. This led to the need for space adjacent to the bema for the preparation of the Gifts, the prothesis, and for keeping of sacred vessels and for storage of the Gospels and other religious items, the diaconicon (literally the 'deacon's place').

Certainly by the ninth century in Byzantine churches the preparation of the bread and wine for the Divine Liturgy came to occupy its own chamber, the prothesis, on the north side of the bema. In most cases the prothesis and bema are joined by an arched opening. The *proskomedía* is the Office of Oblation conducted at the table of oblation in the prothesis that represents the cave of Bethlehem where Jesus Christ was born. The wine is contained in an enamelled chalice and the bread (*prósphoro*) is placed on a silver or gold round plate called a paten (*dískos*). The bread is cut by a special liturgical knife called symbolically the spear. There is a cruciform piece of metal called the asterisk or star that is positioned over the bread on the paten. Special linen cloths are placed over the sacred vessels, one over the asterisk and paten and another over the chalice, to protect them. Both are covered by a rectangular veil that is embroidered and tasselled known as the *aër*. In the diaconicon are kept the incense and charcoal and place to heat the water to be added to the wine in the chalice (the *zéon*) for Holy Communion. The diaconicon sometimes contains a sink with a special drain where clergy can wash their hands before serving the Divine Liturgy or to wash holy objects.

By the eleventh century the Byzantine liturgy had reached its penultimate stage of growth before reaching the final form as the Eastern Orthodox liturgy. Besides the changes mentioned above there were other developments. The prothesis became more elaborate when sometime after the tenth century it became customary to place a veil over the paten and another over the chalice and both covered by a large veil, the *aër*. The *aër* was carried in the Great Entrance procession and placed over the Eucharistic elements after they were placed on the Holy Table. There are different interpretations as to the significance of this largest of the three veils. Some view it as the shroud of Christ and others as the stone that sealed the sepulcher of Christ. Initially the *aër* was made of plain linen or silk but in the late twelfth century began to be embroidered with images. Another change was the replacement of the antiphons with typical psalms (*typiká*) in some churches that was influenced by liturgical practice in the monasteries. Also, as fewer people by this time received communion they were given as a substitute *antídoron*, 'instead of the gifts'. It consisted of the remains of the bread that had been blessed but not consecrated and kept aside in a bowl or salver until the conclusion of the liturgy. The *antídoron* was distributed after the final prayer, a practice that appeared about the ninth or tenth centuries.

In the eleventh century the rite of Constantinople came to be known as the Byzantine rite or as the Orthodox liturgy. It replaced the traditional liturgies of Alexandria, Antioch and Jerusalem and became uniform within the Eastern Empire and even spreading to the new churches founded among the Slav people. The liturgy was that of St Chrysostom, given this name to the Liturgy of the Holy Apostles in Constantinople in the seventh century, and is the one used today on most Sundays in Eastern Orthodox churches. The rite of St Basil is used on only a few occasions in the year, during Lent and on other special days. To the layperson there appears to be little difference between the two rites. There is a wonderful illustration of St Basil celebrating the liturgy in a twelfth-century liturgical roll in the library of the monastery of St John on the island of Patmos.

After the eleventh century there were three changes to the liturgy worth noting. First, priests now regularly took place in the procession of the Great Entrance carrying the unconsecrated gifts whereas before it was just the deacons. The gifts of the bread on the paten, wine and water in the chalice, the spear and spoon were now all veiled and covered with the *aër*. The procession was also more elaborate with liturgical fans, candles and incense. Second, commemorations were made during the procession. The earliest reference to the custom dates from the twelfth or thirteenth century. Third, the priest instead of the deacon began to take paten and chalice and put them on the Holy Table. If a bishop was present he was the one to do so. The Great Entrance in Hagia Sophia in Constantinople must have been splendid when the emperor participated in the liturgy. He would have been at the head of a vast procession of robed clergy and members of the court that headed to the Beautiful Doors of the bema.

The major change after the eleventh century, however, was to the Little Entrance and the Great Entrance. At some point in time these two grand processions were abbreviated so that by the fourteenth century they were merely symbolic. The two processions now began where they ended, in the bema. They never reverted to the older practice of beginning outside the church and then processing through the naos. It has been

1106. St Basil's Liturgy. Imaginary architectural setting, the Theotokos in the semi-circular apse, large 'O' symbol indicating beginning of the prothesis prayer, St Basil holding the Gospels book, Holy Table with chalice and paten, two deacons each with liturgical fans and a square embroidered 'carpet' an indication of twelfth-century Islamic influence

suggested that the change may have occurred after the occupation of Constantinople by the Fourth Crusaders in 1204 when a short-lived Latin Patriarchy was established and the rites and beliefs of the Church of Rome imposed.

By the fourteenth century the Orthodox liturgy had reached the full term of its development. Although a basic uniformity in the liturgy was celebrated in all the churches in the Byzantine world, local variations continued to exist. How the rites as well as the ceremonials were to be observed were set down in writing in the *Diátaxis* by Philotheos Kokkinos while he was a monk on Mount Athos. Later as Patriarch of Constantinople (1353–54 and 1364–1376) he was able to ensure the widespread distribution of the *Diátaxis* that led to a uniform order in the liturgy in the Greek and Slav churches. This was reinforced after the invention of the printing press in the sixteenth century when the first printed service books contained the text headings and comments of the *Diátaxis*. Today the manner in which the Eastern Orthodox liturgy is celebrated is the same as that described in the in mid-fourteenth-century *Diátaxis* of Philotheos, save for a few details. While the Divine Liturgy remained the same in monastery churches and those in city and village churches there were numerous other services conducted by the monks. These made use of the double narthex and the chanting apses.

From the seventh to the fourteenth century, then, the process of change in the liturgy of Eastern Orthodoxy was one of adjustments and elaborations to reach an eventual uniformity. In the West, on the other hand, there were local traditions of performing the mass with no overall uniformity as each church made changes as it saw fit. Western rites were more complicated and diverse than those of the East. A principal difference was the Western custom of varying prayers according to the calendar and changing the Eucharistic prayer depending on the liturgical occasion. Also the Roman rite had a more didactic character with less room for symbolic action than in the Eastern liturgy. A further divergence occurred with the introduction of reforms and the Gregorian chant by Pope Gregory the Great (served 590–604) into the Western Mass. This form became standard when Charlemagne (742–814) as King of the Franks (768–800) and Emperor of the Holy Roman Empire (800–814) imposed the Roman rite throughout his Western and Central Europe dominions. In the sixteenth century the Latin Mass was codified at the Council of Trent and remained largely unchanged until the liturgical reforms that took place in the middle of the twentieth century.

1107. Monastery service in progress showing monks standing along the wall in the outer and inner narthexes (black circles), others (figures) in the *chorastasíes*, priests censing and conducting the service in the bema

Interpretations of the Liturgy

During Byzantine times the term liturgy referred specifically to the ritual of the Eucharist, often called the Divine Liturgy (*e theía leitourgía*), which still today has two forms, that attributed to John Chrysostom and the other to Basil the Great. As it has just been seen the Byzantine or Eastern Orthodox liturgy reached its final form by the end of the fourteenth century and was uniform, except for minor local variations, throughout the Byzantine Empire, the Balkans and Russia. The question is, though, what does the liturgy *mean?* This is a question that has been addressed by many learned theologians. Among the first theologians to address the question was Origen, who lived in Alexandria early in the third century, followed by Dionysios the Areopagite writing in the fifth century or early sixth century. Origen, a theologian, wrote about the symbolic interpretation of the liturgy building upon an earlier tradition. This was founded on the mystery of Christ, both his divinity and humanity, that became an integral part of Byzantine and subsequent Orthodox theology. In Dionysios' treatise *The Ecclesiastical Hierarchy* the Eucharist liturgy is taken to mean the sacrament of union with God and is called the rite of *sýnaxis*.

The union with God is represented by the blessing of the holy bread and cup by the bishop and clergy. Celebration of this sacrament is meant to be a visible and tangible sign of spiritual realities and a symbol of a divine mystery. In mid-eleventh century there coexisted at least three major interpretations of the symbolic significance of the Eucharist liturgy. These were the *Mystagogia* (628–630) written by Maximus the Confessor for monks, the *Ecclesiastical History and Mystical Contemplation* (715–730) of Patriach Germanos for laypeople, and the *Protheoria* (1054–1067) by Nicholas of Andida for the clergy. Finally there was Nicholas Cabasilas in the fourteenth century whose work is titled *Commentary on the Divine Liturgy* and in the fifteenth century Symeon of Thessaloniki who wrote two works, *Interpretation of the Church and the Liturgy* and later *On the Holy Liturgy*.

Maximus the Confessor in his *Mystagogia* provides the first full-scale interpretation of the Eucharist liturgy. It is assumed to be based on the rite of Constantinople and he draws on the writings of others including Dionysius the Areopagite's *Ecclesiastical Hierarchy*. Maximus intends to lead his readers to a knowledge of the mystery of God, which though hidden can be known by revelation. He is also the first commentator to give an interpretation of the church as a building as well as of the liturgy that is celebrated in it. For Maximus the church is composed of stones and souls and is an image of the world which is made up of things visible and invisible. The bema, reserved for priests and ministers, represents symbolically the invisible, spiritual universe while the naos, reserved for the faithful people, represents the material world. The church is also the image of man in which the bema represents man's soul, the naos his body, and the Holy Table his spirit that unites the two. He gives a twofold explanation of the liturgy itself. First, it represents the whole history of God's plan from the incarnation to the second coming of Christ to save mankind. The entry of the bishop into the church signifies the first coming of Christ and his entry into the bema and ascent to his throne the ascension of Christ to heaven to occupy the heavenly throne. The entry of people into the church signifies the passage from the world of evil and ignorance into a place of virtue and knowledge. The readings provide instruction to wage spiritual warfare and the psalms signify joy of the good things revealed by God. The proclamation of the Gospel signifies the end of the world and the descent of the bishop from his throne symbolizes the second coming of Christ to judge the world. The closing of the church doors and the dismissal of the catechumens signifies the ending of the material world and the entry of the faithful into the spiritual world. This begins with the Eucharist prayer and participation in the mystery of God with the climax in the distribution of the sacrament. The second explanation of the liturgy given by Maximus is that it has more special significance as the Eucharist symbolizes the mystical ascent of the soul to God.

The *Mystagogia* of Maximus helped establish a tradition and a way of understanding the liturgy that became part of Eastern Orthodoxy. This is reflected in the second part of the title of the work *Ecclesiastical*

1108. Celestial Divine Liturgy by the Holy Trinity. Christ officiating in the presence of God the Father, the Holy Spirit, archangels, angels and prophets (Painting by Michael Damaskinos)

History and Mystical Contemplation by Germanos, Patriach of Constantinople. He continued the approach of Dionysios the Areopagite and Maximus the Confessor in recognizing the symbolic aspects of the service. Nicholas of Andida in this *Protheoria* depicts the liturgy as a series of images representing in order the life and work of Christ. He followed Maximus in his understanding of church buildings as sacred space.

The Byzantine tradition of liturgical interpretations culminated in two writers, Nicholas Cabasilas and Symeon, Archbishop of Thessaloniki. Nicholas Cabasilas, a fourteenth-century lay theologian, in his *Commentary on the Divine Liturgy*, maintained the interpretation of the liturgy as a symbolic representation of the historic life of Jesus Christ. The central act of the liturgy is in the transformation of the elements into the body and blood of Christ. He was very clear that this act of consecration was sacramental and real, not symbolic. Symeon, a monk who later served as Archbishop of Thessaloniki (1416/7–1429), wrote within the Alexandrian tradition in contrast to Cabasilas who followed the holy fathers of Antioch. For Symeon, as he wrote in *Interpretation of the Church and the Liturgy* and later *On the Holy Liturgy,* the liturgy is made up of

1109. Liturgy of the Just and Damned. Christ with archangels and angels in heavenly clouds above overseeing a moment in the Divine Liturgy of a congregation of the 'just' with the 'damned' below in hell

symbols that contain a hidden reality and it is necessary to understand their meaning. Properly understood, the liturgy reveals the incarnation, passion, death, resurrection and glorification of Christ and the anticipation of the ultimate reality of the heavenly Kingdom.

At the time Nicholas Cabasilas and Symeon of Thessaloniki commented on the liturgy, that is the fourteenth and fifteenth centuries, its development had in all essentials come to an end. Since their day little has changed. Although Easter Orthodoxy today consists of independent churches what unites them is the same way the liturgy is celebrated with only minor variations and in their own language. The liturgy follows a set structure or order with a commitment to its apostolic origins and the Jewish form of biblical worship. Its features are permanence and relative changelessness, the determination to remain loyal to the past.

Processions

From the fourth until at least the twelfth if not the fourteenth century in some places, processions were a dominant feature of the eastern Eucharist liturgy. There were once five processions in all. First there was the Little Entrance, as it was called later, when the bishop and clergy entered the church from the narthex through the central Royal Doors and then they proceeded through the naos to the bema where the Holy Table was located. At the head of the procession was a deacon holding aloft the book of Gospels accompanied by other deacons with candles and incense. The second procession occurred when the deacon took the book of Gospels from the Holy Table and proceeded along the solea to the ambo in the middle of the naos where he would do the reading. The movement from the Holy Table and back was simple at first but with more grandeur over time. The third procession was the Great Entrance itself. Deacons would enter the church from outside bearing the gifts of bread and wine which they handed to the bishop at the Holy Table. Over time this procession became the grandest of all with pomp and circumstance. Less formal was the fourth procession. After the consecration men and women would proceed to separate sides of the sanctuary barrier to receive communion. The fifth and final procession was at the conclusion of the service when the clergy would exit the church in a formal group. Unfortunately, detailed descriptions of all these processions are lacking but it can be imagined what impressive ceremonials they must have been. Today, not counting the informal communion line-up, only two of the five grand ceremonies, the Little Entrance and the Great Entrance, remain. Even so, the most striking visual action in present-day Eastern Orthodox liturgies is these two processions, despite their abbreviated form of what were once majestic ceremonies.

Chapter Seven

SYMBOLISM IN ARCHITECTURE AND ART

In the previous chapters symbolism was touched upon. But as it such a significant aspect of Byzantine architecture and art a deeper understanding of the role of symbolism is desirable. As symbolism involves attributing meanings or significance to objects, events or relationships the question that arises is what exactly is the meaning or *significance* of particular symbols because of this attribution. For Byzantine sacred architecture and art the key is to know what was the attribution, what was ascribed to the church building, its components, and to religious images. It would be natural to do that from a modern perspective but to do so what would be lost are the meanings or significance people in Byzantine times themselves attributed to their architecture and art. How then to know what the relevant views of those living during the Byzantine era were? Due to the immense research efforts of John Wilkinson recorded in his book *From Synagogue to Church* this becomes a feasible effort. The last chapter of his book contains translated extracts from 24 ancient documents and from these portions can be found that refer to the design of churches. Wilkinson groups his extracts by source in a chronological sequence, from Exodus in the Old Testament to a manuscript of the late sixteenth century. Twelve of the documents[1] are found useful for the purpose here, but the most informative are three: the *Ecclesiastical History* by Eusebius (c.AD263–339), the *Mystagogia* of Maximus the Confessor (c.580-662) and the *Eucharist* by Symeon of Thessaloniki (c.1381/7–1429). In contrast to Wilkinson's order by source and date, the selected extracts on church design below are arranged in the same sequence of architectural components as presented in Chapter 2 of this book. No attempt is made here to explain the meanings of the texts but merely to provide the reader with an inkling as to how Byzantine people of the time viewed sacred Christian architecture and art. Words in parenthesis are not part of the original texts but added by translators to improve meanings. Explanatory words by this author are in square brackets. The reader is forewarned of the jarring effect of setting side by side ancient texts from different authors each with their own style of writing.

From Texts

The Spatial Division of the Church
' … the holy Church of God is a figure and image of the universe … Like the universe it … is divided into a place which is allotted exclusively to the priests and ministers (called the sanctuary) [*hierateíon*], and the place where all the faithful people are allowed to enter (called the Temple) [naos] … the church which we build is like the Church "not built by human hands", for the sanctuary represents the world above, allotted to the powers above, and the nave the lower world, inhabited by those whose lot it is to live by the (five) senses … To those who can see it this way, the whole of the spiritual world is imprinted on the world of the senses by symbolic figures … Once again, in another mode of the mystical sense, he said that the holy Church of God is like a human bring. It has the sanctuary as soul, the holy altar as mind, and the Temple as body …'

Laying the Church Foundation
'The Godly High Priest assembles the group of clergy and ministers together at the agreed site ... and they place one stone in the middle of the sanctuary as an example of the spiritual stone hewn from the holy Mountain [Mount Zion] ... and they take twelve stones which are first washed with water, then with wine. These figure the 12 Apostles, whose feet the Lord washed in the Upper Room ... Indeed these stones are placed at the four corners of the church to indicate their directions towards the four corners of the world ... Then he [the Bishop] asks to be given the tool for digging, and draws on the site the measure of the size of the building ... Immediately [after the Anointment, Psalms, the Readings, the Gospel] the Bishop takes a hoe, and first digs the consecrated ground himself, and afterwards gives it to the workmen. [Then] they start holding the service in the place of the altar since it is here that the fulfilment of the mystery is completed.'

'The first to have built a church according to the plan we know today was the apostle James, according to the instructions of Simon Cephas [St Peter]. This plan is that of the ancient Temple [of Jerusalem] which Melchizedek [the priest who brought out bread and wine and blessed Abraham in the Book of Genesis] had built before the Kings came to alter it. The church is the likeness of the world: at its east end the sanctuary is like Paradise where our father Adam was.'

Forecourt and Courtyard
'He (Bishop of Tyre) did not wish those who entered the gates to go directly into the building with unholy or unclean feet. So between the outer entry and the Temple he left a large space as he could. He adorned the four sides of this area with colonnades (*stóai tetrágona*), and all round it he placed latticed chancels. They were of medium height, and joined the columns which rose above them. Thus the middle space was fenced in, and the court inside it was open to the sky, full of air and sunlight ... There he has placed a symbol of holy cleansing, for in front of the Temple he provided great fountains of flowing water (*krénai*), so that anyone who was going further into the sacred enclosure could wash themselves.'

The church and forecourt at Tyre were part of a larger complex (*exóthen perívolos*) surrounded by a wall that included other buildings such as a bishopric. 'Let the house of the bishop be beside that place which is called the forecourt. Also that of the widows who are called "those that sit in front". Also let that of the priests and deacons be behind the baptistery. Let the deaconesses abide beside the door of the Lord's house. Let the church have a house for entertaining nearby, where the chief deacon shall entertain strangers.'

Narthex
'Beyond this splendid court the Bishop (of Tyre) has made a many-doored entry into the Temple [naos]. In fact he set three doors in the east wall. The central one, which was greater and wider than the others, he decorated with bronze plates, nails of iron and raised patterns. This door was like a queen [Bride of Christ] with her guards on either side ... Let a church then be thus: with three entries in type of the Trinity.'

Naos
'Behold! Its ceiling (at the new church at Edessa) is stretched out like the sky and without columns it is arched and simple. And it is also decorated with golden mosaic, as the firmament is with shining stars. And its lofty dome – behold, it resembles the highest heaven. And like a helmet it is firmly placed on its lower (part). The splendor of its broad arches – they portray the four ends of the earth. They resemble

by the variety of their colours the glorious rainbow. Other arches surround it like crags jutting out from a mountain upon, by and through which its entire ceiling is fastened on the vaults. Its marble resembles an image not made by hands, and its walls are suitably overlaid (with marble). And from its brightness, polished and white, light gathers in it like the sun.'

'(Syriac canon) Let the church have a room for the catechumens, which shall also be the room of the Exorcists: Let it not be detached from the church, but placed so that those who have entered it can hear the readings and spiritual songs of praise and the Psalms ... Let all the places be lighted, both for a symbol and also for reading ... Moreover the Temple [naos] stands for the whole earth, but the Place of Men is the east side of Earth towards Eden, and the Place of Women is to the west ... The men stand on the south side and the women on the north.'

Aisles
'The number of the aisles was arranged to match the doors, and they were divided by two colonnades. Above them he (the Bishop of Tyre) has designed the house [naos] with openings which give a great deal of light, for he has constructed the windows from carved wood and decorated frames.'

Holy Bema [Sanctuary]
'The Sanctuary [bema] is a raised place, and the throne on which Christ, the King of All, presides with his apostles ... When the Bishop finished the Temple [naos], he placed at its head a seat to honour the presidents, and on either side of it other benches in strict order. In the center he added the place of the altar, the Holy of Holies. To make this inaccessible to the congregation he surrounded it with wooden rails [templon], and anyone who examines them will be amazed at the consummate mastery of the carving. Nor did the Bishop neglect to make the floor (*édafos*), with fine marble in excellent designs ... Between the nave [naos] and the sanctuary [bema] are three steps ... The altar [Holy Table] in the center of the sanctuary [bema] resembles the Tomb of Christ ... The ciborium above the altar is like the Tabernacle which sheltered the Ark of the Covenant ... The sanctuary is a sign of the heaven of heavens, and the Holy of Holies which is there, into which the all-holy Jesus ascended bodily.'

Apse
'The apse is like both the cave in Bethlehem where Christ was born, and the cave where he was buried: as the evangelist says, "There was a cave quarried out from the rock, and there they laid Jesus" ... One light shines forth also in its sanctuary [bema] by three open windows. And announces to us the mystery of the Trinity, of the Father, and the Son, and the Holy Spirit ... And the light of its three sides abides in many windows. It [the three sides] portrays the Apostles, Our Lord, the prophets, martyrs and confessors.'

Galleries
'That the female congregation should not be mingled with the men, though there is room enough on the ground for both without crowding, you [most probably the bishop of St Stephen at Gaza] have constructed a double women's gallery (*gynaikōnitis*), its length and width equal to those of the aisles below, but somewhat inferior in height to the extent that the columns supporting the roof are shorter than the ones beneath them.'

Holy Table
'The Holy Table is the place of the Tomb where Christ was buried, and on it is set forth the true and heavenly bread … It is also the throne of God on which he is seated … At this Table also at his mystic Supper he sat in the midst with his disciples, and he took bread and wine, and said to them, "Take this, eat and drink it. This is my body and blood" … The persons who approach the altar [Holy Table] in the sanctuary [bema] and gather round it are like the disciples surrounding the table of the last supper, and because they must surround it the Jacobites and the Melkites place the altar near the center of the dome [semi-dome of the apse]. The Nestorians place the altar at the end of it to signify that it is the climax … the Altar truly is the Table of Christ, the throne of glory, the dwelling of God, and the Tomb and monument of Christ and his resting place … Let the altar have a veil of pure linen, for it is without spot.'

Ciborium
'The ciborium above the altar [Holy Table] is like the Tabernacle that sheltered the Ark of the Covenant … The ciborium symbolizes the place where Jesus was crucified, for the place where he was buried (the altar) was "close at hand" and might overhang it. It is arranged in the church to symbolize Jesus' Crucifixion, Burial, and Resurrection. It is also symbolically linked to the Ark of the Covenant of the Lord, which Scripture says was the Holy of Holies …'

Diaconicon
'Let the house of the offering and the treasury be all of it beside the diaconicon … Let the diaconicon be on the right of the right-hand entrance, that the "eucharists" or offerings may be seen. Let there be a forecourt with a portico going round to the diaconicon.'

Synthronon
'Let there be a throne by the altar [Holy Table]. On the right and the left let there be places for the presbyters, so that those who are most exalted and honoured, and those who labour in the Word, may sit on the right, but those who are of middle age on the left. But let that place where the throne is to be raised three steps, for there the altar should be … The structure of nine steps that are placed in the sanctuary of (the church) together with the synthronos portrays the throne of Christ and the nine orders of angels … In heaven a central throne and on each side four living creatures and round the central throne twenty four thrones for the elders.'

Templon and Iconostasis
'The rails [templon] indicate in which place one should pray. Outside them is the place of the laity, and inside is the Holy of Holies, only accessible to the priests. Indeed those rails are also like the bronze rails in the Holy Tomb, placed there to prevent people from simply wandering in … The curtain at the gate of the sanctuary [bema] represents the cherubim who guard the gate of Paradise after Adam had left it.'

'The First Entry signifies the Resurrection and the Ascension of the Saviour, and the shutting and opening of the royal [should be holy] doors of the (sanctuary) the entry into Heaven … After (the departure of the) catechumens is the great Second Entry, which signifies the glorious Second Appearance of Christ … The gates (of the sanctuary) are shut [for] nor can the highest things be seen by us, for we are the imperfect who dwell below…'

Solea
'The pair of partitions running between the sanctuary [bema] and the ambo are like the garden which lay between the Tomb and the Place of Crucifixion … Between these partitions runs the "Desert", the way the priests and deacons take to go and read the holy books. It is the path taken by our Lord when he went to the Mountain to teach his law to mankind. Each partition has an empty space, as a symbol that the doors of penitence are open, and that this entry is open to any who desire it.'

Ambo
'Let the place of reading be a little outside the altar [Holy Table] … Readers and singers go up on the platform, the old custom as recorded by Ezra [Book of Ezra in the Hebrew Bible], "Ezra the scribe stood on a wooden platform which he had made for his speeches" … The ambo is placed in the middle of (the church) on the model of the Upper Room at Zion. And under it are 11 columns, like the eleven apostles that were hidden. The column that is behind the ambo portrays Golgotha in its form. And fastened above it is the cross of light, like our Lord between the thieves … The ambo symbolizes the stone of the Holy Tomb, which the angel rolled back from the door. For the ambo is a hill which stands in a flat and level place … the ambo at the center of the nave, is like Jerusalem, which is the center of the earth, and like the place where our Lord was crucified. It is called Golgotha, that is to say, the place where the head of our father Adam was buried … There are two places on the rights and the left of the ambo and they are like the two places where our Saviour taught his disciples about his law. In the first of these the Old Testament is read, in the second the Epistles of Paul and the Acts, and the Gospel is read in the middle.'

Orientation
'Then he erected a vast lofty entry gate (*propýlon*) to face the very rays of the rising sun, providing those who were standing outside an ample view of what lay within … it is from the east that we are expecting the bright dawn of Christ's second appearance.'

While the Wilkinson documents provide the view of various Byzantines on architecture in their own words, the anthology contained in *The Art of the Byzantine Empire, 312–1453: Sources and Documents* by Cyril Mango can be used to obtain extracts related to art. Of the numerous extracts the following are of particular interest.

Eusebius, *Letter to Constantia* (sister of Constantine the Great)[2]
'You also wrote me concerning some supposed image of Christ … His face shone like the sun and His garments like light.'

St Gregory of Nyssa, *Laudatio S. Theodori*[3]
' … he (the painter) wrought by means of colours as if it were a book that uttered speech, and so … even of if it is silent, is capable of speaking from the wall and being of the greatest benefit.'

Choricus, *Laudatio Marciani*, I, 17 ff.[4]
Choricus provides a very lengthy description of the church built in Gaza during the reign of Justinian, probably before 536, built by the governor of Palestine and Marcian, the bishop of Gaza.

'If we attempted to describe the entirety of its work (i.e. of painting) which adorns the church all round, we would have to compose a speech altogether too long for this festive occasion. Hence, I shall set aside the pictures (*historiai*) that are on the walls, and shall pass up to the ceiling.' The description is of a painting of the Nativity next which consists of 'an ass and a cow, a manger, an infant and a maiden who is lying down on a couch, her left hand placed under her right elbow, her cheek resting on her right hand. What is the meaning of this representation? ... Her face [the Virgin] is not altered with the pallor of one who has just given birth ... [for as she is] deemed worthy of supernatural motherhood, she was justly spared its natural pains. Why then the manger? What are we to say of the cow and the ass? These, we are told, had been prophesied by sages of yore, and so it came to pass. Their ears ringing with a sound from heaven, the shepherds ... raise their necks to heaven and strain their ears in the direction of the sound ...'

Agathias *Anthologia graeca*, I, 34[5]
'On an image of the archangel Michael at Platê (a quarter of Constantinople). The wax, greatly daring, has represented the invisible, the incorporeal chief of the angels in the semblance of his form ... The eyes [of the mortal man beholding the image] encourage deep thoughts, and art is able by means of colours to ferry over (to its object) the prayer of the mind.'

Vita S. Pancratii [6]
The scene is set in Pontus where the apostle Peter built a church and appointed a bishop. St Peter instructs the painter Joseph '"Make me the image of Our Lord Jesus Christ so that, on seeing the form of His Face, the people may believe all the more and be reminded of what I have preached to them" ... And having taken thought, Peter made the entire picture-story (*historia*) of the incarnation of Our Lord Jesus Christ, beginning with the angel's drying "Hail" to the Virgin (the Annunciation), and ending with the Ascension of Our Lord Jesus Christ, and he commanded that churches should be decorated with this story. This is what the apostles did in all the cities and villages from Jerusalem as far as Antioch. From this time onward ..., they were depicted on panels and parchment (*chartiá*), and were given to the bishops who, upon completing the construction of a church, depicted them both beautifully and decorously ...'

St John Damascene, *De imag. orat.*, III, 16 ff [7]
' ... what is the purpose of an image? Every image is declarative and indicative of something hidden ... inasmuch as a man has no direct knowledge of the invisible ... the image has been invented for the sake of guiding knowledge and manifesting publicly that which is concealed ...'

Constantinus Rhodius, *Descr. of the Church of the Holy Apostles* [8]
' In the middle of the costly ceiling, it (the church) bears a representation of Christ as if He were the sun, a wonder exceeding all wonders; next, like the moon, that of the stainless Virgin, and, like the stars, those of the wise Apostles.'

Ulpius (or Elpius) the Roman, *Concerning Bodily Characteristics* [9]
One of eleven descriptions of Fathers of the Church is that of 'Gregory of Nazianzus (Patriarch of Constantinople 379–81): not a tall man, somewhat sallow but pleasing, flat-nosed, straight eyebrows, gentle and kindly expression, although one of his eyes, namely the right one, was rather stern, being contracted in the corner by a scar; beard not long but fairly thick, bald, white-haired, the tip of his beard having a smoky appearance.'

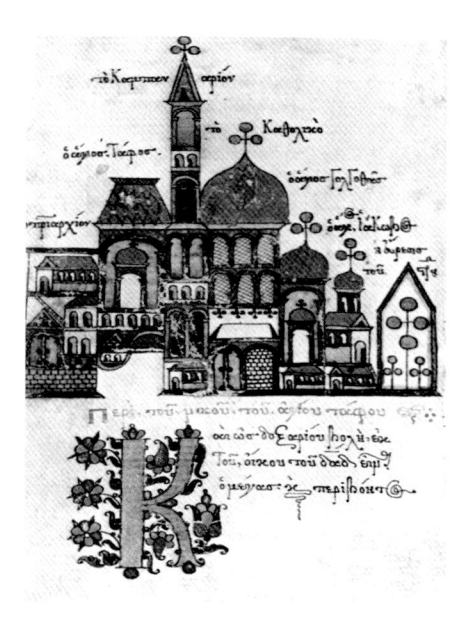

1110. Church of the Holy Sepulcher, Jerusalem. Representation in a manuscript (Monastery of Gregoriou, Mount Athos)

1111. Church of St Savvas in Palestine. Representation of the church in a manuscript (Monastery of Dochiariou, Mount Athos)

Further Reflections

There is no doubt that the Constantinian basilican churches reflected physical and philosophical features of the imperial court. Christian services borrowed several features from imperial court ceremonies particularly liturgical rituals, such as the processional entry into the church, which paralleled formal performances before the emperor or his magistrate. Other features from the imperial court were the vestments of high magistrates, ritual gestures such as bowing and kissing the ring, the use of candles, and the accommodation of the bishop on an elaborate throne. The audience hall of the earthly emperor became the assembly hall of the Christians and that of the 'Emperor of Heaven' with Jesus increasingly viewed over the coming centuries as the King of Heaven. The union of earthly and divine power in the church and the imitation of ceremonial pomp of the state in the liturgy were to demonstrate the legitimacy of Christianity.

As seen in a previous chapter, the Eucharist liturgy developed from the simple *agápe* meal in the first century to reach its authoritative form as the Byzantine rite by the seventh century. During the Golden Age from Emperor Constantine until Emperor Justinian the congregational churches – most commonly with a longitudinal basilica plan – were created around the liturgy of the Eucharist. The ceremonial of the liturgy involved movement and action with pronounced entrances and exits with the liturgy a determining factor in new architectural developments by the end of the Golden Age. In particular the longitudinal axis of the basilica with a forecourt at the western end and the apse at the eastern end reflected this relationship. As the entrance procession of the clergy formed in the narthex the congregation gathered in the forecourt where the colonnades offering shelter. The many doors from the narthex into the naos, usually three in number, allowed the congregation to enter the naos quickly and be in their places by the time the clergy procession reached the bema and the bishop began the service with a blessing.

Preparation of the Gifts, the Prothesis and the Diaconicon
In the East the practice was for people arriving at church with gifts of bread and wine to leave them outside before they entered. In Constantinople at the Great Church begun by Constantine it is supposed that they left the gifts in the small building, known as the *skevophylákion* (the storage place for sacred vessels and books) at the northeast corner. It is in this building that the preparation of the bread and wine took place before they were brought in by the deacons. While the bishop in the church recited the prayer of the catechumens, deacons went to the *skevophylákion* to collect the paten and chalice, or patens and chalices. They returned in solemn procession accompanied by candles, incense and fans and then proceeded through the holy doors in the middle of the icon-screen to deposit the gifts on the Holy Table. It is assumed that this manner of preparation of the gifts of bread and wine and the procession at the Great Church was repeated at other churches. That the bread and wine were brought in from outside is supported by the statement written in 630 by the patriarch Sergios, a contemporary of Maximus, that 'at the time of the bringing in (*eisagésthai*) of the pre-sanctified gifts from the *skevophylákion* to the bema a hymn was sung'. There is no literary evidence as to which door of the church they entered from the *skevophylákion*. It is surmised that as the main doors of the church in the narthex were closed after the dismissal of the catechumens the Entrance of the Mysteries must have been through the side doors. In the two surviving *skevophylákia*, one at Hagia Sophia in Constantinople and the other at St John at Ephesus, the buildings were on the north side of the church which would mean that the doors on that side were the ones used.

After the formal preparation of the gifts was performed they were brought into the church in a procession of deacons, escorted by candles, incense and liturgical fans, known as the Great Entrance. What had begun as a simple but significant ceremony centuries earlier was now becoming quite elaborate and ritualized, sometime between Maximus writing around 628 to 630 and Patriarch Germanos who served from 715 to 730, and destined to be more so over the coming centuries. Germanos observed that by his time the bread or *prósphoro* was pierced by a liturgical spear, a symbolic act, and placed on a paten in the *skevophylákion* accompanied by the prayer of oblation in what came to be known as the rite of *prósthesis*. Included in the rite was the mixing of water and wine in a chalice. An early Christian text in Greek describes this brief rite as the 'Prayer which the priest says in the *skevophylákion* after the bread has been placed on the *dískos* [paten]'.

Churches without separate external *skevophylákia* were built with two side apsed chambers flanking the larger bema apse. This arrangement became known as the tripartite apse scheme and probably came about in the second half of the sixth century during the reign of Justin II (565–78). The northern apse came to be used as and called the *prósthesis* while the southern one, the *diacónicon*, came to be used for the storage of vestments, books and other liturgical equipment. This new architectural arrangement meant, first, that the preparation of the bread and wine took place in the church and, secondly, it was performed by a priest and not a deacon. In churches where there was only a single central apse for the Holy Table the prothesis was a side niche or side table. This meant that the processions finished where they began, depriving the ceremonial movements of all practical significance.

In the West the organization of the offering and distribution of communion was different. It appears that the ends of the side aisles adjacent to the sanctuary were closed off by a low railing. There people would leave the bread offering and small flasks of wine with the deacons. Men presented their offerings

1112. SS Peter and Paul holding a model of a centralized (hexagonal) church

1113. SS Peter and Paul with a model of a church

1114. A centralized (circular) church. (Detail from Akathistos Hymn Icon, Kefalonia)

at the end of the right-hand aisle and women the left-hand aisle. Deacons placed the bread in linen cloths held between two acolytes and poured the wine into chalices and then placed the offering gifts on the altar in the central apse. With the Eucharistic prayer the bread and wine were consecrated. Then the bishop administered the consecrated bread and wine to the clergy from his throne, the *cathedra*. Afterwards the clergy in turn administered communion at the railing at the closed end of each aisle, the men on the right aisle and the women on the left aisle. This arrangement between a liturgical ritual and architectural space continued in Rome until the ninth century.

Entrance Procession and the Narthex
In earlier times there was another difference between the East and West which had to do with when the service began. In the East the clergy assembled in the narthex and the people in the forecourt. The mosaic panels in San Vitale in Ravenna depict such an assembly of the Emperor and the clergy. Once the clergy entered the naos in stately procession the people would go in. To the layperson this entry symbolized an entrance into the divine life. In contrast, in the West people assembled in church first to await and greet the clergy as they arrived. But by the end of the eighth century it seems that even in the East people waited in the church and the service began when the clergy entered formally.

For the first few centuries the book of Gospels had been carried in the entry procession from outside the church. But by the ninth century the 'entrance' was carried out within the church itself in what came to be called the 'Little Entrance' in the Eastern liturgy. The book of Gospels was now carried from the Holy Table in the bema out through the north door of the iconostasis onto the solea then through the Beautiful Gate back again to the Holy Table. At the same time it seems that the 'Great Entrance' too was changed from an external to an internal procession. The procession of gifts of bread and wine also began in the bema but in contrast to the Little Entrance passed through the naos before the return to the bema.

The reduction in the scale of the processions may have been partially responsible for the elimination of the *skevophylákion*. It has been argued by some scholars that it was the reverse, that during the crusader occupation of Constantinople and the uncertain times this was the reason that the grand processions were limited to internal processions.

Relics, the Central Plan and the Dome
The veneration of the relics of martyrs brought about the central type church plan with the dome becoming the dominant architectural feature of the central plan. Circular funerary churches or *martyria* were usually built over or near the graves of martyrs with memorial services held on the anniversary of their martyrdom. At first the central plan of the imperial mausoleum was adopted for the Christian martyrium and also the baptistery. That the circular form of the Roman mausoleum could serve the function of both baptism and dying can be explained by the theology of baptism according to the apostle Paul who said: 'We were therefore buried with him through baptism into his death' (Romans 6:4). This difficult concept has been interpreted to mean that the act of entering and then coming out of the water symbolizes Jesus' death and burial, followed by his resurrection and a new life in Christ. The dome was considered the celestial canopy from which Christ ruled and oversaw the liturgical drama below.

Mystery, the Iconostasis and the Holy Table
Initially there was no solid barrier between the bema and the naos, only a low railing that defined a space for the clergy. It was meant to be a barrier to access to the bema by the laity. In time the simple rail or *templon* was replaced by short columns and then images began to be placed top of the bar resting on the columns. This icon-screen or *iconostasis* between the bema and naos later was increased in height to allow curtains to hide from the worshippers the mysteries, that is, the consecration of the gifts on the Holy Table. The belief was that the Eucharist was the special function of the clergy alone and was to be hidden from the laity which led to the use of a veil to hide the bema during the consecration of the sacrament. Later the veil became a curtain drawn across the central doorway of the iconostasis and even later the curtain was replaced by wooden doors. The first occurrence of the solid barrier between the laity and the consecrated sacrament seems to be in Emperor Justinian's glorious rebuilding of Hagia Sophia at Constantinople and copied in churches elsewhere in the Byzantine world. It would appear, according to one scholar, that the screen's main feature (apart from the decoration with icons, which may be a later development) was originally nothing but a straightforward copy of the traditional back-scene of the Byzantine theatre with its three double-doors. This idea was not inappropriate as it may seem as the Byzantine rite had by this time taken on some of the characteristics of a drama.

The custom of concealing the bema during the *anaphóra* (when the offerings of bread and wine are consecrated as the body and blood of Christ) by means of a curtain, first appeared in monastic circles in Syria around the fourth century. No more could the worshippers participate visually in the offering of the gifts. As Niketas Stethatos, a monk of the monastery of Stoudios in Constantinople, wrote, doors or curtains were used to close off the bema to view from the naos so that laymen could not 'contemplate the mysteries of God' that was alone open to priests. Eventually the icon-screen became solid sometime around the eleventh or twelfth century, perhaps even as late as the fourteenth. For a few centuries already the most important prayers of the service had been inaudible to the congregations and now the actions of the clergy at this point in the service were to be invisible as well. In modern Eastern Orthodox churches the veil is only a relic of its former self, a mere door-curtain inside the central gates of a solid screen, whose outer face is covered with sacred icons.

The separation of the bema and naos was addressed by Symeon of Thessaloniki (served as Archbishop 1416/7–1429) who wrote that the church building although a physical entity also 'has grace from on high: for it is consecrated by the mystical prayers of the bishop, and anointed with sacred oil, and is wholly the dwelling of God. Not everyone can go everywhere in it: some parts are for the priests, some for the laity.' Furthermore, he wrote, the three spaces of the church – bema, naos and narthex – have multiple meanings. The three signify the Trinity while the bema represents what is above the heavens, the naos the things in heaven, and the narthex what is on earth. These spaces represent Christ who is both divine and human, invisible and visible, and they also represent man who is both soul and body. Symeon further considered that the under-cover of the Holy Table symbolized the rock where Christ was buried while the rich top pointed to his grave clothes and his glorification. He then explained that incense represents the fragrant grace of the Holy Spirit while the candles denote the illumination given by the Holy Spirit. For him the ambo stood for the stone rolled over the entrance to the tomb. Symeon further pointed out that the vestments of the clergy have special meanings and all the ornamentation of the church represents the beauty of creation.

Beyond Byzantium in nearly every setting where people organized cult centres some form of barrier or screen was used to separate the divine from the profane. Recognition of the threshold aspect of the barrier or screen was far more critical than its material and perhaps its form. As Mircea Eliade, a leading twentieth-century interpreter of religious experience, eloquently wrote that between the Sacred and the Profane there is a threshold that represents a boundary, a frontier that distinguishes and opposes these two worlds but, at the same time paradoxically, is the place where the two worlds communicate. In Byzantine churches the iconostasis separates the world of the laity from the world of the clergy but at the same time the icons of the Theotokos and St John act as intercessors to connect the faithful to the spiritual world.

An alternative interpretation of the Holy Table is that while the pagan altar was used for bloody animal sacrifices this was replaced in the Christian rite by a holy table that signified the human sacrifice of the crucified Jesus. The Table becomes a different kind of altar, one to prepare the Eucharist, the bread that represents the body of Jesus and wine mixed with water that symbolizes his blood.

Teaching and the Synthronon
At the back of the bema apse there was in some churches the synthronon, a semi-circular bench for the clergy with the bishop's throne in the centre. This arrangement of the bishop seated in the centre of a semi-circle of his clergy and teaching was meant to convey to the faithful a representation of Christ seated in the semi-circle of his disciples. Over time the synthronon disappeared and in some cases only a simple bench was provided. The bishop's throne has now moved out of the sanctuary to a place on the south side of a widened solea for practical reasons – he could be heard better from this location rather than from the rear of the bema.

One known representation in Byzantine art that actually shows a bishop preaching from the synthronon is a picture of Pentecost in which all Twelve Apostles are shown preaching simultaneously. The representation appears in a manuscript by Gregory of Nazianzus, known as the Paris Psalter in the Bibliothèeque Nationale, which depicts the apostles seated on a semi-circular bench raised one step. Each apostle appears to be holding a Gospel book or scroll and gesturing vigorously. At the centre instead of the single elevated bishop's place is a vision of the *hetoimasía*, the Word enthroned with the Holy Spirit, hovering above their heads. Below the preachers on either side stand the crowds, labelled ΦΥΛΑΙ (*FYLAI*) and ΓΛΩCΑΙ (GLOSAI), that is people of every race and tongue who listen to the preaching, each in the language of their native land.

Second Coming of the Messiah and Orientation

In Christian churches orientation is dependent on the direction in which the bema faces. It appears that the bemas of early Christian churches before and after Constantine were at the east end whereas in Constantine's time they were at the west end. In the churches founded by Constantine, such as St Peter's, St Paul, St Lorenzo, the Anastasis and the basilicas at Tyre and Antioch, they each had a western bema. It would seem that Constantine returned to the traditional orientation of ancient Greek temples which had entrance doors on the east through which the rising sun on the festival day of the god or goddess could shine through and illuminate the statue of the deity at the western end of the naos. After the death of Constantine, though, the practice of orientating the churches reverted to the east as recorded in the *Apostolic Constitutions*.

The east is the place of the rising sun and for early Christians this was a fitting symbol of the appearance of Christ as the Messiah in his Second Coming or appearance (*parousía*). Scant evidence for an eastern orientation in the earliest Christian places of assembly is from literary references in Tertullian. In his *Apologeticus,* written in 197, he wrote that the idea of Christians as sun-worshippers 'has no doubt originated from our being known to turn to the East in prayer'. Tertullian observed that prayer to the east as being an apostolic tradition and that it expressed the expectation that Christ will appear as the Rising Sun that will never set. Clement of Alexandria in his work *Stromata* (*c*.203–211) affirmed that 'prayers are made looking towards the sunrise to the east. Whence also the most ancient temples looked towards the west, that people might be taught to turn to the east when facing the images.' It is known that in ancient pagan temples cult statues where at the west end of the temple and that is the direction in which people had to look to see them. Clement is indicating that in Christian churches, on the other hand, people ought to face east and that is the direction in which the Holy Table should be located. Patriarch Germanos in his *Ecclesiastical History and Mystical Contemplation* explained prayer is made toward the east because 'the comprehensible sun of righteousness, Christ our God, appeared on earth in those regions of the east where the perceptible sun rises'. He no doubt refers to Jerusalem as being in the east as the Christians early on named the city the Heavenly Jerusalem from which the Messiah came once and will come again.

Archaeological evidence from the house church at Dura-Europos is that the raised platform on which no doubt the Holy Table was placed was at the east end of the room that was used for liturgical gatherings. When the building was remodelled for use by the Christians a major component was the creation of an enlarged area for assembly but no area for the ritual meal. This suggests the separation of the Eucharist ritual from the *agápe* dinner up to the time of Paul when the Eucharist and the dinner were held together around a table. That the ritual and the dinner had become separate is evident from church orders such as the *Didache* and the *Apostolic Tradition* of Hippolytus, as well as Paul's letter to the Corinthians where he distinguishes between the meal eaten together and the partaking of the symbolic bread and wine from the Lord's cup.

The relationship between the liturgy and orientation in Christian church architecture is further manifest from a Syriac text of the late third century, the *Didascalia Apostolorum*. In the words of this text 'First, let the church (*oîkos*) be elongated, turned to the east, and let it have the *pastophoria* on either side, toward the east.' The bishop's throne was to be placed in the middle of the bema towards the east with the presbyters (*presvytéres*) on either side of him. The lector was to be in the middle 'on an eminence [ambo]' to read the scriptures. When the congregation stands up to pray the rulers may stand up first, followed in turn by the men and then the women. 'For it is required that you pray toward the east, as knowing that which is written: "Give ye glory to God, who rideth upon the heaven of heavens toward the east."' (Psalm 68:33).

When Procopius in his book *Edifices* refers to the eastern part of the sixth-century church of Hagia Sophia he wrote that it is 'that part which faces the rising sun, that portion of the building in which they perform the mysteries in worship of God.' In his description of the church of St Anthemios he depicted the holy bema as 'an inaccessible place [for the layperson], in which the sacred mysteries are rightfully celebrated, along the side facing the rising sun.'

Religious Symbolism and Spiritual Art
Patriarch Germanos envisaged the church building as an 'earthly heaven wherein the heavenly God dwells and walks about'. Byzantine and later Eastern Orthodox art decorative programme was developed to support this idea so that the faithful could apprehend it. Upon entering a church the faithful take a candle, light it and place it next to the icon stand, or *proskynetárion*, on which is set an icon. The icon represents a sacred person, or persons, or an event celebrated by the particular church. Most often this is after whom or which the church was named. The faithful person makes the sign of the cross, kisses the icon and says a brief prayer. This series of acts represent honourable veneration (*timitikí proskýnesis*) of the icon and should not be taken as worshipping (*latreía*) of the icon. The honour which is given to the icon is regarded as being passed over to the prototype. In the narthex above the main doors into the naos, the Royal Doors (*Vasíleion Pýlin*), Jesus as Teacher is represented blessing and holding the Gospel on which is inscribed either 'I am the door' (John 10:9) or 'I am the light of the world' (John 12:34, 46) or 'I am the way and the truth and the life.' (John 4:6). In domed churches the dome it is seen as the symbol of heaven and, in most cases, contains the Pantokrator, a figure that represents a triple theological significance – Creator, Saviour and Judge. Earth and heaven are united by the semi-dome of the apse which contains an image of the Theotokos holding the child Jesus and escorted by two archangels. She is the one who unites the upper world of heaven with the lower level of the earth by means of the divine child in her arms. As the holy bema stands for heaven the images represent acts of salvation whereas the images in the naos, which stands for the material world, denotes the stages leading to salvation. On entering a basilica type church the worshipper's gaze is guided to the spiritual end and Holy Table located in the bema by the two parallel rows of columns one either side of the naos. Around the middle of the fourth century the figures of Christ and the apostles began to be depicted from a figurative to a more spiritual manner. Christ, in particular, was also shown more 'in majesty' following the way emperors were portrayed.

An exciting exhibition was held at the Museum of Byzantine Culture in Thessaloniki between November 2009 and January 2010 titled *Architecture as Icon: Perception and Representation of Architecture in Byzantine Art*. There were displays of architecture in icons, mosaics, wall paintings, manuscript illustrations, engravings, stone reliefs, pottery, coins, and liturgical utensils and as objects in metalwork, ivory carvings, reliquaries and models. It was made clear in the exhibition that buildings in Byzantine art were deliberately not depicted realistically and often no distinction was made between exterior and interior space as space was regarded as infinite. Of special interest here are the symbolic aspects of Byzantine sacred architecture. Previously mention has been made of the emphasis on the number three. First of all in architecture there was the division of Byzantine church buildings into three distinct spaces – narthex, naos and bema. Then there were the three entrance doors in the narthex and the triple windows in the bema apse. In the typical Byzantine decorative art programme there were the three tiers of wall paintings on the naos walls as well as the three tiers of panels on the back wall of the apse. Although not a direct correlation the allusion of the number three is to the Holy Trinity. In the fully developed scheme of the Byzantine church the interior of the building is an image of the universe with three levels of being one above the other.

1115. Incense Burner with five domes I

1116. Incense Burner with five domes II

1117. Reliquary I. (Monastery of Dochiariou, Mount Athos)

The highest level is the uncreated heavenly world of divine being. Architecturally this world is represented in the dome or high vaults with Christ as Pantokrator, the all-ruler, at the centre of the heavens and the universe. Below him are archangels or angels, sometimes apostles or prophets, who act as intermediaries between the world of time and space below with the timeless divine world. The second level below is that of the world of paradise as it was created 'in the beginning' one in which people will be 'saved' after the 'fall' by the events in the life of Christ. Usually 12 main scenes from his life are depicted on the straight wall of the naos that point the way to salvation and the 'return to paradise'. The third level is that of human existence on earth depicting saints and martyrs whose state of being the worshipper is encouraged to aspire to.

1118. Reliquary II. (Hosios Nifon)

1119. Tabernacle. (San Giovanni in Laterno)

The theme of the exhibition was to transmit the idea that in Byzantine art, architecture conveyed spiritual concepts through stylized physical forms and that architecture as background was significant and not just space filling. Of the many examples of architectural symbolism evident in the exhibition one is that inevitably church buildings in all the art media are more often than not shown the same size or even smaller than human beings. A church building was understood as

THE TWELVE GREAT FESTIVALS IN BYZANTINE ICONOGRAPHY
(*Dodekaórton*)
AS DEPICTED ON THE ICONOSTASIS OF THE KATHOLIKON, MONASTERY OF STAVRONIKITA, MOUNT ATHOS
[Actually 15 in a row not shown as such here]
Source: Patrinellis et al Plates 5 to 19

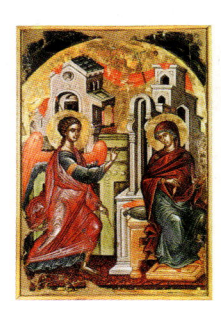

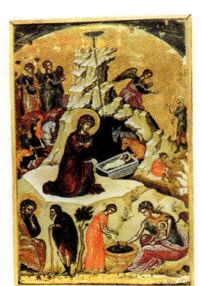

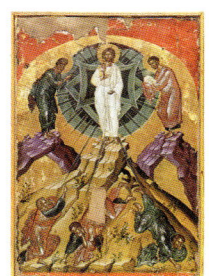

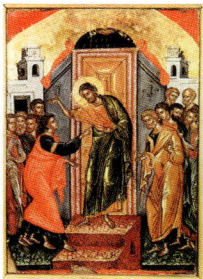

1. The Annunciation
2. The Nativity
3. The Presentation
4. The Baptism
5. The Metamorphosis
6. The Raising of Lazarus
7. Entrance of the Palms
8. The Crucifixion
9. The Resurrection
10. The Holy Tomb
11. The Theophany
12. The Touch of Thomas
13. The Ascension
14. Pentecost
15. Koimisis Theotokou

1120. *Dodekaórton* (*Katholikon* iconostasis, Monastery of Stavronikita, Mount Athos)

being symbol of the heavenly house of God and as such scale was unimportant. Another example is in the three-dimensional miniature church models, even those based on real buildings, were meant to be spiritual symbols and not physical representations. Philosophically the distinction in Byzantine art is that humans can appreciate beauty (*to kalón*) but could only aspire to absolute beauty (*to kállos*) which is divine. The Byzantines interpreted the space of the church as an image of God, an imitation of the cosmos and a symbol of indivisible divine space. Sophronios, patriarch of Jerusalem, went further to explain that not only does the church imitate the heavenly temple but that the priests in celebrating the liturgy in the church imitate the angels of God in heaven.

The vision of Thomas of Marga, a ninth-century Nestorian bishop living in an area near Mosul and author of an important monastic history in Syriac titled *The Book of Governors*, best captures the entire spiritual experience of sacred architecture: 'Every time I am in church for the service of the Holy Mysteries, my mind is lifted up above the sight of the liturgical actions, and above the church and its congregation, to the things which are in heaven. … The church of my thoughts is that of Jerusalem which is upon the earth. The bema in it is Zion. The altar [Holy Table] in it represents the Ark of the Old Covenant, the throne of Christ at the time of his dispensation here … The path from the bema to the dome beyond is the narrow path [solea] which goes up to heaven. The three steps which are in front of the bema are the third heaven, to which the blessed Apostle Paul was taken up … [and a] lattice which surrounds the door of the chancel [bema] and the veils on it. The chancel is the place above the heavens; the ciborium is the heaven of heavens and the veils on it are symbols of the hiddenness of the Godhead even from the angels. The altar is the throne of the Godhead, and the priests are the angels … The light in the chancel represent the divine glory and the god-given knowledge of all things which makes the spiritual beings sparkle and shine … The sweet-smelling incense filling our Holy Temple is our knowledge of the future and our insight into things which are hidden … I forget myself when I am exalted to the immaterial assemblies of spiritual beings. My intellect passes from the symbols to the supernal things which are symbolized.'

EPILOGUE

In the Prologue to this book I began this journey through Byzantine sacred architecture, spiritual art, liturgy and symbolism in my ancestral island of Ithaka. Now that the journey is ended it is time to reflect on it. Just as a poem of Konstantine Kavafy was at the start, let another poem of his be at the close.

Three verses from his poem titled *Ithaka* are:

> When you set out on the journey to Itháki,
> then pray that the road is long,
> full of adventure, full of discovery.
> ...
> Itháki has given you a marvelous journey.
> Without her you would never have taken to the road.
> But she has nothing more to give you now.
> ...
> And poor though you may find her, Itháki has not deceived you.
> For as you have become so wise, with so much experience,
> you must surely understand by now what Ithákes mean.

[From the poem *ITHAKI*, 1911, translated by the author]

1121. St Saviour in Chora, Constantinople, East Elevation. Apse Semi-dome and Naos Dome (centre), Parekklesion (left), Annex (right)

NOTES

PREFACE

1. Translation by George Gingras, *Egeria: Diary of a Pilgrimage*.

CHAPTER 2: SACRED ARCHITECTURE

1. Quotation from Eusebius, *Ecclesiastical History*. English translation by Kirsopp Lake. London: William Heinemann, 1926, 8:1.5.

CHAPTER 3: SPLENDID CHURCHES

1. In *Vita Basilii*, pp. 321 ff. Life of the Emperor Basil I written by or under the supervision of Constantine VII. It constitutes Book V of Theophanes Continuates. Reproduced in an anthology by Cyril Mango *The Art of the Byzantine Empire 312–1453: Sources and Documents*, p.192.
2. The existing and active monasteries of Mount Athos are (excluding *sketes*):
    East coast from south to north: Megistis Lavra, Karakalou, Iveron, Stavronikita, Pantokratoros, Vatopedi, Esfigmenou.
    West coast from south to north: St Paul, Dionysios, Gregoriou, Simonopetra, Xeropotamou, Panteleimon, Xenophontos, Dochiariou
    Inland: Philotheou, Koutloumoussi, Konstamonitou, Zographou, Chelandari.
3. The existing and active monasteries of Meteora in historical order are:
    St Stephen, Holy Trinity, Varlaam, Great Meteoron, Roussanou, St Nicholas
4. The monasteries of Mystras once were (excluding chapels): Evangelistria, Brontochion, SS Theodoroi, Hodegetria also known as Aphentiko, Perivleptos, Pantanassa.

CHAPTER 5: PLACES OF SPLENDID SPIRITUAL ART

1. Mouriki, Doula. 'The Iconography of the Mosaics', Chapter Two in Belting et al., pp. 43– 73.

CHAPTER 7: SYMBOLISM

1. Main and subsidiary documents used by Wilkinson are:
    Eusebius. *Ecclesiastical History*. 10.4. Translated from the edition of E. Schwartz and T. Mommsen. Berlin-Leipzig, 1908, pp. 862–83.
    Maximus the Confessor. *Mystagogies*. Translated from the edition by S. Soteropoulos *E Mystagogía tou Hagíou Máximou tou Homologētou*, Athens, 1978.
    Symeon of Thessaloniki. *The Eucharist*. Edited by Jassy Dositheus, 1683. Reprinted in *Patrologiae cursus completus*. 155. Jacques-Paul Migue. Series graeca (Paris, 1844–1866).

A Syrian Nestorian. *Anonymi Auctoris Exposito Officiorum Ecclesiae, Georgio Arbelensi vulgo adscripta*. I and II, Rome, 1913.

Amalarius of Metz. *The Services of the Church*. III, *Patrologiae cursus completus*. Jacques-Paul Migue. Series latina (Paris, 1844–1864).

Choricus, *Laudatio Marciani*, II, 28 ff.

Germanos, *Church Symbolism*. Translated from the text edited by F. E. Brightman, *Journal of Theological Studies*, 10, 1908, pp. 248–67 and 387–97.

John of Odzun. *Laying the Foundations*. Translated by Robert Thomson.

John the Divine. *Apocalypse* (in Greek but also known as the Book of Revelation).

Syriac Canons and Liturgy. *Testamentum Domini*. Translated mainly by J. Cooper and A. J. Maclean, *The Testament of the Lord*, Edinburgh 1902.

The New Church at Edessa. Translation by Cyril Mango, *The Art of the Byzantine Empire, 312–1453: Sources and Documents*, pp. 57–60.

Thomas of Marga. *The Book of Governors*. 15, based on the translation by E. A. Wallis Budge. London, 1893, Vol. 2, pp. 540–7.

Yahya ibn Jarir. *The Book of the Counsellor*. Chapter 29, translated by J. Khouri-Sarkis in *L'Orient Syrien*, 12, 1967, pp. 303–31.

2. Pitra, J. B. *Speicilegium Solesmense,* I, Paris (1852), p. 383 ff.
3. *Patrologiae cursus completus*. 46, 737. Jacques-Paul Migue. Series graeca (Paris, 1844–1866).
4. Foerster, R. (ed.). *Choricii Gazaei Opera*. Leipzig, 1929.
5. English translation by W. R. Paton. New York: Loeb Classical Library, 1916–1918. 5 volumes.
6. Usener, H. *Kleine Schriften,* IV. Berlin-Leipzig,1913, 418 ff.
7. *Patrologiae cursus completus*. 94, 1337 ff. Jacques-Paul Migue. Series graeca (Paris, 1844–1866).
8. Legrand, E. (ed.). *Revue des études greques,* IX (1896), p. 32 ff.
9. Chatzidakis, M. (ed.). *Epetêris Hetair. Byzant. Spoudón,* XIV, 1938, p. 393 ff.

FURTHER READING

CHAPTER 1: CHURCH AND STATE

Benko, Stephen. *Pagan Rome and the Early Christians.*
Brown, Peter Robert Lamont. *The World of Late Antiquity, AD 150–750.*
Cameron. Averil. *The Mediterranean World in Late Antiquity AD 395–600.*
Cochrane, Charles Norris. *Christianity and the Classical Culture: A Study of Thought and Action from Augustus to Augustine.*
Cormack, Robin and Maria Vassilaki(eds). *Byzantium 330–1453.*
Elsner, Jaś. *Imperial Rome and Christian Triumph: The Art of the Roman Empire AD 100–450.*
Freeman, Charles. *The Closing of the Western Mind. The Rise of Faith and the Fall of Reason.*
Frend, W.H.C. *The Rise of Christianity.*
Gregory, Timothy E. *A History of Byzantium.*
MacMullen, Ramsay. *Christianizing the Roman Empire AD 100–400.*
Norwich, John Julius. *A Short History of Byzantium.*

CHAPTER 2: SACRED ARCHITECTURE

Buchwald, Hans. *Form, Style and Meaning in Byzantine Church Architecture.*
Cavernos, Constantine. *Byzantine Church Architecture.*
Davies, John Gordon. *The Origin and Development of Early Christian Church Architecture.*
Fletcher, Bannister. 'The Byzantine Empire', Chapter 10 in *A History of Architecture.*
Grabar, André. *Early Christian Art: From the Rise of Christianity to the Death of Theodosius.*
———. *The Golden Age of Justinian: From the Death of Theodosius to the Rise of Islam.*
Krautheimer, Richard. *Early Christian and Byzantine Architecture.*
Mango, Cyril. *Byzantine Architecture.*
Ousterhout, Robert. *Master Builders of Byzantium.*
White, L. Michael. *The Social Origins of Christian Architecture.*

CHAPTER 3: SPLENDID CHURCHES

Acheimastou-Potamianou, Myrtali. *Mystras: Historical and Archaeological Guide.*
Bouras, Charalambos. *Byzantine and Post-Byzantine Architecture in Greece.*
Brandenburg, Hugo. *Ancient Churches of Rome from the Fourth to the Seventh Century: The Dawn of Christian Architecture in the West.*
Buchwald, Hans. *Form, Style and Meaning in Byzantine Church Architecture.*
Bustacchini, Gianfranco. *Ravenna: Mosaics, Monuments and Environment.*
Büyükkolanci, Mustafa. *The Life and Monument of St John.*
Davies, John Gordon. *The Origin and Development of Early Christian Church Architecture.*
Dupré, Judith. *Churches.*
Grundmann, Stefan (ed.). *The Architecture of Rome.*

Kadas, Sotiris. *Mount Athos: An Illustrated Guide to the Monasteries and their History.*
Krautheimer, Richard. *Early Christian and Byzantine Architecture.*
Mathews, Thomas F. *The Early Churches of Constantinople: Architecture and Liturgy.*
Mainstone, Rowland J. *Hagia Sophia: Architecture, Structure and Liturgy of Justinian's Great Church.*
Mango, Cyril. *Byzantine Architecture.*
Mastrogiannopoulos, Elias. *The Byzantine Churches of Greece and Cyprus.*
Molho, M. *The Monuments of Thessaloniki.*
Orlandos, A. *Byzantine Architecture.*
Ousterhout, Robert. *Master Builders of Byzantium.*
Theotechni, Sister. *Meteora.*
Van Millingen, Alexander. *Byzantine Churches in Constantinople: Their History and Architecture.*
Webb, Matilda. *The Churches and Catacombs of Early Christian Rome.*

CHAPTER 4: SPIRITUAL ART

Beckwith, John. *Early Christian and Byzantine Art.*
Cavernos, Constantine. *Orthodox Iconography.*
Cormack, Robin. *Byzantine Art.*
———. *Icons.*
Eastmond, Antony and James, Liz (eds). *Icon and Word: The Power of Images in Byzantium.*
Grabar, André. *Christian Iconography: A Study of Its Origins.*
———. *Early Christian Art: From the Rise of Christianity to the Death of Theodosius.*
———. *The Golden Age of Justinian: From the Death of Theodosius to the Rise of Islam.*
Hutte, Irmgard. *The Universe History of Art and Architecture: Early Christian and Byzantine.*
Kalokyris, Constantine D. *The Essence of Orthodox Iconography.*
Mango, Cyril. *The Art of the Byzantine Empire 312–1453: Sources and Documents.*
Ouspensky, Leonid and Vladimir Lossky. *The Meaning of Icons.*
Rice, David Talbot. *The Art of Byzantium.*
Schug-Wille, Christa. *Art of the Byzantine World.*
Syndicus, Eduard. *Early Christian Art.*

CHAPTER 5: PLACES OF SPLENDID SPIRITUAL ART

Acheimastou-Potamianou, Myrtali. *Icons of the Byzantine Museum of Athens.*
———. *Mystras: Historical and Archaeological Guide.*
Belting, Hans, Mango, Cyril, Mouriki, Doula. *The Mosaics and Frescoes of St Mary Pammakaristos (Fethiye Camii) at Istanbul.*
Bourboudakis, Manilos (ed.). *Icons of the Cretan School.*
Bustacchini, Gianfranco. *Ravenna: Mosaics, Monuments and Environment.*
Cattani, Riccardo. *St John Lateran.*
Drandaki, Anastasia. *The Origins of El Greco Icon Painting in Venetian Crete.*
Evans, Helen C., and White, Bruce. *St Catherine's Monastery, Sinai, Egypt.*
Ferracane, Seby e Meli, Tony. *Monreale: Il Duomo.*
Gallio, Paola. *The Basilica of St Praxedes.*
Gerardi, M. *San Clemente Roma.*
Grabar, André. *Christian Iconography: A Study of Its Origins.*
———. *Early Christian Art: From the Rise of Christianity to the Death of Theodosius.*
———. *The Golden Age of Justinian: From the Death of Theodosius to the Rise of Islam.*
Gramiccia, Anna. *Tesori Medioevali della Republica di Macedonia.*
Kadas, Sotiris. *Mount Athos: An Illustrated Guide to the Monasteries and their History.*

Kostof, Spiro. *Caves of God: The Monastic Environment of Byzantine Cappadocia.*
Lazarides, Paul. *The Monastery of Hosios Loukas.*
Maguire, Ann Terry and Henry. *Dynamic Splendour: The Wall Mosaics in the Cathedral of Eufrasius at Poreč.*
Mastrogiannopoulos, Elias. *Byzantine Churches of Greece and Cyprus.*
Papaioannou, Evangelos. *The Monastery of St Catherine Sinai.*
Plakogiannakis, Kimonos Emmanouel. *Agio Oros: O Promachonas tis Orthodoxias.*
Syndicus, Eduard. *Early Christian Art.*
Theotechni, Sister. *Meteora.*
Tsigaridas, Efthymios. *Latomou Monastery.*
Vicchi, Roberta. *The Major Basilicas of Rome.*
Vio, Ettore. *The Basilica of St Mark in Venice.*
Yucel, Erdem. *Hagia Sophia.*
Webb, Matilda. *The Churches and Catacombs of Early Christian Rome.*
Weitzmann, Kurt. *The Icon: Holy Images – Sixth to Fourteenth Century.*

CHAPTER 6: LITURGY

Dix, Dom Gregory. *The Shape of the Liturgy.*
Doig, Allan. *Liturgy and Architecture: From the Early Church to the Middle Ages.*
Kilde, Jeanne Halgren. *Sacred Power, Sacred Space: An Introduction to Christian Architecture and Worship.*
Mathews, Thomas F. *The Early Churches of Constantinople: Architecture and Liturgy.*
Meyendorff, John. *Byzantine Theology: Historical Trends and Doctrinal Themes.*
Oakley, Austin. *The Orthodox Liturgy.*
Schmemann, Alexander. *The Eucharist: Sacrament of the Kingdom.*
Wainwright, Geoffrey and Westerfield Tucker, Karen B. (eds). *The Oxford History of Christian Worship.*
Ware, Timothy (Bishop Kallistos). *The Orthodox Church.*
White, Michael L. *The Social Origins of Christian Architecture, Volume II.*
Wybrew, Hugh. *The Orthodox Liturgy: The Development of the Eucharistic Liturgy in the Byzantine Rite.*

CHAPTER 7: SYMBOLISM

Davies, John Gordon. *The Origin and Development of Early Christian Church Architecture.*
Dix, Dom Gregory. *The Shape of the Liturgy.*
Doig, Allan. *Liturgy and Architecture: From the Early Church to the Middle Ages.*
Mathews, Thomas F. *The Early Churches of Constantinople: Architecture and Liturgy.*
White, L. Michael. *The Social Origins of Christian Architecture.*
Wilkinson, John. *From Synagogue to Church: The Traditional Design. Its Beginning, Its Definition, Its End.*
Wybrew, Hugh. *The Orthodox Liturgy: The Development of the Eucharistic Liturgy in the Byzantine Rite.*

BIBLIOGRAPHY

Acheimastou-Potamianou, Myrtali. *Icons of the Byzantine Museum of Athens.* Athens: Archaeological Receipts Fund, 1998.
———. *Mystras: Historical and Archaeological Guide.* Athens: Hesperos Editions, 2003.
Arcidiocesi di Monreale (PA). *Monreale: Il Duomo.* Palermo: Casa Editrice Mistretta, N.D.
Armstrong, Gregory T. 'Constantine's Churches: Symbol and Structure'. *The Journal of the Society of Architectural Historians,* 33(1), March 1974, pp. 5–16.
Bahat, Dan. *Carta's Historical Atlas of Jerusalem.* Jerusalem: Carta Jerusalem, 1973.
Baldovin, John. *The Urban Character of Christian Worship: The Origins, Development and Meaning of Stational Liturgy.* Orientalia Christiana Analecta, 228. Roma. Rome: Pontifical Oriental Institute Press, 1987. (Reprint 2002.)
Beckwith, John. *Early Christian and Byzantine Art.* New York: Penguin Books, 1979.
Belting, Hans, Mango, Cyril and Mouriki, Doula. *The Mosaics and Frescoes of St Mary Pammakaristos (Fethiye Camii) at Istanbul.* Washington, DC: Dumbarton Oaks Center for Byzantine Studies, 1978.
Benko, Stephen. *Pagan Rome and the Early Christians.* Bloomington, IN: Indiana University Press, 1984.
Borboudakis, Manolis (ed.). *Icons of the Cretan School.* Crete: Ministry of Culture, 1993.
Brown, Peter Robert Lamont. *The World of Late Antiquity, AD 150–750.* NY: Norton, 1989.
Blunt, A. W. F. *The Apologies of Justin Martyr.* Cambridge, 1911 (Edition Gustav Kruger. Freiburg: J.C.B.Mohr 1891)
Brandenburg, Hugo. *Ancient Churches of Rome from the Fourth to the Seventh Century: The Dawn of Christian Architecture in the West.* Translated from the German. Turnout, Belgium: Brepols Publishers, 2004.
Bouras, Charalambos. *Byzantine and Post-Byzantine Architecture in Greece.* Athens: Melissa Publishing House, 2006.
Bouyer, Louis. *Literature and Architecture.* Notre Dame, IN: University of Notre Dame Press, 1967.
Boyd, Susan A. 'Art in the Service of the Liturgy', in Linda Safran (ed.), *Heaven on Earth: Art and Church in Byzantium.* Philadelphia, PA: University of Pennsylvania Press, 1998, pp. 152–85.
Brubaker, Leslie. *Vision and Meaning in Ninth-Century Byzantium.* Cambridge: Cambridge University Press, 1999.
———. *The Cult of the Mother of God in Byzantium.* Burlington, VT: Ashgate, 2011.
Buchwald, Hans. *Form, Style and Meaning in Byzantine Church Architecture.* Ashgate Variorum, 1999.
Bustacchini, Gianfranco. *Ravenna: Mosaics, Monuments and Environment.* Ravenna: Cartolibreria Salbaroli, N.D.
Büyükkolanci, Mustafa. *The Life and Monument of St John.* Selçuk-Izmir: Efes 2000 Foundation, 2001.
Cameron. Averil. *The Mediterranean World in Late Antiquity AD 395–600.* NY: Routledge, 1993.
Cameron, Averil and Hall, Stuart G. *Eusebius: Life of Constantine.* Oxford: Oxford University Press, 1999.
Cattani, Riccardo. *St John Lateran.* Roma: Macart S.r.I, 2008.
Cavernos, Constantine. *Guide to Orthodox Iconography.* Belmont, MA: The Institute of Byzantine and Modern Greek Studies, 1993. (Two volumes.)
———. *Orthodox Iconography.* Belmont, MA: The Institute of Byzantine and Modern Greek Studies, 2007 (Sixth Printing).
———. *Byzantine Church Architecture.* Belmont, MA: The Institute of Byzantine and Modern Greek Studies, 2007.
Chatzitryphonos, Evangelia and Ćurčić, Slobodan. *Architektoniki os Eikona (Architecture as Icon: Perception and Representation of Architecture in Byzantine Art).* Thessaloniki: Museum of Byzantine Culture, 2009.
Cobb, Peter. 'The Architectural Setting of the Liturgy', in Jones, Cheslyn, Wainwright, Geoffrey and Yarnold, Edward (eds), *The Study of the Liturgy.* NY: Oxford University Press, 1978, pp. 528–54.
Cochrane, Charles Norris. *Christianity and the Classical Culture: A Study of Thought and Action from Augustus to Augustine.* Oxford: Oxford University Press, 1944.
Constantine VII Porphyrogenitus. *The Book of Ceremonies* (translated by W.R. Lethaby and H. Swainson), in *The Church of Santa Sophia, Constantinople.* London and New York: Macmillan, 1894.

Cormack, Robin. *Byzantine Art.* Oxford: Oxford University Press, 2000.
———. *Icons.* Cambridge, MA: Harvard University Press, 2007.
Cormack, Robin and Vassilaki, Maria (eds). *Byzantium 330–1453.* London: Royal Academy of Arts, 2008.
Crook, John. *The Architectural Setting of the Cult of Saints in the Early Christian West, c. 300–1200.* Oxford: Clarendon Press, 2000.
Ćurčić, Slobodan and Hadjitryphonos, Evangelia. *Architecture as Icon: Perception and Representation of Architecture in Byzantine Art.* Princeton, NJ: Princeton University Art Museum, 2010.
Dark, Ken and Ozgumus, Ferudun. 'New Evidence for the Byzantine Church of Holy Apostles from Fatih Camii, Istanbul', *Oxford Journal of Archaeology,* 21(4), 2002, pp. 393–413.
Davies, John Gordon. *The Origin and Development of Early Christian Church Architecture.* New York: Philosophical Library, 1953.
Deichmann, Friedrich Wilhelm. *Fruhchristliche Kirchen in Rom.* Basel: I M Amerbach Verlag, 1948.
Demus, Otto. *The Church of San Marco in Venice: History, Architecture, Sculpture.* Washington, DC: Dumbarton Oaks, 1960.
———. *Byzantine Mosaic Decoration.* Boston, MA: Boston Book & Art Shop, 1964. Third Impression.
Dietz, Maribel. *Wandering Monks, Virgins, and Pilgrims: Ascetic Travel in the Mediterranean World AD 300–800.* University Park, PA: The Pennsylvania State University Press, 2005.
Dix, Dom Gregory. *The Shape of the Liturgy.* London: Continuum Books, 2005. (3rd edn.)
Doig, Allan. *Liturgy and Architecture: From the Early Church to the Middle Ages.* Burlington, VT: Ashgate Publishing Company, 2008.
Drandaki, Anastasia. *The Origins of El Greco Icon Painting in Venetian Crete.* New York: Alexander S. Onassis Public Benefit Foundation, 2009.
Dupré, Judith. *Churches.* New York: HarperCollins, 2001.
Duval, Noel. 'L'Architecture chrétienne et les pratiques liturgiques en Jordanie en rapport avec la Palestine', in Painter, Kenneth (ed.). *Churches Built in Ancient Times: Recent Studies in Early Christian Archaeology.* London: Society of Antiquaries, Accordia Research Centre, 1994, pp. 149–212.
Eastmond, Antony and James, Liz (eds). *Icon and Word: The Power of Images in Byzantium.* Aldershot: Ashgate, 2003.
Ebersolt, Jean and Thiers, Adolphe. *Les Eglises de Constantinople.* Paris: Ernest Leroux, Editeur, 1913. (Two volumes.)
Ehrman, Bart D. *Lost Christianities: The Battles for Scripture and the Faith we never knew.* New York: Oxford University Press, 2004.
Elsner, Jaś. *Imperial Rome and Christian Triumph: The Art of the Roman Empire AD 100–450.* Oxford: Oxford University Press, 1998.
Eusebius of Caesarea. *Ecclesiastical History.* (Translated by Samuel Parker.) London: George Sawbridge, 1703.
———. *Vita Constantini.* (Translated by A.C. McGiffert.) Library of the Nicene and Post Nicene Fathers, Volume Two. Oxford: Oxford University Press, 1900.
Evans, Helen C., and White, Bruce. *St Catherine's Monastery, Sinai, Egypt.* New York: The Metropolitan Museum of Art, 2004.
Ferguson, Everett. *Church and State in the Early Church.* New York: Garland, 1993.
Fletcher, Bannister. 'The Byzantine Empire', Chapter 10 in *A History of Architecture* (19th edn), John Musgrove (ed.), pp. 268–306. London: Butterworth, 1987.
Freely, John and Cakmak, Ahmet S. *Byzantine Monuments of Istanbul.* Cambridge: Cambridge University Press, 2004.
Freeman, Charles. *The Closing of the Western Mind. The Rise of Faith and the Fall of Reason.* New York: A. A. Knopf, 2003.
Frend, W.H.C. *The Rise of Christianity.* Philadelphia: Fortress Press, 1984.
Galavaris, Giorgios. *Zografiki Vyzantinon Cheirografon.* Athinai: Ekdotike Athenon S.A., 2006.
Gallio, Paola. *The Basilica of St Praxedes.* Genova: B.N. Marconi, 1998.
Gerardi, M. *San Clemente Roma.* Roma: Collegio S. Clement, 1992.
Germanos of Constantinople. *On the Divine Liturgy.* Meyendorff, Paul. Crestwood, NY: St Vladimir's Seminary Press, 1984.
Gerstel, Sharon E. J. *Beholding the Sacred Mysteries: Programs of the Byzantine Sanctuary.* Seattle: University of Washington Press, 1999.
Gerstel, Sharon E. J. 'Civic and Monastic Influences on Church Decoration in Late Byzantine Thessalonike', Dumbarton Oaks Papers, No. 57, Washington, DC: Dumbarton Oaks Research Library and Collection, 2003.
Gerstel, Sharon E. J. (ed.). *Thresholds of the Sacred: Architectural, Art Historical, Liturgical, and Theological Perspectives on Religious Screens, East and West.* Washington: DC: Dumbarton Oaks Research Library Collections, 2006.

Gingras, George E. *Egeria: Diary of a Pilgrimage*. New York: Newman Press, 1970.
Grabar, André. *The Golden Age of Justinian: From the Death of Theodosius to the Rise of Islam*. Translated by Stuart Gilbert and James Emmons. New York: Odyssey Press, 1967.
———. *Christian Iconography: A Study of Its Origins*. Princeton, NJ: Princeton University Press, 1968a.
———. *Early Christian Art: From the Rise of Christianity to the Death of Theodosius*. (Translated by Stuart Gilbert and James Emmons.) New York: Odyssey Press, 1968b.
Gramiccia, Anna. *Tesori Medioevali della Republica di Macedonia*. Roma: Edizioni De Luca, 1999.
Gregory, Timothy E. *A History of Byzantium*. Malden, MA: Blackwell Publishing, 2005.
Grundmann, Stefan (ed.). *The Architecture of Rome*. (Translated by Bruce Almberg et al.) Stuttgart: Axel Menges, 1998.
Hamilton, John Arnott. *Byzantine Architecture and Decoration*. New York: Charles Scribner's Sons, 1934.
Hammond, Peter. *Liturgy and Architecture*. London: Barrie & Rockliff, 1960.
Harris, Jonathan. *Constantinople: Capital of Byzantium*. New York: Continuum US, 2007.
Hatlie, Peter. *The Monks and Monasteries of Constantinople, ca. 350–850*. Cambridge, Cambridge University Press, 2007.
Hetherington, Paul. *Byzantium: City of Gold, City of Faith*. London: Orbis Publishing, 1983.
Hoddinott, R. F. *Early Byzantine Churches in Macedonia and Southern Serbia*. London: Macmillan & Co., 1963.
Hübsch, Henri. *Monuments de l'Architecture Chrétienne depuis Constantin*. Paris: Morel, 1866.
Hutte, Irmgard. *The Universe History of Art and Architecture: Early Christian and Byzantine*. New York: Universe Books, 1988.
Johnson, Mark J. (ed.) *Approaches to Byzantine Architecture and its Decoration: Studies in Honour of Slobodan Curcic*. Burlington, VT: Ashagate, 2012.
Kartsonis, Anna. 'The Responding Icon', in Safran, Linda (ed.), *Heaven on Earth: Art and Church in Byzantium*. Philadelphia, PA: University of Pennsylvania Press, 1998, pp 58–80.
Kavafis, K. P. *Ta Poiemata*. Athena: Ypsilon / Biblia, 1990.
Kadas, Sotiris. *Mount Athos: An Illustrated Guide to the Monasteries and their History*. Athens: Ekdotike Athenon S.A., 1980.
Kalokyris, Constantine D. *The Essence of Orthodox Iconography*. Translated by Peter Chamberas. Brookline, MA: Holy Cross Orthodox Press, 1985.
Kalopissi-Verti, Sophia. 'The Proskynetaria of the Templon and Narthex: Form, Imagery, Spatial Connections, and Reception', in Gerstel, Sharon E.J. (ed.), *Thresholds of the Sacred: Architectural, Art Historical, Liturgical, and Theological Perspectives on Religious Screens, East and West*. Washington: DC: Dumbarton Oaks Research Library Collections, 2006, pp. 107–34.
Kilde, Jeanne Halgren. *Sacred Power, Sacred Space: An Introduction to Christian Architecture and Worship*. Oxford: Oxford University Press, 2008.
Kiliçkaya, Ali. *Hagia Sophia and Chora*. Istanbul: Silk Road Publications, N.D.
Kinross, Lord. *Hagia Sophia*. Segrate-Milano: Arnoldo Mondadori Editore, 1972.
Kitzinger, E., *Byzantine Art in the Making*. London: Faber & Faber, 1977.
Kleinbauer, W. Eugene, White, Anthony and Matthews, Henry. *Hagia Sophia*. London: Scala Publishers Ltd., 2004
Kostof, Spiro. *Caves of God: The Monastic Environment of Byzantine Cappadocia*. Boston, MA: MIT Press, 1978.
Krautheimer, Richard. *Corpus Basilicarum Christianarum Romae: The Early Christian Basilicas of Rome (IV–IX) centuries*. Citta del Vaticano: Pontifico Instituto di Archaeologia Cristiana, 1937–1977. (Five volumes.)
———. *Early Christian and Byzantine Architecture*. Baltimore, Maryland: Penguin Books, 1965. (Reprinted 1967.)
Lazarides, Paul. *The Monastery of Hosios Loukas*. Athens: Hannibal Publishing House, N.D.
Longo Editore. *Ravenna Felix*. Ravenna: A. Longo Editore, 1977.
Lymberopoulou, Angeliki (ed.). *Images of the Byzantine World: Visions, Messages and Meanings. Studies Presented to Leslie Brubaker*. Farnham: Ashgate Publishing Company, 2011.
MacMullen, Ramsay. *Christianizing the Roman Empire AD 100–400*. New Haven: Yale University Press, 1984.
McDonald, William L. *Early Christian and Byzantine Architecture*. New York: George Braziller, 1962.
McGilchrist, Nigel. *Greek Islands*: London: Genius Loci Publications, 2010. (20 volumes). 14: Chios.
Maguire, Ann Terry, and Henry. *Dynamic Splendor: The Wall Mosaics in the Cathedral of Eufrasius at Poreč*. University Park, PA: The Pennsylvania State University Press, 2007. (Two volumes.)
Mainstone, Rowland J. *Hagia Sophia: Architecture, Structure and Liturgy of Justinian's Great Church*. London: Thames and Hudson, 1988.
Mango, Cyril. *The Art of the Byzantine Empire 312–1453: Sources and Documents*. Englewood Cliffs, New Jersey: Prentice-Hall, Inc. 1972.

Mango, Cyril. *Byzantine Architecture*. Milano: Electa Editrice, 1978.

———. *Byzantium: The Empire of New Rome*. London: Scribner, 1980.

———. *The Art of the Byzantine Empire 312–1453: Sources and Documents*. Toronto: Medieval Academy of America, 1986. Reprinted 1993a.

———. *Studies on Constantinople*. Aldershot: Variorum, 1993b.

Marchini, Giuseppe. *The Baptistery, the Cathedral and the Museum of the Opera del Duomo*. Becocci Editore: Florence, 1972.

Mastrogiannopoulos, Elias. *The Byzantine Churches of Greece and Cyprus*. Translated by N. and M. Logiades. Brookline, MA: Holy Cross Orthodox Press, 1984.

Mathews, Thomas F. *The Early Churches of Constantinople: Architecture and Liturgy*. University Park: The Pennsylvania State University Press, 1971.

———. *The Byzantine Churches of Istanbul: A Photographic Survey*. University Park: The Pennsylvania State University Press, 1976.

Matthiae, Guglielmo. *Le Chiese di Roma dal IV al X Secolo*. Cappelli Editore, 1962.

Maximus the Confessor. 'The Church's Mystagogy', in *Selected Writings of St Maximus Confessor*. G. C. Berthold. New York: Paulist Press, 1985.

Meyendorff, John. *Byzantine Theology: Historical Trends and Doctrinal Themes*. New York: Fordham University Press, 1979 (2nd edn).

Molho, M. *The Monuments of Thessaloniki*. Thessaloniki: Molho Publications, N.D.

Moschopoulos, George. *Cephalonia: Ecclesiastical Art*. Argostoli: Local Historic Archives, 1993 (2nd edn).

Mylonas, Paul M. *Athos and its Monastic Institutions through Old Engravings and Other Works of Art*. Athens, 1963.

———. *Atlas of the Twenty Sovereign Monasteries: Topography and Historical Architecture*. Tubingen: Wasmuth, 2000. Volume One, Part One.

Neumayer, Heinrich. *Byzantine Mosaics*. New York, NY: Crown Publishers, Inc., 1964.

Norwich, John Julius. *A Short History of Byzantium*. New York: Alfred A. Knopf, 1997.

Oakley, Austin. *The Orthodox Liturgy*, London: A. R. Mowbray, 1958.

Orlandos, A. *Byzantine Architecture*. Athens: Archaeological Society, 1998.

———. *E Xylostegos Palaiochristianiki Vasili tis Mesogeiakis Lekanis*. Athene, 1952. (Two volumes.)

Ouspensky, Leonid and Lossky, Vladimir. *The Meaning of Icons*. (Translated by G.E.H. Palmer and E. Kadloubovsky.) Boston, MA: Boston Book and Art Shop, 1956.

Ousterhout, Robert. 'The Holy Space: Architecture and the Liturgy', in Safran, Linda (ed.), *Heaven on Earth: Art and Church in Byzantium*. Philadelphia, PA: University of Pennsylvania Press, 1998, pp. 81–120.

———. *Master Builders of Byzantium*. Philadelphia, PA: University of Pennsylvania Museum of Archaeology & Anthropology, 2008.

Oxford Dictionary of Byzantium. Alexander P. Kazhdan (ed. in chief). Oxford: Oxford University Press, 1991. (Three volumes.)

Painter, Kenneth (ed.). *Churches Built in Ancient Times: Recent Studies in Early Christian Archaeology*. London: Society of Antiquaries, Accordia Research Centre, 1994.

Paluzzi, Carlo Galasci. *Roma Cristiana: Le Chiese di Roma dal IV al X Secolo*. Rom: Cappelli Editore, 1962.

Papaioannou, Evangelos. *The Monastery of St Catherine Sinai*. St Catherine Monastery, N.D.

Patricios, Nicholas N. *Kefallinia and Ithaki: A Historical and Architectural Odyssey*. Danbury, CT: Rutledge Books Inc., 2002.

Patrinelis, Christos, Karakatsanis, Agapis, and Theochari, Maria. *Moni Stavronikita*. Athina: Ethniki Trapeza tis Ellados, 1974.

Paul the Silentiary. (Translated by W.R. Lethaby and H. Swainson). In *The Church of Santa Sophia, Constantinople*. London and New York: Macmillan, 1894.

Peschlow, Urs. 'Dividing Interior Space in Early Byzantine Churches: The Barriers between the Nave and Aisles', in Safran, Linda (ed.), *Heaven on Earth: Art and Church in Byzantium*. Philadelphia, PA: University of Pennsylvania Press, 1998, pp. 53–72.

Peeters, C.J.A.C. *De Liturgische Dispositie van het Vroegchristelijk Kerkgebow*. Assen: Van Gorcum & Comp., 1969.

Pelekanidis, Styliaonos. *Meletes Palaiochristianikis kai Byzantinis Archaiologias*. Thessaloniki: Institute for Balkan Studies, 1977.

Plakogiannakis, Kimonos Emmanouel. *Agio Oros: O Promachonas tis Orthodoxias*. Thessaloniki: Schema Chroma, 2003.

Procopius. *Edifices*. (Translated by H.B. Dewing and Glanville Downey.). Cambridge, MA: Cambridge University Press. 1950.

Quattrini, Paola, Rizzi, Elsa and Zanzoterra, Simonetta. *Chiese a Pianta Centrale: Romae Dintorni*. Roma: Istituto Poligrafico e Zecca dello Stato, 2008.

Restle, Marcell. *Studien zur fruhbyzantinischen Architecktur Kappadokiens.* Wien: Berlag der Osterreichischen Akademie der Wissenschaften, 1979. Band 3.

Rice, David Talbot. *The Art of Byzantium.* New York: Harry N. Abrams, Inc., 1959.

———. *The Byzantines.* London: Thames & Hudson, 1962.

Runciman, Steven. *Mistra: Byzantine Capital of the Peloponnese.* London: Thames & Hudson, 1980.

———. *Byzantine Style and Civilization.* New York: Viking Penguin, 1987.

St John of Damascus. *On the Divine Images.* Translated by D. Anderson. Crestwood, NY: St Vladimir's Seminary Press, 1980.

St Theodore the Studite. *On the Holy Icons.* Translated by C. P. Roth. Crestwood, NY: Vladimir's Seminary Press, 1981.

Safran, Linda (ed.). *Heaven on Earth: Art and Church in Byzantium.* Philadelphia, PA: University of Pennsylvania State Press, 1998.

Ševčenko, Nancy P. 'Illuminating the Liturgy: Illustrated Service Books in Byzantium', in Safran, Linda (ed.), *Heaven on Earth: Art and Church in Byzantium.* Philadelphia, PA: University of Pennsylvania Press, 1998, pp. 186–228.

———. *The Celebration of the Saints in Byzantine Art and Liturgy.* Burlington, VT: Ashgate, 2012.

Schmemann, Alexander. *The Eucharist: Sacrament of the Kingdom.* Translated by Paul Kachur. Crestwood, NY: St Vladimir's Seminary Press, 1988.

Schug-Wille, Christa. *Art of the Byzantine World.* Translated by E. M. Hatt. New York: Harry N. Abrams, Inc., 1969.

Sherrard, Philip. *Athos: The Holy Mountain.* Woodstock, NY: The Overlook Press, 1985.

Smith, Janet Charlotte. *A Study of Architectural Form and Function: The Side Chambers of Fifth and Sixth Century Churches in Ravenna and Classe.* Philadelphia: University Philosophy Faculty, 1987.

St Symeon of Thessalonika. *The Liturgical Commentaries.* (Edited and translated by Steven Hawkes-Teeples.) Toronto: Pontifical Institute of Medieval Studies, 2011.

Stephenson, Paul (ed.). *Byzantine World.* New York, NY: Routledge, 2010.

Stewart, Cecil. *Early Christian, Byzantine and Romanesque Architecture.* New York: David McKay Company, Inc. 1964. (Fourth Impression.) Volume II of Simpson's History of Architectural Development.

Syndicus, Eduard. *Early Christian Art.* (Translated by J. R. Foster.) New York: Hawthorn Books, 1962.

Taft, Robert. *The Great Entrance.* Orientalia Christiana Analecta 200. Rome: Pontifical Institute of Oriental Studies, 1975.

———. *The Liturgy of the Great Church: an Initial Synthesis of Structure and Interpretation on the Eve of Iconoclasm.* Dumbarton Oaks Papers 34–5, 1980–1.

Tertullian. *Apology.* (Translated by S. Thelwall.) In Alexander Roberts and James Donaldson (eds), *The Anti-Nicene Fathers.* Volume III: *Latin Christianity: Its Founder, Tertullian.* Grand Rapids, Michigan: Eerdmans, 1978.

Theotechni, Sister. *Meteora.* (Translated by K. Koini-Moraitis.) Athens: Eptalofos S.A., 1981.

Tsigaridas, Efthymios. *Latomou Monastery.* Thessaloniki: Institute of Balkan Studies, 1988.

Van Millingen, Alexander. *Byzantine Churches in Constantinople: Their History and Architecture.* London: Macmillan & Co., Limited, 1912.

Vassilaki, Maria (ed.). *Mother of God: Presentations of the Virgin in Byzantine Art.* Milan: Skira Editore S.p.A, 2000.

———. *The Hand of Angelos: An Icon Painter in Venetian Crete.* Burlington, VT: Ashgate, 2010.

Vicchi, Roberta. *The Major Basilicas of Rome.* Florence: Scala Group, 1999.

Villard, Ugo Monneret de. *Le Chiese della Mesopotamia.* Roma: Pont. Institutum Orientalium Studiorum, 1940.

Vio, Ettore. *The Basilica of St Mark in Venice.* New York: Riverside Book Company, 1999.

Wainwright, Geoffrey and Westerfield Tucker, Karen B. (eds). *The Oxford History of Christian Worship.* Oxford: Oxford University Press, 2006.

Ward-Perkins, J. B. 'Memoria, Martyr's Tomb and Martyr's Church', in Paul Corby Finney (ed.), *Art, Archaeology and Architecture of Early Christianity.* Volume XVIII, Studies in Early Christianity. New York: Garland Publishing, 1993.

Ware, Timothy (Bishop Kallistos). *The Orthodox Church.* Harmondsworth: Penguin Books, 1993 (2nd edn).

Webb, Matilda. *The Churches and Catacombs of Early Christian Rome: A Comprehensive Guide.* Brighton: Sussex Academic Press, 2001.

Webb, Ruth. 'The Aesthetics of Sacred Space: Narrative, Metaphor, and Motion in *Ekphraseis* of Church Buildings'. Dumbarton Oaks Papers, No. 53, Washington, DC: Dumbarton Oaks Research Library and Collection, 1999.

Weitzmann, Kurt. *The Icon: Holy Images – Sixth to Fourteenth Century.* New York, George Braziller, 1978.

Wharton, Epstein, A. 'The Rebuilding and Redecoration of the Holy Apostles in Constantinople'. *Greek, Roman and Byzantine Studies* 23, pp.79–92.

White, L. Michael. *The Social Origins of Christian Architecture.* Valley Forge, PA: Trinity Press International, 1997. (Two volumes.)

Whittow, Mark. *The Making of Byzantium, 600–1025.* Berkeley, CA: University of California Press, 1996.

Wilkinson, John. *From Synagogue to Church: The Traditional Design. Its Beginning, Its Definition, its End.* London: RoutledgeCurzon, 2002.

Wybrew, Hugh. *The Orthodox Liturgy: The Development of the Eucharistic Liturgy in the Byzantine Rite.* Crestwood, NY: St Vladimir's Seminary Press, 1990.

Xydis, St. 'The Chancel Barrier, Solea and Ambo of Hagia Sophia'. *Art Bulletin,* 29, 1947, pp. 1–24.

Yarwood, Doreen. 'Part Two – Byzantine and Medieval Architecture: Early Christian and Byzantine 325–1453 AD', in *The Architecture of Europe.* London: Chancellor Press, 1974.

Yucel, Erdem. *Hagia Sophia.* Istanbul: K.D.V. Dahildir, N.D.

ILLUSTRATIONS, CREDITS AND SOURCES

Note to illustrations: Every effort has been made to trace the holders of copyright material and obtain official permission to reproduce the works illustrated. The author and publisher will be glad to provide full acknowledgement of the provenance of unattributed copyright material in all future printings and editions.

CHAPTER 1: CHURCH AND STATE

1. Constantine Augustus (Author)
2. The Byzantine World under Justinian I (National Geographic Society)
3. Byzantine Empire territory before and after Justinian I (By permission of John Wiley & Sons)
4. Byzantine Empire territory in the ninth century (By permission of John Wiley & Sons)
5. Emperor Constantine with a model of the city of Constantinople (Author)
6. Emperor Justinian with a model of the church of Hagia Sophia (Author)
7. Church and State (Robert Cormack and Maria Vassilaki, 2008)
8. Map of Byzantine Constantinople (Map redrawn by author after Paul Stephenson)
9. Byzantine Constantinople. Artist's view of the Great Palace (National Geographic Society)
10. Mosaic map of the Holy City of Jerusalem (André Grabar / Odyssey Press / Western Publishing Group, Inc.)
11. Map of Jerusalem. Location of churches and monasteries (Map redrawn by author after Dan Bahat)
12. Map of Thessaloniki. Location of churches and monasteries (By permission of Oxford University Press, Inc.)
13. Map of Rome. Location of Early Christian churches (André Grabar / Odyssey Press / Western Publishing Group, Inc.)
14. Tetrarchy emperors in red porphyry stone (Paul Hetherington / De Agostini Editore, S.p.A., Novara)
15. Battle of Milvian Bridge (Lord Kinross / Arnoldo Mondadori Editore, Milano)
16. Mummy Panel, Hawara (Robert Cormack and Maria Vassilaki, 2008)
17. Funeral Portrait, Egypt (Robert Robert Cormack and Maria Vassilaki, 2008)
18. Tomb of the Aurelii, Rome (André Grabar / Odyssey Press / Western Publishing Group, Inc.)
19. Catacomb Coemeterium Majus, Rome (André Grabar / Odyssey Press / Western Publishing Group, Inc.)
20. Catacomb SS Pietro e Marcellino (André Grabar / Odyssey Press / Western Publishing Group, Inc.)
21. Catacomb fresco of Christ (André Grabar / Odyssey Press / Western Publishing Group, Inc.)
22. Catacomb Commodila, Rome (By permission of George Braziller, Inc.)
23. Santa Maria Nova, Rome (Guglielmo Matthiae / Cappelli Editore, Roma)
24. Santa Maria Antiqua in Forum, Rome (Author)
25. Santa Maria Antiqua in Forum, Rome (Guglielmo Matthiae / Cappelli Editore, Roma)
26. Santa Maria Domnica Apse, Rome (Maria Vassilaki / Skira Editore S.p.A., Milano)
27. Good Shepherd statue, Lateran Museum, Rome (Guglielmo Matthiae / Cappelli Editore, Roma)
28. Thessaloniki, Early Christian cemetery (Author)
29. Thessaloniki, Early Christian cemetery (Author)
30. Thessaloniki, Early Christian cemetery (Author)
31. Thessaloniki, Early Christian cemetery (Author)
32. Emperor Justinian I (Courtesy of Cartolibreria Salbaroli, Ravenna)
33. Empress Theodora, wife of Justinian I (Courtesy of Cartolibreria Salbaroli, Ravenna)
34. Heavenly ladder of St John Klimakos (Robert Cormack and Maria Vassilaki, 2008)
35. St Athanasios (Philip Sherrard / Takis Zervoulakos)
36. Emperor Nikephoros Phokas (Philip Sherrard / Takis Zervoulakos)

37. Emperor John Tzimiskes (Philip Sherrard / Takis Zervoulakos)
38. Monastery of Megistis Lavra, Mount Athos (Courtesy of Professor Emeritus Konstantinos P. Mylonas)
39. Monastery of Panteleimon, Mount Athos (Courtesy of Professor Emeritus Konstantinos P. Mylonas)
40. Monastery of Stavronikita, Mount Athos (Christos Patrinelis et al. / Ethniki Trapeza tis Ellados)
41. Monastery of St Catherine, Sinai (Robert Cormack and Maria Vassilaki, 2008)
42. Monastery of Dionysiou, Mount Athos (Courtesy of Professor Emeritus Konstantinos P. Mylonas)
43. Monastery of Dochiariou, Mount Athos (Courtesy of Professor Emmanuelle Plakoyiannaki)
44. Monastery of Kastamonitou, Mount Athos (Courtesy of Professor Emeritus Konstantinos P. Mylonas)
45. Monastery of Koutloumoussi, Mount Athos (Courtesy of Professor Emeritus Konstantinos P. Mylonas)
46. Monastery of Panteleimon, Mount Athos (Courtesy of Professor Emeritus Konstantinos P. Mylonas)
47. Monastery of Xeropotamou, Mount Athos (Courtesy of Professor Emeritus Konstantinos P. Mylonas)
48. Monastery of Zografou, Mount Athos (Courtesy of Professor Emmanuelle Plakoyiannaki)
49. Monastery of Megistis Lavra, Mount Athos (Philip Sherrard / Takis Zervoulakos)
50. Iconoclasts obliterating an image of Christ with whitewash (Lord Kinross / Arnoldo Mondadori Editore, Milano)
51. Iconoclastic mosaic cross (John Freely and Ahmet S. Cakmak)
52. Emperor Leo V (Paul Hetherington / De Agostini Editore, S.p.A., Novara)
53. Emperor Theophilos (Paul Hetherington / De Agostini Editore, S.p.A., Novara)
54. Triumph of Orthodoxy Icon (Maria Vassilaki / Skira Editore S.p.A., Milano)
55. Emperor Leo VI (BKG, Istanbul)
56. Emperor Alexander (Courtesy of Scala Publishers Ltd.)
57. Emperor Michael IV Paphlagon (Paul Hetherington / De Agostini Editore, S.p.A., Novara)
58. Emperor Constantine IX Monomachos (Paul Hetherington / De Agostini Editore, S.p.A., Novara)
59. Crown of Emperor Constantine Monomachos (David Talbot Rice)
60. Empress Zoe 'The Most Pious Augusta' (Paul Hetherington / De Agostini Editore, S.p.A., Novara)
61. Emperor Nikephoros Botaneiates (David Talbot Rice)
62. Emperor Nikephoros Botaneiates (Giorgios Galavaris / Ekdotike Athenon S.A.)
63. Emperor Alexios I Komnenos (Lord Kinross / Arnoldo Mondadori Editore, Milano)
64. Emperors John II and Alexios I Komnenoi (Giorgios Galavaris / Ekdotike Athenon S.A.)
65. Empress Eirene (Paul Hetherington / De Agostini Editore, S.p.A., Novara)
66. Emperor Alexios II Komnenos (Sotiris Kadas / Ekdotike Athenon S.A.)
67. Latin Emperor Baldwin (Lord Kinross / Arnoldo Mondadori Editore, Milano)
68. Portraits of a Palaiologos prince and princess (David Talbot Rice)
69. John Katakouzenos (David Talbot Rice)
70. Theodore Metochites (David Talbot Rice)
71. Theodore Komnenos Doukas and wife Evdokia (Giorgios Galavaris / Ekdotike Athenon S.A.)
72. Evangelist Matthew (Giorgios Galavaris / Ekdotike Athenon S.A.)
73. Evangelist Mark (Giorgios Galavaris / Ekdotike Athenon S.A.)
74. Evangelist Luke (Giorgios Galavaris / Ekdotike Athenon S.A.)
75. Evangelist John (Giorgios Galavaris / Ekdotike Athenon S.A.)
76. First Ecumenical Council (Manolis Borboudakis / 13th Ephorate, Crete)
77. Second Ecumenical Council, Constantinople (David Talbot Rice)
78. Seventh Ecumenical Council (Courtesy of the Holy Monastery – Holy Meteora)
79. St John Chrysostom (Lord Kinross / Arnoldo Mondadori Editore, Milano)
80. King William II crowned by Christ (Archidiocesi di Monreale / Casa Editrice Mistretta)
81. King William II (Archidiocesi di Monreale / Casa Editrice Mistretta)
82. Creation of light (Archidiocesi di Monreale / Casa Editrice Mistretta)
83. Separation of the waters (Archidiocesi di Monreale / Casa Editrice Mistretta)
84. Creation of dry land (Archidiocesi di Monreale / Casa Editrice Mistretta)
85. Creation of the stars (Archidiocesi di Monreale / Casa Editrice Mistretta)
86. Creation of the fish and birds (Archidiocesi di Monreale / Casa Editrice Mistretta)
87. Creation of the animals and humankind (Archidiocesi di Monreale / Casa Editrice Mistretta)
88. The Creator rests (Archidiocesi di Monreale / Casa Editrice Mistretta)

ILLUSTRATIONS, CREDITS AND SOURCES

CHAPTER 2: SACRED ARCHITECTURE

89. Titulus San Clemente, Rome (Michael L. White)
90. Titulus San Clemente, Rome (Michael L. White)
91. Titulus Byzantis, Rome (After Michael L. White)
92. House-Church, Qirqbize, Syria (Michael L. White)
93. Hall-church, Musmiyeh, Roman Syria (By permission of George Braziller, Inc.)
94. Octagonal hall-church, Philippi, Greece (Michael L. White)
95. Aula Ecclesiae, San Crisogono, Rome (Michael L. White)
96. Aula Ecclesiae, San Crisogono, Rome (After Michael L. White)
97. Aula Ecclesiae, St Martino ai Monti (André Grabar / Odyssey Press / Western Publishing Group, Inc.)
98. Aula Ecclesiae, Basilica Eufrasiana, Parentium (Michael L. White)
99. Insula-church 'Julianos's', Umm el-Jimal, Syria (Michael L. White)
100. Insula-church 'Julianos's', Umm el-Jimal, Syria (Michael L. White)
101. Insula-church, SS Giovanni e Paolo, Rome (Michael L. White)
102. House-church, Dura-Europos (Michael L. White)
103. House-church, Dura-Europos (Michael L. White)
104. House-church, Dura-Europos (By permission of Oxford University Press, Inc.)
105. Model of centralized temple of Minerva Medica, Rome (By permission of George Braziller, Inc.)
106. Basilica Constantiniana (Lateran), Rome (Henri Hübsch / Morel, Paris)
107. Basilica Ulpia, Rome (Bannister Fletcher / Butterworth-Heinemann)
108. Basilica Maxentius, Forum Rome (Author)
109. Basilica Maxentius, Rome (Bannister Fletcher / Butterworth-Heinemann)
110. Basilica of Constantine, Rome (Bannister Fletcher / Butterworth-Heinemann)
111. Trier Basilica of Constantine (Bannister Fletcher / Butterworth-Heinemann)
112. Trier Basilica of Constantine (Cyril Mango / Electa Editrice, Milano)
113. Church Kh. el-Karak, Lake Tiberius (After Noel Duval / Society of Antiquaries, London)
114. Timelines chart of the seven Byzantine church types 300–1453 (Author from various works)
115. Dome of Hagia Eirene, Constantinople (Jean Ebersolt and Adolphe Thiers / Ernest Leroux, Paris)
116. Central and subsidiary domes, St Saviour in Chora, Constantinople (Jean Ebersolt and Adolphe Thiers / Ernest Leroux, Paris)
117. Hagia Sophia, Constantinople (Courtesy of Hans Buchwald from Friedrich Wilhelm Deichmann / Amerbach-Verlag, Basel)
118. St Theodore, Constantinople (Jean Ebersolt and Adolphe Thiers / Ernest Leroux, Paris)
119. First approach circle to square (John Arnott Hamilton / B. T. Batsford Ltd., London)
120. Second approach circle to square (John Arnott Hamilton / B. T. Batsford Ltd., London)
121. A squinch (Courtesy of Austrian Academy of Sciences)
122. Third approach circle to square (Cecil Stewart)
123. Pendentives merged with dome [cupola] (Cecil Stewart)
124. Pendentives surmounted by semi-circular dome [cupola] (Cecil Stewart)
125. Pendentives surmounted by semi-circular dome [cupola] on a drum (Cecil Stewart)
126. San Saba, Rome (Author)
127. Basilica plan type – St John Studios, Constantinople (Jean Ebersolt and Adolphe Thiers / Ernest Leroux, Paris)
128. Basilica type – Santa Sabina, Rome (Friedrich Wilhelm Deichmann / Amerbach-Verlag, Basel)
129. Basilica type aisles – Santa Maria Maggiore, Rome (Friedrich Wilhelm Deichmann / Amerbach-Verlag, Basel)
130. Mosaic showing a Basilica, Tabarka, Tunisia (Richard Krautheimer)
131. Cross-in-square plan type – Prophets, Gerasa (Cyril Mango / Electa Editrice, Milano)
132. Typical cross-in-square church, Greece (Rowland J. Mainstone)
133. Cross-in-square column type – Theotokos Pammakaristos, Constantinople (Hans Belting, Cyril Mango and Doula Mouriki / Dumbarton Oaks)
134. Cross-in-square column type – Theotokos Pammakaristos, Constantinople (Hans Belting, Cyril Mango and Doula Mouriki / Dumbarton Oaks)
135. Cross-in-square column type – Theotokos Pammakaristos, Constantinople (Hans Belting, Cyril Mango and Doula Mouriki / Dumbarton Oaks)
136. Cross-in-Square column type – Theotokos Pammakaristos, Constantinople (Hans Belting, Cyril Mango and Doula Mouriki / Dumbarton Oaks)
137. Cross-in-square compressed type – St Saviour in Chora, Constantinople (Ali Kiliçkaya / Silk Road Publications, Istanbul)
138. Cruciform plan type – St Babylas, Antioch (Richard Krautheimer)

139. Cruciform type – Mausoleum of Galla Placidia, Ravenna (Courtesy of Angelo Longo Editore, Ravenna)
140. Cruciform type – Archiepiscopal Chapel, Ravenna (Courtesy of Angelo Longo Editore, Ravenna)
141. Centralized square plan type – Koimisis tis Theotokou, Nicaea (Alexander Van Millingen / Project Guttenberg Ebook #290775)
142. Centralized circular type – Santo Stefano, Rome (André Grabar / Odyssey Press / Western Publishing Group, Inc.)
143. San Vitale, Ravenna (Courtesy of Cartolibreria Salbaroli, Ravenna)
144. Centralized Tetraconch plan type – Holy Apostles, Athens (By permission of John Wiley & Sons)
145. Centralized type – Holy Apostles, Constantinople (Courtesy of the National Library of Russia, St Petersburg)
146. Centralized type – detail from the icon of SS Peter and Paul icon (Galleria dell'Academia di Belle Arti, Florence # 9382)
147. Domed basilica plan type – Hagia Sophia, Constantinople (R.F. Hoddinott)
148. Domed basilica type – Hagia Sophia, Constantinople (By permission of George Braziller, Inc.)
149. Converted plan type – Parthenon, Athens (Courtesy of Hans Buchwald from Friedrich Wilhelm Deichmann / Amerbach-Verlag, Basel)
150. Converted type – Duomo Siracusa, Ortegia (Author)
151. Converted type – Duomo Siracusa, Ortegia (Author)
152. Athonite plan type – *Katholikon* of Megistis Lavra, Mount Athos (Courtesy of Professor Emeritus Konstantinos P. Mylonas)
153. Typical Athonite Spatial Components, Mount Athos (Courtesy of the Institute for Byzantine and Modern Greek Studies)
154. Typical Basilica Spatial Components – St John Stoudios, Constantinople (Courtesy of the Institute for Byzantine & Modern Greek Studies)
155. Athonite type *Chorostasía* – Prophet Elijah, Thessaloniki (Author)
156. Athonite type. Wooden model, Monastery of Xeropotamou, Mount Athos (Courtesy of Professor Emeritus Konstantinos P. Mylonas)
157. Typical spatial division – basilica type shown (Author)
158. Typical basilica (Noel Duval / Society of Antiquaries, London)
159. Typical bema (C.J.A.C. Peeters / Van Gorcum BV)
160. Qirk-Bizzeh, Plan of Church (C.J.A.C. Peeters / Van Gorcum BV)
161. Qirk-Bizzeh, Stage One (C.J.A.C. Peeters / Van Gorcum BV)
162. Qirk-Bizzeh, Stage Two (C.J.A.C. Peeters / Van Gorcum BV)
163. Qirk-Bizzeh, Stage Three (C.J.A.C. Peeters / Van Gorcum BV)
164. Quirk-Bizzeh. Development stages I to V (Michael L. White)
165. 'Atrium'. The forecourt of Hagia Eirene, Constantinople (Thomas F. Mathews)
166. Forecourt. San Clemente, Rome (Bannister Fletcher / Butterworth-Heinemann)
167. Reconstruction of monumental gateway entrance (Rowland J. Mainstone)
168. Outer narthex, Hagia Sophia, Constantinople (Rowland J. Mainstone)
169. Inner narthex, Hagia Sophia, Constantinople (Courtesy of Scala Publishers Ltd.)
170. Inner narthex, Hagia Sophia, Constantinople (Rowland J. Mainstone)
171. Byzantine column capital topped by an 'impost' (Courtesy of Cartolibreria Salbaroli, Ravenna)
172. Byzantine column capital with floral decoration (Courtesy of Cartolibreria Salbaroli, Ravenna)
173. Byzantine column capital with imperial monogram (David Talbot Rice)
174. Naos column capital with imperial monogram (Courtesy of Dr Mustafa Büyükkolanci)
175. Nave column capital with 'impost' above (Author)
176. Transept Ionic type column capital (Courtesy of Austrian Academy of Sciences)
177. Typical Byzantine Corinthian-type column capitals with Christian symbols (Cecil Stewart)
178. Corinthian-style column capital (After Friedrich Wilhelm Deichmann / Amerbach-Verlag, Basel)
179. *Stasídia* (Philip Sherrard / Takis Zervoulakos)
180. Marble floor with intricate geometrical patterns (Alvise Passigli)
181. Detail of marble floor pattern (Alvise Passigli)
182. Marble floor with elaborate geometrical patterns (B. N. Marconi, Genova)
183. Interior marble wall surfaces and floor (Robert Cormack and Maria Vassilaki, 2008)
184. Marble paneled narthex wall (Author)
185. Bema with low templon screen (Rowland J. Mainstone)
186. Reconstructed plan of bema (Thomas F. Mathews)
187. Diagram of a North African bema (C.J.A.C. Peeters / Van Gorcum BV)
188. Diagram of a North African bema (C.J.A.C. Peeters / Van Gorcum BV)
189. North African solea and central bema (C.J.A.C. Peeters / Van Gorcum BV)

190. Broad solea and ambo (C.J.A.C. Peeters / Van Gorcum BV)
191. Solea with central ambos on both sides (Cecil Stewart)
192. Exterior of the *skevophylákion* (Rowland J. Mainstone)
193. Interior of the *skevophylákion* (Rowland J. Mainstone)
194. Triple apse array, Constantinople churches (Thomas F. Mathews)
195. Variations in apse layouts, North Syria (Thomas F. Mathews)
196. Remains of triple semi-circular apses (Richard Krautheimer)
197. Holy Table with baldachin with *confessione* below (C.J.A.C. Peeters / Van Gorcum BV)
198. Martyrium, shrine or *tropaion* (C.J.A.C. Peeters / Van Gorcum BV)
199. Galleries (Rowland J. Mainstone)
200. Holy Table (Alvise Passigli)
201. Holy Table (C.J.A.C. Peeters / Van Gorcum BV)
202. Tomb below the Holy Table (C.J.A.C. Peeters / Van Gorcum BV)
203. Synthronon (Thomas F. Mathews)
204. Synthronon (Cyril Mango / Electa Editrice, Milano)
205. Synthronon, plan and elevation (Thomas F. Mathews)
206. Synthronon and bema (Cyril Mango / Electa Editrice, Milano)
207. Ivory paneled throne (Courtesy of Angelo Longo Editore, Ravenna)
208. Templon (C.J.A.C. Peeters / Van Gorcum BV)
209. Reconstructed templon (C.J.A.C. Peeters / Van Gorcum BV)
210. Templon (C.J.A.C. Peeters / Van Gorcum BV)
211. Iconostasis (Christos Patrinelis et al. / Ethniki Trapeza tis Ellados)
212. Iconostasis (Author)
213. Iconostasis (Gerasimos Karavias)
214. Iconostasis (George Moschopoulos / Topiko Istoriko Archeio Kefalonias)
215. The Beautiful Gate (Robert Cormack and Maria Vassilaki, 2008)
216. The Beautiful Gate (Author)
217. The Beautiful Gate (Author)
218. Ambo sketch (C.J.A.C. Peeters / Van Gorcum BV)
219. Ambo side view (C.J.A.C. Peeters / Van Gorcum BV)
220. Gospel ambo (Bannister Fletcher/Butterworth-Heinemann)
221. Ambo (Thomas F. Mathews)
222. Ambo (Author)
223. St Efimia, Constantinople (John Freely and Ahmet S. Cakmak)
224. St Efimia, Constantinople (Thomas F. Mathews)

CHAPTER 3: SPLENDID CHURCHES

225. San Giovanni in Laterno, Rome (Friedrich Wilhelm Deichmann / Amerbach-Verlag, Basel)
226. San Giovanni in Laterno, Rome (Richard Krautheimer)
227. San Giovanni in Laterno (Author)
228. Old St Peter's on the Vatican hill, Rome (Friedrich Wilhelm Deichmann / Amerbach-Verlag, Basel)
229. Old St Peter's, Rome (Richard Krautheimer)
230. Old St Peter's, Rome (Richard Krautheimer)
231. Rome, plan type – original basilicas I (Author from various works)
232. Rome, plan type – original basilicas II (Author from various works)
233. Rome, plan type – converted buildings I (Author from various works)
234. Rome, plan type – converted buildings II (Author from C.J.A.C. Peeters / Van Gorcum BV)
235. Rome, plan type – converted buildings III (Author from Bannister Fletcher / Butterworth-Heinemann)
236. Rome, plan type – converted buildings IV (Author from various works)
237. Rome, plan type – converted buildings V (Author from various works)
238. Santa Balbina, Rome (Author)
239. Santa Balbina, Rome (Author)
240. Santa Balbina, Rome (Author)
241. Santa Balbina, Rome (Author)
242. Santa Balbina, Rome (Author)
243. Santa Balbina. Rome (Author)
244. Santa Balbina, Rome (Author)
245. San Giorgio in Velabro, Rome (Author)
246. San Giorgio in Velabro, Rome (Author)
247. San Giorgio in Velabro, Rome (Author)
248. San Giorgio in Velabro, Rome (Author)
249. San Giorgio in Velabro, Rome (Author)
250. San Giorgio in Velabro, Rome (Author)
251. San Giorgio in Velabro, Rome (Author)
252. San Clemente, Rome (Author)
253. San Clemente, Rome (Author)
254. San Clemente, Rome (Author)
255. San Crisogono, Rome (Author)
256. San Crisogono, Rome (Author)

257.	San Crisogono, Rome (Author)	296.	San Lorenzo Fuori le Mura, Rome (Richard Krautheimer)
258.	Santa Maria Egiziaca, Rome (Author)	297.	San Lorenzo Fuori le Mura, Rome (Author)
259.	San Saba, Rome (Author)	298.	San Lorenzo Fuori le Mura, Rome (Author)
260.	San Saba, Rome (Author)	299.	San Lorenzo Fuori le Mura, Rome (Author)
261.	San Saba, Rome (Author)	300.	San Lorenzo Fuori le Mura, Rome (Author)
262.	SS Giovanni e Paolo, Rome (Author)	301.	San Lorenzo Fuori le Mura, Rome (Author)
263.	SS Giovanni e Paolo, Rome (Author)	302.	San Lorenzo Fuori le Mura, Rome (Author)
264.	SS Giovanni e Paolo, Rome (Author)	303.	San Lorenzo Fuori le Mura, Rome (Author)
265.	San Martino, Rome (Guglielmo Matthiae / Cappelli Editore, Roma)	304.	San Paolo Fuori le Mura, Rome (Cecil Stewart)
266.	Rome, plan type – superimposed basilicas I (Author from various works)	305.	San Paolo Fuori le Mura, Rome (Richard Krautheimer)
267.	Rome, plan type – superimposed basilicas II (Author from various works)	306.	San Paolo Fuori le Mura, Rome (Friedrich Wilhelm Deichmann / Amerbach-Verlag, Basel)
268.	Rome, plan type – superimposed basilicas III (Author from various works)	307.	Santa Maria Maggiore, Rome (Guglielmo Matthiae / Cappelli Editore, Roma)
269.	Santa Sabina, Rome (Richard Krautheimer)	308.	Santa Maria Maggiore, Rome (André Grabar / Odyssey Press / Western Publishing Group, Inc.)
270.	Santa Sabina, Rome (Richard Krautheimer)	309.	Santa Maria Maggiore. Rome (Author)
271.	Santa Sabina, Rome (Author)	310.	Santa Maria Maggiore, Rome (Author)
272.	Santa Sabina, Rome (André Grabar / Odyssey Press / Western Publishing Group, Inc.)	311.	San Giovanni a Porta Latina, Rome (Author)
273.	Santa Sabina, Rome (Author)	312.	San Giovanni a Porta Latina, Rome (Author)
274.	Santa Sabina, Rome (Author)	313.	San Giovanni a Porta Latina, Rome (Author)
275.	Santa Sabina, Rome (Author)	314.	San Giovanni a Porta Latina, Rome (Author)
276.	Santa Sabina, Rome (Author)	315.	San Giovanni a Porta Latina, Rome (Author)
277.	Santa Sabina, Rome (Author)	316.	San Giovanni a Porta Latina, Rome (Author)
278.	Santo Stefano Rotondo, Rome (Bannister Fletcher / Butterworth-Heinemann)	317.	San Giovanni a Porta Latina, Rome (Author)
		318.	San Giovanni a Porta Latina, Rome (Author)
279.	Santo Stefano Rotondo, Rome (André Grabar / Odyssey Press / Western Publishing Group, Inc.)	319.	San Giovanni a Porta Latina, Rome (Author)
		320.	Santa Maria Domnica, Rome (Guglielmo Matthiae / Cappelli Editore, Roma)
280.	Santa Prassede, Rome (Author)	321.	Santa Maria in Cosmedin, Rome (Author)
281.	Santa Prassede, Rome (Author)	322.	Santa Maria in Cosmedin, Rome (Author)
282.	Santa Prassede, Rome (Author)	323.	Santa Maria in Cosmedin, Rome (Author)
283.	San Sebastiano, Rome (Richard Krautheimer)	324.	Santa Maria in Cosmedin, Rome (Author)
284.	Rome, plan type – eastern-influenced basilicas I (Author from various works)	325.	Santa Maria in Cosmedin, Rome (Author)
285.	Rome, plan type – eastern-influenced basilicas II (Author from various works)	326.	Santa Maria in Cosmedin, Rome (Author)
286.	Rome, plan type – eastern-influenced basilicas III (Author from various works)	327.	Santa Maria in Cosmedin, Rome (Author)
		328.	Mausoleum, Santa Costanza, Rome (By permission of George Braziller, Inc.)
287.	Sant'Agnese Fuori le Mura, Rome (Author)	329.	Mausoleum, Santa Costanza, Rome (Friedrich Wilhelm Deichmann / Amerbach-Verlag, Basel)
288.	Sant'Agnese Fuori le Mura, Rome (Author)		
289.	Sant'Agnese Fuori le Mura, Rome (Author)	330.	Mausoleum, Santa Costanza, Rome (Friedrich Wilhelm Deichmann / Amerbach-Verlag, Basel)
290.	San Lorenzo Fuori le Mura, Rome (Author)		
291.	San Lorenzo Fuori le Mura, Rome (Bannister Fletcher / Butterworth-Heinemann)	331.	Mausoleum, Santa Costanza, Rome (Richard Krautheimer)
292.	San Lorenzo Fuori le Mura, Rome (Author)	332.	San Angelo, Perugia, Italy (André Grabar / Odyssey Press / Western Publishing Group, Inc.)
293.	San Lorenzo Fuori le Mura, Rome (Author)		
294.	San Lorenzo Fuori le Mura Rome (Author)	333.	Italy and region, early churches I (Author from various works)
295.	San Lorenzo Fuori le Mura, Rome (Friedrich Wilhelm Deichmann / Amerbach-Verlag, Basel)	334.	Italy and region, early churches II (Author from various works)

335. Plan of St Mark's, Venice (Author from David Talbot Rice)
336. St Mark's, Venice (By permission of George Braziller, Inc.)
337. St Mark's, Venice (By permission of George Braziller, Inc.)
338. St Mark's, Venice (Judith Dupré)
339. Constantinople, plan type – basilicas (Author from various works)
340. St John Stoudios, Constantinople (Richard Krautheimer)
341. St John Stoudios, Constantinople (By permission of George Braziller, Inc.)
342. Constantinople, plan type – domed basilicas (Author from various works)
343. Hagia Eirene, Constantinople (After Jean Ebersolt and Adolphe Thiers / Ernest Leroux, Paris)
344. Hagia Eirene, Constantinople (After Jean Ebersolt and Adolphe Thiers / Ernest Leroux, Paris)
345. Hagia Eirene, Constantinople (After Jean Ebersolt and Adolphe Thiers / Ernest Leroux, Paris)
346. Hagia Eirene, Constantinople (After Jean Ebersolt and Adolphe Thiers / Ernest Leroux, Paris)
347. Hagia Eirene, Constantinople (Author)
348. Hagia Eirene, Constantinople (Author)
349. Hagia Eirene, Constantinople (Author)
350. Hagia Eirene, Constantinople (Author)
351. Hagia Eirene, Constantinople (Richard Krautheimer)
352. Hagia Eirene, Constantinople (Cyril Mango / Electa Editrice, Milano)
353. Hagia Sophia, Constantinople (Richard Krautheimer)
354. Hagia Sophia, Constantinople (By permission of George Braziller, Inc.)
355. Hagia Sophia, Constantinople (John Freely and Ahmet S. Cakmak)
356. Hagia Sophia, Constantinople (André Grabar / Odyssey Press / Western Publishing Group, Inc.)
357. Hagia Sophia, Constantinople (Cyril Mango / Electa Editrice, Milano)
358. Hagia Sophia, Constantinople (John Freely and Ahmet S. Cakmak)
359. Hagia Sophia, Constantinople (Scala)
360. Hagia Sophia, Constantinople (Scala)
361. Hagia Sophia, Constantinople (Author)
362. Constantinople, plan type – cruciform and converted (Author from various works)
363. Constantinople, plan type – cross-in-square I (Author from various works)
364. Constantinople, plan type – cross-in-square II (Author from various works)
365. Constantinople, plan type – cross-in-square III (Author from various works)
366. SS Peter and Mark, Constantinople (Jean Ebersolt and Adolphe Thiers / Ernest Leroux, Paris)
367. SS Peter and Mark, Constantinople (Jean Ebersolt and Adolphe Thiers / Ernest Leroux, Paris)
368. SS Peter and Mark, Constantinople (Author)
369. SS Peter and Mark, Constantinople (Author)
370. SS Peter and Mark, Constantinople (Author)
371. St John the Forerunner Troullo, Constantinople (John Freely and Ahmet S. Cakmak)
372. St John the Forerunner Troullo, Constantinople (John Freely and Ahmet S. Cakmak)
373. St Theodosia, Constantinople (John Freely and Ahmet S. Cakmak)
374. Myrelaion, Constantinople (Author)
375. Myrelaion, Constantinople (Author)
376. Myrelaion, Constantinople (Author)
377. Myrelaion, Constantinople (Author)
378. Myrelaion, Constantinople (Author)
379. Theotokos Panachrantos, Constantinople (Jean Ebersolt and Adolphe Thiers / Ernest Leroux, Paris)
380. Theotokos Panachrantos, Constantinople (Jean Ebersolt and Adolphe Thiers / Ernest Leroux, Paris)
381. Theotokos Panachrantos, Constantinople (Author)
382. Theotokos Panachrantos, Constantinople (Author)
383. Theotokos Panachrantos, Constantinople (Author)
384. Theotokos Panachrantos, Constantinople (Author)
385. Theotokos Panachrantos, Constantinople (Author)
386. Theotokos Panachrantos, Constantinople (Author)
387. Theotokos Panachrantos, Constantinople (Author)
388. Theotokos Panachrantos, Constantinople (Author)
389. Theotokos Panachrantos, Constantinople (Author)
390. Theotokos Pammakaristos, Constantinople (Jean Ebersolt and Adolphe Thiers / Ernest Leroux, Paris)
391. Theotokos Pammakaristos, Constantinople (Jean Ebersolt and Adolphe Thiers / Ernest Leroux, Paris)
392. Theotokos Pammakaristos, Constantinople (By permission of George Braziller, Inc.)
393. Theotokos Pammakaristos, Constantinople (Author)
394. Theotokos Pammakaristos, Constantinople (Author)
395. Theotokos Pammakaristos, Constantinople (Author)
396. Theotokos Pammakaristos, Constantinople (Author)
397. St Saviour Pantepoptes, Constantinople (Jean Ebersolt and Adolphe Thiers / Ernest Leroux, Paris)
398. St Saviour Pantepoptes, Constantinople (Jean Ebersolt and Adolphe Thiers / Ernest Leroux, Paris)
399. St Saviour Pantepoptes, Constantinople (Author)

400.	St Saviour Pantepoptes, Constantinople (Author)	432.	SS Sergius and Bacchus, Constantinople (Jean Ebersolt and Adolphe Thiers / Ernest Leroux, Paris)
401.	St Saviour Pantepoptes, Constantinople (Author)		
402.	St Theodore, Constantinople (Jean Ebersolt and Adolphe Thiers / Ernest Leroux, Paris)	433.	SS Sergius and Bacchus, Constantinople (Author)
403.	St Theodore, Constantinople (Jean Ebersolt and Adolphe Thiers / Ernest Leroux, Paris)	434.	SS Sergius and Bacchus, Constantinople (Author)
404.	St Theodore, Constantinople (Jean Ebersolt and Adolphe Thiers / Ernest Leroux, Paris)	435.	SS Sergius and Bacchus, Constantinople (By permission of George Braziller, Inc.)
405.	St Theodore, Constantinople (Jean Ebersolt and Adolphe Thiers / Ernest Leroux, Paris)	436.	SS Sergius and Bacchus, Constantinople (Author)
406.	St Theodore, Constantinople (Jean Ebersolt and Adolphe Thiers / Ernest Leroux, Paris)	437.	SS Sergius and Bacchus, Constantinople (Richard Krautheimer)
407.	St Theodore, Constantinople (Author)	438.	SS Sergius and Bacchus, Constantinople (Author)
408.	St Theodore, Constantinople (Author)	439.	SS Sergius and Bacchus, Constantinople (Author)
409.	St Theodore, Constantinople (John Freely and Ahmet S. Cakmak)	440.	SS Sergius and Bacchus, Constantinople (Author)
		441.	SS Sergius and Bacchus, Constantinople (Author)
410.	St Theodore, Constantinople (Author)	442.	SS Sergius and Bacchus, Constantinople (Author)
411.	St Theodore, Constantinople (Author)	443.	SS Sergius and Bacchus, Constantinople (Author)
412.	St Theodore, Constantinople (Author)	444.	SS Sergius and Bacchus, Constantinople (Author)
413.	Theotokos Kyriotissa, Constantinople (Richard Krautheimer)	445.	St Saviour in Chora, Constantinople (Author)
		446.	St Saviour in Chora, Constantinople (Author)
414.	Theotokos Kyriotissa, Constantinople (Author)	447.	St Saviour in Chora, Constantinople (Author)
415.	Theotokos Kyriotissa, Constantinople (Author)	448.	St Saviour in Chora, Constantinople (Author)
416.	Theotokos Kyriotissa, Constantinople (Author)	449.	St Saviour in Chora, Constantinople (Author)
417.	Theotokos Kyriotissa, Constantinople (Author)	450.	St Andrew in Krisei, Constantinople (Author)
418.	Theotokos Kyriotissa, Constantinople (Author)	451.	St Andrew in Krisei, Constantinople (Author)
419.	Theotokos Kyriotissa, Constantinople (Author)	452.	St Andrew in Krisei, Constantinople (Author)
420.	St Saviour Pantokrator, Constantinople (Jean Ebersolt and Adolphe Thiers / Ernest Leroux, Paris)	453.	St Andrew in Krisei, Constantinople (Author)
		454.	St Andrew in Krisei, Constantinople (Author)
421.	St Saviour Pantokrator, Constantinople (Jean Ebersolt and Adolphe Thiers / Ernest Leroux, Paris)	455.	St Andrew in Krisei, Constantinople (Author)
		456.	St Andrew in Krisei, Constantinople (Author)
422.	St Saviour Pantokrator, Constantinople (Jean Ebersolt and Adolphe Thiers / Ernest Leroux, Paris)	457.	St Andrew in Krisei, Constantinople (Author)
		458.	St Andrew in Krisei, Constantinople (Author)
423.	St Saviour Pantokrator, Constantinople (Jean Ebersolt and Adolphe Thiers / Ernest Leroux, Paris)	459.	St Andrew in Krisei, Constantinople (Author)
		460.	St Andrew in Krisei, Constantinople (Author)
424.	St Saviour Pantokrator, Constantinople (Jean Ebersolt and Adolphe Thiers / Ernest Leroux, Paris)	461.	Panagia Mouchliotissa (Author)
		462.	Panagia Mouchliotissa (Author)
425.	St Saviour Pantokrator, Constantinople (John Freely and Ahmet S. Cakmak)	463.	Panagia Mouchliotissa. Segmented central dome of naos (Author)
426.	St Saviour Pantokrator, Constantinople (John Freely and Ahmet S. Cakmak)	464.	Golgotha – Holy Sepulcher Jerusalem (By permission of George Braziller, Inc.)
427.	Constantinople, plan type – centralized (Author from various works)	465.	Holy Land. Constantinian churches I (Author from various works)
428.	SS Sergius and Bacchus, Constantinople (Jean Ebersolt and Adolphe Thiers / Ernest Leroux, Paris)	466.	Holy Land, Constantinian churches II (Author from various works)
		467.	'New Church' Tokalikilise, Cappadocia (Robert Cormack, 2000)
429.	SS Sergius and Bacchus, Constantinople (Jean Ebersolt and Adolphe Thiers / Ernest Leroux, Paris)	468.	Sivri cross-in-square church, Cappadocia (Courtesy of Austrian Academy of Sciences)
430.	SS Sergius and Bacchus, Constantinople (Jean Ebersolt and Adolphe Thiers / Ernest Leroux, Paris)	469.	Basilica, Der Turmanin, Syria (By permission of George Braziller, Inc.)
431.	SS Sergius and Bacchus, Constantinople (Jean Ebersolt and Adolphe Thiers / Ernest Leroux, Paris)	470.	St Simeon Church, Aleppo, Syria (By permission of George Braziller, Inc.)

ILLUSTRATIONS, CREDITS AND SOURCES

471. Alaban, Cilicia (Cyril Mango / Electa Editrice, Milano)
472. Near East, plan type – basilicas (Author from various works)
473. Near East, plan pype – cross-in-square (Author from various works)
474. Near East, plan types – centralized; cruciform; domed basilica (Author from various works)
475. North Africa, Byzantine church plans (Author from various works)
476. Thessaloniki, plan type – basilicas (Author from various works)
477. St Demetrios, Thessaloniki (André Grabar / Odyssey Press / Western Publishing Group, Inc.)
478. St Demetrios, Thessaloniki (Cyril Mango / Electa Editrice, Milano)
479. St Demetrios, Thessaloniki (Author)
480. St Demetrios, Thessaloniki (Author)
481. St Demetrios, Thessaloniki (Author)
482. Theotokos Acheiropoietos, Thessaloniki (Author)
483. Theotokos Acheiropoietos, Thessaloniki (Author)
484. Theotokos Acheiropoietos, Thessaloniki (Author)
485. Theotokos Acheiropoietos, Thessaloniki (Cyril Mango / Electa Editrice, Milano)
486. Theotokos Acheiropoietos, Thessaloniki (André Grabar / Odyssey Press / Western Publishing Group, Inc.)
487. Theotokos Acheiropoietos, Thessaloniki (Author)
488. Theotokos Acheiropoietos, Thessaloniki (Author)
489. Theotokos Acheiropoietos, Thessaloniki (Author)
490. Theotokos Acheiropoietos, Thessaloniki (Author)
491. Theotokos Acheiropoietos, Thessaloniki (Author)
492. Taxiarchis, Thessaloniki (Author)
493. Taxiarchis, Thessaloniki (Author)
494. Taxiarchis, Thessaloniki (Author)
495. St Nicholas Orphanos, Thessaloniki (Author)
496. Thessaloniki, plan type – cross-in-square (Author from various works)
497. Panagia Chalkeon, Thessaloniki (Author)
498. Panagia Chalkeon, Thessaloniki (Author)
499. Panagia Chalkeon, Thessaloniki (Author)
500. Panagia Chalkeon, Thessaloniki (Author)
501. Panagia Chalkeon, Thessaloniki (Author)
502. Holy Apostles, Thessaloniki (Richard Krautheimer)
503. Holy Apostles, Thessaloniki (Richard Krautheimer)
504. Holy Apostles, Thessaloniki (Author)
505. Holy Apostles, Thessaloniki (Author)
506. Holy Apostles, Thessaloniki (Author)
507. Holy Apostles, Thessaloniki (Author)
508. Holy Apostles, Thessaloniki (Author)
509. Holy Apostles, Thessaloniki (Author)
510. Holy Apostles, Thessaloniki (Author)
511. Holy Apostles, Thessaloniki (Author)
512. Holy Apostles, Thessaloniki (Author)
513. Holy Apostles, Thessaloniki (Author)
514. Holy Apostles, Thessaloniki (Author)
515. Holy Apostles, Thessaloniki (Author)
516. Holy Apostles, Thessaloniki (Author)
517. Thessaloniki, plan type – cruciform / athonite (Author from Charalambos Bouras, Courtesy of Melissa Publishing House, Athens)
518. Prophet Elijah, Thessaloniki (Author)
519. Prophet Elijah, Thessaloniki (Author)
520. Prophet Elijah, Thessaloniki (Author)
521. Prophet Elijah, Thessaloniki (Author)
522. Prophet Elijah, Thessaloniki (Author)
523. Thessaloniki, plan type – centralized (Author from various works)
524. St Catherine, Thessaloniki (Author)
525. St Catherine, Thessaloniki (Author)
526. St Catherine, Thessaloniki (Author)
527. St Catherine, Thessaloniki (Author)
528. St Catherine, Thessaloniki (Author)
529. St Catherine, Thessaloniki (Author)
530. Thessaloniki, plan type – converted (Author from various works)
531. St George Rotunda, Thessaloniki (Author)
532. St George Rotunda, Thessaloniki (By permission of George Braziller, Inc.)
533. St George Rotunda, Thessaloniki (Author)
534. St George Rotunda, Thessaloniki (Author)
535. Thessaloniki, plan type – domed basilica (Author from various works)
536. Hagia Sophia, Thessaloniki (Author)
537. Hagia Sophia, Thessaloniki (Richard Krautheimer)
538. Hagia Sophia, Thessaloniki (Author)
539. Hagia Sophia, Thessaloniki (Author)
540. Hagia Sophia, Thessaloniki (Author)
541. Hagia Sophia, Thessaloniki (Author)
542. Hagia Sophia, Thessaloniki (Author)
543. Greece and Balkans, Byzantine church plans I (Author from various works)
544. Greece and Balkans, Byzantine church plans II (Author from various works)
545. Athens, Panagia Kapnikarea (Author)
546. Athens, SS Theodorii (Author)
547. Athens, Theotokos Gorgoepikoos (Author)
548. Athens, Holy Apostles (Author)
549. Athens, Holy Trinity (Author)
550. Parigoritissa, Arta (John Arnott Hamilton / B. T. Batsford Ltd., London)
551. Parigoritissa, Arta (John Arnott Hamilton / B. T. Batsford Ltd., London)

552. Hagia Sophia, Ohrid (David Talbot Rice)
553. Basilica Eufranius, Parentium (Porec) (Courtesy of Henry Maguire)
554. Mausoleum of Theodoric, Ravenna (Richard Krautheimer)
555. Orthodox Baptistery, Ravenna (Cyril Mango / Electa Editrice, Milano)
556. Orthodox Baptistery, Ravenna (By permission of George Braziller, Inc.)
557. Orthodox Baptistery, Ravenna (Cyril Mango / Electa Editrice, Milano)
558. Orthodox Baptistery, Ravenna (Richard Krautheimer)
559. Mausoleum of Galla Placidia, Ravenna (By permission of George Braziller, Inc.)
560. Mausoleum of Galla Placidia (Cyril Mango / Electa Editrice, Milano)
561. Mausoleum of Galla Placidia, Ravenna (Richard Krautheimer)
562. San Vitale, Ravenna (By permission of George Braziller, Inc.)
563. San Vitale, Ravenna (André Grabar / Odyssey Press / Western Publishing Group, Inc.)
564. San Vitale, Ravenna (Courtesy of Cartolibreria Salbaroli, Ravenna)
565. San Vitale, Ravenna (Courtesy of Cartolibreria Salbaroli, Ravenna)
566. San Vitale, Ravenna (Richard Krautheimer)
567. San Vitale, Ravenna (Courtesy of Angelo Longo Editore, Ravenna)
568. Sant'Apollinare in Classe, Ravenna (Richard Krautheimer)
569. Sant'Apollinare in Classe, Ravenna (Cyril Mango / Electa Editrice, Milano)
570. Sant'Apollinare Nuovo, Ravenna (Courtesy of Cartolibreria Salbaroli, Ravenna)
571. Sant'Apollinare Nuovo, Ravenna (Courtesy of Cartolibreria Salbaroli, Ravenna)
572. San Giovanni Evangelista, Ravenna (Richard Krautheimer)
573. Ravenna, Byzantine Church Plans (Author from various works)
574. Plan of a Typical Monastery (By permission of John Wiley and Sons)
575. Byzantine Monasteries – *Katholika* Plans I (Author from various works)
576. Byzantine Monasteries – *Katholika* Plans II (Author from various works)
577. Byzantine Monasteries – *Katholika* Plans III (Author from various works)
578. Byzantine Monasteries – Chios (Author from Nigel McGilchrist)
579. Monastery of St Catherine, Sinai (Richard Krautheimer)
580. Mount Athos, Church of the Protaton (Author)
581. Mount Athos, Church of the Protaton (Philip Sherrard / Takis Zervoulakos)
582. Mount Athos, Chelandari (Author)
583. Mount Athos, Chelandari (Author)
584. Mount Athos, Dionysiou (Sotiris Kadas / Ekdotike Athenon S.A.)
585. Mount Athos, Esfigmenou (Courtesy of Professor Emeritus Konstantinos P. Mylonas)
586. Mount Athos, Iveron (Author)
587. Mount Athos, Iveron (Author)
588. Mount Athos, Karakalou (Author)
589. Mount Athos, Karakalou (Author)
590. Mount Athos, Koutloumoussi (Author)
591. Mount Athos, Megistis Lavra (Author)
592. Mount Athos, Megistis Lavra (Sotiris Kadas / Ekdotike Athenon S.A.)
593. Mount Athos, Panteleimon (Author)
594. Mount Athos, Pantokrator (Author)
595. Mount Athos, Pantokrator (Author)
596. Mount Athos, Simonos Petra (Courtesy of Professor Emeritus Konstantinos P. Mylonas)
597. Mount Athos, Stavronikita (Sotiris Kadas / Ekdotike Athenon S.A.)
598. Mount Athos, Stavronikita (Author)
599. Mount Athos, Stavronikita (Author)
600. Mount Athos, Vatopedi (Author)
601. Mount Athos, Vatopedi. Monks' wing (Author)
602. Mount Athos, Vatopedi (Author)
603. Mount Athos, Vatopedi (Author)
604. Mount Athos, Vatopedi (Author)
605. Mount Athos, Xenophontos (Author)
606. Mount Athos, Xenophontos (Author)
607. Mount Athos, Xenophontos (Author)
608. Mount Athos, Xenophontos (Author)
609. Mount Athos, Xenophontos (Author)
610. Mount Athos, Xeropotamos (Author)
611. Mount Athos, Zographou (Author)
612. Mount Athos, Skiti Profiti Ilias (Author)
613. Mount Athos, Drum and Dome Roof I (Author)
614. Mount Athos, Drum and Dome Roof II (Author)
615. Mount Athos, Drum and Dome Roof III (Author)
616. Mount Athos, Drum and Dome Roof IV (Author)
617. Mount Athos, *Phiale* I (Author)
618. Mount Athos, *Phiale* II (Author)
619. Mount Athos, Small chapel in courtyard (Author)
620. Mystras, Metropolis (Myrtali Acheimastou-Potamianou / Hesperos Editions)

ILLUSTRATIONS, CREDITS AND SOURCES

621. Mystras, Metropolis (Myrtali Acheimastou-Potamianou / Hesperos Editions)
622. Mystras, Aphendiko (Myrtali Acheimastou-Potamianou / Hesperos Editions)
623. Mystras, Hodegetria (Myrtali Acheimastou-Potamianou / Hesperos Editions)
624. Mystras, Hodegitria (Myrtali Acheimastou-Potamianou / Hesperos Editions)
625. Mystras, Pantanassa (Myrtali Acheimastou-Potamianou / Hesperos Editions)
626. Meteora, Roussanou (Courtesy of the Holy Monastery – Holy Meteora)
627. Stiris, Hosios Loukas (Courtesy of Hannibal Publishing House, Athens)
628. Daphni, Koimisis tis Theotokou (David Talbot Rice)
629. St John at Ephesus (Author after Dr Mustafa Büyükkolanci)
630. St John at Ephesus (Courtesy of Dr Mustafa Büyükkolanci)
631. St John at Ephesus (Courtesy of Dr Mustafa Büyükkolanci)
632. St John at Ephesus (Courtesy of Dr Mustafa Büyükkolanci)
633. St John at Ephesus (Courtesy of Dr Mustafa Büyükkolanci)
634. St John at Ephesus (Courtesy of Dr Mustafa Büyükkolanci)
635. St John at Ephesus (Courtesy of Dr Mustafa Büyükkolanci)
636. St John at Ephesus (Courtesy of Dr Mustafa Büyükkolanci)
637. St John at Ephesus (Courtesy of Dr Mustafa Büyükkolanci)
638. St John at Ephesus (Courtesy of Dr Mustafa Büyükkolanci)
639. St John at Ephesus (Author)
640. St John at Ephesus (Courtesy of Dr Mustafa Büyükkolanci)
641. St John at Ephesus (Courtesy of Dr Mustafa Büyükkolanci)

CHAPTER 4: SPIRITUAL ART

642. Tomb of Aureli, Rome (André Grabar / Odyssey Press / Western Publishing Group, Inc.)
643. Cemetery below St Peter's, Rome (André Grabar / Odyssey Press / Western Publishing Group, Inc.)
644. Catacomb of SS Pietro e Marcellino, Rome (André Grabar / Odyssey Press / Western Publishing Group, Inc.)
645. Catacomb of SS Pietro e Marcellino, Rome (André Grabar / Odyssey Press / Western Publishing Group, Inc.)
646. Catacomb of Goirdani, Rome (André Grabar / Odyssey Press / Western Publishing Group, Inc.)
647. Catacomb Commodila, Rome (Guglielmo Matthiae / Cappelli Editore, Roma)
648. Catacomb of Trasona, (André Grabar / Odyssey Press / Western Publishing Group, Inc.)
649. House of the Scribes, Dura-Europos (André Grabar / Odyssey Press / Western Publishing Group, Inc.)
650. Santa Pudenziana, Rome (Tipolitografica Trullo)
651. SS Cosma e Damiano, Rome (Heinrich Neumayer)
652. SS Cosma e Damiano, Rome (Friedrich Wilhelm Deichmann / Amerbach-Verlag, Basel)
653. Santa Maria Maggiore, Rome (Friedrich Wilhelm Deichmann / Amerbach-Verlag, Basel)
654. Santa Maria Maggiore, Rome (Friedrich Wilhelm Deichmann / Amerbach-Verlag, Basel)
655. Hagia Sophia, Constantinople (Courtesy of Scala Publishers Ltd.)
656. Hagia Eirene, Constantinople (John Freely and Ahmet S. Cakmak)
657. Empress Theodora and son Michael III (Robert Cormack, 2000)
658. Christ. Monastery of St Catherine, Sinai (Giorgios Galavaris / Ekdotike Athenon S.A.)
659. Theotokos. Monastery of St Catherine, Sinai (Giorgios Galavaris / Ekdotike Athenon S.A.)
660. Macedonian style (George Moschopoulos / Topiko Istoriko Archeio Kefalonias)
661. Cretan style (Courtesy of His Eminence Metropolitan Dorotheos II of Syros)
662. Western influence (Manolis Borboudakis / 13th Ephorate, Crete)
663. Ionian School, Kefalonia (George Moschopoulos / Topiko Istoriko Archeio Kefalonias)
664. Ionian School, Monastery of Sission, Kefalonia (George Moschopoulos / Topiko Istoriko Archeio Kefalonias)
665. Ionian School, Kefalonia (George Moschopoulos / Topiko Istoriko Archeio Kefalonias)
666. The iconographer Fotis Kontoglou (Author)
667. Narthex with wall paintings (Courtesy of Professor Emmanuelle Plakoyiannaki)

668. Dome (Courtesy of the Holy Monastery – Holy Meteora)
669. Apse semi-dome (Courtesy of DK Publishing)
670. Apse semi-dome (Courtesy of DK Publishing)
671. Festivals icon (Paul Hetherington / De Agostini Editore, S.p.A., Novara)
672. Bema apse (Otto Demus / Boston Book and Art Shop)
673. Prothesis (Myrtali Acheimastou-Potamianou / Hesperos Editions)
674. Diaconicon vault (Myrtali Acheimastou-Potamianou / Hesperos Editions)
675. Diaconicon apse semi-dome (Myrtali Acheimastou-Potamianou / Hesperos Editions)
676. Synthronon symbolism (Christos Patrinelis et al. / Ethniki Trapeza tis Ellados)
677. Iconostasis (Helen Evans / Metropolitan Museum of Art)
678. Iconostasis (Courtesy of Hannibal Publishing House, Athens)
679. Iconostasis Beautiful Gate (Courtesy of the Holy Monastery – Holy Meteora)
680. Panel Icon (Courtesy of Professor Emmanuelle Plakoyiannaki)
681. Triumphal Arch (Friedrich Wilhelm Deichmann / Amerbach-Verlag, Basel)
682. Portrait. Emperor Constantine (Philip Sherrard / Takis Zervoulakos)
683. Christ and his Mother (George Moschopoulos / Topiko Istoriko Archeio Kefalonias)
684. Scene of the Good Shepherd (Courtesy of Cartolibreria Salbaroli, Ravenna)
685. Symbol of the Good Shepherd (André Grabar / Odyssey Press / Western Publishing Group, Inc.)
686. Early Christian symbol, the Chi Rho (Courtesy of the Institute for Balkan Studies, Thessaloniki)
687. Christian symbols (Pont. Commis. Di Archeologica Sacra, Roma)
688. Tree of Life (Collegio San Clemente, Roma)
689. Three stars on the Theotokos image (Manolis Borboudakis / 13th Ephorate, Crete)
690. Macedonian style icon (Courtesy of the Byzantine and Christian Museum, Athens)
691. Cretan style icon (By permission of George Braziller, Inc.)
692. Elongated figures (Courtesy of the Byzantine and Christian Museum, Athens)
693. Stylized facial features (Courtesy of the Byzantine and Christian Museum, Athens)
694. Christ blessing (Manolis Borboudakis / 13th Ephorate, Crete)
695. Orant (Guglielmo Matthiae / Cappelli Editore, Roma)
696. Halo (By permission of George Braziller, Inc.)
697. Nimbus (Edizioni D'Arte Marconi)
698. Garment depiction (Courtesy of Hannibal Publishing House, Athens)
699. Mountains and trees (Giorgios Galavaris / Ekdotike Athenon S.A.)
700. Inscription IC XC (Courtesy of the Byzantine and Christian Museum, Athens)
701. Inscription O ΩN (Manolis Borboudakis / 13th Ephorate, Crete)
702. Inscription MP OY (By permission of George Braziller, Inc.)
703. Maria Regina (O.Gra.Ro., Roma)
704. Theotokos *Hodegétria* (Courtesy of the Byzantine and Christian Museum, Athens)
705. Theotokos *Eleoúsa* (Courtesy of the Byzantine and Christian Museum, Athens)
706. Theotokos *Glykophiloúsa* (Courtesy of Professor Emmanuelle Plakoyiannaki)
707. Theotokos *Paramýthia* (Courtesy of Professor Emmanuelle Plakoyiannaki)
708. Theotokos *Foverá Prostasía* (Courtesy of Professor Emmanuelle Plakoyiannaki)
709. Theotokos *Geróntissa* (Courtesy of Professor Emmanuelle Plakoyiannaki)
710. Theotokos *Koúkou* (Courtesy of Professor Emmanuelle Plakoyiannaki)
711. Theotokos *Tríche*, (Courtesy of Professor Emmanuelle Plakoyiannaki)
712. Theotokos *Nicopeía* [Bringer of Victory] (Alvise Passigli)
713. XEIP. Signature of iconographer Ieremias (Manolis Borboudakis / 13th Ephorate, Crete)
714. Media – Mosaic (St Andrew Greek Orthodox Church of Kendall)
715. Media – Mosaic (Kina Italia)
716. Media – Mosaic (Heinrich Neumayer)
717. Media – Wall Painting (Courtesy of Professor Emmanuelle Plakoyiannaki)
718. Media – Encaustic (Robert Cormack and Maria Vassilaki, 2008)
719. Media construction – Mosaic (H. P. L'Orange / Henry Maguire)
720. Iconographer Manuel Panselinos (Courtesy of Professor Emmanuelle Plakoyiannaki)
721. Iconographer Andreas Ritzos (Maria Vassilaki / Skira Editore S.p.A., Milano)
722. Iconographer Theophanes (Courtesy of the Holy Monastery – Holy Meteora)
723. Iconographer Michael Damaskinos (George Moschopoulos / Topiko Istoriko Archeio Kefalonias)
724. Iconographer Frangos Katelanos (Courtesy of the Holy Monastery – Holy Meteora)

725. Iconographer Stephanos Tzankarolas (George Moschopoulos / Topiko Istoriko Archeio Kefalonias)
726. Iconographer Angelos Akotantos (Courtesy of the Byzantine and Christian Museum, Athens)
727. Iconographer Theodoros Poulakis (George Moschopoulos / Topiko Istoriko Archeio Kefalonias)
728. Iconographer Emmanuel Tzanes (Courtesy of the Byzantine and Christian Museum, Athens)

CHAPTER 5: PLACES OF SPLENDID SPIRITUAL ART

729. San Giovanni in Via Latina, Rome (Guglielmo Matthiae / Cappelli Editore, Roma)
730. Santa Costanza, Rome (Guglielmo Matthiae / Cappelli Editore, Roma)
731. Santa Costanza, Rome (Author)
732. Santa Costanza, Rome (Author)
733. Santa Costanza, Rome (Author)
734. San Giovanni in Laterno (Author)
735. San Giovanni in Laterno (Author)
736. Santa Pudenziana, Rome (Basilica di St Pudenziana)
737. Santa Sabina, Rome (Friedrich Wilhelm Deichmann / Amerbach-Verlag, Basel)
738. Santa Sabina, Rome (Friedrich Wilhelm Deichmann / Amerbach-Verlag, Basel)
739. SS Cosma e Damiano, Rome (Guglielmo Matthiae / Cappelli Editore, Roma)
740. SS Cosma e Damiano, Rome (Heinrich Neumayer)
741. SS Cosma e Damiano, Rome (Courtesy of Arnaldo Vescovo)
742. SS Cosma e Damiano, Rome (Courtesy of Arnaldo Vescovo)
743. Santa Maria Maggiore, Rome (Basilica Liberiana, Roma)
744. Santa Maria Maggiore, Rome (Basilica Liberiana, Roma)
745. Santa Maria Maggiore, Rome (Basilica Liberiana, Roma)
746. Santa Maria in Domnica, Rome (Heinrich Neumayer)
747. Santa Maria Antiqua, Rome (Guglielmo Matthiae / Cappelli Editore, Roma)
748. San Paolo Fuori le Mura, Rome (Author)
749. San Paolo Fuori le Mura, Rome (Author)
750. San Paolo Fuori le Mura, Rome (Author)
751. San Paolo Fuori le Mura, Rome (Author)
752. San Paolo Fuori le Mura, Rome (Author)
753. San Paolo Fuori le Mura, Rome (Author)
754. Santa Cecilia, Rome (Edizioni D'Arte Marconi)
755. Santa Cecilia, Rome (Edizioni D'Arte Marconi)
756. Santa Cecilia, Rome (Edizioni D'Arte Marconi)
757. Santa Cecilia, Rome (Edizioni D'Arte Marconi)
758. Santa Cecilia, Rome (Edizioni D'Arte Marconi)
759. Santa Cecilia, Rome (Edizioni D'Arte Marconi)
760. Santa Cecilia, Rome (Edizioni D'Arte Marconi)
761. Sant'Agnese Fuori le Mura (Author)
762. Sant'Agnese Fuori le Mura (Author)
763. Sant'Agnese Fuori le Mura (Author)
764. Sant'Agnese Fuori le Mura (Author)
765. San Lorenzo Fuori le Mura, Rome (Author)
766. San Lorenzo Fuori le Mura, Rome (Author)
767. Santa Maria in Trastevere, Rome (Bnm Genova)
768. Santa Maria in Trastevere, Rome (Bnm Genova)
769. Santa Maria in Trastevere, Rome (Author)
770. Santa Maria in Trastevere, Rome (HeinrichNeumayer)
771. Santa Prassede, Rome (Edizioni D'Arte Marconi)
772. Santa Prassede, Rome (Basilica di St Prassede)
773. Santa Prassede, Rome (Basilica di St Prassede)
774. Santa Prassede, Rome (Author)
775. Santa Prassede, Rome (Author)
776. Santa Prassede, Rome (Basilica di St Prassede)
777. Santa Prassede, Rome (Heinrich Neumayer)
778. Santa Prassede, Rome (Edizioni D'Arte Marconi)
779. Santa Prassede, Rome (Edizioni D'Arte Marconi)
780. Santa Prassede, Rome (Basilica di St Prassede)
781. Santa Prassede, Rome (Author)
782. Santa Prassede, Rome (Edizioni D'Arte Marconi)
783. Santa Prassede, Rome (Basilica di St Prassede)
784. Santa Prassede, Rome (Edizioni D'Arte Marconi)
785. Santa Prassede, Rome (Edizioni D'Arte Marconi)
786. San Marco, Rome (Author)
787. San Clemente, Rome (Kina Italia)
788. San Clemente, Rome (Collegio San Clemente)
789. San Clemente, Rome Collegio San Clemente)
790. San Clemente, Rome (Collegio San Clemente)
791. San Clemente, Rome (Kina Italia)
792. Santa Balbina, Rome (Author)
793. Santa Balbina, Rome (Author)
794. Santa Maria in Cosmedin, Rome (Guglielmo Matthiae / Cappelli Editore, Roma)
795. San Crisogono, Rome (Author)
796. San Crisogono, Rome (Author)
797. San Giorgio in Velabro, Rome (Author)
798. San Giorgio in Velabro, Rome (Author)
799. San Giovanni a Porta Latina, Rome (Author)
800. San Giovanni a Porta Latina, Rome (Author)
801. San Giovanni a Porta Latina, Rome (Author)
802. SS Nereo ed Achilleo, Rome (Author)

803. SS Nereo ed Achilleo, Rome (Author)
804. SS Nereo ed Achilleo, Rome (Author)
805. San Pietro in Vincoli, Rome (Author)
806. San Saba, Rome (Author)
807. San Saba, Rome (Author)
808. Baptistery San Giovanni, Florence (Giuseppe Marchini / Editrice Giusti di Becocci, Firenze)
809. Baptistery San Giovanni, Florence (Rolf C. Wirtz)
810. Baptistery San Giovanni, Florence (Giuseppe Marchini / Editrice Giusti di Becocci, Firenze)
811. Baptistery San Giovanni, Florence (Giuseppe Marchini / Editrice Giusti di Becocci, Firenze)
812. Baptistery San Giovanni, Florence (Rolf C. Wirtz)
813. Mausoleum of Galla Placidia, Ravenna (Courtesy of Cartolibreria Salbaroli, Ravenna)
814. Mausoleum of Galla Placidia, Ravenna (Courtesy of Angelo Longo Editore, Ravenna)
815. Mausoleum of Galla Placidia, Ravenna (Courtesy of Angelo Longo Editore, Ravenna)
816. Sant'Apollinare Nuovo, Ravenna (Courtesy of Cartolibreria Salbaroli, Ravenna)
817. Sant'Apollinare Nuovo, Ravenna (Courtesy of Cartolibreria Salbaroli, Ravenna)
818. Sant'Apollinare Nuovo, Ravenna (Courtesy of Angelo Longo Editore, Ravenna)
819. Sant'Apollinare Nuovo, Ravenna (Heinrich Neumayer)
820. Sant'Apollinare Nuovo, Ravenna (Courtesy of Angelo Longo Editore, Ravenna)
821. Sant'Apollinare Nuovo, Ravenna (Courtesy of Angelo Longo Editore, Ravenn)
822. Sant'Apollinare Nuovo, Ravenna (Courtesy of Cartolibreria Salbaroli, Ravenna)
823. San Vitale, Ravenna (Courtesy of Cartolibreria Salbaroli, Ravenna)
824. San Vitale, Ravenna (Courtesy of Angelo Longo Editore, Ravenna)
825. San Vitale, Ravenna (Courtesy of Cartolibreria Salbaroli, Ravenna)
826. San Vitale, Ravenna (Henry Maguire / Ins. Arch. Germ. Rome)
827. San Vitale, Ravenna (Courtesy of Angelo Longo Editore, Ravenna)
828. Sant'Apollinare in Classe, Ravenna (Courtesy of Angelo Longo Editore, Ravenna)
829. Sant'Apollinare in Classe, Ravenna (Heinrich Neumayer)
830. Sant'Apollinare in Classe, Ravenna (Courtesy of Cartolibreria Salbaroli, Ravenna)
831. Sant'Apollinare in Classe, Ravenna (Courtesy of Angelo Longo Editore, Ravenna)
832. Archiepiscopal Chapel, Ravenna (Courtesy of Angelo Longo Editore, Ravenna)
833. Archiepiscopal Chapel, Ravenna (Courtesy of Angelo Longo Editore, Ravenna)
834. Archiepiscopal Chapel, Ravenna (Courtesy of Angelo Longo Editore, Ravenna)
835. Archiepiscopal Chapel, Ravenna (Courtesy of Angelo Longo Editore, Ravenna)
836. Arian Baptistery, Ravenna (Courtesy of Cartolibreria Salbaroli, Ravenna)
837. Arian Baptistery, Ravenna (Courtesy of Angelo Longo Editore, Ravenna)
838. Orthodox Baptistery, Ravenna (Courtesy of Angelo Longo Editore, Ravenna)
839. Orthodox Baptistery, Ravenna (Courtesy of Angelo Longo Editore, Ravenna)
840. Orthodox Baptistery, Ravenna (Courtesy of Cartolibreria Salbaroli, Ravenna)
841. Orthodox Baptistery, Ravenna (Courtesy of Cartolibreria Salbaroli, Ravenna)
842. St Mark's, Venice (Richard Krautheimer)
843. St Mark's, Venice. Narthex dome (Otto Demus / Boston Book and Art Shop)
844. St Mark's, Venice. Narthex dome (Otto Demus / Boston Book and Art Shop)
845. St Mark's, Venice. Narthex dome (Otto Demus / Boston Book and Art Shop)
846. St Mark's, Venice. Narthex dome (Otto Demus / Boston Book and Art Shop)
847. St Mark's, Venice. Domes (Alvise Passigli)
848. St Mark's, Venice. Pentecost dome (Otto Demus / Boston Book and Art Shop)
849. St Mark's, Venice. Ascension dome (Otto Demus / Boston Book and Art Shop)
850. St Mark's, Venice. Emmanuel dome (Otto Demus / Boston Book and Art Shop)
851. St Mark's, Venice. Christ Pantokrator (Alvise Passigli)
852. St Mark's, Venice. Altar (Alvise Passigli)
853. Basilica Eufrasiana, Parentium (Porec) (Renco Kosinozic / Henry Maguire)
854. Basilica Eufrasiana, Parentium (Porec) (Renco Kosinozic / Henry Maguire)
855. Basilica Eufrasiana, Parentium (Porec) (Courtesy of Henry Maguire)
856. Ohrid (Maria Vassilaki / Skira Editore S.p.A., Milano)
857. St George Rotunda, Thessaloniki (Author)
858. St George Rotunda, Thessaloniki (Author)
859. St George Rotunda, Thessaloniki (Author)
860. St George Rotunda, Thessaloniki (Author)
861. St George Rotunda, Thessaloniki (Author)
862. St George Rotunda, Thessaloniki (Author)

ILLUSTRATIONS, CREDITS AND SOURCES 433

863. St Saviour Latomos, Thessaloniki (Courtesy of the Institute for Balkan Studies, Thessaloniki)
864. St Saviour Latomos, Thessaloniki (Courtesy of the Institute for Balkan Studies, Thessaloniki)
865. St Saviour Latomos, Thessaloniki (Courtesy of the Institute for Balkan Studies, Thessaloniki)
866. St Saviour Latomos, Thessaloniki (Courtesy of the Institute for Balkan Studies, Thessaloniki)
867. St Saviour Latomos, Thessaloniki (Courtesy of the Institute for Balkan Studies, Thessaloniki)
868. St Saviour Latomos, Thessaloniki (Courtesy of the Institute for Balkan Studies, Thessaloniki)
869. St Saviour Latomos, Thessaloniki (Courtesy of the Institute for Balkan Studies, Thessaloniki)
870. St Saviour Latomos, Thessaloniki (Courtesy of the Institute for Balkan Studies, Thessaloniki)
871. St Saviour Latomos, Thessaloniki (Courtesy of the Institute for Balkan Studies, Thessaloniki)
872. St Saviour Latomos, Thessaloniki (Courtesy of the Institute for Balkan Studies, Thessaloniki)
873. St Saviour Latomos, Thessaloniki (Courtesy of the Institute for Balkan Studies, Thessaloniki)
874. St Saviour Latomos, Thessaloniki (Courtesy of the Institute for Balkan Studies, Thessaloniki)
875. St Saviour Latomos, Thessaloniki (Courtesy of the Institute for Balkan Studies, Thessaloniki)
876. St Saviour Latomos, Thessaloniki (Courtesy of the Institute for Balkan Studies, Thessaloniki)
877. St Saviour Latomos, Thessaloniki (Courtesy of the Institute for Balkan Studies, Thessaloniki)
878. St Demetrios, Thessaloniki (Author)
879. St Demetrios, Thessaloniki (Heinrich Neumayer)
880. St Demetrios, Thessaloniki (Molho Publications, Thessaloniki)
881. St Demetrios, Thessaloniki (Molho Publications, Thessaloniki)
882. St Demetrios, Thessaloniki (Author)
883. St Demetrios, Thessaloniki (Molho Publications, Thessaloniki)
884. Hagia Sophia, Thessaloniki (Author)
885. Hagia Sophia, Thessaloniki (Courtesy of the Institute for Balkan Studies, Thessaloniki)
886. Hagia Sophia, Thessaloniki (Author)
887. Hagia Sophia, Thessaloniki (Author)
888. Hagia Sophia, Thessaloniki (Author)
889. Hagia Sophia, Thessaloniki (Author)
890. Hagia Sophia, Thessaloniki (Courtesy of the Institute for Balkan Studies, Thessaloniki)
891. St Catherine, Thessaloniki (Author)
892. Holy Apostles, Thessaloniki (Hans Belting, Cyril Mango and Doula Mouriki / Dumbarton Oaks)
893. Holy Apostles, Thessaloniki (Author)
894. Holy Apostles, Thessaloniki (Author)
895. Vatopedi, Mount Athos (Courtesy of Professor Emmanuelle Plakoyiannaki)
896. Ravdouchou *kélli*, Mount Athos (Sotiris Kadas / Ekdotike Athenon S.A.)
897. Ravdouchou *kélli*, Mount Athos (Sotiris Kadas / Ekdotike Athenon S.A.)
898. Vatopedi, Mount Athos (Author)
899. Vatopedi, Mount Athos (Author)
900. Vatopedi, Mount Athos (Author)
901. Vatopedi, Mount Athos (Author)
902. Vatopedi, Mount Athos (Author)
903. Vatopedi, Mount Athos (Author)
904. Vatopedi, Mount Athos (Author)
905. Vatopedi, Mount Athos (Author)
906. Vatopedi, Mount Athos (Author)
907. Vatopedi, Mount Athos (Author)
908. Vatopedi, Mount Athos (Author)
909. Vatopedi, Mount Athos (Author)
910. Vatopedi, Mount Athos (Author)
911. Vatopedi, Mount Athos (Author)
912. Vatopedi, Mount Athos (Author)
913. Vatopedi, Mount Athos (Author)
914. Church of the Protaton, Mount Athos (Author)
915. Church of the Protaton, Mount Athos (Author)
916. Church of the Protaton, Mount Athos (Author)
917. Church of the Protaton, Mount Athos (Author)
918. Church of the Protaton, Mount Athos (Author)
919. Church of the Protaton, Mount Athos (Author)
920. Church of the Protaton, Mount Athos (Author)
921. Church of the Protaton, Mount Athos (Author)
922. Church of the Protaton, Mount Athos (Author)
923. Chelandari, Mount Athos (Author)
924. Chelandari, Mount Athos (Author)
925. Esfigmenou, Mount Athos (Author)
926. Esfigmenou, Mount Athos (Author)
927. Esfigmenou, Mount Athos (Author)
928. Philotheou, Mount Athos (Author)
929. Philotheou, Mount Athos (Author)
930. Megistis Lavra, Mount Athos (Sotiris Kadas / Ekdotike Athenon S.A.)
931. Stavronikita, Mount Athos (Author)
932. Stavronikita, Mount Athos (Christos Patrinelis et al. / Ethniki Trapeza tis Ellados)
933. Stavronikita, Mount Athos (Christos Patrinelis et al. / Ethniki Trapeza tis Ellados)
934. Stavronikita, Mount Athos (Christos Patrinelis et al. / Ethniki Trapeza tis Ellados)
935. Stavronikita, Mount Athos (Christos Patrinelis et al. / Ethniki Trapeza tis Ellados)

936. Xenofondos, Mount Athos (Courtesy of Professor Emmanuelle Plakoyiannaki)
937. Xenofondos, Mount Athos (Courtesy of Professor Emmanuelle Plakoyiannaki)
938. Dochiariou, Mount Athos (Author)
939. Dochiariou, Mount Athos (Author)
940. Dochiariou, Mount Athos (Author)
941. Dochiariou, Mount Athos (Author)
942. Dochiariou, Mount Athos (Author)
943. Mount Athos as the 'Garden of Panagia' (Author)
944. Chelandari, Mount Athos (Sotiris Kadas / Ekdotike Athenon S.A.)
945. Iveron, Mount Athos (Sotiris Kadas / Ekdotike Athenon S.A.)
946. Megistis Lavra, Mount Athos (Sotiris Kadas / Ekdotike Athenon S.A.)
947. Stavronikita, Mount Athos (Courtesy of Professor Emmanuelle Plakoyiannaki)
948. Megistis Lavra, Mount Athos (Courtesy of Professor Emmanuelle Plakoyiannaki)
949. Koutloumoussi, Mount Athos (Author)
950. Koutloumoussi, Mount Athos (Author)
951. Koutloumoussi, Mount Athos (Author)
952. Koutloumoussi, Mount Athos (Author)
953. Koutloumoussi, Mount Athos (Author)
954. Koutloumoussi, Mount Athos (Author)
955. Koutloumoussi, Mount Athos (Author)
956. Koutloumoussi, Mount Athos (Author)
957. Koutloumoussi, Mount Athos (Author)
958. Koutloumoussi, Mount Athos (Author)
959. Great Meteoron, Meteora (Courtesy of the Holy Monastery – Holy Meteora)
960. St Nicholas Anapafsis, Meteora (Courtesy of the Holy Monastery – Holy Meteora)
961. St Nicholas Anapafsis, Meteora (Courtesy of the Holy Monastery – Holy Meteora)
962. St Nicholas Anapafsis, Meteora (Courtesy of the Holy Monastery – Holy Meteora)
963. St Nicholas Anapafsis, Meteora (Courtesy of the Holy Monastery – Holy Meteora)
964. St Nicholas Anapafsis, Meteora (Courtesy of the Holy Monastery – Holy Meteora)
965. St Nicholas Anapafsis, Meteora (Courtesy of the Holy Monastery – Holy Meteora)
966. Varlaam, Meteora (Courtesy of the Holy Monastery – Holy Meteora)
967. Hosios Loukas, Stiris (Courtesy of Hannibal Publishing House, Athens)
968. Hosios Loukas, Stiris (Otto Demus / Boston Book and Art Shop)
969. Hosios Loukas, Stiris (Courtesy of Hannibal Publishing House, Athens)
970. Hosios Loukas, Stiris (Courtesy of Hannibal Publishing House, Athens)
971. Hosios Loukas, Stiris (Courtesy of Hannibal Publishing House, Athens)
972. Hosios Loukas, Stiris (Courtesy of Hannibal Publishing House, Athens)
973. Hosios Loukas, Stiris (Courtesy of Hannibal Publishing House, Athens)
974. Hosios Loukas, Stiris (Courtesy of Hannibal Publishing House, Athens)
975. Hosios Loukas, Stiris (Courtesy of Hannibal Publishing House, Athens)
976. Hosios Loukas, Stiris (Courtesy of Hannibal Publishing House, Athens)
977. Hosios Loukas, Stiris (Courtesy of Hannibal Publishing House, Athens)
978. Hosios Loukas, Stiris (Courtesy of Hannibal Publishing House, Athens)
979. Hosios Loukas, Stiris (Courtesy of Hannibal Publishing House, Athens)
980. Hosios Loukas, Stiris (Courtesy of Hannibal Publishing House, Athens)
981. Hosios Loukas, Stiris (Courtesy of Hannibal Publishing House, Athens)
982. Hosios Loukas, Stiris (Courtesy of Hannibal Publishing House, Athens)
983. Hosios Loukas, Stiris (Courtesy of Hannibal Publishing House, Athens)
984. Hosios Loukas, Stiris (Courtesy of Hannibal Publishing House, Athens)
985. Hosios Loukas, Stiris (Courtesy of Hannibal Publishing House, Athens)
986. Metropolis, Mystras (Myrtali Acheimastou-Potamianou / Hesperos Editions)
987. Hodegetria, Mystras (Myrtali Acheimastou-Potamianou / Hesperos Editions)
988. Hodegetria, Mystras (Myrtali Acheimastou-Potamianou / Hesperos Editions)
989. Hodegetria, Mystras (Myrtali Acheimastou-Potamianou / Hesperos Editions)
990. Hodegetria, Mystras (Myrtali Acheimastou-Potamianou / Hesperos Editions)
991. Perivleptos, Mystras (Myrtali Acheimastou-Potamianou / Hesperos Editions)
992. Pantanassa, Mystras (Myrtali Acheimastou-Potamianou / Hesperos Editions)
993. Pantanassa, Mystras (Myrtali Acheimastou-Potamianou / Hesperos Editions)
994. SS Theodoroi, Mystras (Myrtali Acheimastou-Potamianou / Hesperos Editions)
995. Metropolis, Mystras (Myrtali Acheimastou-Potamianou / Hesperos Editions)

996. Athens. Map of Byzantine churches (By permission of Oxford University Press, Inc.)
997. Holy Apostles, Athens (Author)
998. Holy Apostles, Athens (Author)
999. Theotokos Gorgoepikoos, Athens (Author)
1000. Daphni, Athens (After Otto Demus / Boston Book and Art Shop)
1001. Daphni, Athens (Heinrich Neumayer)
1002. Daphni, Athens (Courtesy of Holy Cross Orthodox Press)
1003. Daphni, Athens (David Talbot Rice)
1004. Daphni (Otto Demus / Boston Book and Art Shop)
1005. Kaisariani, Athens (After John Arnott Hamilton / B.T. Batsford Ltd., London)
1006. Holy Trinity, Athens (Author)
1007. Nea Moni, Chios (After Otto Demus / Boston Book and Art Shop)
1008. Constantinople. Location of major landmarks (Map redrawn by author after Rowland J. Mainstone)
1009. Hagia Sophia, Constantinople (BKG, Istanbul)
1010. Hagia Sophia, Constantinople (Courtesy Scala Publishers Ltd.)
1011. Hagia Sophia, Constantinople (Author)
1012. Hagia Sophia, Constantinople (Author)
1013. Hagia Sophia, Constantinople (Author)
1014. Hagia Sophia, Constantinople (Author)
1015. Hagia Sophia, Constantinople (Erdem Yucel / K.D.V. Dahildir, Istanbul)
1016. Hagia Sophia, Constantinople (BKG, Istanbul)
1017. Hagia Sophia, Constantinople. Theotokos and Christ Child (Ali Kiliçkaya / Silk Road Publications, Istanbul)
1018. Hagia Sophia, Constantinople (Author)
1019. Holy Saviour in Chora, Constantinople (Richard Krautheimer)
1020. Holy Saviour in Chora, Constantinople (Ali Kiliçkaya / Silk Road Publications, Istanbul)
1021. Holy Saviour in Chora, Constantinople (Ali Kiliçkaya / Silk Road Publications, Istanbul)
1022. Holy Saviour in Chora, Constantinople (Ali Kiliçkaya / Silk Road Publications, Istanbul)
1023. Holy Saviour in Chora, Constantinople (Author)
1024. Holy Saviour in Chora, Constantinople (Author)
1025. Holy Saviour in Chora, Constantinople (Heinrich Neumayer)
1026. Holy Saviour in Chora, Constantinople (Ali Kiliçkaya / Silk Road Publications, Istanbul)
1027. Holy Saviour in Chora, Constantinople (Author)
1028. Holy Saviour in Chora, Constantinople (Author)
1029. Holy Saviour in Chora, Constantinople (Ali Kiliçkaya / Silk Road Publications, Istanbul)
1030. Holy Saviour in Chora, Constantinople (BKG, Istanbul)
1031. Holy Saviour in Chora, Constantinople (Author)
1032. Holy Saviour in Chora, Constantinople (Author)
1033. Holy Saviour in Chora, Constantinople (Author)
1034. Holy Saviour in Chora, Constantinople (Author)
1035. Holy Saviour in Chora, Constantinople (Ali Kiliçkaya / Silk Road Publications, Istanbul)
1036. Holy Saviour in Chora, Constantinople (Ali Kiliçkaya / Silk Road Publications, Istanbul)
1037. Parekklesion, Theotokos Pammakaristos, Constantinople (Hans Belting, Cyril Mango and Doula Mouriki / Dumbarton Oaks)
1038. Parekklesion, Theotokos Pammakaristos, Constantinople (Author)
1039. Parekklesion, Theotokos Pammakaristos, Constantinople (Hans Belting, Cyril Mango and Doula Mouriki / Dumbarton Oaks)
1040. Parekklesion, Theotokos Pammakaristos, Constantinople (Hans Belting, Cyril Mango and Doula Mouriki / Dumbarton Oaks)
1041. Parekklesion, Theotokos Pammakaristos, Constantinople (Hans Belting, Cyril Mango and Doula Mouriki / Dumbarton Oaks)
1042. Parekklesion, Theotokos Pammakaristos, Constantinople (Hans Belting, Cyril Mango and Doula Mouriki / Dumbarton Oaks)
1043. Parekklesion, Theotokos Pammakaristos, Constantinople (Hans Belting, Cyril Mango and Doula Mouriki / Dumbarton Oaks)
1044. Parekklesion, Theotokos Pammakaristos, Constantinople. Theotokos (Hans Belting, Cyril Mango and Doula Mouriki / Dumbarton Oaks
1045. Parekklesion, Theotokos Pammakaristos, Constantinople (Hans Belting, Cyril Mango and Doula Mouriki / Dumbarton Oaks)
1046. Parekklesion, Theotokos Pammakaristos, Constantinople (Hans Belting, Cyril Mango and Doula Mouriki / Dumbarton Oaks)
1047. Parekklesion, Theotokos Pammakaristos, Constantinople (Hans Belting, Cyril Mango and Doula Mouriki / Dumbarton Oaks)
1048. Parekklesion, Theotokos Pammakaristos, Constantinople (Author)
1049. Parekklesion, Theotokos Pammakaristos, Constantinople (Author)
1050. Parekklesion, Theotokos Pammakaristos, Constantinople (Hans Belting, Cyril Mango and Doula Mouriki / Dumbarton Oaks)
1051. Parekklesion, Theotokos, Pammakaristos, Constantinople (Hans Belting, Cyril Mango and Doula Mouriki / Dumbarton Oaks)
1052. Parekklesion, Theotokos, Pammakaristos, Constantinople (Hans Belting, Cyril Mango and Doula Mouriki / Dumbarton Oaks)

1053. Parekklesion, Theotokos, Pammakaristos, Constantinople (Author)
1054. Parekklesion, Theotokos Pammakaristos, Constantinople (Hans Belting, Cyril Mango and Doula Mouriki / Dumbarton Oaks)
1055. Parekklesion, Theotokos Pammakaristos, Constantinople (Hans Belting, Cyril Mango and Doula Mouriki / Dumbarton Oaks)
1056. Parekklesion, Theotokos Pammakaristos, Constantinople (Hans Belting, Cyril Mango and Doula Mouriki / Dumbarton Oaks)
1057. Parekklesion, Theotokos Pammakaristos, Constantinople (Hans Belting, Cyril Mango and Doula Mouriki / Dumbarton Oaks)
1058. Parekklesion, Theotokos Pammakaristos, Constantinople (Hans Belting, Cyril Mango and Doula Mouriki / Dumbarton Oaks)
1059. Parekklesion, Theotokos Pammakaristos, Constantinople (Hans Belting, Cyril Mango and Doula Mouriki / Dumbarton Oaks)
1060. Parekklesion, Theotokos Pammakaristos, Constantinople (Hans Belting, Cyril Mango and Doula Mouriki / Dumbarton Oaks)
1061. Parekklesion, Theotokos Pammakaristos, Constantinople (Hans Belting, Cyril Mango and Doula Mouriki / Dumbarton Oaks)
1062. Parekklesion, Theotokos Pammakaristos, Constantinople (Hans Belting, Cyril Mango and Doula Mouriki / Dumbarton Oaks)
1063. St Catherine, Mount Sinai (Helmut Buschhausen / Henry Maguire)
1064. St Catherine, Mount Sinai (By permission of George Braziller, Inc.)
1065. St Catherine, Mount Sinai (By permission of George Braziller, Inc.)
1066. St Catherine, Mount Sinai (By permission of George Braziller, Inc.)
1067. St Catherine, Mount Sinai (By permission of George Braziller, Inc.)
1068. Bawit, Egypt (André Grabar, 1968)
1069. Bawit, Egypt (Robert Cormack, 2000)
1070. Cathedral, Cefalu (Otto Demus / Boston Book and Art Shop)
1071. Cathedral, Cefalu (Otto Demus / Boston Book and Art Shop)
1072. Capella Palatina, Palermo (Heinrich Neumayer)
1073. Cathedral, Monreale (Archidiocesi di Monreale / Casa Editrice Mistretta)
1074. Cathedral, Monreale (Author)
1075. Cathedral, Monreale (Archidiocesi di Monreale / Casa Editrice Mistretta)
1076. Cathedral, Monreale (Author)
1077. Cathedral, Monreale (Otto Demus / Boston Book and Art Shop)
1078. Cathedral, Monreale (Casa Editrice Mistretta di Giuseppe Mistretta)
1079. Cathedral, Monreale (Otto Demus / Boston Book and Art Shop)
1080. Cathedral, Monreale (Archidiocesi di Monreale / Casa Editrice Mistretta)
1081. Cathedral, Monreale (Archidiocesi di Monreale / Casa Editrice Mistretta)
1082. Cathedral, Monreale (Archidiocesi di Monreale / Casa Editrice Mistretta)
1083. Cathedral, Monreale (Archidiocesi di Monreale / Casa Editrice Mistretta)
1084. Cathedral, Monreale (Archidiocesi di Monreale / Casa Editrice Mistretta)
1085. Cathedral, Monreale (Archidiocesi di Monreale / Casa Editrice Mistretta)
1086. Cathedral, Monreale (Archidiocesi di Monreale / Casa Editrice Mistretta)
1087. Cathedral, Monreale (Archidiocesi di Monreale / Casa Editrice Mistretta)
1088. Cathedral, Monreale (Archidiocesi di Monreale / Casa Editrice Mistretta)
1089. Cathedral, Monreale (Archidiocesi di Monreale / Casa Editrice Mistretta)
1090. Cathedral, Monreale (Archidiocesi di Monreale / Casa Editrice Mistretta)
1091. Cathedral, Monreale (Archidiocesi di Monreale / Casa Editrice Mistretta)
1092. Cathedral, Monreale (Archidiocesi di Monreale / Casa Editrice Mistretta)
1093. Cathedral, Monreale (Author)
1094. Cathedral, Monreale (Author)
1095. Cathedral, Monreale (Author)
1096. Cathedral, Monreale (Author)

CHAPTER 6: LITURGY

1097. Christ in a mandorla (Robert Cormack and Maria Vassilaki, 2008)
1098. Book of Gospels, cover (Robert Cormack and Maria Vassilaki, 2008)
1099. Gospels book cover [Megistis Lavra, Mount Athos] (Sotiris Kadas / Ekdotike Athenon S.A.)
1100. Paten (Lord Kinross / Arnoldo Mondadori Editore, Milano)
1101. Chalice of Emperor Romanos I (Lord Kinross / Arnoldo Mondadori Editore, Milano)
1102. Triptych (Paul Hetherington / De Agostini Editore, S.p.A., Novara)
1103. Paten (Robert Cormack and Maria Vassilaki, 2008)
1104. First entrance procession with Emperor Justinian (Author)
1105. First entrance procession with Empress Theodora (Author)
1106. St Basil's Liturgy (Giorgios Galavaris / Ekdotike Athenon S.A.)
1107. Monastery service in progress (Courtesy of Professor Emeritus Konstantinos P. Mylonas)
1108. Celestial Divine Liturgy (Manolis Borboudakis / 13th Ephorate, Crete)
1109. Liturgy of the Just and Damned (Courtesy of Dr Svetlana Rakic)

CHAPTER 7: SYMBOLISM

1110. Holy Sepulcher (Sotiris Kadas / Ekdotike Athenon S.A.)
1111. St Savvas in Palestine (Sotiris Kadas / Ekdotike Athenon S.A.)
1112. SS Peter and Paul I (Maria Vassilaki / Skira Editore S.p.A., Milano)
1113. SS Peter and Paul II (Maria Vassilaki / Skira Editore S.p.A., Milano)
1114. A centralized [circular] church (George Moschopoulos / Topiko Istoriko Archeio Kefalonias)
1115. Incense Burner with five domes I (Robert Cormack and Maria Vassilaki, 2008)
1116. Incense Burner with five domes II (Lord Kinross / Arnoldo Mondadori Editore, Milano)
1117. Reliquary (Monastery of Dochiariou, Mount Athos) (Sotiris Kadas / Ekdotike Athenon S.A.)
1118. Reliquary (Hosios Nifon) (Courtesy Professor Emeritus Konstantinos P. Mylonas)
1119. Tabernacle (Author)
1120. *Dodekaórton* (Author from Christos Patrinelis et al. / Ethniki Trapeza tis Ellados)

1121. St Saviour in Chora (Jean Ebersolt and Adolphe Thiers / Ernest Leroux, Paris)

COLOUR PLATES: ARCHITECTURE (appear between pp. 244–45)

I. Typical Domed Byzantine Church (Giorgios Galavaris / Ekdotike Athenon S.A.)
II. Rome, Sant'Agnese Fuori le Mura (Author)
III. Rome, San Lorenzo Fuori le Mura (Author)
IV. Rome, Santa Sabina (Author)
V. Ravenna, San Apollinare in Classe (Courtesy of Cartolibreria Salbaroli, Ravenna)
VI. Constantinople, Hagia Sophia (Author)
VII. Constantinople, Hagia Sophia (Judith Dupré)
VIII. Constantinople, Hagia Sophia (Courtesy the Scala Group)
IX. Constantinople, Hagia Sophia (André Grabar / Odyssey Press / Western Publishing Group, Inc.)
X. Constantinople, Hagia Sophia (Courtesy the Scala Group)
XI. Constantinople, Hagia Eirene (John Freely and Ahmet S. Cakmak)
XII. Constantinople, Pammakaristos (Paul Hetherington / De Agostini Editore, S.p.A., Novara)
XIII. Constantinople, Pammakaristos (Author)
XIV. Constantinople, Pammakaristos (Author)
XV. Thessaloniki, St Demetrios (Author)
XVI. Thessaloniki, Acheiropoietos (Author)
XVII. Thessaloniki, Holy Apostles (Author)
XVIII. Stiris, Hosios Loukas (Robert Cormack, 2000)
XIX. Stiris, Hosios Loukas (Courtesy of Hannibal Publishing House, Athens)
XX. Mystras, SS Theodoroi (Author)

COLOUR PLATES: ART (appear between pp. 372–73)

XXI.	Coptic icon (Author)	XXXII.	The Crucifixion (Author)
XXII.	San Cosma (Courtesy of Arnaldo Vescovo)	XXXIII.	The Holy Trinity by Theophanes Bathas-Strelitzas (Author)
XXIII.	Theotokos and Christ Child icon (Basilica Liberiana, Roma)	XXXIV.	Archangel Michael icon by Frangos Katelanos (Author)
XXIV.	Enthroned Theotokos and Christ Child (Heinrich Neumayer)	XXXV.	Christ Pantokrator icon by Michael Damaskinos (Author)
XXV.	Christ from the Deësis mosaic (Author)	XXXVI.	Theotokos *Hodegétria* icon by Michael Damaskinos (Author)
XXVI.	Theotokos *Hodegétria* icon (Author)		
XXVII.	Christ icon (By permission of George Braziller, Inc.)	XXXVII.	Three Hierarchs icon by Michael Damaskinos (Author)
XXVIII.	St Nicholas icon (By permission of George Braziller, Inc.)	XXXVIII.	St Anthony icon by Michael Damaskinos (Author)
XXIX.	Christ *despotikó* icon (Christos Patrinelis et al. / Ethniki Trapeza tis Ellados)	XXXIX.	Enthroned Christ icon by Emmanuel Tzanes (Author)
XXX.	Theotokos *despotikó* icon (Christos Patrinelis et al. / Ethniki Trapeza tis Ellados)	XL.	Enthroned Theotokos icon by Emmanuel Tzanes (Author)
XXXI.	Christ portable icon (Sotiris Kadas / Ekdotike Athenon S.A.)		

INDEX

The page numbers in bold refer to illustrations

Acts, 38, 374
aër., 383
Against Heresies, 31
agápe meal, 38, 374, 400
Agathias, 394
agioreitikos, 62
Agrippa, Marcus, 103
Alaric the Visigoth, 16, 91, 217
Alexandria, 14, 15, 33
anaphorá, 374, 398
Anastasis, 59, 81, 183, 184, **336**, 350, **351**, 371
An Exact Exposition of the Orthodox Faith, 276
Annunciation, 82, **83**, 258, **328**, **371**
antídoron, 383
Antioch, 5, 14, 39
Apologists, 31
Apostle
    John, 237, **301**
    Paul, 5, 188, 282, 285, 286, **287**, **291**, **292**, **307**, **308**, **322**, **336**, 354, 355, **369**, **371**, 374, **397**
    Peter, 8, **272**, **282**, **285**, 286, **287**, **289**, **292**, **296**, **307**, **308**, **321**, **326**, 354, 364, 365, **369**, 397
Apostoleíon, 146, 148
Apostolic Constitutions, 75, 377, 400
Apostolic Tradition, 375, 400
Aquileia, 312
Archangel
    Gabriel, **332**, **345**, 360, 366
    Michael, **27**, **329**, **351**, **352**, 360
    Raphael, **358**, 360
    Uriel, 360
Archbishop
    Apollinaris, 217

Maximian, 81
Symeon of Thessaloniki, 387, 389, 399
archeiropoíetos, 195, 250
architect
    Anthemius of Tralles, 138, 146
    Bernini, 90
    Borromini, **90**
    Bramante, 90
    Brunelleschi, Filippo, 53
    della Porta, Giacomo, 53
    Isidorus of Miletus, 138, 146
    Michelangelo, 53, 90
    Raphael, 90, 105
    Sansovino, Andrea, 127
    Stephanos, 223
Architecture as Icon, 401
architekton, 138
Ascension, 198, 256, 277, **310**, **342**, 370
Athens, 254, 342–46
    Map of Byzantine churches, **343**
Augusta, 283
    Helena, 182, 223, 363
    Zoe, 27, 348
Augustus, 10
aula ecclesiae, 39
Aula Ecclesiae
    Eufrasiana, Parentium, **41**
    San Crisogono, **40**, **41**
    San Martino ai Monti, **41**

baptism of Jesus, 360, **361**, 370
baptismal fonts, 85
baptistery
    Arian, **307**, **308**
    Lateran, **266**
    Olympas, 136
    Orthodox, 218, **308**

San Giovanni, **300**, **301**
St John, Ephesus, 242
Basilica
    A, Beyazit, Constantinople, **84**
    B, Nikopolis, **78**
    basilica (βασιλικόν), 46
    Constantine, Trier, **46**
    Constantiniana, 44, **45**, **46**, 89
    Maxentius, **45**
    Olympia, **81**
    Tyre, 86
    Ulpia, **45**
Bawit, 365
Beautiful Gate, 82, **255**, 258, **260**, **328**
Belisarius, 16, 217
Bethlehem, **121**, 182–83, 285, 305
Bishop
    Athanasius, 33
    Clement, 86, 374, 400
    Cyprian, 72
    Cyril, 377
    Dionysios, 376
    Ecclesius, **304**
    Ioannis, **318**
    Irenaeus, 31, 375
    Isaac, 39
    Maximian, **307**
    Maximianus, 219
    Paulinus, 86
    Theodore, 380
    Theoteknos, 64
    Thomas of Marga, 404
Book of Gospels, 33, 75, 79, 85, 257, **266**, **288**, **354**, **376**, 381, 388, 397
    Canonical, 375
Book of Revelation, 79, 237
Brandenburg, Hugo, 88, 90, 91

Buchwald, Hans, 55, 188
Byzantine church architectural fixtures, 78
    Ambo, 83, 84, **85**, 115, **129**, 145, 382, 393
    Baldachino, 47, 78
    Bishop's Throne, 79, **81**, **101**, **307**, 378, 386, 391, 399
    Ciborium, 47, 78, 391, 392
    Holy Table, 78, 391, 392, 398
    Iconostasis, 81, **82**, **83**, 258, **260**, 392, 398
    Synthronon, 79, **80**, **259**, 392, 399
    Templon, 44, **73**, 81, **82**, **128**, 258, 392
Byzantine church architecture
    Arcade, **54**, 55, **77**, **101**, 106, 111, 112, **119**, 125, **194**, 196, **221**, **299**, **303**
    Column capital, **69**, **70**, 102, 103, 104, 107, **122**, **123**, 141, 144, **162**, 166, 174, 195, 210, 213, 220, 241
    Cupola, 53
    Dome, 51, **143**, **157**, **158**, **176**, **182**, **255**, 300, **308**, **309**, **310**, **311**, **331**, **339**, **341**, **343**, **354**, **355**
    Pendentive, 51, **52**, **53**, **256**, **345**
    Squinch, 51, **52**
Byzantine church space division, 389
    Aisles, **45**, 46, 47, **54**, 55, 56, **65**, **91**, **194**, 211, 391, 396
    Apse, **45**, 46, 53, **54**, **57**, **63**, 76, 86, 87, 248, 252, 277, 391
    Bema, 72, 73, 391
    (βῆμα), 46
    Diaconicon, 75, 76, **128**, 258, 383, 392, 396
    Forecourt and Courtyard, 66, **67**, **91**, 140, **213**, 390
    Foundation, 390
    Galleries, 77, **121**, **194**, 391
    Naos, 69, **111**, **120**, **123**, **124**, **125**, **133**, **137**, **143**, **221**, 390
    (ναός), 47
    Narthex, 67, **68**, **144**, **165**, **178**, **208**, 277, 390
    litî, 62, 68, 180
    Pastophoria, 75
    Prothesis, 75, 76, **128**, **258**, 373, 382, 383, 396
    Solea, 74, 393
    Transept, 77
Byzantine church type definition
    Athonite, 62
    Basilica, 54
    Centralized, 58
    Converted Temple, 61
    Cross-in-Square, 55
        compressed type, 56
        four-pier type, 55
    Cruciform, 58
    Domed Basilica, 61
    Timelines Chart, 48
Byzantine Monasteries
    Architecture, 223–37
    Art, 321–42
Byzantine Spiritual Art
    Decorative Scheme, 255–60
    Epochs, 246–55
    Iconography, 260–75
    Texts, 276–77
Byzantium, 1, 22, 29, 44

Cabasilas, Nicholas, 387
Caesar, 10
Cakmak, Ahmet, 134
Cappadocia, 361
Catacomb
    Aurelii, **12**, **246**
    Callistus, 279
    Coemeterium Majus, **12**
    Commodila, **13**, **247**
    Domitilla, 279
    Goirdani, **247**
    Priscilla, 269, 279
    SS Pietro e Marcellino, **12**, **246**
    St Sebastiano, **262**
    Trasona, **247**
catacombs, 9, 12, 261
catechoúmenon, 77
cathedra, 81
cathedral at
    Cefalu, **366**
    Monreale, 36, 366, **367**, **368**, 370, **372**
    Ortegia, Siracusa, 62, 105
Cavallini, Pietro, 286, **287**, **289**, 290
Chalcedonians, 33
chalice, **379**, 383
chapel
    Archiepiscopal, **58**, **81**, **307**
    Palatina, **255**, **367**
    San Zeno, **287**, **293**
Chi Rho, 11, 12, **15**, 102, 122, **262**, **289**, **297**
Choniates, Niketas, 29
Choricus, 393
chorostasía, 62, 385
Christ
    'Chalke' composition, **353**
    in a mandorla, 356, **364**, 365, **374**
    Pantokrator, 61, **255**, 256, **268**, 287, 288, 311, 314, **328**, 334, **336**, 338, **339**, **341**, **343**, **344**, 349, **355**, 356, 365, **366**, **367**, 368, 401, 402
    Yperagáthos, **357**
Chronographia, 180
church at
    Alaban, **188**
    Aleppo, **187**
    Aphendelli, **82**
    Aquileia, **262**
    Cappadocia, 361
    Cefalu, **255**
    Dermech, **74**
    Der Turmanin, **187**
    Jerusalem, 362
    Lake Tiberius, **47**
    Madaba, 362
    Myrelaion, 154, **155**, **156**
    Qirk-Bizzeh, **65**, **66**
    Sbeita, **76**
    Sivri, **187**
    Tabarka, **55**
    Tokali, **187**, 361
Church History, 31–37
church of
    Aphendiko, **235**
    Archangel Michael, 166
    Beta Ghiorghis, 188
    Blachernitissa, 180
    Eufrasiana, 217, **312**, 313
    Golgotha, 183, **184**, **185**, **186**
    Hagia Eirene, **23**, 33, 34, **50**, **67**, **80**, 136, 138, **140**, **141**, **142**, **250**, 349
    Hagia Sophia I, Constantinople, 136
    Hagia Sophia II, Constantinople, 136
    Hagia Sophia, Constantinople, **50**, 53, **61**, **67**, **68**, **69**, **72**, **75**, **84**,

138, 142, **143**, **144**, **145**, **249**, **347**, **348**, **350**
Hagia Sophia, Ohrid, **217**, 263, 313
Hagia Sophia, Thessaloniki, **84**, 211, **213**, **319**, **320**
Holy Apostles, Athens, **60**, **216**, **343**
Holy Apostles, Constantinople, **60**, 146
Holy Apostles, Thessaloniki, 198, **200**, **201**, **202**, **203**, **321**
Holy Saviour in Chora. *See* St Saviour in Chora
Holy Sepulcher, Jerusalem, **395**
Holy Theotokos Blachernae. *See* Blachernitissa
Holy Trinity, Athens, **216**
Koimisis tis Theotokou, Anogi, **83**
Koimisis tis Theotokou, Nicaea, **59**
Nea Ekklesia, Constantinople, 153, 349
Nea Ekklesia, Jerusalem, 184
Panagia Chalkeon, 198, **200**, 320
Panagia Kapnikarea, **216**, 342
Panagia Mouchliotissa, 181, **182**
Panagia, Stiris, 334
Pantanassa, **236**
Parigoritissa, **216**, **217**
Prophet Elijah, **63**, **205**, **206**
Prophets, Gerasa, **56**
Protaton, **228**, 273, 324, **325**, **326**
San Clemente, **67**, **74**, **84**, 99, **103**, **104**, **262**, **295**, **296**
San Cosmedin, **297**
San Crisogono, 102, **104**, **297**
San Giorgio in Velabro, **101**, **102**, **103**, **297**
San Giovanni a Porta Latina, 123, **125**, **126**, **127**, **298**
San Giovanni Evangelista, **221**
San Giovanni in Laterno, 89, **280**, 281
San Giovanni in Via Latina, **279**
San Lorenzo Fuori le Mura, **85**, 115, **120**, **121**, **122**, **123**, **260**, 286, **289**
San Lorenzo Maggiore, Milan, 300
San Marco, Rome, 107, 288, **294**
San Martino ai Monti, 39, **107**
San Nicola in Carcere, 105
San Paolo Fuori le Mura, 119, **123**, **284**, **285**, 286
San Pietro in Vincoli, **299**
San Saba, **54**, **106**, **299**
San Sebastiano, **115**
San Silverstro in Capite, 99
San Vitale, Ravenna, **60**, **69**, **219**, **220**, 263, **304**, **305**
San Vitale, Rome, 99
Sant'Agnese Fuori le Mura, **70**, 114, **119**, 286, **288**
Sant'Angelo in Pescheria, 99
Sant'Angelo, Perugia, **130**
Sant'Apollinare in Classe, **221**, **306**
Sant'Apollinare Nuovo, **221**, 223, **303**, **304**
Santa Balbina, **100**, **101**, **296**, **297**
Santa Cecilia, 107, **285**, **286**, **287**
Santa Maria ad Martyres, 104
Santa Maria Antiqua, **13**, 127, **284**
Santa Maria del Fiore, 53
Santa Maria della Navicella, 127
Santa Maria Domnica, **14**
Santa Maria Egiziaca, 105
Santa Maria in Cosmedin, 127, **128**, **129**
Santa Maria in Domnica, 127, **284**
Santa Maria in Trastevere, **269**, 286, **289**, **290**
Santa Maria Maggiore, **55**, 122, **124**, **249**, **282**, **283**
Santa Maria Nova, **13**, 99
Santa Prassede, **71**, 114, **115**, 129, **266**, 286, **290**, **291**, **292**, **293**, **294**
Santa Pudenziana, **249**, **280**, 281
Santa Sabina, **54**, 111, **112**, **113**, **281**
Sant'Apollinare in Classe, 305
Sant'Apollinare Nuovo, 302
Santi Cosma e Damiano, 105, **249**, 281, **282**
Santi Giovanni e Paolo, 38, **106**, **107**
Santi Nereo ed Achilleo, 103, **298**, **299**
Santo Stefano alle Carozze, 105
Santo Stefano Rotondo, **59**, 113, **114**
SS Peter and Mark, 148, **152**, **153**
SS Peter and Paul, Constantinople, **60**, 168
SS Peter and Paul, Gerasa, **74**
SS Sergius and Bacchus, 168, **171**, **172**, **173**, **174**
SS Theodorii, Athens, **216**
St Andrew in Krisei, 175, **177**, **178**, **179**, **181**
St Babylas, **58**
St Catherine, Sinai, **83**, **260**, **264**, **364**
St Catherine, Thessaloniki, 206, **208**, **320**
St Clement, 314
St Demetrios (Metropolis), Mystras, **235**, **236**, **258**
St Demetrios, Thessaloniki, **77**, 188, **194**, **195**, **318**
St Efimia, 34, **80**, **82**, 87, 179
St Eleftherios, Athens. *See* Theotokos Gorgoepikoos
St George in the Phanar, 181
St George Rotunda, **210**, 314, **315**
St George, Athens, **344**
St George, Jordan, 184
St John Stoudios, **54**, **63**, **73**, **79**, **136**, **137**
St John the Forerunner Troullo, 148, **153**
St John, Ephesus, **69**, **70**, 237–43, **239**, **240**, **241**, **243**
St Nicholas Orphanos, **198**
St Nicholas, Myra, **80**
St Nicholas, Svoronata, **83**
St Panteleimon, Thessaloniki, 206
St Peter's (new), 53
St Peter's (old), 44, **77**, 90, **91**
St Polyektos, 137
St Savvas, **395**
St Saviour in Chora, 30, **50**, **57**, **174**, **176**, 349, **351**, 353, **354**, **355**
St Saviour Latomou, 203, 314, **316**, **317**
St Saviour Pantepoptes, 159, **162**, **163**
St Saviour Pantokrator, 165, **168**, **169**
St Theodore, **50**, 162, **164**, **165**, **166**
St Theodosia, 148, **154**
St Mark's, Venice, **71**, **78**, **133**, 308, **309**, **310**, **311**
Taxiarchis, ix, **198**
the Nativity, 182, **185**, **186**

Theotokos Acheiropoietos, **195, 196**, 197
Theotokos Chalkoprateia, 137, 180
Theotokos Diaconissa. *See* Theotokos Kyriotissa
Theotokos Eleousa, 165
Theotokos Gorgoepikoos, **216**, 343, **344**
Theotokos Hodegetria, **236**
Theotokos Kyriotissa, 163, **166**, **167**, **168**
Theotokos Pammakaristos, **56, 57**, 156, **160, 161, 162, 355, 356, 357, 358, 359, 360**
Theotokos Panachrantos, 156, **157, 158, 159**
Transfiguration of the Saviour, Thessaloniki, 206
Transfiguration of the Saviour, Vlatades, 203
cloisonné, 72
Codex Barberini, 382
Commentary on the Divine Liturgy, 387
Constantinople, 1, 14, 17, 22, 29, 34, 44, 54
 Church type, 134–82
 Great Palace, **6**, 134
 Location of churches and monasteries, **5, 347**
 Spiritual Art, 346–61
Corinth, 8
Council of
 Arles, 8
 Hieria, 23, 34, 181, 250
 Jerusalem, 375
 Trullo, 250, 261
Cretan style, **264**, 326, 330
Crete, 253, 362
Crucifixion, **328, 336, 379**
Crusade
 First, 26
 Fourth, 29, 136, 137, 142, 148, 251, 384

Davies, John, 84
De idololatria, 375
Deacons' Doors, 82
Deësis, **325, 329, 348**, 349
despotikaí, 82, 258

Diátaxis, 263, 384
Didache, 400
Didascalia Apostolorum, 375, 400
Dionysios of Fourna, 276, 277, 330, 385
Dionysius the Areopagite, 386
Divine Liturgy, 385, **386**
domus ecclesiae, 38
Domus Faustae, 89
double narthex, 63, 68, 180
Doukas, Theodore Komnenos, **31**
Dupré, Judith, 103, 188
Dura-Europos, 361
 House of the Scribes, **247**
 house-church, 39, 247, 400

Early Christian and Byzantine Architecture, 187
Early Christianity, 5–9
ecclesia, 38
Ecclesiastical Hierarchy, 385, 386
Ecclesiastical History, 31, 40, 44, 389
Ecclesiastical History and Mystical Contemplation, 382, 386, 400
Ecumenical Council
 First (Nicaea), 11, **33**, 380
 Second (Constantinople), 33, **34**
 Third (Ephesus), 34, 380
 Fourth (Chalcedon), 34, 380
 Fifth (Constantinople), 34, 380
 Sixth (Constantinople), 34, 380
 Seventh (Nicaea), **34**, 79, 250, 276, 380
Edessa, 5, 39, 390
Edict
 of Milan, 11, 14, 38, 85, 99, 248
 of Tolerance, 11
Edifices, 16, 138, 146, 238, 401
Egeria, xii, 81, 184, 377
egg tempera, 272
Ekphrasis on the Church of the Holy Apostles, 146
Eliade, Mircea, 399
Emperor
 Alexander, **25**
 Alexios I Komnenos, 27, **28**
 Alexios II Komnenos, **28**
 Arcadios, 1, 136
 Aurelian, 39
 Baldwin, **29**
 Basil I, 18, 25, 152, 153, 175, 180, 349

Basil II, **4**, 25, 26, 188
Constantine, 1, **4**, 10, 11, 12, 14, 33, 38, 44, 46, 89, 90, 115, 119, 129, 136, 146, 148, 182, 183, **261**, 347, 400
Constantine IV, 34
Constantine V, 23, 34, 181, 250
Constantine VI, 23
Constantine VII Porphyrogennetos, 25, 154
Constantine IX Monomachos, **26**, 348, **350**
Constantine XI, 340
Constantius II, 136, 146
Decius, 9
Diocletian, 9, 10, 40, 105, 188
Domitian, 8, 237
Galerius, 188, 210
Hadrian, 103, 183
Herakleios, 3
Honorius, 1, 119, 217, 301
Isaac I Komnenos, 174, **353**, 355
John II Komnenos, 27, **28**, 165, 349
John Katakouzenos, **30**
John Tzimiskes, **19**
Julian, 33
Justin I, 16
Justin II, 16, 180
Justinian, **4**, 16, 17, 34, 49, 134, 136, 138, 146, 168, 174, 182, 223, 237, 240, 301, 363
Leo I, 148
Leo III, 23, 24, 250
Leo IV, 23
Leo V, 24, 251, **348**
Leo VI, **25**, 155
Licinius, 10, 11
Marcian, 34
Maximian, 10
Maximinus, 8
Michael III, 24
Michael IV Paphlagon, **26**
Michael VII Doukas, 156
Michael VIII Palaiologos, 30, 156
Michael IX Palaiologos, 157
Nero, 8
Nikephoros Botaneiates, **27**
Nikephoros Phokas, **19**, 223
Romanos I Lekapenos, 154
Romanos II, **4**
Romanos IV Diogenis, 26

Romulus Augustulus, 16
Septimius Serverus, 8
Theodosius I, 1, 3, 14, 15, 33, 34, 137, 248
Theodosius II, 34, 136, 237
Theophilos, **24**
Trajan, 374
Valerian, 9
Zeno, 16
Empress
   Aelia Eudocia, 362
   Anna Dalassena, 159, 160
   Eirene, 23, 24, **28**, 34, 250, 349, **350**
   Eirene Komnena, 165
   Eudoxia, 136
   Maria Dukaina, 174
   Maria Palaelogina, 181
   Pulcheria, 137, 180
   Theodora, 16, **17**, 24, 156, 240, **250**, **272**
   Zoe, 25, **27**, 348, **350**
encaustic, 273
Enneads, 276
Ephesus, 5, 15
epískopos, 374
Eucharist, 389
Eucharist liturgy, 375, 377, 378, 382
Eusebius, 10, 31, 33, 40, 44, 64, 79, 86, 146, 183, 184, 389, 393
evangélion, 375
Evangelist
   John, **32**, 256
   Luke, **32**, 256
   Mark, **32**, 256
   Matthew, **32**, 256
Explanation of Orthodox Iconography, 276
Explanation of the Art of Painting, 276

Fall of Constantinople, *4*, 278
First Apology, 375
Florence, 300
Freely, John, 134

Galbius and Candidus, 148
Gate of Persecution, 238
Genseric, 91
George the Monk, 180
Gibbon, Edward, 3
Glavas, Michael, 357

Gnostics, 31
Good Shepherd, 12, **14**, **262**, **302**
Gospel
   of John, 237, 256, 401
Great Church of the Holy Wisdom. *See* church of Hagia Sophia, Constantinople
Great Entrance, 381, 384, 396
Grundmann, Stefan, 88

hall-church
   Musmiyeh, Syria, **40**
   Philippi, Greece, **40**
Hatlie, Peter, 180
Hermeneía, 330
Hippolytus, 375, 400
History and Mystical Contemplation, 387
Holy Communion, **379**, 380, 383
Holy Sepulcher, Jerusalem, 113
horos, 51
horrea ecclesiae, 39
house-church
   Dura-Europos, **43**, **44**
   Qirqbize, Syria, **40**

icon (*eíkon*), 260
Iconoclasm, 22–24
iconoclasts, **23**, 250, 276
iconodules, 276
iconographer
   Akotantos, Angelos, 30, **275**, 363
   Astrapas, Michael, 314
   Damaskinos, Michael, 33, **253**, **274**, **328**, **338**, 363, **386**
   Dikotaris, Giorgios and Frangos, 334
   Eftychius, 314
   Ionian School, **253**
   Katelanos, Frangos, 273, **275**, 327, **334**
   Klontzas, George, 363
   Kontoglou, Fotis, **254**, 274, 276, 277
   Matsoukas, G., **253**
   Ouspensky, Leonid, 274
   Panselinos, Manuel, 273, **274**, 324
   Poulakis, Theodoros, **275**
   Ritzos, Andreas, 30, 273, **274**
   Theophanes, 273, **274**, 326, 327, **331**, **333**, **334**
   Theotokopoulos, Domenikos ('El Greco'), **252**, 363

Tzanes, Emmanuel, **275**, **334**
Tzankarolas, Stephanos, **253**, **275**
Tzorzis, 327
I C X C, 265, **268**
igoúmenos, 18
   Philotheos, 334
   St Theodore, 136
incense burner, **402**
insula-church
   Santi Giovanni e Paolo, Rome, **43**
   Umm el-Jimal, Syria, **41**, **42**
Interpretation of the Church and the Liturgy, 387
Ithaki, 88, 405
ΙΧΘΥΣ, 305

Jerusalem, **6**, **7**, 14, 26, 81, **120**, 182–84, 285, 362
John of Damascus. *See* St John Damascene
Justin Martyr, 375

Karyes, 324
katathésis, 79
katechetís, 376
katholikon, 22, 62, 67
   Holy Trinity, **346**
   Kaisariani, **345**
   Hosios Loukas, **266**
Kavafis, Konstantine, x, 405
Kedrenos, Giorgios, 180
Kefallinia, 88
King William II, **35**, 36, 367, **371**
Koimisis tis Theotokou, **252**, **275**, **283**, **355**, 356
koinonía, 376
Komnenoi dynasty, 27, 278
Krautheimer, Richard, 187
kyriakón, 64

Ladder of Divine Ascent, 18
Lalibela, **188**
Last Judgment, 256, 350
Last Supper, **253**, **303**, **370**, 373, 374
Late Antiquity, 10–17
lectors, 85
leitourgía, 376
Leontius, 188
Liber Pontificalis, 44, 70
Life of Constantine, 31

litì. See Byzantine church space division: Narthex
Little Entrance, 381, **382**, 384
Liturgy of
St Basil, **384**
St Chrysostom, **384**
the Catechumens, 376
the Faithful, 376
the Just and Damned, **387**
Livos, Constantine (Lips), 155

Macedonian dynasty, 25, 49
Macedonian style, **264**, 324, 333
Madaba, 362
Map, 184
Maderno, Stefano, 107
Mango, Cyril, 49, 393
Manzikert, 26
Marcion, 31
Maria Regina, 269
Marinus, 64
Marmara, 240
martyrium, 76
Mathews, Thomas, 134
Mausoleum of
Galla Placidia, **58**, 218, **219**, **262**, 301, **302**
San Vittore, 299
Santa Costanza, **70**, 129, **130**, **279**, **280**
Theodoric, **218**
Maximus the Confessor, 381, 386, 389
McGilchrist, Nigel, 88
mechanikos, 138
Mesarites, Nicholas, 146, 352
Meteora, 235, 332–34
Metochites, Theodore, 30, **31**, 174, 349, 354
Metropolis. *See* church of St Demetrios, Mystras
Milan, 15, 299
Milvian Bridge, **10**
Monastery of
All Saints, Varlaam, 333
Aphendiko. *See* Panagia Hodegetria
Chelandari, **228**, **326**
katholikon, **234**
Daphni, 237, **344**
katholikon, **345**
Dionysiou, **20**, 228
Docheriou, **20**
Doupiani, 332
Esfigmenou, **229**, **327**
Great Meteoron, **333**
Hodegetria, **236**, **339**, **340**
Hosios Loukas, **237**, 334–39, **336**, **337**
katholikon, **72**, **257**, **260**, **335**
Hosios Meletios, **223**
Iveron, **229**
katholikon, **234**
Karakallou, **229**
Kastamonitou, **21**
Koutloumoussi, **21**, **229**, **235**, **330**, **331**, **332**
katholikon, **234**
Megistis Lavra, 18, **19**, **22**, **223**, **230**, 232, **322**, **327**
katholikon, **63**
Nea Moni, Chios, 339
katholikon, **227**, **346**
Panagia Hodegetria, 340
Pantanassa, **236**, 341, **342**
Panteleimon, **19**, **21**, **230**
Pantokratora, **230**, **272**
Perivleptos, 340
Philotheou, **327**
Roussanou, **236**, 334
Simonos Petra, **230**
SS Theodoroi, Mystras, **342**
St Apollo, 365
St Catherine, Sinai, 18, **20**, 223, **228**, **251**, **266**, 363
St Demetrios, **342**
St Jeremiah, 365
St Nicholas Anapafsis, **333**, 334
St Stephen, 332
katholikon, **260**
Stavronikita, **20**, **82**, **231**
katholikon, **260**
Vatopedi, **231**, **232**, **321**, **322**, **323**, **324**
Xenophontos, **232**, **233**
katholikon, **234**
Xeropotamou, **21**
katholikon, **64**
Zografou, **22**, **233**
Monasticism, 17–22
Monophysites, 33
Monreale, 366–72, **371**
Mount Athos, 223, 321–32
Athonite Spatial Components, **63**
Garden of Panagia, **330**
MP ΘΥ, **269**
Mystagogia, 381, 386, 389
Mystagogical Catecheses
Cyril, 377, 380
Theodore, 380
mystagogikaí, 377
Mystras, 236, 339–42

Naples, 247
nave. *See* Byzantine church space division: Naos
Naxos, 88
Nazarene painting, 254
Necropolis, 90, **246**
Nestorians, 33, 392
New Apostoleion, 146
Nicene Creed, 33, 381
Nicholas of Andida, 386
Nika Rebellion, 17, 136, 137, 138

Ο ΩΝ, **268**
Odoacre, 16
Ohrid, 313
On the Holy Liturgy, 387
orant, **247**, 265, **266**
Ordines Romani, 70
orientation, 85, 393, 400
Origen, 34
Orologian Gate, 142, 347
órthros, 376
Ostrogoths, 16
Ousterhout, Robert, 134, 154

Pala d'Oro, **311**, 312
Palace of
Antiochus, 179
Hormisdas, 168
Palaiologos dynasty, 30, 278
Panagias tis Karyótissas, 328
Pantheon, 53, 103, 104
parekklésion, 63, 64, **160**, **161**, **202**, **208**, **331**, 349, **351**, **356**, **357**, **358**, **359**, **360**
Parentium (Porec), 312
Parousía (Second Coming of Christ), 281, 400
Parthenis, Kostis, 254
Parthenon, **61**
pastophoria. *See* Byzantine church space division: Diaconicon and Prothesis

paten, **379**, 383
Patriarch
    Cyril I, 366
    Germanos, 276, 382, 386, 387, 396, 400, 401
    Philotheos, 263, 384
    Photius, 349
    Sergios, 396
Patricios, Nicholas, 88
Patrizio, Giovanni, 122
Paul the Silentiary, 140, 145, 381
Pentecost, **368**, 399
phiale, 67, 235
    Iveron, **234**
    Koutloumoussi, **234**
plan type
    basilicas
        Constantinople, 135
        Near East, **189**
        Rome, **92**, **93**
        Thessaloniki, **193**
    centralized
        Constantinople, **170**
        Thessaloniki, **207**
    centralized, cruciform and domed basilica
        Near East, 191
    converted
        Rome, **94**, **95**, **96**, **97**, **98**
        Thessaloniki, **209**
    cross-in-square
        Constantinople, **149**, **150**, **151**
        Near East, **190**
        Thessaloniki, **199**
    cruciform / athonite
        Thessaloniki, **204**
    cruciform and converted
        Constantinople, **147**
    domed basilica
        Constantinople, 139
        Thessaloniki, **212**
    Eastern-influenced basilicas
        Rome, **116**, **117**, **118**
    superimposed basilicas
        Rome, **108**, **109**, **110**
Platytéra, **213**, 257, 259, 278, 319, 338, **339**, 340, **341**, **343**, **344**, 348
Pliny, 374
Plotinus, 276
Pope
    Boniface IV, 103
    Damasus, 91
    Felix IV, 105, 282
    Gregory I, 16, 385
    Gregory IV, 107
    Hadrian I, 127
    Honorius I, 114, 286, **288**
    Honorius III, 115
    Innocent II, 113
    John VIII, 105
    Julius II, 90
    Leo I, 91, 248
    Leo III, 24
    Leo X, 127
    Liberius, 122
    Mark, 107
    Miltiades, 89
    Nicholas V, 113
    Paschal I, 107, 127, 129, **266**, 285, **287**, **291**, **292**
    Paschal II, 99
    Pelagius, 286
    Pelagius II, 115
    Simplicius, 113
    Siricius, 99, 119
    Sixtus III, 91, 122, 269, 282
    Symmachus, 286, **288**
presbytéros, 374
Princess
    Anicia Juliana, 137
    Arcadia, 175
    Theodora Raoulaina, 175
processions, 387, 397
Procopius, 16, 17, 51, 138, 146, 172, 238, 401
Prokonnesian marble, 241
prophet
    Daniel, **338**
    Elijah, **264**, **328**
    Ezekiel, 314, **316**
    Ezra, 393
    Habakkuk, 314, **316**
    Isaiah, **334**
    King David, **327**
    King Solomon, **327**
    Micah, **356**
    Moses, **266**
    Zachariah, **356**
    Zephaniah, **356**
propylaeum, 184
proskomedía, 75, 376, 383
proskýnesis, 250
proskynetárion, 259, **331**
prósphoro, 376, 383
Protheoria, 386
psáltes, 62

Ravenna, 1, 15, 217
    Church type, 217–23
    Spiritual Art, 301–08
reliquary, **402**
Resurrection. *See Anastasis*
Revelations, 268
Rhodius, Constantinus, 394
Romans, 38, 398
Rome, 14
    Church types, 88–133
    Location of early Christian churches, **9**
    Spiritual Art, 279–99
Royal Doors, 68, 142, 256, 347, 378, 387, 401

Sakkara, 365
Salonika, 8
sanctuary. *See* Byzantine church space division: Bema
Schola cantorum, 74, 99, **295**
Sigma Court, 87
skéte, 64, 322
    Profiti Ilias, **233**
skevophylákion, 75, 373, 398
St
    Agatha, 285
    Agnese, 286, **288**, **294**
    Ambrose, 299
    Anthony, 17, **359**
    Antipas, **359**, 364
    Apa Mena, **365**
    Apollinaris, **306**
    Arsenios, **360**
    Athanasios, **18**, 223, 257, **332**
    Athanasios the Athonite, **261**, 322, **325**
    Basil of Caesarea, 17, 34, 257, **265**, 276, 378
    Benedict of Nursia, 18
    Cecilia, 285, **287**
    Clemente, **296**
    Cosmas, **282**
    Damian, **282**
    Demetrios, **318**, **329**
    Efthymios, **360**

George, **329**
Giuleta, **284**
Gregory, **265**
Gregory of Agrigentum, **360**
Gregory of Armenia, **340**, **359**, **360**
Gregory of Nazianzus, 34, 81, 257, 276, 394
Gregory of Nyssa, 34, 245, 276, 393
Hermagoras, 312
Hyppolitus, 286
Ignatios Theophoros, **359**
John Chrysostom, **27**, 34, **35**, 81, 257, **265**, 267, **338**, 378
John Damascene, 23, 250, 260, 276, 394
John Klimakos, 18, **360**
John the Forerunner, 156, 259, 265, **267**, 277, **320**, **325**, **349**, **357**, **358**
John the Theologian, **328**, **335**
Kyrillos, **296**
Lorenzo, 286
Loukas, **335**
Marco, **294**
Methodios, **296**
Moses, **332**
Nicholas, **328**, **329**, **334**, **338**
Nilus, 276
Pachomius, 17
Photios, 260
Prassede, **291**
Pudenziana, **292**
Sebastiano, **299**
Stephen, 113, 286
Theodore, 282
Trifon, **329**
Valerian, 285, **287**
Vitalis, **304**
Zeno, **292**
stasídia, **70**

Stephen the Great, 254
Stethatos, Niketas, 260, 398
Stromata, 400
sýnaxis, 376, 385

tabernacle, 79, **402**
Tacitus, 374
temple of Minerva Medica, **45**
Tertullian, 374, 375, 400
tesserae, 271, **273**
tetrarchy, 10
The Art of the Byzantine Empire, 393
The Book of Governors, 404
the Nativity, **345**
The Orthodox Liturgy, 378
Theodoric, 16, 105, 217
Theophanes, 180
Theotokos, 34
 E Geróntissa, **271**, 330
 Elaiovrýtissa, 270
 Eleoúsa, 269, **270**, **351**, **352**
 Esfagméni, 270
 Foverá Prostasía, **271**, **332**
 Glykophiloúsa, 270
 Hodegétria, 269, **270**, **338**
 Kardiótissa, **275**
 Koúkou, 271
 Koukouzelíssa, **330**
 Nicopeía, **271**, 312
 Paráklesis, 263
 Paramýthia, **271**
 Phaneroméni, **253**
 Portaïtissa, 328, **330**
 Pyrovolítheisa, 270
 Tríche, **271**
 Zoodóchos Pigí, **340**
Theotokos and Christ Child, **332**, **350**, **352**, **364**, 365, **369**
Thessaloniki, 15, 26, 27
 Church type, 188–213

Early Christian cemetery, **15**, **262**
Location of churches and monasteries, **8**
Spiritual Art, 314–21
Thiersch, Ludwig, 254
titulus
 Byzantii, 38
 Clementis, 38, 99
 Esquitii, 39
 Fasciolae, 103
 Sabina, 112
Trier, 46
triple apses, 76, 396
triptych, **379**
Triumph of Orthodoxy, 24
Twelve Great Festivals, 256, **257**, 259, **403**
typikón, 18, 223
Tyre, 390

Ulpius, 394

Van Millengen, Alexander, 134
Vandals, 16
Venice, 308–12
Via
 Cornelia, 279
 Latina, 280
Victory of the Icons, **251**, 268

Webb, Matilda, 88
Weitzmann, Kurt, 30
Wilkinson, John, 389
Wybrew, Hugh, 378

Zakynthos, 254
zeon, 381
Zoodóchos Pigí, 340

XEIP, 270, **272**